# CAREER
## Counseling

# CAREER
# Counseling

Foundations, Perspectives, and Applications

## Second Edition

### DAVID CAPUZZI

Walden University
Johns Hopkins University
Portland State University

### MARK D. STAUFFER

Walden University
Oregon State University

Routledge
Taylor & Francis Group
New York   London

Routledge
Taylor & Francis Group
711 Third Avenue
New York, NY 10017

Routledge
Taylor & Francis Group
27 Church Road
Hove, East Sussex BN3 2FA

© 2012 by Taylor & Francis Group, LLC
Routledge is an imprint of Taylor & Francis Group, an Informa business

Version Date: 2011902

International Standard Book Number: 978-0-415-88594-2 (Hardback)

**Library of Congress Cataloging-in-Publication Data**

Career counseling : foundations, perspectives, and applications / [edited by] David Capuzzi and Mark D. Stauffer. -- 2nd ed.
     p. cm.
Includes bibliographical references and index.
ISBN 978-0-415-88594-2 (hardcover : alk. paper)
    1. Vocational guidance. I. Capuzzi, Dave. II. Stauffer, Mark D.

HF5381.C265233 2011
331.702--dc23                                                                              2011022956

**Visit the Taylor & Francis Web site at**
**http://www.taylorandfrancis.com**

**and the Routledge Web site at**
**http://www.routledgementalhealth.com**

# Contents

## PART 1    *Foundations of Career Counseling*

## PART 2    *Skills and Techniques*

# Preface

The profession of counseling has been described as one in which counselors interact with clients to assist them in learning about themselves, their families, and their styles of interacting with others at home, at work, and in their communities for the purpose of discovering the most meaningful way to view themselves, and those they interact with, on a daily basis. Counselors in school, mental health, rehabilitation, hospital, private practice, and a variety of other settings must be thoroughly prepared to support clients in their quest to develop their identities, capacities, and abilities to cope with the rapid sociocultural, technological, and economic changes that are occurring in the 21st century. Professional organizations, accrediting bodies, licensure boards, and graduate preparation programs and departments are stressing the importance of developing standards for the education and supervision of counselors with both the knowledge and the skills base needed to support clients in the discovery process that affects their future and their lifestyle planning. As the profession has matured, more and more emphasis has been placed on the importance of preparing counselors to work holistically with their clients as they search for meaning in their lives.

One of the primary ways individuals develop a sense of identity and meaning is through their careers and the relationship that career choices and pathways have with personality traits, values, interests, communication styles, preferred living and working environments, and uses of leisure time. Viewing career in this manner is certainly holistic and demands that the counselor approach career and lifestyle planning with clients in a most comprehensive, personal, and developmental way. Counselors engaged in career and lifestyle planning with clients must be thoroughly prepared conceptually and able to translate concepts that will be helpful to clients through the use of relevant skills and techniques. They must also develop the contextual perspectives needed for competent practice as well as the unique requirements of clients representative of specific populations.

The content of this textbook is derived from the standards and competencies developed by professional associations and groups such as the National Career Development Association, the Association for Counselor Education and Supervision, the National Occupational Information Coordinating Committee, and the Council for the Accreditation of Counseling and Related Educational Programs. Reviews of the most current journal and textbook information on career and lifestyle planning have also been used in the process of identifying the content areas included in the 18 chapters of the book. This book also reflects our view that counselors must be prepared in a holistic manner because career and lifestyle planning with clients is inherently related to their search for identity and meaning for their lives.

The book is unique in both format and content. The contributed author format provides state-of-the-art information from experts who are recognized nationally and internationally for their expertise, research, and publications related to career and lifestyle planning. The content provides readers with information from areas not always addressed in introductory texts. Examples of these areas include chapters on career and lifestyle planning with clients in mental health, rehabilitation, and couples and family counseling settings as well as discussion of gender issues in career and lifestyle planning. Chapters focused on career and lifestyle planning with ethnic and minority clients and clients with addictive behaviors provide perspectives often overlooked in texts of this kind. Both the format and the content enhance the book's readability and interest for the reader and should engage and motivate graduate students in counseling and aligned professions.

The book is designed for graduate students who are taking a preliminary course in career and lifestyle planning in a Council for the Accreditation of Counseling and Related Educational Programs or equivalent graduate program. It presents a comprehensive overview of the foundations of career counseling, the skills and techniques needed for career counseling, and contextual perspectives on career and lifestyle planning. We, as editors, know that one text cannot adequately address all the factors that make up the complex and holistic aspects of career and lifestyle planning with clients. We have, however, attempted to provide readers with a broad perspective based on current professional literature and the rapidly changing world we live in at this juncture of the new millennium. We highlight the major features of the text next.

## Overview

The format for the coedited textbook is based on the contributions of authors who are recognized, nationally and internationally, for their expertise, research, and publications. With few exceptions, each chapter contains case studies that illustrate the practical applications of the concepts presented as well as interesting sidebars that contain information related to the chapter content, case studies, or awareness-building exercises. Most chapters refer the reader to Web sites containing information that supplements the information already presented. Students will find it helpful to use the study material contained in the Web-assisted site maintained by Routledge. Professors may want to make use of the PowerPoint slides developed for each of the chapters as well as the test manual that can be used to develop quizzes and exams on the book's content. These resources can be accessed at http://www.routledgementalhealth.com/career-counseling-9780415885942.

The text is divided into three parts: Foundations of Career Counseling; Skills and Techniques; and Contextual Perspectives on Career and Lifestyle Planning.

Part 1, Foundations for Career Counseling (Chapters 1–5), begins with information dealing with the historical perspectives that serve as the foundation for current approaches to career and lifestyle planning with clients. Key players, legislation, theories, institutions and professional organizations, licensure and accreditation issues, and world events are all chronicled and discussed to provide the reader with the contextual background needed to assimilate subsequent chapters. Chapters focused on theoretical perspectives, holistic views of career and lifestyle planning, multicultural theories, and ethical and legal issues in career counseling are also included in this first section of the book.

Part 2, Skills and Techniques (Chapters 6–10), presents information on the skills and techniques counselors must acquire to do competent work with clients requesting assistance with career and lifestyle planning. Individual and group assessment and appraisal, using technology, information, and other resources; development of comprehensive plans of action for clients; program promotion, management, and implementation; and supervision, coaching, and consultation provide the content of the five chapters in this part of the text. All of these chapters provide overviews and introduce readers to the skills and techniques that can be used in the career counseling process in a variety of settings.

Part 3, Contextual Perspectives on Career and Lifestyle Planning (Chapters 11–18), presents information relative to career and lifestyle planning with clients in schools; mental health; vocational rehabilitation; couples, marriage, and family settings; and addictions counseling settings. Two chapters on gender issues in career counseling and college career counseling, whether traditional, hybrid, or online, are also highly relevant.

## New to the Second Edition

- Chapter 3, "Toward a Holistic View: Decision-Making, Postmodern, and Emerging Theories"
- Chapter 11, "Career Counseling: Kindergarten Through Eighth Grade"
- Chapter 12, "High School Career Counseling: Preparing Youth for College, Careers, and Other Alternatives"
- Chapter 13, "College Career Counseling: Traditional, Hybrid, and 100% Online Campuses"
- Informational sidebars to encourage the visual learner and encourage additional contemplation of chapter content
- Integration of updated and current research from peer-reviewed journals and new textbooks
- An Instructor's Manual that includes journaling, group work, and experiential exercises for additional classroom assignments.

Every attempt was made by the editors and contributors to provide the reader with current information in each of the 18 areas of focus. Our hope is that this second edition of *Career Counseling: Foundations, Perspectives, and Applications* will provide the beginning graduate student counselor with the foundation needed for supervised practice in the arena of career and lifestyle planning with clients.

# Acknowledgments

We would like to thank the authors who contributed their time, expertise, and experience to the development of this textbook. They have done a superb job of addressing the basics of career and lifestyle planning with clients. We also thank those who provided the external reviews of the second edition of this text; their critiques and suggestions were invaluable in the process of bringing this textbook to its current stage of development. We also extend our thanks to our families and our colleagues, who supported our efforts. Special thanks to Dana Bliss, and other staff at Routledge, for their encouragement, creativity, and diligent efforts that culminated in the publication of our book.

**David Capuzzi and Mark D. Stauffer**

# Editors

**David Capuzzi, PhD, NCC, LPC,** is professor emeritus at Portland State University, Portland, Oregon; senior faculty associate in the Department of Counseling and Human Services, Johns Hopkins University, Baltimore, Maryland; and a member of the core faculty in the PhD in Counselor Education and Supervision program, School of Counseling and Social Service, Walden University. Previously, he served as an affiliate professor in the Department of Counselor Education, Counseling Psychology, and Rehabilitation Services at Pennsylvania State University, University Park. He is past president of the American Counseling Association, formerly the American Association for Counseling and Development.

From 1980 to 1984, Dr. Capuzzi edited *The School Counselor.* He authored a number of textbook chapters and monographs on the topic of preventing adolescent suicide and is coeditor and author with Dr. Larry Golden of *Helping Families Help Children: Family Interventions With School Related Problems* (Charles C. Thomas Publishing, 1986) and *Preventing Adolescent Suicide* (Routledge, 1988). He coauthored and edited with Douglas R. Gross *Youth at Risk: A Prevention Resource for Counselors, Teachers, and Parents* (American Counseling Association, 1989, 1996, 2000, 2004, 2008); *Introduction to the Counseling Profession* (Allyn & Bacon, 1991, 1997, 2001, 2005, 2009); *Introduction to Group Work* (Love Publishing, 1992, 1998, 2002, 2006, 2010); and *Counseling and Psychotherapy: Theories and Interventions* (Prentice Hall, 1995, 1999, 2003, 2007, 2011). Other texts are *Approaches to Group Work: A Handbook for Practitioners* (Prentice Hall, 2003), *Suicide Across the Life Span* (American Counseling Association, 2006), and *Sexuality in Counseling* (Nova Science Publications, 2002). the last coauthored and coedited with Larry Burlew. He has coedited three textbooks in the counseling field with Dr. Mark D. Stauffer, *Introduction to Group Work* (Love Publishing, 2010); *Career Counseling: Foundations, Perspectives, and Applications* (Allyn & Bacon, 2006); and *Foundations of Addictions Counseling* (Prentice Hall, 2008, 2012). He has authored or coauthored articles in a number of American Counseling Association–related journals.

A frequent speaker and keynoter at professional conferences and institutes, Dr. Capuzzi has also consulted with a variety of school districts and community agencies interested in initiating prevention and intervention strategies for adolescents at risk for suicide. He has facilitated the development of suicide prevention, crisis management, and postvention programs in communities throughout the United States; provides training on the topics of youth at risk and grief and loss; and serves as an invited adjunct faculty member at other universities as time permits.

An American Counseling Association fellow, he is the first recipient of the association's Kitty Cole Human Rights Award and a recipient of the Leona Tyler Award in Oregon. In 2010, he received the association's Gilbert and Kathleen Wrenn Award for a Humanitarian and Caring Person.

**Mark D. Stauffer, PhD, NCC,** received his doctoral degree from the Department of Teacher and Counselor Education at Oregon State University, Corvallis. He specialized in couples, marriage, and family counseling during his graduate work in the Counselor Education Program at Portland State University, Portland, Oregon, where he received his master's degree. He was a Chi Sigma Iota International fellow and was awarded the American Counseling Association's Emerging Leaders Training Grant. He is glad to be a member of the National Career Development Association.

Dr. Stauffer has worked in the Portland Metro Area in Oregon at crisis centers and other nonprofit organizations, working with individuals, couples, and families affected by addictions. He has studied and trained in the Zen tradition and presents locally and nationally on meditation and mindfulness-based therapies in counseling. He continues to maintain a small private practice on top of his teaching assignments.

In the realm of counselor education and supervision, Dr. Stauffer is a contributing instructor at Oregon State University for the Department of Teacher and Counselor Education and at Walden University in the PhD in Counselor Education and Supervision Program, School of Counseling and Social Service. He enjoys working with school and mental health–track counselors as well as with doctoral students in their development as personal and career counselors. Dr. Stauffer was also an instructor for Portland Community College's Career and Guidance Department, Portland, Oregon, where he taught 100-level career-related courses. Currently, his passion is examining methods and technology for instruction and supervision in 100% online and hybrid formats.

He has coedited three textbooks in the counseling field with Dr. David Capuzzi: *Introduction to Group Work* (Love Publishing, 2010), *Career Counseling: Foundations, Perspectives, and Applications* (Allyn & Bacon, 2006), and *Foundations of Addictions Counseling* (Prentice Hall, 2008, 2012).

# Contributors

**Anne S. Bartone, MSW,** received her MSW from Binghamton University, State University of New York, in 2006. She is currently a first-year doctoral student in the counseling psychology PhD program at Tennessee State University, Nashville. She plans to pursue a career as a practitioner on completing her degree. Her primary research interests include multicultural issues, issues of grief and loss, and cross-cultural happiness.

**Deborah P. Bloch, PhD,** obtained a BA in English from Brooklyn College, Brooklyn, New York, and went on to earn her MS in counselor education from Saint John's University and a PhD in organizational studies from New York University, both in New York City, New York. In 2009, she graduated from the University of San Francisco's Master's in Fine Arts program in writing. Retired from both the University of San Francisco, San Francisco, California, and the City University of New York, Dr. Bloch has released seven books in the field of career development, and her work has appeared in numerous professional journals, including the *International Journal of Information Management, Career Development Quarterly, World Futures,* and the *Journal of Spirituality, Leadership, and Management.*

**Sibyl Camille Cato, PhD,** attended Truman State University, Kirksville, Missouri, for her undergraduate work and the University of Arizona, Tucson, for her master's degree in school counseling. She received her PhD in counselor education from the Ohio State University, Columbus. Her research interests include the Council for the Accreditation of Counseling and Related Educational Programs and historically Black colleges and universities, school counselor supervision, and school counseling in urban settings. Dr. Cato was a school counselor at Carson Middle School, Tucson, Arizona. She is a member of the American Counseling Association, Association of Counselor Education and Supervision, American School Counseling Association, and Association of Multicultural Counseling and Development. She has presented at the Association of Counselor Education and Supervision national conference and the Transforming School Counseling national conference, and has also made various presentations in Columbus, Ohio. Dr. Cato also serves on the editorial board of the *Journal of Humanistic Counseling Education and Development.*

**Jeffrey D. Cook, PhD,** is Assistant Professor in the graduate counseling program at Saint Mary's College of California, Moraga. Dr. Cook received his doctorate in counselor education from Oregon State University, Corvallis. In addition to his counseling degrees, he received his Master's of Divinity from Denver Seminary, Littleton, Colorado. Dr. Cook is a licensed professional counselor (Oregon) and a national certified counselor. His academic focus is in family systems, intercultural counseling, and group counseling.

Before full-time academic work, he worked in private practice with a focus on trauma, shame, and couples, and worked as a school counselor and career counselor in a university setting.

**Mary M. Deacon, PhD,** received a PhD in counselor education and supervision from the Curry School of Education, University of Virginia, Charlottesville. She has a master's degree in professional counseling, clinical track, from Liberty University, Lynchburg, Virginia, and a BS in chemistry from Central Michigan University, Mount Pleasant. Her counseling experiences include providing career, mental health, and substance abuse counseling in university and community mental health settings. She is also an adjunct professor of psychology and counseling at Liberty University. Her teaching and research interests include the areas of girls' and women's career development, gender equity, and multicultural competency. She has presented at national and local conferences on career counseling-related topics. In addition, Dr. Deacon is a national certified counselor.

**Rebecca M. Dedmond, PhD,** is Director of the School Counseling Program at the Alexandria Center, George Washington University, Alexandria, Virginia. Her research focuses on drop-out prevention. She wrote and validated the nationally recognized Standards for Freshman (eighth and ninth grade) Transition Courses. She directs the Freshman Transition Initiative and presents her model program to administrators and leaders throughout the country (http://www.freshmantransition.com). Dr. Dedmond was the career supervisor for the Commonwealth of Virginia and has served as a leader in career services in Ghana, West Africa, the U.S. Virgin Islands, and throughout the United States. She contributes to the counseling profession by serving in national professional organizations and by writing articles, books, training guides, and career products.

**Dennis W. Engels, PhD,** is past president, Texas Counseling Association; past president and charter fellow, National Career Development Association; editor emeritus, *Counseling and Values,* the journal of the Association for Spiritual, Ethical, and Religious Values in Counseling; past chair, American Counseling Association Council of Journal Editors; senior associate editor, *Journal of Counseling and Development;* and former secretary and newsletter editor, Association for Counselor Education and Supervision. He served for 30 years on the editorial boards of the *Journal of Counseling and Development, Counselor Education and Supervision,* and *Career Development Quarterly* and has extensive experience with accreditation. His research and scholarly interests center on career development, decision making, ethics, human resource development, multipotentiality, organizational and disciplinary history, and strategic and operational planning.

**Kathy M. Evans, PhD,** Associate Professor at the University of South Carolina, Columbia, received her PhD from the Pennsylvania State University. Dr. Evans has more than 40 publications including her career text *Gaining Cultural Competence in Career Counseling* and her most recent book, coauthored with Elizabeth Kincade and Susan Seem, *Introduction to Feminist Therapy* (Wadsworth Publishing, 2007). Her research, writing, and teaching focus on culture, career, family, and women's issues in counseling.

**Rich W. Feller, PhD,** is Professor of counseling and career development and University Distinguished Teaching Scholar at Colorado State University, Fort Collins. President-elect of the National Career Development Association, an NCDA Fellow and recipient of the Eminent Carer Award in 2009, and recipient of the Eminent Career Award in 2009, he is coauthor of *Knowledge Nomads and the Nervously Employed* (Caps Press, 2005). *A Counselor's Guide to Career Assessment Instruments,* (National Career Development Association, 2009), and *Career Transitions in Turbulent Times* (Counseling and Psychological Services, 1996), and the Harrington-O'Shea Career Decision Making System. His research in using technology and media to advance career development has resulted in his coauthoring the Web sites CDM Internet (http://www.cdminternet.com) and STEMCareer (http://www.stemcareer. com), the *CDM Video Tour of Your Tomorrow,* and the *Making the Most of Your Abilities* video series. He has consulted on six continents and in 49 states with clients including the National Aeronautics and Space Administration, National Science Foundation, the United Nations, and major corporations.

**Francesca G. Giordano, PhD,** is Program Director for the Master's of Arts in Counseling Psychology, the Family Institute, Northwestern University, Evanston, Illinois. Before joining the Family Institute, she was a professor of counseling in the Department of Counseling, Adult, and Health Education at Northern Illinois University, DeKalb. She is also a licensed clinical professional counselor in the State of Illinois. For the past 17 years, she has been an administrator and counselor educator with a specialization in mental health, consultation, and ethics. She is the vice-chair, Illinois Professional Counselor Licensing and Disciplinary Board; past board member of the Illinois Mental Health Counselors Association; and president-elect, Illinois Counseling Association. She is also a highly successful workshop presenter and offers workshops for the Illinois Mental Health Counselors Association, including an exam preparation workshop for the clinical professional counselor license and workshops on legal and ethical issues. She was the coproject director on two national grants targeting the career development needs of underserved populations. One grant has been funded to develop an online workforce transitions program for welfare-to-work participants. The second grant has been funded to offer community development programming and mental health services for a housing project in Rockford, Illinois. She is the coeditor of the *Journal of Counseling in Illinois.* She consults with mental health centers in the areas of effective treatment planning, ethical issues, anger, and therapeutic change. In 1998, she received the Counselor Educator of the Year award from the American Mental Health Counselors Association; in 2002, she received the Distinguished Service award from the Illinois Mental Health Counselors Association; in 2006, she received the Counselor Educator of the Year award from the Illinois Counselor Education and Supervision Association; and in 2009, she received the

C.A. Michelman award for outstanding service to the counseling profession. She also maintains an active clinical practice specializing in sexuality counseling, anger management, career development, and relationship restoration in couples.

**Matthew V. Glowiak, MS,** received a BA in psychology from the University of Illinois, Urbana–Champaign, and a master's degree in mental health counseling from Walden University. As a scholar–practitioner, his professional passion has centered on advocacy with youth and children as well as Alcohol and Other Drugs group counseling. In 2004 to 2005, Glowiak interned with the Champaign County Juvenile Offender Outreach program, where he mentored adjudicated juveniles facing incarceration. Glowiak is currently pursuing a doctoral degree in counselor education and supervision at Walden University, with an emphasis in consultation. His professional focus is on publishing, licensure, national certification, and counselor education.

**Jane Goodman, PhD,** is professor emerita of counseling and summer director of the Adult Career Counseling Center at Oakland University, Rochester, Michigan. Previously, she was a career counselor and organizational consultant at a counseling–consulting center. She received her bachelor's degree in sociology from the University of Chicago, Chicago, Illinois, and her doctoral and master's degrees in counseling from Wayne State University, Detroit, Michigan. She has been active in professional associations for more than 25 years and was the 2001–2002 president of the American Counseling Association. Her published works include three books, several guides or monographs, and many book chapters and journal articles, primarily in the area of career development and adult transitions.

**Mary H. Guindon, PhD,** is retired former chair of and associate professor in the Department of Counseling and Human Services, Johns Hopkins University, Baltimore, Maryland. A licensed psychologist and licensed clinical professional counselor, Dr. Guindon maintains a private practice in executive, personal, and career coaching; consulting; and counselor supervision. She holds a PhD from the University of Virginia, Charlottesville. She is the author of *A Counseling Primer: An Orientation to the Profession* (2011) and author–editor of *Self-Esteem Across the Lifespan: Issues and Interventions* (2010), both published by Routledge/Taylor & Francis.

**Henry L. Harris, PhD,** is an associate professor in and department chair of the Department of Counseling, University of North Carolina at Charlotte. He is also a military veteran, a licensed North Carolina secondary school counselor, and a licensed professional counselor in the States of Georgia and North Carolina.

**Barbara Herlihy, PhD, NCC, LPC,** is university research professor in the Counselor Education Program, University of New Orleans, New Orleans, Louisiana. She is the coauthor of three current textbooks on ethical issues in counseling and is author or coauthor of numerous articles and book chapters on the topics of gender issues in counseling, ethics, social justice and multicultural competence, feminist therapy, and supervision.

**Cheryl Holcomb-McCoy, PhD,** is currently Professor and Chair of the Department of Counseling and Human Services, Johns Hopkins University, Baltimore, Maryland. Previously, Dr. Holcomb-McCoy held appointments as Associate Professor of counselor education, University of Maryland, College Park, and Assistant Professor and Director of the School Counseling Program, Brooklyn College of the City University of New York. Academically, Dr. Holcomb-McCoy earned a PhD in counseling and educational development from the University of North Carolina at Greensboro and an MEd in school counseling and a BS in early childhood education, both from the University of Virginia, Charlottesville. Her areas of research specialization include the measurement of multicultural self-efficacy and cultural competence in school counseling, best practices in urban school counselor preparation, and the examination of school counseling programs that influence students' college readiness. Dr. Holcomb-McCoy has authored more than 50 articles in refereed national journals and is the author of the best-selling book *School Counseling to Close the Achievement Gap: A Social Justice Framework for Success* (Corwin Press, 2007). She has served as guest editor for the *Professional School Counseling* journal and is currently an associate editor of the *Journal for Counseling and Development*. In 2009, she was awarded the Mary Smith Arnold Anti-Oppression Award at the American Counseling Association conference in Charlotte, North Carolina.

**Brian Hutchison, PhD, NCC,** is Assistant Professor and school counseling program coordinator, the University of Missouri—St. Louis. He has several publications pertaining to career development and counseling and continues to pursue a research agenda focused on these areas with urban and low-social-class populations. Hutchison is currently president of the Missouri Career Development Association, an ad hoc reviewer for the *Career Development Quarterly*, a member of the National Career Development Association International Career Issues Committee, and principal developer of the Cultural School Counselor Web site training Web site (http://www.culturalcompetentschoolcounselor.com).

**Clint Limoges, MA,** is currently a PhD student at Walden University. Mr. Limoges earned his master's degree in community counseling from Henderson State University, Arkadelphia, Arkansas. Mr. Limoges is a licensed professional counselor and a national certified pastoral counselor. He is currently a school-based mental health counselor at Harmony Grove Middle School, Haskell, Arkansas. In addition to counseling, his professional experiences include pastoral ministry and teaching.

**Ellen Hawley McWhirter, PhD,** is Professor of counseling psychology, University of Oregon, Eugene. She received a BA from the University of Notre Dame, Notre Dame, Indiana, and a master's degree in counseling and a PhD in counseling psychology from Arizona State University, Tucson. Dr. McWhirter is the author of *Counseling for Empowerment* (1994, American

Counseling Association), coauthor of *At Risk Youth: A Comprehensive Response* (4th ed., 2007, Brooks/Cole), and author or coauthor of more than 50 articles and book chapters. Her scholarship addresses adolescent career development and at-risk adolescents. She is a fellow of the Society for Counseling Psychology.

**Jerry A. Olsheski, PhD,** is Associate Professor emeritus of rehabilitation counseling, Ohio University, Athens. Dr. Olsheski has extensive experience in the field of rehabilitation counseling and has worked as a counselor, supervisor, administrator, and educator. Before his appointment at Ohio University, he served as the director of disability management services at the University of Cincinnati Center for Occupational Health, Cincinnati, Ohio. Dr. Olsheski is a licensed professional counselor and certified rehabilitation counselor. He has provided numerous disability management consultation services to employers, unions, and rehabilitation professionals throughout the United States.

**Jackie J. Peila-Shuster, PhD,** an assistant professor of counseling and career development at Colorado State University, Fort Collins, also teaches courses in adult development and aging. With a master's degree in counseling and career development and a BS in occupational therapy, her areas of interest include career counseling, counselor education, retirement, and strengths-based approaches to career and life planning. Her publications include contributions to *Explorations in Diversity* (Brooks Cole, 2010) and *Experiential Activities for Teaching Multicultural Competence* (American Counseling Association, 2011). Her current research involves strengths-based interventions, positive emotions, and retirement self-efficacy.

**Michelle Perepiczka, PhD,** earned her PhD in counselor education from the Texas A&M University—Commerce. A core faculty member in the Mental Health Counseling Program of Walden University, Dr. Perepiczka is a licensed mental health counselor, certified school counselor, registered play therapist, and national certified counselor with 5 years of experience in community and school counseling settings. In addition to teaching, her professional experiences include providing counseling services to children and adolescents who have experienced various forms of abuse, serving as a school counselor in a disciplinary alternative program, and supervising students in a university counseling center. Her primary areas of interest include counselor wellness and development, wellness assessment, and humanism.

**Manivong J. Ratts, PhD,** is Assistant Professor and School Counseling Program director, Department of Counseling and School Psychology, Seattle University, Seattle, Washington. He received his PhD in counselor education and supervision from Oregon State University, Corvallis. He also holds an associate's degree from Yakima Valley Community College, Yakima, Washington; a bachelor's degree in psychology from Western Washington University, Bellingham; and a master's degree in counseling from Oregon State University. He is a national certified counselor and a licensed school counselor, and he serves on the editorial board of various peer-reviewed journals. Dr. Ratts' writing and research is in the area of social justice, multicultural competence, and social justice advocacy. Specifically, his teaching, scholarship, and service are focused on helping emerging counselors to become change agents and advocates for social justice. He conducts diversity and social justice workshops for K–12 school districts and community agencies. He is president-elect of Counselors for Social Justice, a division of the American Counseling Association, and founder of Seattle University Counselors for Social Justice (http://www.sucsj.org), an advocacy organization that addresses issues of equity affecting individuals, communities, and schools). He also operates a part-time private clinical practice in Seattle.

**KristiAnna Santos, MA,** is a doctoral student in counselor education and supervision at the University of Texas at San Antonio. She received her master's degree in counseling from Seattle University, Seattle, Washington, where she was one of the initial members of the university's branch of Counselors for Social Justice. She received her BA in American studies and psychology from the University of Notre Dame, Notre Dame, Indiana. She has previously worked with the children of Asian immigrants at Seattle's Asian Counseling and Referral Center and has provided career counseling services to college students in Texas. Santos is a native of Guam, and her research interests include multicultural counseling, career development, and social justice issues, particularly with respect to Pacific Islanders.

**Leanne Schamp, PhD, LMFT,** received her PhD in counselor education and supervision from Oregon State University, Corvallis, and her MA in marriage and family therapy from George Fox University, Newberg, Oregon. She is a licensed marriage and family therapist in Oregon, where she has practiced in agency, nonprofit, and private practice settings. She has been active in providing resources and education for the local community by presenting multiple types of workshops and through networking local faith communities with secular agencies for support in mental health issues, domestic violence, and child abuse prevention. While providing clinical services to couples, individuals, and families regarding a variety of concerns, Dr. Schamp has focused her clinical practice on the treatment of issues related to intimate partner violence, specifically with women of faith. Her clinical and research interests include intimate partner violence, integration of spirituality and counseling, integration of mental health and career counseling, multiculturalism, and clinical supervision. She is currently Director, Clinical Mental Health Counseling Program & Counseling Center, and Assistant Professor in the Clinical Mental Health Counseling program, Northwest Christian University, Eugene, Oregon.

**Donald A. Schutt, Jr., PhD,** has been the director of human resource development in the Office of Human Resources, University of Wisconsin—Madison, since January 1998. In this position, he manages the development and delivery of centralized professional and career development workshops for more than 18,000 employees at the University of Wisconsin—Madison.

In the past 15 years, he has presented more than 500 workshops focusing on a variety of topics including leadership development, management strategies, employee relations, innovative strategies for teaching career development program design and evaluation, and professional and career development concepts. In addition, he has written four books focusing on creating and implementing career development systems for individuals in organizations. Schutt is a licensed professional counselor in the State of Wisconsin as well as a national certified counselor, a master career development professional, and an International Public Management Association certified specialist in organizational and employee development. In addition, Schutt has a certificate in strategic human resources management from Cornell University, Ithaca, New York, and Six Sigma Green Belt certification from the Wisconsin School of Business, University of Wisconsin—Madison. His educational background includes a PhD and MA in counselor education from the University of Iowa, Iowa City, and a BA in journalism and economics from the University of Wisconsin—Madison.

**Pat Schwallie-Giddis, PhD,** a past president of the National Career Development Association, has been recognized as a champion of counseling and career development throughout the United States. She has spoken to groups of professionals in almost every state as well as in Germany, Australia, and Russia. She is currently an associate professor in and chair of the Department of Counseling and Human Development at the George Washington University, Washington, DC. Schwallie-Giddis formerly served as the associate and interim executive director of the American Counseling Association. She received her PhD in counseling and human systems at Florida State University, Tallahassee, in 1991, where she was later honored as distinguished educator of the year. In 2000, she was also recognized as a distinguished educator by the University of Wisconsin—Platteville, where she received her master's degree. Other awards for her service to the field of counseling include the Carl D. Perkins Legislative Award and the Spirit of America Award.

**David S. Shen-Miller, PhD, MSW,** is Assistant Professor of counseling psychology, Tennessee State University, Nashville. He received his master's degree in social work from the University of Texas and his doctoral degree in counseling psychology from the University of Oregon, Eugene, under the advisement of Dr. Linda Forrest. From 2003 to 2006, he served as the director of the University of Oregon Men's Center and has engaged in clinical, administrative, and research work related to men's health. His clinical interests include working with the intersections of male identity and mental health, racial and ethnic identity development, and other aspects of multicultural counseling. He conceptualizes and conducts his research and clinical practice in an ecological framework. His research interests include the psychology of men and masculinity, men's health and occupational behaviors, diversity and multicultural issues in supervision and training, and problems of professional competence in training.

**Donna S. Sheperis, PhD,** earned her PhD in counselor education from the University of Mississippi, Oxford. A core faculty member in the Mental Health Counseling Program of Walden University, Dr. Sheperis is a licensed professional counselor, national certified counselor, and approved clinical supervisor with 20 years of experience in community counseling settings. In addition to teaching, her professional experiences include providing vocational preparation for individuals with developmental disabilities, working with children and adolescents in residential group home settings, serving as the adult outpatient services coordinator in a community mental health setting, operating a behavioral assessment private practice, and supervising students in a university counseling center. Her primary areas of interest include mental health and coping, counselor development, ethics, and supervision.

**Marie F. Shoffner Creager, PhD,** is Associate Professor of counselor education, Commonwealth University, Richmond, Virginia. Dr. Shoffner received her PhD and MEd in counselor education and an ME in electrical engineering from the University of Virginia and a BS in mathematics from the College of William and Mary, Williamsburg, Virginia. She has investigated the career development of women and students of color in science, technology, engineering, and mathematics. She has written on career development and career counseling, collaboration among school personnel, school counseling, and the career development of girls and women. She was president of the Association for Assessment in Counseling and Education in 2009 and 2010; has held several other positions in state and national organizations; has presented at national, regional, and state conferences; and serves on several editorial boards, including those of the *Career Development Quarterly* and the *Journal of Career Development.* Dr. Shoffner is a national certified counselor and a national certified school counselor.

**Laura R. Simpson, PhD, LPC,** is core faculty for counselor education and supervision at Walden University. Dr. Simpson has been a counselor educator since 2005, supported by 21 years as a mental health clinician. She is a licensed professional counselor, national certified counselor, and approved clinical supervisor. Dr. Simpson maintains a private practice and serves on the Mississippi Licensed Professional Counselors Board of Examiners as well as the executive board of the Mississippi Counseling Association and Mississippi Licensed Professional Counselor Association. She has presented research on the state, national, and international levels and published scholarly writings for professional counseling journals and textbooks. Research interests include counselor wellness and secondary trauma, spirituality, crisis response, cultural diversity, and supervision.

**Shelby E. Strong, MA,** holds her Master's in Education and Human Development in School Counseling from the George Washington University, Washington, DC. As an undergraduate at Johns Hopkins University, Baltimore, Maryland, she worked for 4 years as an internship assistant at the Homewood Career Center, which fostered her initial interest in career counseling. She served as the 2009–2010 intern for the American School Counseling Association, where she served as a member of the National Alliance of Pupil Services Organizations, attended meetings of the Committee for Education Funding, and lobbied for greater school counselor inclusion in the Elementary and Secondary Education Act reauthorization. She is now preparing to enter the field as a school counselor with a focus on career counseling across the lifespan.

**Zarus E. P. Watson, PhD, LPC,** is an associate professor and program coordinator of the Counselor Education Program, University of New Orleans, New Orleans, Louisiana. He received his BA from Tulane University, New Orleans and his MA and PhD in counselor education/research methods from the University of New Orleans. Dr. Watson is also the research director of the UNO Research Center for Multiculturalism and Counseling. His areas of research includes journal and chapter publications in regards to social systems theory, systemic conditioning mechanisms, identity development, transgenerational trauma, and multicultural issues in organizations, socially ascribed groups and communities. Dr. Watson has consulted in business and industry in the areas of contextual program evaluation, task group functionality, executive coaching, and organizational diagnostics utilizing a "systems-as-client" approach. In addition, he has over sixty presentations covering culture and socialization processes across multiple settings, groups and contexts. Dr. Watson is the past president of the Louisiana Association of Multicultural Counseling and Development and is a licensed professional counselor.

**Chris Wood, PhD, NCC, NCSC,** is an Associate Professor with the counseling program in the New College Institute at Old Dominion University, Chester, Virginia . He has been an Associate Professor at Seattle University and, prior to his tenure there, was a faculty member at The Ohio State University, Columbus, Ohio, and the University of Arizona, Tuscon. He is past President of the Western Association for Counselor Education & Supervision (WACES). Dr. Wood is the Associate Editor for the *Professional School Counseling* journal and has published articles in *Professional School Counseling,* the *Journal of Counseling & Development,* the *Journal of College Counseling, Counselor Education & Supervision,* and *The Elementary School Journal* as well as numerous book chapters. Chris Wood is the head editor for sixth edition of the National Career Development Association (NCDA) publication, *A Counselor's Guide to Career Assessment Instruments* (with Hays) and co-editor for the third edition of *Critical Incidents in School Counseling* (with Tyson). Dr. Wood has previous experience as a high school counselor, a school counseling/guidance department chair, a counselor/group leader at a residential youth facility for troubled teens, and a career counselor at an alternative school serving grades 7-12.

**Anita Young, PhD,** is Assistant Professor, Counseling and Human Services Department, and Chi Sigma Iota chapter faculty advisor, Johns Hopkins

University, Baltimore, Maryland. She earned her PhD from Ohio State University, Columbus. Dr. Young is a former teacher, school counselor, and district school counseling administrator. Her research interests are cultivating school counselor leadership, examining best school counseling practices, and using accountability strategies to ensure equitable services and success for all students. She has coauthored publications designed to train school counselors to use data and accountability strategies to address educational issues. In addition to American School Counselor Association National Model presentations, she has presented numerous workshops on closing the achievement gap and increasing postsecondary opportunities for all students. She has served on state and national school counseling committees. Dr. Young is also a former American School Counselor Association District Supervisor of the Year recipient.

# PART 1

# FOUNDATIONS OF CAREER COUNSELING

CHAPTER 1

# Historical Influences on the Evolution of Vocational Counseling

David S. Shen-Miller, Ellen Hawley
McWhirter, and Anne S. Bartone

## Contents

> Far and away the best prize that life offers is the chance to work hard at work worth doing.
>
> **—Teddy Roosevelt**

All career and vocational theories develop within a historical context. Examining the historical roots and development of different vocational theories provides a basis for understanding their lineage, a context for how they develop over time, and a sense of their connection to U.S. history and prevailing culture. In this chapter, we examine major influences on U.S. vocational counseling theory and practice in an effort to present a contextual portrait of the field and its growth. This portrait includes key figures, legislation, institutions and professional organizations, licensure and accreditation, and world events.

As an example of contextual influences that have shaped the history of vocational counseling, Gysbers, Heppner, Johnston, and Neville (2003) identified five tenets that influenced the development of career counseling research, theory, and practice in the United States: (1) individualism and autonomy, (2) affluence, (3) an open structure of opportunity based on assumptions of merit, (4) work as the central role in people's lives, and (5) the logical, linear, and progressive development of work and career (pp. 53–57). These tenets reflect the U.S. mainstream culture's assumptions that (a) the individual is the primary unit of focus, (b) individuals make career choices (vs. family or collectivist decision making), (c) individuation represents psychological progress and development, (d) volition and unconstrained choices guide occupational decisions, (e) the world of work operates as a meritocracy free from biases (e.g., racism, sexism), and (f) work is the most important aspect of people's lives. These assumptions rely on a static work culture and environment that no longer exists, even for those who once enjoyed its benefits, and completely ignore the realities of many others (Gysbers, Heppner, Johnston, & Neville, 2003).

The analysis by Gysbers, Heppner, Johnston, and Neville (2003) provided an excellent example of the extent to which the aims and beliefs of career counseling have been influenced by larger social forces. It also illustrates why career counseling has failed to benefit many who have sought its services and why many have not viewed career counseling as useful or relevant. Throughout the history of vocational counseling, there have been those who have argued that a critical dimension of career counseling practice involves identifying and transforming the structures and practices that perpetuate occupational stratification, inequality, and workplace injustices (e.g., Blustein, Juntunen, & Worthington, 2000; Blustein, McWhirter, & Perry, 2005; O'Ryan, 2003).

In this chapter, we trace the emergence and development of vocational and career guidance over nine historical stages. We determined these stages through consideration of the works of Pope (2000) and Aubrey (1977). Within each stage, we present a sampling of historical events, legislation, and educational and vocational trends that contributed to the development of career guidance and counseling. These events should be viewed as a launching point for further inquiry rather than as a definitive catalogue of the influences on the field.

We begin with a few key definitions. On the basis of Richardson (1993) and Blustein et al. (2005), we define *work* as a central human activity, paid or unpaid, that is designed to fulfill the tasks of daily living and ensure survival. We define *career* as a subset of work that is characterized by volition, pay, and hierarchical and thematic relationships among various jobs that may or may not constitute a career, and, finally, we define *vocation* as a more general term that subsumes both work and career. These contemporary definitions are sometimes at odds with the language used over the course of time in vocational counseling. In recognition of changing terms over time, we also offer the broader definition of *career* offered by the National Vocational

Guidance Association in 1973: "a time-extended working out of a purposeful life pattern through work undertaken by the individual" (as cited in Casell & Samples, 1976, p. 3) that exists over the course of the life span and highlights the relation between work and identity.

## Stage 1: The Beginning (1890–1914)

The mid- and late 1800s ... [were] marked by a devastating civil war, periods of economic depression, the closing of the American frontier, unbridled growth of large metropolitan areas, large waves of uneducated and unskilled immigrants, a war with the fading Spanish empire, unchecked expansion of family fortunes through business and industry, abrupt and unforeseen modes of communication and transportation, legal freeing of millions of former slaves without concomitant economic and social autonomy, the challenge to established religions by social and biological Darwinism, the rapid spread of compulsory school attendance laws, concentration of job opportunities in large cities, growth of state and federal government to cope with the earlier enlargement of corporate and industrial complexes, the struggle of women for basic human rights, and, the increased exploitation of many segments of the United States population by unscrupulous hucksters and entrepreneurs. (Aubrey, 1977, pp. 288–289)

As captured in this summary by Aubrey (1977), the years in which vocational guidance emerged in the United States were marked by large-scale economic and demographic changes that followed the Industrial Revolution. The second major immigration wave in the United States was marked by mass movement into the cities from rural areas in the United States and abroad and included people from many nations, members of ethnic minority groups, farmers, Southerners, and youth (DeBell, 2001; McLemore, Romo, & Baker, 2001; Pope, 2000). This immigration was accompanied by xenophobic social movements as well as restrictive immigration legislation after World War I, and continued through the Depression and World War II (McLemore et al., 2001). There was little sympathy for the plight of new arrivals, many of whom found work only in the most abysmal conditions (e.g., Sinclair, 1905). Labor unions emerged in the middle of the 1800s and grew in strength to become important political forces by the turn of the century (Brecher, 1997; DeBell, 2001).

The turn-of-the-century job market was characterized by changes in required job skills (DeBell, 2001). Although most opportunities for employment consisted of unskilled labor in the major industries of mining, railroads, factories, and mills (Baker, 2002; Pope, 2000), rising industrialization offered a number of new occupations and opportunities (Watkins, 1992). Implementation of Frederick Taylor's (1911) theory of scientific management radically increased worker productivity but was criticized as dehumanizing (Harris, 2000). The emergence of large organizations and subsequent prohibition against individuality and self-expression effected a shift in the relationship between identity and work. Romantic-era sentiments about expressing one's core identity through "vocational passion" were replaced by more pragmatic definitions of identity based on one's place within an organization (Savickas, 1993, p. 206), which shifted the locus of work identity from "a calling from God" (internal) to "what your neighbors call you" (external), which Savickas (1993, p. 206) linked with the emergence of the "career ladder."

### SIDEBAR 1.1   A Job versus A Calling

Jobs are not big enough for people. It's not just the assembly line worker whose job is too small for his spirit, you know? A job like mine, if you really put your spirit into it, you would sabotage immediately. You don't dare. So you absent your spirit from it. My mind has been so divorced from my job, except as a source of income, it's really absurd.

As I work in the business world, I am more and more shocked. You throw yourself into things because you feel that important questions—self-discipline, goals, a meaning of your life—are carried out in your work. You invest a job with a lot of values that the society doesn't allow you to put into a job. You find yourself like a pacemaker that's gone crazy or something. You want it to be a million things that it's not and you want to give it a million parts of yourself that nobody else wants there. So you end up wrecking the curve or else settling down and conforming. (Terkel, 1974, p. 521)

Events such as the Triangle Shirtwaist Fire of 1911 and the publication of Upton Sinclair's *The Jungle* (1905) brought the extreme conditions of the workplace to the attention of the general public. Although middle- and upper-class White women did not enter the labor force in large numbers until World War II, many women worked to stave off extreme poverty and compensate for widespread male unemployment and underemployment (Peterson & Gonzales, 2000). Children were also present in the labor force in great numbers and were subjected to terrible working conditions, in part because of the absence of child labor laws (Aubrey, 1977; Baker, 2002). The first national child labor law was not passed until 1908 (DeBell, 2001). Today, although labor laws protect the majority of U.S. children, others continue to be exposed to abysmal working conditions, such as migrant farmworker children (Tucker, 2000) and those forced into the child sex industry (Estes & Weiner, 2002).

The Protestant work ethic and social Darwinism were dominant sociocultural influences of the time. These philosophies conveyed that hard work inevitably leads to success and that the strongest and hardest working achieve the most success. The Protestant work ethic has been critiqued for its limited multicultural relevance and "disrespect for immigrant work habits" (Peterson & Gonzales, 2000, p. 51) and for ignoring social and political restrictions on individual occupational success as well as the reality that opportunities are not made available on an equal basis to all (Gysbers, Heppner, & Johnston, 2003; Peterson & Gonzales, 2000).

These social, political, and economic changes in which the nation was embroiled gave rise to two movements that were essential to the history of vocational guidance: the progressive movement and the educational reform movement. The progressive movement arose from the idea that science and technology should be used to benefit the common good and move toward human perfection (Baker, 2002). Made up of reformists who worked to alleviate negative social conditions, the progressive movement was based on beliefs that the government should help individuals and communities (Pope, 2000) and targeted women's suffrage, regulation of industry and educational reform, and enactment of child labor laws as major goals (Baker, 2002).

The educational reform movement emerged in response to vast increases in school enrollment. Mass immigration into the cities, changes in child labor laws, and the need for more highly educated workers all increased the size of school classrooms, and student diversity expanded considerably with respect to language, background, education, and aptitude (Aubrey, 1977; Baker, 2002). These changes in student composition meant that old methods of teaching were no longer as effective, leading to a call for widespread educational reform in academic content and teaching practices (Baker, 2002). Factory and corporate schools emerged to meet the increasing need to train workers (Harris, 2000). Although focused on skill-specific training, many corporate schools "taught everything from basic English to specific, production-related technical skills" (Harris, 2000, p. 5) and may also have served a larger acculturative function.

## Vocational Guidance: Beginnings

The ideals of the progressive and educational reform movements were perhaps best reflected in the work of Frank Parsons, a Boston-based attorney. Noting Parsons' own journey from engineer to lawyer to professor to mayoral candidate to godfather of vocational guidance, Watkins (1992) joked that Parsons himself was a man desperately in need of career guidance. Through his work at the Vocation Bureau of the Civic Service House in Boston, Massachusetts, Parsons responded to changing needs in industry and the workforce by focusing on the school-to-work transition of children (Blustein et al., 2000; Super, 1955).

The Civic Service House had been a place for self-governing clubs of immigrants and socialites interested in civic action and justice to meet as they worked to help individuals who formerly had little or no hope of rising above their social and economic status (Brewer, 1942; Hartung & Blustein, 2002; Pope, 2000; Zytowski, 2001). Part of the Civic Service House included the Breadwinner's College (later, Institute), which provided primary and continuing education for interested members (Brewer, 1942; Zytowski, 2001). One of the first instructors at the Breadwinner's College was the civic-minded Parsons, who was a professor and dean of liberal arts (Brewer, 1942). In 1906, Parsons delivered "The Ideal City," a lecture detailing the need to counsel young people about vocational decisions as a means of empowering them and working toward social justice (Brewer, 1942; O'Brien, 2001). The lecture generated tremendous interest and led to the formation of the Vocation Bureau (Brewer, 1942; Zytowski, 2001).

The Vocation Bureau is generally considered the formative site of the U.S. vocational guidance movement (Hartung & Blustein, 2002). The bureau provided assistance to students, trained the first vocational counselors, facilitated the school-to-work transition, and focused on the development of vocational choice (Baker, 2002; Zytowski, 2001). Parsons' (1909) *Choosing a Vocation* served as a foundation for vocational guidance throughout the remainder of the century (Hartung & Blustein, 2002; Watkins, 1992). In it, he recommended a three-step model: (1) evaluating individuals' interests, abilities, values, and skills; (2) identifying requirements of various occupations; and (3) matching individuals to suitable occupations via true reasoning. Each step was designed to achieve harmonious results and establish labor efficiency. Over time, this approach has become known as *trait and factor theory.*

Although Parsons intended to address the social problems of his day scientifically (Hartung & Blustein, 2002; Savickas, 1993), by contemporary standards his techniques for career guidance would be considered commonsense pragmatics rather than empirically driven (Aubrey, 1977). Nonetheless, his emphasis on assessment had a major influence on the subsequent development of vocational assessment tools (Watkins, 1992).

A year after Parsons died in 1908, he was honored at the first vocational conference in Boston. This conference initiated steps toward the creation of a guidance counselors' organization (Aubrey, 1977), resulting in the 1913 formation of the National Vocational Guidance Association (NVGA) in Grand Rapids, Michigan (Gibson & Mitchell, 1999; Pope, 2000). In the same year, the U.S. Department of Labor was formed, and it began to gather workforce statistics (Pope, 2000). For the founders of the NVGA, it was a time "of growth and high hopes for vocational guidance" (Pope, 2000, p. 197).

### Simultaneous Efforts

As Parsons was promoting vocational guidance in Boston, a school administrator named Jesse Davis was making the first citywide efforts to incorporate guidance into schools in Grand Rapids, Michigan. Davis began teaching vocational guidance in the schools during one class period per week (Aubrey, 1977; Brewer, 1942). He advocated a study of the self and occupations that was similar to Parsons' approach. Believing that properly minded youth would choose civic-minded careers, Davis focused on the development of moral consciousness, character, and ethical behavior as a means to affect career choices (Aubrey, 1977). He conceptualized vocational guidance in terms of finding one's calling (Gibson & Mitchell, 1999). A progressive who was instrumental in the formation of the NVGA, Davis served as its second president (Pope, 2000).

There were two distinct tracks toward high school graduation: college preparatory and vocational education. John Dewey's (1916) farsighted advocacy for integrating the two tracks was an effort to discourage replication of class distinctions (Blustein et al., 2000) and discrimination based on an individual's job (the discriminatory "occupationism" described by Krumboltz, 1991, p. 310). Today, the two-track system still exists, as does the debate over its logic and consequences (Blustein et al., 2000; Hartung & Blustein, 2002). Failure to interrupt the reproduction of poverty through vocational and educational guidance practices has led Baker (2002) and others (Blustein, 2006; Hawks & Muha, 1991; O'Brien, 2001) to suggest that vocational guidance has drawn away from its social justice goals over time.

Other vocational theorists of the time included Anna Reed, Eli Weaver, and David Hill. Only Hill articulated a need for diversity in education and vocational guidance (Gibson & Mitchell, 1999). Anna Y. Reed, head of a voluntary bureau in Seattle, Washington, engaged in work similar to Parsons', but her emphasis was on the employers and positions rather than the individual, working to match youth to existing jobs (Gibson & Mitchell, 1999). Across the United States, cities and schools were forming departments and courses on vocational guidance, ranging from Reed's Seattle bureau to the efforts of Eli Weaver, who incorporated vocational guidance into the public schools in New York City (Brewer, 1942). By 1910, some form of vocational guidance was being offered in schools in more than 35 cities, and the first university course in the subject was taught in 1911 at Harvard University (Aubrey, 1977). Yet vocational guidance was about to gain even more momentum: World War I, the increased presence of vocational guidance in schools, and drives for empirical testing would increase the awareness and perceived legitimacy of the field.

## Stage 2: Calls for Measurement and Vocational Guidance in the Schools (1914–1929)

World War I involved the mobilization of 4,355,000 U.S. soldiers. Of this group, a vast number died or were wounded, presenting significant economic and vocational challenges for returning veterans and their family members (Strachan, 2003). The war and its aftermath were the dominant contextual influences in this time period. Also during this era, women gained the right to vote, Henry Ford was selling cars for $290, Frank Lloyd Wright was designing homes in California and Japan, the first skyscrapers were under construction, and James Langston Hughes published his first book of poetry.

The postwar period saw a surge in testing in public and private education (Super, 1955). Increases in student diversity and the importance of literacy skills in the workplace translated into more attention to vocational guidance (Pope, 2000). The United States' involvement in World War I, coupled with ongoing, large-scale immigration, fueled legislative action such as the Immigration Act of 1917, the Emergency Quota Act of 1921, and the Immigration Act of 1924 (McLemore et al., 2001). On the basis of the "national origins principle" that promoted the immigration of certain "superior and preferable" groups, legislation was enacted from 1917 to 1924 that established and enforced quota-based restrictions that continued through the Depression and World War II (DeBell, 2001; McLemore et al., 2001).

### Vocational Instruments

The early years of the vocational guidance movement were characterized by debate between advocates for experiential self-assessment (e.g., "What kinds of things are you skilled at doing?") and advocates for empirical testing to increase the reliability and validity of existing assessments (American Psychological Association [APA], 1956; Aubrey, 1977; Super, 1955). Calls for the scientific evaluation of assessment tools began as early as 1911 and were echoed in government (Baker, 2002), paralleling a shift from knowledge via individual experience (i.e., subjectivity) to an emphasis on science and objectivity (Savickas, 1993). Psychometrics (the field concerned with design and analysis of the measurement of human characteristics) took on great significance at this time in developing vocational and intellectual assessments and establishing the credibility of vocational guidance as a profession (Aubrey, 1977; Watkins, 1992). The move toward credibility was also supported at this time by publication of the NVGA's "Principles and Practices of Vocational Guidance" (Pope, 2000). Information about the history of credentialing career counselors can be found in Engels, Minor, Sampson, and Splete (1995).

The debate over experiential self-assessment versus increased empirical testing was ultimately (and perhaps prematurely) resolved by the onset of World War I. The U.S. Army needed to quickly place thousands of men into positions for which they had the skills or aptitude (Super, 1983). Standardized objective tests suitable for group administration, such as the Army Alpha and Army Beta tests, were developed on the basis of pioneering work in intelligence testing by Binet and Terman, among others (Super, 1983). The predecessors of today's Army General Classification Test (the Armed Services Vocational Aptitude Battery) were administered to more than 2 million men during World War I (Baker, 2002; Seligman, 1994; Walsh & Betz, 1995). In 1927, E. K. Strong published the Strong Vocational Interest Blank for Men (Strong, 1927; Walsh & Betz, 1995), a measure that remains one of the most widely used career instruments today (Seligman, 1994). The use of standardized tests for admissions and placement decisions spread into higher education as army psychologists obtained postwar employment in colleges and universities and has similarly continued through the present (Gibson & Mitchell, 1999; Williamson, 1965). Despite controversy over the accuracy and validity of intelligence measurement, including criticism of the use of testing results to justify the inequitable treatment of ethnic minorities and immigrants in the education system (McLemore et al., 2001; Williamson, 1965), widespread use of such testing continued, and the debate regarding its validity continue today (Suzuki, Prevost, & Short, 2008).

## Vocational Legislation

As veterans began returning home wounded in body, mind, or both, the United States faced the challenge of how to provide them with a means of self-support or, if employment was not an option, some other form of assistance. This situation inspired the vocational rehabilitation movement (P. P. Heppner, Casas, Carter, & Stone, 2000). The Vocational Rehabilitation Act of 1918 provided job training for returning veterans. The Veterans' Bureau was created as part of the Veteran's Administration in 1921 and provided vocational rehabilitation and education programming for disabled veterans of World War I (Gibson & Mitchell, 1999). In the civic sector, the Smith-Hughes Act of 1917 provided funding for vocational education and guidance programs in elementary and secondary schools (Pope, 2000), and in 1921 the Workers

Education Bureau and the first Labor Extension Program at the University of California, Berkeley, were initiated. Also by 1921, workmen's compensation (begun in 1910 in New York) had spread to 45 states (Danek et al., 1996).

## Vocational Education and Organization

From 1910 to 1920, vocational guidance became entrenched in the school systems in Boston and Philadelphia, Pennsylvania (1915); Chicago, Illinois (1916); South Bend, Indiana, and Berkeley (1919); and Detroit, Michigan (1920; Brewer, 1942). During this time, the organization of vocational guidance programs remained inconsistent because of the general lack of understanding that the comprehensive experience of vocational guidance included integrating research, practice trials, choices, readjustment, and guidance (Brewer, 1942). As a result, some individuals wanted to focus on placement, and others favored gathering information and safeguarding children's rights (Brewer, 1942).

In industry, corporate schools such as the Carnegie Corporation's American Association for Adult Education continued to operate (Harris, 2000). Organized labor continued trying to meet the needs of workers and employers, walking the fine line between advocating for training versus education and determining how aggressive to make its demands and actions (Brecher, 1997; Harris, 2000). Corporate schools had a similar struggle regarding what level of education to provide for their workers. The American Association for Adult Education's idea that adult education should create informed citizens and "maintain social stability" (Harris, 2000, p. 32) parallels Dewey's (1916) notions as well as contemporary debates about whether education should be used to challenge class distinctions (Blustein et al., 2000).

This period included more organization in the vocational guidance profession; for example, the NVGA produced its first journal, *Vocational Guidance*, in 1915. In 1924, the National Civilian Rehabilitation Association (renamed the National Rehabilitation Association in 1927) convened for the first time (P. P. Heppner et al., 2000). As the use of and reliance on standardized testing increased, attention to contextual factors important in selecting an occupation decreased, as did the counseling dimension of vocational guidance (Aubrey, 1977). Aubrey (1977) noted that this shift paralleled the general reliance on authority and rigidity that was the spirit of the postwar period in the United States. The emphasis on testing increased over the course of the next decade, as Americans looked to vocational guidance to ease the crises created by the mass unemployment of the Great Depression (Super, 1955).

## Stage 3: The Great Depression and the Expectations of a Nation (1929–1939)

During this era, Europe and the United States experienced widespread economic depression. Abysmal working and living conditions as well as civil and social unrest across the world did nothing to abate mass levels of immigration into the United States, although this wave of immigrants did not find the conditions of which they had dreamed. To address the vast unemployment and underemployment that accompanied the Great Depression, the Roosevelt administration's New Deal created public programs for employment through the Civilian Conservation Corps, established in 1933, and the Works Progress Administration, established in 1935 (Pope, 2000).

During this period, unions became much more organized. One of the first to appear was the Knights of Labor. Aspiring to social justice, this union emphasized rallying people around their identities as workers first: "The Order tried to teach the American wage-earner that he was a wage-earner first and a bricklayer, carpenter, miner, shoemaker … a Catholic, Protestant, Jew, white, black, Democrat, Republican after" (Ware, 1964, as quoted in Brecher, 1997, p. 43). Women, too, were subjected to terrible working conditions and participated in organized action (Brecher, 1997). Although the Knights of Labor aspired to goals that were congruent with those of the common worker, not all unions were so fair minded. For example, emerging unions affiliated with the American Federation of Labor "generally included only highly skilled craft workers, excluding—in practice and often by deliberate intent—African Americans, women, many immigrants, and non-craft workers" (Brecher, 1997, p. 69). Thirty years later, craft unions and the construction industry in Philadelphia would catch President Nixon's eye as strongholds against affirmative action and would be targeted in his Philadelphia Order (Brunner, n.d.).

### SIDEBAR 1.2 The Decline of Manual Labor

I'm a dying breed. A laborer. Strictly muscle work … pick it up, put it down, pick it up, put it down. We handle between forty and fifty thousand pounds of steel a day. (Laughs) I think this is hard to believe—from four hundred pounds to three- and four-pound pieces. It's dying.

You can't take pride any more. You remember when a guy could point to a house he built, how many logs he stacked. He built it and he was proud of it. I don't really think I could be proud if a contractor built a home for me. I would be tempted to get in there and kick the carpenter in the ass (laughs), and take the saw away from him. 'Cause I would have to be part of it, you know.

It's hard to take pride in a bridge you're never gonna cross, in a door you're never gonna open. You're mass-producing things and you never see the end result of it. (Terkel, 1974, p. xxxi)

Organized labor was by no means a cure-all for worker problems. Disaffection with the slow and careful progress of the unions and fears of collaboration between union leaders and owners were part of the dynamic of the time (Brecher, 1997). Citizen self-help organizations began to form, such as the Unemployed Council in Chicago and the Unemployed Citizens League in Seattle (Brecher, 1997). Seen in the light of these citizen activities, the New Deal may have been motivated as much by fear of mass uprisings as by humanitarian concerns over job losses (Brecher, 1997; Pope, 2000). Also at this time, the child study movement of the 1930s continued to raise expectations of teacher accountability and responsibility (Gibson & Mitchell, 1999).

## Vocational Legislation

Vocational guidance had established its utility through testing and placement success during World War I. Now the nation looked to vocational guidance to help with the employment crisis of the Depression (Herr & Shahnasarian, 2001; Super, 1955). Vocational education legislation continued with the George-Reed (1929), George-Ellzey (1934), and George-Deen (1936) Acts, each of which continued financial support for vocational guidance works that had begun with the Smith-Hughes Act of 1917 and provided funding for education in agriculture and home economics (Herr & Shahnasarian, 2001; Pope, 2000). The George-Deen Act led to the creation of the Occupational and Informational Guidance Branch of the U.S. Office of Education and provided states with funding for education supervisors and guidance in the schools (Hoyt, 2001). Greater numbers of supervisors and guidance counselors in the schools meant greater entrenchment in the schools. The efforts of the progressives finally came to fruition with the passage of the Fair Labor Standards Act of 1938, which explicitly outlawed exploitative child labor (Pope, 2000). Under the New Deal, the U.S. Department of Labor also developed offices for job placement and guidance for unemployed Americans in 1933 (Gibson & Mitchell, 1999) and developed the U.S. Employment Service, the National Employment Counseling Association, and employee assistance programs. The Social Security Act became law in 1935, providing a guaranteed source of retirement income to all Americans who qualified (Pope, 2000; Seligman, 1994).

## Vocational Instruments and Organization

The psychometrics movement continued during this period through the Minnesota Employment Stabilization Research Institute (Super, 1955; Watkins, 1992). Led by a number of vocational psychology trailblazers including E. G. Williamson, John Darley, and Donald Paterson, the institute responded to the educational and vocational needs of unemployed Americans as it developed psychometric tests (Watkins, 1992). The institute's work sparked interest in public and private vocational guidance centers, and the U.S. Employment Service soon took over to expand the institute's research and practical applications into the larger society (Super, 1955). This expansion strengthened connections among education, psychometrics, social work, and vocational guidance, as well as the organizational power of the NVGA (Super, 1955).

This era was also marked by the publication of E. G. Williamson's (1939) trait and factor manual *How to Counsel Students*, which focused on the importance of testing and measurement in the tradition of Parsons (Gibson & Mitchell, 1999). In 1939, the U.S. Department of Labor produced the *Dictionary of Occupational Titles* (U.S. Department of Labor, 1940), an encyclopedic and highly organized classification system of occupations that provided extensive information about the nature of occupational activities, worker traits, work settings, and educational and training requirements (Sharf, 2002). The *Dictionary of Occupational Titles* provided for the first time a common organizational framework for occupations, which arrived just in time for the United States' involvement in World War II, with the associated masses of people entering (and leaving) the military and the workforce. The *Dictionary of Occupational Titles* was updated continuously until 1991, when it was replaced by the online data base O*NET (http://online.onetcenter.org/).

## Stage 4: World War II, More Testing, and Major Theoretical Influences (1940–1957)

The United States' entry into World War II coincided with the end of the Great Depression. Preparation for and engagement in the war and responding to its aftermath resulted in labor and population booms, increased access to free public education, and entry of middle-class White women into the labor force in greater numbers than ever before (Aubrey, 1977; Seligman, 1994). During the war, most women found jobs in heavy industry, and the government provided some day care and household assistance as incentives (Faludi, 1991). After the war, most of those same women were rushed out of heavy industry. Those who continued working were often forced to accept lower paying, lower status clerical and administrative positions as a result of the political and social realities of the time. Despite this, women's participation in the labor market continued to grow (Faludi, 1991).

Personal freedom and autonomy were dominant national themes (Aubrey, 1977). Counseling psychology emerged as a new specialty in this time period, a combination of vocational guidance, psychometrics, and guidance that emphasized a holistic perception of the individual (Gelso & Fretz, 2001; Super, 1955). The vocational needs of women of color and working-class women continued to be ignored in research and practice literature, even as they continued to be a significant part of the workforce (Seligman, 1994). The power of organized labor continued to grow, and approximately one third of the labor force was unionized in 1955 (DeBell, 2001).

### Vocational Theory

Vocational guidance theory was also changing. The growing dominant culture themes of increased personal autonomy and self-determination were incongruent with the assumptions of unchangeable personal qualities that were the basis for trait and factor guidance (Aubrey, 1977). Theoretical writings on vocational guidance were losing ground to counseling in the professional and practice literature, and during the 1950s vocational guidance began to include a more developmental focus (Aubrey, 1977). Even labels were changing, as *vocational guidance* began to be replaced by terms such as *career counseling* and *career development* (Pope, 2000).

Developmental stage theories from related disciplines sparked changes in vocational guidance theory (Gibson & Mitchell, 1999). For example, Erikson's (1950) *Childhood and Society* articulated eight stages of psychosocial development and focused on the domains of ideology, family, and vocation. His influence can be seen in theories such as those of Ginzberg, Ginsburg, Axelrad, and Herma (1951); Super (1953, 1990); and Gottfredson (1981, 1996). Ginzberg et al. (1951) combined trait and factor theory with Erikson's work to describe decision making as a developmental process involving personal–environmental factors (Sharf, 2002).

Erikson's (1950) work also influenced Donald Super (Sharf, 2002). Super, a vocational psychologist whose work spanned six decades, created an integrative model of vocational development across the life span focused on ideas of self-concept and career maturity (Sharf, 2002; Super, 1990). In later revisions of his model, Super emphasized how identity and vocational self-concept development influenced the adoption of occupational and other life roles (Gibson & Mitchell, 1999). These adaptations paralleled later revisions of Ginzberg et al.'s (1951) model and eventually led to Person × Environment theory (Gibson & Mitchell, 1999).

Around the same time, Maslow (1954) proposed with his landmark hierarchy of needs that human needs were satisfied in a hierarchical progression. This theory influenced Anne Roe (1956, 1957), whose developmental theory of occupational classification and selection included a strong emphasis on parent–child interaction (Sharf, 2002). Roe's system for categorizing occupations was followed by Holland's (1959) theory of personality types and occupational classification. Holland continued working on his model for more than four decades; his theory had a strong trait and factor influence, focusing on matching internal qualities and workplace environment. Later revisions of the model included concepts of consistency, congruence, and differentiation (Holland, 1997).

In addition to developmental approaches, the growth of interpersonal counseling and psychotherapy had an enormous impact on vocational guidance (Aubrey, 1977). Carl Rogers's (1939, 1951) groundbreaking work on genuineness, empathic responses, and unconditional positive regard for clients reflected the national spirit of self-determination, personal autonomy, and empowerment (Aubrey, 1977). His techniques were incorporated into vocational guidance and have in fact been credited with changing its primary focus (Super, 1955). Specifically, the importance of psychometrics and testing were displaced by emphasis on clients' personal experience (Gibson & Mitchell, 1999; Super, 1955). Whereas in the past, career counselors focused on finding solutions to their clients' vocational problems, Rogers's work (alongside that of Erikson, Maslow, and others) led to greater focus on counseling the person and understanding the individual problem as just one aspect of living. In other words, vocational guidance began to be grounded in the context of clients' lives (Super, 1955).

## Vocational Instruments

As with World War I, involvement in World War II prompted the need for assessments to assist in placing large numbers of personnel into appropriate jobs in the armed forces (Super, 1983). After the war, the mental health and vocational needs of returning veterans—and the workers they inadvertently displaced—became evident. The Armed Services Vocational Aptitudes Battery was developed at this time by the U.S. Department of Defense (Sharf, 2002). Major tools also developed during this time included the Army

General Classification Test (replacing the Alpha Test), the General Aptitude Test Battery (Dvorak, 1947), and the *Occupational Outlook Handbook* (Super, 1983; U.S. Department of Labor, 1949). The early stages of development of the Myers-Briggs Type Indicator, a popular personality indicator based on Jung's theory, commenced during this time period. Refinement and revision of the Strong Interest Inventory continued, with separate scales for women added in 1933 (Sharf, 2002; Strong, 1943, 1955; Walsh & Betz, 1995).

## Vocational Legislation and Organization

After World War II, major legislation addressed the needs of veterans. The Servicemen's Readjustment Act of 1944 (known as the GI Bill) allocated funding for college, job training, and home ownership (Faludi, 1999), and the George-Barden Act of the same year provided funding to train school counselors in higher education settings and create Veterans Administration counseling centers (Gibson & Mitchell, 1999; Hoyt, 2001). This funding increased certification and the professionalization of career guidance (Herr & Shahnasarian, 2001) and promoted occupational training and education for veterans. In 1947, the Feingold Report recommended that guidance be applicable to other areas of life beyond education for all students, not just those whose educational careers seemed promising. (Feingold, 1947).

Changes in theory and instruments resulted in political and organizational realignments within vocational guidance as well as changes in the primacy of vocational guidance (Super, 1955). The APA's Division of Counseling and Guidance (Division 17) was established in 1946 by E. G. Williamson and John Darley, but its name changed to the Division of Counseling Psychology in 1952 (APA, 1956; Super, 1955). Many academic departments restructured to increase focus on counseling psychology doctoral programs. More intensive training of counseling psychologists led to supplantation of vocational counselors in some circles (Super, 1955). For example, in 1952 the Veterans Administration replaced the title of *vocational counselor* with *counseling psychologist* (APA, 1956).

In part because of a desire to project a stronger identity, the NVGA merged with the Guidance Supervisors and Counselor Trainers and the American College Personnel Association to form the American Personnel and Guidance Association (APGA) in 1952 (Super, 1955). Unfortunately, consolidation into APGA resulted in a more than 50% decline in membership in the NVGA (Pope, 2000), perhaps because of the heterogeneous membership of NVGA, with many members "whose primary affiliation is elsewhere" (Super, 1955, p. 6). At the international level, 1951 saw the formation of the International Association for Vocational Education and Guidance, a nongovernmental organization committed to the development of the profession and provision of high-quality and appropriate guidance services worldwide.

Even as vocational guidance struggled to maintain its identity within psychology, the field continued to grow, with greater emphasis on training, educational requirements, and interdisciplinary influences. And the looming threat of war with the Soviet Union began to shape developments in important ways.

## Stage 5: 1958–1970—The Space Race, Civil Rights, and the Great Society

The launching of Sputnik I by the Soviet Union demonstrated technological advances that caught the immediate attention of the United States. Concerned that the country was lagging behind in science and technology, the United States initiated a series of legislative actions intended to increase the quality and quantity of U.S. scientists (Borow, 1974). The National Defense Education Act (NDEA) of 1958 provided mass funding for vocational guidance in the schools, in the hope that new school personnel would greatly increase the number of talented young men and women pursuing higher education in math and science (Pope, 2000). After President Kennedy's assassination, President Lyndon Johnson carried forward his vision by initiating the War on Poverty and the creation of the Great Society.

This period also increased the emphasis on finding meaning in work, because "many young people wanted jobs that ... would allow them to change the world for the better" (Pope, 2000, p. 200). Striving for meaning in work developed alongside resurging commitment to social justice. The 1960s saw a rising national awareness of the major social, educational, and economic inequalities that existed across ethnic, racial, and gendered domains; this awareness was accompanied by growing mistrust of and unease with major U.S. institutions, including the government and the military (Dixon, 1987; Borow, 1974). Throughout the decade, various civil rights movements emerged, growing from an original focus on African Americans to a focus on a broader sector of people challenged by inequity and injustice, including gays and lesbians, people with disabilities, other racial and ethnic minorities, and women (P. P. Heppner et al., 2000). Mass action for these causes ranged from sit-ins to mass riots (Borow, 1974). In addition, the conflict in Southeast Asia and very high levels of unemployment in the United States contributed to mass action and civil unrest (Pope, 2000). It did not take long for the government to connect civil unrest with increasing number of out-of-school youth and a lack of employment opportunities (Herr, 1974).

### SIDEBAR 1.3    Think About This: Affirmative Action

President Lyndon Johnson's Great Society initiative sought to end poverty and racial injustices and to address other social justice problems of that time. In the late 1960s, he issued Executive Order 11246 (affirmative action), which required employers to hire without regard to race, ethnicity, religion, gender, or nationality. Given a pool of candidates with comparable qualifications for a position, affirmative action requires that employers hire a candidate from a group (i.e., women, racial or ethnic minorities) that has been underrepresented in the workplace. The policy was created to help eliminate past and present discrimination. Do you agree with the affirmative action policy? Why or why not? Do you believe it has changed the landscape of work opportunity in the United States? In what ways? Which view do you believe most Americans have on this policy?

### Vocational Theory

During the 1960s, contributors to APGA literature voiced sentiments reminiscent of the 1947 Feingold report by advocating guidance for every student rather than limiting focus to college-bound students (Aubrey, 1977). The developmental focus continued in the counseling and guidance literature as well, including Wrenn's (1962) *The Counselor in a Changing World;* Tiedeman and O'Hara's (1963) model of self-development, cognitive development, and career decision making; and Lofquist and Dawis's (1969) trait- and factor-based work adjustment theory (Gibson & Mitchell, 1999). This decade was the first in which attention was paid to the career development of people with disabilities who were not veterans (Szymanski, Hershenson, Enright, & Ettinger, 1996). Simultaneously, researchers began to examine populations other than men for the first time; Terman and Oden (1959) published a landmark study of a sample of gifted students, finding that although gifted male students largely grew up to become physicists, physicians, and lawyers, the majority of gifted female students became housewives and secretaries.

## Vocational Instruments

Instruments that drew heavily on personality and development continued to develop. The Myers-Briggs Type Indicator (Myers, 1962) test was published in 1962, and the Kuder Occupational Interest Scale followed in 1966 (Sharf, 2002; Walsh & Betz, 1995). In the late 1960s, career counselors began using computer technology, beginning with the System of Interactive Guidance and Information and the Computerized Vocation Information System (Harris-Bowlsbey, 2003).

## Vocational Legislation and Organization

As with the social climate during the Roosevelt administration, civil disorder and crises likely prompted the Kennedy and Johnson administrations to use vocational legislation to respond to great forces for social change (Herr, 1974; Pope, 2000). Legislation during this stage was significant in three important ways: (1) Minority groups and women began to be directly involved in vocational legislation (e.g., the emergence of affirmative action); (2) contextual factors such as educational, social, and cultural barriers to vocational success began to be overtly considered; and (3) vocational guidance became even more integral to legislation aimed at reducing economic or occupational woes. The years from 1960 to 1979 have been described as a "boom for counseling" (Pope, 2000, p. 208). Others agreed:

> To a degree unparalleled in … American history, vocational guidance and counseling became identified consistently in federal or in state legislation as a vital part of the manpower policies designed to respond to human needs in the occupational and economic arenas. (Herr, 1974, p. 33)

The Area Redevelopment Act of 1961 and the Manpower Development and Training Act of 1962 focused on attracting jobs to impoverished areas, followed by provisions for worker assistance and job skills (Herr, 1974). Beginning with the Manpower Development and Training Act, legislative efforts acknowledged the existence of social and political barriers to occupational success and involved active recruitment strategies (Herr, 1974). The Vocational Education Act of 1963 had as its goal the improvement of the kinds and quality of vocational education and training available to all students and directed funds toward retraining adult workers displaced by technological change (Pope, 2000). In 1963, the Community Mental Health Centers Act initiated rehabilitative services for people with mental illness (Gibson & Mitchell, 1999).

Title VII of the Civil Rights Act of 1964 outlawed discrimination in employment on the basis of race, color, religion, sex, and national origin. It applied to direct treatment in the workplace and to indirect discrimination such as hiring or workplace practices or procedures (Peterson & Gonzales, 2000). In 1965, President Lyndon Johnson signed into law Executive Order 11246, which enforced equality in hiring and employment of people of color, or affirmative action. Just before enacting the order, President Johnson noted in a commencement address at Howard University in Washington, DC, that

> you do not wipe away the scars of centuries by … taking a man who for years has been hobbled by chains, liberate him, bring him to the starting line of a race, saying, "you are free to compete with all the others," and still justly believe you have been completely fair … This is the next and more profound stage of the battle for civil rights. (Brunner, n.d.)

This order was amended 2 years later to include discrimination on the basis of gender (Brunner, n.d.), and discrimination on the basis of age was similarly protected against in the 1967 Age Discrimination in Employment Act.

In 1965, legislation increased funding for the Vocational Rehabilitation Administration, acknowledging the influence of social and environmental factors on vocational development and opportunity (Herr, 1974). Similarly, the Economic Opportunity Act of 1964 created a wealth of programs, including Job Corps, Neighborhood Youth Corps, VISTA, Youth Opportunity Centers, the U.S. Employment Service Human Resource Development Program, Head Start, and New Careers Program (Herr, 1974; Pope, 2000). The Social Security Act amendments of 1967 contained a Work Incentive Program for education and training of and support for welfare recipients to find work, and the Elementary and Secondary Education Act of 1969 provided aid for children in impoverished areas (Herr, 1974; Pope, 2000).

### National Defense Education Act of 1958

The single greatest influence on the profession and practice of career guidance in this era was the NDEA (Hoyt, 2001). The NDEA funded and trained educators and counselors to identify and encourage young people to enroll in science and math classes (Pope, 2000). In addition, money from the act affected accreditation and licensure consolidations for school counselors (Gibson & Mitchell, 1999). Combined with other legislation, the NDEA sparked a 400% increase in the number of school counselors from 1958 to 1967 (Aubrey, 1977), normalized the presence of guidance counselors and testing in the schools (Gibson & Mitchell, 1999), and funded an entire generation of counselors, counselor educators, and counseling psychologists.

The increased visibility and prominence of vocational counseling in everyday life, including school, community, and public and private organizations, led the U.S. Employment Service to develop the subprofession of career counseling (Hoyt, 2001). At the same time, school counselors formed a Guidance Division of the American Vocational Association, the NVGA celebrated its 50th anniversary as an organization, and its membership began to recover from the losses sustained in the merger with APGA (Hoyt, 2001; Pope, 2000). In 1964, the American School Counselor Association clarified the roles and functions of school counselors in its Policy for Secondary School Counselors (Gibson & Mitchell, 1999).

Aubrey (1977) suggested that the consolidation and expansion of vocational guidance during this period led to more opportunities and possibilities than ever before. This growth in turn led to a critical need for self-examination and clarity regarding future directions, such as the nature of clientele served and methodologies used. Such activities continued into the next stage.

### SIDEBAR 1.4   Think About This: NDEA Then and Now

The National Defense Education Act (NDEA) was signed into law on September 2, 1958, and provided funding to private and public institutions at all levels of education. The NDEA was also the impetus for an increase in the number of students attending college, particularly in math, science, and counseling and guidance-related careers. What do you think was the impact of the NDEA on U.S. society? How did the passage of the NDEA fit with the other social realities (e.g., hiring discrimination, limited job opportunities for women) of the time? What are some historical antecedents of this law?

## Stage 6: The Boom Years Continue

The 1970s witnessed the decline of President Johnson's Great Society. The disaffection toward and mistrust of the government of the 1960s continued during Watergate and the end of the Vietnam War. Rising unemployment and an unstable economy contributed to a growing sense of apathy toward the government and its institutions (Aubrey, 1977). Vocational services remained essential elements of social change legislation (and funding) in career development and education for people at multiple levels of the educational system (Blustein et al., 2000). Vocational counselors and theorists began making efforts to focus on the needs of women, ethnic minorities, and people with disabilities, although research on these and other dimensions of diversity would not receive significant attention until the 1980s and 1990s.

### Vocational Theory

Bandura's (1969) introduction of social learning theory in his *Principles of Behavior Modification* contained promising new directions for vocational counseling (Sharf, 2002). His subsequent work on constructs such as self-efficacy expectations (e.g., Bandura, 1977, 1986) prompted research and theoretical developments that eventually became the foundation for social cognitive career theory (Hackett & Betz, 1981; R. W. Lent, Brown, & Hackett, 1994). Krumboltz (e.g., 1979, 1996; Krumboltz, Mitchell, & Gelatt, 1975) applied social learning theory to career counseling and career decision making. Krumboltz conceptualized learning as an interaction between genetic and environmental factors, integrating aspects of Bandura's work with other theories that attended to the role of the environment.

Stage theories of career development of the 1940s through 1970s progressed to broader conceptualizations of careers across the life span (Gibson & Mitchell, 1999), such as Gysbers and Moore's (1973) life career development theory that focused on interactions of all aspects of an individual's life (Gysbers, Heppner, & Johnston, 2003). This theory fused environmental and developmental concepts, suggesting that counselors conceptualize career and work as the intersection of the roles, life stages, personal factors, individual differences (e.g., race, ethnicity, socioeconomic status, sexual orientation), settings, and events that occur over a person's lifetime (Gysbers, Heppner, & Johnston, 2003). Life career development theory became even more inclusive with its 1992 revision, incorporating larger societal-level factors (Gysbers, Heppner, & Johnston, 2003). At the end of the decade, Herr (1979) published *Guidance and Counseling in the Schools*.

## Vocational Instruments

Development of computer-based assessments continued with SIGI Plus, DISCOVER, the Career Information System, and the Guidance Information System (Harris-Bowlsbey, 2003). The profession began to critique and test its assessments for cross-cultural relevance, addressing issues such as comfort with test items, generalizability concerns, data interpretation and language problems, and cultural differences in disclosing information (Betz & Fitzgerald, 1995; Fouad, 1993). Theories of vocational behavior and development were critiqued for failing to address differences across domains of identity such as gender, sexual orientation, race or ethnicity, or level of physical ability (Fouad, 1993), and researchers began to pay attention to the vocational development and concerns of racial and ethnic minorities and of women (Fitzgerald & Betz, 1983; Smith, 1983).

## Vocational Legislation and Organization

In 1971, the U.S. Office of Education dedicated $9 million to developing models of career education (Gibson & Mitchell, 1999). Career education incorporated career development (i.e., decision making and planning) and occupational skill-based training into the regular school curriculum, making it a necessary part of everyday life for all students—both college and work bound (Blustein et al., 2000). This funding ushered in a new age of popularity for vocational counseling ranging from 1974 to 1982: "In less than a decade, more than ten major national associations endorsed career education, hundreds of publications on career education were published and distributed, and an astounding array of proponents and interpreters of the career education concept emerged" (Gibson & Mitchell, 1999, p. 312). During this period, interest in career counseling grew significantly among school counselors.

Emerging vocational legislation was more inclusive of women and people with disabilities. In 1974, the Women's Educational Equity Act provided grant funding for girls and women, and in 1972 the 1965 Higher Education Act was amended and updated to ensure that equality in community services and educational opportunities would continue (Hansen, 2003; Herr, 1974). These amendments also created the U.S. Office of Education Bureau of Occupation and Adult Education and extended funding for the Vocational Education Act Amendments of 1968 (Herr, 1974). The Equal Employment Opportunities Commission, which had been criticized for its lack of enforcement authority, was granted expanded legislative authority and joined together with the Departments of Justice and Labor, the Civil Service Commission, and the Civil Rights Commission to form the Equal Employment Opportunity Coordinating Council (U.S. Equal Employment Opportunities Commission, 2004). During this period, legislation also addressed rights for individuals with disabilities, including the 1973 Rehabilitation Act for people with disabilities and the Education for All Handicapped Children Act of 1977 (Danek et al., 1996).

During this decade, vocational legislation continued to focus on job placement (vs. career counseling), emphasizing return to work with minimum loss of wages (Danek et al., 1996). The military influence on vocational counseling continued with the Vietnam Veterans Readjustment Assistance Act of 1974, which extended services to veterans with minor injuries; the major focus of this act and its ensuing amendments has been to provide veterans with skills to gain stable employment (Danek et al., 1996). In 1976, amendments to the Vocational Education Acts of 1963 and 1968 created the National and State Occupational Information Coordinating Committees. These committees consolidated service delivery across federal and state agencies, increasing the availability of information about the world of work (Pope, 2000).

In the 1970s, guidance counselors also began to explore public perceptions of their functions and responsibilities, such as the direction, success, and occupational choices of their students and their credibility as a profession (Gibson & Mitchell, 1999). This examination continued during the 1970s and 1980s and led to more accountability, data-based programs, and objective assessments (Gibson & Mitchell, 1999). It also led to proposed competencies for the profession. Pope and Russell (2001) noted that a number of position papers from 1973–1980 preceded these competencies, including the AVA-NVGA Position Paper on Career Development; the APGA Position Paper on Career Guidance; the ACES Position Paper on Counselor Preparation for Career Development, the AIR Report on Competencies Needed for Planning, Supporting, Implementing, Operating, and Evaluating Career Guidance Programs; and the APGA Career Education Project. This list in turn led to the first specialty recognized by the National Board of Certified Counselors (Engels et al., 1995; Pope, 2000) and in 1983 to the first National Career Counselor Exam (Pope, 2000). Yet even as the field continued to respond to demands for accountability and credibility, an infrastructure that had traditionally excluded groups of people was struggling to come to terms with diverse clients and members.

## Stage 7: Inclusion of a Wider Culture (1980–1989)

Growing recognition of the diverse composition of U.S. society continued into the 1980s amid the second largest wave of immigration in U.S. history (DeBell, 2001). Legislation, grants, research, new theories, and critiques and adaptations of existing theories increasingly included attention to the needs of diverse populations (P. P. Heppner et al., 2000). At the same time, the field was still overwhelmingly made up of and governed by White counselors and psychologists.

Decreasing power of organized labor occurred alongside increased need for technological skills and contract labor, both of which were beginning to emerge as transforming factors (Brecher, 1997; DeBell, 2001). High unemployment rates, calls for educational reform in standards and teaching, and increased focus on schools as the arena for improvement (Blustein et al., 2000) revived Parsons-era expectations placed on teachers and schools. Socially, this stage was marked by a backlash against changes in social norms that accompanied women's entry into the workplace in greater numbers than ever before (Faludi, 1991).

### Vocational Theory

Vocational theorists increased attention to family influences and the growing diversity of the workforce, moving in the direction of more holistic models. Hackett and Betz (1981) applied Bandura's self-efficacy construct (Bandura, 1977) to understanding women's and men's math-related confidence and performance, and Mitchell and Krumboltz (1984) applied self-efficacy to career decision making (Shoffner, 2006). Isaacson (1985) described learning theory as the basis for vocational identity, focusing on genetic and environmental factors (Gibson & Mitchell, 1999). Miller-Tiedeman and Tiedeman (1990) developed life career theory, a holistic integration of life and career decision-making development (Peterson & Gonzales, 2000).

Critiques that existing theories did not address the vocational development of individuals with disabilities began to emerge (Szymanski et al., 1996). Publications addressing the needs of women and minorities appeared in greater number, such as Betz and Fitzgerald's (1987) *Career Psychology of Women*. Gottfredson's (1981) theory of circumscription and compromise combined developmental progression with self-concept and the influence of gender role and social class issues. Later scholars (e.g., Bowman, 1995) applied this theory to ethnic minority women. Astin (1984) presented a model of career choices and behavior that included interaction among psychological, cultural, and environmental factors. In her model, Astin incorporated constructs of motivation, expectations, and sex role socialization with notions of the real and perceived structure of opportunity. Farmer (1985) examined the career choices and aspirations of girls and ethnic minority adolescents. Brown-Collins and Sussewell (1986) created the developmental multiple self-referent model for African American women, later adapted by Gainor and Forrest (1991) to conceptualize the different types of self-identity that may influence or arise from the workplace experiences of African American women.

## Vocational Legislation and Organization

The legislative focus on providing youth with vocational training continued. The Job Training Partnership Act (JPTA) of 1982 established local, state, and federal agencies to foster collaboration among schools, employers, and communities to facilitate youth's entry into the workforce (Gibson & Mitchell, 1999). Like its predecessor, the Manpower Development and Training Act of 1962, the Job Training Partnership Act focused on job training as a means to overcome economic and social barriers to employment (Danek et al., 1996). The Comprehensive Employment and Training Act of 1973 was continued by the Job Training Partnership Act of 1982; both acts provided federal assistance to state and local governments to develop job training for lower income youth and adults (Gibson & Mitchell, 1999). In 1984, the Carl D. Perkins Vocational Education Act supported the development of programs that would facilitate self-assessment, career planning and decision making, and job skills for underserved populations (Gibson & Mitchell, 1999). Efforts to connect homeless youth with schools were supported via the Homeless Assistance Act of 1987 (Gibson & Mitchell, 1999), and support for education and training in high-tech occupations followed in 1988 with the Omnibus Trade and Competitiveness Act (Pope, 2000). During this stage, the Department of Labor and the National Occupational Information Coordinating Committee awarded money to develop career and guidance information systems, which led to computer-based career services and guidance systems (Gibson & Mitchell, 1999).

This new golden age of career counseling was accompanied by a number of important conferences (Gibson & Mitchell, 1999), including the 20/20 Conference: Building Strong School Counseling Programs in 1987, the National Career Development Association (NCDA) Diamond Jubilee Conference, and the first conference of the Association for Counselor Education and Supervision in 1988. This last conference established task forces to study national world of work concerns (Gibson & Mitchell, 1999). Finally, in 1984 the NVGA officially changed its name to the NCDA (Pope, 2000).

## Stage 8: 1990–2005

Steady declines in wages for skilled and semiskilled labor that began in the 1970s continued into the 1990s, precipitating increased attention to the school-to-work transition. Presidential candidate Bill Clinton included these issues in his 1992 campaign agenda (Blustein et al., 2000). As workplace environments changed and changes in the very nature of work began to accelerate, different skills were needed (Savickas, 1993). Discrimination and sexual harassment in the workplace also received national media attention, as both the appointment of Justice Clarence Thomas to the U.S. Supreme Court and the U.S. Navy's Tailhook Convention in 1991 were marked by allegations of sexual harassment. These controversies highlighted the seriousness, prevalence, and need for prevention and protective measures for sexual harassment in the workplace. The NCDA and the National Occupational Information Coordinating Committee funded Gallup Organization studies about attitudes toward work and schools. This period saw a continued focus on women and minorities, the rise of career services available in different forms (e.g., Internet), and international expansion of theory and service delivery (Pope, 2000).

### SIDEBAR 1.5  Think About This: Sexual Harassment in the Workplace

Workplace environments changed drastically in the early 1990s. Discrimination and sexual harassment issues received national attention. In 1998, the U.S. Supreme Court increased employer liability for sexual harassment of their employees. In a study released in 2010, the Society for Human Resource Management reported that 62% of companies offered sexual harassment prevention training programs, and 97% had a written sexual harassment policy (Sexual Harassment Support, 2010). Despite these changes, researchers have estimated that only between 5% and 15% of harassed women formally report harassment to their employers or employment agencies (Sexual Harassment Support, 2010). What are some reasons for these persistently low rates? Also, according to a recent sociological study, women in supervisory positions are the most likely targets of sexual harassment (McLaughlin, Uggen, & Blackstone, 2009). Why do you think this is the case? What other forms of workplace harassment do you think might be occurring that are similarly underreported?

## Vocational Theory

Research on women and career development continued during this period as vocational counseling continued to attend to the effects of discrimination on work behavior, performance, and satisfaction (P. P. Heppner et al., 2000). During the 1990s, the first vocational texts for members of ethnic minority groups were published (e.g., Fouad & Bingham, 1995; Leong, 1995). Continued lack of inclusivity in U.S. career counseling (Betz & Fitzgerald, 1995) inspired the modification and development of theories, including Blustein and Spengler's (1995) domain-sensitive approach and Gysbers and Moore's (1973) life career development theory (Gysbers, Heppner, & Johnston, 2003). R. W. Lent et al. (1994) applied Bandura's social cognitive theory (Bandera, 1986) to the development of career-related interests, goals, and attainments in a model that incorporates contextual factors such as supports and barriers.

The validity of contemporary career development theories for ethnic minorities; gay, lesbian, and bisexual people; and people from many other groups was continuously challenged (Chung, 1995). Advocates suggested a need for theory that integrated aspects of racial and ethnic identity development, self-identity development, and career development (e.g., Bowman, 1995; Osipow & Littlejohn, 1995). Osipow and Littlejohn (1995) stated that changes in the workplace were dramatic enough to require modification of vocational theories even for the White male population on which they had been based. These authors suggested that creating an inclusive environment and valuing multicultural contributions would be more productive than promoting assimilation. Efforts toward contextual understanding of career choice and development continued with a special issue of the *Career Development Quarterly* in which authors addressed socioeconomic status (E. B. Lent, 2001), sexual orientation (Chung, 2001), and sociopolitical context and issues of power (Santos, Ferreira, & Chaves, 2001). The *Journal of Career Assessment* had special issues on career assessment issues of women of color and White women (1997). A special issue in 2000 focused on Internet counseling in the next millennium (2000). Betz's (2008) review of the career development and vocational behavior literature noted advances in research on Holland's theory, the theory of work adjustment, and social cognitive career theory. The work of Tracey and colleagues (e.g., Darcy & Tracey, 2007) suggested that Holland's six themes (realistic, investigative, artistic, social, enterprising, and conventional [RIASEC]) may be better described as a circular (rather than hexagonal) pattern across genders, ethnicities, and nationalities. Moreover, researchers found the RIASEC structure to be more fitting for participants in Western than non-Western cultures (Yang, Stokes, & Hui, 2005). With respect to the theory of work adjustment, correspondence between people and their work environment was related to satisfaction with work among samples of African American workers (Lyons & O'Brien, 2006) and gay and lesbian workers (Lyons, Brenner, & Fassinger, 2005), suggesting cross-cultural applicability to the theory of work adjustment's major hypothesis (Lyons et al., 2005). Finally, social cognitive career theory continues to generate a considerable amount of research, including examination of the model in different contexts and with more diverse samples. For instance, R. W. Lent et al. (2005) found that students at historically Black universities reported higher self-efficacy and outcome expectations than did those at predominately White universities (Betz, 2008).

Over time, vocational research has focused more on understanding career development and decision making than on specific intervention techniques, resulting in gaps between theory and practice that have affected legislative efforts (Niles, 2003; Whiston, 2003). In this stage, researchers began to devote increased attention to career counseling outcome research (Brown & Krane, 2000; Brown & McPartland, 2005; Whiston, Brecheisen, & Stephens, 2003). In their meta-analysis of career counseling interventions, Brown and Krane (2000) found that career interventions likely to produce the greatest effects include (a) written exercises, (b) individualized assessment interpretation and feedback, (c) current information on the world of work, (d) models of effective strategies, and (e) opportunities to build support. Despite this important contribution to the field, Whiston et al. (2003) contended, "Career counselors do not know what works with which clients under what conditions" (p. 37). Women and minorities continued to be underrepresented in career counseling research (Savickas, 2003; Tang, 2003; Whiston et al., 2003), making it difficult to apply research findings to the work world.

## Vocational Legislation and Organization

The Americans With Disabilities Act of 1990 represented comprehensive civil rights legislation for individuals with disabilities (Danek et al., 1996).

This bill reworked the Rehabilitation Act of 1973 and made federal funding available for private, public, and nonprofit agencies to teach employment skills and end discrimination (Danek et al., 1996). The Higher Education Act, the Elementary and Secondary Education Act, and the Carl D. Perkins Act were all reauthorized in 1990 (Pope, 2000), and the 1975 Education for All Handicapped Children Act was restructured into the Individuals With Disabilities Education Act of 1990, to include attention to the school-to-work transition (Danek et al., 1996).

At this time, the U.S. Task Force on Education issued a call for reform targeting transferable skills and lifetime learning habits, which led to the creation of the Secretary's Commission for Achieving Necessary Skills to identify competencies and foundations of learning for preparing youth for competition in a global market (Blustein et al., 2000). The School-to-Work Opportunity Act of 1994 and the Workforce Investment Act of 1998 also provided opportunities to facilitate students' movement from school to work (Herr & Niles, 1998; Pope, 2000). The latter act funded partnerships for students, parents, schools, government agencies and local businesses (Blustein et al., 2000), whereas the School-to-Work Opportunity Act focused on career counseling and exploration in schools to provide students with accurate and realistic knowledge and skills (Gibson & Mitchell, 1999). The School-to-Work Opportunity Act represented an alliance between the U.S. Departments of Labor and Education (Gibson & Mitchell, 1999) and prefaced the Personal Responsibility and Work Opportunity Reconciliation Act of 1996. This act affected government assistance by restructuring work, establishing time limits for receiving government aid, and mandating that welfare recipients find jobs.

The Personal Responsibility and Work Opportunity Reconciliation Act replaced the Aid to Families With Dependent Children program and the Job Opportunities and Basic Skills Training program (Peterson & Gonzales, 2000). It included the Workforce Initiative and the Welfare to Work programs, the latter of which set a 5-year limit on the Temporary Assistance to Needy Families program (Pope, 2000). The Workforce Initiative program focused on finding work for and training individuals on the job, regardless of the match. This approach had dramatic implications for career counselors because it was a complete departure from the foundations on which the profession was based (Blustein et al., 2000; Pope, 2000). The negative impact of these acts on families on welfare, and those affected by domestic violence, have been documented (Anelauskas, 1999; Faludi, 1991; Kaplan, 1997).

In 1996, the APA Division of Counseling Psychology's Special Interest Group on Vocational Behavior and Career Intervention became the Society for Vocational Psychology (P. P. Heppner et al., 2000). In 1995, the NCDA adopted a comprehensive nondiscriminatory policy to include sexual orientation as a protected category, and in the same year the NCDA changed the composition of its board of directors to include more applied workers (Pope, 2000). The NCDA followed in 1997 with competency and performance indicators and ethical standards for career counseling on the Internet (Hansen,

2003; NCDA, 1997; Niles, 2003). In 1998, the NCDA and the Association for Counselor Education and Supervision formed a joint Commission on Preparing Counselors for Career Development in the 21st Century (Hansen, 2003; Savickas, 2003). Although many of the described trends in the world of work developed over time, these changes, along with increasingly vast amounts of available information, have strained career counseling services and models, leading to new challenges for workers and career counselors in the next millennium.

## Stage 9: The Present

The changes wrought in the U.S. economy and the world of work by the Information Age have been as profound as those wrought by the Industrial Revolution of the late 18th through 19th centuries, calling to mind the cultural context that prompted the emergence of career counseling (Blustein, 2006; DeBell, 2001; Savickas, 2003). Hansen (2003) noted that the terrorist attacks of September 11, 2001; increasing exposure of corporate corruption; random workplace violence; the passage of the PATRIOT Act; economic recession; and lack of universal health care have all resulted in demoralization and a decreased sense of security among U.S. workers, along with depression, anxiety, and existential crises. Globalization has rendered some jobs obsolete, decreased the security and longevity of others, and increased the importance of adaptability, creative activities, teamwork, technological aptitude, and ability to work quickly without traditional boundaries (Fouad & Kantamneni, 2008; Gysbers, Heppner, & Johnston, 2003; Harris, 2000; Pulakos, Arad, Donovan, & Plamondon, 2000). International expansion of the world of work has been accompanied by issues related to cross-cultural interactions, including acculturation stress, culture shock, and differences in work norms and expectations (Herr, 2003; Niles, 2003; Parmer & Rush, 2003). Around the world, career counselors may need to support clients with international agendas as well as consult colleagues from other countries for service delivery, research, and related issues (Hansen, 2003; Yakushko, Watson, Ngaruiya, & Gonzalez, 2008). The U.S. recession and forecasts for a slow recovery have increased the sense of urgency to respond to the career development needs of youth, adults, and older workers. Nearly 32,000 U.S. military personnel have been wounded in Iraq alone since 2003 (British Broadcasting Corporation, 2010), many of whom are and will be seeking employment. Individualist models are being supplanted by interdependent approaches that include attention to market forces, an international economy, and lower agency on the part of the individual (Savickas, 1993; 2000).

Downsizing, specialization and outsourcing, valuing skill and performance over loyalty and tenure, and increased use of temporary labor have led to fewer benefits for a majority of workers (Gysbers, Heppner, & Johnston, 2003; Harris, 2000). At the same time, increasing access to and use of technologies are changing the landscape of work and posing new challenges and opportunities for career counselors (Bloch, 2006; Harris-Bowlesby, 2003;

Whiston, 2003; and Chapter 7). Internet job search sites are significant aspects of the vocational world, providing assistance to those searching for employment. Sites such as Hotjobs.com (http://www.hotjobs.com) and Monster.com (http://www.monster.com) are meant to streamline job search efforts, offering information about job openings, résumé posting services, tips for writing résumés, and other career advice. Although individuals are not required to pay a fee for using these services, registration is required (Bloch, 2006). A special issue of the *Journal of Career Assessment* (2000) was dedicated to career assessment via the Internet.

---

**SIDEBAR 1.6   Think About This: Predicting the Future of Career Counseling**

The Information Age has brought great change to the world of work. Recent developments include the online placement of occupational information systems such as O*NET and the *Occupational Outlook Handbook* (U.S. Department of Labor, 1949), as well as Internet job search sites. Monster.com, for instance, has revolutionized the way in which some people search for jobs. What are the pros and cons of such advancements? How do you think technology will continue to change the field of career counseling over the next 10 years? How do you think that social networking sites are influencing job searches today?

---

## Vocational Instruments

One contemporary focus in vocational assessment is the validation of measures across cultural groups, investigating whether the constructs assessed are equivalent between populations that differ with respect to ethnicity or national setting (e.g., Miller, Roy, Brown, Thomas, & McDaniel, 2009; Nota, Heppner, Soresi, & Heppner, 2009). In addition, attention has focused on measurement of social class (Fouad & Fitzpatrick, 2009; Thompson & Subich, 2006, 2007). Career counselors have also begun to explore the influence of poverty and social class on world-of-work concerns (Blustein, 2006), and tools need to be developed to explore the complex role of social class in shaping a person's life trajectory and both perceived and actual structures of opportunity.

## Vocational Theory

Career theorists and practitioners are striving to meet these challenges. Vocational psychology and career counseling scholars have emphasized the importance of exploring the meaning of work in people's lives (Blustein, 2006, 2008; Fouad, 2007). Savickas (2000, 2005) proposed a constructivist approach to career development that is responsive to the increasingly multicultural and globalized world of work. On the basis of an adaptation and expansion of Super's developmental theory (1990), Savickas (2005) presented a constructivist career theory with 16 theoretical propositions. Griffin and Hesketh (2005) proposed updates to the theory of work adjustment to facilitate worker adaptation and adjustment to these contemporary workplace demands. Goodman, Schlossberg, and Anderson (2006) focused on theory and practice for career counseling with adults in transition. Recently, John Krumboltz (2009) proposed happenstance theory, advocating that career counselors refrain from emphasizing career decisions in a constantly changing world-of-work landscape and focus instead on encouraging clients to engage in activities that reward interests and foster skill development, to seek opportunities for further exploration and learning, and to take advantage of happenstance events that can lead to work-related opportunities (Krumboltz, 2009).

Career theorists have also attended to the importance of culture and cultural diversity. Fouad and Kantamneni (2008) proposed an integrative career development model of vocational development that incorporates a rich variety of contextual and identity factors, and Blustein et al. (2005) proposed an emancipatory communitarian approach to vocational theory development that attends to social inequities, structural injustice, and the working lives of marginalized people. The literature has seen a resurgence in research on links among career counseling, advocacy, and social justice, such as integrating the competencies for advocacy and multicultural counseling with career counseling (Ali, Liu, Mahmood, & Arguello, 2008; Toporek, 2005), becoming involved with legislative action (Fassinger, 2001), or combining teaching, research, and service delivery to high-risk populations (Blustein, 2001; Chronister & McWhirter, 2003; O'Brien, 2001).

A cultural formulation approach to career counseling proposed by Leong, Hardin, and Gupta (2010), as described by Leong (2010), incorporates into career assessment and counseling these elements: discussion of cultural identity, cultural conception of career problems, cultural context and psychosocial environment, and cultural dynamics in the career counselor–client relationship. In a special issue of the *Journal of Career Development* (Leong, 2010), the cultural formulation approach was applied to working with Asian American, Latino, American Indian, and Black clients, as well as international students. Recent texts on career counseling have focused on women (Walsh & Heppner, 2006) and poor and working-class individuals (Blustein, 2006). Attention to the role of social class is increasing (Diemer & Ali, 2009; Fouad & Fitzpatrick, 2009). Changes in the workplace have contributed to changing social definitions and expectations associated with gender roles (M. J. Heppner & Fu, 2011; Park, Smith, & Correll, 2010). Increases in equality in the workplace have led to more role sharing in households as well as changes in family composition and work–family conflicts (Gilbert & Rader, 2008; Higgins, Duxbury, & Lyons, 2010; Perrone, 2009; Perrone, Wright, & Jackson, 2009; Schultheiss, 2009). Conceptions of mothering (Schultheiss, 2009) and fathering (M. J. Heppner & Heppner, 2009) as work that matters have received increasing attention. Career counselors are attempting to address the concerns of individuals who are working longer, those interrupting their careers for child rearing, and those dealing with unemployment, underemployment, and midlife career changes (Bobek & Robbins, 2005). Vocational and career professionals are challenged to continue efforts to make career education and counseling services beneficial to specific populations, such as people with HIV/AIDS (Parmer & Rush, 2003), immigrants (Yakushko et al., 2008), and transgender people (Budge, Tebbe, & Howard, 2010; O'Neil, McWhirter, & Cerezo, 2008).

At the same time, more is needed. Workers who are not engaged in careers remain on the margins of contemporary vocational theories, research, and practice (Blustein et al., 2005). Vocational and career professionals are challenged to continue efforts to make career education and counseling services beneficial to broader populations. Vocational research has focused more on understanding career development and decision making than on specific intervention techniques, resulting in a gap between theory and practice that affects legislative efforts (Niles, 2003; Whiston, 2003).

## Vocational Legislation and Organization

Career counseling became institutionalized as a part of governmental initiatives for change in the 20th century, and legislative efforts consistently relied on vocational counseling to ease social, political, and economic transitions and remediate social injustices (Herr, 2003). Career counselors and vocational psychology scholars are becoming actively involved in contributing to legislative efforts and raising legislator awareness of research and practice issues salient to career counseling (e.g., Blustein, 2006; Blustein et al., 2005; Hansen, 2003; Herr, 2003; Pope, 2003). Despite major changes in theory and practice toward holistic career counseling, most government programs have continued to focus on matching people to jobs (Hansen, 2003), and "voids in legislation" (Herr, 2003, p. 14) have led to uninformed efforts, duplication of services, and incoherent services. The Society for Vocational Psychology's biennial conference in fall 2011 will focus on increasing communication between vocational psychology researchers and practitioners and state and national legislators and policymakers.

The critical role of vocational guidance in responding to societal problems of economic crises and social inequity is also recognized at the international level (e.g., International Association for Educational and Vocational Guidance, 2009). U.S. participation in international career counseling conferences has increased significantly. The NCDA and the International Association for Educational and Vocational Guidance (IAEVG) held their first joint symposium in 2004 in San Francisco; in 2007, a second joint symposium took place in Padua, Italy, with the Society for Vocational Psychology as a third partner (Trusty & Van Esbroek, 2009). A third joint symposium took place in San Francisco in 2010, and in 2013 a joint International Association for Educational and Vocational Guidance–Society for Vocational Psychology– NCDA symposium will precede the NCDA's 100th anniversary conference in Boston. The 2010 San Francisco conference drew participants from 26 countries. In addition, in 2005 both the *Career Development Quarterly* and the *International Journal for Educational and Vocational Guidance* published special issues with an international focus (Trusty & Van Esbroek, 2009).

Finally, guidelines for career guidance and counseling practice are helping to increase the visibility of the career counseling and guidance profession at national and international levels. The NCDA developed a statement on career counseling competencies in 1997 and in 2009 approved the *Minimum Competencies for Multicultural Career Counseling* (NCDA, 2009). In 2003, the IAEVG General Assembly approved the *International Competencies for Educational and Vocational Guidance Practitioners* (IAVEG, 2003). In addition, as of this writing, a draft of *Guidelines for Integration of Vocational Psychology Into Professional Psychology Practice* (Fouad, Juntunen, & Whiston, 2010) has been approved by the Society for Vocational Psychology and the Society for Counseling Psychology and is under review by all of APA's divisions. These guidelines are intended to increase awareness of and resources for addressing the interface of work and personal lives in applied psychology practice.

## Summary

Career counseling has changed significantly since its inception while preserving many of its fundamental elements. The field originated to assist youth in the process of identifying work for which they were suited. As the value of this endeavor became widely recognized, vocational guidance units were added to school curricula. Vocational guidance served both those who are work bound and those who are college bound, although in fact the two groups often received very different types of training, and distinctions between the two groups have yet to be addressed adequately within the field. Early calls for measurement in vocational guidance coincided with World War I, which generated the need to match large numbers of soldiers with suitable positions.

Legislative efforts over time have demonstrated recognition of the positive effects of vocational guidance, and guidance has increasingly been seen as a means to alleviate social problems. This phenomenon was particularly apparent during the Great Depression, President Johnson's Great Society, and after the Soviet Union's 1957 launch of Sputnik. During World War II, vocational guidance again played an important role in the placement of soldiers into appropriate positions. The writings and theories of Carl Rogers, Erik Erikson, and Abraham Maslow influenced vocational theory as counselors began to understand vocational problems contextually and work with clients holistically.

Since the 1960s, critics have identified the lack of attention to the vocational needs and development of major groups such as women; ethnic and racial minorities; gay, lesbian, and bisexual people; and people with disabilities. Although attention to cultural, linguistic, and other types of diversity has certainly increased, more attention needs to be paid to theory development, assessment, research, and practice to increase the relevance and utility of vocational psychology to the U.S. population.

Toward the end of the 20th century, career theories continued to develop contextually and holistically. The beginning of the 21st century has witnessed changes in the job marketplace, including the rapid expansion of required skills, changing work environments, and the transformation of work from one format to another. These changes parallel some that were set in motion more than 100 years ago, when vocational guidance began. The Web sites listed in the next section provide additional information relating to the chapter topics.

## Useful Web Sites

- American Psychological Association: *Making "Welfare to Work" Really Work*, a report from the APA Task Force on Women, Poverty, and Public Assistance: http://www.apa.org/pi/women/programs/poverty/welfare-to-work.aspx
- American Psychological Association: Workplace issues: http://www.apa.org/topics/workplace/index.aspx
- Center for the Study of Career Development and Public Policy at Penn State: *Career Policy Related Legislation,* the Center for the Study of Career Development and Public Policy: http://www.ed.psu.edu/educ/cscdpp/career-policy-related-legislation
- The GoodWork Project http://www.goodworkproject.org
- International Association for Educational and Vocational Guidance: http://www.iaevg.org/iaevg/index.cfm?lang=2
- National Career Development Association: http://www.ncda.org
- National Employment Counseling Association: http://www.employ mentcounseling.org/
- Society for Vocational Psychology: http://www.div17.org/vocpsych/

## Concluding Remarks

We have presented an overview of the evolution of vocational guidance and career counseling. In the process, we discovered that writing a book might have been an easier task because of the complexity and density of the historical and contextual information available. We acknowledge the extent to which our worldviews, backgrounds, oversights, and values shaped the development of this chapter. We hope readers will reflect on the influences and factors identified here, as well as the many other influences that could have been included—as we will. Finally, we hope that the material included has provided the reader with a useful background for critical thinking about the theory and practice of career counseling.

## References

Ali, S. R., Liu, W. M., Mahmood, A., & Arguello, J. (2008). Social justice and applied psychology: Practical ideas for training the next generation of psychologists. *Journal for Social Action in Counseling and Psychology, 1*(2). Retrieved from http://www.psysr.org/jsacp/Ali-V1N2-08.pdf

American Psychological Association, Division of Counseling Psychology, & Committee on Definition. (1956). Counseling psychology as a specialty. *American Psychologist, 11,* 282–285.

Anelauskas, V. (1999). *Discovering America as it is.* Atlanta, GA: Clarity Press.

Astin, H. S. (1984). The meaning of work in women's lives: A sociopsychological model of career choice and work behavior. *Counseling Psychologist, 12,* 117–126. doi: 10.1177/0011000084124002

Aubrey, R. F. (1977). Historical development of guidance and counseling and implications for the future. *Personnel and Guidance Journal, 55,* 288–295.

Baker, D. B. (2002). Child saving and the emergence of vocational psychology. *Journal of Vocational Behavior, 60,* 374–381. doi: 10.1006/jvbe.2001.1837

Bandura, A. (1969). *Principles of behavior modification.* New York: Holt, Rinehart & Winston.

Bandura, A. (1977). *Social learning theory.* Englewood Cliffs, NJ: Prentice Hall.

Bandura, A. (1986). *Social foundations of thoughts and action: A social cognitive theory.* Englewood Cliffs, NJ: Prentice Hall.

BBC News Middle East. Iraq war in figures. (2010, September). Retrieved from: http://www.bbc.co.uk/news/world-middle-east-11107739

Betz, N. E. (2008). Advances in vocational theories. In S. D. Brown & R. W. Lent (Eds.), *Handbook of counseling psychology* (3rd ed., pp. 357–374). Hoboken, NJ: Wiley.

Betz, N. E., & Fitzgerald, L. F. (1987). *The career psychology of women.* Orlando, FL: Academic Press.

Betz, N. E., & Fitzgerald, L. F. (1995). Career assessment and intervention with racial and ethnic minorities. In F. T. L. Leong (Ed.), *Career development and vocational behavior of racial and ethnic minorities* (pp. 263–280). Mahwah, NJ: Erlbaum.

Bloch, D. P. (2006). Using information and technology in career counseling. In D. Capuzzi & M. D. Stauffer (Eds.), *Career counseling: Foundations, perspectives, and applications* (pp. 152–177). Boston, MA: Pearson Education.

Blustein, D. L. (2001). Extending the reach of vocational psychology: Toward an integrative and inclusive psychology of work. *Journal of Vocational Behavior, 59,* 171–182. doi: 10.1006/jvbe.2001.1823

Blustein, D. L. (2006). *The psychology of working: A new perspective for career development, counseling, and public policy.* Mahwah, NJ: Erlbaum.

Blustein, D. L. (2008). The role of work in psychological health and well-being: A conceptual, historical, and public policy perspective. *American Psychologist, 63,* 228–240. doi: 10.1037/0003-066X.63.4.228

Blustein, D. L., Juntunen, C. L., & Worthington, R. L. (2000). The school-to-work transition: Adjustment challenges of the forgotten half. In S. D. Brown & R. W. Lent (Eds.), *Handbook of counseling psychology* (pp. 435–470). New York, NY: Wiley.

Blustein, D. L., McWhirter, E. H., & Perry, J. C. (2005). Toward an emancipatory communitarian approach to vocational development theory. *Counseling Psychologist, 33,* 141–179.

Blustein, D. L., & Spengler, P. M. (1995). Personal adjustment: Career counseling and psychotherapy. In W. B. Walsh & S. H. Osipow (Eds.), *Handbook of vocational psychology* (2nd ed., pp. 295–329). Mahwah, NJ: Erlbaum.

Bobek, B. L., & Robbins, S. B. (2005). Counseling for career transition: Career pathing, job loss, and reentry. In S. D. Brown & R. W. Lent (Eds.), *Career development and counseling: Putting theory and research to work* (pp. 625–650). Hoboken, NJ: Wiley.

Borow, H. (1974). Apathy, unrest and change: The psychology of the 1960s. In E. Herr (Ed.), *Vocational guidance and human development* (pp. 3–31). Boston, MA: Houghton Mifflin.

Bowman, S. (1995). Career intervention strategies and assessment issues for African Americans. In F. T. L. Leong (Ed.), *Career development and vocational behavior of racial and ethnic minorities* (pp. 137–164). Mahwah, NJ: Erlbaum.

Brecher, J. (1997). *Strike!* Boston, MA: South End Press.

Brewer, J. M. (1942). *History of vocational guidance.* New York, NY: Harper.

Brown, S. D., & Krane, N. E. R. (2000). Four (or five) sessions and a cloud of dust: Old assumptions and new observations about career counseling. In S. D.

Brown & R. W. Lent (Eds.), *Handbook of counseling psychology* (pp. 740–766). New York, NY: Wiley.

Brown, S. D., & McPartland, E. B. (2005). Career interventions: Current status and future directions. In W. B. Walsh & M. L. Savickas (Eds.), *Handbook of vocational psychology* (2nd ed., pp. 195–226). Mahwah, NJ: Erlbaum.

Brown-Collins, A. R., & Sussewell, D. R. (1986). The Afro-American woman's emerging selves. *Journal of Black Psychology, 13,* 1–11. doi: 10.1177/009579848601300101

Brunner, B. (n.d.). *Timeline of affirmative action milestones.* Retrieved from http://www.infoplease.com/spot/affirmativetimeline1.html

Budge, S. L., Tebbe, E. N., & Howard, K. A. S. (2010). The work experiences of transgender individuals: Negotiating the transition and career decision-making processes. Journal of Counseling Psychology, 57, 377–393. doi:10.1037/a0020472

Casell, D. A., & Samples, S. (1976). Career Education in Universities. *Journal of Career Development, 3*(1), 3–12.

Chartrand, J. M., & Oliver, L. W. (Eds.). (2000). Introduction to the special issue: Career assessment on the Internet [Special issue]. *Journal of Career Assessment, 8*(1), 1–2.

Chronister, K. M., & McWhirter, E. H. (2003). Women, domestic violence, and career counseling: An application of social cognitive career theory. *Journal of Counseling and Development, 81,* 418–424.

Chung, Y. B. (1995). Career decision making of lesbian, gay, and bisexual individuals. *Career Development Quarterly, 44,* 178–190.

Chung, Y. B. (2001). Work discrimination and coping strategies: Conceptual frameworks for counseling lesbian, gay, and bisexual clients. *Career Development Quarterly, 50,* 33–44.

Cook, E. P., Heppner, M. J., & O'Brien. K. M. (2002). Career development of women of color and White women: Assumptions, conceptualization, and interventions from an ecological perspective. *Career Development Quarterly, 50*(4), 291–305.

Danek, M. M., Conyers, L. M., Enright, M. S., Munson, M., Brodwin, M., Hanley-Maxwell, C., & Gugerty, J. (1996). Legislation concerning career counseling and job placement for people with disabilities. In E. M. Szymanski & R. M. Parker (Eds.), *Work and disability: Issues and strategies in career development and job placement* (pp. 39–78). Austin, TX: Pro-Ed.

Darcy, M., & Tracey, T. (2007). Circumplex structure of Holland's RIASEC interests across gender and time. *Journal of Counseling Psychology, 54,* 17–31. doi: 10.1037/0022-0167.54.1.17

DeBell, C. (2001). Ninety years in the world of work in America. *Career Development Quarterly, 50,* 77–88.

Dewey, J. (1916). *Democracy and education: An introduction to the philosophy of education.* New York, NY: Macmillan.

Diemer, M. A., & Ali, S. R. (2009). Integrating social class into vocational psychology: Theory and practice implications. *Journal of Career Assessment, 17,* 247–265. doi: 10.1177/1069072708330462

Dixon, D. N. (1987). From Parsons to profession: The history of guidance and counseling psychology. In J. Glover & R. Ronning (Eds.), *Historical foundations of educational psychology* (pp. 107–120). New York, NY: Plenum Press.

Dvorak, B. J. (1947). The new U.S.E.S. General Aptitude Test Battery. *Journal of Applied Psychology, 31,* 372–376.

Engels, D. W., Minor, C. W., Sampson, J. P., & Splete, H. H. (1995). Career counseling specialty: History, development, and prospect. *Journal of Counseling and Development, 74,* 134–138.

Erikson, E. H. (1950). *Childhood and society.* New York, NY: Norton.

Estes, R. J., & Weiner, N. (2002). *The commercial sexual exploitation of children in the U.S., Canada, and Mexico.* Retrieved from http://www.sp2.upenn.edu/restes/CSEC.htm

Faludi, S. (1991). *Backlash: The undeclared war against American women.* New York, NY: Crown. doi: 10.2307/1341561

Faludi, S. (1999). *Stiffed: The betrayal of the American man.* New York, NY: William Morrow.

Farmer, H. S. (1985). Model of career and achievement motivation for women and men. *Journal of Counseling Psychology, 32,* 363–390. doi: 10.1037/0022-0167.32.3.363

Fassinger, R. (2001). Using the master's tools: Social advocacy at the national level. In P. Gore & J. Swanson (Chairs), *Counseling psychologists as agents of social change.* Symposium conducted at the Fourth National Conference on Counseling Psychology, March 2001, Houston, TX.

Feingold, G. A. (1947). A new approach to guidance. *School Review, 4,* 542–550.

Fitzgerald, L. F., & Betz, N. E. (1983). Issues in the vocational psychology of women. In W. B. Walsh & S. H. Osipow (Eds.), *Handbook of vocational psychology* (Vol. 1, pp. 83–160). Hillsdale, NJ: Erlbaum.

Fouad, N. A. (1993). Cross cultural vocational assessment. *Career Development Quarterly, 42,* 4–13.

Fouad, N. A. (2007). Work and vocational psychology: Theory, research, and applications. *Annual Review of Psychology, 58.* doi: 10.1146/annurev.psych.58.110405.085713

Fouad, N. A., & Bingham, R. P. (1995). Career counseling with racial and ethnic minorities. In W. B. Walsh & S. H. Osipow (Eds.), *Handbook of vocational psychology* (pp. 331–365). Mahwah, NJ: Erlbaum.

Fouad, N. A., & Fitzpatrick, M. E. (2009). Social class and work-related decisions: Measurement, theory, and social mobility. *Journal of Career Assessment, 17,* 266–270. doi: 10.1177/1069072708330677

Fouad, N. A., Juntunen, C., & Whiston, S. (2010). *Guidelines for integration of vocational psychology into professional psychology practice.* Unpublished draft. Retrieved from http://www.div17.org/vocpsych/Guidelines%20SVP%20August%202010.pdf

Fouad, N. A., & Kantamneni, N. (2008). Contextual factors in vocational psychology: Intersections of individual, group, and societal dimensions. In S. D. Brown & R. W. Lent (Eds.), *Handbook of counseling psychology* (4th ed., pp. 408–425). New York, NY: Wiley.

Gainor, K., & Forrest, L. (1991). African American women's self-concept: Implications for career decisions and career counseling. *Career Development Quarterly, 39,* 261–273.

Gelso, C. J., & Fretz, B. R. (2001). *Counseling psychology* (2nd ed.). Fort Worth, TX: Harcourt Brace. doi: 10.1016/B0-08-043076-7/01354-1

Gibson, R. L., & Mitchell, M. H. (1999). *Introduction to counseling and guidance.* Upper Saddle River, NJ: Merrill.

Gilbert, L. A., & Rader, J. (2008). Work, family, and dual-earner couples: Implications for research and practice. In S. D. Brown & R. W. Lent (Eds.), Handbook of counseling psychology (4th ed., pp. 426–443). New York, NY: Wiley.

Ginzberg, E., Ginsburg, S., Axelrad, S., & Herma, J. (1951). *Occupational choice: An approach to a general theory.* New York, NY: Columbia University Press.

Goodman, J., Schlossberg, N. K., & Anderson, M. L. (2006). *Counseling adults in transition: Linking practice with theory.* New York, NY: Springer.

Gottfredson, L. (1981). Circumscription and compromise: A developmental theory of occupational aspiration. *Journal of Counseling Psychology, 28,* 545–579. doi: 10.1037//0022-0167.28.6.545

Gottfredson, L. S. (1996). Gottfredson's theory of circumscription and compromise. In D. Brown, L. Brooks, & Associates (Eds.), *Career choice and development* (3rd ed., pp. 179–232). San Francisco, CA: Jossey-Bass.

Griffin, B., & Hesketh, B. (2005). Counseling for work adjustment. In S. D. Brown & R. W. Lent (Eds.), Career development and counseling: Putting theory and research to work (pp. 483–505). Hoboken, NJ: Wiley.

Gysbers, N. C., Heppner, M. J., & Johnston, J. A. (2003). *Career counseling: Process, issues and techniques.* Boston, MA: Allyn & Bacon.

Gysbers, N. C., Heppner, M. J., Johnston, J. A., & Neville, H. A. (2003). Empowering life choices: Career counseling in cultural contexts. In N. Gysbers, M. Heppner, & J. Johnston (Eds.), *Career counseling: Process, issues and techniques* (pp. 50–76). Boston, MA: Allyn & Bacon.

Gysbers, N. C., & Moore, E. J. (1973). *Life career development theory: A model.* Columbia: University of Missouri.

Hackett, G., & Betz, N. E. (1981). Self-efficacy approach to the career development of women. *Journal of Vocational Behavior, 18,* 326–339.

Hansen, S. S. (2003). Career counselors as advocates and change agents for equality. *Career Development Quarterly, 52,* 43–53.

Harris, H. (2000). Defining the future or reliving the past? Unions, employers, and the challenge of workplace learning (Information Series No. 380). Columbus, OH: ERIC Clearinghouse on Adult, Career, and Vocational Education. Retrieved from http://www.calpro-online.org/eric/mp_harris_01.asp

Harris-Bowlsbey, J. (2003). A rich past and a future vision. *Career Development Quarterly, 52,* 18–25.

Hartung, P. J., & Blustein, D. L. (2002). Reason, intuition, and social justice: Elaborating on Parsons's career decision making model. *Journal of Counseling and Development, 80,* 41–47.

Hawks, B. K., & Muha, D. (1991). Facilitating the career development of minorities: Doing it differently this time. *Career Development Quarterly, 39,* 251–260.

Heppner, M. J., & Fu, C. C. (2011) The gendered context of vocational self-construction. In P. J. Hartung & L. M. Subich (Eds.), *Developing self in work and career: Concepts, cases, and contexts* (pp. 177–192). Washington, DC: American Psychological Association.

Heppner, M. J., & Heppner, P. P. (2009). On men and work: Taking the road less travelled. *Journal of Career Development, 36,* 49–67. doi: 10.1177/0894845309340789

Heppner, P. P., Casas, J. M., Carter, J., & Stone, G. L. (2000). The maturation of counseling psychology: Multifaceted perspectives, 1978–1998. In S. D. Brown & R. W. Lent (Eds.), *Handbook of counseling psychology* (3rd ed., pp. 3–49). New York, NY: Wiley.

Herr, E. L. (1974). Manpower policies, vocational guidance, and career development. In E. Herr (Ed.), *Vocational guidance and human development* (pp. 32–62). Boston, MA: Houghton Mifflin.

Herr, E. L. (1979). *Guidance and counseling in the schools: The past, present, and future.* Falls Church, VA: American Personnel and Guidance Association.

Herr, E. L. (2003). The future of career counseling as an instrument of public policy. *Career Development Quarterly, 52,* 8–17.

Herr, E. L., & Niles, S. G. (1998). Career: Social action in behalf of purpose, productivity and hope. In C. C. Lee & G. R. Walz (Eds.), *Social action: A mandate for counselors*. Alexandria, VA: American Counseling Association.

Herr, E. L. & Shahnasarian, M. (2001). Selected milestones in the evolution of career development practices in the 20th century. *Career Development Quarterly, 49,* 225–237.

Higgins, C. A., Duxbury, L. E. & Lyons, S. T. (2010). Coping with overload and stress: Men and women in dual-earner families. *Journal of Marriage and Family, 72,* 847–859. doi: 10.1111/j.1741-3737.2010.00734.x

Holland, J. L. (1959). Theory of vocational choice. *Journal of Counseling Psychology, 6,* 35–45. doi: 10.1037/h0040767

Holland, J. L. (1997). *Making vocational choices: A theory of vocational personalities and work environments* (3rd ed.). Odessa, FL: Psychological Assessment Resources.

Hoyt, K. B. (2001). A reaction to Mark Pope's (2000) "A brief history of career counseling in the United States." *Career Development Quarterly, 49,* 374–379.

International Association for Educational and Vocational Guidance. (2003). *International competencies for educational and vocational guidance practitioners.* Retrieved from http://www.iaevg.org/iaevg/nav.cfm?lang=2&menu=1&submenu=5

International Association for Educational and Vocational Guidance. (2009). *Finland Communique: Light and dark times—The value of career guidance in an economic crisis.* Retrieved from http://www.iaevg.org/iaevg/nav.cfm?lang=2&menu=1&submenu=7

Isaacson, L. E. (1985). *Basics of career counseling.* Boston, MA: Allyn & Bacon.

Kaplan, A. (1997). Domestic violence and welfare reform. *Welfare Information Network: Issue Notes, 1*(8). Retrieved from http://www.welfareinfo.org/domesticissue.htm

Krumboltz, J. D. (1979). A social learning theory of career decision making. In A. M. Mitchell, G. B. Jones, & J. D. Krumboltz (Eds.), *Social learning and career decision making* (pp. 19–49). Cranston, RI: Carroll Press.

Krumboltz, J. D. (1991). The 1990 Leona Tyler Award Address: Brilliant insights— Platitudes that bear repeating. *Counseling Psychologist, 19,* 298–315. doi: 10.1177/0011000091192016

Krumboltz, J. D. (1996). A learning theory of career counseling. In M. L. Savickas & W. B. Walsh (Eds.), *Handbook of career counseling theory and practice* (pp. 55–80). Palo Alto, CA: Consulting Psychologists Press.

Krumboltz, J. D. (2009). The happenstance learning theory. *Journal of Career Assessment, 17,* 135–154. doi: 10.1177/1069072708328861

Krumboltz, J. D., Mitchell, A., & Gelatt, H. G. (1975). Applications of social learning theory of career selection. *Focus on Guidance, 8,* 1–16.

Lent, E. B. (2001). Welfare-to-work services: A person centered perspective. *Career Development Quarterly, 50,* 22–32.

Lent, R. W., Brown, S. D., & Hackett, G. (1994). Toward a unified social cognitive theory of career and academic interest, choice and performance. *Journal of Vocational Behavior, 45,* 79–122. doi: 10.1006/jvbe.1994.1027

Lent, R. W., Brown, S. D., Sheu, H. B., Schmidt, J., Brenner, B., Gloster, C. S., & Treistman, D. (2005). Social cognitive predictors of academic interests and goals in engineering: Utility for women and students at historically Black universities. *Journal of Counseling Psychology, 52,* 84–92. doi: 10.1037/0022-0167.52.1.84

Leong, F. T. L. (Ed.). (1995). *Career development and vocational behavior of racial and ethnic minorities.* Mahwah, New Jersey: Erlbaum.

Leong, F. T. L. (2010). A cultural formulation approach to career assessment and career counseling: Guest editor's introduction. *Journal of Career Development, 37*, 375–390. doi: 10.1177/0894845310363708

Leong, F. T. L., and Hartung, P. J. (2000). Cros-cultural career assessment: Review and prospects for the new millennium. *Journal of Career Assessment, 8*(4), 391–401.

Lofquist, L. H. & Dawis, R. V. (1969). *Adjustment to work.* New York: Appleton-Century-Crofts.

Lyons, H., Brenner, B., & Fassinger, R. (2005). A multicultural test of the theory of work adjustment: Investigating the role of heterosexism and fit perceptions in the job satisfaction of lesbian, gay, and bisexual employees. *Journal of Counseling Psychology, 52*, 537–548. doi: 10.1037/0022-0167.52.4.537

Lyons, H., & O'Brien, K. (2006). The role of person–environment fit in the job satisfaction and tenure intentions of African American employers. *Journal of Counseling Psychology, 53*, 387–396. doi: 10.1037/0022-0167.53.4.387

Maslow, A. H. (1954). *Motivation and personality.* New York, NY: Harper & Row.

McLaughlin, H., Uggen, C., & Blackstone, A. (2009). *Sexual harassment, workplace authority, and the paradox of power.* Unpublished manuscript, Department of Sociology, University of Minnesota, Minneapolis.

McLemore, S. D., Romo, H. D., & Baker, S. G. (2001). *Racial and ethnic relations in America.* Needham Heights, MA: Allyn & Bacon.

Miller, M. J., Roy, K. S., Brown, S. D., Thomas, J., & McDaniel, C. (2009). A confirmatory test of the factor structure of the short form of the Career Decision Self-Efficacy Scale. *Journal of Career Assessment, 17*, 507–519. doi: 10.1177/1069072709340665

Miller-Tiedeman, A., & Tiedeman, D. (1990). Career decision-making: An individualistic perspective. In D. Brown, L. Brooks, & Associates (Eds.), *Career choice and development: Applying contemporary theories to practice* (pp. 308–337). San Francisco, CA: Jossey-Bass.

Mitchell, L., & Krumboltz, J. D. (1984). Research of human decision making: Implications for career decision makers and counselors. In D. Brown & R. Lent (Eds.), *Handbook of counseling psychology* (pp. 238–280). New York, NY: Wiley.

Myers, I. B. (1962). *Manual: The Myers-Briggs Type Indicator.* Princeton, NJ: Educational Testing Service.

National Career Development Association. (1997) *Career counseling competencies.* Retrieved from http://associationdatabase.com/aws/NCDA/asset_manager/get_file/3397

National Career Development Association. (2009). *Minimum competencies for multi-cultural career counseling.* Retrieved from http://www.associationdatabase.com/aws/NCDA/asset_manager/get_file/9914/minimum_competencies_for_multi-cultural_career_counseling.pdf

National Vocational Guidance Association, Board of Directors. (1982). Vocational/career counseling competencies. *NVGA Newsletter, 22*(June), 6.

Niles, S. G. (2003). Career counselors confront a critical crossroad: A vision of the future. *Career Development Quarterly, 52*, 70–77.

Nota, L., Heppner, P. P., Soresi, S., & Heppner, M. J. (2009). Examining cultural validity of the Problem-Solving Inventory (PSI) in Italy. *Journal of Career Assessment, 17*, 478–494. doi: 10.1177/1069072709339490

O'Brien, K. M. (2001). The legacy of Parsons: Career counselors and vocational psychologists as agents of social change. *Career Development Quarterly, 50*, 66–77.

O'Neil, M., McWhirter, E. H., & Cerezo, A. (2008). Transgender identities and gender variance in vocational psychology: Recommendations for practice and social advocacy. *Journal of Career Development, 4,* 286–308.

O'Ryan, L. (2003). Career counseling and social justice. *Counselors for Social Justice Newsletter, 4*(1), 1, 3.

Osipow, S. H., & Littlejohn, E. M. (1995). Toward a multicultural theory of career development: Prospects and dilemmas. In F. T. L. Leong (Ed.), *Career development and vocational behavior of racial and ethnic minorities* (pp. 251–262). Mahwah, NJ: Erlbaum.

Park, B., Smith, J. A., & Correll, J. (2010). The persistence of implicit behavioral associations for moms and dads. *Journal of Experimental Social Psychology, 46,* 809–815. doi: 10.1016/j.jesp.2010.04.009

Parmer, T., & Rush, L. C. (2003). The next decade in career counseling: Cocoon maintenance or metamorphosis? *Career Development Quarterly, 52,* 26–34.

Parsons, F. (1909). *Choosing a vocation.* Boston, MA: Houghton-Mifflin.

Perrone, K. M. (2009). Traditional and nontraditional work and family roles for women and men. *Journal of Career Development, 36,* 3–8. doi: 10.1177/0894845309340787

Perrone, K. M., Wright, S. L., & Jackson, Z. V. (2009). Traditional and nontraditional gender roles and work-family interface for men and women. *Journal of Career Development, 36,* 8–24. doi: 10.1177/0894845308327736

Peterson, N., & Gonzales, R. C. (2000). *The role of work in people's lives: Applied career counseling and vocational psychology.* Belmont, CA: Brooks/Cole.

Pope, M. (2000). A brief history of career counseling in the United States. *Career Development Quarterly, 48,* 194–211.

Pope, M. (2003). Career counseling in the twenty-first century: Beyond cultural encapsulation. *Career Development Quarterly, 52,* 54–60.

Pope, M., & Russell, M. (2001, March). *A practitioner's view of career development policy in the United States.* Paper presented at the Second International Symposium on Career Development and Public Policy. March 2001; Vancouver, BC, Canada.

Pulakos, E. D., Arad, S., Donovan, M. A., & Plamondon, K. E. (2000). Adaptability in the workplace: Development of a taxonomy of adaptive performance. *Journal of Applied Psychology, 85,* 612–624. doi: 10.1037//0021-9010.85.4.612

Richardson, M. S. (1993). Work in people's lives: A location for counseling psychologists. *Journal of Counseling Psychology, 40,* 425–433. doi: 10.1037/0022-0167.40.4.425

Roe, A. (1956). *The psychology of occupations.* New York, NY: Wiley.

Roe, A. (1957). Early determinants of vocational choice. *Journal of Counseling Psychology, 4,* 212–217. doi: 10.1037/h0045950

Rogers, C. R. (1939). *Counseling and psychotherapy.* Boston, MA: Houghton Mifflin.

Rogers, C. R. (1951). *Client-centered therapy.* Boston, MA: Houghton Mifflin.

Santos, E. J. R., Ferreira, J. A., & Chaves, A. (2001). Implications of sociopolitical context for career services delivery. *Career Development Quarterly, 50,* 45–55.

Savickas, M. L. (1993). Career counseling in the postmodern era. *Journal of Cognitive Psychotherapy: An International Quarterly, 7,* 205–215.

Savickas, M. (2000). *Renovating the psychology of careers for the 21st century.* In A. Collin & R. A. Young (Eds.), *The future of career* (pp. 53–68). Cambridge, England: Cambridge University Press.

Savickas, M. L. (2003). Advancing the career counseling profession: Objectives and strategies for the next decade. *Career Development Quarterly, 52,* 87–96.

Savickas, M. L. (2005). The theory and practice of career construction. In S. D. Brown & R. W. Lent (Eds.), Career development and counseling: Putting theory and research to work (pp. 42–70). Hoboken, NJ: Wiley.

Schultheiss, D. E. P. (2009). To mother or matter: Can women do both? *Journal of Career Development, 36,* 25–48.

Seligman, L. (1994). *Developmental career counseling and assessment.* Thousand Oaks, CA: Sage.

Sexual Harassment Support. (2010). *Sexual harassment in the workplace.* Retrieved from http://www.sexualharassmentsupport.org/SHworkplace.html

Sharf, R. S. (2002). *Applying career development theory to counseling.* Pacific Grove, CA: Brooks/Cole.

Shoffner, M. F. (2006). Career counseling: Theoretical perspectives. In M. Stauffer & D. Capuzzi (Eds.), *Career and life style planning: Theory and application* (pp. 40–68). Boston, MA: Allyn & Bacon.

Sinclair, U. (1905). *The jungle.* New York, NY: Signet.

Smith, E. J. (1983). Issues in racial minorities' career behavior. In W. B. Walsh & S. H. Osipow (Eds.), *Handbook of vocational psychology* (Vol. 1, pp. 83–160). Hillsdale, NJ: Erlbaum.

Strachan, H. (2003). The first World War: To arms. Oxford, England: Oxford University Press.

Strong, E. K. (1927). *Vocational interest blank.* Palo Alto, CA: Stanford University Press.

Strong, E. K. (1943). *Vocational interests of men and women.* Stanford, CA: Stanford University Press.

Strong, E. K. (1955). *Vocational interests 18 years after college.* Minneapolis: University of Minnesota Press.

Super, D. E. (1953). A theory of vocational development. *American Psychologist, 8,* 185–190. doi: 10.1037/h0056046

Super, D. E. (1955). Transition: From vocational guidance to counseling psychology. *Journal of Counseling Psychology, 2,* 3–9. doi: 10.1037/h0041630

Super, D. (1983). The history and development of vocational psychology: A personal perspective. In W. B. Walsh & S.H. Osipow (Eds.), *Handbook of vocational psychology: Vol. 1. Foundations* (pp. 5–38). Hillsdale, NJ: Erlbaum.

Super, D. E. (1990). A lifespan–lifespace approach to career development. In D. Brown, L. Brooks, & Associates (Eds.), *Career choice and development: Applying contemporary theories to practice* (2nd ed., pp. 197–261). San Francisco, CA: Jossey-Bass.

Suzuki, L. A., Prevost, L., & Short, E. L. (2008). Multicultural issues and the assessment of aptitude. In L. A. Suzuki & J. G. Ponterotto (Eds.), *The handbook of multicultural assessment* (3rd ed., pp. 490–519). San Francisco, CA: Jossey-Bass.

Szymanski, E. M., Hershenson, D. B., Enright, M. S. & Ettinger, J. M. (1996). Career development theories, constructs, and research: Implications for people with disabilities. In E. M. Szymanski & R. M. Parker (Eds.), *Work and disability: Issues and strategies in career development and job placement* (pp. 79–126). Austin, TX: Pro-Ed.

Tang, M. (2003). Career counseling in the future: Constructing, collaborating, advocating. *Career Development Quarterly, 52,* 61–69.

Taylor, F. W. (1911). *The principles of scientific management.* New York, NY: Harper.

Terkel, S. (1974). *Working.* New York, NY: Pantheon.

Terman, L. M. & Oden, M. H. (1959). *Genetic studies of genius: V. The gifted group at midlife.* Stanford, CA: Stanford University Press.

Thompson, M. N., & Subich, L. M. (2006). The relation of social status to the career decision-making process. *Journal of Vocational Behavior, 69,* 289–301. doi: 10.1016/j.jvb.2006.04.008

Thompson, M., & Subich, L. M. (2007). Exploration and validation of the Differential Status Identity Scale. *Journal of Career Assessment, 15,* 227–239. doi: 10.1177/1069072706298155

Tiedeman, D. V., & O'Hara, R. P. (1963). *Career development: Choice and adjustment.* New York, NY: College Entrance Examination Board.

Toporek, R. L. (2005). An integrative approach for competencies: Career counseling, social justice advocacy, and the multicultural counseling competencies. *Career Planning and Adult Development Journal, 21*(40), 34–50.

Trusty, J., & Van Esbroek, R. (2009). IJEVG and CDQ editors' joint statement on the second special international issues. *Career Development Quarterly, 57,* 291–292.

Tucker, L. (2000). *Fingers to the bone: United States failure to protect child farmworkers.* New York, NY: Human Rights Watch.

U.S. Department of Labor. (1940). *Dictionary of occupational titles.* Washington, DC: U.S. Government Printing Office.

U.S. Department of Labor. (1949). *Occupational outlook handbook.* Washington, DC: U.S. Government Printing Office.

U.S. Equal Employment Opportunity Commission. (2004). Retrieved from http://www.eeoc.gov/

Veterans Rehabilitation Act (Smith-Sears Act), Sess. 2, ch. 107, 40 U.S.C. § 617 (1918).

Walsh, W. B., & Betz, N. E. (1995). *Tests and assessment.* Englewood Cliffs, NJ: Prentice Hall.

Walsh, W. B., & Heppner, M. (2006). *Handbook of career counseling for women* (2nd ed.). Mahwah, NJ: Erlbaum.

Watkins, C. E. (1992). Historical influences on the use of assessment methods in counseling psychology. *Counseling Psychology Quarterly, 5,* 177–188. doi: 10.1080/09515079208254460

Whiston, S. C. (2003). Career counseling: 90 years old yet still healthy and vital. *Career Development Quarterly, 52,* 35–42.

Whiston, S. C., Brecheisen, B. K., & Stephens, J. (2003). Does treatment modality affect career counseling effectiveness? *Journal of Vocational Behavior, 62,* 390–410.

Williamson, E. G. (1939). *How to counsel students.* New York, NY: McGraw Hill.

Williamson, E. G. (1965). *Vocational counseling.* New York, NY: McGraw Hill.

Wrenn, C. G. (1962). *The counselor in a changing world.* Washington, DC: American Personnel and Guidance Association.

Yakushko, O., Watson, M., Ngaruiya, K., & Gonzalez, J. (2008). Career development concerns of recent immigrants and refugees. Journal of Career Development, 34, 362–396. doi: 10.1177/0894845308316292

Yang, W., Stokes, G. S., & Hui, C. H. (2005). Cross cultural validation of Holland's interest structure in Chinese population. Journal of Vocational Behavior, 67, 379–396. doi: 10.1016/j.jvb.2004.08.003

Zytowski, D. G. (2001). Frank Parsons and the progressive movement. *Career Development Quarterly, 50,* 57–65.

CHAPTER **2**

# Trait and Factor, Developmental, Learning, and Cognitive Theories

Marie F. Shoffner Creager and Mary M. Deacon

## Contents

The world is changing quickly, and the changes have accelerated during the past 50 years. The world of work is markedly different from that of this generation's parents and grandparents. The current reality includes downsizing and subsequent job loss, rapid technological advancements revolutionizing industries, decreases in job benefits, interdependent global economy, changing demographics, increased self-employment, and fewer low-wage jobs (Carnevale, Smith, & Strohl, 2010a, 2010b; Niles, Engels, & Lenz, 2009; Niles & Harris-Bowlsbey, 2009). The adept career counselor understands and is able to apply various theories to current realities. These theories include well-established as well as emerging career theories. A career counselor must understand the strengths and weaknesses of theories, how to apply them to practice, and how research has supported or failed to support their application to diverse populations.

The career theories that guide career counseling practice can be classified as trait and factor theories; developmental theories; cognitive learning theories and approaches; psychodynamic approaches; contextual, ecological, and sociological theories; and several additional theories such as values-based theory and chance or accident theories. Before describing each of the theories, we first present an analogy developed by a career theorist–practitioner for understanding the utility of various theories of career development and counseling.

## What Good Is a Theory?

A useful theory provides a framework for understanding complex phenomena; a career theory is a way of summarizing what is seen and what is known by constructing explanations for career development and behavior. Drawing on a useful analogy presented by John Krumboltz (1994, p. 9), a theory is "an attempt to represent some aspect of behavior, much in the same way that a map is an attempt to represent some geographic territory" or to represent facts about that territory (e.g., state boundaries, major highways, altitude). Maps vary in purpose and usefulness (e.g., a map of average rainfall in Virginia has a different use than a street map of New York City). To be useful, maps often oversimplify facts and distort certain features (e.g., the Earth is not flat) and reflect current knowledge. Finally, maps must be periodically corrected and updated as new knowledge is accumulated and the world changes (Krumboltz, 1994). In short, "a good theory is a simplified representation of some domain constructed so that users can ask questions about that domain with an increased probability of receiving valuable answers" (Krumboltz, 1994, p. 12). As you read about the various career theories presented in this chapter, keep in mind the specific map to career development and choice that each of the theories offers. Some theories will be better at addressing career choice, others will be better at explaining the development of career interests, and still others will be best at describing work adjustment.

## Trait and Factor Approaches

In 1909, Frank Parsons developed a way of helping young people become successfully employed by matching personal traits with employment factors. For this reason, his three-pronged matching process became known as the trait and factor approach. In this approach, a person first explores individual knowledge, for example, by assessing personal interests, abilities, and skills. Second, a client explores the world of work and looks for jobs that require his or her particular set of knowledge, interests, abilities, and skills. Finally, with a solid base of information, reasoned matching separates best fits from less desirable options (see Figure 2.1). The reasonable assumption is that when people are optimally matched with work environment, they will be more successful and satisfied. This assumption underlies the approach used in all career theories based on matching individuals to work environments. In this section, we present two of the most well-known and well-established matching theories, Holland's (1959) typological theory and Dawis and Lofquist's

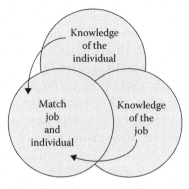

**FIGURE 2.1**   Parsons' trait and factor theory (1909).

theory (Dawis, England, & Lofquist, 1964) of work adjustment (TWA; currently called person–environment correspondence, or PEC).

## Holland's Theory of Personality Types

### *Theoretical Concepts*

John Holland is generally acknowledged as one of the most influential people in the field of career counseling and practice. More empirical studies exist regarding Holland's theory than any other, and more articles have been written about his theory of personality or types than about any other in vocational psychology (Spokane & Cruza-Guet, 2005). Noting Holland's substantive contribution to theory, research, and practice, G. D. Gottfredson and Johnstun (2009) stated,

> Holland's theory, assessment instruments, and intervention tools transformed the delivery of vocational assistance by counselors, schools, and impersonal mechanisms. This occurred because of the organizing power of his theory of persons and environments, the ease with which the theory can be communicated to counselors and clients, and the self-directed nature of the interventions and assessments he developed. (p. 99)

In 1959, Holland presented his theory of career choice. In short, he proposed that individuals choose situations and environments that satisfy their personality (Holland, 1959). He suggested that individuals have a combination of six personality orientations that influence work satisfaction (Holland, Whitney, Cole, & Richards, 1969). The focus of Holland's theory has been on why career choice occurs, and the outcome of that choice, rather than on how or why personality orientations develop. Like other trait and factor approaches, the theory attempts to match individual stable traits (orientations or types) with the characteristics of work environments (Liptak, 2001; Spokane & Cruza-Guet, 2005).

According to Holland's (1959) theory of career choice, occupations are not merely a set of work skills but represent a way of life. Holland's theory of personality types explicitly addresses the influence of behavioral style and personality type on choice of career. In fact, style and type, relatively unchanging traits, are considered the major influence on career choice. Personal interests are a manifestation of one's personality, and this personality leads one to seek satisfaction in work that fits this personality. For example, an individual with an outgoing personality, who likes meeting new people and who is entrepreneurial by nature, might find the most compatible work environment in the context of real estate sales, public relations or marketing for a corporation, or fundraising for a university. This same person would likely be dissatisfied and even unhappy in the work environment of an auditor, a Web designer, or a registrar.

Holland's (1959) theory is based on these four major assumptions:

1) In our culture, most persons can be categorized as one of six types: Realistic, Investigative, Artistic, Social, Enterprising, or Conventional;
2) There are six kinds of environments: Realistic, Investigative, Artistic, Social, Enterprising, or Conventional;
3) People search for environments that will let them exercise their skills and abilities, express their attitudes and values, and take on agreeable problems and roles; and
4) A person's behavior is determined by an interaction between personality and the characteristics of his environment. (Holland, 1973, pp. 2–4)

Holland (1973) further defined these six basic personal orientations and six occupation orientations, based on the belief that people will enter and stay in work that is similar to (or congruent with) their personality type. These types are part of a personal orientation that is based on life experiences and heredity, reflects interests and personality, and is fairly stable. Thus, choice of career is an extension of one's personality type into the world of work—a choice made to satisfy an individual's preferred personal orientation.

### The Six Types

1. *Realistic:* Those who do things. People who are primarily of this type are thought to be good with hands-on, tool-oriented work, such as skilled trades, many technical occupations, and several service occupations. They see themselves as practical, rugged, and mechanical. *Example occupations:* firefighter, auto mechanic, carpenter, forest service technician.
2. *Investigative:* Those who think about things. People who are of this type are thought to be good at solving problems and in scientific occupations and some technical occupations. They see themselves as scientific and precise. They may avoid tasks that seem contrary to inquiry, such as selling, persuading, and advertising. *Example occupations:* professor of history or philosophy, physicist, chemist, doctor.
3. *Artistic:* Those who create things. People who are of this type are thought to be good with creative activities and in artistic, literary, and musical occupations. They see themselves as expressive and independent. *Example occupations:* scenic designer, interior decorator, film editor, animator, journalist.

4. *Social:* Those who help others. People who are of this type are thought to be good with helping people and in social welfare and education occupations. They may avoid jobs that emphasize machinery and tools. *Example occupations:* counselor, nursing, preschool teacher.

5. *Enterprising:* Those who persuade others. People who are of this type are thought to be good at leading, persuading, and selling things and ideas and in sales and managerial occupations. They see themselves as energetic and ambitious. *Example occupations:* land developer, freelance consultant, small business owner and promoter, events coordinator.

6. *Conventional:* Those who organize things. People who are of this type are thought to be good with systemic processes, numbers, records, accounting, and clerical occupations. They may resist work that is ambiguous in process. They may see themselves as orderly and systematic. *Example occupations:* certified public accountant, efficiency expert for a large company, curriculum writer.

### SIDEBAR 2.1   Case Study for Holland's (1959) Theory

Mary has a Holland code of CAR (conventional, artistic, realistic) with C being strong (on a scale from 1 to 10, C is 10); A, less strong (A = 8); and R, weak (R = 2). The other three types are either 0 or 1. Given this profile, and using Holland's circular and hexagonal arrangement or typology, what is Mary's level of consistency? How would you describe her level of differentiation? Can you think of any congruent occupations for Mary? How might you work with her as a career counselor?

Holland's (1959) theory assumes that there are many types of people in the world, not just six types. In fact, a combination and pattern of all six types are used to describe a person's personality. The three dominant types found on assessment results are considered a person's Holland code (e.g., RIC, EAR, SAI). For example, Janeen, who has taken the Self-Directed Search, found that her dominant Holland code was SAI (i.e., she scored highest on social, then artistic, and then investigative). Her counselor might use this personality combination to match her to an occupation that heavily employs SAIs or has an environment that allows an SAI type to thrive. In his later work, Holland (1992) stated that members of a vocation have similar personalities, similar histories of personal development, and similar responses to situations. Therefore, these groups of individuals create work environments characteristic of that vocation (L. S. Gottfredson & Richards, 1999; Holland, 1992; Satterwhite, Fleenor, Braddy, Feldman, & Hoopes, 2009).

In addition, in Holland's (1992) later work, he presented his circular structure and hexagonal description of vocational types (see Figure 2.2). In his circular structure, he posited that the six types can be envisioned as arranged in a circle, with those types more similar to each other being placed closer to each other on this circle and those least similar being placed farthest away from each other. Thus, the realistic and investigative types are adjacent to each other, and realistic and social are far from each other. The order of the six types is therefore realistic, investigative, artistic, social, enterprising, and conventional (RIASEC).

**Steps in Using the SDS**

**Step 1:**
Using the Assessment Booklet,
a person:
- lists occupational
  aspirations
- indicates preferred activities
  in the six areas
- reports competencies in the
  six areas
- indicates occupational
  preferences in the six areas
- rates abilities in the six
  areas
- scores the responses he/she
  has given and calculates six
  summary scores
- obtains a three-letter
  Summary Code from the
  three highest summary
  scores

R = Realistic
I = Investigative
A = Artistic
S = Social
E = Enterprising
C = Conventional

**Step 2:**
Using the Occupations Finder,
a person locates among the
1,335 occupations those with
codes that resemble his/her
Summary Code.

**Step 3:**
The person compares the code
for his/her current vocational
aspiration with the Summary
Code to determine the degree
of agreement.

**Step 4:**
The person is encouraged to
take "Some Next Steps" to
enhance the quality of his/her
decision making.

**FIGURE 2.2** Reproduced by special permission of the Publisher, Psychological Assessment Resources, Inc,. 16204 North Florida Avenue, Lutz, Florida 33549, from the Self-Directed Search Professional's User's Guide by John L. Holland, PhD, Copyright 1985, 1987, 1994, 1997. Further reproduction is prohibited without permission from PAR, Inc.

### Holland Personality Types

Holland's (1959) theory posits four basic theoretical constructs that provide additional information when examining an individual's typology:

1. *Congruence:* Congruence is the level of closeness between an individual's code and a particular work environment. Congruence is calculated using various mathematical formulas to estimate fit (S. D. Brown & Gore, 1994). When the occupation type matches a person's type, there is congruency between that person's type and the occupation, and the person is more likely to be satisfied with his or her occupation. For example, if a person's three primary types are IAR, and the I type is dominant, then there would be congruency between that person's type and a scientific research position, a position that requires investigative skills. However, there would be little congruence between this person's type and a clerical position, a position that requires conventional skills. In fact, job stability and performance, in addition to satisfaction, are influenced by the congruency between personality type and the work environment (Donohue, 2006; Liptak, 2001; Niles & Harris-Bowlsbey, 2009).

2. *Consistency:* The degree to which a person's first two primary types are similar is known as consistency. The closer the top two types are on the hexagonal model, the more consistency there is in the person's style and behavior. For example, in the hexagonal model, someone with a RIA

typology would have a consistent profile, because R, I, and A are close on the model, and R and I are next to each other. However, someone with an RSA typology would have a profile that is not consistent.

3. *Differentiation:* Differentiation is often observed as a difference in scores between the first two letters of the person's type (the person's first and second orientation). Differentiation has less to do with the rank order of a person's type and more to do with the differences found within a person's type. For example, a person with an RIA typology who has high levels of R and much lower levels of I and A is said to have greater differentiation than, for example, a person with an RIA typology whose levels of all three are the same. Therefore, strong differentiation indicates crystallization of interests related to a specific personality orientation. A flat profile on all six types would exhibit the lowest differentiation.

4. *Identity:* Finally, Holland (1985) defined identity as the "possession of a stable and clear picture of one's own goals, interests and talents" (p. 5). Identity can be assessed through Holland's Vocational Identity Scale, which is discussed in Chapter 6. Likewise, work environments that have clarity, stability, and consistency have a clear work identity. A person who demonstrates greater levels of consistency, congruence, and differentiation should have a more clearly defined vocational identity and so may find it easier to find a fitting work environment or field.

### Strengths and Weaknesses

The major strengths of this theory are that it is easy for both counselor and client to understand, it is a practical way of organizing information to help clients find fitting work environments, it is supported by a considerable body of research, and a number of valid, reliable instruments are based on it. Findings suggest that there is a relationship between congruence and job satisfaction, although the relationship is typically small to moderate (Nante, 2010; Spokane, Meier, & Catulago, 2000; Tsabari, Tziner, & Meier, 2005). Research results have supported the ordering and hexagonal structure of RIASEC types based on interest, and results have been mostly supportive of a lack of bias for racial–ethnic groups (Anderson, Tracey, & Rounds, 1997; Day, Rounds, & Swaney, 1998; Fouad, 2002; Fouad, Harmon, & Borgen, 1997; Fouad & Mohler, 2004; Rounds & Tracey, 1996; Ryan, Tracey, & Rounds, 1996; Tang, Fouad, & Smith, 1999; Tang, Pan, & Newmeyer, 2008; Turner & Lapan, 2002, 2003). Researchers have found differences by gender (Fouad, 2007). In addition, the ordering of the types across gender has been confirmed, although women tend to score higher on *S*ocial, *A*rtistic, and *C*onventional, while men tend to score higher on *R*ealistic, *I*nvestigative, and *E*nterprising. This is, however, a reflection of the current work world and not a negative reflection on the theory. It is not always in a circular shape (Darcy & Tracey, 2007; Tracey, 1997).

Perhaps the greatest weakness of Holland's (1959) theory is the simplicity of its application, which can lead to possible misuse of the results. In other words, an unaware or less experienced counselor may allow test results to lead to a limited number of career choice possibilities. To use this chapter's map metaphor, a theory helps conceptualize one reality by distorting information unimportant in other views. In this case, the hexagon used to describe personality types and the world at work (one reality) have inherent distortions. For example, although research consistently confirmed a circular structure, it has not found distances between adjacent types equal (Armstrong, Hubert, & Rounds, 2003; Darcy & Tracey, 2007; Tinsley, 2000). In addition, some counselors may lack appropriate understanding of congruence, consistency, and differentiation, and so may misuse the theory with clients. To be respectful and competent, a counselor continues to challenge the assumptions and weaknesses of a theory.

## Theory of Work Adjustment

### Theoretical Concepts

The TWA (Dawis, England, & Lofquist, 1964) also developed from the trait and factor approach to career counseling. In 1991, the name of the theory was changed to PEC (Dawis & Lofquist, 1993; Lofquist & Dawis, 1991), although PEC is similar to its original presentation. TWA focuses on the person's adjustment to work, and PEC focuses on the fit of a person with a particular work environment. In both, a person chooses work that fulfills personal values and needs (e.g., good pay, health benefits, close to home) and jobs (employers) employ and reward workers on the basis of the worker's satisfactoriness (i.e., skilled, efficient, profitable to the company). Correspondence between the person and the environment leads to success and satisfaction.

TWA distinguishes between the satisfaction of the person and the satisfaction of the employer (environment), by reserving the term *satisfaction* for a person's perception of the ways the environment is meeting his or her needs and the term *satisfactoriness*, for the environment's (employer's) satisfaction with the person. TWA suggests that people have two types of needs that influence the perception of satisfaction: basic survival needs and psychological needs. Psychological needs include fulfillment of one's aspirations and expectations, and basic needs relate to access to resources such as food, clothing, shelter, and so forth. Therefore, work adjustment is indicated by an individual's overall job satisfaction, satisfaction with the various aspects of the work environment, and satisfaction of basic and psychological needs. Similar to a person's needs, work environments have requirements of the person. In this way, work adjustment is also indicated by supervisors' and coworkers' perceptions of the individual's productivity and efficiency (i.e., the individual's satisfactoriness).

Work adjustment happens when an individual improves or maintains his or her correspondence with the work environment. "The P-E correspondence variable reflects the degree to which each meets the requirements of the other" (Dawis, 2005, p. 6). Work adjustment may happen through change in the individual (e.g., the person's reactivity) or through change in the environment (e.g., person's activeness), or both. Like Holland's (1959) theory, TWA stresses the importance of the person–environment fit in the career choice process and, like various learning theories, acknowledges the important role of reinforcement (Dawis, 2005; Eggerth, 2008; Rounds & Hesketh, 1994). The theory posits that the individual and the work environment continually influence each other; work reinforces the individual career development process, and the individual reinforces the dynamic work environment. For example, when a salesperson is provided a bonus for increased sales, he or she is reinforced to continue or increase behaviors that bring about sales. As the company profits from increased sales, it continues to provide or increase bonuses. The work culture manifests results from this relationship of mutual responsiveness and implies that the person and the work environment act on and react to each other "in a mutual give and take" (Dawis, 2005, p. 4; Dawis & Lofquist, 1984) to achieve and maintain correspondence with each other. This interactive process then provides a perspective of work adjustment as ongoing and ever changing. In summary, satisfaction drives the system, and the satisfaction–dissatisfaction continuum influences the individual's behaviors on the job, as well as the work environment's organizational behavior. Success leads to job tenure and better job performance (Dawis, 2005). As an example, Brian is motivated by his internship experiences as a counselor at Best Practices Counseling Center. His supervisor has asked him to examine the current research on helping veterans with PostTraumatic Stress Disorder (PTSD) return to civilian life and work. Brian invests his energy in this research and grows from the internship site's educational mandate. The center changes as well because it adopts a new evidenced-based protocol for veterans based on Brian's studious work. As a result of Brian's meeting and exceeding the requirements of his job role, Best Practices Counseling Center decides to hire him on completion of his internship.

In applying the TWA or PEC to career choice, the counselor applies a trait and factor model, first assessing the individual and various work environments, as in Figure 2.1, and then determining PEC. The important difference is that this model assumes that both the individual and the work environment are subject to change and influence each other. In applying the theory to work adjustment, the counselor is going beyond trait and factor and is instead attempting to help clients understand what adjustments are needed, which are potential individual changes, and which may be changes needed in the work environment or organization.

Hershenson's (1981, 1996, 2001) TWA approach is somewhat different from Dawis and Lofquist's (1993–2005) conceptualization. Research has supported the utility of Hershenson's developmental approach to explain the interaction among domains within a person and in the work environment (Power & Hershenson, 2003; Strauser & Lustig, 2003). (For further information on this theory, see Chapter 12.)

### SIDEBAR 2.2   Work Personality Style and Adjustment Style

Personality style and adjustment style describe a person's (or environment's) process of adjustment (Dawis, 1994, 1996).

The four style variables relating to the pursuit of meeting needs and requirements are

- *Celerity:* speed of response or interaction
- *Pace:* activity level of interaction
- *Rhythm:* pattern of interaction (e.g., steady, infrequent)
- *Endurance:* sustainability of interaction or tolerance of unsatisfactory situations.

A person's adjustment style includes

- *Flexibility:* threshold for tolerating dissatisfaction before adjusting
- *Perseverance:* ability to sustain adjustment behavior
- *Activeness:* adjustment to environment by attempting change to the environment
- *Reactiveness:* adjustment to environment by changing the person.

### Strengths and Weaknesses

In general, research on TWA in general is supportive of the primary propositions, particularly that PEC variables predict work adjustment outcomes (Dawis, 2005). For example, Bizot and Goldman (1993), in a longitudinal study, found that the correspondence between personal aptitudes and job predicted satisfactoriness, with work satisfaction providing additional explanation for satisfactoriness. They also found that satisfactoriness predicted satisfaction, as did correspondence between current interests and job. These relationships did not hold when original interests (at the beginning of the study) were used rather than current interests as measured 8 years later. In another study, Hesketh, McLachlan, and Gardner (1992) found that the correspondence between work preferences and job perception was correlated with satisfaction, and both satisfaction and performance (satisfactoriness) were related to tenure intentions. Other studies have also supported the predictive influence of person–environment fit on tenure and satisfaction (e.g., Bretz & Judge, 1994). Despite primarily supportive research findings, however, TWA research has faced similar operationalization issues as other fit theories, which may account for the sometimes mixed results and the sometimes low predictive power. Determining how best to measure correspondence continues to be a challenge (Dawis, 2005).

The strength of TWA lies in a solid research foundation that led to the original formulation of the theoretical propositions, operationalized constructs (D. Brown, 2003; Dawis, 2005; Eggerth, 2008), and a continued focus on empirical results to support the theory. Another strength is its applicability to work adjustment issues for various populations (Chiocchio & Frigon, 2006; Degges-White & Shoffner, 2002; Harper & Shoffner, 2004; Lyons, Brenner, & Fassinger, 2005; Withrow & Shoffner, 2006; also see Chapter 15 in this book). One challenge in using this theory with clients in an exploratory phase of career development centers on its complex theoretical formulations, which are often difficult for high school and college students to grasp. When thinking about PEC, it is easier for clients (and sometimes practitioners) to conceptualize types (as in Holland's 1959 theory) than it is to conceptualize the various dimensions delineated in TWA.

In discussing the relevance of the theory to women and members of racial minorities, Dawis (1996) stated that these variables are important background information that may account for structure and styles of personality and adjustment. However, he contended that they do not limit the relevance of TWA, but rather the societal restrictions and socialization that influence the early opportunities of those who have historically been oppressed. (For an example of the use of TWA with lesbian clients, see Degges-White & Shoffner, 2002).

## Values-Based Career Counseling

The values-based approach to career counseling (D. Brown, 1996, 2002; D. Brown & Crace, 1996; Niles & Harris Bowlsbey, 2009) posits that values are the primary salient characteristic of career decision making, more so than individual interests. Values are formed and influenced by external sources and are prioritized by individuals. In this approach, individual–work congruence is a value-based fit reached when the value structure of an individual matches the value structure of the work environment. In some ways, then, values-based career counseling is a form of a trait and factor approach. However, rather than looking at the dimensions of congruence as related to interests or aptitudes, this approach suggests that counselors examine the values that may drive an individual to be drawn to one type of career rather than another (Niles & Harris-Bowlsbey, 2009). Clients can then explore their potential fit to occupational cultures or work environments composed of other individuals with similar values. Because of its relative newness to the career counseling literature, little research on outcomes has been associated with this approach. (For further discussion of cultural and individual values, see Chapter 16.)

## Developmental Theories

Unlike trait and factor approaches, developmental theories provide a framework for understanding the unfolding process of career and career choice over the life span. In this section, we present Donald Super's theory (Super, 1990; Super, Savickas, & Super, 1996) of vocational development and Linda Gottfredson's theory (1981, 1996) of circumscription and compromise. (For further discussion of developmental issues with diverse populations, see Chapters 14, 15, and 16.)

### Theory of Vocational Development
#### *Theoretical Concepts*
In the mid-1950s, Donald Super published works that greatly influenced the way we envision careers. These early works presented a multifaceted developmental career theory built on the tenets of several areas of psychology and on the work of Ginzberg (Ginzberg, Ginsburg, Axelrad, & Herma, 1951). Super (Super, Savickas, & Super, 1996) described his theory as differential, developmental, social, and phenomenological. In a set of propositions, he posited a strong relationship between an individual's personal growth and

his or her career development. He did not focus on choice points (e.g., career choice), as did previous theorists and researchers, but rather on the developmental process of vocational behavior and the relationship of this unfolding process to various life roles (Super, Savickas, & Super, 1996). In addition to supporting the importance of individual abilities and interests, Super contributed to the understanding of the salience of values as providing meaning and purpose. The latest rendition of Super's theory (Super et al., 1996) contains the final set of propositions for this theory.

Super et al. (1996) assumed that an individual's career choice was not merely the result of matching his or her abilities and interests to the world of work, but that it was an expression of the individual's self-concept. Thus, people were satisfied to the degree that they could implement their self-concept through their work choice, thereby connecting with the personal meaning of their abilities, interests, values, and choices (Super et al., 1996).

Another major concept in Super's (1996) theory of career development was that of the life space, which includes the constructs of lifestyle, life roles, life role salience, life structure, and values (see Table 2.1). Super's (1980) life career rainbow represents an individual's life career from birth to death and includes the nine major life roles of child, student, leisurite, citizen, worker, homemaker, spouse (or partner), parent, and pensioner across the four arenas of home, school, work, and community (see Figure 2.3). Over the life span, the role of work is connected to these other roles and to the importance of each role in an individual's life at any particular time (life role salience). These life roles together constitute the lifestyle; the sequence of various life roles over time is the life cycle and provides structure to the

**TABLE 2.1  Super's Life Space and Life Span**

| | |
|---|---|
| Primary life roles | Child, student, leasurite, citizen, worker, homemaker, spouse (or partner), parent, pensioner<br>Life role relates to behaviors, motives, and sentiments more than merely position |
| Life arenas | Home, school, work, community<br>Life roles are exercised in these four arenas. One role can be played out in several theaters |
| Life space | The constellation of life roles played out by individuals in life stages. Life spaces differ between individuals because of personal factors (e.g., interests, needs, values) and situational factors (e.g., family, culture, gender, societal forces) |
| Life role salience | The importance of a role; awareness of which life roles are more or less important |
| Lifestyle | The simultaneous combination of life roles |
| Life cycle | Sequence of life roles |
| Major life stages | Growth, exploration, establishment, maintenance, disengagement or decline |
| Lifespan | The course of life or "maxicycle" stages |
| Life structure | The career pattern that results from role salience and structuring of various life roles |

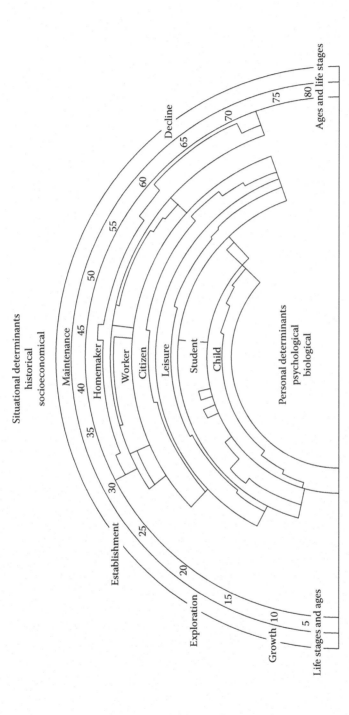

**FIGURE 2.3** Super's (1990) life career rainbow: Six roles in schematic life space. (From "A Lifespan, Life-Space Approach to Career Development," by Super, D. E., In *Career Choice and Development: Applying Contemporary Theories to Practice* [2nd ed., p. 212], by D. Brooks, L. Brown, and Associates [Eds.], 1990, Hoboken, NJ: Wiley & Sons, Copyright 1990 by John Wiley & Sons, Inc.)

life space. The overall structure is called the career pattern, a central aspect of Super's theory.

In his developmental approach to career, Super posited a stage model of vocational choice and development in which he envisioned career choice as a continuous, lifelong progression of stages and substages. Although these stages were initially considered primarily linear and predictable, the revised theory (Super, 1990) included cyclical aspects of the stages and showed how similar developmental challenges with variations are met at each stage. We briefly discuss each of these five stages next.

The growth stage, typically occurring from birth through age 14, includes the substages of curiosity, fantasy, interest, and capacity. Tasks consist of the formation of a self-concept through interaction with adult figures (e.g., parent, guardian, coach) and an orientation to work through chores and responsibilities at school and at home. During this stage, children begin to get a sense of what they are able to do and what interests them. The exploration stage (ages 15–24) includes crystallizing, specifying, and implementing. During this time, the individual begins to connect his or her self-concept to the world of work and to identify types of work through part-time jobs, summer work, and job shadowing. The individual makes the transition from school to work or to further education. There is often a tentative commitment to some beginning jobs and much learning through trial and error about potentially satisfying (or dissatisfying) occupations. The establishment stage (ages 25–44) includes stabilizing, consolidating, and advancing. The individual works to make his or her place in the chosen field of work. This time tends to be productive; the individual pursues advancement (e.g., promotion, additional responsibility) and economic stability. The maintenance stage (ages 45–64) includes the substages of holding, updating, and innovating. The individual maintains his or her level of achievement through the challenges of competition, rapid changes in technology, and family. Often, this stage has considerable professional activity, although it may also become a time of stagnation for some. The final stage, disengagement or decline (from age 65 to death) involves decelerating, retirement planning, and retirement living. During this time, there is a clear change in level of work activity and often greater activity in roles involving family, volunteering, and leisure (Super, 1980). (See Table 2.2.)

In addition to the concepts mentioned earlier, Super is credited with inventing the construct of career maturity (Super et al., 1996). *Career maturity* refers to a person's readiness to handle the challenges involved in exploring and identifying a career choice. The construct of career maturity includes decision-making ability, career exploration, career planning, and an understanding of the world of work and of specific occupations. Successfully navigating any of the five stages or the transitions between stages depends on an individual's career maturity. In determining a client's level of career maturity, the counselor may assess planfulness, exploratory attitudes, decision-making skills, realistic self-appraisal, and the client's knowledge of developmental tasks and of occupations. Career maturity is a psychosocial

**TABLE 2.2   Cycling and Recycling of Developmental Tasks Throughout the Life Span**

| Life Stage | Age | | | |
| | Adolescence (14–25) | Early Adulthood (25–45) | Middle Adulthood (45–65) | Late Adulthood (65 and Older) |
|---|---|---|---|---|
| Decline | Giving less time to hobbies | Reducing sports participation | Focusing on essential activities | Reducing work hours |
| Maintenance | Verifying current occupational choice | Making occupational position secure | Holding own against competition | Keeping up what is enjoyed |
| Establishment | Getting started in a chosen field | Settling down in a permanent position | Developing new skills | Doing things one has always wanted to do |
| Exploration | Learning more about more opportunities | Finding opportunity to do desired work | Identifying new problems to work | Finding a good retirement spot |
| Growth | Developing a realistic self-concept | Learning to relate to others | Accepting one's limitations | Developing non-occupational roles |

*Source:* From "A Life-Span, Life-Space Approach to Career Development," by D. E. Super. In *Career Choice and Development: Applying Contemporary Theories to Practice* (2nd ed., p. 212), by D. Brown, L. Brooks, & Associates (Eds.), 1990, Hoboken, NJ: Wiley. Copyright 1990 by John Wiley & Sons, Inc. Reprinted with permission.

aspect of adolescence, whereas career adaptability is the equivalent construct for most adults (Super et al., 1996).

### Strengths and Weaknesses

Super's developmental theory is a segmented theory rather than a comprehensive theory, which means that many aspects of the theory can stand alone and should be researched separately from the other aspects of the theory. This makes Super's work difficult to research as a whole. However, various segments of the theory can be tested, and the data have generally supported various aspects of Super's model.

Although Super's early theory did not explicitly address the context in which life roles exist, there are clearly contextual factors that affect the career pattern and, in particular, life role salience (Hartung, 2002; Niles & Goodnough, 1996). These factors include the effects of the dominant culture (racial, age, and gender stereotypes and traditional gender and age expectations) and the individual's culture (career beliefs and life themes).

## Theory of Circumscription and Compromise

### Theoretical Concepts

Linda Gottfredson (1981, 1996) is one of the few theoreticians to present a theory on the influence of childhood on career development and career choice. In her original monograph, published in 1981, Gottfredson stated that vocational self-concept begins early in childhood and is defined through four orientations to work (Figure 2.4). She proposed a theory on how children organize their learning about the world of work (L. S. Gottfredson, 2005; Krumboltz, 1994).

### SIDEBAR 2.3  Self-Awareness for Gottfredson's Theory (1981)

Imagine yourself when you were 4 years old, before you entered kindergarten. What do you remember about your perceptions of the world of work? Did you think that certain work or jobs were more powerful? Did jobs that the men around you did seem different than the jobs that women did? If so, how were they different? What about in elementary and middle school (ages 6–10, ages 11–13)? What do you remember about the world of work when you were that age? Were there jobs that you remember thinking, "I can't do that because … "? What were the reasons you gave yourself? When you began to think about your interests and values and the career or work that would fit with them, what careers or jobs might you already have eliminated from consideration? Why do you think they were no longer on your radar?

The first orientation is formed from ages 3 to 5 and is focused on size and power. During this stage, children begin to rule out certain types of careers on the basis of the perceived power of those in that career. This power is often in the form of physical power (e.g., fireman, athlete) or social power and fame (e.g., rock star, movie star). During the next period, ages 6 through 8, children further delineate their occupational space on the basis of sex role. Girls begin to rule out careers that they see as male dominated (e.g., doctor, scientist), and boys rule out careers that they see as female dominated (e.g., nurse, office secretary). From ages 9 through 13, children circumscribe their options on the basis of the prestige and perceived social valuation of occupations. Children now talk about being doctors, lawyers, or crime scene investigators, with the previously delineated sex role restrictions still in place. The final stage begins at about age 14 (early adolescence) and is focused on the unique self, consisting of interests, abilities, and other traits specific to the individual. As children proceed through these stages, they limit or circumscribe an occupational space, referred to as a *region* or *zone of acceptable alternatives*. Occupations and careers that fall out of this region are no longer considered as options (L. S. Gottfredson, 1981). This process is often

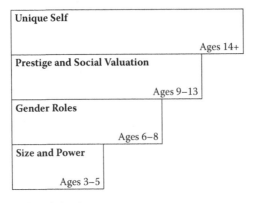

**FIGURE 2.4**  Gottfredson's (1981) development stages.

unconscious, in that these possibilities are often not readily accessible to the individual as possible self schemas.

If, as these children become adolescents and adults and begin to examine options, a particular career or career path that was retained in the zone of acceptable alternatives is no longer an available option, individuals become willing to compromise their acceptable alternatives. Gottfredson (1981) believed that this would happen in the opposite order from the circumscription process. In other words, individuals would first be willing to compromise occupational choices on the basis of their individual interests and abilities (the self) before they would consider compromising occupational prestige and value (L. S. Gottfredson, 1981).

Further development of this theory has posited the idea that one can use schema, especially gender schema, to understand some of these complex processes. In addition, individuals may use an individualized weighting process (for each schema; Vandiver & Bowman, 1996).

### Strengths and Weaknesses

Research has shown that these orientations are important in vocational self-concept development (Hesketh, Elmslie, & Kaldor, 1990) and that children circumscribe their options on the basis of these orientations. In one study, more than 70% of 4- and 5-year-old children aspired to real adult jobs, whereas 11% held fantasy aspirations (Care, Deans, & Brown, 2007). Helwig's (2001) longitudinal study supported Gottfredson's conceptualization (1981) of Stage 3 and Stage 4. However, other research examining the order of compromise has produced mixed results (Blanchard & Lichtenberg, 2003). The circumscription and compromise processes appear to be much more complex than Gottfredson had envisioned in her theory. More research is needed on the theoretical propositions, as well as on interventions designed to address issues of circumscription and compromise.

## Learning and Cognitive Theories

Learning and cognitive approaches to career development and career counseling are based on various learning theories. They focus on the impact of cognition and the effects of learning on career choice and the development process. Some of these theories also consider the factors that affect an individual's learning and thus indirectly affect his or her choices. In this section, we present Krumboltz's (1979; Krumboltz, Mitchell, & Jones, 1976) social learning theory, social cognitive career theory (SCCT), and the cognitive information processing approach.

### Social Learning Theory

#### Theoretical Concepts

The social learning theory of career development was first introduced in the 1970s (Krumboltz, 1979; Krumboltz, Mitchell, & Jones, 1976) as the social learning theory of career decision making. This theory recognized the importance of cognitive processes and behavior in career decision making and explicitly addressed the influence of reinforcement and learning on the career development and choice processes. In 1996, Krumboltz refined aspects of this theory into a learning theory of career counseling (LTCC), which focuses more specifically on cognitive–behavioral interventions and the goals and outcomes of counseling (Krumboltz, 1996; Mitchell & Krumboltz, 1996).

The four primary factors in both the social learning theory of career decision making and LTCC are genetics (gender, race, physical characteristics, specific talents such as music), environment (social, cultural, political, economic, geographic, climate), learning experiences (both instrumental and associative), and task-approach skills (including work habits, performance abilities, and thought processes). Krumboltz (1994) believed that the last two of these four are learned and so can be addressed by counselors. In fact, learning through experiences (both instrumental and associative) and human interaction is the primary focus of career development and decision making according to this theory. An individual will choose an occupation or field of work if he or she has success in tasks believed to be required for that occupation; he or she has observed or been made aware of a role model reinforced for such tasks; others, especially family and friends, have spoken of the advantages of this profession; or he or she observes the positive aspects (in words or in images) associated with the occupation (Krumboltz, 1994).

### SIDEBAR 2.4  Self-Awareness for Krumboltz and Planned Happenstance

How has the unfolding of your career been less than linear, planned, or predictable? Discuss luck and happenstance (being in the right place at the right time; having a particular mentor or role model, etc.). How do you believe you capitalized on these chance experiences? Were there other experiences that you purposefully sought out or planned in terms of your educational and career development and choices? What skills did you need to capitalize on these experiences? Where and how did you learn these skills?

Krumboltz (1996) further identified four important and current needs in today's changing work world. First of all, people need to expand their knowledge, skills, and interests if they are to remain useful employees. Second, people should assume that change will happen and prepare for it, rather than assume work stability; they will often need help in learning how to do so. Third, people need to be empowered and encouraged to expand and change. Last, counselors need to play a primary role in dealing with all career problems, not just the choice of an occupation or career (Krumboltz, 1996). The most useful and effective career counselor today, according to Krumboltz, will be the professional who promotes and encourages client learning. (For an example of the use of LTCC with college athletes, see Shurts & Shoffner, 2004.)

Planned happenstance theory (Mitchell & Krumboltz, 1999) extends LTCC to include the role of chance events and uncertainty in people's careers. For example, a senior chemistry–biology major sees a sign in the chemistry hall inviting dual majors to interview for an intern position at a toxicology lab. She interviews, gets the job, and subsequently changes her career goal from medicine to toxicology. Career counselors rarely discuss unexpected or chance events with their clients, nor do they view uncertainty as a core component of career decision making (Trevor-Roberts, 2006). A planned happenstance intervention helps clients view such unplanned events as new learning experiences. Clients learn how to actively search while remaining open to new unexpected opportunities. Viewing uncertainty as a natural by-product of limited learning opportunities, counselors then help clients move from indecision to open mindedness. This move allows clients to approach the myriad of new situations and changes that people constantly face in a way that encourages growth and further self-definition (Blustein, 1997). Individuals require five skills to capitalize on planned happenstance: curiosity, persistence, flexibility, optimism, and risk taking (Krumboltz & Levin, 2004). The career counselor plays a crucial role in helping clients learn to identify, use, and create further positive chance events.

### Strengths and Weaknesses

Because learning theories, especially LTCC, are most concerned with counselor-facilitated client learning and view clients as dynamic, changing, learning individuals, they have wide applicability to diverse populations (Datti, 2009). LTCC, like SCCT, described later, is grounded in Bandura's (1977, 1986) well-tested general social learning theory, and therefore, many of its foundational premises have been supported (Trusty, 2002, 2004; Trusty & Niles, 2003, 2004; Trusty, Robinson, Plata, & Ng, 2000). However, more research studies, particularly outcome studies, should be conducted on LTCC.

Because of the focus on learning and client adaptability, counselors using LTCC may ignore critical contextual factors (Krumboltz & Henderson, 2002). In particular, it is important that counselors understand and acknowledge the restricted opportunity structure that may have provided differential learning experiences for their clients, with possible long-term consequences and restricted options. Some of these experiences cannot be undone or redone. For example, placement in lower level math classes in middle school and early high school will restrict future options at the postsecondary level. Similarly, a counselor working with a client within an LTCC framework might choose to facilitate the development of coping skills for dealing with institutional barriers rather than attempt to change systemic oppression. Career counselors should not ignore their advocacy role of confronting and working to change systemic attitudes that perpetuate sexism, racism, or other "isms" in education and in the workplace.

## Cognitive Information Processing
### Theoretical Concepts

The cognitive information processing approach to decision making and to career problem solving is designed to enable "individuals to become skillful career problem solvers and decision makers … individuals learn not only how to solve the immediate career problem and make an appropriate decision, but also how to generalize this experience to future career problems" (Peterson, Sampson, Reardon, & Lenz, 2008, p. 1393). The major assumptions of this approach are that

1. Thoughts (cognitions) and emotions (affect) are inseparable in career decision making and problem solving. Emotions can motivate individuals in either positive or negative ways.
2. Career problems are addressed through knowledge (content) and thinking about that knowledge to make choices.
3. Career resources can help individuals organize the vast amount of constantly changing information about the world and about themselves so that they can make informed choices.
4. Information processing skills can be learned and improved so that individuals can become better at making decisions (Peterson et al., 2008).

The cognitive information processing approach involves two primary dimensions, the pyramid of information processing domains and the communication–analysis–synthesis–valuing–execution (CASVE) cycle, which is used to help identify strategies for assessment and screening of career decision-making skills. The pyramid of information processing domains (Figure 2.5) delineates the areas of cognition involved in career decision making. The base of the pyramid (or triangle) is formed by the two components of the knowledge domain: self-knowledge (who am I?) and occupational knowledge (what are my options?). The next domain, resting on the knowledge domain, is the

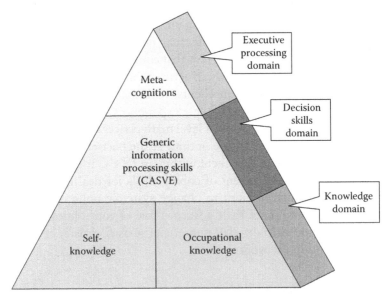

**FIGURE 2.5** Pyramid of information processing domains. (From *Career Development and Services: A Cognitive Approach* [p. 28], by G. Peterson, J. Sampson, & R. E. Reardon, 1991, Florence, KY: Brooks/Cole, Copyright 1991 by Brooks/Cole Publishing Company, a division of Thompson International Publishing, Inc. Adapted with permission.)

decision-making skills domain. This domain involves the information processing skills used in the CASVE cycle (how do I make decisions?), which are discussed later. Finally, the top of the pyramid consists of the executive processing domain (metacognitions). This domain includes self-talk, self-awareness, and cognitive monitoring (Niles & Harris-Bowlsbey, 2009; Peterson et al., 2008; Sampson, Reardon, Peterson, & Lenz, 2004).

The CASVE cycle is a sequential decision-making procedure involving communication (identifying a need, a problem, or a gap between what is and what would be ideal), analysis (identifying what is needed, especially in the way of information, and how to acquire what is needed), synthesis (identifying alternatives and narrowing the list to a set of likely and acceptable alternatives), valuing (prioritizing the alternatives on the basis of the individual's values, the impact on others, and the likelihood of success), and execution (developing strategies as a plan of action and implementing the chosen alternative; Peterson et al., 2008; Reardon, Lenz, Sampson, & Peterson, 2005). The career counselor can help clients learn the components of this cycle and how to use the steps for career choice and decision making. It is hoped that this approach to decision making will continue to be useful to clients in other areas of their lives.

### Strengths and Weaknesses

Cognitive information processing appears to be an excellent approach to use with clients who are motivated to use linear decision-making models. The theoretical propositions are laid out in such a manner that researchers will be able to test them. Although it is still early in the development and investigation of the theory, the few empirical findings to date have focused on dysfunctional career thoughts (Kleiman et al., 2004; Meyer-Griffith, Reardon, & Hartley, 2009; Osborn, Howard, & Leierer, 2007; Paivandy, Bullock, Reardon, & Kelly, 2008).

## Social Cognitive Career Theory

### Theoretical Concepts

SCCT, derived from Bandura's (1977, 1986) general social cognitive theory, focuses on the "(a) formation and elaboration of career-relevant interests, (b) the selection of academic and career choice options, and (c) performance and persistence in educational and occupational pursuits" (Lent, Brown, & Hackett, 1994, p. 79). The primary constructs of SCCT are self-efficacy beliefs, the subjective beliefs that one is able to perform particular tasks; outcome expectations, the beliefs that these behaviors will result in particular outcomes; and goal mechanisms. The framework further describes the influence of person factors, contextual factors, and experiential and learning factors (Bandura, 1977, 1986) on academic and career development and on choice. In fact, SCCT recognizes and addresses the critical importance of individuals' beliefs and perceptions about their skills, potential outcomes, and barriers and supports and their perceived ability to deal with perceived barriers.

In SCCT, learning experiences shape self-efficacy beliefs and outcome expectations and are influenced by factors such as educational opportunity and family context (Ferry, Fouad, & Smith, 2000; Lent et al., 1994; Lent, Brown, & Hackett, 2000; Tang, Pan, & Newmeyer, 2008; Turner, Steward, & Lapan, 2004). Self-efficacy beliefs influence choice, actual performance, and persistence (Bandura, 1977, 1997; Lent et al., 1994) and act as moderators between experience and career interests (Lent et al., 1994). Goal aspirations, and ultimately goal choices, are influenced by interests and by relevant self-efficacy and outcome expectation beliefs. Self-efficacy is believed to have a direct influence on the development of outcome expectations, with both constructs influencing interests and aspirations. In addition, these aspirations are mediated and moderated by perceived barriers, perceived supports, and contextual factors (Lent et al., 2000). Career aspirations and choices, therefore, are not based on interests alone but are also influenced by self-efficacy and outcome expectations, as well as perceived barriers, perceived supports, and other contextual influences. Beliefs about one's ability to cope with various perceived barriers (coping self-efficacy) may also influence an individual's perceived options. (For further discussion of real and perceived barriers, see Chapters 14, 15, and 16.)

### SIDEBAR 2.5  Case Study for Social Cognitive Career Theory

Sue is a 10th grader (16 years old) who would like to go to college to become a pharmacy assistant. Neither her mother nor her father nor anyone in her family has ever been to college. Her father left high school when he was Sue's age. Sue has done well in school but is stuck in her progress toward the next step in her education and career.

Using SCCT, what do you think might be some areas in which Sue might feel a higher level of self-efficacy? In which might she feel a lower level of self-efficacy? What do you believe are some of her outcome expectations for (a) completing high school, (b) getting into college, (c) staying in college, and (d) completing her bachelor's degree and becoming a pharmacy assistant?

If you were a professional school counselor and Sue came to see you regarding her postsecondary school plans, what would be some of the issues you might discuss with her?

Outcome expectations incorporate the concept of values. In other words, the salience of particular outcome expectations, and the strength of these expectations as reinforcers, are individual factors (Lent et al., 1994, 2000). Career-relevant outcome expectations include the anticipation of physical outcomes (e.g., financial gain, lifestyle), the gaining of social approval, and self-satisfaction outcomes (Bandura, 1986; Lent et al., 1994). Research has also indicated two additional categories of outcome expectations: relational outcomes and generativity outcomes (Shoffner, Newsome, & Barrio, 2004).

Before the development of SCCT, Hackett and Betz (1981) asserted that girls' and women's beliefs regarding specific careers, such as mathematics and science, were influenced by low self-efficacy because of gender socialization experiences. This low self-efficacy, in turn, limited their interest in and exploration of these topics. This assertion implied that differential access to sources of self-efficacy and reinforcement limited potential options. Thus, although the constructs of the theory are internal and cognitive, they are highly influenced by socialization and institutional factors that may restrict options and the use of individual strengths and abilities. (See the Theories of Embedded Careers section.)

### Strengths and Weaknesses

This theory has been used to successfully explain the career development of a number of diverse populations, including girls and women (Betz & Hackett, 1987; Evans & Diekman, 2009; Lent & Brown, 2006), members of racial minority groups (Alliman-Brissett & Turner, 2010; Byars & Hackett, 1998; Hackett & Byars, 1996; Lent, Lopez, Lopez, & Sheu, 2008), and gay and lesbian individuals (Morrow, Gore, & Campbell, 1996). Research has consistently demonstrated the important influence of women's beliefs about their ability (self-efficacy) on their choice of nontraditional careers (Betz & Fitzgerald, 1987) and in forecasting science- and mathematics-related interests (Byars-Winston & Fouad, 2008; Lent et al., 1991; Usher & Pajares, 2009) and other career-related choices and performance (Hackett, 1985; Hackett & Lent, 1992; Lent, Shue, et al., 2008). The impact of ability on self-efficacy, and its subsequent influence on outcome expectations and specific interests, has also been supported (Byars-Winston & Fouad, 2008; Fouad & Guillen, 2006; Fouad & Smith, 1996; Lent & Brown, 2006; Lopez et al., 1997; Navarro et al., 2007). Research by Betz and Voyten (1997) has supported the relationship between lower outcome expectations and decreased exploratory behavior. Fouad and Smith (1996) found that self-efficacy significantly but indirectly influenced career-related interests through its relationship to interests and outcome expectations. They also found strong paths between outcome expectations and intentions.

### SIDEBAR 2.6  Self-Awareness for Social Cognitive Career Theory and Barriers

What are some of the barriers that people at lower economic levels might face in their career development? Which of those barriers can be addressed through advocacy? Identify one barrier to full equity in career development and choice that you would like to help to lower or even eradicate. Identify the steps you might take in the next 2 years to begin this process.

Research on the influence of perceived barriers and supports has primarily lent support to the tenets of SCCT (Lent et al., 2001). Both high school and college populations perceive barriers to reaching their educational and career goals (Gushue et al., 2006; McWhirter, 1997; McWhirter et al., 1998; Ojeda & Flores, 2008; Rivera et al., 2007; Swanson & Tokar, 1991; Tien et al., 2009), although the impact of these perceptions on future career choices and goals is not clear. For high school youth, perceived barriers did not explain youth's career exploration activities (Gushue et al., 2006), academic plans, or expectations regarding careers (McWhirter, 1997; McWhirter et al., 1998) but did explain career consideration (Rivera et al., 2007). The theory posits that it is the perception of barriers and not the actual existence or actual strength of these barriers that influence career outcomes (Albert & Luzzo, 1999; Luzzo, 1996). The effect comes from the individual's subjective perception of and response to these barriers. Perceived support from both parents and teachers is instrumental in its effect on career-related outcomes (Lapan, Hinkelman, Adams, & Turner, 1999; McWhirter et al., 1998).

Clearly, there is much in the way of research support for SCCT, which is one of its primary strengths. Given the large body of empirical evidence supporting the utility of the SCCT model of career development, the authors of the *Career Development Quarterly* annual review identified SCCT as one of the most visible and researched career theories (Shoffner Creager, in press). In addition, it is a theory that can be directly and effectively applied to career counseling. A direct focus on perceptions and beliefs regarding self-efficacy, outcomes, barriers, and supports can lead to targeted interventions for providing structured activities for developing self-efficacy in specific areas, for countering erroneous outcome expectations, and for exploring perceived barriers and appropriate coping skills. (For an example of the use of SCCT with first-generation college students, see Gibbons & Shoffner, 2004.)

## Theories of Embedded Career

Similar to Blustein's (1994, 2006) concept of the embedded self, or the self in relationship with others and the environment, career and career development can be viewed as embedded in the larger context of social and environmental interchange and relationship. Several career theories and approaches are focused on the influence of the environment on career development and the individual's internal (meaning making) or external (behavior) outcomes of these relationships. Some of the theories that we have already discussed (e.g., SCCT) could conceivably fall into this category but were not included here because of their primary emphasis on some other aspect of career theory, such as cognition. Theories of embedded career include contextualism, the ecological approach, and sociological theories. There are additional theories similar in their focus on context or system. (See Chapter 6 for a description of complexity theory and Chapter 13 for a presentation of family systems theory.)

### Contextualism

#### *Theoretical Concepts*

Contextual approaches to career theory and career counseling are grounded in constructivist approaches, which state that there is an ongoing, dynamic, and reciprocal interaction between individuals and their environments (their context), which is in contrast to the approaches that have individuals as passive recipients of input and subject to developmental stages and growth (Patton & McMahon, 1999, 2006). This ongoing reciprocal relationship, as delineated in contextualism, is based on individuals' perceptions and the personal meaning assigned to the events and experiences of which they are a part. Therefore, individuals' career development is based in their construction of personal meaning regarding their past memories, present experiences, future aspirations (Savikas, 2005), and actions. Two primary tenets of this theory, then, are that behavior is caused "by the social context in which the behavior occurs" and that "reality is a matter of perception" (Young, Valach, & Collin, 1996, p. x). Thus, the role of the career counselor is to explore the meaning that clients have created and are creating (their narrative) and to facilitate their continued construction of their career path by projecting their narratives into the future (Savickas, 2005). The focus of counseling can be on the three perspectives of action as discussed by Young and Valach (2004): unobservable behavior, unobservable internal processes, and the meaning associated with the results of action, from the point of view of both the client and other observers.

### Strengths and Weaknesses

As with psychodynamic approaches (see the next section), the strength of contextualism from a career counseling perspective is its focus on the client's reality and perception. Its greatest weakness is inherent in most phenomenological approaches. It is difficult to research because the process is at least as important as the outcome, and much of the process is internal to the client. Nonetheless, investigations of its utility in career counseling through outcome research would be helpful in providing evidence that constructivist approaches have some relevance and efficacy. In addition, qualitative methodologies would be useful in helping practitioners know what approaches work best in facilitating and coconstructing clients' meaning making.

## An Ecological Perspective

Similar to the contextual approach, the ecological approach to career counseling conceptualizes clients as within and influenced by their various environments (Cook, Heppner, & O'Brien, 2002, 2005; Patton & McMahon, 2006). This perspective is based on Bronfenbrenner's (1979) ecological model and provides a lens through which to provide service to clients for whom the assumptions of more traditional approaches do not apply. The assumptions of many of the earlier career theories are that the roles of family and of work are separate in clients' lives, that individualism is a driving force for clients, that work is central in clients' lives, that career development is linear and rational, and that the opportunity structure is the same for all individuals (Barrio & Shoffner, 2005; Cook et al., 2002, 2005). Although these traditional theories may still be relevant, it is important for the career counselor to assess, with each individual and unique client, the relevance of any model for that person (Stebleton, 2007, 2010).

**SIDEBAR 2.7   Case Study for Ecological Approach (or Others)**

Johnny, who is 30 years old, is terminally ill. He is at the top of his career as a marketing and advertising representative. He has a sizable income, two young children, and a wife who teaches at the local elementary school. Johnny has just been diagnosed with cancer, with a 30% survival rate and an estimated 2 years to live. What theory and map would be most appropriate to consider in working with this client? Why? What would be your goals as a career counselor? What would be your goals as an advocate? What are some aspects of working with Johnny that might be different if his prognosis was 7 to 10 years? What might be different if his prognosis was a 70% survival rate?

In the ecological approach, the counselor goes beyond the coconstruction of meaning to address specific environmental factors that may be influencing the client's optimal career development (Cook et al., 2005). In other words, an ecological perspective uses interventions focused on changing the individual's interactions with his or her environment. In working with clients, the authors of this approach suggest these main intervention themes: clarifying and affirming life options, managing multiple roles, obtaining needed resources, creating healthy work environments; and linking individuals with role models and mentors. (More information on the ecological approach is presented in Chapter 12.)

## Strengths and Weaknesses

The primary strength of the ecological approach is its recognition of and focus on the ecological systems of which the client is a part. In addition, the approach provides some specific guidelines for working with clients. However, the approach is relatively new, and so there is little research to support its premises and to support the effectiveness of its use in career counseling. However, given its focus on context, this approach offers some promise in addressing the career counseling needs of diverse populations.

## Sociological Theories of Career Development

Sociological theories of career development are founded in sociology and sociological research and center on the domains of status, stratification, and organizational behavior. These theories, more clearly than others, directly address the restrictive or enhancement influence of institutional factors, the influence of parental social status on individual capabilities and opportunity, and the restrictive impact of work system dynamics on financial, social, and psychological choice and satisfaction (Blustein, 2006; Hotchkiss & Borow, 1990).

## Psychodynamic Approaches

Several additional approaches to career development and career counseling, although perhaps not as often used or researched, are important in understanding the various ways to approach career work with clients. Psychodynamic theories of career development focus on issues of ego identity, life scripts, and life themes and are often extensions of the theories of Adler's life themes (1988) and Erikson's (1968) ego identity development. They may also focus on the role of affect in career development, the role of the family of origin in shaping career development and career identity, the interaction between career identity and identity development, and work identity. In summary, these approaches are based on internal structures of motivation and the constructs of identity, lifestyle, the self, and family systems (Bordin, 1990, 1994). The foci of recent psychodynamic career theories have been (a) ego identity in career development (Blustein, 1994) and the impact of relationships on career development (e.g., Blustein, Prezioso, & Schultheiss, 1995; Blustein, Walbridge, Friedlander, & Palladino, 1991; Schultheiss, Kress, Manzi, & Glasscock, 2001); (b) life themes and how clients construct their identity and live out life scripts as extensions of this identity (e.g., Savickas, 1998); and (c) adult play and its implications for career counseling (e.g., Bordin, 1994). (For information regarding Roe's needs theory, another psychodynamic theory, see Chapter 5. Note that postmodern approaches also focus on clients' construction of story and the meaning assigned to various aspects of this story. For an example, see the presentation on narrative approaches in Chapter 3.)

Of the psychodynamic approaches, perhaps that most directly applicable to the work of a career counselor is the application of lifestyle as it influences adulthood and the developing career self. Here, the primary idea is that early recollection can be used to help clients understand their lifestyle. This understanding, then, can help them explore and identify career options that seem to be most appropriate to their lifestyle.

## Strengths and Weaknesses

There is relatively little research on psychodynamic approaches to career counseling. The research that does exist tends to focus on the development of career identity as part of the development of a healthy identity during adolescence and early adulthood or the role of parental influence on early career identity.

Psychodynamic career counseling is best used with verbal clients and is appropriate in addressing gender and cultural issues. The approach tends to be strength based and includes an emphasis on the subjective world of the client; it may thus be one of the more culturally responsive approaches to career counseling work with clients from diverse populations.

The major strength of this approach to career counseling is its focus on clients' constructed understanding of their identity and their past in relation to career exploration and adjustment. This strength, however, is also a major weakness in that it does not lend itself to quantitative methods of research to support its claims. However, qualitative methodologies may be very useful in exploring how individuals construct their identities and develop their life scripts and how these in turn influence their career exploration, their decision making, and ultimately their work adjustment.

## Summary

All of the types of theories discussed in this chapter provide different categories of maps: trait and factor, developmental, learning and cognitive, embedded careers, and psychodynamic. Within these, each theory or approach provides the career theorist, researcher, or practitioner with a guide to aspects of the career development process. Not all of these theories will be equally as applicable across the needs and stages of diverse career clients. This situation is no different from counseling in general. Each counseling intervention should be geared to what will optimize the client's career and work growth. The Web sites listed in the next section provide additional information relating to the chapter topics.

## Useful Web Sites

- Career Key—Holland types: http://www.careerkey.org/english/you/hollands_home.html
- Linda S. Gottfredson's Web page—links to many of her documents: http://www.udel.edu/educ/gottfredson/reprints/
- New Zealand's Career Services site includes illustrations of Super's theory, a career theories overview, and career theory chronological timelines: http://www2.careers.govt.nz/super_theory.html
- Self-Directed Search—Holland's types: http://www.self-directed-search.com/

## References

Albert, K. A., & Luzzo, D. A. (1999). The role of perceived barriers in career development: A social cognitive perspective. *Journal of Counseling and Development, 77,* 431–437.

Alliman-Brissett, A., & Turner, S. (2010). Racism, parent support, and math-based career interests, efficacy, and outcome expectations among African American adolescents. *Journal of Black Psychology, 36,* 197–225. doi: 10.1177/0095798409351830

Anderson, M. Z., Tracey, T. J. G., & Rounds, J. (1997). Examining the invariance of Holland's vocational interest model across gender. *Journal of Vocational Behavior, 50,* 349–364.

Armstrong, P. I., Hubert, L., & Rounds, J. (2003). Circular unidimensional scaling: A new look at group differences in interest structure. *Journal of Counseling Psychology, 51,* 297–308. doi: 10.1037/0022-0167.50.3.297

Bandura, A. (1977). Self-efficacy: Toward a unifying theory of behavioral change. *Psychological Review, 84,* 191–215.

Bandura, A. (1986). *Social foundations of thought and action.* Englewood Cliffs, NJ: Prentice Hall.

Bandura, A. (1997). *Self-efficacy: The exercise of control.* New York, NY: Freeman.

Barrio, C. A., & Shoffner, M. F. (2005). Career counseling with persons living with HIV: An ecological approach. *Career Development Quarterly, 53,* 325–336.

Betz, N. E., & Fitzgerald, L. F. (1987). *The career psychology of women.* San Diego, CA: Academic Press.

Betz, N. E., & Hackett, G. (1987). Concept of agency in educational and career development. *Journal of Counseling Psychology, 34,* 299–308.

Betz, N. E., & Voyten, K. K. (1997). Efficacy and outcome expectations influence career exploration and decidedness. *Career Development Quarterly, 46,* 179–189.

Bizot, E. B., & Goldman, S. H. (1993). Prediction of satisfactoriness and satisfaction: An 8-year follow up. *Journal of Vocational Behavior, 43,* 19–29.

Blanchard, C., & Lichtenberg, J. (2003). Compromise in career decision making: A test of Gottfredson's theory. *Journal of Vocational Behavior, 62*, 250. doi: 10.1016/S0001-8791(02)00026-X

Blustein, D. L. (1994). Who am I? The question of self and identity in career development. In M. L. Savickas & R. W. Lent (Eds.), *Convergence in career development theories: Implications for science and practice* (pp. 139–154). Palo Alto, CA: CPP Books.

Blustein, D. L. (2006). *The psychology of working: A new perspective for career development, counseling, and public policy.* Mahwah, NJ: Erlbaum.

Blustein, D. L. (1997). A context-rich perspective of career exploration across the life role. *The Career Development Quarterly, 45*, 260–274.

Blustein, D. L., Prezioso, M. S., & Schultheiss, D. P. (1995). Attachment theory and career development: Current status and future directions. *Counseling Psychologist, 23*, 416–432.

Blustein, D. L., Walbridge, M. M., Friedlander, M. L., & Palladino, D. E. (1991). Contributions of psychological separation and parental attachment to the career development process. *Journal of Counseling Psychology, 38*, 39–50.

Bordin, E. S. (1990). Psychodynamic models of career choice and satisfaction. In D. Brown, L. Brooks, & Associates (Eds.), *Career choice and development: Applying contemporary theories to practice* (2nd ed., pp. 102–144). San Francisco, CA: Jossey-Bass.

Bordin, E. S. (1994). Work and play. In M. L. Savickas & R. W. Lent (Eds.), *Convergence in career development theories: Implications for science and practice* (pp. 53–61). Palo Alto, CA: CPP Books.

Bretz, R. D., Jr., & Judge, T. A. (1994). Person-organization fit and the theory of work adjustment: Implications for satisfaction, tenure and career success. *Journal of Vocational Behavior, 44*, 32–54.

Bronfenbrenner, U. (1979). *The ecology of human development.* Cambridge, MA: Harvard University Press.

Brown, D. (1996). A holistic, values-based model of career and life role choice and satisfaction. In D. Brown, L. Brooks, & Associates (Eds.), *Career choice and development* (3rd ed., pp. 337–372). San Francisco, CA: Jossey-Bass.

Brown, D. (2002). The role of work and cultural values in occupational choice, satisfaction, and success: A theoretical statement. *Journal of Counseling & Development, 80*, 48–55.

Brown, D. (2003). *Career information, career counseling, and career development* (8th ed.). Boston, MA: Allyn & Bacon.

Brown, D., & Crace, R. K. (1996). Values in life role choices and outcomes: A conceptual model. *Career Development Quarterly, 44*, 211–224.

Brown, S. D., & Gore, P. A. (1994). An evaluation of interest congruence indices: Distribution characteristics and measurement properties. *Journal of Vocational Behavior, 45*, 310–327.

Byars, A. M., & Hackett, G. (1998). Applications of social cognitive theory to the career development of women of color. *Applied and Preventive Psychology, 7*, 255–267.

Byars-Winston, A. M., & Fouad, N. A. (2008). Math and science social cognitive variables in college students: Contributions of contextual factors in predicting goals. *Journal of Career Assessment, 16*, 425–440. doi: 10.1177/1069072708318901

Camp, C. C., & Chartrand, J. M. (1992). A comparison and evaluation of interest congruence indices. *Journal of Vocational Behavior, 41*, 162–182.

Care, E., Deans, J., & Brown, R. (2007). The realism and sex type of four- to five-year-old children's occupational aspirations. *Journal of Early Childhood Research, 5*, 155–168. doi: 10.1177/1476718X07076681

Carnevale, A. P., Smith, N., & Strohl, J. (2010a). *Help wanted: Projections of jobs and education requirements through 2018 (Executive Summary).* Washington, DC: Georgetown University Center on Education and the Workforce. Retrieved from http://www9.georgetown.edu/grad/gppi/hpi/cew/pdfs/ExecutiveSummary-web.pdf

Carnevale, A. P., Smith, N., & Strohl, J. (2010b). *Projections of jobs and education requirements through 2018.* Washington, DC: Georgetown University Center on Education and the Workforce. Retrieved from http://www9.georgetown.edu/grad/gppi/hpi/cew/pdfs/FullReport.pdf

Chiocchio, F., & Frigon, J. (2006). Tenure, satisfaction, and work environment flexibility of people with mental retardation. *Journal of Vocational Behavior, 68,* 175–187. doi: 10.1016/j.jvb.2004.11.004

Chope, R. (2008). Practice and research in career counseling and development— 2007. *Career Development Quarterly, 57,* 98–173.

Cook, E. P., Heppner, M. J., & O'Brien, K. M. (2002). Career development of women of color and White women: Assumptions, conceptualization, and interventions from an ecological perspective. *Career Development Quarterly, 50,* 291–305.

Cook, E. P., Heppner, M. J., & O'Brien, K. M. (2005). Multicultural and gender influences in women's career development: An ecological perspective. *Journal of Multicultural Counseling and Development, 33,* 165–17.

Darcy, M. U. A., & Tracey, T. J. G. (2007). Circumplex structure of Holland's RIASEC interests across gender and time. *Journal of Counseling Psychology, 54,* 17–31. doi: 10.1037/0022-0167.54.1.17

Datti, P. (2009). Applying social learning theory of career decision making to gay, lesbian, bisexual, transgender, and questioning young adults. *Career Development Quarterly, 58,* 54–64.

Dawis, R. V. (1994). The theory of work adjustment as convergent theory. In M. L. Savikas & R. W. Lent (Eds.), *Convergence in career development theories* (pp. 33–44). Palo Alto, CA: CPP Books.

Dawis, R. V. (1996). The theory of work adjustment and person-environment-correspondence counseling. In D. Brown, L. Brooks, & Associates (Eds.), *Career choice and development: Applying contemporary theories to practice* (3rd ed., pp. 75–120). San Francisco, CA: Jossey-Bass.

Dawis, R. V. (2005). The Minnesota theory of work adjustment. In S. D. Brown & R. W. Lent (Eds.), *Career development and counseling: Putting theory and research to work* (2nd ed., pp. 3–23). Hoboken, NJ: Wiley.

Dawis, R. V., England, G. W., & Lofquist, L. H. (1964). A theory of work adjustment. *Minnesota Studies in Vocational Rehabilitation, 15,* 1–27.

Dawis, R. V., & Lofquist, L. H. (1984). *A psychological theory of work adjustment: An individual-differences model and its applications.* Minneapolis: University of Minnesota Press.

Dawis, R. V., & Lofquist, L. H. (1993). From TWA to PEC. *Journal of Vocational Behavior, 43,* 113–121.

Day, S. X., Rounds, J., & Swaney, K. (1998). The structure of vocational interests for diverse racial-ethnic groups. *Psychological Science, 9,* 40–44.

Degges-White, S. D., & Shoffner, M. F. (2002). Career counseling with lesbian clients: Using the theory of work adjustment as a framework. *Career Development Quarterly, 51,* 87–96.

Donohue, R. (2006). Person-environment congruence in relation to career change and career persistence. *Journal of Vocational Behavior, 68,* 504–515. doi:10.1016/j.jvb.2005.11.002

Eggerth, D. (2008). From theory of work adjustment to person-environment correspondence counseling: Vocational psychology as positive psychology. *Journal of Career Assessment, 16,* 60–74. doi: 10.1177/1069072707305771

Erikson, E. H. (1968). *Identity: Youth and crisis.* New York: Norton.

Evans, C. D., & Diekman, A. B. (2009). On motivated role selection: Gender beliefs, distant goals, and career interest. *Psychology of Women Quarterly, 33*(2), 235-249. doi:10.1111/j.1471-6402.2009.01493.x

Ferry, T. R., Fouad, N. A., & Smith, P. L. (2000). The role of family context in a social cognitive model for career-related choice behavior: A math and science perspective. *Journal of Vocational Behavior, 57,* 348–364.

Fouad, N. A. (2002). Cross-cultural differences in vocational interests: Between-group differences on the Strong Interest Inventory. *Journal of Counseling Psychology, 49,* 283–289. doi: 10.1037/0022-0167.49.3.282

Fouad, N. A. (2007). Work and vocational psychology: Theory, research, and applications. *Annual Review of Psychology, 58,* 543–564.

Fouad, N. A., & Guillen, A. (2006). Outcome expectations: Looking to the past and potential future. *Journal of Career Assessment, 14,* 130–142. doi: 10.1177/1069 072705281370

Fouad, N. A., Harmon, L. W., & Borgen, F. H. (1997). Structure of interests in employed male and female members of U.S. racial-ethnic minority and non-minority groups. *Journal of Counseling Psychology, 44,* 339–345.

Fouad, N., & Mohler, C. (2004). Cultural validity of Holland's theory and the Strong Interest Inventory for five racial/ethnic groups. *Journal of Career Assessment, 12,* 423–439. doi: 10.1177/1069072704267736

Fouad, N., & Smith, P. (1996). A test of a social cognitive model for middle school students: Math and science. *Journal of Counseling Psychology, 43,* 338–346. doi: 10.1037/0022-0167.43.3.338

Gibbons, M. M., & Shoffner, M. F. (2004). Prospective first-generation college students: Meeting their needs through social cognitive career theory. *Professional School Counseling, 8,* 91–97.

Ginzberg, E., Ginsburg, S. W., Axelrad, S., & Herma, J. (1951). *Occupational choice: An approach to a general theory.* New York, NY: Columbia University Press.

Gottfredson, G. D., & Johnstun, M. (2009). John Holland's contributions: A theory-ridden approach to career assistance. *Career Development Quarterly, 58,* 99–107.

Gottfredson, L. S. (1981). Circumscription and compromise: A developmental theory of occupational aspirations [Monograph]. *Journal of Counseling Psychology, 28,* 545–579.

Gottfredson, L. S. (1996). Circumscription and compromise: A developmental theory of occupational aspirations. In D. Brown, L. Brooks, & Associates (Eds.), *Career choice and development: Applying contemporary theories to practice* (3rd ed., pp. 170–232). San Francisco, CA: Jossey-Bass.

Gottfredson, L. S. (2005). Using Gottfredson's theory of circumscription and compromise in career guidance and counseling. In S. D. Brown & R. W. Lent (Eds.), *Career development and counseling: Putting theory and research to work* (pp. 71–100). Hoboken, NJ: Wiley.

Gottfredson, L. S., & Richards, J. M., Jr. (1999). The meaning and measurement of environments in Holland's theory. *Journal of Vocational Behavior, 55,* 57–73.

Gushue, G., Clarke, C., Pantzer, K., & Scanlan, K. (2006). Self-efficacy, perceptions of barriers, vocational identity, and the career exploration behavior of Latino/a high school students. *Career Development Quarterly, 54,* 307–317.

Hackett, G. (1985). The role of mathematics self-efficacy in the choice of math-related majors of college women and men: A path model. *Journal of Counseling Psychology, 32,* 47–56.

Hackett, G., & Betz, N. E. (1981). A self-efficacy approach to the career development of women. *Journal of Vocational Behavior, 18,* 326–339.

Hackett, G., & Byars, A. M. (1996). Social cognitive theory and the career development of African American women. *Career Development Quarterly, 44,* 322–340.

Hackett, G., & Lent, R. W. (1992). Theoretical advances and current inquiry in career psychology. In S. D. Brown & R. W. Lent (Eds.), *Handbook of counseling psychology* (2nd ed., pp. 419–451). New York, NY: Wiley.

Harper, M. C., & Shoffner, M. F. (2004). Counseling for continued career development after retirement: An application of the theory of work adjustment. *Career Development Quarterly, 52,* 272–284.

Hartung, P. J. (2002). Cultural context in career theory and practice: Role salience and values. *Career Development Quarterly, 51,* 12–26.

Hartung, P. J. (2009). Practice and research in career counseling and development – 2009. *The Career Development Quarterly, 59,* 98–142.

Helwig, A. A. (2001). A test of Gottfredson's theory using a ten-year longitudinal study. *Journal of Career Development, 28,* 77–95. doi: 10.1023/A:1012578625948

Hershenson, D. B. (1981). Work adjustment, disability, and the three r's of vocational rehabilitation: A conceptual model. *Rehabilitation Counseling Bulletin, 25,* 91–97.

Hershenson, D. B. (1996). Work adjustment: A neglected area in career counseling. *Journal of Counseling and Development, 74,* 442–446.

Hershenson, D. B. (2001). Promoting work adjustments in Workforce Investment Act consumers: A role for employment counselors. *Journal of Employment Counseling, 38,* 28–37.

Hesketh, B., Elmslie, S., & Kaldor, W. (1990). Career compromise: An alternative account to Gottfredson's theory. *Journal of Counseling Psychology, 37,* 49–56.

Hesketh, B., McLachlan, K., & Gardner, D. (1992). Work adjustment theory: An empirical test using a fuzzy rating scale. *Journal of Vocational Behavior, 40,* 318–337.

Holland, J. L. (1959). A theory of vocational choice. *Journal of Counseling Psychology, 6,* 35–45.

Holland, J. L. (1973). *Making vocational choices: A theory of careers.* Englewood Cliffs, NJ: Prentice-Hall.

Holland, J. L. (1985). *Making vocational choices: A theory of vocational personalities and work environments* (2nd ed.). Englewood Cliffs, NJ: Prentice-Hall.

Holland, J. L. (1992). *Making vocational choices: A theory of vocational personalities and work environments* (2nd ed.). Odessa, FL: Psychological Assessment Resources.

Holland, J. L. (1997). *Making vocational choices: A theory of vocational personalities and work environments* (3rd ed.). Odessa, FL: Psychological Assessment Resource.

Holland, J. L., Whitney, D. R., Cole, N. S., & Richards, J. M. (1969). *An empirical occupational classification derived from a theory of personality and intended for practice and research* (ACT Research Reports No. 29). Iowa City, IA: American College Testing Program.

Hotchkiss, L., & Borow, H. (1990). Sociological perspectives on work and career development. In D. Brown, L. Brooks, & Associates (Eds.), *Career choice and development: Applying contemporary theories to practice* (2nd ed., pp. 262–307). San Francisco, CA: Jossey-Bass.

Kleiman, T., Gati, I., Peterson, G., Sampson, J., Reardon, R., & Lenz, J. (2004). Dysfunctional thinking and difficulties in career decision making. *Journal of Career Assessment, 12,* 312–331.

Krumboltz, J. D. (1979). A social learning theory of career decision making. In A. Mitchell, G. Jones, & J. Krumboltz (Eds.), *Social learning and career decision making* (pp. 19–49). Cranston, RI: Carroll Press.

Krumboltz, J. D. (1994). Improving career development theory from a social learning perspective. In M. L. Savickas & R. W. Lent (Eds.), *Convergence in career development theories: Implications for science and practice* (pp. 9–31). Palo Alto, CA: CPP Books.

Krumboltz, J. D. (1996). A learning theory of career counseling. In M. L. Savickas & W. B. Walsh (Eds.), *Handbook of career counseling theory and practice* (pp. 55–80). Palo Alto, CA: Davies-Black.

Krumboltz, J. D., & Henderson, S. J. (2002). A learning theory for career counselors. In S. G. Niles (Ed.), *Adult career development: Concepts, issues and practices* (3rd ed., pp. 39–56). Broken Arrow, OK: National Career Development Association.

Krumboltz, J. D., & Levin, A. S. (2004). *Luck is no accident.* Atascadero, CA: Impact.

Krumboltz, J. D., Mitchell, A., & Jones, G. (1976). A social learning theory of career selection. *Counseling Psychologist, 6,* 71–81.

Lapan, R. T., Hinkelman, J. M., Adams, A., & Turner, S. (1999). Understanding rural adolescents' interests, values, and efficacy expectations. *Journal of Career Development, 26,* 107–124.

Lent, R., & Brown, S. (2006). On conceptualizing and assessing social cognitive constructs in career research: A measurement guide. *Journal of Career Assessment, 14,* 12–35. doi: 10.1177/1069072705281364

Lent, R. W., Brown, S. D., & Hackett, G. (1994). Toward a unifying social cognitive theory of career and academic interest, choice, and performance [Monograph]. *Journal of Vocational Behavior, 45,* 79–122.

Lent, R. W., Brown, S. D., & Hackett, G. (2000). Contextual supports and barriers to career choice: A social cognitive analysis. *Journal of Counseling Psychology, 47,* 36–49.

Lent, R. W., Brown, S. E., Brenner, B., Chopra, S. B., Davis, T., Talleyrand, R., & Suthakaran, V. (2001). The role of contextual supports and barriers in the choice of math/science educational options: A test of social cognitive hypotheses. *Journal of Counseling Psychology, 48,* 474–483.

Lent, R. W., Lopez, F. G., & Bieschke, K. J. (1991). Mathematics self-efficacy: Sources and relation to science-based career choice. *Journal of Counseling Psychology, 38,* 424–430.

Lent, R. W., Lopez, A. M., Jr., Lopez, F. G., & Sheu, H.-B. (2008). Social cognitive career theory and the prediction of interests and choice goals in the computing disciplines. *Journal of Vocational Behavior, 73,* 52–62. doi: 10.1016/j.jvb.2008.01.002

Lent, R. W., Sheu, H.-B., Singley, D., Schmidt, J. A., Schmidt, L. C., & Gloster, C. S. (2008). Longitudinal relations of self-efficacy to outcome expectations, interests, and major choice goals in engineering students. *Journal of Vocational Behavior, 73,* 328–335. doi: 10.1016/j.jvb.2008.07.005

Liptak, J. J. (2001). *Treatment planning in career counseling.* Belmont, CA: Brooks/Cole.

Lofquist, L. H., & Dawis, R. V. (1991). *Essentials of person-environment-correspondence counseling.* Minneapolis: University of Minnesota Press.

Lopez, F. G., Lent, R. W., Brown, S. D, & Gore, P. A. (1997). Role of social-cognitive expectations in high school students' mathematics-related interest and performance. *Journal of Counseling Psychology, 44,* 44–52.

Luzzo, D. A. (1996). Exploring the relationship between the perception of occupational barriers and career development. *Journal of Career Development, 22,* 239–248.

Lyons, H., Brenner, B., & Fassinger, R. (2005). A multicultural test of the theory of work adjustment: Investigating the role of heterosexism and fit perceptions in the job satisfaction of lesbian, gay, and bisexual employees. *Journal of Counseling Psychology, 52,* 537–548.

McWhirter, E. H. (1997). Perceived barriers to education and career: Ethnic and gender differences. *Journal of Vocational Behavior, 50,* 124–140.

McWhirter, E. H., Hackett, G., & Bandalos, D. L. (1998). A causal model of the educational plans and career expectations of Mexican American high school girls. *Journal of Counseling Psychology, 45,* 166–181.

Meyer-Griffith, K., Reardon, R. C., & Hartley, S. L. (2009). An examination of the relationship between career thoughts and communication apprehension. *Career Development Quarterly, 51,* 171–180.

Mitchell, L. K., & Krumboltz, J. D. (1996). Krumboltz' learning theory of career choice counseling. In D. Brown, L. Brooks, & Associates (Eds.), *Career choice and development: Applying contemporary theories to practice* (3rd ed., pp. 233–276). San Francisco, CA: Jossey-Bass.

Mitchell, K., Levin, A., & Krumboltz, J. (1999). Planned Happenstance: Constructing Unexpected Career Opportunities. *Journal of Counseling & Development, 77*(2), 115–124.

Morrow, S. L., Gore, P. A., Jr., & Campbell, B. W. (1996). The application of a sociocognitive framework to the career development of lesbian women and gay men. *Journal of Vocational Behavior, 48,* 136–148.

Nauta, M. (2010). The development, evolution, and status of Holland's theory of vocational personalities: Reflections and future directions for counseling psychology. *Journal of Counseling Psychology, 57,* 11–22. doi: 10.1037/a0018213

Navarro, R. L., Flores, L. Y., & Worthington, R. L. (2007). Mexican American middle school students' goal intentions in mathematics and science: A test of social cognitive career theory. *Journal of Counseling Psychology, 54,* 320–335. doi: 10.1037/0022-0167.54.3.320

Niles, S. G., Engels, D., & Lenz, J. (2009). Training career practitioners. *Career Development Quarterly, 57,* 358–365.

Niles, S. G., & Goodnough, G. E. (1996). Life-role salience and values: A review of recent research. *Career Development Quarterly, 45,* 65–86.

Niles, S. G., & Harris-Bowlsbey, J. (2009). *Career development interventions in the 21st century* (3rd ed.). Upper Saddle River, NJ: Pearson Education, Inc.

Ojeda, L., & Flores, L. (2008). The influence of gender, generation level, parents' education level, and perceived barriers on the educational aspirations of Mexican American high school students. *Career Development Quarterly, 57,* 84–95.

Osborn, D. S., Howard, D. K., & Leierer, S. J. (2007). The effect of a career development course on the dysfunctional career thoughts of racially and ethnically diverse college freshmen. *Career Development Quarterly, 55,* 365–377.

Paivandy, S., Bullock, E. E., Reardon, R. R., & Kelly, F. D. (2008). The effects of decision-making style and cognitive thought patterns on negative career thoughts. *Journal of Career Assessment, 16,* 474–488.

Parsons, F. (1909). *Choosing a vocation.* Boston, MA: Houghton Mifflin.

Patton, W., & McIlveen, P. (2009). Practice and research in career counseling and development—2008. *Career Development Quarterly, 58,* 118–161.

Patton, W., & McMahon, M. (1999). *Career development and systems theory: A new relationship.* Belmont, CA: Brooks/Cole.

Patton, W. A., & McMahon, M. L. (2006). The systems theory framework of career development and counseling: Connecting theory and practice. *International Journal for the Advancement of Counselling, 28,* 153–166. doi: 10.1007/s10447-005-9010-1

Peterson, G., Sampson, J., & Reardon, R. E. (1991). *Career development and services: A cognitive approach.* Pacific Grove, CA: Brooks/Cole.

Peterson, G. W., Sampson, J. P., Jr., Reardon, R. C., & Lenz, J. G. (2008). Cognitive information processing model. In F. T. L. Leong (Ed.), *Encyclopedia of counseling* (pp. 1504–1509). Thousand Oaks, CA: Sage.

Power, P., & Hershenson, D. (2003). Work adjustment and readjustment of persons with mid-career onset traumatic brain injury. *Brain Injury, 17,* 1021. doi: 10.1080/0269905031000110526.

Prediger, D. J. (2000). Holland's hexagon is alive and well—though somewhat out of shape: Response to Tinsley. *Journal of Vocational Behavior, 56,* 197–204.

Reardon, R. C., Lenz, J. G., Sampson, J. P., Jr., & Peterson, G. W. (2005). *Career development and planning: A comprehensive approach* (2nd ed). Pacific Grove, CA: Brooks/Cole.

Rivera, L., Chen, E., Flores, L., Blumberg, F., & Ponterotto, J. (2007). The effects of perceived barriers, role models, and acculturation on the career self-efficacy and career consideration of Hispanic women. *Career Development Quarterly, 56,* 47–61.

Rounds, J. R., & Hesketh, B. (1994). Theory of work adjustment: Unifying principles and concepts. In M. L. Savickas & R. W. Lent (Eds.), *Convergence in career development theories: Implications for science and practice* (pp. 177–186). Palo Alto, CA: CPP Books.

Rounds, J., & Tracey, T. J. (1996). Cross-cultural structural equivalence of RIASEC models and measures. *Journal of Counseling Psychology, 43,* 310–329.

Ryan, J. M., Tracey, T. J. G., & Rounds, J. (1996). Generalizability of Holland's structure of vocational interests across ethnicity, gender, and socioeconomic status. *Journal of Counseling Psychology, 43,* 330–337.

Sampson, J. P., Jr., Reardon, R. C., Peterson, G. W., & Lenz, J. G. (2004). *Career counseling and services: A cognitive information processing approach.* Belmont, CA: Brooks/Cole.

Satterwhite, R., Fleenor, J., Braddy, P., Feldman, J., & Hoopes, L. (2009). A case for homogeneity of personality at the occupational level. *International Journal of Selection & Assessment, 17,* 154–164. doi: 10.1111/j.1468-2389.2009.00459.x.

Savickas, M. L. (1998). Career style assessment and counseling. In T. J. Sweeney (Ed.), *Adlerian counseling: A practitioner's approach* (pp. 329–359). Philadelphia, PA: Accelerated Development.

Savickas, M. L. (2005). The Theory and Practice of Career Construction. In S. D. Brown & R. W. Lent (Eds.) *Career development and counseling: Putting theory and research to work* (pp. 42–70). Hoboken, NJ: John Wiley & Sons.

Schultheiss, D. E. P., Kress, H. M., Manzi, A. J., & Glasscock, J. M. J. (2001). Relational influences in career development: A qualitative inquiry. *Counseling Psychologist, 29,* 214–239.

Shoffner, M. F., Newsome, D. W., & Barrio, C. A. (2004). *Youth's outcome expectations: A qualitative study.* Manuscript submitted for publication.

Shoffner Creager, M. F. (in press). Practice and research in career counseling and development – 2010. *The Career Development Quarterly*.

Shurts, W. M., & Shoffner, M. F. (2004). Providing career counseling for collegiate student-athletes: A learning theory approach. *Journal of Career Development, 31,* 95–109.

Spokane, A. R. (1994). The resolution of incongruence and the dynamics of person-environment fit. In M. L. Savickas & R. W. Lent (Eds.), *Convergence in career development theories: Implications for science and practice* (pp. 119–137). Palo Alto, CA: CPP Books.

Spokane, A. R., & Cruza-Guet, M. C. (2005). Holland's theory of vocational person-alities in work environments. In S. D. Brown & R. W. Lent (Eds.), *Career development and counseling: Putting theory and research to work* (2nd ed., pp. 24–41). Hoboken, NJ: Wiley.

Spokane, A. R., Meir, E. I., & Catalano, M. (2000). Person-environment congru-ence and Holland's theory: A review and reconsideration. *Journal of Vocational Behavior, 57,* 137–187.

Stebleton, M. (2007). Career counseling with African immigrant college students: Theoretical approaches and implications for practice. *Career Development Quarterly, 55,* 290–312.

Stebleton, M. J. (2010). Narrative-based career counseling perspectives in times of change: An analysis of strengths and limitations. *Journal of Employment Counseling, 47*(2), 64–78.

Strauser, D., & Lustig, D. (2003). The moderating effect of sense of coherence on work adjustment. *Journal of Employment Counseling, 40,* 129–140.

Super, D. E. (1980). A lifespan, life space approach to career development. *Journal of Vocational Behavior, 16,* 282–298.

Super, D. E. (1990). A life-span, life-space approach to career development. In D. Brooks & L. Brown, & Associates (Eds.), *Career choice and development: Applying contemporary theories to practice* (2nd ed., pp. 197–261). San Francisco, CA: Jossey-Bass.

Super, D. E., Savickas, M. L., & Super, C. M. (1996). The life-span, life-space approach to careers. In D. Brooks, L. Brown, & Associates (Eds.), *Career choice and development: Applying contemporary theories to practice* (3rd ed., pp. 121–178). San Francisco, CA: Jossey-Bass.

Swanson, J. L., & Tokar, D. M. (1991). College students' perceptions of barriers to career development. *Journal of Vocational Behavior, 38,* 92–106.

Tang, M., Fouad, N. A., & Smith, P. L. (1999). Asian Americans' career choices: A path model to examine factors influencing their career choices. *Journal of Vocational Behavior, 54,* 142–157.

Tang, M., Pan, W., & Newmeyer, M. (2008). Factors influencing high school stu-dents' career aspirations. *Professional School Counseling, 11,* 285–295.

Tien, H.-L. S. (2007). Practice and research in career counseling and development—2006. *Career Development Quarterly, 56,* 98–140.

Tien, H.-L. S., Wang, Y.-F., & Liu, L.-C. (2009). The role of career barriers in high school students' career choice behavior in Taiwan. *Career Development Quarterly, 57,* 274–288.

Tinsley, H. F. A. (2000). The congruence myth: An analysis of the efficacy of the person-environment fit model. *Journal of Vocational Behavior, 56,* 147–179.

Tracey, T. J. G. (1997). The structure of interests and self-efficacy expectations: An expanded examination of the spherical model of interests. *Journal of Counseling Psychology, 44,* 32–43.

Tracey, T. J., & Rounds, J. R. (1993). Evaluating Holland's and Gati's vocational-interest models: A structural meta-analysis. *Psychological Bulletin, 113,* 229–246.

Trevor-Roberts, E. (2006). Are you sure? The role of uncertainty in career. *Journal of Employment Counseling, 43*(3), 98–116.

Trusty, J. (2002). Effects of high school course-taking and other variables on choice of science and mathematics college majors. *Journal of Counseling & Development, 80,* 464.

Trusty, J. (2004). Effects of students' middle-school and high-school experiences on completion of the bachelor's degree. *Professional School Counseling, 7,* 99–107.

Trusty, J., & Niles, S. (2003). High-school math courses and completion of the bachelor's degree. *Professional School Counseling, 7,* 99–107.

Trusty, J., & Niles, S. (2004). Realized potential or lost talent: High school variables and bachelor's degree completion. *Career Development Quarterly, 53,* 2–15.

Trusty, J., Robinson, C., Plata, M., & Ng, K. (2000). Effects of gender, socioeconomic status, and early academic performance on postsecondary educational choice. *Journal of Counseling & Development, 78,* 463–472.

Tsabari, O., Tziner, A., & Meir, E. I. (2005). Updated meta-analysis on the relationship between congruence and satisfaction. *Journal of Career Assessment, 13,* 216–232.

Turner, S. L., & Lapan, R. T. (2002). Career self-efficacy and perceptions of parent support in adolescent career development. *Career Development Quarterly, 51,* 44–55.

Turner, S. L., & Lapan, R. T. (2003). The measurement of career interests among at-risk inner-city and middle-class suburban adolescents. *Journal of Career Assessment, 11,* 405–420.

Turner, S., Steward, J., & Lapan, R. (2004). Family factors associated with sixth-grade adolescents' math and science career interests. *Career Development Quarterly, 53,* 41–52.

Usher, E., & Pajares, F. (2009). Sources of self-efficacy in mathematics: A validation study. *Contemporary Educational Psychology, 34,* 89–101. doi: 10.1016/j.cedpsych.2008.09.002

Vandiver, B. J., & Bowman, S. L. (1996). A schematic reconceptualization and application of Gottfredson's model. In M. L. Savickas & W. B. Walsh (Eds.), *Handbook of career counseling theory and practice* (pp. 155–168). Palo Alto, CA: Davies-Black.

Withrow, R., & Shoffner, M. (2006). Applying the theory of work adjustment to clients with symptoms of anorexia nervosa. *Journal of Career Development, 32,* 366–377.

Young, R. A., & Valach, L. (2004). The construction of career through goal-directed action. *Journal of Vocational Behavior, 64,* 499–514. doi: 10.1016/j.jvb.2003.12.012

Young, R. A., Valach, L., & Collin, A. (1996). A contextual explanation of career. In D. Brown, L. Brooks, & Associates (Eds.), *Career choice and development* (3rd ed., pp. 477–512) San Francisco, CA: Jossey-Bass.

CHAPTER **3**

# Toward a Holistic View
## Decision-Making, Postmodern, and Emerging Theories

Jane Goodman

## Contents

In recent years, a number of people have addressed the idea that career and personal counseling are inseparable (e.g., Bloch & Richmond, 1997; Jepsen, 1992; Looby & Sandhu, 2002). The reader needs only to consider his or her own career to realize how personal it indeed is. Not only are people's careers central to their identity, but they affect and are affected by all of the other areas of their lives. Making a career decision in a vacuum is worse than meaningless, it is counterproductive. Career counselors who ask clients to set aside all other areas of life as they consider their career choices are doing them a serious disservice. It must be said here that clients often err in this regard also. They may resist life planning as being more complex than they wish. The search for simple answers is a common one. Counselors have an obligation to explain the process and explain what makes effective decisions as opposed to merely efficient decisions. In many cases, there may be what can be called an unconscious conspiracy between counselor and client to avoid ambiguity, short circuit the process, and make a quick decision.

Although much career counseling is done in agencies and by counselors in private practice, many counselors assist students with career development, both in the K through 12 system and at colleges and universities. I specifically address student concerns in a section of this chapter, but virtually all of the material presented using the word *client* also applies to students. For purposes of simplicity, I use the word *client* to mean both students and clients.

The personal aspects of career were addressed early in the history of career development theories by Super (1957), particularly in his metaphors of the career rainbow and arch. In his landmark work *The Psychology of Careers*, Super (1957, pp. 3–16) identified several reasons why people work. They include the need to earn a livelihood, for both current needs and security for the future, but they also include the need for recognition as a person, status, and opportunity for self-expression. Super's (1980) life career rainbow includes the roles of child, student, leisurite, citizen, worker, and homemaker. His arch uses the self as its keystone, and personal and societal influences form the pillars.

Many others have pointed out the integration of career and life planning (e.g., Hansen, 1997; Hansen & Suddarth, 2008). Gold, Rotter, and Evans (2002) made a strong case that all career decisions are influenced by one's family and culture. One can follow their logic and assert that the practice of career counseling should, and often has, reflected this change. Many counseling protocols emphasize values that are often considered traditionally male, that is, competition, individual accomplishment, and autonomous decision making. Gold et al. (2002) recommended that career counselors include what are sometimes considered the traditionally feminine values of relational reasoning and interdependence. They recommended a tripartite approach that includes these values and also focuses on the contextual and sociological components of an individual's life space. Evans, Rotter, and Gold's (2002) book *Synthesizing Family, Career, and Culture: A Model for Counseling in the Twenty-First Century* focused on the intersection of these three aspects. As they put it,

> We are not as "individual" as we may think, or even hope, but rather present for counseling as a representative, or reflection of our relational and sociological contexts. What we have learned about ourselves as a family member, son, or daughter, male or female, member of a specific religious group, racial or ethnic group, and so on are vital components of our self definition, in our career concerns as well as general life decisions. (Evans et al., 2002, p. 23)

It is important to consider each individual's culture as one looks at the relationships among family, community, and the individual. One decider may put his or her own autonomy as the first consideration; another may put community needs or family expectations first.

Cohen-Scali (2003), in discussing the influence of family on young adults, put forth the thesis, based on a European longitudinal study, that young people begin to develop their professional identity at a very young age. Deriving first from informal home experiences and developing during the usually more formal experiences of their school years, adolescents form a cognitive map onto which to project their ideas about occupations. Cohen-Scali (2003) stated that this map allows young people to "compare and evaluate professions, their degree of masculinity/femininity, and their degrees of prestige" (p. 240). She concluded that students are socialized for work and then later socialized by work, as they re-form identities through interaction with the work environment. This work implies that school counselors should work with parents to help them help their children to form expanded concepts of their possible professional identities, as well as work directly with the children in the school. I discuss the implications of this work for school counselors in a later section.

Schultheiss (2003) put forth a passionate proposal for a relational approach to career counseling. She suggested that traditional career counseling can be enhanced by this approach, using a relational approach to assessment and intervention. Growing out of feminist and other early work suggesting that connectedness should be held as an equal value to autonomy, she argued that "the goal of integrating relational theory with career theory is to provide a more holistic integrative conceptual framework, or meta-perspective, that recognizes the value of relational connection and, quite simply, the realities of people's lives" (Schulthiess, 2003, p. 304). Similarly, Blustein, Schultheiss, and Flum (2004) argued that a social constructionist perspective allows for a deeper understanding of careers, work, and relationships. In this chapter, I present a variety of ways in which career counselors can move beyond simplistic matching approaches to ones that take this kind of relational holistic view of the career decision-making process.

#### SIDEBAR 3.1 Melissa Winters, Sommelier

Melissa Winters loved her work as a sommelier at a four-star restaurant. She loved creating the wine list and helping customers select wines for what was for many a special occasion. She worked primarily evenings and weekends, which had worked well for her as a young single woman, but she had recently married and wanted to have her evenings free to spend with her new husband, who worked a standard nine-to-five day.

#### SIDEBAR 3.2 Diego Sanchez, Surgeon

Diego Sanchez was a successful and satisfied pediatric surgeon until he developed Parkinson's disease in his early 50s. He could no longer perform surgery because of his tremors. He had worked many years to develop his surgical expertise and was terrified that he would not be able again to find work that he loved.

#### SIDEBAR 3.3 Takesha Jones, Teacher

Takesha Jones had always wanted to be an elementary school teacher. But she completed her training at a time when school districts were laying off, not hiring, teachers. Her friends are telling her to look for a job in business, where they think she would thrive. Should she abandon her dream?

#### SIDEBAR 3.4 James Green, High School Dropout

James Green has just turned 30. He is beginning to question his wisdom in dropping out of high school at age 16 without a diploma. Although he has supported himself reasonably well as a roofer, he is tired of the seasonal uncertainty and the hard physical labor. He wonders, "Is this all there is for me?"

There are thousands, maybe hundreds of thousands of people like Melissa Winter, Diego Sanchez, Takesha Jones, and James Green. They all hope to find work that meets their financial and physical needs, but they also hope to find work that helps to meet their need to find meaning in their lives. In this chapter, I discuss individuals' desire for "right work," the pathways to managing a satisfying career, and the barriers that may be placed in their ways because of world and national economic conditions, poverty, and discrimination.

I follow each of these individuals as I explore finding meaning in work and career, individual choice, the decision-making process, and the balance among work, family, leisure, and community life. Although I recognize that each of these elements overlaps considerably with others, I describe them as though they were discrete. I also look at some pathways and barriers to each individual's successful career development.

## Barriers

Let us begin with the barriers.

### SIDEBAR 3.5  Barrier Activity

As you read this section on barriers, keep a running list of all the barriers described, and add to it barriers faced by you and people whom you know. They could include internal barriers, such as fear of failure or success, and external barrier such as financial resources or discrimination.

Many Americans do not have "liberty and justice for all," as promised in the Pledge of Allegiance. Many are condemned by poverty to poor education, poor prenatal and childhood nutrition, and reduced access to the opportunity structure. Many have reduced intellectual abilities because of pollution and environmental hazards such as lead paint. Others face discrimination because of racism, sexism, ageism, homoprejudice, or handicapping condition. Still others have limited access to jobs, education, or both by virtue of living in a rural area or a community affected by the loss of a major industry. Unskilled or minimally skilled workers are harder hit by these circumstances. In the past 60 years, the United States has moved from an economy in which the majority of jobs were filled by unskilled workers to one in which a high school and often a college degree is necessary. For example, jobs in manufacturing, a traditional employer of unskilled and semiskilled workers, are expected to decline 24% from 2008 to 2018 according to the *Occupational Outlook Handbook* (2010). Furthermore, a shift to a more service-oriented labor force has led to many people working in lower paying jobs, jobs that are part time or temporary, and frequently in jobs without benefits and with uncertain employment futures (Bobek & Robbins, 2005). This enormous change has left many people unprepared to find work that provides an adequate income.

Melissa was fortunate to have no obvious external barriers. She was successful in what has traditionally been a male province and was a middle-class member of the majority in all ways. However, her lifestyle choices were creating a conflict for her—family time versus work she loved. I discuss issues of finding work–life balance later in this chapter. Melissa had found her job as a sommelier by working first as a waitress and learning about wine through on-the-job training. She had no obvious training for other positions. She had no résumé and no serious job-hunting experience.

Diego Sanchez had grown comfortable in his role as a medical doctor. The third child in a large Mexican American family, Dr. Sanchez had worked extremely hard to complete his education. His parents were supportive emotionally but were not able to help him financially. His two older sisters and his two younger brothers were very proud of the doctor in the family. He was ashamed, although he knew it was unreasonable, feeling that he had let them down by becoming ill. He believed that his ethnicity would make it more difficult to make a career change, because he felt it had made it difficult when he originally pursued the surgical branch of medicine. He had not considered career counseling for his problem. He had been raised in a family that believed that getting outside help was a sign of weakness, and although he frequently recommended counseling for his patients, he did not think this advice applied to him. Perhaps more serious for Dr. Sanchez than either of these barriers is the fact that he is older than 50. Workers older than 40 are protected by federal regulations for a reason—age discrimination exists. If Dr. Sanchez is interested in retraining, this barrier may be even higher.

Takesha Jones is an African American woman in her early 20s. She attended private schools because her professional parents were not happy with the public schools in the urban area in which they lived. She has always felt confident about her abilities to succeed in anything she chose, so the circumstances she is now facing are surprising to her. She believed she could overcome any societal barrier, but she does not know what to do with an economic one. Takesha loves the urban area in which she lives and does not want to relocate. She is close to her family and would be unhappy living far away from them. Information that there are teaching jobs in distant states or in rural areas is not reassuring to her. Takesha has no memory of making a conscious decision to become a teacher. It is what she has always known she would do. She has no idea how she might decide on a different occupation.

James Green has created many of his own barriers. Dropping out of school was, he realized in retrospect, a poor decision. He also fathered a child whom he helps to support, although he is no longer married to the child's mother. He has another child with the woman he lives with, and he is also a primary provider for her other two children, although their father does pay some child support. His partner works at a low-paying job that just barely covers the costs of day care for the younger two children. Her job does provide health insurance for her and the three children, but James is not covered under her policy because they are not married. That is another decision facing him. If he leaves his job, should he get married just for health insurance? After his failed first marriage, he is very uncertain about taking the plunge again.

All of these people are faced with internal and external barriers. As I follow them through their career development, I look at career counseling approaches that might assist in them in finding satisfying work and overcoming the barriers that they face. Although it is beyond the scope of this chapter, I believe it is also important for career counselors to advocate efforts on behalf of clients, as well as to teach clients how to advocate on their own behalf. (For more information, see Goodman, Schlossberg, & Anderson, 2006, pp. 251–272, and the American Counseling Association Advocacy Competencies; Ratts, Toporek, & Lewis, 2010.)

## Pathways

Helping individuals find the right path is the goal of most career counseling. For young people, the challenge is to identify first steps; for others, it is to determine where to proceed next. There may be forks in the road, unexpected obstacles, steep hills, or easy slopes. Although the goal may be to identify an occupation or field of study, it is important to remember that this is usually one in a series, not *the* occupation or even the last education and training that will be needed. The Bureau of Labor Statistics (2002) estimated that the average baby boomer in the United States held 9.6 different jobs from the ages of 18 to 36. Peterson (1995) stated that "most people entering the work force today will have three to five careers and eight to ten jobs" (p. xiv). The basic structure of the labor force has also changed. These changes are a result of the combination of changing birthrates, the entry of large numbers of women into the workforce—from 30% in 1950 to an estimated 59.5% in 2008—the aging of the workforce, and its increased diversity (Toossi, 2002). Today's world rarely provides individuals with a job for life. Most will need retraining and will need to make several changes during their working lives. For some clients, this is a relief—making a decision for life can be daunting. For others, it is an added pressure. They resist accepting that they will have to engage in the decision-making process again, probably more than once. In the sections that follow, I discuss aspects of these decisions and present a variety of counseling tools that can be used to promote healthy transitions.

## Finding Meaning in Work and Career

Man's search for meaning (Frankl, 1963) is not a new concept. Perhaps Frost (1930) put it most eloquently in his poem *Two Tramps in Mud Time:*

But yield who will to their separation,
My object in living is to unite
My avocation and my vocation
As my two eyes make one in sight. (p. 314)

People's search for meaning through career is also not a new concept, but it has had a resurgence in recent years. Frankl's (1963) proposition was that meaning is essential to survival. Drawing from his own concentration camp experience, he attempted to understand why some people survived that hell on Earth emotionally intact and why some did not. His observation was that those who were able to find even small amounts of meaning during the experience fared better than those who were not able to. This meaning might have come from helping another, from finding a way to practice one's art, or for most, from a spiritual connection. Frankl's small book has been extremely influential to many individuals involved in helping others. Career counselors can learn much about the human heart and soul from its pages.

Career development was formerly called *vocational guidance,* and the word *vocation* finds its roots in the Latin *vocare,* which means "to call." A vocation was therefore a calling from God. Many people refer to their work as a calling, referring, perhaps unconsciously, to this meaning of the word *vocation.* The recent increased attention to meaning seems to touch a deep chord in individuals. For many others, however, paid work is only a means to an end—survival or paying for necessities so that individuals can engage in what they consider their real work. The poet Wallace Stevens worked as an insurance executive. Another poet, e. e. cummings, sold tokens in the New York City subway. Many artists, musicians, and actors have day jobs to pay the rent. Others find satisfaction in family, in community service, or in personal hobbies. Career counselors must be sensitive to the fact that not all clients are interested in finding meaningful paid jobs. A landmark study by McClelland, Atkinson, Clark, and Lowell (1953) found that although many people are motivated by the need for achievement, many others are motivated by the need for affiliation. For these people, what they do is often less important than with whom they do it. Career counselors, themselves usually in the need achievement category, need to be mindful of the needs of their clients who have different motivational structures. It is also important to pay attention to the variety of worldviews expressed by clients. This variety results not only from cultural diversity but also from generational changes in belief systems. As Anderson (2003) put it,

> There has been a basic shift in the realms of psychology and modern science away from the logical positivism that once shaped people's worldviews. The shift toward postmodernism and social constructionism is an important movement regarding how people view reality. Instead of fundamental and absolute truths, laws and principles, there is now a belief in multiple perspectives and a variety of ways of perceiving. Within the postmodern viewpoint, the context in which individuals live is emphasized and meaning emerges through human relationships, language, culture and personal meaning making. (p. 14)

Sometimes people see this need for meaning more clearly when it is missing.

In researching the phenomenon of burnout through case studies, Malach-Pines and Yafe-Yanai (2001) concluded that career burnout resulted from a failure in the search for meaning through work. They asserted that every person they interviewed who had experienced burnout also experienced a lack of meaning in his or her work. They also asserted that the unconscious often plays a role in career decision making and that taking a psychodynamic or psychoanalytic approach can be a fruitful way to help clients examine causes of burnout, or even career choice. Through case studies, Malach-Pines and Yafe-Yania presented ideas reminiscent of Savickas (1997) that one's symptoms can lead to one's solution, that one's preoccupation can become one's occupation, and that, quoting Satan in Milton's (1940/1667) *Paradise Lost*, "Our torments also may, in length of time, become our elements" (p. 33). Savickas (1997) deconstructed the word *spirituality* to remind people of its origin, which is *breath* or *wind*. If one thinks about the word *inspire*, one can see that its original meaning was "to breathe into." It is now used to mean to hearten, to give confidence to, and to raise one's spirits. Moving beyond matching interests and skills, Savickas distinguished traditional career counseling from "career counseling that attends to the individual's spirit,… [that] addresses how people can use occupations and work for personal and spiritual development" (p. 6).

### SIDEBAR 3.6  Mission Statement

One way to capture what is meaningful to an individual is to have the person write a mission statement. I suggest that you do just that. You may want to consider your values, roles, life purpose, and other areas of importance to you. You may also want to use Hansen's (1997) six areas necessary for integrative life planning (see later in chapter).

It is easy to see how attention to spirituality can relate to an existential worldview, one in which the focus is on experiencing, living in the present, and finding meaning in living (see, e.g., Adler, 1964; May, 1969). However, Gendlin (1973) took a step beyond existentialism to a theory he called experiential psychotherapy. This theory has four bases. Described in a greatly oversimplified manner, they are (1) experiencing, meaning all of the aspects of physical and emotional feelings; (2) interaction, "living in an infinite universe and in situations, a context of other people, of words and signs, of physical surroundings, of past, present, and future" (Gendline, 1973, p. 324); (3) authenticity, by which Gendlin (1973) meant a carrying forward, implying continuity and next steps; and (4) focaling, which he later called focusing (Gendlin, 1981), relating to purpose mediated by values. If career counselors follow Gendlin's ideas, they help their clients both experience the moment fully and plan for a future consistent with their values. It is particularly important for career counselors to help their clients maintain this dual focus on the present and the future.

In an article focusing on existentialism and career development, Cohen (2003) proposed a cyclical four-stage model—responsibility, evaluation, action, and reevaluation. In each stage, one needs to face the existential question "How does this relate to the freedom and responsibility to find and create a meaningful existence?" Central to this model is the assertion that for people to obtain and maintain career satisfaction, they must be satisfied with the "meaning and opportunities for authentic existence that the occupation provides" (p. 195). Cohen asserted that because career decisions are so important, when people fully appreciate both their freedom and responsibility, the decision may evoke deep existential angst. The unconscious conspiracy alluded to earlier can result when the counselor buys into this anxiety and provides solutions for the client. Drawing on the work of philosophers such as Tillich (1952), Heidegger (1949), and Kierkegaard (1950), along with Frankl (1963), Cohen argued that "Who am I?" becomes a question that supersedes "What can I do?" The role of the career counselor then becomes helping individuals identify what will make meaning for them in their life roles as well as in their work roles. The search for meaning as translated into career counseling includes discussing the role of individuals' spirituality, helping them find hope and optimism, and making decisions that enhance the possibilities of finding meaning in work. In the sections that follow, I discuss these three major roles.

## Spirituality

Looby and Sandhu (2002, p. 17) suggested that the current interest in spirituality in the workplace is a result of the increasing levels of isolation and existential frustration during the 1990s. They cited a study by Mitroff and Denton, who interviewed senior executives and human resources professionals. Mitroff and Denton (1999, as cited in Looby & Sandhu, 2002, p. 23) found that "most participants wished to express and develop their whole selves at work." Looby and Sandhu cited increasing workplace violence and other evidence of alienation that suggest that integrating spirituality in the workplace would be a positive step. They proposed 12 standards for what one might call a spiritually competent workplace (pp. 27–28): (1) creativity, encouraging individuals to find new ways of being and doing; (2) communication, fostering teamwork and honest expression; (3) respect, for self and others; (4) partnership, taking responsibility and working together; (5) vision, seeing the possible and desiring to grow; (6) flexibility, readiness to change and resilience; (7) energy, excitement stemming from creativity; (8) fun, enjoying, valuing, and revering each day; (9) finding self, helping individuals be "in harmony with themselves and the universe" (p. 28); (10) values training, ensuring that employees share company values; (11) relational management, creating a trusting and honest environment; and (12) stress management, encouraging employees to lead healthy lives, including a balance between work and personal lives. Whether each aspect relates directly to spirituality, each is certainly a component of a desirable workplace.

On his Web site, Greider (2003) describes the concept of a more spiritual—or perhaps humane—workplace. Discussing his new book, *The Soul of Capitalism* (Greider, 2003), he stated,

> Yes, we are fabulously wealthy as a nation, but are we truly free? How can people be considered free when their daily lives are so closely regimented by the confinements imposed upon them at work, rules that tell them to turn off their brains and take orders, no back talk? The content and conditions of

work for most Americans—even in well-salaried positions—are determined from above by a steep pyramid of distant managers, who are often brutally indifferent to the human consequences or even to what the employees know about how the company functions (and malfunctions). These confining circumstances, once associated with the assembly line, have crept very far up the job ladder. Indeed, the satisfactions inherent in doing a good job—intangible qualities of human fulfillment enjoyed by conscientious workers at every level—have been steadily degraded in recent decades, even for many high-skilled professionals. (p. 1)

Similarly, Kinjerski and Skrypnek (2008) defined spirit at work as involving "profound feelings of well being, a belief that one's work makes a contribution, a sense of connection to others ..., an awareness of a connection to something larger than self, and a sense of perfection and transcendence" (p. 319).

Bloch (1997, 2004) suggested that there are three implications for individuals of trying to find right work, and there are six implications for counselors. Individuals need to understand the "nature of meaning in lifework and its particular relationship to a sense of connectedness and absorbedness" (Bloch, 1997, p. 204). They also need to practice meditation, visualization, or another form of stillness as a way to discover or uncover meaning and spirituality in their own lives. One morning as I was writing this chapter, I took my dog for a walk on a railroad right of way that passes a small woods. As we were returning, I saw a small doe, daintily nibbling the vegetation at the edge of the trees. Quietly, the dog sat, and we both watched the deer as she first watched us, then returned to eating, and finally melted back into the woods. That stillness lasted for hours, as I wondered at my dog's ability to sense the preciousness of the moment, and I treasured the connectedness I had felt.

Finally, individuals need to practice intentionality, a way of using one's mind to influence events. Although this last leg of the client's tripod is counter to linear scientific thinking, Bloch (1997, pp. 197–204) cited a body of literature to make a strong case for its inclusion in one's approach. There are six guidelines for counselors: (1) Accept that each individual is a work in progress; (2) be in harmony with oneself; (3) recognize the uniqueness of each individual; (4) practice intentionality oneself; (5) be open to learning from others' culture and experiences; and (6) see yourself as a teacher. Young (1983), reflecting on her life in an introspective book called *Inscape: A Search for Meaning*, commented that she has experienced life, reflected deeply on it, and lived it. In the foreword, Lotus (1983, p. iv) said, "I am grateful to her for reminding me of the need to deal with life's paradoxes, such as being both a participant in life and an observer of life; making sense of my life while at the same time accepting the mystery of it."

People for whom spirituality is an important component of life decisions often reflect on death and the afterlife as they make decisions for this life. Others talk about living this life to the fullest. A career development activity that resonates with many is composing one's own obituary or imagining what would be on one's tombstone or said at one's wake. The idea behind these kinds of activities is to focus on values and goals.

In discussing life after the Biblical three-score and 10, Heilbrun (1997) said,

> I find it powerfully reassuring not to think of life as borrowed time. Each day one can say to oneself: I can always die; do I choose death or life? I daily choose life the more earnestly because it is a choice. (p. 10)

Heilbrun committed suicide in October 2003 at age 77. Her son Robert was quoted as follows in her obituary: "She had not been ill. She wanted to control her destiny," he said, "and she felt her life was a journey that had concluded" (McFadden, 2003). Although most would probably not agree with Heilbrun's choice to commit suicide, her focus on choosing how to spend each day of life is one that resonates with many.

Others define spirituality more narrowly as they look at the integration of religion into an organization. They describe such activities as breakfast prayer groups, Bible study, and allowing employees time off to celebrate religious holidays, even when they are not national holidays. Given the increased diversity of religious beliefs that comes with the increased diversity of the United States, this latter is becoming more important, while at the same time it is more challenging for managers.

According to Brewer (2001), the connection between work and spirituality relates to a personal sense of life's meaning, an unfolding sense of self and purpose that is expressed and driven by action. She developed the concept of a vocational souljourn paradigm, defined as "the ongoing interior process of discovering meaning, being, and doing and the expression of that discovery in the exterior world of work through four possible paths: job, occupation, career, and vocation" (Brewer, 2001, p. 84). She suggested that one find out during career counseling:

> (a) What is the nature of this client's relationship to work with regard to a whole life? (b) What does this client find meaningful? (c) Who is this person, and how does the wish to implement self in work become expressed? (d) Is this client coming to counseling for change in work/life choices, acceptance of life as it is, or some discovery of life goals and purpose? (p. 84)

These questions could be very useful for Dr. Sanchez as he attempts to find new meaning in his life. He is certainly in a place of finding new life goals and purposes.

## Hope and Optimism

*Hope* has been defined as belief in the face of doubt. For people to be willing to take action on their own behalf, it is essential that they have hope. Without hope, action seems futile, and it is hard to sustain energy when the desired outcome does not seem possible. I next discuss two elements of hope and optimism, self-efficacy beliefs and learned optimism.

### Self-Efficacy Beliefs

The attitude that one can act on one's own behalf, and that it will make a difference, is the core of self-efficacy. Originally proposed by Bandura (1977), self-efficacy theory has become a widely used explanatory system for many behaviors. Career inaction may be attributed to lack of self-efficacy beliefs. It is logical not to act when one believes that it will make no difference. To intervene, therefore, counselors need to help clients develop a sense of efficacy rather than simply exhorting them to try harder. A hallmark of self-efficacy theory, in contrast to self-esteem theory, is that it is situation dependent. A person may have a strong sense of efficacy about his or her ability to relate to people, but poor efficacy beliefs around academic learning.

Brown (1992) asserted that self-efficacy expectations are learned and that therefore new expectations can be learned. There are three keys to self-efficacy—action, effort, and persistence. Counselors can help clients develop a better sense of efficacy through empowering experiences, role models, messages, and emotions. How might one, for example, help James develop a better sense of self-efficacy? A counselor might guess that his school experiences have not left him with a strong sense of academic efficacy. He or she might also guess that James is unsure of his ability to do work greatly different from roofing. Brown would suggest that a counselor help James identify empowering experiences from the past. The counselor might also help him develop new empowering experiences that are related to his current challenges. For example, if James is indeed unsure of his scholastic ability, the counselor might have him enroll in an adult education class in an area in which the counselor suspects he will be comfortable, woodworking perhaps. The object is for the class to be difficult enough to help him improve his expectations, but easy enough that the counselor knows he will succeed.

To help James identify empowering role models, the counselor may need to enlist his assistance. With whom does he identify who has been successful? Again, it is important that these people be close enough to how James sees himself that he can see himself doing what they do. Group counseling is often an appropriate venue for finding role models; often, someone else in the group either is an appropriate role model or knows someone who can fit that bill. It is well known that empowering messages are useful only when they are believed. The messenger needs to be someone believable, the message has be close enough to James's ideas that he can accept its truth, and James has to want to absorb this new self-image. If all of these conditions are met, James may enhance his self-efficacy beliefs in a new arena. Fourth, Brown (1992) suggested that emotions also need to be empowering. If James's stress is overpowering, he will not have the energy to change his beliefs; if he does not care enough, he may not be willing to do the work to change them. Brown says that people need to have dreams—what they want—and turn them into visions—what they will attain. Sometimes the dream itself is an achievement.

### Learned Optimism

Seligman (1998, pp. 217–220) has suggested that optimism is a critical life skill and that it can be learned. Seligman proposed teaching skills that transform pessimists into optimists. The first skill is distraction, which is a process of shifting focus away from distressing thoughts toward more positive ones. The admonition "Don't think about it" does not seem to work. The admonition "Think about something positive instead" actually does seem to work. Dr. Sanchez might, for example, change "I am worthless if I am no longer a surgeon" to "I have a renewed opportunity to contribute to developing new physicians through my teaching." I am reminded poignantly of the scientist in Levinson's (1978) *The Seasons of a Man's Life.*

> He had given up the image of himself as a youthful hero going out to save the world, but had not yielded to the threatening specter of the dried-up, dying old man. He accepted himself as a middle aged man of considerable achievement, experience and integrity.... He was content to make a modest social contribution as parent, concerned citizen, scientist, teacher, and mentor to the younger generation. He had a sense of well being. (p. 277)

One can only hope that Dr. Sanchez can reach such comfort. This kind of reframing, if not used punitively, can help clients learn to be more optimistic. It is punitive if one tries to gloss over the challenges, struggle, and grief that change can bring. It is encouraging if one helps people move on after a time of mourning for what is lost.

Reframing can help James Green change the view that "work is simply drudgery. No one in my family likes their work. I don't expect to either" to "I would like to be the first in my family to have a satisfying career. What can I do to increase the likelihood of that happening?"

Seligman's (1998) second technique is disputation, which is a process of actually arguing with a thought—either internal self-talk or negative statements that have been made by others. Three of Seligman's suggestions for disputation are

1. *Evidence:* Encourage clients to ask themselves, "What is the actual evidence that this thought or accusation is true?" Find contrary evidence. For example, if clients are thinking that because they performed poorly on a test, they are terrible students, remind them of all of the tests they have done well on or remind them that they perform better in practical situations. Dr. Sanchez may need to remind himself of what he knows as a medical professional—that Parkinson's is not something he brought on himself.
2. *Alternatives:* Encourage clients to ask themselves, "What are the alternative explanations for this event?" James Green may need to consider that he was young when he dropped out of school and that he is now more mature.
3. *Implications:* Encourage clients to consider their catastrophic expectations and then examine whether they are really likely. Takesha Jones

could find out whether it is true that school districts are not hiring anyone at all. Perhaps certain fields such as mathematics or special education are still good career avenues.

## Decision-Making Process

Many authors have described decision-making strategies. Some are logical and sequential; some draw more on feelings and intuition. Contrary adages abound: He who hesitates is lost; look before you leap; you cannot cross a chasm in a single bound; you must let go of the trapeze to grasp the next one. Napoleon is supposed to have said, "Take time to deliberate, but when the time for action has arrived, stop thinking and go in" (Safire & Safir, 1982). You have read or will read elsewhere in this volume about several theories of career development. In recent years, some authors have instead focused their attention on strategies of career counseling. These strategies are not atheoretical but rather describe processes that are guides for the practitioner. I describe several of these approaches here: planned happenstance, positive uncertainty, learned optimism, and some of the so-called postmodern approaches.

## Planned Happenstance

Originally developed by Mitchell, Levin, and Krumboltz (1999), planned happenstance proposes that "chance favors the prepared mind" (a quote attributed to Pasteur). Most schoolchildren have heard the story of Archimedes running naked through the streets of Sicily shouting "Eureka," having discovered specific gravity while in the bath. Deriving inspiration from such stories and others such as the development of Velcro, Post-Its, Wite-Out, and penicillin, Mitchell et al. encouraged counselors to teach their clients to develop their curiosity. Clients are helped to "generate, recognize, and incorporate chance events into their career development" (Mitchell et al., 1999, p. 117).

Mitchell et al. (1999) reframed indecision as open mindedness. They suggested that counselors teach clients to embrace uncertainty, to see it as part of the process of discovery, and to resist premature foreclosure in decision making. The authors argued that the usual response to indecision is discomfort and that clients are urged by internal and external forces to have definite plans. I am reminded here of the unconscious conspiracy alluded to earlier—the pressure felt by client and counselor to reduce ambiguity and seek a finite plan. Career counseling is seen as a step in making those plans. The perhaps paradoxical intervention of encouraging indecision can create discomfort in and resistance from clients who want clarity and closure. It requires a leap of faith and trust in both the counselor and the process. Mitchell et al. (1999) proposed five skills to promote using chance events to increase career options:

1. Curiosity: exploring new learning opportunities
2. Persistence: exerting effort despite setbacks

3. Flexibility: changing attitudes and circumstances
4. Optimism: viewing new opportunities as possible and attainable
5. Risk Taking: taking action in the face of uncertain outcomes. (p. 118)

Melissa Winter's career dilemma provides a good opportunity to demonstrate how one might operationalize these principles. Melissa's counselor can help her identify how chance has helped her in the past to find satisfying work, and she can be reassured that her anxiety is normal. Let us follow Melissa through the experience of implementing a planned happenstance approach to her decision. First, a counselor can teach her career exploration skills that include practicing curiosity.

### SIDEBAR 3.7 Discovering a Curiosity

Go out and discover a curiosity. For 1 week, keep a running tally of all the things you wonder about. They may be person related (Why is Doug always so grumpy?), work related (Why do we need to log all phone calls?), or just related to everyday life (Why do dogs dislike cats?). At the end of the week, choose one and search out an answer. The goal of this activity is to increase your awareness of the world around you and engage problem-solving skills.

She might, for example, be asked to spend a week noting things she wonders about. She might then choose one of those things to explore more fully and actually research (K. E. Mitchell, personal communication, June 1997). If any of these explorations have a career focus, wonderful; if not, they can be seen as training her curiosity muscles. Second, she can be asked to identify when in her past life she needed to be persistent, how she overcame frustration and disappointment, and how she maintained her efforts even in the face of difficulties. She may well need to call on these strengths again, so it is important for her to identify and own them. Next, the counselor should encourage Melissa to be flexible. She is motivated by her commitment to her marriage to find day work. She will probably not be able to find a sommelier job without weekend and evening work. So she needs to look beyond her comfort level. There may be other wine-related jobs; there may be other jobs in which she can work only some nights or weekends; there may be jobs that use her transferable skills, the ability to learn and understand complex ideas or to relate well to people. Melissa has many options if she will open her mind to them. If Melissa is willing to retrain, this is another arena for flexibility.

To help Melissa embrace or learn optimism, the counselor may follow Seligman's (1998) suggestions, described earlier. Finally, to help Melissa take advantage of her risk-taking skills, the counselor could have her list all the risks she has taken in the past—physical, emotional, and intellectual—as well as the more specific career risks. She could then assess which have paid off for her, which have not, and why. Doing so may give her a more confident sense of how and when she can take risks and encourage her to use this confidence in her current situation.

It would certainly be a disservice to unemployed clients who need work immediately to refuse to help them make short-term plans. It is more appropriate to help them with both short- and long-term goals, that is, finding immediate work to satisfy life needs while continuing the career exploration process that could lead to more satisfying work in the long term. Maslow's (1954) hierarchy suggests that one must meet physiological, safety, and belonging needs before one can look to satisfy the need for self-esteem and importance, let alone information, understanding, beauty, and self-actualization. To push clients to try to reach self-actualization when they are worried about their next meal is not only cruel but is unlikely to achieve its aim.

## Positive Uncertainty

In positive uncertainty, Gelatt (1991) influentially proposed a method of fostering career resilience with his series of paradoxes related to career decisions: (a) Be focused and flexible about what you want, (b) be aware and wary about what you know, (c) be objective and optimistic about what you believe, and (d) be practical and magical about what you do (pp. 7–10). His approach is one of "using *both* [italics added] rational and intuitive techniques" (book cover) to make decisions. How does one implement these paradoxes in working with clients?

More recently, (2010) has taken the idea of uncertainty and extended it to beliefs about everything, not just career choices. His thesis is that having tentative beliefs serves people better than certainty because it allows them to admit new information. He extends this philosophy well beyond career development, but the application to career is also important. He states that "the minute you make up your mind that the way you see things makes a difference, it will make a difference in the way you see things and do things" (p. 1). In his process of illumination, he proposed that

> the way we see the problem IS the problem. If we see the problem is not our problem, or a solution is not possible, or we don't know what to do, then we ignore it. We don't seek solutions, or we expect someone else to solve it. We need to make up our minds that the way **we see things** makes a difference. (http://gelattpartners.com/hbspoi/poiinanutshell.html, 2010)

Today's world requires that people plan for a lifetime of self-managed careers. The mutual loyalty bonds that tied employer and employee are much less strong than perhaps they once were. Individuals leave employment, and employers let people go, with great regularity. It is a rare day that the newspapers do not announce another round of layoffs.

Power and Rothausen (2003) suggested that "the flexibility needed by employers has translated into insecurity, financial pressures, overwork, and increased risk to income and quality of work life for many middle class workers and especially for older workers, women, and minorities" (p. 160). As Herr, Cramer, and Niles (2004, p. 69) so eloquently put it,

> Many persons in the twenty-first century will need to learn how to change with change, accept ambiguity and uncertainty, negotiate job or career changes multiple times in their working lifetimes, be able to plan and act

on shifting career opportunities … and have the motivation to be career resilient—to persist in the face of change and unplanned for problems and difficulties. (from Herr, 2001, p. 208)

Power and Rothausen (2003) proposed a new model for working with middle-class, mid-career workers. They stated that this group, about 60% of U.S. workers, is that most affected by these labor market changes (p. 158). The model presumes that people are satisfied in their jobs; if not, they suggested that other career models are more appropriate. The three core concepts are (1) defining work as a set of activities that can provide value for many employers and that provide meaning for oneself, which is distinguished from a traditional definition that includes a specific function for a specific employer, that is, a position; (2) identifying the future requirements to do the work, which assumes self-management of one's career and therefore of the training and education necessary to maintain or update skills rather than depending on an employer for such training, as well as a commitment to keep up with current information relating to trends to foresee the need for a career transition; and (3) choosing a developmental direction that defines a phase of 3 to 5 years in the future. Power and Rothausen provided a series of questions for use by career counselors for each of these tasks. For example, they would ask a person in the defining work stage, "With what activity or effort at work do you most identify? About what do you feel passionate to learn more? What activities fire your interest and imagination?" (p. 178). In the identifying future requirements stage, they would ask, "What are the future challenges in doing this work? What are the performance benchmarks for this work? What technological changes will have a major impact on this work?" (p. 178). In determining developmental direction, they suggested determining whether the person's development is job oriented, work maintenance oriented, or work growth oriented and planning accordingly (p. 175).

Casto (2003, p. 1) stated,

> My own concept of career is like a wardrobe, where you "try on" different outfits throughout your lifetime, and continue to check the mirror to see if it still fits and matches your current style and taste. In the modern world of work, you will need to find work that is "suited" to you. Think of your life's work as your wardrobe. It is ever-changing as you move through life, changing as your styles and interests change. Throughout the process, you will be tailoring yourself to fit different roles, and to meet changing work styles and expectations.

A number of catch phrases have sprung up to describe this phenomenon, for example "You, Inc." The idea is that individuals are responsible for their own career planning and career management. They are, in effect, their own corporation. It has been suggested, therefore, that individuals not wait for a crisis to engage in career development activities.

The concept of the preventative check-up, or dental, model (Goodman, 1991, 1992) has been used as a way of describing ongoing career development activities. The premise behind much school-based career counseling is that once people become adults, they are prepared to be henceforth self-directed and independent in managing their lives. The dental model proposes that one's need for career assistance does not end with completion of one's formal education. It suggests that people need to see career counselors as they see dentists, for regular checkups and routine maintenance throughout their lives, to navigate successfully in today's rapidly changing world. During check-ups, individuals might get assistance in analyzing employment trends in their own or related industries, and they might assess their own interests and values to determine whether there is still a good fit with their current situation. Often, individuals change as they mature, leading to a desire for different work. Lifestyle changes can also influence career satisfaction. An income, for example, that was satisfying for a young, single person may now be inadequate to support young children and defray the costs of child care or to send older children to college. The long hours necessary to earn that kind of income may no longer be necessary when children are grown, and people may wish to trade money for more leisure or more job flexibility. In addition, many career counselors have found that intrapersonal needs have changed. Jung (1959) talked about the move to androgyny, where men seek out and find their so-called feminine side and women their so-called masculine side. Goodman and Waters (1985, p. 95) termed this development the time of "affective men and effective women."

This development can also lead to what has been termed the dromedary camel syndrome, or the out-of-sync career commitment curve (Goodman & Waters, 1985). The two-humped camel symbolizes traditional women's career commitment graph, on which there is often a declining career commitment—although not always declining work hours—during the child-rearing years. Although this may be changing somewhat, anecdotal evidence still supports the thesis that many women stay home, work part time, or otherwise reduce their career investment during the years in which their children are young. The one-humped dromedary symbolizes men's more predictable career trajectory. A problem may arise for dual-career couples when a traditional man's declining curve crosses his partner's second climb. Her enhanced career investment may come at the exact time as his is declining. Career counselors working with couples doing retirement planning may want to keep this potential conflict in mind.

Gelatt's (1991) thesis is that whatever approach one uses, one must be both decisive and flexible about change. In the best-seller *Who Moved My Cheese?* Johnson (1998) presented an allegory of mice that resist change to the point of starvation and compared them with mice that accept change and move on. The lessons learned by the resilient mouse are (1) change happens, (2) anticipate change, (3) monitor change, (4) adapt to change quickly, (5) change, (6) enjoy change, and (7) be ready to quickly change again and again. The underlying message is not only that change is constant, but also that one must embrace change and see it as leading to more positive outcomes. In *Going to Plan B,* Schlossberg and Robinson (1996) discussed the resilience that is required when anticipated things do not happen—nonevents, in their terminology. They posited a series of responses—acknowledging, easing, refocusing, and reshaping—that are necessary to cope with these nonevents.

The vast amount of information available on the Internet has created a dilemma for many career decision makers. People who try to get all the information before deciding can become paralyzed by the amount available. Furthermore, the information is not always accurate. There are no fact checkers on the Internet. Gelatt's edict to be wary takes on particular significance on light of this explosion of (often inaccurate) information. Gelatt's (1991) final directive, to be practical and magical about what one does, encourages people to be creative, to dream the impossible dream, while keeping their feet on the ground, to mix a metaphor. Although I do not believe the adage "If you dream it, you can do it," I do believe that if you cannot dream something, you cannot do it. Sitting home and waiting for magic to happen will probably not help someone to reach goals, but being in the right place at the right time is more likely if one is in lots of places.

Langer (1997) expressed a similar worldview as she discussed mindful learning. She stated that people must appreciate "both the conditional, or context-dependent nature of the world and the value of uncertainty" (p. 15). She described three characteristics of her approach: "the continuous creation of new categories; openness to new information; and an implicit awareness of more than one perspective" (p. 4). Dependence on context is one of the hallmarks of the postmodern approaches that I discuss next.

## Postmodern Approaches

### Narrative

Perhaps the most influential career counseling approach to be brought forth in recent years is that of using narrative as a basis for the career counseling interview. Because it can encompass any of the techniques described earlier, it can be seen as a way of integrating many perspectives. Drawing on its roots in the ancient tradition of storytelling, the narrative approach simply proposes that counselors have clients tell their stories. These stories can then be used to develop themes and to understand individuals at a deeper level. Savickas (2001) described four levels of career theories. The first relates to vocational personality types. Chiefly associated with John Holland's (1959) RIASEC (realistic, investigative, artistic, social, enterprising, and conventional) codes, types have been shown to have cross-cultural validity, to have a high amount of heritability, to relate to an individual, and to be relatively context free. The second type identified by Savickas (2001) is defined as being connected to contextual factors such as historical context as well as relating to an individual's personal life space and is usually called career concerns. The third type is identified as being related to career narratives. Narratives "compose a life.… They give a life meaningful continuity over time" (Savickas, 2001, p. 310). Savickas warned that narratives are particularly appropriate for middle-class people who probably have more career options but recommended them nonetheless as a useful counseling approach. Savickas's fourth level, which is beyond the scope of this discussion, is designed to describe the process of continuity and change in career development.

Several people have proposed techniques designed to elicit these stories. Savickas (2003, p. 1) recommended asking the following questions:

1. Who do you admire? Who would you pattern your life after? Who did you admire growing up? How are you like this person? How are you different from this person?
2. Do you read any magazines regularly? Which ones?
3. What do you like to do in your free time?
4. Do you have a favorite saying or motto?
5. What are (were) your three favorite subjects in school? What subjects do (did) you hate?
6. What is your earliest recollection?

Using these questions, counselors can help their clients construct a narrative, looking for themes, patterns, continuities, and discontinuities. Others have suggested having clients divide their lives into chapters or acts in a play. Jepsen (1992) suggested that the client then simultaneously becomes the play's star, playwright, director, and audience.

### Integrative Life Planning

Hansen (1997, 2002, 2008) suggested another postmodern approach. Her holistic approach, summarized by the phrase "weaving our lives into a meaningful whole," includes

1. Finding work that needs doing
2. Attending to our health
3. Connecting family and work
4. Valuing pluralism and diversity
5. Managing transitions and organizational change
6. Exploring spirituality and life purpose. (Hansen, 2002, p. 61)

Let us look at what applying these tasks might look like for Takesha Jones. Takesha found work that needed doing, but she also needs to find someone to employ her to do the work. Just because many people live in substandard housing or drive on potholed roads does not mean that there is money to solve these problems. If Takesha wants to work as a teacher, she will have to find somewhere else to work, find another way to earn a living and teach on a voluntary basis during her leisure hours, or, as suggested earlier, specialize in an area in which there are openings. Another way for Takesha to approach her dilemma is to look at the underlying values beneath her desire to teach. Is it because she loves the act of teaching, because she loves children, or perhaps because she sees teaching as a way of making a difference in a troubled world? Or are there other reasons? All of these would help her apply Hansen's (1997) first principle. What about the second? I have thus far only discussed Takesha's occupational decisions. One would need to know more about the rest of her life. A counselor might use Savickas's (2003) questions or Super's (1957) rainbow to help Takesha explore other areas of her life. Hansen's (1997) third principle involves negotiating the balance of family and work. This issue concerns both time and emotional involvement. As seen with Melissa, a work schedule can in itself conflict with family life and could also create health issues, relating to Hansen's second task. Total work hours are also an issue for many. There are only 168 hours in a week. Having clients construct a time pie can help them assess whether they are content with the current distribution. As they plan for future jobs, they can insert the time commitment for the work into their pie to assess the fit. Including aspects such as time spent commuting, required overtime, or work brought home as this assessment is made is important. Many men and women choose jobs with less commitment during the time their children are small or when they begin to think about transitioning toward retirement. Health issues may also be part of a decision to work fewer hours. Part of the dual-career negotiation process may be whether either or both members of the couple will make what may be seen as a sacrifice during these years. Both members of the couple will need to look at reduced income if one works fewer hours or not at all. Single parents obviously have an even harder time balancing work and family needs. Many people later in their lives and careers find themselves taking care of aging or ill parents or other relatives. Career counselors must keep these and similar issues in mind when helping clients choose occupations to pursue. Takesha has none of these issues at present, but she hopes someday to marry and have children. Her desire to be a teacher is partly predicated on the understanding that she will have a work schedule similar to that of her children.

Hansen (1997) suggested that individuals express their values of pluralism and inclusivity in their life career decision making. Following on the understanding that the world is more interconnected than ever before, she stated that this globalism dictates

> a new philosophy of career planning in which the focus is not so much on individual occupational choice for personal satisfaction and livelihood as on multiple choices over a lifetime not only for individual wholeness but for life with meaning, that is for work that benefits self and community. (Hansen, 1997, p. 3)

This same idea has been expressed as the development among nations that parallels individual development, from dependence (childhood), to counter-dependence (adolescence), to independence (young adulthood), to interdependence (maturity). This paradigm shift is reflected in the conflict often experienced by first-generation Americans, when their parents hold to cultural beliefs of putting the family or the community first and children are encouraged to be autonomous and individualistic in their decision making. Hansen, provocatively, has suggested that people need to move to embrace the former cultural stance. For Takesha, this approach fits with her own belief system. Part of her reason for wanting to teach is to be part of her community and to make a difference for children who perhaps did not have her advantages of educated parents and private school.

Takesha's current transition is one of finishing school and seeking her first full-time career position. Although graduation is called commencement, underlining its place in the beginning of a new life stage, it is also an ending. For students like Takesha, who loved school, it is an ending faced with some sadness. Takesha's counselor needs to help her manage her feelings about her transition as well as the decisions about her future. (For more on managing transitions, see the section on Schlossberg's transition theory [Goodman et al., 2006] elsewhere in this chapter.) Although Takesha is not yet in an organization, it would not be remiss for her counselor to help her be aware of the changes she will face and to arm her for the predictable upheaval in any organization in which she finds herself.

Finally, it is important that Takesha be given the opportunity to explore her own spirituality and life purpose. As I discussed earlier in the section on spirituality, the existential quest for meaning is important for many. One might guess, given Takesha's altruistic goals, that she would value finding meaning in work.

### Constructivist Theories

The hallmark of constructionist approaches is their nonlinear nature. As eloquently described by Peavy (1998), a constructiveness counseling session is

> a workshop where the counselor and the client jointly build understandings of the client's relations with significant aspects of his or her immediate milieu, [and] make plans and projects which the client can use to navigate and participate in social life successfully and with meaning. (p. 47)

Peavy proposed that the counseling process be jointly constructed with the client and that the focus be on clients' understanding of themselves and their life space. He used the term *bricolage* to emphasize the construction process, that is, brick by brick, with the bricks being the clients' life experience and the counselor being the mason. Constructivism assumes a paradigm shift from looking at behavior to looking at action and meaning; from determining causation to assessing reciprocal influence; from believing in one reality to holding that there are multiple realities; and from seeing the self as determined to seeing the self as a work in progress, constructed (p. 45). Constructivist counselors use narrative approaches to enter their clients' life space, to develop mutual trust and respect, and to explore possible career paths. They assume that counselors are culturally competent, that is, that they have knowledge of and respect for cultural differences, that they have an understanding of the sociopolitical context in which their clients live, and that they allow for nonlinear emergent conversations.

Another postmodern theory is that of Pryor, Amundson, and Bright (2008), who have adapted the physical theories of complexity and chaos to the career counseling arena. Arguing that life is unpredictable, context dependent, and nonlinear, they proposed a series of characteristics for career counseling that focuses on possibilities rather than the certainties implied by matching models. The emergent decision-making perspective has the following characteristics:

- assuming personal responsibility
- making choices
- refusing to let fear conquer action
- maintaining positive action
- looking to the future with optimism and excitement
- searching for new and enlightening knowledge
- adopting multiple descriptions simultaneously
- recognizing and welcoming uncertainty
- working with incomplete knowledge and recognizing it will always be so
- following your curiosity
- taking risks
- learning from failure
- pursuing your passion
- listening to your intuitive self
  (Pryor et al., 2008, p. 312)

One can see the parallels with positive uncertainty (Gelatt, 1991) and happenstance theory (Mitchell et al., 1999), but my opinion is that chaos theory adds a depth and dimension that can help counselors assist their clients to gain comfort within the ambiguity of today's world of work.

## School-Based Career Counseling
### Kindergarten to Grade 12

This volume has a separate chapter on schools, so here I discuss only briefly how the concepts outlined in this chapter can be implemented in that setting. Providing career development activities for young people that focus on matching interests, abilities, and educational aims with specific job titles is efficient. Indeed, students need to identify a target for that first job. However, it is also important to teach them about self-assessment and decision making and to encourage them to broaden their thinking beyond job titles to their role in constructing a career and a life. Some of the ideas presented earlier in this chapter—for example, positive uncertainty and planned happenstance—are particularly appealing to young people and should be married to the more logical sequential approaches normally followed. It is also important to remember that students, like anyone, have spiritual beliefs and values that they should include in their decision making.

## College and University

Many students at this level never seek out the assistance of a career counselor or see their academic advisor for more than a signature on a program plan. Nonetheless, most colleges and universities have available excellent career decision-making courses or individual career assistance. Although students may have matriculated as part of a career plan, this time is also when these plans need to be changed, whether because the student has been unsuccessful in a chosen area, has discovered that it is not what he or she truly loves, or changed his or her goals for higher education, career assistance can be critical in helping the student achieve a successful outcome. The need for concrete plans leads many students into premature foreclosure, that is, making a decision without the information base or self-knowledge to make a good decision. Nationally, fewer than half of students who enter college complete their plans (Ingham Intermediate School District, 1998). For some, this noncompletion may be an appropriate alteration of plans, but for many it is a failure that haunts them throughout their lives. All of the suggestions in this chapter can be followed in working with this population.

## Adult Career Transitions

Goodman et al. (2006) proposed a so-called "4-S" system of looking at transitions that included four basic elements: the situation, the self, available support, and strategies. This taxonomy is actually an assessment system, but it can be used to structure a counseling interview, and it provides a broad-enough base to encompass many of the aspects of career decision making discussed earlier. I discuss each of these elements in turn, using James Green as the client.

What is James's situation? He is working at a job that no longer satisfies his physical or financial needs. He is also unhappy with the insecurity of the seasonal nature of his work, so one could say that his emotional needs are also unsatisfied. James has several children he helps to support, and he is facing a decision about marriage. The timing of the possible transition is good, in that it is his choice, not a choice imposed on him. It is in his control, and there does not seem to be a need for an immediate decision. James has the luxury, unlike someone who is unemployed, of making a more thoughtful decision than his first career decision, that is, dropping out of high school.

What about James's self? He has probably been impulsive in his decision to leave school and perhaps in his early marriage. He seems to be more mature now and more thoughtful about his life course. He is responsible about paying child support and also helps support his partner's other two children. He is apparently in good physical health. Nothing is known about James's emotional or mental health, nor about his interests, skills, abilities, or other personal characteristics, such as willingness to take risks or values such as desire for autonomy or prestige. These are all aspects of James that a counselor will need to find out in interviews, perhaps by engaging James in a narrative and hearing his story. A counselor may also try to ascertain whether James left school because learning was difficult for him. If so, and if getting more education turns out to be a goal for James, he may need to look at some kind of learning support.

Regarding James's support system, he lives with a woman and their child, as well as her other children. Nothing else is known about James's life space. Does he have an extended family with whom he is close? Do they live nearby? What about his friendships? A counselor might ask James to complete an extended genogram, including not only family but other important people in his life. A counselor might also suggest that James look at his stress system. These people are sometimes the same as those in a support system, and comparing the two can be helpful in understanding James's life space. A counselor may suspect, as mentioned earlier, that James's school experience implies that he does not find paper and pencil the best way to learn. If that is the case, the counselor may want to ask James to create a family sculpture (Satir, 1964) instead of writing a genogram or to find another kinesthetic way of assessing his support.

One way that I have found useful would be to simply have James draw a circle, with himself in the middle, and list his supports as spokes of the wheel, identifying the role they play as he goes. It is important to encourage him to look also at non–people supports such as exercise, faith, a pet, or memories. He might also list the more pragmatic support aspects such as a working car, good health, and so forth. Such an activity may help him realize the amount of support he has or recognize that he does not have the support he would like and to learn some support access skills.

Finally, what strategies is James using to manage his anticipated transition? Goodman et al. (2006) indicated that there are three categories of strategies. What can James do to change his situation? What can he do to change the meaning of his situation? How can he manage the concomitant stress? Let us address each in turn. James wants a new job and a new line of work. He needs strategies for decision making and most probably for pursuing further education, at least as far as a high school diploma or a GED. He may need to learn job search techniques and all that they entail. Goodman et al.'s model would imply that a counselor first find out what strategies James already knows and then develop a plan for filling in the gaps. Changing the meaning of a situation is a delicate task. One does not want to run the risk of trivializing James's problems with a clichéd response such as "When life gives you lemons, make lemonade." James can, however, perhaps grow to see that he does have an opportunity to create a more satisfying and meaningful life. His coming to a career counselor in the first place indicates a readiness to look at change. A counselor needs to capitalize on that readiness. Discussion of his strengths, his support, and so forth as outlined in previous sections can be brought into this part of the model. Last, James needs to either access or learn stress management techniques.

Adults who experience career transitions must often also develop a new work or professional identity. Identity renegotiation theory (Blume, 2010), although originally applied to family interventions, offers an insight into the challenges faced by individuals whose work role changes their sense of self. "Identity renegotiation theory defines identities as interpersonal narratives rather than internal realities. Identities are described as continually changing, co-constructed by storytellers and audiences and susceptible to social power and influence" (Blume, 2010, p. 103). Career counselors can use this understanding to assist their clients in accepting and managing this renegotiation.

## Summary

In the foregoing, I have discussed the centrality of individuals' careers to their lives. I have talked about how counselors can help their clients find personal meaning in work and have identified a number of strategies to assist in that process. Barriers and pathways to succeeding in this quest were described, as were methods of integrating the ideas behind self-efficacy and learned optimism theories into the career counseling process.

I also presented the concepts of spirituality, hope, and optimism and a variety of decision-making processes: planned happenstance, positive uncertainty, and the postmodern approaches of narrative, integrative life planning, and constructivism. I also briefly described school-based career counseling and adult transitions. By following four cases, I have demonstrated the application of several of these concepts and theories. The Web sites listed in the next section provide additional information relating to the chapter topics.

## Useful Web Sites

- The Career Key. http://www.careerkey.org/english/
- Center for Spirituality at Work. http://www.cfsaw.org/index.htm
- Oakland University, Kresge Library. http://library.oakland.edu/research/careers/index.htm
- Sunny Hansen. http://www.sunnyhansenbornfree.com
- Team Builders Plus. http://www.teambuildinginc.com/article_spirituality.htm
- U.S. Department of Labor, Bureau of Labor Statistics. http://www.bls.gov/oco/

## References

Adler, A. (1964). *Superiority and social interest*. Evanston, IL: Northwestern University Press.

Anderson, M. L. (2003). *Spirituality and coping with work transitions.* Unpublished dissertation proposal, Oakland University.

Bandura, A. (1977). Self-efficacy: Toward a unifying theory of behavioral change. *Psychological Review, 84,* 191–215.

Bloch, D. P. (1997). Spirituality, intentionality and career success: The quest for meaning. In D. P. Bloch & L. J. Richmond (Eds.), *Connections between spirit and work in career development* (pp. 185–208). Palo Alto, CA: Davies Black.

Bloch, D. P. (2004). Spirituality, complexity and career counseling, *Professional School Counseling,7*(5), 343–350.

Bloch, D. P., & Richmond, L. J. (Eds.). (1997). *Connections between spirit and work in career development.* Palo Alto, CA: Davies Black.

Blustein, D. L., Schultheiss, D. E. P., & Flum, H. (2004). Toward a relational perspective of the psychology of careers and working: A social constructionist analysis. *Journal of Vocational Behavior, 64,* 423–440.

Blume, T. (2010). Counseling for identity renegotiation. *Identity: An International Journal of Theory and Research, 10,* 92–105.

Bobek, B. L., & Robbins, S. B. (2005). Counseling for career transition: Career pathing, job loss, and reentry. In S. D. Brown & R. W. Lent (Eds.), *Career development and counseling: Putting theory and research to work* (pp. 625–650). Hoboken, NJ: Wiley.

Brewer, E. W. (2001). Vocational souljourn paradigm: A model of adult development to express spiritual wellness as meaning, being, and doing in work and life. *Counseling and Values, 45,* 83–92.

Brown, M. (1992, November). *Self efficacy.* Oral presentation to the Michigan Association of Counseling and Development, .

Bureau of Labor Statistics. (2002). *News: United States Department of Labor* (USDL Publication No. 02-497). Washington, DC: United States Government Printing Office.

Casto, M. L. (2003, October 16). What is a career anyway? *Career Convergence.* Retrieved from http://associationdatabase.com/aws/NCDA/pt/sd/news_article/4789/_self/layout_ccmsearch/false

Cohen, B. N. (2003). Applying existential theory and interventions to career decision-making. *Journal of Career Development, 29,* 195–209.

Cohen-Scali, V. (2003). The influence of family, social, and work socialization on the construction of the professional identity of young adults. *Journal of Career Development, 29,* 237–249.

Evans, K. M., Rotter, J. C., & Gold, J. M. (Eds.). (2002). *Synthesizing family, career, and culture: A model for counseling in the twenty-first century.* Alexandria, VA: American Counseling Association.

Frankl, V. E. (1963). *Man's search for meaning: An introduction to logotherapy.* New York, NY: Washington Square Press.

Frost, R. (1930). *The poems of Robert Frost.* New York: Random House.

Gelatt, H. B. (1991). *Creative decision making: Using positive uncertainty.* Los Altos, CA: Crisp.

Gendlin, E. T. (1973). Experiential psychotherapy. In R. Corsini (Ed.), *Current psychotherapies* (pp. 317–352). Itasca, IL: F. E. Peacock.

Gendlin, E. T. (1981). *Focusing.* New York: Bantam.

Gold, J. M., Rotter, J. C., & Evans, K. M. (2002). Out of the box: A model for counseling in the twenty-first century. In M. K. Evans, J. C. Rotter, & J. M. Gold (Eds.), *Synthesizing family, career, and culture: A model for counseling in the twenty-first century* (pp. 19–33). Alexandria, VA: American Counseling Association.

Goodman, J. (1991). Career development for adults in organizations and in the community. In *The national career development guidelines: Progress and possibilities* (pp. 25–36). Washington, DC: National Occupational Information Coordinating Committee.

Goodman, J. (1992). The key to pain prevention: The dental model for counseling. *American Counselor, 1*(2), 27–29.

Goodman, J., Schlossberg, N. K., & Anderson, M. L. (2006). *Counseling adults in transition: Linking practice with theory* (3rd ed.). New York, NY: Springer.

Goodman, J., & Waters, E. B. (1985). Conflict or support: Work and family in middle and old age. *Journal of Career Development, 12,* 92–98.

Greider, W. (2003). The question of power. Retrieved October 16, 2003, from http://williamgreider.com/article.php?article_id=13

Hansen, L. S. (2002). Integrative life planning (ILP): A holistic theory for career counseling with adults. In S. Niles (Ed.), *Adult career development: Concepts, issues, and practices* (pp. 57–75). Tulsa, OK: National Career Development Association.

Hansen, L. S. (1997). *Integrative life planning: Critical tasks for career development and changing life patterns.* San Francisco, CA: Jossey-Bass.

Hansen, L. S. (2002). Integrative life planning (ILP): A holistic theory for career counseling with adults. In S. Niles (Ed.), *Adult career development: Concepts, issues, and practices* (pp. 59–76). Tulsa, OK: National Career Development Association.

Hansen, L. S., & Suddarth, B. (2008). Integrative life planning. *Career Developments, 24*(4), 5–9.

Heidegger, M. (1949). *Existence and being.* Chicago, IL: Regency.

Heilbrun, C. G. (1997). *The last gift of time: Life beyond sixty.* New York, NY: Dial.

Heilbrun, R. (2003). Retrieved from http://www.nytimes.com/2003/10/11/obituaries/11HEIL.html

Herr, E. L. (1992). Counseling for personal flexibility in a global economy. *Educational and Vocational Guidance, 53,* 5–16.

Herr, E. L., Cramer, S. H., & Niles, S. G. (2004). *Career guidance and counseling through the lifespan: Systematic approaches* (6th ed.). Boston, MA: Pearson.

Holland, J. L. (1959). A theory of vocational choice. *Journal of Counseling Psychology, 6,* 35–45.

Ingham Intermediate School District. (1998). *Career preparation: Careers by choice, not by chance.* Mason, MI: Author.

Jepsen, D. A. (1992, March). Understanding careers as stories. In M. Savickas (Chair), *Career as story.* Presented at a symposium at a meeting of the American Association for Counseling and Development, Baltimore, MD.

Johnson, S. (1998). *Who moved my cheese?* New York, NY: Putnam.

Jung, C. G. (1959). *Basic writings.* New York, NY: Random House.

Kierkegaard, S. (1950). *The point of view.* London, England: Oxford University Press.

Kinjerski, V., & Skrypnek, B. J. (2008). Four paths to spirit at work: Journeys of personal meaning, fulfillment, well-being, and transcendence through work. *Career Development Quarterly, 56,* 319–329.

Langer, E. J. (1997). *The power of mindful learning.* Reading, MA: Addison-Wesley.

Levinson, D. J. (1978). *The seasons of a man's life.* New York, NY: Ballantine.

Looby, E. J., & Sandhu, D. S. (2002). Spirituality in the workplace: An overview. In D. S. Sandhu (Ed.), *Counseling employees: A multifaceted approach* (pp. 17–46). Alexandria, VA: American Counseling Association.

Lotus, A. (1983). Foreword. In C. I. Young, *Inscape: A search for meaning* (unpaginated). Rochester, MI: Continuum Center, Oakland University.

Malach-Pines, A., & Yafe-Yanai, O. (2001). Unconscious determinants of career choice and burnout: Theoretical model and counseling strategy. *Journal of Employment Counseling, 38,* 170–184.

Maslow, A. H. (1954). *Motivation and personality.* New York, NY: Harper & Row.

May, R. (1969). *Love and will.* New York, NY: W. W. Norton.

McClelland, D. C., Atkinson, J. W., Clark, R. A., & Lowell, E. L. (1953). *The achievement motive.* Englewood Cliffs, NJ: Prentice-Hall.

McFadden, R. D. (2003, October 11). Carolyn Heilbrun, Pioneering Feminist Scholar, Dies at 77 [Obituary]. *The New York Times,* p. 1.

Milton, J. (1940). *Paradise lost.* New York, NY: Heritage Press (Original work published in 1667).

Mitchell, K. E., Levin, A. L., & Krumboltz, J. D. (1999). Planned happenstance: Constructing unexpected career opportunities. *Journal of Counseling and Development, 2,* 115–124. *Occupational Outlook Handbook,* http://bls.gov/oco/oco2003.htm#industry, retrieved October 26, 2010.

Peavy, V. (1998). A new look at interpersonal relations in counseling. *Educational and Vocational Guidance Bulletin, 62,* 45–50.

Peterson, L. (1995) *Starting out, starting over.* Palo Alto, CA: Davies-Black.

Power, S. J., & Rothausen, T. J. (2003). The work-oriented midcareer development model. *Counseling Psychologist, 31,* 157–197.

Pryor, R. G. L., Amundson, N. E., Bright, J. E. H. (2008). Probabilities and possibilities: The strategic counseling implications of the chaos theory of careers. *Career Development Quarterly, 56,* 309–318.

Ratts, M. J., Toporek, R. L., & Lewis, J. A. (2010). *ACA advocacy competencies: A social justice framework for counselors.* Alexandria, VA: American Counseling Association.

Safire, W., & Safir, L. (1982). *Good advice.* New York, NY: Wings Books.

Satir, V. (1964). *Conjoint family therapy.* Palo Alto, CA: Science & Behavior.

Savickas, M. L. (1997). The spirit in career counseling: Fostering self completion through work. In D. P. Bloch & L. J. Richmond (Eds.), *Connections between spirit and work in career development* (pp. 185–208). Palo Alto, CA: Davies Black.

Savickas, M. L. (2001). Toward a comprehensive theory of career development: Dispositions, concerns, and narratives. In F. T. L. Leong & A. Barak (Eds.), Contemporary models in vocational psychology: A volume in honor of Samuel Osipow (pp. 295–320). Mahwah, NJ: Erlbaum.

Savickas, M. L. (2003, September 4). *The career theme interview.* Oral presentation to the International Association of Educational and Vocational Guidance, Berne, Switzerland.

Schlossberg, N. K., & Robinson, S. P. (1996). *Going to plan B.* New York, NY: Simon & Schuster.

Schultheiss, D. E. P. (2003). A relational approach to career counseling: Theoretical integration and practical application. *Journal of Counseling and Development, 81,* 301–310.

Seligman, M. E. P. (1998). *Learned optimism* (2nd ed.). New York, NY: Pocket Books.

Super, D. E. (1957). *The psychology of careers.* New York, NY: Harper.

Super, D. E. (1980). A life-span, life space approach to career development. *Journal of Vocational Behavior, 16,* 282–298.

Tillich, P. (1952). *The courage to be.* New Haven, CT: Yale University Press.

Toossi, M. (2002). A century of change: The U. S. labor force, 1950–2050. *Monthly Labor Review, 125*(5), 15–28.

Young, C. I. (1983). *Inscape: A search for meaning.* Rochester, MI: Oakland University, Continuum Center.

CHAPTER 4

# Career Counseling Without Borders
*Moving Beyond Traditional Career Practices of Helping*

Manivong J. Ratts and KristiAnna Santos

## Contents

The advent of the multicultural and social justice counseling movements has led to increased attention to the effectiveness of career counseling with diverse populations and the influence of sociopolitical forces on career development. This concern has led to the need for multiculturally and advocacy-competent career interventions (Toporek, 2006) and to questions regarding how the career counseling field can be used as a vehicle to promote social justice. The need to deliver multiculturally and advocacy-competent career counseling, to explore equity of career services, and to promote access to career resources is becoming increasingly apparent. As their clientele become ever more diverse, career counselors are realizing that traditional career methods of helping are limiting.

**SIDEBAR 4.1   Advent of the Multicultural and Social Justice Counseling Movements**

The earlier theories and approaches to career counseling, many of which are still in use today, were developed before there was much emphasis in the counseling profession on the differing needs of diverse populations. This emphasis has changed as a result of the efforts of some of the divisions of the American Counseling Association (e.g., the Association for Multicultural Counseling and Development and Counselors for Social Justice) as well as the interests of recent presidents of the American Counseling Association.

**111**

Moreover, counselors recognize the impact that oppressive environmental factors have on clients' ability to achieve their career goals and desires and, because of the empathy they have developed for their clients, are called to move outside the comfort of their office settings (Pope & Pangelinan, 2010). Career counselors also recognize that promoting issues of career equity and access to career resources further enhances their work with clients. In this chapter, we (a) provide an introduction to multicultural and social justice counseling concepts, (b) provide a framework for infusing multiculturalism and social justice into career counseling, and (c) explore the implications of multiculturalism and social justice in career counseling.

## Background

The demographic changes in the U.S. population have led to an increased commitment to multicultural career development theories (Sue, Parham, & Santiago, 1998). The demographic shift in the U.S. population means that increasing numbers of diverse clients are entering the workforce and, thus, are likely to seek career counseling. The shift from a homogeneous to a heterogeneous population means that career counselors must also shift their approach to career counseling. Western theories of career development have been found to be ineffective with diverse populations because of their lack of attention to cultural and contextual factors (Cook, Heppner, & O'Brien, 2005). Career counselors operating from a multicultural framework need to be sensitive to clients' culture and their social context. We provide a context for understanding multiculturalism and social justice in these ways:

- Clarifying key concepts and reviewing the history of multiculturalism and social justice issues in the career counseling field
- Increasing understanding of how multiculturalism and social justice influence career options and functioning
- Increasing awareness of how multiculturalism and social justice influence the career counseling process
- Presenting several perspectives on multicultural and social justice career interventions
- Suggesting ways to develop self-awareness, knowledge of diverse populations, and social justice–relevant career counseling skills.

## Definitions

Issues of multiculturalism and social justice are complex and can be difficult to implement in career counseling. Part of this difficulty stems from a lack of a common language when communicating important multicultural and social justice career counseling issues. For the purposes of this chapter, we provide key concepts and definitions as a foundation for understanding the multicultural and social justice perspectives in career counseling.

The term *multiculturalism* has historically been used to refer to racial and ethnic individual and group differences. However, a broader and more inclusive definition includes, but is not limited to, sexual orientation, gender, disability status, economic status, age, and religion (Pope, 1995).

### SIDEBAR 4.2  Broadening Multiculturalism

It is interesting to note that even as recently as 20 years ago, many counseling professionals had a very narrow conception of the meaning of *multiculturalism*. Characteristics such as sexual orientation, gender, disability status, economic status, age, and religion were not considered aspects of diversity and were not taken into consideration during the process of career counseling.

*Race* is a social construct that categorizes individuals on the basis of skin pigmentation and other physical attributes. *Ethnicity* has to do with an individual's identification with a cultural group on the basis of factors such as country of origin, language, sociopolitical history, and religion. The term *diversity* refers to individual and group differences based on factors such as race, ethnicity, gender, sexual orientation, economic class, religion, spiritual orientation, age, and disability status, to list a few (Adams et al., 2010).

Working with culturally diverse clients requires an understanding of their culture. Kehe and Smith (2004) described *culture* as the "characteristics, values, behaviors, products, and worldviews of a group of people with a distinct sociohistorical context" (p. 329). Aspects of culture can be observable or unobservable. Observable aspects of a client's culture include, but are not limited to, clothing, foods, traditions, languages, and customs. Unobservable aspects of culture may include gender role expectations, family structure, communication styles, and orientation to time.

Sue and Sue (2008) contended that human beings have individual, group, and universal dimensions of existence. *Individual existence* refers to the uniqueness of a person, which may include unique values, beliefs, and individual ways of being that make a person different from others. *Group dimensions of existence* refers to the commonalities of experience individuals have as a result of being a member of a racial–ethnic, sexual orientation, gender, religious, or economic social identity group. *Universal dimensions of existence* are the needs that all human beings have regardless of individual or group needs. These needs may include the need for food, shelter, and safety.

Operating from a multicultural and social justice framework in career counseling also requires an understanding of oppression. Hardiman and Jackson (1982) added,

Oppression exists when one social group exploits another social group for its own benefit. Oppression is distinct from a situation of simple brute force or control. It is first and foremost a systematic phenomenon that involves ideological domination, institutional control, and the promulgation of the dominant group's ideology of domination and culture on the oppressed. Oppression is simply not an ideology or set of beliefs that asserts one group's superiority over another. Nor is it random acts of discrimination or harassment toward members of the subordinate group. It is a *system* of domination with many interlocking parts. (p. 2)

Ratts (2011) contended that oppression can be an impediment to career development. For this reason, career counselors need to consider how they incorporate social justice into their practice. Fouad, Gerstein, and Toporek (2006) defined social justice as "the distribution of advantages and disadvantages within a society" (p. 1). In career counseling, it involves promoting equitable access to career resources and ensuring that career opportunities are available to all clients. Chang, Crethar, and Ratts (2010) contended that social justice counseling is both a goal and a process. The goal of social justice counseling is to create a socially just world in which all individuals have the opportunity to fulfill their career goals, which means ensuring that clients have equitable access to resources such as food, shelter, health care, employment, education, and career opportunities. The process of achieving social justice should be transparent and collaborative and involve clients throughout the career counseling process.

Career counselors who operate out of a social justice framework are often referred to as *social change agents*. In the career counseling field, social change agents use advocacy with, and on behalf of, clients to promote issues of career equity and access. *Advocacy* is the process of taking action to empower clients (Toporek, 2000).

## Multicultural and Social Justice Career Counseling Perspectives
### Multicultural Career Counseling

Descriptions of multicultural counseling have evolved over time. Arredondo, Toporek, Brown, Jones, and Locke (1996) described multicultural counseling as "preparation and practices that integrate multicultural and culture-specific awareness, knowledge, and skills into counseling interactions" (p. 42). Recently, Rubel and Ratts (2007) described multicultural counseling as

> a helping process that relies on both universal and culture-specific techniques to meet goals that are consistent with client values; recognizes individual, group and universal dimensions of client identity; and integrates client worldview into the assessment, diagnosis, and treatment of client's and client systems. (p. 50)

Inherent within these definitions is the assumption that cultural variables and the sociopolitical context influences all aspects of the counseling process.

The 1950s is referred to as the birth of the multicultural counseling movement because increasing numbers of counseling professionals began then to recognize the diversity of the country (Jackson, 1995). Because of widespread racial segregation and discrimination during this era, counseling with African American clients typically involved assimilation into the White dominant culture.

Not until the 1960s, a period characterized by social unrest and political upheaval, did multicultural counseling literature begin to materialize

(Ponterotto, Casas, Suzuki, & Alexander, 2010). Counseling professionals began to openly challenge racist counseling practices and the White establishment, which led to the formation of the Association for Non-White Concerns, an organization that primarily focused on the needs of African Americans. Not until 1972 did the Association for Non-White Concerns become recognized as an official division of the American Personnel and Guidance Association, the precursor to the American Counseling Association (ACA). The 1970s also saw a broadening of the multicultural counseling movement to include other underrepresented racial–ethnic groups, women, and people with disabilities.

The 1990s saw the maturation of the multicultural counseling movement with the creation of the Multicultural Counseling Competencies by Sue, Arredondo, and McDavis (1992). The Multicultural Counseling Competencies encompass three areas: (1) counselors' awareness of their cultural values, biases, and assumptions; (2) counselors' understanding of the worldview of the culturally different client; and (3) counselors' development and use of culturally appropriate intervention strategies and techniques (Sue et al., 1992). Each area is further divided into three primary domains: knowledge, skills, and awareness (Arthur & McMahon, 2005), creating a 3 × 3 matrix guiding the Multicultural Counseling Competencies.

### SIDEBAR 4.3  Influence of Multiculturalism and Social Justice Counseling

Even though the birth of the multicultural movement can be traced back to the 1950s, not until the development of the multicultural competencies in the 1990s did expectations for counselors in this regard really gain momentum. The development of these competencies, counselor licensure, and the accreditation of counselor education programs and departments are three of the most significant and influential movements of the past few decades.

The Multicultural Counseling Competencies were created in an effort to reduce bias in counseling and to provide consistency across practices, and they offered helping professionals a framework to develop cultural competencies. The notion that standards of cultural knowledge and conduct exist has led to the creation of career development models that meet the needs of diverse clients (Vespia, Fitzpatrick, Fouad, Kantamneni, & Chen, 2010) and to the development of culturally appropriate interventions and strategies (Arthur & McMahon, 2005).

The evolution of the multicultural counseling perspective in the general counseling field, coupled with the changing demographics of the U.S. population, has given rise to the multicultural career perspective (Swanson, 1993). The multicultural career perspective has led to concerns about whether use of traditional career development theories is effective with diverse clients. Cook et al. (2005) questioned the relevancy of traditional career theories with diverse clients because the values inherent within these theories were often in direct conflict with the values of diverse clients. Vespia et al. (2010) concurred, adding that traditional career development theories promoted "masculine and Western European values of individuality, self-determination, the centrality of work, separation between work and family, and a linear career development process" (p. 54). Similarly, Hartung (2002) was concerned that the career development field's overemphasis on "person variables" (p. 12) such as clients' abilities, needs, and interests has contributed to the lack of attention to clients' cultural background and the extent to which environmental barriers impede career development. For this reason, career counselors have often been ill equipped when they used Western theories of career development that were in conflict with the values of diverse clients.

### SIDEBAR 4.4  Multicultural Career Counseling

Career counselors working through a multicultural lens might use the knowledge, skills, and awareness they have of their client's background and culture to understand the contextual factors that might hinder, or support, the client's career development. Asking questions about the client's family, support system, and personal values might assist the counselor in gaining a more accurate picture of his or her career goals. Rather than using traditional standardized assessment instruments, the career counselor might interview the client regarding the career issues he or she deems important, being sure to include questions about his or her environment and how this might affect the client.

The multicultural counseling perspective has led to countless calls for career strategies that integrate the multicultural perspective. Brown (2007) added that a key element of multicultural career counseling is to operate from a cultural framework throughout the career counseling process, which includes identifying how culture affects the client–counselor relationship, identifying the decision-making process, establishing culturally appropriate career goals and interventions, and using advocacy when necessary. Osipow (1983) suggested using a systems theory approach to help contextualize the career needs of diverse clients. Arthur and McMahon (2005) also believed a systems approach to career counseling was important because it emphasized "both the parts within a whole system and view the whole system as greater than the sum of its parts" (p. 209). A systems approach to career counseling illuminates the context in which clients live. In so doing, it offers career counselors a comprehensive understanding of the dynamic interaction between clients and their surroundings. Although considerable gains have been made in the area of multicultural counseling, Vera and Speight (2003) contended that it is limited in helping clients address systemic issues, and they have called for a greater focus on social justice and advocacy in counseling.

### SIDEBAR 4.5  Immigrant Career Experiences

It is important to note that the career needs of individuals of different ages also vary across groups. For example, new immigrants who are professionals in their home countries might experience problems obtaining specific licensures or certifications necessary for practicing their occupation. Additionally, certain groups might lack knowledge of the English language, which might be problematic in attaining job placement, or even in identifying career goals.

## Social Justice Career Counseling

The field of career counseling has roots in social justice that can be traced back to the early 1900s, beginning with the work of Frank Parsons. Known as the father of vocational guidance, Parsons helped immigrants seek employment by challenging systemic barriers that hindered their career opportunities

(Kiselica & Robinson, 2001). Parsons was a tireless social change agent who chose to not accept the status quo by sitting on the sidelines and remaining silent. Instead, he championed closing the career gap between the rich and the poor by helping those who were disempowered find better career opportunities (Fouad, 2006). Parson's work is noted because he realized that helping clients with vocational and career issues meant that counselors needed to work with, and on behalf of, clients. Parsons' work was foundational to setting the stage for vocational and career counselors to advocate for social justice at the social and political levels.

The Great Depression of the 1930s was a challenging time for career and vocational professionals who sought to help individuals find work. The collapse of the economy meant that many Americans were out of work and needed assistance with developing skills to become sufficiently employed. After World War II, vocational and career counselors worked tirelessly to develop training programs for returning soldiers to help them find employment (Fouad, 2006). As a result of the United States' social and political landscape, career counselors continuously found themselves being called to not only work individually with clients, but also engage in advocacy in the social and political realms to address issues of inequity and access that obstruct individuals' career development. The advocacy work of vocational and career counselors at the systems level helped to strengthen individual work with clients.

Not until the 1970s did social justice scholarship began to appear in the counseling literature (Rubel & Ratts, 2007). The rise in the social justice counseling literature had to do with the social and political unrest across the United States in the 1960s. Individuals from marginalized communities voiced their concerns over the lack of access to career opportunities and inequitable career resources. African American clients did not have access to career opportunities equal to those of their White counterparts; women were counseled into low-paying administrative jobs; clients living in generational poverty did not have access to quality career resources; and same-sex benefits were not widely available to lesbian, gay, bisexual, and transgender workers.

The social and political upheaval of the 1960s was an impetus for such landmark policies as the Equal Pay Act of 1963, which prohibited wage inequities based on sex; the Civil Rights Act of 1964, which banned discrimination in employment based on race, color, religion, sex, or national origin; and the Age Discrimination in Employment Act of 1967, which prohibits employment discrimination against individuals age 40 and older.

Despite antidiscrimination employment policies, career counselors continued to find it difficult to assist clients from marginalized communities with career issues in the 1980s and 1990s. For example, people with disabilities were not considered a protected group and often had limited career options. Not until 1990, with the passage of the Americans With Disabilities Act, did people with disabilities become a protected group. Similarly, lesbian, gay, bisexual, and transgender clients continued to experience overt forms of heterosexism that negatively limited their career options.

In spite of the advocacy work career counselors were doing, the training career counselors received in their training programs was not adequately equipping them to deal with the social and political realities often faced by clients. For example, school counselors working in low-income schools realized that the dearth of career resources left their clients with limited career information and networking opportunities that had a drastic impact on their career options. Counselors working in agencies realized that they were ill equipped to deal with the systemic barriers their clients presented in therapy.

### SIDEBAR 4.6 Advocacy Examples

Advocacy in career counseling might be as simple as finding a mentor for a Hispanic woman who is uncertain about entering the engineering field. It can also include talking with prospective employers about the various environmental barriers that might keep certain individuals from applying for certain jobs. Advocacy in career counseling can take various forms, and it is vital that career counselors understand how they can work as social justice advocates on behalf of their clients.

In 1998, Lee and Walz published a landmark book titled *Social Action: A Mandate for Counselors*. The authors of this book recognized the importance of social advocacy in counseling and challenged all counselors to make social advocacy more prominent in their work with clients. In 1999, Loretta Bradley was elected ACA president and made advocacy a central theme of her leadership. Her leadership culminated in the publication of the book *Advocacy in Counseling: Counselors, Clients, and Communities* in 2000. In 2000, Jane Goodman, then president of the ACA, commissioned a task force to develop advocacy competencies for the profession. The task force developed the ACA Advocacy Competencies in 2001. The ACA Advocacy competencies provide a framework for career counselors to enact advocacy strategies. The ACA adopted the Advocacy Competencies (Lewis, Arnold, House, & Toporek, 2002) in 2003 as a response to the growing need for counselors to implement advocacy interventions.

The Advocacy Competencies consist of three levels of intervention (Ratts, Toporek, & Lewis, 2010): client–student, school–community, and the public arena. Each level is divided into two domains that assist a counselor in acting with, and on behalf of, the client. The client–student advocacy level includes the client–student empowerment and client–student advocacy domains. At this level, career counselors recognize the impact that social, political, economic, and cultural factors have on an individual's career development. Career counselors use direct interventions to identify clients' strengths and help to identify barriers and potential allies. The school–community level includes the community collaboration and systems advocacy domains. At this level, career counselors are aware of how environmental factors negatively affect career development and choose to respond to these barriers by collaborating with community organizations and advocating to remove unnecessary career barriers. The public arena level includes the public information and social–political advocacy domains. At this level, career counselors might take action against societal and normative career barriers by taking the issue public and by advocating politically against the presence of social injustices.

**SIDEBAR 4.7   Integrating Advocacy in Counselor Education**

Learning how many counselor education programs and departments have developed internship experiences designed to hone the advocacy skills of counselor candidates would be interesting. In today's increasingly diverse society, it would be unusual for practicing counselors to have a caseload devoid of clients who had experienced oppression and discrimination in the process of attempting to enter a career field or become upwardly mobile once established in an occupation.

## Connecting the Multicultural and Social Justice Career Perspectives

Given the historical and philosophical underpinnings of multicultural and social justice, understanding the complementary nature of the career counseling field's two perspectives is important. When combined, both perspectives can strengthen the work of career counselors (Ratts, 2011). The multicultural perspective helps career counselors develop insight into how social, political, economic, and cultural forces influence the career development process. Understanding the sociopolitical nature of career development often leads career counselors to recognize that they cannot continue to do the same things if they want to help culturally diverse clients. Increased understanding of the sociopolitical context of client problems can often serve as a gateway to social justice advocacy.

Ratts (2011) viewed multiculturalism and social justice as "two sides of the same coin" (p. 35). In other words, both multiculturalism and social justice are necessary when working with culturally diverse clients. Rubel and Ratts (2007) added that the multicultural perspective is about social justice. They believed the multicultural and social justice perspectives shared common assumptions: the need

- To view clients within the context of their environment
- To explore whether client problems are connected to oppressive social, political, and economic conditions
- To move beyond traditional models of helping when working with culturally diverse clients.

The similarities between multiculturalism and social justice led Toporek (2006) to connect the two perspectives by linking the Multicultural Counseling Competencies and Advocacy Competencies with the Career Development Competencies of the National Career Development Association. This innovative approach offers career counselors a framework to implement multicultural and social justice competencies. Similarly, in an effort to connect the multicultural and social justice perspectives, Ratts (2011) developed the multicultural and advocacy dimensions model. This model lays the groundwork for developing culturally and advocacy-responsive counseling services. It can help career counselors in their work to develop into multiculturally and advocacy-competent helping professionals.

## Career Counseling With Diverse Clients

Working out of a multicultural and social justice career framework means doing things differently. The process of stepping outside of one's training and practice to do things differently is difficult. To ease this transition, in this section of the chapter we provide a framework for work with diverse clients, reconceptualizing the counseling relationship, suggesting the goals and overall process of career counseling, and describing interventions and strategies to accomplish these goals.

## Understanding Clients Through a Sociopolitical Framework

Both the multicultural and the social justice career perspectives stress the importance of understanding how social, political, and economic forces influence career development and opportunities. An intrapsychic model of career counseling, which often ignores the social milieu, has its limits. The rationale is that clients, and the career issues they present, cannot be understood in a vacuum. Clients bring to counseling a host of environmental factors that can have an impact on their career development. Bringing this fact to clients' awareness and helping them make sense of their world is critical so that they can make well-informed career decisions. Clients who become aware of their situation within the context of their environment begin to see their world differently. Friere (1993) referred to this process as *conscientizaco*. Clients who experience *conscientizaco*, especially those from marginalized groups, begin to realize that many of the career obstacles they experience have to do with how the world is structured. For diverse clients, this realization can be overwhelming. Knowing that their career options are limited or that they face obstacles that individuals from privileged groups do not can lead to feelings of anger and hopelessness. For example, clients born into generational poverty may feel overwhelmed when presented with information regarding the cost of a college education. For this reason, it is important for multicultural and social justice career counselors to help diverse clients develop the skills to navigate their world (Ratts, 2008). Equipping diverse clients with accurate information regarding financial aid, connecting them with financial resources and scholarships, and walking them through the process of applying for financial assistance can be empowering for clients in generational poverty.

## Understanding Career Clients Through Identity Development

The use of identity development models has been important within the multicultural and social justice counseling fields (Sue & Sue, 2008). Identity development models were created to understand the impact of oppression on racial (Atkinson, Morten, & Sue, 1989; Helms & Cook, 1999), sexual (Cass, 1979), and gender (Worell & Remer, 2003) identity development. Identity development models help explain the influence of complex phenomena such as racism, sexism, and heterosexism on human development (Wijeyesinghe & Jackson, 2001).

Many identity development models follow a similar arrangement. They explain human behavior and perception in linear stages, with each stage reflecting a different way of seeing and experiencing the world. The first stage typically describes a person who is unaware of certain aspects of his or her identity. The latter stages tend to describe a person who has an integrated sense of who he or she is in relation to the world.

Identity development models are helpful in understanding the extent to which clients are affected as a result of living in a society in which access to career resources and opportunities are influenced by factors such as race, class, gender, and sexual orientation. It is a useful tool because it allows insight into how aware culturally diverse clients are of how race, class, gender, and sexual orientation influence their career development. Identity development models also allow counselors to see clients from a broader perspective that goes beyond just looking at their values, interests, personality, and skills.

## Understanding Career Clients Through Worldview

According to Sue and Sue (2008), worldview "determines how people perceive their relationship to the world (nature, institutions, other people, etc.)" (p. 293) and "is highly correlated with a person's cultural upbringing and life experiences" (p. 293). Moreover, worldview allows counselors to gain insight into how culturally diverse clients perceive their ability to be in control of their life and the extent to which they feel responsible for their life.

It is important to understand the concept of worldview because clients from diverse groups hold worldviews that differ from those of the dominant culture. For example, the dominant belief in the United States is that through hard work people can achieve their career aspirations. However, culturally diverse clients do not always hold this belief because they see that systemic barriers can be an impediment to their hard work. Therefore, understanding the worldview of culturally diverse clients can help career counselors gain insight into how clients perceive themselves in relation to the world of work. Moreover, worldview can help career counselors understand the extent to which clients feel in control of their career options and the degree to which they feel responsible for their career choices.

## Developing Multicultural and Social Justice Career Competence

Developing into effective multiculturally and social justice–competent career counselors requires a habit of mind. Operating out of a multicultural and social justice career framework does not just happen. It takes intentionality and a willingness to do things differently. It means expanding one's horizons and being willing to examine current practices and traditional methods of helping. It involves ethical and reflective practice and being cognizant of how one conducts oneself with culturally diverse clients. It requires counselors to move beyond the traditional office setting and use social advocacy to alter oppressive environmental barriers that hinder clients' career development.

Multicultural and social justice competence is a developmental and life-long process. It is not something that occurs overnight, and it goes beyond coursework. A combination of self-reflection, education, and lived experiences allows career counselors to develop the awareness, knowledge, and skills to be competent helping professionals. Being a culturally competent change agent is a way of being that goes beyond what counselors do with clients in the office setting.

Living out multicultural and social justice ideals in all aspects of life can also strengthen the important work career counselors do with clients. This work requires a personal and professional commitment to cultural competence and to addressing issues of career equity. Whether one is at the grocery store or working with a client, living out multicultural and social justice ideals is a must.

## Implications for Practice

Culturally diverse clients bring with them a unique set of career problems that traditional ways of helping cannot always address. Career counselors can be responsive to the unique needs of culturally diverse clients by using culturally appropriate techniques while also being cognizant of whether client problems warrant individual counseling or advocacy.

Often, multicultural and social justice perspectives require a new way of practicing that may be counter to one's training and ways of practicing. Questioning tradition and the way things have always been done can be difficult. It means being willing to take a risk, being ridiculed, and opening oneself to criticism. Therefore, developing patience and possessing the ability to effectively communicate the advantages of a multicultural and social justice perspective to clients, counselors, families, and the community is critical to its adoption.

### SIDEBAR 4.8   Risk to Counsel

Given the changing times in which we live, some important qualities that counselors in the new millennium must possess are high self-esteem, the ability to communicate articulately, and the willingness to take risks. Often, a counselor new to a system must be willing to work tirelessly with supervisors and peers who may not be willing to depart from traditional approaches to career counseling because of lack of awareness, poorly developed advocacy skills, or apprehension about change. Counselors must be willing to advocate for their clients when their clients' rights are violated or ignored even when it means taking risks in the context of their own work setting.

Multicultural and social justice career counseling has many benefits. Working from a multicultural and social justice framework ensures that client problems will be viewed with a wider lens that includes the social milieu, thus providing career helping professionals with a more comprehensive understanding of the issues with which clients present. In turn, this understanding can lead to culturally sensitive career interventions that take into consideration clients' sociocultural history. Counselors would also be more equipped to deal with the complex systemic career barriers with which clients often present because they have attained a certain level of multicultural and social justice awareness, knowledge, and skills.

## Summary

The advent of the multicultural and social justice counseling movements has led to increased attention to the effectiveness of career counseling with diverse populations and the influence of sociopolitical forces on career development. This concern has led to the need for multiculturally and advocacy-competent career interventions. In this chapter, we (a) provided an introduction to multicultural and social justice counseling concepts, (b) provided a framework for infusing multiculturalism and social justice in career counseling, and (c) explored the implications of multiculturalism and social justice in career counseling.

## References

Adams, M., Blumenfeld, W. J., Castaneda, R., Hackman, H. W., Peters, M. L., & Zuniga, X. (Eds.). (2010). *Readings for diversity and social justice* (2nd ed.). New York, NY: Routledge.

Age Descrimination Act of 1967, Pub. L. No. 90–202, § 29 Stat. 621 (1967).

Americans with Disabilities Act of 1967, Pub. L. No. 101–336, § 2, 104 Stat. 328 (1991).

Arredondo, P., Toporek, R., Brown, R., Jones, J., & Locke, D. C. (1996). Operationalization of the multicultural counseling competencies. *Journal of Multicultural Counseling and Development, 24,* 42–78.

Arthur, N., & McMahon, M. (2005). Multicultural career counseling: Theoretical applications of the systems theory framework. *Career Development Quarterly, 53,* 208–222.

Atkinson, D. R., Morten, G., & Sue, D. W. (1989). A minority identity development model. In D. R. Atkinson, G. Morten, & D. W. Sue (Eds), *Counseling American Minorities* (pp. 35–52). Dubuque, IA: W. C. Brown.

Brown, D. (2007). *Career information, career counseling, and career development* (9th ed.). Boston, MA: Pearson.

Cass, V. (1979). Homosexual identity formation: A theoretical model. *Journal of Homosexuality, 4,* 219–235.

Chang, C. Y., Crethar, H. C., & Ratts, M. J. (2010). Social justice: A national imperative for counselor education and supervision. *Counselor Education and Supervision, 50,* 82–87.

Civil Rights Act of 1964, Pub. L. No. 88–352, § 78 Stat. 241 (1964).

Cook, E. P., Heppner, M. J., & O'Brien, K. M. (2005). Multicultural and gender influences in women's career development: An ecological perspective. *Journal of Multicultural Counseling and Development, 33,* 165–179.

Equal Pay Act of 1963, Pub. L. No. 88–38, § 29 Stat. 206 (1963).

Fouad, N. A. (2006). Social justice in career and vocational aspects of counseling psychology. In R. L. Toporek, L. H. Gerstein, N. A. Fouad, G. Roysircar, & T. Israel (Eds.), *Handbook for social justice in counseling psychology: Leadership, vision, and action* (pp. 251–255). Thousand Oaks, CA: Sage.

Fouad, N. A., Gerstein, L. H., & Toporek, R. L. (2006). Social justice and counseling psychology in context. In R. L. Toporek, L. H. Gerstein, N. A. Fouad, G. Roysircar, & T. Israel (Eds.), *Handbook for social justice in counseling psychology: Leadership, vision, and action* (pp. 1–16). Thousand Oaks, CA: Sage.

Friere, P. (1993). *Pedagogy of the oppressed* (Rev. ed.; M. B. Ramos, Trans. & ed.). New York, NY: Continuum.

Hardiman, R., & Jackson, B. (1982). Oppression: Conceptual and developmental analysis. In M. Adams, P. Brigham, P. Dalpes, & L. Marchesani (Eds.), *Social diversity and social justice—Diversity and oppression: Conceptual frameworks* (pp. 1–6). Dubuque, IA: Kendall/Hunt.

Hartung, P. J. (2002). Cultural context in career theory and practice: Role salience and values. *Career Development Quarterly, 51,* 12–25.

Helms, J. E., & Cook, D. A. (1999). *Using race and culture in counseling and psychotherapy.* Needham Heights, MA: Allyn & Bacon.

Jackson, M. L. (1995). Multicultural counseling: Historical perspectives. In J. G. Ponterotto, J. M. Casas, L. Suzuki, & C. M. Alexander (Eds.), *Handbook of multicultural counseling* (pp. 3–16). Thousand Oaks, CA: Sage.

Kehe, J., & Smith, T. (2004). Glossary. In T. B. Smith (Ed.), *Practicing multiculturalism: Affirming diversity in counseling and psychology* (pp. 325–337). Boston, MA: Pearson Education.

Kiselica, M. S., & Robinson, M. (2001). Bringing advocacy counseling to life: The history, issues, and human dramas of social justice work in counseling. *Journal of Counseling and Development, 79,* 387–398.

Lee, C. C., & Walz, G. R. (Eds). (2000). *Social action: A mandate for counselors.* Alexandria, VA: American Counseling Association.

Lewis, J., Arnold, M. S., House, R., & Toporek, R. (2002). ACA Advocacy Competencies. pp 1–2; retrieved from http://www.counseling.org/Publications.

Osipow, S. H. (1983). *Theories of career development.* Englewood Cliffs, NJ: Prentice Hall.

Ponterotto, J. G., Casas, J. M., Suzuki, L. A., & Alexander, C. M. (Eds.). (2010). *Handbook of multicultural counseling* (3rd ed.). Thousand Oaks, CA: Sage.

Pope, M. (1995). The "salad bowl" is big enough for us all: An argument for the inclusion of lesbians and gay men in any definition of multiculturalism. *Journal of Counseling and Development, 73,* 301–304.

Pope, M., & Pangelinan, J. S. (2010). Using the ACA advocacy competencies in career counseling. In M. J. Ratts, R. L. Toporek, & J. A. Lewis (Eds.), *ACA advocacy competencies: A social justice framework for counselors* (pp. 209–223). Alexandria, VA: American Counseling Association.

Ratts, M. J. (2008). A pragmatic view of social justice advocacy: Infusing microlevel social justice advocacy strategies into counseling practices. *Counseling and Human Development, 41,* 1–8.

Ratts, M. J. (2011). Multiculturalism and social justice: Two sides of the same coin. *Journal of Multicultural Counseling and Development, 39,* 24–37.

Ratts, M. J., Toporek, R. L., & Lewis, J. A. (Eds.). (2010). *ACA advocacy competencies: A social justice framework for counselors.* Alexandria, VA: American Counseling Association.

Rubel, D., & Ratts, M. (2007). Diversity and social justice issues in counseling and psychotherapy. In D. Capuzzi & D. R. Gross (Eds.), *Counseling and psychotherapy: Theories and interventions* (4th ed., pp. 47–67). Upper Saddle River, NJ: Pearson Education.

Sue, D. W., Arredondo, P., & McDavis, R. J. (1992). Multicultural counseling competencies and standards: A call to the profession. *Journal of Multicultural Counseling and Development, 20,* 64–89.

Sue, D. W., Parham, T. A., & Santiago, G. B. (1998). The changing face of working in the United States: Implications for individual, institutional, and societal survival. *Cultural Diversity and Ethnic Minority Psychology, 4,* 153–164.

Sue, D. W., & Sue, D. (2008). *Counseling the culturally diverse: Theory and practice* (5th ed.). New York, NY: Wiley.

Swanson, J. L. (1993). Integrating a multicultural perspective into training for career counseling: Programmatic and individual interventions. *Career Development Quarterly, 42,* 41–50.

Toporek, R. (2000). Developing a common language and framework for understanding advocacy in counseling. In J. Lewis & L. Bradley (Eds.), *Advocacy in counseling: Counselors, clients, and community* (pp. 5–14). Greensboro, NC: CAPS.

Toporek, R. L. (2006). An integrative approach for competencies: Career counseling, social justice advocacy, and the multicultural counseling competencies. *Career Planning and Adult Development Journal, 21*(4), 34–50.

Vera, E. M. & Speight, S. L. (2003), Multicultural competence, social justice, and counseling psychology: Expanding our roles. *The Counseling Psychologist, 31*(3), 253–272.

Vespia, K. M., Fitzpatrick, M. E., Fouad, N. A., Kantamneni, N., & Chen, Y. L. (2010). Multicultural career counseling: A national survey of competencies and practices. *Career Development Quarterly, 59,* 54–71.

Wijeyesinghe, C., & Jackson, B. (Eds.). (2001). *New perspectives on racial identity development: A theoretical and practical anthology.* New York, NY: NYU Press.

Worell, J., & Remer, P. (2003). *Feminist perspectives in therapy: Empowering diverse women* (2nd ed.). Hoboken, NJ: Wiley.

# CHAPTER 5

# Ethical and Legal Issues in Career Counseling

Henry L. Harris and Dennis W. Engels

## Contents

Ethical and legal guidelines, along with principles, codes, and statutes, govern and enhance the work of career counselors, career facilitators, and others working in career development. In this chapter, based on the National Career Development Association's (NCDA; 2007) Ethical Standards, we review selected ethical standards, principles, and issues and legal concerns related to career development and career counseling as means to discerning and discussing implications for work and life today, with special emphasis on how these considerations and implications affect the work of career counselors, career development workers, and their clients. We also discuss elements of the Multicultural Counseling Competencies developed by Arredondo et al. (1996) in the context of NCDA's (2007) Ethical Standards. We also include three case studies and three self-awareness activities designed to stimulate thinking.

## Establishment of Ethical Standards

In counseling and counseling specialties, a code of ethics is the foundation needed to develop competent trustworthy professionals and ensure client success. Ethical guidelines in the helping profession were formally established in 1953 when the American Psychological Association published its first code of ethics (Neukrug, 2011). The National Association of Social Workers followed in 1960, and in 1961 the American Counseling Association (ACA) developed guidelines for ethical behavior as well. Even though ethical guidelines for these organizations (see ACA, 2005; American Psychological Association, 2002; National Association of Social Workers, 2008) have experienced major revisions over the years to reflect the changing values of society and organizations, they share many similarities (Neukrug, 2011).

Regardless of the organization, ethical standards are designed to (a) protect public consumers and improve delivery of services, (b) promote accountability and stability of the organization by enforcing established standards, (c) educate members about what is considered desired ethical conduct, (d) provide a framework in the ethical decision-making process when ethical dilemmas arise, and (e) protect professionals delivering services from licensure board complaints and malpractice suits from consumers (Corey, Corey, & Callanan, 2011; Herlihy & Corey, 2006; Van Hoose & Kottler, 1985). Ethical codes, although extremely important, are not without limitations. Most often, the public is not involved in creating the guidelines, and there may be situations in which the codes prove difficult to enforce. Conflicts may also arise when differences between the codes and the law are apparent or when differences exist between the professional's personal values and the codes (Neukrug, 2011). Ethical codes are considered a crucial resource for successful organizations, and professionals should work to understand the intentions of the standards by attending to both the letter and the spirit of the code (Herlihy & Corey, 2006; Neukrug, 2011).

## Definitions of Key Terms

When evaluating human behavior, human values, and relationships, the words *ethical, moral,* and *legal* are often used in a reciprocal manner because they typically involve judgments about what is right or wrong or good or bad. Although the words share some similarities, they have different definitions and different interpretations of the definitions.

### SIDEBAR 5.1  Case Study: What Would You Do?

Imagine yourself walking down the street as you return from a disappointing job interview and seeing someone in front of you drop what appears to be a dollar bill. The individual keeps walking; you quickly pick up the money and notice it is much more than you had expected—two $100 bills. What would you do? Would you keep the money? Would you return it to the person who dropped it? If you decide to keep the money, will you have broken a law? If you were an unemployed single parent with dwindling resources and two small children, would this affect your decision? If the person who dropped the money was neatly dressed and appeared to be wealthy, would this make a difference in your reasoning? Regardless of the circumstances, how do individuals in society make such decisions? How are decisions influenced by individual morals, ethics, and the law?

## Morals

Morality is generally concerned with how people conduct themselves and is based on a personal value system heavy influenced by one's culture (Remley & Herlihy,

2007). Results from the Fitzpatrick (2007) National Cultural Values Survey found that the majority of Americans believe the nation is in a moral decline. Of those surveyed from all major demographic groups, 74% believe moral values in the United States are weaker than they were 20 years ago; after parents and families, the media are the second greatest influence on moral values. The report also indicated that although respondents placed a high value on classical virtues such as truthfulness, thrift, industry, and charity, 33% admitted that, if receiving unemployment benefits, they would work under the table and not disclose this information. Twenty-five percent also indicated that they would not alert the restaurant if an item was left off their bill (Fitzpatrick, 2007).

A more recent survey revealed that Americans are three times more likely to describe the current state of moral values in the United States as poor than as excellent or good. Additionally, 76% indicated that moral values are getting worse, and some blamed parenting, poor government leaders, Americans failing to embrace God, rising crime rates, and the breakdown of traditional two-parent families (Jones, 2010). It is essential to keep in perspective that moral judgments and decisions vary individually, culturally, generationally, and from one society to another.

## Ethics

Ethics can be variously defined as "the study of standards of conduct and moral judgment; moral philosophy, ... the system or code of morals of a particular person, religion, group, profession, etc." (*Webster's New World College Dictionary*, 1999, p. 488) or as "a set of moral principles, ... rules of conduct governing a particular group, ... moral principles, as of an individual: *His (her) ethics forbade cheating*" (*Merriam-Webster's Collegiate Dictionary*, 2000, p. 453). Philosophers also remind one that ethics is an area of philosophy that examines virtue, character, and the good life (Mann & Kreyche, 1966) while the counselor attends to his or her motives and activities and goals.

Beauchamp and Childress (1994), Welfel (2002), Urofsky and Engels (2003), and many others have discussed the importance of counselors enhancing their ethical capacity by understanding ethical foundations, including philosophical origins in moral philosophy and related ethical theory. Freeman (2000) and Freeman, Engels, and Altekruse (2004) also articulated and advocated counselor commitment to wisdom, insight, good judgment, and morality in applying professional skill and knowledge. In addition to the fundamental importance of an individual professional's responsibility for ethical behavior, we should also note that standards, including ethical standards, are predicated on minima, or the least one must do (Council for the Accreditation of Counseling and Related Educational Programs, 2005), and counselors can and should stay mindful of ethical principles as means to go beyond minimal ethical requirements (Engels, 1981).

## Laws

Laws are agreed-on general or specific rules imposed by society typically in response to events or circumstances in which society believes regulation is needed. For people to live together as a group, laws are designed to place societal needs over individual desires, yet at the same time protect individual rights from the action of others. Laws are generated in the courtroom in the form of decisions or when elected government officials decide to enact new laws, and if or when individuals fail to abide by the principles of the law, punishment may follow (Levin, 2010; Remley & Herlihy, 2007).

**SIDEBAR 5.2   Moral Awareness and Economics—Golden Parachutes**

A *golden parachute* is defined as an employment contract that provides extraordinary benefits to top executives of a company if the company merges with or is sold to another firm. The package might include stock options and bonus or severance pay when the executive's job ends at the company (Golden Parachute, 2010). In the past, Lee Raymond, former Exxon/Mobile executive, received a $351 million exit package; Richard Fuld of Lehman Brothers, a $299.2 million exit package; Kenneth Lewis of Bank of America, a $120.2 million exit package; James Dimon of JPMorgan Chase, $25.5 million exit package; and Daniel Mudd of Fannie Mae, a $22.4 million exit package (Young, Lehman, McGregor, Polek, 2007). What are your thoughts about individuals receiving such packages? Morally, did these individuals do anything wrong from your perspective? If you were a top executive, would you negotiate this type of package in your contract?

In summary, professional ethics for career counselors encompass individual practitioner knowledge of, skill in, and commitment and adherence to professional organizational standards as a basis for wise moral, ethical, and legal decisions in professional practice. In attending to the vital importance of wisdom and the importance of philosophical bases for ethics and ethical behavior for individual professionals, Freeman et al. (2004) also pointed out that wisdom and principles could be lost by too narrow a focus on situational details and specific counselor knowledge and skills. Hence, counselors need to focus on ethical principles, the most fundamental of which are nonmaleficence and beneficence, "do no harm" and "do good."

# Ethical Standards in Career Counseling

As noted in the Preamble of the ACA's (2005) Code of Ethics and the NCDA's (2007) Ethical Principles, counselors and career counselors are dedicated to promoting the worth, dignity, uniqueness, and potential of every person whom they counsel. These noble and inspiring human principles and characteristics have been a long-standing positive traditional base for and a consensus goal of members of ACA, NCDA, and all ACA divisions, branches, and entities and of the National Board for Certified Counselors (1991), and worth and dignity are major points as well in Principle E of the American Psychological Association's 2003 *Ethical Principles of Psychologists and Code of Conduct* (APA, 2002).

The NCDA's (2007) Ethical Principles have five major purposes: (1) support the mission of NCDA, (2) define ethical practices and behaviors expected of association members, (3) serve as a guide to help those receiving career-related services understand their rights and responsibilities, (4) make clear to all members and those served the nature of commonly prescribed ethical responsibilities, and (5) serve as guide to fully help members promote the core values of the profession and also assist them in developing a professional course of action that will most effectively serve individuals using career services (NCDA, 2007). The latest revision of the NCDA Ethical Principles occurred in 2007, and because the career counseling literature is not replete with articles on ethical issues in career development (e.g., Chung & Gfroerer, 2003; Niles, 1997; Pate & Niles, 2002), we briefly discuss important highlights of each section of the NCDA Ethical Principles and review some key ethical issues. Given the racial and ethnic diversification of the United States, we also discuss the Association of Multicultural Counseling and Development's Multicultural Counseling Competencies (the Competencies; Arredondo et al., 1996) in the context of the NCDA Ethical Principles as well.

## Section A: The Professional Relationship

This section of the codes outlines responsibilities and expected behaviors of professionals and furthermore says that professionals must perform at the highest level of their ability, practice ethical behavior at all times, be accountable for professional behavior at all times, and refrain from falsifying or exaggerating professional qualifications or abilities. Additionally, career professionals must only pursue positions for which they are qualified and recognize and address personal limits of skill and knowledge. Career counselors must also help clients who cannot afford their fee to find services at a more acceptable cost; if bartering is considered, it should only occur if the relationship is not exploitive, it is an accepted practice among career professionals in the community, and cultural factors are taken into consideration, along with knowledge of legal implications (NCDA, 2007).

On the basis of census data projections, by the year 2050 the U.S. population will experience a racial transformation and consist of 46% Caucasians, 30% Hispanics, 12% African Americans, 8% Asians, 3% multiracial, 0.8% American Indian/Alaska Natives, and 0.2% Native Hawaiian and Pacific Islanders (U.S. Census Bureau, 2008). It is safe to assume that many of these individuals from the various racial and ethnic groups will be employed in the workforce, seeking employment, and using career counseling services. Therefore, it is imperative for career counselors to respect the cultural diversity of their clients and develop an awareness of their own values, attitudes, and beliefs when providing services. These NCDA standards are very similar to the Association of Multicultural Counseling and Development's Competencies (Arredondo et al., 1996), which also call for counselors to develop awareness of how racism, oppression, stereotyping, and discrimination affect them personally and in the work environment. When appropriate, career professionals should attempt to remove systemic barriers that affect client development and develop cultural sensitivity when providing services to culturally diverse clients.

**SIDEBAR 5.3  Case Study**

A colleague of Michael's consistently makes jokes or comments about some of the clients being served in the career center. Michael also notices most of the jokes and comments are directed toward a specific group of individuals. Michael's colleague has indicated that he intends no harm and this is just a part of his cultural upbringing. Michael, even though he feels it is inappropriate, has sometimes found himself laughing along with a supervisor at some of the jokes and comments. Michael would like to express his objections but is somewhat concerned about the outcome. He has applied for a higher position within the company and does not want to jeopardize his potential promotion with any controversy. "Only a few people are hearing this and no one is being harmed" is the thought that has been running through Michael's head. What should Michael do? Are the colleague's and supervisor's actions unethical? Are Michael's actions unethical? What should Michael do in this situation? What would you do if you were in Michael's shoes?

In summary, career counselors must remain conscious of their potential impact on clients' lives and provide culturally appropriate career counseling services to clients in a manner that will enhance their growth and development. This section and the overall standards make it abundantly clear that career counselors are ethically obligated to serve their clients. Career counselors are clearly responsible and accountable to the employees and dependents whom they counsel, as well as to their employer (NCDA, 2007).

## Section B: Confidentiality, Privileged Communication, and Privacy

The Confidentiality, Privileged Communication, and Privacy section details expected behaviors within the counselor–client dyad or group, including the career professional's primary commitment and responsibility to respect client integrity and welfare. When working with clients from culturally diverse backgrounds, career professionals should be sensitive to and aware of their client's unique cultural background and also understand how this might affect confidentiality. Confidentiality of all information obtained in the relationship must be a top priority; however, in the case of a client who is an imminent danger to him- or herself or others, the counselor has the responsibility to notify appropriate authorities. Career counselors may also be justified in disclosing confidential information if they have a client who discloses that he or she has a life-threatening or communicable disease that others may possibly be in danger of contracting (NCDA, 2007).

Client records should always be kept in a secure location with only authorized individuals having access. When transmitting confidential information (i.e., computer, e-mail, voice mail, text messages, or other forms of technology), the counselor must also confirm that the information is appropriate and nondiscriminatory. The counselor must have knowledge, including hands-on use and search experience, and assurance that the information is current, accurate, and relevant whatever the electronic method of delivery. Additionally, the counselor must determine whether the client is capable (emotionally, intellectually, and physically) of using the application (NCDA, 2007).

## Section C: Professional Responsibility

The Professional Responsibility section outlines professionals' responsibilities in dealing with the public and other professionals as they are encouraged to provide communication that is reliable, accurate, and open. Career professionals must also possess knowledge, understand, and follow the NCDA (2007) Ethical Standards. They should only practice in areas in which they have received education, appropriate training, and supervision. Career professionals are encouraged to consistently evaluate their effectiveness and improve their skills by engaging in peer group supervision when needed, participating in continuing education, and consulting with other professional colleagues. Similarly, the Competencies (Arredondo et al., 1996) also encourage culturally skilled counselors to seek appropriate training, consultative, and educational experiences as a method to improve their overall effectiveness in working with culturally diverse populations.

Career professionals attempt to promote change within the individual, group, institution, and society in an ethically and culturally responsive manner. The goal is to improve the quality of life for those being served, which may be most effectively accomplished when career professionals engage in appropriate self-care activities. Career counselors should always present their educational degrees and credentials accurately and never engage in sexual harassment or discriminate against an individual on the basis of ethnicity, race, sexual orientation, mental or physical disability, religion, gender, gender identity, language, socioeconomic status, age, marital status, or physical appearance. The ultimate goal of this section is to encourage professional conduct by career counselors (NCDA, 2007).

## Section D: Relationship With Other Professionals

The primary purpose of this section of the standards is to encourage career professionals to construct appropriate communication and working relationships with individuals from within and outside of the profession to create and provide beneficial services to clients (Makela, 2009; NCDA, 2007). Counseling professionals serving as consultants need to be honest and straightforward in communicating in language that is easily understood. Everyone involved should be informed about the reasons for services to be provided, possible risks and rewards, confidentiality limits, and cost. Career professional consultants in a collaborative effort with the individuals or group being serviced are encouraged to develop a clear definition of the problem, articulate goals for change, and use culturally responsive interventions. Culturally responsive interventions are used by skilled counselors who possess knowledge of possible bias when using assessment instruments and during their interpretation and are consciously aware of the individual cultural aspects of the client (the Competencies; Arredondo et al., 1996).

According to C. C. Lee and Hipolito-Delgado (2007), *advocacy* is defined as the act of taking action to produce some type of environmental change on behalf of clients. Career professionals respond as advocates when they alert their employers to inappropriate practices or policies that are potentially disruptive to clients and the services being provided. If employers fail to take appropriate action after being notified, career professionals may consider taking further action that might include voluntarily seeking employment elsewhere or contacting state licensure or national accrediting boards.

Thompson and Cummings (2010) encouraged career counselors to advocate more for individuals participating in career counseling who have criminal records by examining policies that may contribute to unpredictable economic resources and recidivism. They further stated that career counselors have the ability to accomplish this because they are "well equipped with skills and resources required to draw awareness to individuals in the community needing attention and that such involvement aligns closely with the profession's ethical principles, strengths-based perspective, and social justice agenda" (p. 16). O'Neil, McWhirter, and Cerezo (2008) advised career professionals to advocate for transgender individuals by providing sensitivity training and workplace education to help coworkers, employers, and supervisees establish and maintain a healthy work environment. Transgender people can also be supported when career professionals support legislation, social events, and political functions aimed at creating ways to eliminate the discriminatory behavior they encounter. This form of action supports one of main goals of this section, to provide effective services to clients.

### SIDEBAR 5.4 Awareness

As you envision yourself in the role of a career counselor, what are some worthy causes in the area of career development that you could see yourself participating in as an advocate? First, explore your definition of an advocate. What are some issues that you are passionate about? Have you ever decided to advocate for a specific reason? If not, what has kept you from doing so? As a career counselor, how can you make a difference in helping those without a voice be heard? What are the risks involved when advocating? What are some of the potential benefits of advocating?

## Section E: Evaluation, Assessment, and Interpretation

The Evaluation, Assessment, and Interpretation section emphasizes a very common area of career counseling practice and an area in which career counselors have considerable expertise, for example, regarding core aspects of instrument validity and reliability. One example of areas in which career counselors can help the public and policymakers might be in terms of the technical and human complexities seen in assessment. Schultz and Schultz (2002), in reminding psychologists to protect client worth, dignity, and welfare, noted the importance of counselor competence and adherence to formal assessment protocols and compliance with a producer's guidelines for using career assessment instruments. In this regard, counselors provide raw scores only to professionals who are qualified to properly interpret results and to ensure an understandable interpretation of results to the client. Schultz and Schultz provided an excellent example of problems that can arise in career assessment when they addressed the need for respect of and privacy regarding intimate personal issues. They cited the *Soroka v. Dayton-Hudson* case, wherein the California Court of Appeals held that unless an employer could prove the direct relationship of an applicant's sexual habits and religious faith to the job sought, an employment screening instrument's questions regarding sex and religion violated an applicant's privacy rights (Schultz & Schultz, 2002, pp. 121–122). Certainly, cultural awareness of such ethical, legal, and moral complexities can help counselors see the need for formal preparation and continuing education in ethics. Better articulation of these issues could afford strong platforms for career counselors advocating credentialing and other public policy requirements aimed at protecting clients. Another example related to assessment might focus on the appearance of software-based assessment reports that appear to be highly personalized or culturally insensitive when they are really prepackaged and software driven. Counselors certainly need to understand this categorical reality of software-driven reports and need to be vigilant regarding client deference to the seemingly highly personalized objectivity of such reports, lest clients or counselors put too much faith in these categorical assessments.

Additionally, counselors need to understand and clarify for clients that counselors use relatively few tests. Although there are technical and semantic reasons for noting that most of the instruments counselors use are not tests, the important technical and ethical reason to clarify this point for clients focuses on the testlike appearance of most of these instruments and the high likelihood that clients will regard assessment results as some objective and valid set of test results. For example, an interest inventory printout, while appearing highly personalized and highly objective, could be inferred by clients as a set of objective competency test results rather than as a set of categorical statements related to interests. Additionally, clients might easily fail to appreciate that these instruments point out an apparent commonality of client interest with interests of the norming occupational groups rather than explicit client interest in any specific occupation. Career professionals would do well to seek out an appropriate battery of assessment instruments rather than relying on and giving clients a sense of relying on one or two instruments.

## Section F: Use of the Internet in Career Services

In today's technology-driven world, Americans are using computers and other forms of digital technology at a greater rate than ever before. According to Pierce (2010), the Internet is used by more than 80% of Americans and individuals spend an average 19 hours per week online. When it comes to purchasing goods online, 59% of Internet users indicated that they purchased books or clothes online, followed by gifts (55%), travel (53 %), and electronics and appliances (47%). Given the high Internet use, consumers are also purchasing other services online, including various forms of career-related services (i.e., career counseling, career coaching, resume critiques, career assessments, career transitions, one-on-one consultation services, career workshops, job searches) that are being offered via the Internet. Multiple ways of communicating online include e-mail, discussion boards, video and audio recordings, podcasts, Web sites, instant messages, and virtual rooms (Venable, 2010). In their survey of counselor education professionals, Lewis and Coursol (2007) found that 83% of the respondents indicated that they were open to addressing career issues using online counseling. It is also interesting to note that, when comparing text-based chat applications, videoconferencing, and e-mail, participants selected videoconferencing as the most appropriate format. Regardless of the delivery format, career counselors must deliver these services in an ethically responsive manner and always inform prospective clients about the potential advantages and disadvantages. They must make sure clients will benefit from this type of career service and have the intellectual, emotional, and physical capability required (NCDA, 2007). Career counselors must also be mindful of how age may affect Internet use because 17% of Americans between the ages of 36 and 55 are not Internet users (Pierce, 2010).

Informed consent and confidentiality is paramount for career professionals providing online career-related services. They should always maintain a secure Web site, validate the accuracy of all information posted on the site, and provide their credentials to all prospective clients. Fees for services provided should be clearly stated and easy to locate. Furthermore, career professionals should inform clients about the difficulty of maintaining absolute confidentiality when using online resources, inform clients of their rights, discuss alternate forms of delivery along with potential cultural barriers, and make sure clients are aware of dangers of authorized and unauthorized users. As online career counseling becomes used more often, it would be wise for career professionals to investigate its impact on clients, their expectations of the experience, and their level of satisfaction (Lewis & Coursol, 2007).

## Section G: Supervision, Training, and Teaching

Supervision, training, and teaching are considered important aspects of career professionals. Hart (1982) defined *supervision* as a continuing educational process in which the individual serving in the role as supervisor helps another person in the role of supervisee develop suitable professional behavior by examining the supervisee's professional activities. According to Bradley and Kottler (2001), supervision is an aspect of training that is designed to promote competence and facilitate professional and personal development. One of the major responsibilities of career professionals is to oversee client welfare and supervise services provided to students and other career professionals for whom they are responsible. This aspect of the code is accomplished when supervisors meet with supervisees to consult, make live observations, and review cases. Career counselor supervisors are aware of limitations that could prevent their supervisees from being successful and are encouraged to seek consultation when difficult decisions may have to be made concerning a supervisee's performance. They have also received specific training in supervision, maintain appropriate credentials, adhere to maintaining sound ethical relationships with their supervisees, and are conscious of the difference in power between themselves and supervisees (NCDA, 2007).

Career professionals are aware of the impact of diversity on the relationship developed with supervisees and should strive to be culturally competent. When people are culturally competent, they have developed an awareness of their own person assumptions, understand the worldviews of culturally diverse clients, and are obligated to develop culturally appropriate methods of responding (Toporek, Gerstein, Foud, Roysicar-Sowdowsky, & Israel, 2005). In their qualitative study, Ancis and Marshall (2010) examined the perspectives of trainees regarding their supervisor's multicultural competence in supervision. They discovered that (a) supervisees described their supervisors as being accepting, open, and genuine about their own cultural background and biases; (b) supervisees were encouraged to develop an increased level of self-awareness by understanding the impact of their own personal cultural experiences and biases in their work experiences with clients; (c) supervisors openly discussed the limits of their knowledge with the supervisees and provided them with relevant resources; and (d) supervisees described their supervisors as being aware of the impact of oppression and racism and communicating this during supervision, which had a positive impact on client outcome. The results of this study clearly reflect Standard G.11.c—Multicultural/Diversity Competence (NCDA, 2007), which calls for educators to train culturally competent students by helping them to gain awareness, knowledge, and skills in the Competencies' culturally responsive practice.

As teachers and trainers, career professionals are responsible for possessing expected levels of knowledge about the profession's ethical, legal, and regulatory perspectives. In addition, they are responsible for applying this knowledge to help supervisees and students become aware of their responsibilities, in particular the importance of following the NCDA (2007) Ethical Standards. When teaching specific theoretical techniques to students, teachers and trainers should communicate both the risks and the benefits of using such techniques in a sound ethical manner. Career professionals seek appropriate placement sites for students and clearly articulate throughout the training program well-defined methods of evaluation, expected competency levels, and a time frame in which evaluations will be completed (NCDA, 2007).

## Section H: Research and Publication

The Research and Publication section outlines guidelines for research within the field of career counseling, including human participants guidelines, informed consent, and the principal investigator's ethical competence and acknowledgment of responsibility. Research results are reported in a manner that decreases the possibility that they are misleading or distorted. Career professionals specifically make known to the public all variables and conditions that may have affected data interpretation or study outcome. Original data are made available to others who may desire to replicate the study, while ensuring that participants' identities are protected. If participants personally indicate involvement in a research study, appropriate steps are taken to minimize potential harm and protect their identity. Investigators must be familiar with the research being addressed, cite the previous research conducted in the area, and disseminate results that hold promise for improving the field, even when the results are negative (NCDA, 2007).

One major concern related to research and publication can center on giving credit to all contributors to published works, in proportion with author or creator contribution. One important means of attending to this issue is to approach it in a manner similar to the informed consent with which counselors enter into counseling relationships with clients. The key ethical point is that the list of authors or creators should reflect the sequence and level of contribution to the work.

**SIDEBAR 5.5  Case Study**

A career professional submits a manuscript to a major career counseling journal for publication, and it is eventually accepted. Once published, a former student enrolled in a doctoral counseling program reads the article and notices some striking similarities between the published article and a paper she wrote while a student in his class. She is thrilled to see this publication because it addresses a topic that she is passionate about, yet disappointed to not have been recognized as a contributing author. The publication is beginning to receive rave reviews, and her friends have encouraged her to inform her advisor and possibly contact the author. What would you do if you were the student? What would be your major concerns? Would you discuss this with your advisor or contact the author? What are the risks of and potential benefits for everyone involved? As the author, how would you respond if you were contacted by the student? Has an ethical or legal violation occurred? For classroom discussion, one group of students should respond as the student and another group should respond as the author. Both groups are encouraged to pay close attention to the NCDA (2007) Ethical Standards during the discussion.

## Section I: Resolving Ethical Issues

The final section, Resolving Ethical Issues, notes the importance of career professionals adhering to the NCDA (2007) Ethical Standards. They are responsible not only for conducting themselves in their professional work environment in a moral, ethical, and legally responsive manner, but also for holding other career professionals to the same standards. An ethical dilemma is defined as a conflict that requires a decision or action from among two or more morally acceptable courses of action (Hamric, Spross, & Hanson, 2000). When career professionals are faced with ethical dilemmas, they take appropriate actions to resolve them. For example, if another colleague is suspected of making an ethical violation, career professionals are encouraged to first attempt to resolve the issue informally with the individual, providing confidentiality rights are not violated. Consultation with knowledgeable colleagues is also suggested because the next step in resolving an ethical dilemma could involve reporting an ethical violation.

Career coaching appears to be one area in which more attention relating to ethics is warranted. Perhaps most notably, NCDA needs to continue attending to important ethical issues related to career coaching. According to Chung and Gfroerer (2003), void of professional and legal regulations, almost anyone can practice career coaching without training. Although some improvements have been made concerning career coaching qualifications (i.e., Certified Career Coach, Certified Workforce Development Coach, Certified Career Management Coach, Certified Job Search Strategist, Certified Professional Career Coach, Certified Employment Interview Professional, and Master Career Director), certification requirements vary tremendously (Coaching Certifications, 2010). Professional identity and credentials are the most important matters for career counselors and the career counseling profession as designations and credentials proliferate nationally and internationally.

Career development facilitators, unlike career coaches, have specific standards and required training that must be completed to receive this credential. They perform a variety of career-related roles ranging from group facilitator to resource career development coordinator. Individuals are required to receive 120 class or instructional hours of training in the area of career development. This training must also be provided by a nationally qualified and trained instructor. Because of the number of people providing career counseling services who lack the proper training and standards, the Career Development Facilitator credential was specifically created for these individuals to provide quality training (Career Development Facilitator, 2010).

Suffice it to say, credentialing is a matter of utmost ethical concern and one essential aspect of professional ethics for career counselors. Without question, NCDA has been proactive in attempting to resolve the ethical dilemma around individuals practicing in the career counseling arena without the appropriate credentials. Regardless of the issue, when ethical dilemmas arise, the counselor should (a) identify and define the problem, (b) consider the moral principles involved, (c) become aware of feelings he or she is personally experiencing, (d) consult with colleagues or experts in the field, (e) include the client in the decision-making process, (f) determine desired outcomes, (g) consider possible actions that must be taken, and finally (h) make the decision and then act on it (Remley & Herlihy, 2007). Furthermore, during the ethical decision-making process, Knapp and VandeCreek (2007) encouraged individuals to respect their clients' cultural values because clients may sometimes present values that conflict with Westernized U.S. values. If or when this happens, counselors should seek a therapeutic solution that meets the cultural value system of all involved by engaging in a genuine, respectful dialogue. Knapp and VandeCreek also indicated that if a serious threat exists to a fundamental value and an acceptable solution cannot be agreed on, "it may be appropriate to allow Western notions of beneficence to temporarily trump the respect of autonomy" (p. 665).

As one can see, many of these standards are general enough to be relative to any field of counseling; however, it is important to note how these standards are the foundation of this specialty and are vital to a successful career practice, with guidelines for providing the highest quality of services to clients and, in turn, to society as a whole. Career counselors have a primary responsibility to their clients in addition to any other parties who might be involved in paying for the career counseling.

Although the NCDA (2007) Ethical Standards are relatively clear and regularly reviewed by NCDA's ethics committee, ethical standards are likely to have some purposeful and principled ambiguity. It would be impossible and imprudent to try to cover every possible ethical issue, and trying to make the standards extremely prescriptive would likely happen at the risk of missing general principles, while also risking a minimalization of the complexities of human development and behavior. Moreover, career counselors who hold professional credentials and membership in multiple professional organizations incur multiple ethical and legal obligations, which can add substantial complexity, contradictions, and dilemmas to ethical decision making and practice, especially when these different ethical codes conflict. Adding legal requirements adds yet more complexity, as do additional factors, such as stipulations by a counselor's employer, leading to important implications of ethically and legally serving one's employer. Central among these issues is the need for counselors to always be committed to serving clients in a culturally responsive manner.

## Perspectives on Ethical, Legal, and Practice Issues

Although some ethical and legal decisions seem clear, straightforward, and intuitive in terms of appropriate professional counselor action requirements, ultimately all ethical decisions require individual counselor judgment, and many decisions, situations, and actions lack clarity and call for more than simply looking at the literal standards or the law for wise professional judgment. To illustrate some of the complexity for counselors considering ethical and legal issues in career counseling and career development, Engels, Wilborn, and Schneider (1990) used a 2 × 2 table to juxtapose the terms *ethical* and *legal*.

| 1. Ethical and legal | 3. Legal, not ethical |
|----------------------|-----------------------|
| 2. Ethical, not legal | 4. Not legal, not ethical |

As one can see in this illustration, counseling intentions and behaviors in Quadrant 1 that are clearly both legal and ethical (e.g., providing professional counseling services consistent with one's expertise, experience and credentials) tend to seem somewhat straightforward. Decisions and behaviors based in Quadrant 1 might not constitute the same level of problem or quandary for practitioners as those more nebulous choices and actions represented in Quadrants 2 and 3.

## Complexities

Nebulous ethical and legal issues in career development abound, as one looks at Quadrants 2 and 3, reflecting the complexity of human circumstances, issues, and actions while also appreciating the many gray areas of even the first and the final quadrants. Among many examples one could use to highlight the complexity of discerning issues and acting ethically, one could note a number of concerns.

For example, in Quadrant 2, the ethical–not legal quadrant, informing a potential victim that a client intends that person physical harm would comply with the majority decision in *Tarasoff v. Regents of the University of California* (1974, 1976), while violating a long-standing Texas statute based on the primacy of confidentiality and a client's right to privacy (Mappes, Robb, & Engels,1985), a stance that was reaffirmed in *Thapar v. Zezulka* (1999). A minority opinion in the Tarasoff case agreed with the majority opinion of the Texas Supreme Court ruling in *Thapar v. Zezulka* (1999), stating that a mental health professional can be liable for violating a client's right to an assumption of privacy if a counselor were to warn a potential victim after a client makes threats toward a specific person or people. In the face of two so completely different majority legal conclusions regarding a counselor's ethical duty to warn, counselors need to consider such a matter very carefully. In addressing such quandaries, knowledge of ethical or moral theory could help career counselors find personal ethical peace and a basis for action, a matter we address later in this chapter.

An example of Quadrant 3, the legal–not ethical quadrant, would be engaging in consensual sexual relations with a current adult client, which could be legal but would not be ethical. Another example could be a counselor openly displaying specific religious information in his or her private practice office while knowingly serving clients of a different religion. A prudent rule of thumb is to stay vigilant about the focus of counseling and one's professional obligation to prizing and enhancing client worth, dignity, uniqueness, and potential. Doing so is the first step to helping counselors stay focused and avoid such possible human temptations in the intensely personal work of career counseling, when clients are sometimes especially vulnerable. Clarity of focus and goals for career counseling, starting with informed consent, can help counselors and clients stay focused on productive counseling relationships.

Falling into Quadrant 4, the not legal–not ethical quadrant, physically harming a client, sexually exploiting a juvenile client, falsely advertising one's credentials or expertise, charging for services not performed, and providing services while one's license is suspended would all seem to be examples of practices that are simultaneously unethical and illegal. Similar to Quadrant 1, Quadrant 4 may be illustrative of less complex issues than those represented in Quadrants 2 and 3; however, it is clear that one can see considerable gray areas and complexity across all four quadrants and, by extension, across much of the work of career development professionals. Again, these examples only serve to highlight the myriad concerns, issues, and difficulties of professional ethical decision making and behavior in all counseling, including career counseling.

Further complicating the matter for career development practice is the existence of many career development practitioner competency bases, credentials, and designations, including paraprofessionals and some practitioners with no counseling credentials or formal preparation who offer services similar to services offered by professional career counselors. We join Pate and Niles (2002) in delimiting the scope of this discussion to professional career counselors, career development professionals, and paraprofessionals, such as career development facilitators, who are working under the supervision of a professional career counselor. As noted in the earlier discussion of career coaching, these areas of concern are ongoing, with profound ethical issues requiring career counselor vigilance and advocacy for ethical practice.

Pate and Niles (2002) offered yet another important gray area in noting that many career counselors and career development professionals provide professional services that may or may not be considered counseling, such as time management, educational advising, career placement, résumé editing, and other services aimed at improving client employability skills. Pate and Niles wondered whether a career counselor at a university counseling center who edits a student's résumé incurs the same level of ethical accountability as would be incurred in career or mental health counseling. Determining whether and which ethical standards pertain to these activities is a matter that merits considerable attention by practitioners and researchers.

## Addressing Ethical and Legal Career Issues

Seen in the light of this array of complex issues, concerns, and activities, there is a strong need for career counselors to be aware of legal and ethical issues and to be familiar with laws and personal and organizational ethical standards and guidelines as bases for ethical decision making and legal and ethical behavior. By extension, counselor educators need to be cognizant of this complexity, knowledge, and skill in helping aspiring career counselors explore, acquire, commit to, and comply with professional ethics. Professional organizations such as NCDA also need to continue working to educate policymakers, the public, members, and others on legal and ethical matters related to all facets of career counseling and career development.

Although these implications may seem self-evident, and although the counseling literature has an abundance of resources attending to ethics, in writing this chapter we found relatively few recent articles, chapters, and other sources dedicated to ethical and legal issues in and implications for career counseling. In the *Career Development Quarterly*'s annual review of 1996 research and practice in career counseling and career development (Niles, 1997), professional ethics was one of the few areas noted as needing attention from career professionals. Whiston and Brecheisen's (2002) review of 2001 career research in the literature noted some attention to ethical issues regarding facets of assessment and electronic- and technology-based career counseling and career development work, but made no mention of attention to other ethical aspects of career development. More recent annual reviews of research in the *Career Development Quarterly* revealed a significant deficit in the attention focused on ethical and legal aspects of career development (Patton & McIlven, 2008; Tien, 2007).

Hansen (2003), Savickas (2003), and Whiston (2003) alerted readers to works advocating for the larger and higher moral plain in addressing sociopolitical issues, such as exposing and removing barriers to individual human and career growth for people who are economically disadvantaged and widening the scope of populations served by career counseling and career development professionals. This charge is critical for career professionals because the racial and ethnic composition of the workforce will change dramatically in the near future. Hispanics and Asians are the fastest growing populations in the workforce, and by 2050 both groups are projected to account for 24% and 8%, respectively, of the total labor force. However, in contrast, the African American labor force population is projected to increase from 11% to only 14%, and the non-Hispanic

Caucasian workforce share is projected to drop to just more than 50% (Lee & Mather, 2008). Women made up 46% of the workforce in 2007, yet the wage disparity between women's and men's earnings still exists. In 2007, female workers earned 77% of Caucasian men's median income, and the gap widened even more when race was factored into the equation. Asian, Caucasian, African American, and Hispanic women earn 82%, 74%, 63%, and 52%, respectively, of Caucasian men's earnings, reflecting to some degree both gender and racial inequality. Overall, women are clearly underrepresented in many higher paying career fields related to engineering, mathematics, science, technology, and upper-level managerial business positions (Lee & Mather, 2008).

These large scale socio-political issues call for greater attention, which will require individual and organizational advocacy; one method of advocacy is via public policy. Career professionals, NCDA, and other professional associations have much to offer in helping to formulate and refine public policy related to all aspects and segments of the workforce. Arguably, the best mode of articulation of and advocacy for individual practitioners to affect policy is membership in professional associations and participation in these associations' public policy initiatives.

Problems and issues of human disempowerment—such as sexual harassment, unethical supervisory behavior, unfair hiring, unfair promotion practices, workplace violence, exploitation, illegal treatment of nonresident workers, multicultural and diversity issues, and misuse of assessment—are among many social, personal, and personnel areas that could benefit from ethical career counselor attention in the form of counselor advocacy for workers at all levels and in the form of career counselor private and public policy initiatives. As noted earlier, with the exception of ethical issues related to assessment and electronic or Web-based counseling, we found relatively few recent works on career-specific ethical issues, such as those presented earlier; hence, it seems appropriate to recommend that career counseling professionals, researchers, and professional organizations refocus and devote conscious attention to ethical and legal issues as a means to clearly articulate public policy needs and priorities.

### SIDEBAR 5.6 Awareness Exercise

For the next few weeks, make a conscious observation about the type of people who work in specific career occupations. Pay close attention to factors such as race, gender, ethnicity, and location of business. For example, if you visit a public school setting, what do you notice about the race and gender of the employees? When visiting a grocery store or a fast food restaurant, what do you observe about the workers? If you visit your physician or dentist, make an observation here as well. How does the location in which you shop affect the diversity of the workers? If you watch television, observe the type of occupations individuals are portrayed as working in. After completing your observations, what did you notice? Did you observe racial or gender trends of individuals working in specific occupations? How did the location affect the diversity of the workforce you observed? How could your observation affect your approach as a career counselor?

## Legal Issues

Typically, one incurs legal liability or accountability under the law as one increases one's expertise and competence. In our increasingly litigious society, all counselors are well advised to carry liability insurance and to become familiar with laws specific to the counselor's primary duties, such as, for example, career counselors serving as expert witnesses regarding worker disability or divorce and spousal support mediation while always remembering the counselor's primary ethical obligation to the client. Although some career counselors also have ethical and legal obligations to employers and third-party payers, responsibilities and obligations to the client must not be diminished or subordinated. These and other legal matters can constitute powerful negative reinforcers, thus prompting counselors to avoid lawsuits. These issues could also serve as positive reinforcers to increase a counselor's desire to behave ethically as a solid defense, should a counselor be sued. Suffice it to say, one must be aware of and have access to someone knowledgeable of all pertinent legislation related to the area in the country or world in which one functions and that is relevant to the services one offers. Legal care and similar legal advice and access resources, available via some professional organizations, can be excellent member services for professional organizations. Moreover, one's ability to note how one's behavior complies with official ethical standards and principles or legal guidance could afford a major basis for a plausible defense in a lawsuit.

## History and Precedents for Looking Forward

Just as Frank Parsons, Jesse Davis, and other career practitioners led the way to founding the National Vocational Guidance Association (now NCDA) in 1913 as the first national counseling association, career practitioners have long addressed and anticipated many issues in counseling and counselor ethics. One poignant example of career counseling's early and long-standing attention to and leadership in major counseling advances and issues is manifest in software-based interactive guidance systems, such as JoAnn Harris Bowlsbey's pioneering work in developing and implementing the Computerized Vocational information System in the early 1970s. This long history of computer-based guidance systems affords a useful context of knowledge and experience to help counselors in other specialties assuage the 1990s' and current perception of urgency regarding unprecedented ethical issues emerging in the face of extensive use of Web-based assessment and counseling and other Internet services.

Because many concerns regarding counseling via the Internet emerged in the 1990s, career counselors familiar with computer-based interactive guidance information systems, such as the Computerized Vocational information System, CHOICES, DISCOVER, SIGI-PLUS, VISIONS, and VISIONS PLUS, among others, could afford other counselors a sense of context and perspective on the basis of those earlier computer software–based career systems. In effect, there were numerous precedents for and much experience in affording clients counselor-originated service via software in an electronic platform more than 20 years in advance of counselor use of the Internet for counseling, affording career counselors a more incremental perspective for

Web-based and other electronic approaches to counseling. Suffice it to say, in our dynamic and sometimes turbulent world, career counseling's vanguard activities make it a most important specialty for clients and for counselors in other specialties, and ethics is a highly important element of and for this and all facets of career counseling.

Among pertinent historical counseling landmarks noted in any outline of the history of career counseling are the initial ideas of Frank Parsons (1909) that, arguably, started contemporary counseling by helping clients understand and find means for some influence and autonomy over their role in the world of work. Theories of career development, choice, and counseling have emerged to support and define this career counseling specialty, as have career counseling competencies, credentialing, and standards for ethics and for career counselor preparation and respect for clients (Engels, 1994; Engels, Minor, Sampson, & Splete,1995; Smith, Engels, & Bonk, 1985). Ironically, many counselor educators seem not to realize or appreciate the parallel centrality of work in the thinking of such mainstream counseling pioneers as Adler, Freud, and Jung, but each of those pioneers noted and attended to work and career because of the primal importance of work in life.

## Moral and Other Philosophical Bases for Ethical Practice

Welfel and Lipsitz (1983), Welfel (2002), and Kitchener (1984a), among others, noted that counselors need to know themselves well and need some knowledge of moral principles to make personal sense of the ethical standards while also addressing conflicts within, among, and between codes of ethics or between ethics and law. Bersoff and Koeppl's (1993) attention to the consensus nature of a profession's ethical standards serves as another reminder that ethical standards represent the least one must do. Moreover, they also noted the importance of career counselors seeking insight into personal, societal, and client ethical and moral principles and values. Central among these principles are veracity, or truthfulness (Meara, Schmidt, & Day 1996); core principles of autonomy, nonmaleficence, beneficence, and justice (Beauchamp & Childress, 1994); and fidelity (Kitchener, 1984b, 1991, 1996), as well as a counselor's personal integrity, good judgment, and wisdom or prudence.

## Conclusion

Until career counselors can find means to the admittedly difficult learning tasks of acquiring fuller insight and empowerment in these and other moral bases for ethical motivation and practice, all counselors might benefit from close attention to the models of those who delve more deeply into those philosophical bases and those offering sound approaches to ethical practice (Neukrug, Lovell, & Parker, 1996; Savickas, 1995). Welfel (2002), for example, afforded counselors an insightful and comprehensive model for and 10-step approach to ethical decision making, moving from ethical dedication and appreciation for underlying moral bases for counseling and ethical behavior to good scrutiny of current standards, pertinent laws, professional research, and advice to consciously deliberate and make a decision, followed by substantial processing regarding the specific focus of this decision, as well as implications for the future. Some more fundamental guidance also comes from standards and these models. Emanating from the NCDA and ACA ethical standards is a clear message that career counselors should network. Having a trusted local colleague or two for confidential consultation on vital ethical issues is fundamental. Through participation in local chapters of state counseling organizations, new career counselors can seek mentors and veteran career counselors can mentor and also establish peer networks. ACA's Web site, ethics committee, and professional staff services also include resources for members seeking ethical advice. NCDA's 2004 introduction of a national mentoring model, including participation of past presidents, eminent career award winners, NCDA fellows, and other career professionals, holds great promise as another excellent networking resource. Attention to models, resources, and approaches such as these might go far in helping career counselors promote client worth, dignity, uniqueness, and potential.

## References

American Counseling Association. (2005). *ACA code of ethics*. Alexandria, VA: Author. Retrieved from http://www.counseling.org/Resources/CodeOfEthics/ TP/Home/CT2.aspx

American Psychological Association. (2002). Ethical principles of psychologists and code of conduct. *American Psychologist, 57*, 1060–1073. Retrieved from http:// www.apa.org/ethics/code/index.aspx

Ancis, J. R., & Marshall, D. S. (2010). Using a multicultural framework to assess supervisees' perceptions of culturally competent supervision. *Journal of Counseling and Development, 88*, 277–284.

Arredondo, P., Toporek, R., Brown, S., Jones, J., Locke, D. C., Sanchez, J., & Stadler, H. (1996). *Operationalization of the multicultural counseling competencies*. Alexandria, VA: Association for Multicultural Counseling and Development.

Beauchamp, T. L., & Childress, J. F. (1994). *Principles of biomedical ethics* (4th ed.). New York, NY: Oxford University Press.

Bersoff, D. N., & Koeppl, P. M. (1993). The relation between ethical codes and moral principles. *Ethics and Behavior, 3*, 345–357.

Bradley, L. J., & Kottler, J. A. (2001). Overview of counselor supervision. In L. J. Bradley & N. Ladany (Eds.), *Counselor supervision: Principles, process, and practice* (3rd ed., pp. 3–27). Philadelphia, PA: Brunner-Routledge.

*Career development facilitator*. (2010). Retrieved from http://associationdatabase.com/ aws/NCDA/pt/sp/facilitator_overview

Chung, B. Y., & Gfroerer, M. C. A. (2003). Career coaching: Practice, training, professional, and ethical issues. *Career Development Quarterly, 52*, 141–152.

*Coaching certifications*. (2010). Retrieved from http://www.certifiedcareercoaches.com/ certifications.php

Corey, G., Corey, M. S., & Callanan, P. (2011). *Issues and ethics in the helping profession* (8th ed.) Belmont, CA: Brooks/Cole.

Council for the Accreditation of Counseling and Related Educational Programs. (2005). *CACREP manual*. Alexandria, VA: Author.

Engels, D. W. (1981). Maximal ethics in counselor education. *Counseling and Values, 26,* 48–54.

Engels, D.W. (Ed.). (1994). *The professional practice of career counseling and consultation: A resource document.* Alexandria, VA: National Career Development Association.

Engels, D. W., Minor, C. W., Sampson, J. P., & Splete, H. H. (1995). Career counseling specialty: History, development, and prospect. *Journal of Counseling and Development, 74,* 134–138.

Engels, D. W., Wilborn, B. L., & Schneider, L. J. (1990). Ethics curricula for counselor preparation programs. In *Ethical standards casebook* (pp. 111–126). Alexandria, VA: American Association for Counseling and Development.

Fitzpatrick, B. (2007). *National cultural values survey.* Alexandria, VA: Division of Media Research Center, Culture and Media Institute.

Freeman, S. J. (2000). *Ethics: An introduction to philosophy and practice.* Belmont, CA: Wadsworth/Thomson Learning.

Freeman, S. J., Engels, D.W., & Altekruse, M. K. (2004). Foundations for ethical standards and codes: The role of moral philosophy and theory in ethics. *Counseling and Values, 48,* 163–173.

Golden parachute. (2010). In *Business glossary.* Retrieved from http://www.allbusiness .com/glossaries/golden-parachute/4946770-1.html

Hamric, A. B., Spross, J. A., & Hanson, C. M. (2000). *Advanced nursing practice: An integrative approach.* Philadelphia, PA: W. B. Saunders.

Hansen, L. S. (2003). Career counselors as advocates and change agents for equality. *Career Development Quarterly, 52,* 43–53.

Hart, G. (1982). *The process of clinical supervision.* Baltimore, MD: University Park Press.

Herlihy, B., & Corey, G. (2006). *ACA ethical standards case book* (6th ed.). Arlington, VA: American Counseling Association.

Jones, J. M. (2010). *Americans' outlook for U.S. morality remains bleak.* Retrieved from http://www.gallup.com/poll/128042/americans-outlook-morality-remains-bleak.aspx

Kitchener, K. S. (1984a). Ethics and counseling psychology: Distinctions and directions. *Counseling Psychologist, 12,* 15–18.

Kitchener, K. S. (1984b). Intuition, critical-evaluation and ethical principles: The foundation for ethical decisions in counseling psychology. *Counseling Psychologist, 12,* 43–55.

Kitchener, K. S. (1991). The foundations of ethical practice. *Journal of Mental Health Counseling, 13,* 236–246.

Kitchener, K. S. (1996). There is more to ethics than principles. *Counseling Psychologist, 24,* 92–97.

Knapp, S., & VandeCreek, L. (2007). When values of different culture conflict: Ethical decision making in a multicultural context. *Professional Psychology: Research and Practice, 38,* 660–666.

Lee, C. C., & Hipolito-Delgado, C. P. (2007). Introduction: Counselors as agents of social justice. In C. C. Lee (Ed.), *Counseling for social justice* (2nd ed., pp. 13–28). Alexandria, VA: American Counseling Association.

Lee, M. A., & Mather, M. (2008). U.S. labor force trends. *Population Bulletin, 63,* 3–20.

Levin, A. V. (2010). Do I have an ethical dilemma? *Oman Journal of Ophthalmology, 3,* 49–50.

Lewis, J., & Coursol, D. (2007). Addressing career issues online: Perceptions of counselor education professionals. *Journal of Employment Counseling, 44,* 146–153.

Makela, J. P. (2009). *A case study approach to ethics in career development: Exploring shades of gray.* Broken Arrow, OK: National Career Development Association.

Mann, J. A., & Kreyche, G. F. (Eds.). (1966). *Reflections on man: Readings in philosophical psychology from classical philosophy to existentialism.* New York, NY: Harcourt Brace & World.

Mappes, D., Robb, G., & Engels, D. (1985). Ethical and legal issues in counseling and psychotherapy. *Journal of Counseling and Development, 64,* 246–252.

Meara, N. M., Schmidt, L. D., & Day, J. D. (1996). Principles and virtues: A foundation for ethical decisions, policies, and character. *Counseling Psychologist, 24,* 4–77.

*Merriam-Webster's Collegiate Dictionary* (6th ed.). (2000). Random House, NY: Random House.

National Association of Social Workers. (2008). *Code of ethics.* Retrieved from http://www.naswdc.org/pubs/code/default.asp

National Board for Certified Counselors, Inc. (1991). *Ethical standards.* Greensboro, NC: Author.

National Career Development Association. (2007). *National Career Development Association ethical standards.* Retrieved from http://associationdatabase.com/aws/NCDA/asset_manager/get_file/3395/code_of_ethicsmay-2007.pdf

Neukrug, E. S. (2011). *Counseling theory and practice.* Belmont, CA: Brooks/Cole Cengage Learning.

Neukrug, E. S., Lovell, C., & Parker, R. J. (1996). Employing ethical codes and decision-making models: A developmental process. *Counseling and Values, 40,* 98–106.

Niles, S. G. (1997). Annual review: Practice and research in career counseling and development—1996. *Career Development Quarterly, 46,* 115–141.

O'Neil, M. E., McWhirter, E. H., & Cerezo, A. (2008). Transgender identities and gender variance in vocational psychology: Recommendations for practice, social advocacy, and research. *Journal of Career Development, 38,* 286–308.

Parsons, F. (1909). *Choosing a vocation.* Boston: Houghton-Mifflin.

Pate, R. H., & Niles, S. G. (2002). Ethical issues in career development interventions. In S. G. Niles & J. Harris-Bowlsbey. *Career development interventions in the 21st century.* Columbus, OH: Prentice Hall.

Patton, W., & McIlveen, P. (2009). Annual review: Practice and research in career counseling and development—2008. *Career Development Quarterly, 58,* 118–161.

Pierce, J. (2010, July 23). *2010 USC Annenberg Digital Future Study finds strong negative reaction to paying for online services.* Retrieved from http://www.digitalcenter.org/pdf/2010_digital_future_final_release.pdf

Remley, T. P., & Herlihy, B. (2007). *Ethical, legal, and professional issues in counseling* (2nd ed.). Upper Saddle River, NJ: Pearson Prentice Hall.

Savickas, M. L. (1995). Constructivist counseling for career indecision. *Career Development Quarterly, 43,* 363–373.

Savickas, M. L. (2003). Advancing the career counseling profession: Objectives and strategies for the next decade. *Career Development Quarterly, 51,* 87–96.

Schultz, D., & Schultz, M. E. (2002). *Psychology and work today* (8th ed.). Upper Saddle River, NJ: Pearson Education.

Smith, R., Engels, D., & Bonk, E. (1985). The past and future of the National Vocational Guidance Association: History at the crossroads. *Journal of Counseling and Development, 63,* 420–424.

Tarasoff v. Regents of the University of California, 13 Cal. 3d 177, 529 P.2d 553 (1974), vacated.

Tarasoff v. Regents of the University of California, 17 Cal. 3d 425, 551 P.2d 334, 131 Cal. Rptr.14 (1976).

Thapar v. Zezulka, 994.S.W.2d 635, 637 (Tex. 1999).

Thompson, M. N., & Cummings, D. L. (2010). Enhancing the career development of individuals who have criminal records. *Career Development Quarterly, 58,* 209–218.

Tien, H. S. (2007). Practice and research in career counseling and development— 2006. *Career Development Quarterly, 56,* 98–140.

Toporek, R. L., Gerstein, L. H., Foud, N. A., Roysicar-Sowdowsky, G., & Israel, T. (Eds.). (2005). *Handbook for social justice in counseling psychology: Leadership, vision, and action.* Thousand Oaks, CA: Sage.

Urofsky, R. I., & Engels, D. W. (2003). Philosophy, moral philosophy, and counseling ethics: Not an abstraction. *Counseling and Values, 47,* 118–130.

U.S. Census Bureau. (2008). *Distribution of U. S. population by race/ethnicity, 2010 and 2050.* Washington, DC: U.S. Government Printing Office.

Van Hoose, W. H., & Kottler, J. (1985). *Ethical and legal issues in counseling and psychotherapy* (2nd ed.). San Francisco, CA: Jossey-Bass.

Venable, M. A. (2010). Using technology to deliver career development services: Supporting today's students in higher education. *Career Development Quarterly, 59,* 87–96.

*Webster's New World College Dictionary* (4th ed.). (1999). New York, NY: Macmillan.

Welfel, E. R. (2002). *Ethics in counseling and psychotherapy: Standards, research, and emerging issues* (2nd ed.). Pacific Grove, CA: Brooks/Cole.

Welfel, E. R., & Lipsitz, N. E. (1983). Wanted: A comprehensive approach to ethics research and education. *Counselor Education and Supervision, 22,* 320–332.

Whiston, S. C. (2003). Career counseling: 90 years old yet still healthy and vital. *Career Development Quarterly, 52, 35–42.*

Whiston, S. C., & Brecheisen, B. K. (2002). Annual review: Practice and research in career counseling and development—2001. *Career Development Quarterly, 51,* 98–145.

Young, L., Lehman, P., McGregor, J., & Polek, D. (2007, November 26). How golden are their parachutes? *BusinessWeek, 1*(4060), p. 34.

PART **2**

# SKILLS AND TECHNIQUES

# CHAPTER 6

# Individual and Group Assessment and Appraisal

Donna S. Sheperis, Michelle Perepiczka, and Clint Limoges

---

## Contents

Career assessment tools are appraisal methods specifically designed to enhance the career decision-making process. Although some instruments serve more general purposes, in this chapter we focus on career counseling applications. Career counselors use assessment methods to identify information salient to clients' career decisions. Additionally, many instruments serve as predictive indicators of potential occupational performance and clients' work-related satisfaction. Assessment tools are to be used as a component of the career counseling process, never to serve as a substitute for counseling.

This chapter was organized to provide counselors with a general understanding of a broad range of career appraisal methods. The psychometric concepts we discuss provide the foundation for understanding career appraisal. Instruments presented in this chapter include those created in direct support of theories of career counseling as well as those developed to measure specific career-related constructs. We provide for each assessment a description of the instrument and its uses as well as information regarding its availability. Although we do not present an exhaustive list of tools, we present some of the more commonly used ones. We hope that career counselors will find these tools suitable to a wide variety of applications.

## Psychometric Concepts

Mental health professionals who use career assessments must have a general working knowledge of concepts such as reliability, validity, and standard error of measurement if they are to use these instruments competently. Each concept provides a layer of protection for test users administering, scoring, and interpreting results from various aptitude, achievement, interest, value, maturity, and personality tests in an appropriate manner while adhering to high ethical and culturally competent practice.

Reliability is a measure of test score consistency. All reliability values represent correlation coefficients that range from 0 to 1. One type is *test–retest reliability*, which is a measure of a test's stability over time (i.e., between the initial administration of a test and administration occurring weeks or months later) as evidenced by a correlation coefficient called the *stability coefficient*. A second type of reliability is called *equivalent forms reliability*. Equivalent forms reliability yields a measure of the relationship between two sets of scores derived from a group of individuals taking similar forms of a test at or about the same time. The result is defined as the coefficient of equivalence. Finally, a third form of reliability termed *internal consistency*, or *item response consistency*, offers a correlation coefficient that indicates the degree of relationship among items measuring the same construct within the instrument. The correlation coefficient resulting from this analysis is dependent on the type of item being used. You may see Cronbach's alpha (Cronbach, 1951) or the Kuder–Richardson formula (Kuder & Richardson, 1937) used as internal consistency coefficients depending on what item format was used in the test.

Another related concept, the standard error of measurement, provides a means for the practical interpretation of reliability. This concept assists clients in understanding that their scores have some inherent variability associated with them and provides an estimate of the range of possible scores if the person was to take an instrument over and over again. Classical test theory assumes that no score is perfect and that some source of measurement error is always associated with the test setting as a result of the test taker and the administrative conditions. For example, a test taker may misinterpret the meaning behind a particular question on a test or find the test location unsatisfactory. This type of test variability causes an examinee's obtained score on a test to be different from his or her true score. As a matter of fact, test theory assumes that a person's true score is normally distributed around one's observed score with the standard error measurement serving as the standard deviation for a person's scoring distribution. Therefore, 68% of the time one's true score falls within one standard error of measurement above and below one's observed score. For example, if Jim receives a 60 on the Career Resiliency Inventory and the manual states the standard error of measurement for the test is 4, then Jim's true score will fall between 56 and 64 approximately 68% of the time. Standard error of measurement is dependent on two factors: the standard deviation of the test scores and the reliability coefficient associated with those scores. The standard error of measurement can range from 0 to the standard deviation of scores for a given test. The size of the standard error of measurement and the reliability associated with it provide some support for the validity of the test.

**SIDEBAR 6.1   Validity Visual**

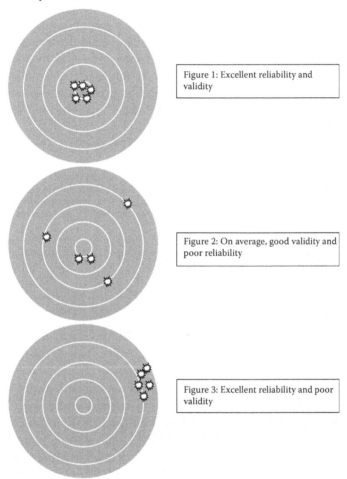

Figure 1: Excellent reliability and validity

Figure 2: On average, good validity and poor reliability

Figure 3: Excellent reliability and poor validity

Validity defines the accuracy and integrity of a test by providing evidence that the test truly measures what it is supposed to measure. Most test manuals recognize three main types of validity: content, criterion, and construct. *Content validity* is evidence obtained from experts in the field of a particular content domain (e.g., career interest) that ensures that the test measures the domain it was intended to assess. Content experts review and verify that all the items on a test adequately and appropriately represent the defined domain to be evaluated.

*Criterion validity* is a second form of validity that takes test scores on a domain to be measured, such as career readiness, and relates them to a practical criterion (e.g., frequency of career exploration activities) either in the present or in the future. For instance, aptitude test scores provide a means to predict future abilities or behaviors perhaps in college or on the job.

A final major type of validity, known as *construct validity*, provides evidence that the personal trait or characteristic measured by a test or scale truly measures the construct it is supposed to measure (factorial validity), correlates highly with other tests purported to measure the same or similar constructs (convergent validity), and correlates minimally with other tests that measure dissimilar constructs (divergent validity). For example, an assessment may be developed to measure mathematical ability. Using the concepts of construct validity, one would assume that this assessment would truly measure mathematical ability as opposed to artistic aptitude, would correlate highly with other assessments of mathematical ability, and would not correlate highly with measures that assess for unrelated skills and abilities.

### SIDEBAR 6.2  Case Study 1: Reliability and Validity Section

You are a career counselor working with Steven, a 30-year-old man looking for a career change after working for a few years after college graduation. He is currently in a human relations position, which he finds very unsatisfying and frustrating. Steven chose this field because he scored high on subscales related to this field on a previous assessment in college. You and the client choose to complete new assessments as part of the counseling process. You choose an aptitude assessment with high reliability and validity. You report that he has a high aptitude for scientific tasks and low aptitude for human services work. Steven is shocked to hear this because he was previously told the opposite, which highly influenced his career choice. You examine his previous records and discover that the prior assessment had low reliability and validity. How would you explain the conflicting results to Steven?

## Norms and Scoring

Test norms are descriptive statistical data derived from a representative group of scores to serve as a comparison for individuals taking the test. Norms provide crucial information for test interpretation purposes. Often, raw scores on a test are transformed into percentiles or standard scores. Both types of transformed scores describe a means of relating where one's score falls in comparison to those of others who took the test. For instance, a person who scores at the 50th percentile scored higher than 50% of the people who took the test in the norming group. Similarly, standard scores are transformed raw scores that usually provide simple integer values for the means and standard deviations calculated from the scores of the norming group for ease of test interpretation. Typical standard scores on career inventories are $z$ scores (fixed $M = 0$, fixed $SD = 1$), $T$ scores (fixed $M = 50$, fixed $SD = 10$), stanines (fixed $M = 5$, fixed $SD = 2$), and sten scores (fixed $M = 5.5$, fixed $SD = 2$). Standard scores are referenced to how many standard deviations a score is above and below the mean, which, if the scores are normally distributed, can be referenced to the standard normal curve.

One area of primary importance for test administrators is cultural competence, which is illustrated by the question, "Does my examinee match the norming group for the test in age, gender, race, socioeconomic status, geographical location, education level, job or career type, and other relevant demographic characteristics?" Norms many times try to use a national sample based on the proportions of the most recent national census data breakdown, which may sound like a good idea but may in fact not be representative of one's local population. For example, one would be cautious in using a U.S. nationally normed career interest inventory with college-bound Chinese students thinking of attending a university in the United States and then returning to China to seek work opportunities. Another example would be using an aptitude inventory based on national norms to predict GPA for a group of 12th-grade high school students in the southern United States at a particular university in their first semester.

It is important to realize that norms do not always represent mainstream groups; rather, they may be representative of former substance abusers, high school dropouts, children with learning disabilities, nontraditional students, and other more atypical groups. Some norms may be typical of student abilities at particular grade levels, such as grade norms for achievement tests, and others are more representative of one's specific age, such as age norms for maturity or developmental types of tests. The development of local norms for specific job placement issues may be more relevant than national or general norms, but most counselors do not have the resources or the time to create these norms. For this reason, counselors must be cautious in extrapolating results from career-related tests especially if norms are inconsistent with a client's background.

## Ethical Considerations

In addition to competence in the arena of psychometric properties for career instruments, counselors need to have awareness of the applicable ethical codes and standards related to assessment, scoring, interpretation, and test development. In its ethics code, the American Psychological Association (2010) offers 11 separate subcategories under the heading of assessment. The American Counseling Association (2005) has a similar section in its ethics code dealing with evaluation, assessment, and interpretation, identifying 13 standards of ethical assessment practice. The National Board of Certified Counselors (2005) has also developed 15 standards in a section of its code titled "Measurement and Evaluation." Specific areas of appropriate test use covered by these three professional codes include informed consent or orientation, obsolete data or testing materials, test security or copyright requirements, classification and diagnosis of examinees, qualifications or training requirements, and standards for appropriate test selection.

One additional set of standards provided by the Joint Committee on Testing Practice emphasized test development to a greater degree than the codes already mentioned in this section. The *Code of Fair Testing Practices in Education* (2004) recognizes ethical competencies for developers and users of educational tests in the areas of development and selection, interpretation, fairness, and informed practice.

### SIDEBAR 6.3 Self-Awareness 1: Ethical Considerations

Imagine you are a counselor intern at a career counseling agency. Your supervisor has a new client for you who wants to take a career battery. You are not trained in administering or scoring this assessment. However, you remember a lot of information from your career counseling course. Your supervisor tells you he believes in you but cannot provide additional supervision or training before the interview because of the fast pace of the office. You are unsure of your ethical responsibility as an intern. You want to gain the experience, but you do not want to harm the client. You desire additional supervision but do not want to cross your supervisor. What would you consider in this situation? What would you choose to do? How comfortable would you feel handling this situation?

## Use of Assessments in Career Counseling

Career assessments are used by counselors functioning in a variety of settings. To use such assessments, counselors must have both competency and privilege. Competency simply means that the counselor has the aptitude, training, and ability to conduct the assessment at hand. Competency is typically based on training and education. A second issue of concern related to assessment is privilege. Although a test developer and publisher may determine that a counselor is competent to administer a certain assessment, state law may say otherwise. Other helping professions have successfully lobbied to prevent counselors from conducting assessments in many states. The Fair Access Coalition on Testing is a multidisciplinary board dedicated to providing access to assessments on the basis of competency, not legislation.

Keeping this in mind, a counselor pursuing a master's degree in counseling will likely be able to administer the assessments discussed in this chapter. Therefore, it is important to consider when and how such practices should occur as well as how the results should be presented to the client. Often, one's career is viewed as a means to personal satisfaction and growth in addition to the fulfillment of material needs (Drummond & Ryan, 1995). As such, informal career assessments will take place in virtually every counseling relationship because life concerns may be exacerbated or directly influenced by career-related issues.

To solicit pertinent information, a thorough intake assessment should include questions about work and work history. Responses to these items may lead the counselor to further investigate a client's employment status, either informally via interview or formally through the use of career inventories. Even if the counselor is not performing career counseling services per se, career assessments may prove beneficial to the therapeutic growth of the client. As in any counseling relationship, the practitioner must take care to focus on the whole person, including his or her career and lifestyle needs.

It is both necessary and ethical to involve the client in the assessment process. Clients may not have an understanding of the rationale for assessment and will rely on the counselor to provide the information needed for them to feel secure about the process. Although the counselor may be comfortable with the intent and purpose of the assessment, the counselor is responsible for helping the client feel comfortable. During the intake or when preparing the client for assessment, the counselor will explain the purpose and nature of the assessments, the amount of time the assessments will take, how the assessments will be scored, and what will happen with the interpretive data. This way, the client can ask questions and join the counselor in the assessment process.

A counselor's particular work setting will probably dictate the degree to which career assessments are used in the counseling process. High school counselors will most certainly use a battery of instruments to assess academic achievement and occupational interest at some point in a student's academic life. Counselors involved in human resource programs may find that much of their work involves career counseling and the assessments that accompany that effort. Finally, counselors in private practice or other settings may find that career assessment is a necessary part of their work.

In addition to competency in the administration and scoring of recommended instruments, the ethical provision of career assessment services includes reviewing the assessment needs and outcomes with the client. The client must have an understanding of what the instrument is intended to assess and what it will and will not provide in terms of outcome information. An orientation session offered by the test administrator discussing the purpose and rationale for each instrument is suggested for all clients involved. Additionally, the counselor must provide informed consent regarding confidentiality and the storage of assessment records. Finally, the counselor must explain the client's rights and responsibilities in a testing situation (*Code of Fair Testing Practices in Education*, 2004).

On completion of the assessment or assessments, the counselor will likely conduct an interpretation session with the client. During this session, the counselor will thoroughly review test score ranges, including the standard error of measurement, before sharing the results. When presenting results, it is important for the counselor to communicate them in a way the client will understand, without using too much technical language. The counselor should check in with the client frequently to determine how the information is being received. The counselor will help the client extract his or her individualized meaning from the instrument and frame it in the context of the client's experience. Client questions should be solicited and a thorough summary of the results provided. Finally, the counselor and client will want to work together to develop career goals based on the information gleaned from the assessment process.

### SIDEBAR 6.4   Tips for Communicating Assessment Results to Clients

When you are explaining and discussing the interpretation of the assessments with a client, remember these tips:

- Best practice is to communicate the results of assessments in a timely manner. Try to have assessments scored and interpreted within a reasonable time frame.
- Counselors should disclose information from an assessment to the client. Results should only be communicated to other individuals or groups when an appropriate release of information is provided by the client. In terms of minors, those with disabilities, or other clients who may have difficulty understanding the results, the assessment results should be communicated to

caregivers who have appropriate rights to the information (American Counseling Association, 2005).

- Consider addressing the client's anxiety level at the start of the session to help the client feel comfortable. A client may be apprehensive when waiting to hear results on aptitude or achievement assessments.
- At the start of the discussion, remind the client of the construct that was measured and explain the meaning. Review the purposes and scope of each assessment completed. Review the limitations, potential risks, and benefits of incorporating assessments into therapeutic work.
- Communicate your findings using language that the client understands. Talk at the client's level without talking over or under the client's head. When possible, try to avoid use of unneeded technical terms. If you use technical terms, then be sure to explain them (e.g., percentages and percentiles can be confusing).
- Consider the client's readiness to hear particular results. Be sure to appropriately prepare the client as best as possible.
- If you choose to discuss the statistics of the results, then be sure to personalize the results and provide examples of the meaning of the numbers.
- Give guidance and support to your client during the discussion. Check on the client's level of understanding periodically as well as his or her emotional reaction to the findings.
- When talking about the results, keep in mind that the test is not the person. Talk with the client about the results instead of talking at the client.
- Work collaboratively with the client to increase his or her participation in the session. Communicate results in a way that the client feels he or she knows him or herself and is not being told about him- or herself. Explore what results seem to fit well with the client's understanding of him- or herself as well as what seems to not be the best fit.
- Be sure to address how the results may not be appropriate in various cultural contexts.
- Communicate results from a strength-based perspective while being realistic about the client's aptitudes, interests, and motivation.
- Inquire about the client's interpretations of what the assessments mean to him or her in the career process.
- A second session to discuss the client's reactions to and insights into the information would be ideal (Hood, 2001).
- Provide the client with the Layperson's Guide to Counselor Ethics (American Counseling Association Ethics Committee, 2009).

## Assessments Developed to Support Theories

A number of dominant theories have emerged in the field of career counseling. Many of them have previously been discussed in this text. In the course of theory development, assessment tools were developed to aid in the application of such theories to the career counseling process. The instruments in this section were developed specifically in support of a particular career theory.

### Holland's Theory

John Holland (1997) developed a typological approach to career choice, identifying personality characteristics of individuals and of various environments. He believed that both these traits and settings could be classified into six categories: realistic, investigative, artistic, social, enterprising, and conventional (RIASEC). Vocational and avocational settings were basically defined by the codings of those people of whom they consisted. Holland (1994c, 1997) used a pictorial graphic of a hexagon to serve as a visual aid to emphasize the interrelationships between the letters assigned to each of the points on it in a circular-type arrangement. For example, adjacent points on the hexagon, such as R and C, indicate more compatibility in personality traits and work duties than, say, R and S, which tend to be more diametrical opposites on the hexagon. These more adjacent categories were considered to have more consistency and overlap in their characteristics than those that were not.

Holland (1997) also felt that individuals would actively seek out environments that matched their personality styles. For instance, individuals who are considered to be S, or social, personality types tend to display an interest in helping others. These individuals typically search for social environments in which their talents and abilities seem to have the best fit and thus provide the most personal satisfaction. Holland (1997) looked at three-letter preference codes for each personality and environment to evaluate the degree of match between them, which he defined as their congruence. The goal of career counseling in this approach is to increase self- and career knowledge to promote effective career decision making, leading to the best possible match between the person and his or her environment.

Counselors using the Holland approach often use various inventories to assess individual and job characteristics for goodness-of-fit purposes to promote personal satisfaction and success. Next, we describe some common inventories developed by Holland and others to assess personality characteristics and their relationship to career choice.

### Self-Directed Search

The Self-Directed Search (SDS) was initially developed to deal with vocational problems, but it also provides a way for students and adults to have a career counseling experience when they do not have access to a counselor or through personal choice (Holland, Powell, & Fritzsche, 1997). A self-administered and self-scored instrument, the SDS consists of two booklets, an assessment booklet and the Occupation Finder, used to determine one's summary code and to identify possible career options. For instance, in an SDS, a typical assessment booklet evaluates a person's activities, competencies, occupations, and self-estimates in 228 items (Holland, 1994a). Aside from these sections, this booklet also provides a means for individuals to write down their future career aspirations (Occupational Daydreams section) before completing the assessment for comparison purposes. The associated Occupation Finder booklet has 1,309 occupations listed by three-letter summary codes (Holland, 1994a). See the case study provided in Table 6.1.

Other instruments related to Holland's theory include the Vocational Preferences Inventory, Career Attitudes and Strategies Inventory, and the Strong Interest Inventory (SII). Each was either authored by John Holland himself or supports his RIASEC framework.

### Vocational Preferences Inventory

A forerunner to the SDS, the Vocational Preferences Inventory was used to help develop Holland's theory and the typology underlying his career choice classification system (Holland, Fritzsche, & Powell, 1997). The inventory assesses

## TABLE 6.1  Case Study

John, a white 17-year-old high school junior, is considering options for college. He has been interested in meteorology since middle school. He purchased some weather instruments with his weekly allowance at that time so he could chart weather data and even provides weather information from time to time to a television station in a nearby major city. Besides tracking the weather, John's hobbies include computers, running, and reading self-help psychology books. John has been using a Web authoring software program his father purchased for him last year to create Web pages for himself and a few of his friends. He appears to have a knack for this. In addition, running has always been an outlet he's enjoyed, especially since joining the cross-country team at his high school. John also enjoys reading self-help psychology books when time permits because he says it make him feel better when he reads them.

John has received As in math and science but Bs in English and history. Last marking period, he received a C in English literature because he was just plain bored with the class.

John also values helping others by volunteering in a local soup kitchen once a month with his family in an outreach program provided by his church. His parents have encouraged him to get more involved with a local peer group in the social service area. John's father has carved out a career in copper tubing sales for a regional distributor, and his mom has worked in the nursing field since his preschool years. Both his parents have attended college to obtain associate's degrees in their respective fields. John has an older brother, Sam, age 19, who has already gone off to college at an aeronautical university, desiring a career as an airline pilot. His younger brother Pete, age 15, is opting to not go to college because he wants to pursue a military career as a mechanic.

John's grandparents were immigrants from Austria who were factory workers and coal miners with no formal education past the sixth grade. They have lived their entire lives in a coal mining town in the northeastern part of the United States.

John has been troubled lately by his inability to commit to a career path because his senior year is just 4 months away. So he decides to make an appointment with his school guidance counselor, Mrs. Catwick. During the meeting, Mrs. Catwick discusses John's concerns with him and then encourages him to take SDS Form R (Holland, 1994b), stating, "This may help you to consider what occupations may be of interest to you and how strongly you feel about each of them." John sits down and fills the inventory out under her guidance.

John first lists his Occupational Daydreams (Holland, 1994b), or the occupations he has most thought about for the future, and then uses the SDS Occupation Finder (Holland, 1994a) to identify the most relevant three-letter RIASEC codes for each one:

| Occupation | Code |
|---|---|
| Meteorologist | IRS |
| Counselor | SIA |
| Computer Programmer | IRC |

At the request of Mrs. Catwick, John also looks up the occupation codes for his parents so he can understand the influence each has had on his career decision-making process. Mrs. Catwick discusses this with him.

| Occupation | Code |
|---|---|
| Father: Sales representative | ESR |
| Mother: Licensed practical nurse | SAC |

John goes on to complete the SDS Assessment Booklet, identifying the activities that he likes or dislikes and feels competent in or not, and recognizing the interest or disinterest he has in various occupations. He then rates his abilities and skills in 14 different areas, such as mechanical, teaching, managerial, sales, and clerical. His results pertaining to the six Holland types (realistic, investigative, artistic, social, enterprising, and conventional) are as follows:

**TABLE 6.1 Continued**

|  | R | I | A | S | E | C |
|---|---|---|---|---|---|---|
| Activities | 2 | 8 | 2 | 6 | 1 | 1 |
| Competencies | 5 | 7 | 3 | 4 | 1 | 4 |
| Occupations | 3 | 6 | 7 | 4 | 1 | 2 |
| Self-Estimates 1 | 4 | 5 | 2 | 4 | 2 | 2 |
| Self-Estimates 2 | 3 | 5 | 2 | 5 | 1 | 2 |
| Total Scores | 17 | 31 | 16 | 23 | 6 | 11 |
| Summary Code | ISR |  |  |  |  |  |

Mrs. Catwick has John now look up in the Occupational Finder (Holland, 1994a) the jobs listed under his summary code, ISR, as well as any jobs that pique his interest under all of the three-letter permutations of this code type: IRS, SIR, SRI, RIS, and RSI. She explains to John that investigative (I) types like himself find investigative jobs most satisfying, which include scientific occupations and some technical ones. Social (S) types enjoy social jobs and prefer education-oriented or social service positions. This second type was somewhat less important to John than the investigative type. Finally, realistic (R) types like realistic jobs and prefer skilled trades, service occupations, or technical positions. The R type was the one of the three types (ISR) that least resembled his personality characteristics but provided a better fit than any of the artistic, enterprising, and conventional occupations (Holland, 1994c). John developed the following list of jobs that he would like to investigate further.

| Code | Occupation | DOT Code | ED |
|---|---|---|---|
| ISR | Exercise physiologist | 076.121-018 | 5 |
| IRS | Meteorologist | 025.062-010 | 5 |
| IRS | Internet–intranet administrator |  | 4 |
| RIS | Forester | 040.167-010 | 5 |
| RSI | Data communications or telecommunications analyst | 031.262-010 | 5 |

*Note:* DOT = *Dictionary of Occupational Titles;* ED = education level required.

Mrs. Catwick also helps John to recognize that the three occupations on his Occupational Daydreams list (Holland, 1994b) are pretty consistent with his results on the SDS because of his strong to moderate interest in investigative (I) and social (S) activities. She provides additional information on his list of preferred occupations, indicating that an educational level code of 5 means that a college education or an advanced degree is needed for those particular occupations. She also encourages him to go online at http://www.onetonline.org to read up on the job descriptions also found in the *Dictionary of Occupational Titles* (U.S. Department of Labor, 1991) for each of his identified occupations. Finally, she hands John a copy of *You and Your Career* (Holland, 1994c) to reinforce the material discussed in the counseling session and schedules a follow-up appointment with him.

**Questions for Discussion**

1. What other experiences or sources of information would you consider for John when discussing John's career options?
2. How would you process John's family vocational history with him? What kind of relevance does it have for him at this point?

*(continued)*

**TABLE 6.1 Continued**

3. What kind of strategy would you have to work on with John in the follow-up session?
4. The SDS is one part of the career counseling process for John. Describe in a step-by-step manner your own career counseling approach to working with John.
5. Pick an ethical code that can be accessed online—that of the American Psychological Association (http://www.apa.org/ethics/code2002.html), American Counseling Association (http://www.cacd.org/codeofethics.html), or National Board for Certified Counselors (http://www.nbcc.org/Assets/Ethics/nbcc-codeofethics.pdf). What particular standards are most important for Mrs. Catwick to consider when administering, scoring, and interpreting the SDS with John?

personality and interest on 11 scales including Realistic, Investigative, Social, Conventional, Enterprising, Artistic, Self-Control, Masculinity–Femininity, Status, Infrequency, and Acquiescence (Holland, 1985).

### Career Attitudes and Strategies Inventory

The Career Attitudes and Strategies Inventory is a 130-item inventory targeting employed and unemployed adults. It was developed to evaluate some general obstacles, attitudes, feelings, and experiences that might influence a person's career selection. Scores are charted on a profile sheet in nine areas of career adaptation: job satisfaction, work involvement, skill development, dominant style, career worries, interpersonal abuse, family commitment, risk-taking style, and geographical barriers (Holland & Gottfredson, 1994). A supplemental checklist of 21 career obstacles (e.g., health and emotional difficulties) that many people worry about is also provided as part of the test package.

*Authors:* John L. Holland, Amy B. Powell, Barbara A. Fritzsche (SDS); John
        L. Holland (Vocational Preferences Inventory, Career Attitudes
        and Strategies Inventory); Gary Gottfredson (Career Attitudes
        and Strategies Inventory)
*Availability:* SDS, Vocational Preferences Inventory, and Career Attitudes
        and Strategies Inventory
        Psychological Assessment Resources, Inc.
        16204 N. Florida Ave.
        Lutz, FL 33549
        (800) 899-8378
        http://www.parinc.com

### Strong Interest Inventory

The SII is a 317-item inventory evaluating an individual's interest in various occupations, school subjects, activities, types of people, and other preferences (Donnay, Thompson, Morris, & Shaubhut, 2004). Results yield information about a person's preferences in six general occupational themes based on Holland's RIASEC classification and 25 subthemes (e.g., artistic–culinary arts, investigative–science) on the Basic Interest Scales. Additional scales include the 211 occupational scales and four new personal style scales.

*Authors:* E. K. Strong, David P. Campbell, and Jo-Ida C. Hansen
*Availability:* SII

        Consulting Psychologists Press Inc.
        1055 Joaquin Rd., 2nd floor
        Mountain View, CA 94043
        (800) 624-1765
        http://cpp.com

## Super's Life Span Theory

Super's life span theory (Super & Osborne, 1992) is a developmental approach to career counseling. Maintaining that individuals go through various career stages established by internal and external forces rather than tied to chronological age, Super's theory offers clients the opportunity to identify and organize those factors that influence them. Assessment tools are important to this endeavor. Super and his colleagues developed many of the instruments associated with this theory. Super believed that interests and preferences are "to be viewed in the light of career maturity, the salience of life roles, and the values sought in life as moderator variables" (Super & Osborne, 1992, p. 74). Measures associated with this theory include appraisals of interest, values, and roles.

### Interest

Super recommended beginning an assessment battery with the SII (described in the previous section). This measure provides information related to the client's interest in multiple occupational themes. As such, it is an elemental measure of clients' interests that functions well within Super's theory.

### Values

Two instruments are available through this theory to measure values. The Work Values Inventory and the Values Scale were developed to measure both intrinsic and extrinsic values related to motivation. Clients are affected by both their internal needs and the external means by which they satisfy those needs. For the client seeking a first job or considering changing jobs, exploration of these values can be a meaningful starting point for counseling.

### Work Values Inventory

The 72-item Work Values Inventory also measures both extrinsic and intrinsic values associated with work environment and satisfaction (Zytowski, 2006). Intended for students in Grades 7 through adulthood, the Work Values Inventory measures 12 work values such as achievement, creativity, income, challenge, and prestige. Each scale contains three items to be considered on a 5-point Likert scale ranging from *unimportant* (1) to *very important* (5; Zytowski, 2006). Easily administered and hand scored, this measure is a useful complement to other career considerations.

*Author:* Donald Super
*Availability:* Kuder Assessments

302 Visions Pkwy.
Adel, IA 50003
(800) 314-8972
http://www.kuder.com/solutions/kuder-assessments.html

## Values Scale

The Values Scale measures 21 values intended to help clients discern the importance of work within other life roles. Focusing on both intrinsic and extrinsic values, the Values Scale measures ability utilization, advancement, authority, creativity, lifestyle, personal development, physical activity, risk, social interaction, social relations, working conditions, cultural identity, physical prowess, and economic security (Drummond, 2000). Developed for clients from high school age through adulthood, the provided normative data can facilitate discussion of client values and career options. Used in this manner, the Values Scale is an effective tool to narrow the field of desirable positions (Schoenrade, 2002).

*Authors:* Donald E. Super and Dorothy D. Nevil
*Availability:* Psychometrics Canada Ltf.
7125 77th Ave.
Edmonton AB T6B 0B5, Canada
(800) 661-5158
http://www.psychometrics.com

## Theory of Work Adjustment

The theory of work adjustment, an outgrowth of landmark research at the University of Minnesota, is concerned with the relationship between the individual and the work environment (Dawis, 1980). The individual brings a set of needs to the employment setting that are greater than the need for an income. According to this theory, clients come to understand the many and varied reasons they choose work, including such desires as status, sense of accomplishment, and a reputable employer. In turn, the employment setting has requirements of the individual that must be met. In the theory of work adjustment, the client's skills and needs interact with the workplace requirements and methods of reinforcement. The client's satisfaction with the work and the satisfactoriness of the client to the organization ultimately leads to the client's length of employment or tenure (Dawis, 1980). For example, a client with high satisfaction for the work who is not able to meet the needs of the workplace, or who is not satisfactory to the organization, will have a briefer tenure than an employee who is a better match to the workplace. Within the structure of the theory of work adjustment, a number of assessment tools have emerged.

### Needs–Values

The Minnesota Importance Questionnaire was designed to measure the client's work needs and values to determine worker satisfaction in adults ages 16 and older. Additionally, the individual's preferred methods of reinforcement emerge with this instrument. Two forms are available, including a paired form, which allows the client to select one of two options, or a ranked form, which presents items on the basis of need and asks the client to rank order groups of items (Benson, 1988). Machine scored and suitable for group administration, this instrument surveys 20 needs: ability utilization, achievement, activity, advancement, authority, company policies and practices, compensation, coworkers, creativity, independence, moral values, recognition, responsibility, security, social service, social status, supervision–human relations, supervision–technical, variety, and working conditions. Six values are appraised: achievement, altruism, autonomy, comfort, safety, and status. From this, a prediction of satisfaction with particular occupations can be made (Layton, 1992).

### Job Satisfaction

The Minnesota Satisfaction Questionnaire is a measure of client satisfaction with an occupation. Similar to the Minnesota Importance Questionnaire, the Minnesota Satisfaction Questionnaire measures adults' satisfaction in their current employment setting on the same 20 needs subscales listed earlier (Thompson & Blain, 1992).

### Other

The Minnesota Job Description Questionnaire (n.d.) was developed to assess how well a particular work setting meets the 20 needs found on the Minnesota Importance Questionnaire and the Minnesota Satisfaction Questionnaire (Sharf, 2009). Additionally, the Minnesota Occupational Classification System delineates more than 1,700 occupations in terms of occupational ability patterns and occupational reinforcer patterns to facilitate client and counselor exploration of a suitable career path based on client preferences (Sharf, 2009).

*Availability:* Minnesota Importance Questionnaire, Minnesota Satisfaction
        Questionnaire, and Minnesota Job Description Questionnaire
        Vocational Psychology Research
        University of Minnesota—Twin Cities
        N620 Elliot Hall
        75 East River Rd.
        Minneapolis, MN 55455-0344
        (612) 625-1367
        http://www.psych.umn.edu/psylabs/vpr/default.htm

### Abilities

No aptitude scales were developed in support of this theory, but the General Aptitude Test Battery, a widely used measure of abilities discussed later in this chapter, is often used to provide information about the client's aptitude for a particular work setting (Sharf, 2009).

## Krumboltz

Krumboltz's learning theory of career counseling (Krumboltz, Mitchell, & Gelatt, 1976) is a practical theory that focuses on clients and the experiences that have shaped their career beliefs and choices. Initially developed by Krumboltz et al. in 1976, the learning theory of career counseling is built on factors influencing clients seeking career counseling. These factors include personal characteristics and environmental events outside of clients' control and learning opportunities and skills acquired throughout their lives (Mitchell, Levin, & Krumboltz, 1999). The learning theory of career counseling holds that assumptions made by clients about these factors influence career choice (Krumboltz, 1994). Counselors working within this theory help clients to identify assumptions or beliefs and facilitate an understanding of their influence on career preference and choices.

Career choice in the learning theory of career counseling is considered a continuous process influenced by ongoing learning experiences. As such, assessment is considered to be another learning experience. The theory suggests the use of aptitude tests to determine task approach skills and interest inventories to serve as starting points for dialogue about career preference. The learning theory of career counseling considers the role of the counselor to be that of an educator, or catalyst for awareness, rather than a "matchmaker" (Mitchell et al., 1999).

The primary assessment tool in the learning theory of career counseling is the Career Beliefs Inventory (CBI).

### Career Beliefs Inventory

The CBI was developed by Krumboltz (1994) to help clients become aware of attitudes or beliefs that may be interfering with their attainment of career goals. It is best used at the beginning of the counseling process and has proved particularly useful for the high school and college populations as well as with clients considering a midlife career change (Krumboltz, 1994). The 96-item instrument assesses client beliefs on five subscales: My Current Career Situation, What Seems Necessary for My Happiness, Factors That Influence My Decisions, Changes I Am Willing to Make, and Effort I Am Willing to Initiate.

Rather than defining particular occupations suited to the client, the CBI outcomes integrate career and personal counseling topics that will help define optimal career paths. The focus is on investigating assumptions or beliefs that may interfere with client career choices rather than merely pairing client interests with job codes. The test manual states, "What appears to be inappropriate or self-defeating behavior may become understandable when one discovers the assumptions and beliefs on which each person operates" (Krumboltz, 1991, p. 1). Success is defined in the CBI as helping clients to develop the self-awareness needed to create satisfying career paths for themselves. In this theoretical model, such success includes ongoing learning and increased satisfaction in both clients' work and personal lives (Krumboltz, 1998).

The contention is that the CBI transcends traditional career assessment because of the multidimensional focus of engaging the client about the why along with the what of career choice (Krumboltz, 1994). Given that it measures different constructs than other instruments available to career counselors, the CBI may be most useful as a complement to other traditional interest and ability assessments (Walsh, 1995).

*Availability:* CBI
Consulting Psychologists Press Inc.
3803 E. Bayshore Rd.
P.O. Box 10096
Palo Alto, CA 94303
(800) 624-1765
http://cpp-db.com

**SIDEBAR 6.5  Self-Awareness 2: Krumboltz**

You are working as a career counselor in a community college. You had four sessions with Alex, who is 21 years old, unemployed with no work history, and Caucasian and from an affluent family. You follow Krumboltz's learning theory of career counseling in session and completed the CBI with the client. You discover that the client has unrealistic beliefs about careers. He wants to put forth little effort and make few to no changes, is motivated to maximize free time as well as income, and views most jobs as undesirable. His resistance is very frustrating for you. How would you engage in self-care inside and out of the session to be proactive with managing your countertransference?

## Cognitive Information Processing Theory

The cognitive information processing theory model was developed to help adolescents and adults achieve an optimal level of career problem-solving and decision-making skills in support of their career choices (Peterson, Sampson, Peterson, Reardon, & Lenz, 2003). Career choice is viewed as a problem-solving activity through new learning in the areas of self-knowledge, occupational knowledge, information processing abilities (decision-making skills), and metacognitive awareness. Learning is also emphasized in a seven-step counseling sequence: initial interview, preliminary assessment, problem definition and analysis, goal formulation, individual learning plan creation, execution of the learning plan, and a review–generalization phase of treatment (Sampson, Reardon, Peterson, & Lenz, 2003). In this model, career-related problems are viewed as gaps between an existing situational state and an ideal one. For example, one common type of gap may be a client's struggle between knowing he or she has to make a job choice and then feeling he or she has in fact made an appropriate one; however, a preliminary assessment of client readiness is necessary before problem-related activities begin in the cognitive information processing approach. An additional element of cognitive information processing is to reserve expensive staff resources for those with more complex needs and allow clients with high levels of readiness to engage in self-help services (Sampson, Peterson, Reardon, & Lentz, 2003).

One of the instruments specifically developed to address readiness is the Career Thoughts Inventory.

### Career Thoughts Inventory

The Career Thoughts Inventory is an instrument devised within the cognitive information processing framework, measuring client mental readiness or dysfunction in the areas of decision-making confusion, commitment and anxiety, and external conflict (Sampson, Peterson, Lenz, Reardon & Saunders, 1996a). The 48-item inventory targets high school and college students as well as general adult populations to explore their ability to cognitively focus on the career decision-making process, understand how their anxiety contributes to career indecisiveness, and assess their ability to differentiate between their own perceptions of career options and the influences of significant others. A workbook serves as an adjunct to the test and provides exercises to assist individuals in identifying and working through dysfunctional thought patterns that get in the way of career choice (Sampson, Peterson, Lenz, Reardon, & Saunders, 1996b). The instrument is meant to be self-administered and self-scored, but professional assistance is recommended to double check the scoring and to aid the client in interpretation (Fontaine, 1999).

*Authors:* James Sampson, Gary Peterson, Janet Lenz, Robert Reardon, and Denise Saunders
*Availability:* Career Thoughts Inventory
        Psychological Assessment Resources, Inc.
        P.O. Box 998
        Odessa, FL 33556
        (800) 899-8378
        http://www.parinc.com

One other instrument not specifically linked to the cognitive information processing model but used to help assess career decision-making status is the My Vocational Situation inventory.

### My Vocational Situation

The My Vocational Situation was developed for people Grade 9 through adult to assess three potential problem areas in career decision making: vocational identity, personal or environmental barriers, and the need for information or training. The instrument is self-administered and self-scored (Kapes & Mastie, 2002).

*Authors:* John Holland, Denise Daiger, and Paul Power
*Availability:* My Vocational Situation
        Consulting Psychologists Press Inc.
        1055 Joaquin Rd., 2nd floor
        Mountain View, CA 94043
        (800) 624-1765
        http://cpp.com

## Roe's Theory

Anne Roe (1956) developed a psychoanalytic theory of career development and career choice based on human needs related to early childhood experiences. A person's attachment history with his or her parents were thought to shape his or her personal and relational preferences (e.g., attitudes, interests, abilities, desire for closeness) in adulthood, especially in influencing one's vocational choice. An important theme of Roe's work was the assumption that as a result of his or her upbringing, a person develops a relational life pattern either toward other people or away from them. Occupations were then grouped according to these criteria as either person oriented or non-person oriented (Roe, 1956). The former highlighted occupational classifications such as service, business contact, organization, general culture, and arts and entertainment. Non–person-oriented categories included positions in science, technology, and the outdoors (e.g., farming, forestry). Roe created a two-dimensional career classification system based on a person's affinity to connect with others (fields) and his or her motivation to achieve status in a particular occupational setting (levels). The levels dimension evidenced more of a person's internal drive or motivation to find satisfaction with life at higher levels of self-actualization, similar to the process identified by Maslow's hierarchy of needs. Roe (1957) considered six occupational levels ranging from unskilled through professional and managerial positions.

Roe's classification scheme has led to the development of a number of career assessment instruments based on her ideas. Two of them are the Vocational Interest Inventory and the Career Occupational Preference System—Professional Level Interest Inventory.

### Vocational Interest Inventory

The Vocational Interest Inventory measures a person's interest intensity in the eight occupational fields already mentioned (e.g., service, business contact, organization) for Roe's (1956) classification system. Consisting of two 56-item sections, the Vocational Interest Inventory is used to evaluate the occupational and activity preferences of later high school students to assist them in choosing a college major. Although the inventory was intended to be self-administered and self-interpreted, computer-generated reports appear to offer extensive information, identifying job listings related to the highest scores on the test, education levels needed to obtain them, and a ranking of 25 college majors related to the taker's mean profile (Herman, 1998; Law, 1998).

*Author:* Patricia Lunneborg
*Availability:* Vocational Interest Inventory
Western Psychological Services
625 Alaska Avenue
Torrance, CA 90503-5124
(800) 648-8857
http://www.wpspublish.com

### Career Occupation Preference System—Professional Level Interest Inventory

The Career Occupational Preference System—Professional Level Interest Inventory was developed to measure career interest for those seeking professional career status (Albanese, 2001). College-bound high school students, college students, and adult professionals benefit from a set of inventories and resource materials that help them not only to identify career options related to their personal preferences but also to review a wealth of in-depth information about a number of career alternatives.

*Authors:* Lisa Knapp-Lee, Lila Knapp, and Robert Knapp
*Availability:* Educational and Industrial Testing Service
　　　　　P.O. Box 7234
　　　　　San Diego, CA 92167
　　　　　(800) 416-1666
　　　　　http://www.edits.net/index2.htm

## Assessments by Type

Not all career appraisal methods have been created to support theories of career counseling. The majority of instruments available to counselors were developed to measure specific constructs salient to the career decision-making process. The instruments in this section are presented by type, or the construct they were designed to measure.

## Assessments of Aptitude, Ability, or Achievement

An *aptitude* is defined as an ability, tendency, or capacity that is inherited or is the result of environment and life experiences (Zunker & Osborn, 2005). Whether such traits are natural or acquired, a measure of aptitude has some ability to predict how well clients will do in a particular activity (Worthen, White, Fan, & Sudweeks, 1999). Aptitude tests are more sophisticated than intelligence tests in that they measure more specialized constructs and a broader array of experiences relevant to traditional achievement tests (Harrington & Schafer, 1996). Measures of aptitude and ability are cornerstones of career counseling assessment practices; high school students frequently take one or more of these instruments before graduation to assist them in determining their vocational direction. Often, the appraisals are group administered and computer scored to aid the school counselor in mass administration and interpretation. Additionally, measures of skills and abilities serve clients beyond the high school population who are interested in determining suitability for a given occupation. As such, career counselors may consider using these appraisals as a supplement to other inventories.

In a survey conducted by Kapes and Mastie (2002) of professionals using aptitude measures, the most commonly used instruments were the Differential Aptitude Test, the General Aptitude Test Battery, and the Armed Services Vocational Aptitude Battery. Those and other commonly used aptitude tests are discussed in this section.

### Differential Aptitude Test

The Differential Aptitude Test is actually a battery of aptitude tests providing scores for the subtests of Verbal Reasoning, Numerical Ability, Abstract Reasoning, Clerical Speed and Accuracy, Mechanical Reasoning, Space Relations, Spelling, and Language Usage. It is designed for group administration and use with students in Grades 8 to 12 or other young adult populations. The combined Verbal Reasoning and Numerical Ability score serves as the best indicator of academic and vocational interest and provides the basis for advising (Pennock-Román, 1988). Counselors will want to work with clients using the available Differential Aptitude Test Individual Report because the clear narrative interpretations provide the greatest impact for the client (Wang, 2002).

*Authors:* G. K. Bennet, H. G. Seashore, and A. G. Wesman
*Availability:* Pearson Assessments
        19500 Bulverde Rd.
        San Antonio, TX 78259
        (800) 627-7271
        http://www.pearsonassessments.com

### General Aptitude Test Battery

The General Aptitude Test Battery (Keesling & Healy, 1988) is a broad measure of nine occupational aptitudes such as general learning and manual dexterity. This test is intended for students in Grades 9 to 12 as well as adults and can be group administered. Developed by the U.S. Employment Service primarily for administration through local State Employment Security agencies, qualified schools and other organizations may obtain permission to administer this assessment. The General Aptitude Test Battery is designed to help clients compare their abilities with those of employed adults. This awareness serves as a springboard for career counseling using the General Aptitude Test Battery.

*Availability:* Local employment service agency or U.S. Employment Service
        Western Assessment Research and Development Center
        140 East Third St.
        Salt Lake City, UT 84111
        http://www.uses.doleta.gov

### Armed Services Vocational Aptitude Battery

Developed by the U.S. Department of Defense, the Armed Services Vocational Aptitude Battery (U.S. Military Entrance Processing Command, 2002) is designed for high school seniors and is provided at no cost to schools through a cooperative venture. Results of this widely used instrument yield students' abilities in three areas: academic, verbal, and mathematical. Resultant Armed Services Vocational Aptitude Battery scores are compared with those of other students nationally. The instrument is designed to facilitate self-awareness, career exploration, and career planning with suggestions for suitable occupations, including military careers (U.S. Military Entrance Processing Command, 2002).

*Availability:* Local high school or
    Department of Defense
    Defense Manpower Data Center
    Personnel Testing Division
    99 Pacific St., Suite 155A
    Monterey, CA 93940
    (408) 583-2400
    https://www.dmdc.osd.mil/appj/dwp/index.jsp

Other aptitude tests include the Wonderlic Basic Skills Test, the Scholastic Assessment Test (SAT) and ACT Assessment, the Graduate Record Examination, and the Miller Analogies Test.

### Wonderlic Basic Skills Test

The Wonderlic Basic Skills Test is a measurement of verbal skills, including the Word Knowledge, Sentence Construction, and Information Retrieval subtests, and quantitative skills, including the Explicit Problem Solving, Problem Solving, and Interpretive Problem Solving subtests. Intended for group or individual administration, the Wonderlic Basic Skills Test is suitable for assessing job readiness in teenage and young adult populations and has significant potential for providing clients with information about their career decisions (Hanna & Hughey, 2002). Additionally, this instrument has been approved by the U.S. Department of Education as a means of qualifying students for Title 10 federal financial assistance. This instrument can be computer scored by the counselor with appropriate software. A desirable feature of this instrument is that falsified answer sheets are easily identified during scoring, and the computer report will indicate to the administrator that the client should be retested (Donlon, 1998).

*Availability:* Wonderlic, Inc.
    400 Lakeview Parkway,
    Suite 200Vernon Hills, IL 60061
    (877) 605-9496
    http://www.wonderlic.com

### Scholastic Assessment Test and ACT Assessment

The SAT and ACT Assessment are measures of readiness for undergraduate school. Minimum scores on these instruments often serve as gatekeepers to colleges and universities in the admissions process. The SAT results in a score ranging from 600 to 2,400, which is the combination of three 800-point subtests in mathematics, critical reading, and writing. The ACT was introduced in the late 1950s as a competitor to the SAT and is composed of four subtests: English, math, reading, and science reasoning. The maximum average composite score on the ACT is 36, which corresponds with a 2,400 on the SAT. The average ACT score in 2009 was 21.1 (ACT, 2009).

*Availability:* SAT
Educational Testing Service
College Board Programs
Princeton, NJ 08541
http:// www.ets.org

ACT National Office
2201 North Dodge St.
P.O. Box 168
Iowa City, IA 52243-0168
(319) 337-1000
http://www.act.org

### Graduate Record Examination

The Graduate Record Examination is an assessment of readiness for graduate school. Used to help distinguish between students of similar backgrounds, the Graduate Record Examination General Test measures skills acquired throughout the educational process that are common to all fields of study. Analytical writing, verbal, and quantitative skills are also measured. Administered by the Educational Testing Service, the GRE is provided in computer or paper form through local testing centers worldwide.

*Availability:* GRE-ETS
P.O. Box 6000
Princeton, NJ 08541-6000
(800) 473-2255
www.gre.org

### Miller Analogies Test

The Miller Analogies Test was developed more than 70 years ago to assess readiness for graduate school, often as an alternative to the Graduate Record Examination. Its aim is to differentiate between high-functioning graduate applicants by testing cognitive complexity (Ivens, 1995). Clients are presented with 100 analogies requiring swift responses in a 50-minute time period. Its usefulness is limited to clients looking at the potential for graduate school in their career decisions and to the programs to which they apply.

*Availability:* Pearson Assessments
19500 Bulverde Rd.
San Antonio, TX 78259
(800) 627-7271
http://pearsonassessments.com

**SIDEBAR 6.6   Self-Awareness 3: Assessments of Aptitude, Ability, and Achievement**

You work as a school counselor in a poor neighborhood in a rural town that has a high unemployment rate. The students in the area are predominately African American and Hispanic. Job opportunities for the graduating seniors are very limited, and few students choose to go or can afford to go to college. Your principal encourages every senior to take the Armed Services Vocational Aptitude Battery and to be open to military service as a career choice. You notice that military recruiters begin to heavily attempt to recruit the students for active duty. There is a backlash from the community because parents are concerned that the only option their children have is to serve the military and go to war. The principal looks to you and so do the parents. How would you respond in this situation?

## Assessments of Interests

An important factor in career decision making is the concept of client interests. Generally defined as a set of beliefs or attitudes toward a given activity, interest is linked to motivation to engage in some form of that activity (Drummond, 2000). Career instruments that measure interest have long been a part of developmental, life-span theorists. Previously in this chapter, we discussed the use of the SII and the SDS often associated with Holland's (1997) typology theory as well as the Vocation Interest Inventory and the California Occupational Preference Survey often associated with Roe's (1956) psychoanalytic theory. Other measures of interest are available to career counselors for use in defining what clients are attracted to in their work and in their personal lives. Because of the idiosyncratic nature of the information being gathered, these instruments are typically in the form of a self-report questionnaire. They often serve as only one piece of information in the career decision-making puzzle. Three interest inventories are widely used: the Kuder Occupational Interest Survey, the Kuder General Interest Survey, and the Career Assessment Inventory.

### *Kuder Occupational Interest Survey*

The Kuder Occupational Interest Survey, Form DD, relates client interests to interests typical of 126 occupational groups. Appropriate for clients from 10th grade through adult, the instrument requires clients to rate 100 activity triads in terms of which activity of the three the client prefers. This method of rating preference is to elicit patterns of interest rather than intensity of that interest (Kelly, 2002). Validity of this instrument is strong, with more than half of study participants winding up in a career field suggested by their outcomes on this measure (Worthen et al., 1999).

*Author:* G. Frederic Kuder
*Availability:* National Career Assessment Services, Inc.
601 Visions Pkwy.
P.O. Box 277
Adel, IA 50003
(800) 314-8972
http://www.kuder.com

### *Kuder General Interest Survey, Form E*

The Kuder General Interest Survey was developed to measure the general interests of a younger population than the Kuder Occupational Interest

Survey (Pope, 1995). The Kuder General Interest Survey is written at a sixth-grade level and measures broad occupational themes in 10 areas including outdoor, mechanical, computational, scientific, persuasive, artistic, literary, musical, social service, and clerical. The instrument can be administered in small classroom settings or with larger groups and can be self- or machine scored. Like the Kuder Occupational Interest Survey, clients select the one of three activity choices they like the best and the one they like the least, in an effort to elicit preferences. The Kuder General Interest Survey is typically used by school counselors to stimulate general career discussion rather than focus on specific career decisions (Pope, 2002).

*Author:* G. Frederic Kuder
*Availability:* National Career Assessment Services, Inc.
    302 Visions Pkwy.
    P.O. Box 277
    Adel, IA 50003
    (800) 314-8972
    http://www.kuder.com

### Career Assessment Inventory

The Career Assessment Inventory was originally developed for use with clients interested in occupations that did not require a post–high school education (Kehoe, 1992). An enhanced version has broadened the measurement to include professional occupational interests, but the Career Assessment Inventory is targeted to non–baccalaureate degree seekers (Miner & Sellers, 2002). Using Holland's (1997) organizing themes as a foundation, this instrument is patterned after the SII and is intended for clients ages high school through adult. The Career Assessment Inventory is easily administered to groups, and a local machine-scoring or scoring service scoring is available.

*Author:* Charles B. Johansson
*Availability:* Pearson Assessments
    19500 Bulverde Dr.
    San Antonio, TX 78259
    (800) 627-7271
    (800) 632-9011 (fax)
    http://pearsonassessments.com

### Chronicle Career Quest

The Chronicle Career Quest was developed to help students assess career opportunities. Structured in concert with the U.S. Employment Service *Guide for Occupational Exploration*, the instrument focuses on 12 *Guide for Occupational Exploration* (Employment and Training Administration, 1979) interest clusters: artistic, scientific, plants and animal, protective, mechanical, industrial, business detail, selling, accommodating, humanitarian, leading influencing, and physical performing. The Chronicle Career Quest was designed for group administration with clients from seventh grade through adult and is interpreted through the resulting Career Paths Occupational Profile. Useful as both a stand-alone measure of vocational interest as well as a part of a larger career battery, the Chronicle Career Quest directs clients toward various career interests and educates individuals on the career options available to them (Daniel & Thompson, 1995).

*Author:* Chronicle Guidance Publications, Inc.
*Availability:* Chronicle Guidance Publications, Inc.
66 Aurora St.
Moravia, NY 13118-1190
(800) 622-7284
http://www.chronicleguidance.com

### Campbell Interests and Skills Survey

The Campbell Interests and Skills Survey is a vocational interest and skills inventory used with college-bound or college-educated English- or Spanish-speaking clients. Along with measuring clients' attraction to (interest in) a particular occupation, the Campbell Interests and Skills Survey also measures how well clients perceive they can actually do the skills necessary for the job (Pugh, 1998).

*Author:* David Campbell
*Availability:* Psychological Corporation
P.O. Box 599700
San Antonio, TX 78259
(800) 627-7271
(800) 232-1223 (fax)
http://psychcorp.pearsonassessments.com

## Assessments of Values

Closely related to interest and personality, values are integral components of client decision making. Values are generally defined as cognitive, emotional, and behavioral factors that manifest themselves as beliefs (Zunker & Osborn, 2005). Their role in career decision making can be highlighted through the use of a variety of established instruments in the field. These instruments may help counselors "stimulate discussions of values and their relationship to career decision-making" (Zunker & Osborn, 2005, p. 160). The previously discussed Values Scale and the Salience Inventory from Super's life span theory (Super & Osborne, 1992) of career counseling as well as the Minnesota Importance Questionnaire from the theory of work adjustment are excellent examples of values instruments available to career counselors. Other quality measures of values include the Survey of Personal Values, Career Orientation and Evaluation Survey, and Rokeach Values Survey.

### Survey of Personal Values

The Survey of Personal Values is a measure of how individuals cope with daily life problems and stressors. Intended for high school and adult populations, this measure surveys values related to practical mindedness, achievement, variety, decisiveness, orderliness, and goal orientation. This self-administered instrument, which can be quickly hand scored, may be most useful in the area of personnel selection as well as career guidance (Erchul, 1989). Its companion test, the Survey of Interpersonal Values, provides additional information related to the client's approach to interpersonal relationships.

*Author:* Leonard V. Gordon
*Availability:* Vantage, Inc.
    Suite 1600
    One North Dearborn
    Chicago, IL 60602
    (800) 922-7343
    http://www.pearsonreidlondonhouse.com

### Career Orientation Placement and Evaluation Survey

The Career Orientation Placement and Evaluation Survey is an instrument intended for the junior high through community college population. One element of the larger Career Occupational Preference System, the Career Orientation Placement and Evaluation Survey is designed to measure individual values that relate to occupational motivation (Wickwire, 2002). Seven work values are presented to clients using these forced-choice options: investigative versus accepting, practical versus carefree, leadership versus supportive, orderliness versus flexibility, recognition versus privacy, aesthetic versus realistic, and social versus reserved. A self-interpretive scoring guide and profile relates scores to specific occupational clusters (Wickwire, 2002).

*Author:* Lisa Knapp-Lee, Robert R. Knapp, and Lila F. Knapp
*Availability:* Educational and Industrial Testing Service
    P.O. Box 7234
    San Diego, CA 92167
    (800) 416-1666
    http://www.edits.net/copes.html

### Rokeach Values Survey

The Rokeach Values Survey is a two-part instrument that offers clients the opportunity to rank order lists of values to facilitate the discernment of important values for the client. "Terminal" or desired end-state values such as freedom, happiness, national security, and true friendship are ranked. Also ranked are instrumental values that indicate a client's beliefs about conduct such as ambition, cheerfulness, and courage. Through these rankings, the Rokeach Values Survey provides information useful for exploration of the client's value system as well as on changes within the values system (Sanford, 1995).

*Author:* Milton Rokeach
*Availability:* Consulting Psychologists Press Incorporated
    3803 E. Bayshore Rd.

P.O. Box 10096
Palo Alto, CA 94303
(800) 624-1765
http://cpp-db.com

## Assessments of Career Maturity

Career maturity inventories grew out of developmental approaches to career counseling, including Super's life span theory (Super & Osborne, 1992). *Career maturity* generally refers to the clients' ability to make reasoned career choices on the basis of their skills, readiness, awareness, and experience (Levinson & Ohler, 1998). Zunker and Osborne (2005) cited this category of inventories as one of the greatest growth areas in the field of career assessment. The Career Thoughts Inventory from the theory of cognitive information processing is a career maturity assessment previously discussed in this chapter. Other examples include the Career Maturity Inventory and Career Factors Inventory.

### Career Maturity Inventory

The Career Maturity Inventory is designed to measure attitudes toward career choice as well as competency to make career decisions. The Career Maturity Inventory is considered one of the foremost career maturity instruments (McDivitt, 2002). Intended for students in Grades 6 to 12, the Career Maturity Inventory is made up of two separate 25-item tests. An Attitude Scale measures true or false responses to various work-related statements. A Competence Test measures knowledge considered necessary to make effective career decisions. Suitable for group administration, the inventory can be hand scored or sent to a machine-scoring service for interpretation. Scores on each test as well as responses to individual items can illuminate clients' needs and serve as the basis for counseling.

*Authors:* John O. Crites and Mark L. Savikas
*Availability:* Careerware, A Bridges Transition company
3534 Hayden Ave.
Culver City, CA 90232
(800) 281-1168
http://www.bridges.com

### Career Factors Inventory

The Career Factors Inventory is designed to assess career indecision in clients ages 13 to adult. It focuses on the emotional and informational factors influencing decision-making abilities (Chartrand & Robbins, 1990). Consisting of 21 items responded to on a Likert scale, the Career Factors Inventory is self-scorable and provides profile scores for the scales Need for Career Information, Need for Knowledge, Career Choice Anxiety, and Generalized Indecisiveness. This simple and practical measure of career indecision can be swiftly administered and is helpful in counseling settings in which readiness to make career decisions is a concern (D'Costa, 2001).

*Authors:* Judy M. Chartrand, Steven B. Robbins, and Weston H. Morrill
*Availability:* Consulting Psychologists Press Inc.
          3803 E. Bayshore Rd.
          P.O. Box 10096
          Palo Alto, CA 94303
          (800) 624-1765
          http://cpp-db.com

## Assessments of Personality

Measures of personality have long held interest for career counselors because such instruments serve the utilitarian function of illuminating client traits, attitudes, and motivations. Such information is helpful to counselors working with clients about career choices and changes and attempting to predict career fit or satisfaction. Research is limited, however, regarding the relationship between personality factors and career satisfaction. Consequently, such instruments should be used with care and never as a single measure of career need. Rather, personality assessments provide counselors and clients with a point of reference when exploring potential career options.

### Sixteen Personality Factor Questionnaire and Personal Career Development Profile

The Sixteen Personality Factor Questionnaire is an objective test of a broad base of personality traits and attributes across 16 dimensions. Intended for use with high school, college, and adult populations, the Sixteen Personality Factor Questionnaire is suitable for group or individual administration. The machine-scored profile and interpretive report provide an abundance of information for the counselor working with career choice decisions. Supplemental to the Sixteen Personality Factor Questionnaire is the Personal Career Development Profile, a career-focused computer interpretation of the Sixteen Personality Factor Questionnaire. This profile provides information about occupational interest patterns, leadership abilities, and career lifestyle preferences (McLellan, 1995)

*Authors:* Raymond Cattell (Sixteen Personality Factor Questionnaire); Verne
        Walter (Personal Career Development Profile)
*Availability:* Institute for Personality and Ability Testing
        1801 Woodfield Dr.
        Savoy, IL 61874
        (800) 225-4728
        http://www.ipat.com

### Myers-Briggs Type Indicator

One of the most widely used measures of personality preferences available to counselors, the Myers-Briggs Type Indicator provides scores on the dichotomies of Extraversion–Introversion, Sensing–Intuition, Thinking–Feeling, and Judging–Perceiving (Myers, McCaulley, Quenk, & Hammer, 1998). The publisher claims that clients taking the Myers-Briggs Type Indicator will generate the same three to four type preference structure 75% to 90% of the time (http://www.myersbriggs.org). Available for both computer and hand scoring, the Myers-Briggs Type Indicator is best used in situations in which the focus is on increasing a client's self-understanding (Mastrangelo, 2001). The manual provides information regarding occupational information and Myers-Briggs Type Indicator typology that may prove valuable to the career counseling process.

*Author:* K. C. Briggs, I. B. Myers, M. H. McCaulley, N. L. Quenk, & A. L. Hammer
*Availability:* Consulting Psychologists Press Inc.
1055 Joaquin Dr., 2nd floor
Mountain View, CA 94043
(800) 624-1765
http://cpp.com

### Student Styles Questionnaire

The Student Styles Questionnaire is designed to measure personal learning styles and preferences for junior and senior high school students. The instrument is based on Jungian constructs, making it similar in design to the Myers-Briggs Type Indicator. Designed for group or individual administration, with hand- and machine-scoring options, the Student Styles Questionnaire provides scores for eight dimensions: extroverted–introverted, practical–imaginative, thinking–feeling, and organized–flexible. The Student Styles Questionnaire is intended for use in school settings to identify learning styles, gifted students, and students with high-risk behaviors. Counselors may also use information gleaned from the instrument to facilitate vocational and educational choices (Schraw, 2001).

*Authors:* Thomas Oakland, Joseph Glutting, and Connie Horton
*Availability:* Pearson Assessments,
19500 Bulverde Rd.
San Antonio, TX 78259
(800) 872-1726
http://pearsonassessments.com

### Comprehensive Personality Profile

The Comprehensive Personality Profile was designed to measure compatibility between clients and specific occupations. Consisting of a series of 88 true–false questions, this machine-scored instrument provides clients with an assessment of their personal characteristics and ideal characteristics of given jobs. The Comprehensive Personality Profile is intended for adults, is machine scored, and can be administered to individuals or groups. The general focus of the Comprehensive Personality Profile is on occupations in the service industry, including positions in sales or customer service (Cohn, 2001).

*Author:* Larry L. Craft
*Availability:* Wonderlic, Inc
      1795 N. Butterfield Rd.
      Libertyville, IL 60048-1238
      (888) 397-8519
      http://www.wonderlic.com

### Jackson Personality Inventory—Revised

The Jackson Personality Inventory—Revised measures a range of personality variables in adolescents and adults. An intended primary use of this measure is career counseling related to hiring decisions (Zachar, 1998). The instrument is divided into five clusters: analytical, emotional, extraverted, opportunistic, and dependable. The interpretive information found in the computer-scored profile provides a basis for career counseling.

*Author:* Douglas Jackson
*Availability:* Sigma Assessment Systems
      P.O. Box 610757
      Port Huron, MI 48061-0984
      (800) 265-1285
      http://www.sigmaassessmentsystems.com

### NEO Personality Inventory—Revised

The NEO Personality Inventory—Revised was first developed in 1985 and consists of 243 items designed to provide a description of personality in relation to clinical and nonclinical populations (Sigma Assessment Systems, 2011). The instrument is based on five primary factors: Neuroticism, Extraversion, Openness to Experience, Agreeableness, and Conscientiousness. Each factor contains a number of subscales, which the publisher terms *facets,* that further describe the characteristics of the individual's personality. The publisher has reported high internal consistency and longitudinal stability coefficients. The assessment can be used with adults and older adolescents.

*Authors:* Paul T. Costa and Robert R. McRae
*Availability:* Sigma Assessment Systems
      P.O. Box 610757
      Port Huron, MI 48061-0984
      (800) 265-1285
      http://www.sigmaassessmentsystems.com

## Computer-Assisted Career Guidance Systems

With the advent of widely available assessment technology, career assessments built on computer foundations have emerged as a specialized area of career counseling. Often used to supplement existing career counseling methods, computer-assisted career guidance systems (CAGS) may be used in test administration, scoring, profiling, interpreting, or multimedia interpretation (Sampson, 2000). CAGS are beneficial to career counselors because they can rapidly and efficiently update large quantities of information not feasible with paper-and-pencil instruments (Gati, Saka, & Krausz, 2001). In a recent review of a comprehensive compilation of career assessment tools, roughly half of the instruments used computer assistance in some form (Sampson, Lumsden, & Carr, 2002).

We must note that CAGS function best in addition to the counselor's services to the client, not as a replacement for the counselor (Sampson et al., 2002). Counselors may best serve clients by explaining the computer application before testing, intervening at selected points during testing to ensure the client is gaining maximum benefit from the process, and following up during the interpretive phase to ensure the client integrates new information (Zunker & Osborn, 2005). As with any assessment tool, counselors must be thoroughly familiar with CAGS before using them in practice. Some of the more popular computer-based tools for career counseling are presented here.

### DISCOVER

DISCOVER is a broad application to career planning for clients high school age through adult. Clients enter "halls" within a virtual World of Work center where they complete self-assessments, choose occupations, plan their educations, and plan for work (Zunker & Osborn, 2005). Clients are assessed using the Inventory of Work Related Abilities and the Inventory of Work Preferences (ACT, 2001). The results are interpreted through the World-of-Work Map, an extension of Holland's (1994c, 1997) hexagon, to provide a comprehensive yet easy-to-understand overview of the work world (ACT, 2001).

*Availability:* ACT
    500 ACT Dr.
    P.O. Box 168
    Iowa City, IA 52243-0168
    (319) 337-1000
    http://www.act.org

### Choices Planner for Career Transitions

Choices Planner for Career Transitions is intended for clients in postsecondary institutions seeking ongoing educational or occupational direction. Using the Choices Planner for Career Transitions Road Map, the user participates in guided career exploration. The program connects to an Internet component allowing clients access to college links, financial aid sources (Zunker & Osborn, 2005), and more than 965 O*NET occupations (O*NET Resource Center, 2010). Site licensing makes Choices Planner for Career Transitions an affordable option for school and college counselors.

*Availability:* Bridges Transition Co.
3534 Hayden Ave.
Culver City, CA 90232
(800) 281-1168
http://bridges.com

### SIGI PLUS System of Interactive Guidance Information

The SIGI PLUS provides counselors with a more comprehensive assessment tool for career decision making (Educational Testing Service, 1990; Zunker & Osborn, 2005). Created with multiple modules, the use of which can be varied to meet the needs of the test taker or client, SIGI PLUS contains a self-assessment, a search for compatible career options, and information needed to prepare for and make tentative career plans (Kivlighan & Johnston, 1994). Updated annually by the Educational Testing Service, SIGI PLUS is available in PC, Internet, or institutional intranet versions (Zunker & Osborn, 2005).

*Availability:* Educational Testing Service
Rosedale Rd.
Princeton, NJ 08541
(800) 257-7444
http://www.ets.org/sigi

### Career Key

The Career Key is available free via the Internet at http://www.ncsu.edu/careerkey. Clients can take the assessment online or print and complete a paper version. Because the Career Key is offered as a public service by the author, duplication of the instrument for group administration is possible (Jones, 2003). Clients rate 24 statements about their activities, values, interests, and preferences as well as their interest in 42 occupations. The results are then interpreted in terms of Holland's (1997) six personality types as they relate to career decision making (Levinson & Zeman, 2002). The Web site offers supplemental information useful to career counselors including the Career Key Professional Manual and career information resources (Jones, 2003).

*Author:* Lawrence K. Jones
*Availability:* North Carolina State University
520C Poe Hall
P.O. Box 7801
Raleigh, NC, 27695
(919) 515-6359
http://www.ncsu.edu/careerkey

### O*NET Work Importance Profiler

The O*NET Work Importance Profiler is a free computerized self-assessment that assists clients in determining satisfying occupations on the basis of the type of job and the client's work values (O*NET Resource Center, 2011).

Clients taking the Work Importance Profiler rank and rate 21 work needs that measure achievement, independence, recognition, relationships, support, and working conditions. The results provide a window into more than 800 occupations via O*NET OnLine.

*Availability:* O*NET Project
U.S. Department of Labor, Employment and Training
Administration Room N5637, 200 Constitution Ave., NW
Washington, DC 20210
http://www.onetcenter.org/WIP.html

### COIN

The COIN Career Guidance System was developed to assist high school through adult populations with a series of career exploration tools. The instruments provided include a self-assessment and the ability to match clients to an occupation specific to their interests and geographical location. Additionally, this product has the capability to integrate scores from other career inventories the client may have taken such as the SDS, CDM, Armed Services Vocational Aptitude Battery, Career Occupational Preference System, and CAPS.

*Availability:* COIN Educational Products
10 Estes Street
Ipswich, MA 01938
(800) 653-2726
http://coin3.com

### Magellan

Magellan, an interactive CAGS for school-based application, contains eight assessments related to career choice. Developed to pique student interest in career decision making, this lively tool contains occupational video clips, career biographies, and a large occupational database. Also linked to the *Guide for Occupational Exploration* and the *Occupational Outlook Handbook*, Magellan is most appropriate for middle and high school career counseling settings.

*Availability:* Valpar International Corp.
2440 N. Coyote Dr., Suite 127
Tucson, AZ 85745
(800) 633-3321
http://valparint.com

## Qualitative Assessment

Although most of this chapter has been dedicated to the use of standardized instruments, such approaches may leave some clients feeling more like test takers than active participants in their own career futures (Croteau & Slaney, 1994). A more flexible and unique process of career counseling and assessment can occur through the use of qualitative methods. Typically presented in the form of simulations, games, or card-sorting activities, qualitative methods are emerging as feasible options for career counselors (Croteau & Slaney, 1994). Goldman (1992) outlined several general traits of qualitative tools, including their more informal manner, minimal need for statistical expertise, enhanced level of client involvement, tendency to be open ended and flexible, and applicability to group settings.

Counselors must take care when selecting qualitative methods. These exercises are not intended to replace standardized assessment measures (Goldman, 1992). Qualitative methods require that counselors possess a unique knowledge base related to the use of these tools. Additionally, excellent interpersonal skills are needed because of the increased dependence on the collaborative client–counselor relationship (Okocha, 1998). Finally, the lack of standardized interpretation assistance for qualitative activities places the responsibility for facilitating career exploration and decision making on the counselor (Goldman, 1992).

Numerous methods that are traditionally considered therapeutic may be used by career counselors as qualitative assessments. One example is Life Lines, in which clients recall and chart significant life events, resulting in individualized descriptions of client interests and values (Goldman, 1992). Likewise, an occupational genogram elicits information about career choices in the client's family of origin (Okocha, 1998). A third type of qualitative measure is the card sort.

### Career Values Card Sort

The Career Values Card Sort Planning Kit was designed for adults to foster an understanding of values critical to client satisfaction. During the activity, the client sorts 41 occupational values into degrees of interest. These prioritized values are then compared with corresponding career exploration concerns that facilitate the client's awareness of how values affect work decisions. This learning activity is most helpful as an exploratory measure rather than as a predictive tool (Kinnier, 1998).

*Author:* Richard L. Knowdell
*Availability:* Career Research and Testing, Inc.
    2081 Bering Dr. #f
    San Jose, CA 95131-2012
    (800) 469-3560
    http://www.careertrainer.com

**SIDEBAR 6.7  Case Study 2: Qualitative Assessments**

You have a 40-year-old Native American female client named Jamie. She spent all of her life on her tribe's reservation. She chose to move off the reservation to explore new opportunities. As a first step, she wants to learn more about her aptitude for a career in business management. You choose to assess her qualitatively to account for cultural diversity. As part of the assessment, you ask the following question: "What would be the first step you would take in developing a new program for a large business?" The common categories for coding answers are related to program evaluation, program curriculum construction, and needs assessment. Jamie states that she would seek guidance from elders in the community about the first step. You find this pattern in many of her answers. How would you interpret these responses in terms of the client's aptitude for a business management career?

## Assessments of Special Populations

Career counselors need to be aware of their clients' special needs, cultural background, and experience and how these relate to the formation of their vocational identities. What may appear typical of the majority culture might not be generalizable to those who are different in race, language, acculturation, and geography. Career counselors must take into consideration the characteristics of a career instrument's norming group. They must seek out research supporting its relevance to their targeted population and engage in a thorough analysis of the implications of intervening with this particular instrument with their particular group.

Earlier in this chapter, we emphasized the importance of comparing and contrasting the make up of a test's norming group with a client's demographic profile. Often, counselors must make subjective decisions regarding the relevance of a particular career inventory or technique and its applicability to their current client population. Frequently, few guidelines are offered to determine when a client's characteristics are too divergent for use with a particular career assessment tool.

Leung (1996) offered six guidelines for career assessment with ethnic minorities that may be applicable for special testing populations in general. First, counselors must have adequate training in multicultural counseling, including awareness of the most recent research on cross-cultural assessment for ethnic minorities. Second, test selection must ensue only after client needs are thoroughly assessed and related to the purpose, structure, norms, psychometric properties, and limitations of each instrument. Third, assessment of the cultural histories of minority clients must recognize the large within-group differences generic to each ethnic group. Fourth, counselors must be aware of the client's verbal and nonverbal responses when test data are presented to ensure proper test interpretations by each client. Fifth, assessment data, scores, and individual item responses can be used as stimuli to promote further exploration of the client's career development. Finally, career assessment can serve to empower clients to take control of their lives through the role they play and the choices they make in the career counseling process.

Some commonly used instruments already discussed in this chapter that have some research supporting their potential appropriateness with multicultural populations include the SII, SDS, My Vocational Situation, and Career Maturity Inventory (Leung, 1996). Other instruments that may prove useful when working with multicultural populations are acculturation inventories such as the Cross-Cultural Adaptability Inventory (Kelley & Myers, 1995) and the Suinn–Lew Asian Self-Identity Acculturation Scale (Suinn, Rickard-Figueroa, Lew, &Vigil, 1987).

*Authors:* Colleen Kelley and Judith Meyers
*Availability:* Cross-Cultural Adaptability Inventory

Pearson Assessments
5601 Green Valley Dr.
Bloomington, MN 55437
(800) 627-7271
(800) 632-9011 (fax)
http://pearsonassessments.com

Finally, one other instrument that may be applicable not only to multicultural clients but also to those populations with varying degrees of physical, emotional, verbal, and cognitive limitations is the Wide Range Interest and Opinion Test.

### Wide Range Interest and Opinion Test

The Wide Range Interest and Opinion Test is a pictorial instrument intended for educationally or culturally disadvantaged clients or with those whose severe disabilities render other interest inventories unfeasible (Zunker & Osborn, 2002). Similar to other interest inventories, the test taker selects the most and least preferred choices from a series of triads. The stimulus items were redrawn in the late 1970s to enhance inclusion of gender and cultural minorities (Hsu, 1985). The instrument may be administered individually or in groups, is machine scored, and is intended for ages 5 to adult. Results provide scores for 18 occupational clusters such as art, office work, and biological science (Zunker & Osborn, 2005).

*Authors:* Joseph Jastak and Sarah Jastak
*Availability:* Psychological Assessment Resources, Inc.
      16204 N. Florida Ave.
      Lutz, FL 33549
      (800) 889-8378
      http://www. parinc.com

#### SIDEBAR 6.8   Case Study 3: Assessments of Special Populations

You have a client, Deo, who is a 55-year-old man who recently immigrated to the United States from a conflict area in Uganda. The client is bilingual with English as his second language. In your conversations with him, you found his use of the English language to be adequate. In Uganda, he is considered well educated with a doctoral degree. In the United States, Deo's education is not recognized because the universities he attended are not formally accredited. The client would like to complete a career interest test to assist his job search in this country. You have one test available that included a norm group of 50-year-old African American men born in the United States who had an undergraduate education and spoke English as their primary language. Consider whether this test would be an appropriate fit for Deo. If so, would you need to make any accommodations? If not, what type of normative group would you look for in a different interest test?

## Additional Assessments

Counselors engaging in career exploration anticipate that clients are in need of employment. In this chapter, we have largely focused on assessments that help clients understand their preferences and abilities and facilitate the counselor matching those preferences and abilities to occupations. Not all clients in need of career assessment are seeking work. Other populations that may present for assessment are employed people who are good at what they do but are simply stressed, overworked, or burned out. In such cases, assessments of stress and burnout may be indicated. Although an exhaustive review of such tools is beyond the scope of this chapter, one example is the Maslach Burnout Inventory.

### Maslach Burnout Inventory

The Maslach Burnout Inventory is a unique tool designed to measure three general constructs: emotional exhaustion (feeling overextended at work), depersonalization (lack of caring toward recipients of one's work), and personal accomplishment (feelings of success and competence). Although the inventory does not generate an overall score of burnout, the three subscores can be useful in understanding the client's experience of on-the-job burnout. Reliability is judged to be adequate with high internal consistency, and validity is indicated on the basis of a number of small studies correlating this construct of burnout with other measures (Fitzpatrick, 2005).

## Summary

From standardized to qualitative, computer assisted to pen and paper, career assessment instruments are available in a variety of forms to meet the unique needs of career counselors and their clients. Although no one type of assessment is superior, each has its own advantages and limitations. Counselors must be well-informed consumers of career assessment products to make appropriate decisions regarding their applicability to the unique needs of their clients. The Web sites listed in the next section provide additional information relating to the chapter topics.

 ## Useful Web Sites

- American School Counselor Association. A variety of support materials for counselors practicing in a school setting: http://www.school counselor.org/
- America's Career InfoNet. Comprehensive site providing links to basic employment outlook and trend data, assessment resources, and local job banks: http://www.careerinfonet.org
- Career Communications, Inc. Listing of career resource materials, including self-assessments as well as those administered by professionals: http://www.careerbookstore.com/assessment_testing.shtml
- Career Consciousness, Inc. Links to instructional materials, reference books, and numerous assessment tools including purchasing information: http://www.careercc.com/links/
- Clearinghouse on Assessment and Evaluation. The Code of Fair Testing Practices in Education provides guidelines for professionals and consumers of testing services: http://ericae.net/code.txt

- Fair Access Coalition on Testing. Site includes testing guidelines and news about restricted test lists by state: http://www.fairaccess.org/home
- National Career Development Association. The home page of the National Career Development Association, a division of the American Counseling Association, which provides support and resources to career professionals and the public: http://www.ncda.org/

## Acknowledgment

The authors would like to acknowledge the contribution that Scott D. Rasmus made to the first edition version of this chapter.

## References

ACT. (2001). *DISCOVER: Research support for DISCOVER assessment components.* Retrieved from http://www.act.org/discover/pdf/research_support.pdf

ACT. (2009). *ACT profile report—National graduating class 2009.* Iowa City, IA: Author.

Albanese, M. A. (2001). Review of the Career Occupational Preference System Professional Level Interest Inventory (COPS-P). In B. S. Plake & J. C. Impara (Eds.), *Fourteenth mental measurements yearbook* (Vol. 65, pp. 225–227). Lincoln, NE: Buros Institute of Mental Measurements.

American Counseling Association. (2005). *American Counseling Association code of ethics.* Alexandria, VA: Author.

American Counseling Association Ethics Committee. (2009). The layperson's guide to counselor ethics. Retrieved from http://www.counseling.org/resources/CodeofEthics/TP/Home/CT2.aspx

American Psychological Association. (2010). 2010 amendments to the 2002 "Ethical principles of psychologist and code of conduct." *American Psychologist, 65*, 493.

Benson, P. G. (1988). Minnesota Importance Questionnaire. In J. T. Kapes & M. M. Mastie (Eds.), *A counselor's guide to career assessment instruments* (2nd ed., pp. 144–149). Alexandria, VA: National Career Development Association.

Chartrand, J. M. & Robbins, S. B. (1990). Using multidimensional career decision instruments to assess career decidedness and implementation. *Career Development Quarterly, 39*, 166–178.

*Code of fair testing practices in education.* (2004). Washington, DC: Joint Committee on Testing Practices.

Cohn, S. (2001). Review of the Comprehensive Personality Profile. In B. S. Plake & J. C. Impara (Eds.), *Fourteenth mental measurements yearbook* (Vol. 92, pp. 310–313). Lincoln, NE: Buros Institute of Mental Measurements.

Cronbach, L. J. (1951). Coefficient alpha and the internal structure of tests. *Psychometrika, 16*, 197–334.

Croteau, J. M., & Slaney, R. B. (1994). Two methods of exploring interests: A comparison of outcomes. *Career Development Quarterly, 42*, 252–262.

Daniel, L. G., & Thompson, D. (1995). Review of the Chronicle Career Quest™. In J. C. Conoley & J. C. Impara (Eds.), *Twelfth mental measurements yearbook* (Vol. 79, pp. 193–197). Lincoln, NE: Buros Institute of Mental Measurements.

Dawis, R. V. (1980). Personnel assessment from the perspective of the theory of work adjustment. *Public Personnel Management, 9*, 268–273.

D'Costa, A. (2001). Review of the Career Factors Inventory. In B. S. Plake & J. C. Impara (Eds.), *Fourteenth mental measurements yearbook* (Vol. 63, pp. 219–221). Lincoln, NE: Buros Institute of Mental Measurements.

Donlon, T. F. (1998). Review of the Wonderlic Basic Skills Test. In J. C. Impara & B. S. Plake (Eds.), *Thirteenth mental measurements yearbook* (Vol. 362, pp. 1137–1139). Lincoln, NE: Buros Institute of Mental Measurements.

Donnay, D., Thompson, R., Morris, L., & Shaubhut, N. (2004). *Technical brief for the newly revised Strong Interest Inventory assessment: Content reliability and validity.* Palo Alto, CA: Consulting Psychologist Press.

Drummond, R. J. (2000). *Appraisal procedures for counselors and helping professionals* (4th ed.). Upper Saddle River, NJ: Merrill.

Drummond, R.J., & Ryan, C.W. (1985). *Career counseling: A developmental approach.* Upper Saddle River, NJ: Merrill.

Educational Testing Service. (1990). *SIGI PLUS counselor's manual.* Princeton, NJ: Author.

Employment and training Administration (DOL), W.C. (DOL), Washington, DC. (1979). Guide for Occupational Exploration. *Occupational Outlook Quarterly, 24*(1): pp. 26–28.

Erchul, W. P. (1989). Review of the Survey of Personal Values. In B. S. Plake & J. C. Ingram (Eds.), *Tenth mental measurements yearbook* (Vol. 354, pp. 800–801). Lincoln, NE: Buros Institute of Mental Measurements.

Fitzpatrick, R. (2005). Review of the Maslach Burnout Inventory. In R. A. Spies & B. S. Plake Eds.), *The sixteenth mental measurements yearbook.* Lincoln, NE: Buros Institute of Mental Measurements. Retrieved from Mental Measurements Yearbook with Tests in Print database.

Fontaine, J. H. (1999). Review of the Career Thoughts Inventory. In B. S. Plake & J. C. Impara (Eds.), *Fourteenth mental measurements yearbook* (Vol. 63, pp. 228–230). Lincoln, NE: Buros Institute of Mental Measurements.

Gati, I., Saka, N., & Krausz, M. (2001). "Should I use a computer-assisted career guidance system?" It depends on where you career decision-making difficulties lie. *British Journal of Guidance & Counselling, 29,* 301–321.

Goldman, L. (1992). Qualitative assessment: An approach for counselors. *Journal of Counseling & Development, 70,* 616–622.

Hanna, G. S., & Hughey, K. F. (2002). Wonderlic Basic Skills Test. In J. T. Kapes & E. A. Whitfield (Eds.), *A counselor's guide to career assessment instruments* (4th ed., pp. 178–182). Alexandria, VA: National Career Development Association.

Harrington, T. F., & Schafer, W. D. (1996). A comparison of self-reported abilities and occupational ability patterns across occupations. *Measurement and Evaluation in Counseling and Development, 28,* 180–191.

Herman, J. (1998). Review of the Vocational Interest Inventory and exploration. In J. C. Impara & B. S. Plake (Eds.), *Thirteenth mental measurements yearbook* (Vol. 357, pp. 1083–1084). Lincoln, NE: Buros Institute of Mental Measurements.

Holland, J. L. (1985). *Vocational Preferences Inventory manual.* Palo Alto, CA: Consulting Psychologist Press.

Holland, J. L. (1994a). *The Occupation Finder—Form R* (4th ed.). Lutz, FL: Psychological Assessment Resources.

Holland, J. L. (1994b). *Self-Directed Search: Assessment booklet—Form R* (4th ed.). Lutz, FL: Psychological Assessment Resources.

Holland, J. L. (1994c). *You and your career—Form R* (4th ed.). Lutz, FL: Psychological Assessment Resources.

Holland, J. L. (1997). *Making vocational choices* (3rd ed.). Odessa, FL: Psychological Assessment Resources.

Holland, J. L., Fritzsche, B. A., & Powell, A. B. (1997). *Self-Directed Search: Technical manual.* Lutz, FL: Psychological Assessment Resources.

Holland, J. L., & Gottfredson, G. D. (1994). *Career Attitudes and Strategies Inventory: An inventory for understanding adult careers.* Odessa, FL: Psychological Assessment Resources.

Holland, J. L., Powell, A. B., & Fritzsche, B. A. (1997). *Self-Directed Search: Professional users guide.* Lutz, FL: Psychological Assessment Resources.

Hood, A. B. (2001). Communicating assessment results in the counseling interview. Retrieved from Ebscohost and from http://eric.ed.gov

Hsu, L. M. (1985). Review of the Wide Range Interest-Opinion Test. In J. V. Mitchell (Ed.), *Ninth mental measurements yearbook* (Vol. 2, pp. 1737–1739). Lincoln, NE: Buros Institute of Mental Measurements.

Ivens, S. H. (1995). Review of the Miller Analogies Test. In J. C. Conoley & J. C. Impara (Eds.), *Twelfth mental measurements yearbook* (Vol. 235, pp. 617–620). Lincoln, NE: Buros Institute of Mental Measurements.

Jones, L. K. (2003). *The Career Key.* Retrieved from http://www.ncsu.edu/careerkey

Kapes, J. T., & Mastie, M. M. (2002). *A counselor's guide to career assessment instruments* (4th ed.). Alexandria, VA: National Career Development Association.

Keesling, J. W., & Healy, C. C. (1988). The General Aptitude Test Battery. In J. T. Kapes & M. M. Mastie (Eds.), *A counselor's guide to career assessment instruments* (2nd ed., pp. 71–75). Alexandria, VA: National Career Development Association.

Kehoe, J. F. (1992). Review of the Career Assessment Inventory. In B. S. Plake & J. C. Ingram (Eds.), *Eleventh mental measurements yearbook* (Vol. 59, pp. 148–151). Lincoln, NE: Buros Institute of Mental Measurements.

Kelley, C., & Meyers, J. (1995). *Cross-Cultural Adaptability Inventory.* Bloomington, MN: Pearson Assessments.

Kelly, K. R. (2002). Kuder Occupational Interest Survey. In J. T. Kapes & E. A. Whitfield (Eds.), *A counselor's guide to career assessment instruments* (4th ed., pp. 265–275). Alexandria, VA: National Career Development Association.

Kinnier, R. T. (1998). Review of the Career Values Card Sort. In B. S. Plake & J. C. Impara (Eds.), *Thirteenth mental measurements yearbook* (Vol. 47, pp. 183–185). Lincoln, NE: Buros Institute of Mental Measurements.

Kivlighan, D. M., Jr., & Johnston, J. A. (1994). Who benefits from computerized counseling? *Journal of Counseling & Development, 72,* 289–293.

Krumboltz, J. D. (1991). *Manual for the Career Beliefs Inventory.* Palo Alto, CA: Consulting Psychologists Press.

Krumboltz, J. D. (1994). The Career Beliefs Inventory. *Journal of Counseling & Development, 72,* 424–429.

Krumboltz, J. D. (1998). Debate: Counsellor actions needed for the new career perspective. *British Journal of Guidance & Counselling, 26,* 559–565.

Krumboltz, J. D., Mitchell, A., & Gelatt, H. G. (1976). Applications of social learning theory of career selection. *Focus on Guidance, 8,* 1–16.

Kuder, G. F., & Richardson, M. W. (1937). The theory of estimation of test reliability. *Psychometrika, 2,* 151–160.

Law, J. (1998). Review of the Vocational Interest Inventory and exploration. In J. C. Impara & B. S. Plake (Eds.), *Thirteenth mental measurements yearbook* (Vol. 408, pp. 1083–1084). Lincoln, NE: Buros Institute of Mental Measurements.

Layton, W. L. (1992). Review of the Minnesota Importance Questionnaire. In J. T. Kramer & J. C. Conoley (Eds.), *Eleventh mental measurements yearbook* (pp. 544–546). Lincoln, NE: Buros Institute of Mental Measurements.

Leung, S. A. (1996). Vocational assessment across cultures. In L. A. Suzuki, P. J. Meller, & J. G. Ponterotto (Eds.), *Handbook of multicultural assessment* (pp. 475–508). San Francisco, CA: Jossey-Bass.

Levinson, E. M., & Ohler, D. L. (1998). Six approaches to the assessment of career maturity. *Journal of Counseling & Development, 76,* 475–483.

Levinson, E. M., & Zeman, H. L. (2002). A critical evaluation of the Web-based version of the Career Key. *Career Development Quarterly, 5,* 26–36.

Mastrangelo, P. M. (2001). Review of the Myers-Briggs Type Indicator. In B. S. Plake & J. C. Impara (Eds.), *Fourteenth mental measurements yearbook* (Vol. 251, pp. 818–819). Lincoln, NE: Buros Institute of Mental Measurements.

McDivitt, P. J. (2002). Career Maturity Inventory. In J. T. Kapes & E. A. Whitfield (Eds.), *A counselor's guide to career assessment instruments* (4th ed., pp. 336–342). Alexandria, VA: National Career Development Association.

McLellan, M. J. (1995). Review of the 16-Personality Factor Questionnaire Fifth Edition. In J. C. Conoley & J.C. Impara (Eds.), *The twelfth mental measurements yearbook.* Lincoln, NE: Buros Institute of Mental Measurements. Retrieved from Mental Measurements Yearbook with Tests in Print database.

Miner, C. U., & Sellers, S. M. (2002). Career Assessment Inventory. In J. T. Kapes & E. A. Whitfield (Eds.), *A counselor's Guide to career assessment instruments* (4th ed., pp. 202–209). Alexandria, VA: National Career Development Association.

*Minnesota Job Description Questionnaire.* (n.d.). Retrieved from http://www.psych.umn.edu/psylabs/vpr/mjdqinf.htm

Mitchell, K. E., Levin, A. S., & Krumboltz, J. D. (1999). Planned happenstance: Constructing unexpected career opportunities. *Journal of Counseling & Development, 77,* 115–124.

Myers, I. B., McCaulley, M. H., Quenk, N. L., & Hammer, A. L. (1998). *Manual: A guide to the development and use of the Myers-Briggs Type Indicator* (3rd ed.). Palo Alto, CA: Consulting Psychologists Press.

National Board of Certified Counselors. (2005). *National board for certified counselor code of ethics.* Charlotte, NC: Author.

Okocha, A. A. G. (1998). Using qualitative appraisal strategies in career counseling. *Journal of Employment Counseling, 35,* 151–160.

O*NET Resource Center. (2010). *About O*NET.* Retrieved from http://www.onet-center.org/overview.html

O*NET Resource Center. (2011). *O*NET Work Importance Profiler.* Retrieved from http://www.onetcenter.org/WIP.html

Pennock-Román, M. (1988). Differential Aptitude Test. In J. T. Kapes & M. M. Mastie (Eds.), *A counselor's guide to career assessment instruments* (2nd ed., pp. 65–68). Alexandria, VA: National Career Development Association.

Pope, M. (1995). Review of the Kuder General Interest Survey. In J. C. Conoley & J. C. Impara (Eds.), *Twelfth mental measurements yearbook* (Vol. 209, pp. 543–545). Lincoln, NE: Buros Institute of Mental Measurements.

Pope, M. (2002) Kuder General Interest Survey. In J. T. Kapes & E. A. Whitfield (Eds.), *A counselor's guide to career assessment instruments* (4th ed., pp. 257–264). Alexandria, VA: National Career Development Association.

Pugh, R. C. (1998). Review of the Campbell Interests and Skills Inventory. In J. C. Impara & B. S. Plake (Eds.), *The thirteenth mental measurements yearbook.*

Lincoln, NE: Buros Institute of Mental Measurements. Retrieved from Mental Measurements Yearbook with Tests in Print database.

Roe, A. (1956). *Psychology of occupations.* New York, NY: Wiley.

Roe, A. (1957). Early determinants of vocational choice. *Journal of Counseling Psychology, 4,* 212–217.

Sampson, J. P., Jr. (2000). Using the Internet to enhance testing in counseling. *Journal of Counseling & Development, 78,* 348–356.

Sampson, J. P., Lumsden, J. A., & Carr, D. L. (2002). Computer-assisted career assessment. In J. T. Kapes & E. A. Whitfield (Eds.), *A counselor's guide to career assessment instruments* (4th ed., pp. 202–209). Alexandria, VA: National Career Development Association.

Sampson, J. P., Peterson, G. W., Lenz, J. G., Reardon, R. C., & Saunders, D. E. (1996a). *Career Thoughts Inventory.* Odessa, FL: Psychological Assessment Resources.

Sampson, J. P., Peterson, G. W., Lenz, J. G., Reardon, R. C., & Saunders, D. E. (1996b). *Improving your career thoughts: A workbook for the Career Thoughts Inventory.* Odessa, FL: Psychological Assessment Resources.

Sampson, J. P., Peterson, G. W., Reardon, R. C., & Lenz, J. G. (2003). *Key elements of the CIP approach to designing career services.* Unpublished manuscript, Florida State University, Center for the Study of Technology in Counseling and Career Development, Tallahassee. Retrieved from http://www.career.fsu.edu/documents/cognitive%20information%20processing/Key%20Elements.htm

Sampson, J. P., Jr., Reardon, R. C., Peterson, G. W., & Lenz, J. G. (2004). *Career counseling and services: A cognitive information processing approach.* Pacific Grove, CA: Brooks/Cole.

Sanford, E. E. (1995). Review of the Rokeach Values Scale. In J. C. Conoley & J. C. Impara (Eds.), *Twelfth mental measurements yearbook* (Vol. 334, pp. 879–880). Lincoln, NE: Buros Institute of Mental Measurements.

Schoenrade, P. (2002). Review of the Values Scale. In J. T. Kapes & E. A. Whitfield (Eds.), *A counselor's guide to career assessment instruments* (4th ed., pp. 298–302). Alexandria, VA: National Career Development Association.

Schraw, G. (2001). Review of the Student Styled Questionnaire™. In B. S. Plake & J. C. Impara (Eds.), *Fourteenth mental measurements yearbook* (Vol. 375, pp. 1197–1199). Lincoln, NE: Buros Institute of Mental Measurements.

Sharf, R. (2009). *Applying career development theory to counseling* (5th ed.). Pacific Grove, CA: Brooks/Cole.

Sigma Assessment Systems. (2011). *NEO Personality Inventory—Revised.* Retrieved from http://www.sigmaassessmentssystems.com/assessments/neopi3.asp

Suinn, R. M., Rickard-Figueroa, K., Lew, S., & Virgil, P. (1987). The Suinn-Lew Asian Self-Identity Acculturation Scale: An initial report. *Educational and Psychological Measurement, 47,* 401–407.

Super, D. E., & Osborne, W. L. (1992). Developmental career assessment and counseling: The C-DAC model. *Journal of Counseling & Development, 71,* 74–83.

Thompson, J. M., & Blain, M. D. (1992). Presenting feedback on the Minnesota Importance Questionnaire and the Minnesota Satisfaction Questionnaire. *Career Development Quarterly, 41,* 62–66.

U.S. Department of Labor. (1991). *Dictionary of occupational titles* (4th ed., revised; Stock No. 1191-295-302). Washington, DC: U.S. Government Printing Office.

U.S. Department of Labor. Bureau of Labor Statistics. (1949). *Occupational outlook handbook.* Washington, DC: U.S. Government Printing Office.

U.S. Military Entrance Processing Command. (2002). *ASVAB Student & Parent Guide*. North Chicago, IL: Author.

Walsh, B. D. (1995). The Career Beliefs Inventory: A review and critique. *Measurement and Evaluation in Counseling and Development, 28*, 61–62.

Wang, L. (2002). Differential Aptitude Test. In J. T. Kapes & E. A. Whitfield (Eds.), *A counselor's guide to career assessment instruments* (4th ed., pp. 123–131). Alexandria, VA: National Career Development Association.

Wickwire, P. N. (2002). COPSystem. In J. T. Kapes & E. A. Whitfield (Eds.), *A counselor's guide to career assessment instruments* (4th ed., pp. 210–217). Alexandria, VA: National Career Development Association.

Worthen, B. R., White, K. R., Fan, X., & Sudweeks, R. R. (1999). *Measurement and assessment in schools* (2nd ed.). New York, NY: Longman.

Zachar, P. (1998). Review of the Jackson Personality Inventory—Revised. In B. S. Plake & J. C. Impara (Eds.), *Thirteenth mental measurements yearbook* (Vol. 162, pp. 555–561). Lincoln, NE: Buros Institute of Mental Measurements.

Zunker, V. G., & Osborn, D. S. (2005). *Using assessment results for career counseling* (7th ed.). Pacific Grove, CA: Brooks/Cole.

Zytowski, D. G. (2006). *Super's Work Values Inventory—Revised: Technical manual version 1.1*. Adele, IA: Kuder.

CHAPTER 7

# Using Information and Technology

Brian Hutchison, Mark D. Stauffer, and Deborah P. Bloch

## Contents

On October 4, 1957, the Soviet Union launched a metal sphere measuring 23 inches in diameter and weighing 185 pounds into low Earth orbit. The sphere housed a radio transmitter that sent signal pulses back to Earth for 22 days, where scientists received them. These pulses were used to measure density and other atmospheric attributes (Gaddis, 2005). This technological event marked not only significant scientific, geopolitical, and social change but also the advent of the technology-based career development and intervention paradigms seen at the dawn of the 21st century.

The reader might wonder why initial space exploration a half century ago affects today's career counselor. In response to the Sputnik launch, the United States embarked on a competitive period of significant innovation and development (e.g., the space race). Concomitant with a focus on technology was the investment in career development and education via the National Defense Education Act of 1958 (National Defense of Education Act of 1958, P.L. 85-864, § 72 Stat. 1580). Although the primary purpose of this bill was to encourage interest in mathematics and science careers, the law provided the focus and funding necessary for the development of counselor education programs and an employment market that matured into the career counseling profession of today (Hutchison, Niles, & Trusty, 2008).

In many ways, the profession of career development and counseling has marched in lockstep with the late 20th- and early 21st-century technology boom. This trend is seen in the use of early mainframe computer technology for the development of computer-assisted career guidance systems in the 1960s and 1970s, the proliferation of Internet-based career information delivery systems (CIDS) in the 1990s and early 2000s, and the current innovative use of synchronous technologies such as chats and social media to deliver counseling interventions. The speed with which innovation and change occur provides a challenge to both the readers and writers of this chapter; how does one effectively keep abreast of available technology tools while making decisions that best benefit clients?

In this chapter, we provide an answer to this essential question. First, we explore the relationship between a client and technology systems as it influences the efficacy of career counseling interventions. Second, we describe the implications this relationship has for an individual counselor's choices when incorporating technology into the practice of counseling. Third, we provide a comprehensive overview of Internet-based CIDS, which currently serve as the backbone of systematic, comprehensive career development programs in the United States. Finally, we turn to the search for employment with a discussion of how using technology can enhance the job search. This section includes suggestions for effectively using job search Web sites and creating an electronic résumé. In the end, we hope that readers will be prepared with a foundation to ethically explore, choose, and incorporate technology into their career practice.

## Working With a Client's Unique Relationship With Technology

The role of the career counselor is to open the world and its connections through career information. Opening connections means helping clients make sense of the ever-changing dynamics of the world. Too often clients see themselves as isolated. Sometimes they have a sense of connection to a family or community and to a particular occupation, employer, or industry. However, opening various connections in the world means enabling clients to look at career information in its broadest sense—from specific job descriptions to an understanding of how they are a gift to the world of work.

## Understanding a Client's Relationship to Technology

Adept counselors apply interventions that are personally and culturally appropriate for clients (Sue, Arredondo, & McDavis, 1992). This is true not only in cross-cultural mental health counseling, but also when using career information and technology as part of an intervention strategy. Career counselors explore important questions about clients' relationship to career information and technology. Do they have access to the Internet from a home-based computer? What level of acceptance or resistance to various technologies do they experience? Do they feel the need to print something out rather than read it online? Do they have a mobile Internet device? What is the quality, not just the quantity, of digital media use? Do they enjoy social networking sites related to career (e.g., LinkedIn)? Such questions relate directly to the lived experiences and culture of the client.

## Access, Literacy, and Use Patterns

A counselor will work with a client base that represents a spectrum of digital literacy, access, and use patterns. For example, one client may be skilled in Web site construction and may know how to share a résumé over the Internet using a Blackberry, whereas the next may prefer to call job prospects found in the local print newspaper from a land-line phone. Counselors need to help clients land jobs, make network connections, and disseminate important career information with those who are markedly different in their approach to and use of information and technology. Skilled counselors not only prepare for differences in client use of career information and technology but also assess for these differences using formal or informal assessment. Assessment may occur as part of an intake or include a more comprehensive format.

### Digital Literacy

One way to understand clients' relationship to technology is to examine their digital literacy.

> Digital literacy has been variously defined in the literature, but all definitions agree that it is more than the ability to read and write. Students [clients] must be able to gather information from any format and, more importantly, make sense of that information, use it, and communicate it to others. (Stripling, 2010, p. 16)

As an example, to explore the concrete meaning of digital literacy, we examined the University of Washington's Health Services self-assessment tool (Revere, D., 2005. Unpublished instrument. Digital literacy self-assessment: University of Washington. Retrieved from http://courses.washington.edu/hsstudev/studev/self-assess.html). It divides digital literacy into the following categories:

1. General computer knowledge (e.g., mouse drag and drop)
2. File management knowledge (e.g., saving files, unzipping files)
3. System maintenance and security (e.g., adding hardware to a computer, creating a backup, Internet security)
4. Word processing skills (e.g., creating a table, using a spellchecker, using "save as")
5. Communications skills (e.g., attaching documents to e-mail, using electronic mailing lists, asynchronous and synchronous conferencing)

6. Web skills (e.g., using a search engine, bookmarking sites, saving material from the Web)
7. Databases, searching, and information integrity (e.g., searching large databases, evaluating the validity of Web material)
8. Spreadsheets (e.g., sorting columns, using autosum)
9. Presentation skills (e.g., using design templates, creating slides).

## Digital Access

A client may be literate in digital media but lack access. Digital access concerns ownership of hardware and software but also relates to items such as download speeds and how up-to-date one's hardware and software are. For example, consider these three combinations and how they affect the ability to access career-related searches and perform job exploration: (1) 5-year-old desktop computer hardware and software on dial-up Internet service; (2) 2-year-old desktop computer hardware, new computer software, and high-speed Internet; and (3) high-end new laptop computer with 4G wireless Internet connection in an urban setting. One must also consider that with the advent of Internet- and multimedia-enabled smartphones (e.g., iPhone, Droid), the many barriers between information systems and communication technologies can be negligible with the right access hardware and software.

Privileges such as access have costs. A counselor will want to know what the true cost to a client is, as well as ways to increase access with fewer costs. For example, it is important to note what community resources are available, such as public-access technology available at the local library (Bertot, 2009). The process of obtaining access may also incur time costs to a client. Furthermore, the cost of access relates to a client's ability to upgrade technology to be current with changing trends and advances.

### SIDEBAR 7.1  Assessing Clients' Digital Access and Literacy

As an experiment, use a search engine (i.e., Google, Yahoo) to find and examine career counseling intake forms at career counseling Web sites (e.g., enter "career counseling intake form"). Do intake forms assess for digital literacy, access, and preferences? You may find that many have no simple questions related to clients' access (e.g., do you have regular access to a computer or Internet?), let alone digital literacy or use patterns and preferences (e.g., do you prefer to be contacted by phone or e-mail?). What would you want to know about client use patterns, digital literacy, and access?

## Are There Generational Differences?

Age and generation may influence abilities, use patterns, and familiarity with various technologies. Some professional literature has echoed a commonly held belief that clients with exposure to computer and Internet advances during their formative developmental years have a different relationship to technology and are set apart from older generations in their experiences with technology. For example, Prensky (2001a, 2001b) suggested that those born after 1980 are "digital natives" and those born before this date are "digital immigrants." The idea is that those born after 1980 developed in an era with access to digital media and spent considerable time during their formative years exploring digital devices and media. Furthermore, Blowers (2010) commented, "Attitudes and perceptions related to digital privacy, identity, creativity, piracy, and advocacy also help to set younger generations apart" (p. 8).

Other literature has suggested that an emphasis on age and generational influences may be exaggerated or focused on the wrong variables (Brown & Czerniewicz, 2010; Salajan, Schonwetter, & Cleghorn, 2010). For example, when examining information and communication technology competency, Guo, Dobson, and Petrina (2008) suggested that "there was no statistically significant difference ... in scores between digital natives and digital immigrants" (p. 251). In many cases, other cultural factors (e.g., socioeconomic status, affluent nation status) will be more important in gauging digital literacy and access. As career counselors work with clientele from across the life span and from various cultures, they prepare for possibilities but assess for a client's unique relationship to career information systems and technology.

## Assessing and Working With Resistance

An emotional response to technology can hinder a client's career discovery process. Career counselors often need to explore acceptance of and resistance to using technology. The word *resistance* as used here differs from some clinical uses; resistance is not a marker of client stubbornness toward progress. Resistance may be a natural adaptive process or even neutral, neither good nor bad. Regardless, the career counselor works with resistance to encourage alliance and resolution. Safran and Muran (2000) suggested "allying with resistance" by framing resistance as an adaptive response to painful feelings (p. 26). Although Safran and Muran's suggestions were directed toward the psychotherapeutic process of alliance, the same concept applies to the career counselor. In this manner, a counselor creates a space to join clients in their struggle rather than challenging it as a client maladaptive response. A career counselor may want to first intervene in relation to resistance before beginning a new career information system or introducing career interventions using technology. For example, a counselor might validate and process a client's sense of feeling overwhelmed by Internet use before beginning Internet job-search strategies, or a counselor might normalize and investigate procrastination related to word processor use before formatting a résumé. Clients accept or resist new information systems and technology for various reasons (Kim & Kankanhalli, 2009; Lapointe & Rivard, 2005). For example, one early model, the technology acceptance model proposed by Davis (1989), suggested that perceived usefulness of a technology and a belief that a technology is easy to use influences intentions. The perceptive counselor will be aware of the possible causes of resistance and respond appropriately.

### SIDEBAR 7.2   Tips on Using This Material in Counseling

The adage suggests, practice breeds familiarity. Before working with clients, counselors-in-training should prepare by checking out the Web sites cited in this chapter. The material in this chapter is hard to integrate or use without exploring Internet resources, so consider exploring while reading this chapter. Here are a few tips to better integrate site-specific knowledge:

1. Consider reading through the section as a whole and then returning to the start of the section.
2. Then work at your computer, opening and exploring the sites as you read along.
3. Connect this exploration with your motivation to work with clients. Imagine how you might use each site with various clients.
4. Open a word-processing file into which you can copy the addresses or URLs of interesting sites and add notes.

Keep notes on specific sites for future counseling. For example, take notes on the level of assistance needed by clients to use a site, the site's appropriateness for specific cultural populations, or how a site addresses important career issues (e.g., job searches).

## Technology-Assisted Counseling

Counselor intentionality has been described as "acting with a sense of capability and deciding from a range of alternative actions" (Ivey, 1994, p. 11). Among the range of alternative actions from which a counselor may choose when working directly with clients are theoretical orientation, treatment planning options, in-session techniques, assessments, and out-of-session homework and tasks. In recent years, much attention has been given to the proliferation of technology as it affects each of these therapeutic choices. Specifically, the evolution of technology-assisted counseling options has led to a multitude of ethical considerations when working with clients who are not seated in the same room as their counselor during interventions. Given the depth and breadth of technological options available to a practicing counselor, it is imperative that decisions about the delivery of counseling services are approached with the same intentionality as other therapeutic choices (National Board for Certified Counselors [NBCC], 2007).

### Ethical Considerations

Ethical decisions are those made with a set of standards in mind (Remley & Herlihy, 2007). Counselors evaluate these judgments as good or bad for clients within the ethical codes of their professional organization (e.g., American Counseling Association, American Psychological Association, NBCC). Three tools that professional organizations use to communicate about ethical practice are taxonomies, written standards, and credentialing. A *taxonomy* is a system of classification used to differentiate between entities within a closed system. Standards are statements intended to delineate acceptable levels of practice within a system, including situation-specific behaviors. Credentialing is used to identify professional areas of competence and communicate this capability within the profession and to the general public (Remley & Herlihy). The NBCC provides guidance to counselors considering the use of technology as a primary means of service delivery from afar.

### Taxonomy of Counseling

Counseling is the "application of mental health, psychological, or human development principles, through cognitive, affective, behavioral, or systemic intervention strategies that address wellness, personal growth, or career development, as well as pathology" (NBCC, 2007, p. 1). Traditionally, counseling has been performed face-to-face with the client, couple, or group with whom a counselor is working. This face-to-face counseling remains the most common mode of intervention delivery.

Technology-assisted distance counseling (TDC) describes the provision of counseling services to individuals, couples, or groups from afar by using telephone, computer, and Internet technologies. Communication from afar can include what is read (text), what is heard (live or prerecorded audio), and what is seen and heard (via live or prerecorded video). The interaction process of counseling may be synchronous (little or no time delay between client and counselor responses) or asynchronous (a time delay between client and counselor responses). Synchronous methods of distance counseling include individual, couple, and group telecounseling (speaking via the telephone); individual, couple, and group chat-based counseling (reading text in real time using private Internet chat exchanges such as AOL Instant Messenger); and individual, couple, and group video-based Internet counseling (seeing and hearing in real time using private Internet video exchanges such as Skype). E-mail–based Internet counseling and podcasts (prerecorded video messages) are examples of asynchronous methods of distance counseling. Decisions regarding the use of TDC in practice are made after taking into consideration several factors, including counselor and client resources, client needs, client preparedness for interacting with the technology, and a review of ethical standards (NBCC, 2007).

## Standards for the Ethical Practice of Internet Counseling

Owing to the unique nature of Internet counseling, NBCC (2007) has published a standard of ethical practice as an addendum to its Code of Ethics. This set of standards is organized into three different areas for counselors to consider before embarking on the practice of this type of TDC. First, counselors must consider several aspects of the counseling relationship that differ from face-to-face delivery, including

1. Developing necessary protocols (such as code words or numbers) to confirm client identity and age of consent
2. Altering the content of the counseling orientation process to include procedures for contacting the counselor offline, alternative modes of communication in case of technology failure, the potential for misunderstanding when visual cues do not exist, and identifying local resources, including crisis hotlines
3. Meeting the obligation of a culturally competent counselor to make the client aware of free Internet access points within his or her community, to make the counselor's Web site barrier free to people with disabilities, and to make certain that the counselor is aware of clients' local cultural considerations, including language differences, time differences, cultural perspectives, and environmental factors.

As the first point suggests, the assurance of client confidentiality while conducting Internet-based counseling presents unique challenges. This assurance is addressed in the NBCC standards with instructions for counselors to (a) inform clients of encryption methods used to ensure confidentiality and security of information, and (b) inform clients about the storage of session data (text, audio, and video), including where and how long it will be retained. In particular, describing procedures for ensuring the confidentiality and sharing of e-mail data is important.

Finally, the standards address legal and ethical considerations specific to the practice of Internet counseling, including a thorough review of ethical codes and pertinent state or federal laws. Included in these standards is the necessity for Internet-based counselors to post hyperlinks to professional bodies for all licenses and certifications.

## Credentialing for Distance Counselors

The Center for Credentialing and Education, Inc. (http://www.cce-global.org/home), is an affiliate organization of the NBCC that provides a variety of counseling and education credentialing services. Counselors who have a master's degree in counseling or a related field and are licensed to practice in their state or country are eligible to become certified as a distance credentialed counselor after completing a 15-hour training program. Distance credentialed counselors are trained in best practices of technology-assisted methods to include telecounseling, secure e-mail counseling, chat, videoconferencing, and the use of stand-alone distance counseling software programs.

### SIDEBAR 7.3   Casey Decides to Go Virtual

Casey works as a career counselor for the Continuing Education Unit at State University. Recently, State University established a relationship with the State System of Prisons to provide access to bachelor's-level online and distance courses for incarcerated people. Students in the academic unit, the faculty, and staff ask Casey to lead the effort to provide the same level of career development and counseling interventions as for traditional students. Casey meets with the representatives from the State System of Prisons, and they agree that telecounseling is the best modality of service delivery given the resources available.

Using the NBCC ethical guidelines, Casey completes an array of tasks before meeting with her clients via telephone for the first time. These include

1. Visiting with prison officials to identify rooms from which clients may speak on the telephone in private (ensuring confidentiality), ensuring that the correct client is provided access to the dedicated counseling line at the time of his or her appointment (ensuring client identity), and confirming that the dedicated counseling line is not recorded or monitored by prison officials (ensuring data security)
2. Developing an informed consent based on the TDC ethical guidelines developed by NBCC
3. Successfully completing the 2-day distance credentialed counselor training.

It is almost 4:00 p.m.; time for her first telecounseling appointment!

## Evaluating and Choosing Technology for a Counseling Practice

Just as face-to-face counseling choices are made within ethical paradigms in response to client needs, counselors make decisions about TDC in response to client needs or concerns. Distance counseling may be considered as a supplement to or replacement for face-to-face counseling depending on the circumstances that precipitate the choice. TDC may be used to bridge gaps between sessions caused by client or counselor travel, geographic relocation, transportation interruption, or any other acute impediment to the delivery of services. Longer term TDC may provide access to services for populations who otherwise might not be able to participate in counseling. Examples include providing counseling to second-, third-, or swing shift employees who cannot attend sessions during business hours, incarcerated clients, clients who work or attend school abroad, and clients isolated because of travel or geographic restrictions, to name a few.

If the need is present, the counselor is then responsible for making decisions regarding the type of counseling offered, the technology tools used, the security of information and data, and the explanation of these processes to the client. Please see Sidebar 7.4 for a framework one might use to make decisions about technology-assisted counseling.

### SIDEBAR 7.4  Evaluating Technology Needs

It is inevitable that you will incorporate technology into your career counseling practice. The pragmatic, and ethical, question for you as a counselor is, "How do I choose the technology I use in my practice?" There are several pertinent questions to consider when making technology choices. These can be framed into four distinct categories of inquiry:

1. What is purpose of new technology within the scope of my practice?
   - What client needs might be enhanced by incorporating technology?
   - What unmet client needs would be addressed by incorporating technology?
   - How would the technology affect the scope, size, and nature of my practice?
2. How do I prepare to incorporate new technology into my practice?
   - What technology do I use to meet the needs identified in Question 1?
   - What technology resources (e.g., servers, encryption, expertise) are needed to implement the technology?
   - Will I use synchronous or asynchronous methods to best meet my clients' needs?
   - What technical training do I need to use the technology?
   - What credentialing do I need to use the new technology ethically?
3. How do I prepare my clients for the use of the new technology?
   - What are the needs of my clients and market that will be met by the technology?
   - How can I learn about my clients' preparedness for interacting with the technology?
   - How will I introduce and orient my clients to the technology?
4. How will I achieve a personal touch while using the technology?
   - How do I ensure client identity, consent, and confidentiality during counseling?
   - How do I connect with each client on a personal level in my practice?
   - How do I establish rapport and ensure a working alliance during my practice?

## Career Information Systems

In this portion of the chapter, we identify major organized systems for providing career information. Counselors will often find themselves recommending these systems and working with clients to maximize their effectiveness in meeting client needs. An organized system for providing career information includes one or more of these major elements:

- Occupational descriptions and one or more methods for sorting and searching the descriptions

- Information about educational programs and institutions with one or more methods for sorting and searching the information
- One or more instruments for identifying individual interests, skills, or values and relating these to occupational and educational information
- Links among those major elements of the system as well as links between the files within the elements.

Comprehensive systems include all of these elements. Historically, two terms have been used to describe comprehensive systems: *career information delivery systems* and *computer-assisted career guidance systems.* Although the origin of the two terms may be of interest to historians of the field, suffice it to say they are now used interchangeably. For consistency in this chapter, we use the term CIDS.

We first describe CIDS, then systems that provide only occupational information or only educational information. CIDS, themselves, fall into two groups—those offered nationally and those available in particular states or other locales. In other words, after a discussion of the research and evaluation data on CIDS, we describe the potentially confusing mix of systems in this order: national CIDS, state-based CIDS, occupational information systems, and educational information systems.

## Evaluation of CIDS

The National Career Development Association (NCDA) has developed *Guidelines for the Preparation and Evaluation of Career and Occupational Information Literature* (NCDA, 1991), *Guidelines for the Preparation and Evaluation of Video Career Media* (NCDA, 1992), and *Guidelines for the Use of the Internet for Provision of Career Information and Planning Services* (NCDA, 1997). All of these are available on the NCDA Web site (http://associationda tabase.com/aws/NCDA/pt/sp/guidelines). Other organizations have provided ratings of systems from time to time. For example, the *Career Planning and Adult Development Journal* published a special issue, "Using the Internet for Career Development," under the editorship of Hohenshil and Brott in 2002.

However, the professional association that has made the provision of career information its primary business is the Association of Computer-based Systems for Career Information (ACSCI). In 2002, ACSCI published its *Standards Implementation Handbook.* This handbook is in its fourth edition, replacing the standards that originated in 1981 and were revised in 1982 and 1999. These changes reflect both continuity and change—continuity of efforts to explain what is meant by a high-quality CIDS and change that reflects new technology and a growth in the user base for career information.

The standards are organized into four major groups.

1. Core standards apply to all career information products and services. They include the requirements for information, delivery, support, evaluation, disclosure, and confidentiality.

2. Component standards are used to assess the components of a particular system. They include the requirements for assessment, search and sorting, career planning and management, occupational information, industry information, education and training information, financial aid information, and job search information.
3. Integration standards apply to systems with multiple components and include integrity, transparency, and integration of the relationships among components.
4. Comprehensive system standards, or standards for CIDS as defined earlier in this chapter, include requirements for accessibility, privacy and confidentiality, services and support, localization of key information, feedback and evaluation, and accountability.

The standards and checklists for assessing a system are provided in print or online by ACSCI (http://www.acsci.org/standards.asp).

#### SIDEBAR 7.5   Evaluating CIDS

One reaction to the section you are about to read may be "Wow! There are a lot of CIDS on the Internet." As discussed earlier in this chapter, it is imperative that you, the counselor, consider legal and ethical issues and issues of utility when choosing to refer clients to a CIDS. While reviewing CIDS before referring clients to them, keep the following in mind:

1. What client needs am I meeting with my choice of CIDS?
2. Do the research evidence, theoretical perspective, and norm populations meet the needs of my clients?
3. How user friendly is the CIDS for my clients?
   • Are the language, age, and education level appropriate?
   • Does the means of communicating information fit your clients' needs (e.g., text vs. video, static vs. interactive)?
   • Can my clients navigate the system efficiently?
   • Does the system include occupational information about jobs that my clients may desire (e.g., industry, educational preparation, social class)?
4. Does the cost of the CIDS facilitate its use with your clients?

## National CIDS

In writing about resources, particularly electronic resources, there is always a danger that one will inadvertently omit a valuable resource.

We provide a review of these national CIDS:

■ Career Cruising (http://www.careercruising.com)
■ CIS (http://cis.uoregon.edu), available from Into Careers at the University of Oregon
■ COIN Educational Products (http://www.coin3.com)
■ DISCOVER (http://www.act.org/discover), available from ACT
■ eChoices (http://www.echoices.com), available from Bridges.com
■ Keys2Work (http://www.keys2work.com)
■ SIGI PLUS (http://www.ets.org/sigi), available from the Educational Testing Service.

Many of the national CIDS offer a variety of products and modes of delivery, including both Internet-based and CD-ROM systems. One can expect that as technology changes, so will the systems. However, what is at the heart of the systems is not their technology, but what they include.

Occupational information includes a description of the occupation, characteristics of the work being performed, levels of skills and knowledge required, physical demands, entry requirements, wage information, and anticipated demand for the occupation. Educational information includes descriptions of postsecondary educational programs and descriptions of educational institutions that provide the programs. The postsecondary institutions include public and private colleges and universities and, sometimes, technical schools, career schools, and trade schools. Educational institution information usually includes the characteristics that prospective students most often consider important in choosing a place to study, but minimally it includes the location, Web site, and contact person (ACSCI, 2002). Many CIDS also provide information on financial aid, including not only general information on federal assistance but also the specifics of scholarship requirements and grants.

CIDS offer much more than data banks of information. All of the CIDS listed provide methods for self-exploration and for linking self-exploration to lists of occupations. Within occupational information, the systems provide links that allow clients to identify related occupations. In addition, the systems provide for seamless movement from occupational information to educational information. The information and self-exploration can prove useful in many types of phase transitions. The needs at the transition phase from school to additional schooling or work are obvious. In addition, CIDS can prove useful for adults in transition from one occupation to another. CIDS can be used to identify occupations that require skills developed in one job that can be used in another. The occupational descriptions of CIDS can also be used to power a résumé with terms appropriate to a new occupation.

The original CIDS began with the needs of high school students in mind. However, with the growth in technological capacity and the pervasiveness of computers, CIDS have expanded their base. Some CIDS now offer modules that focus on the needs of younger students and decisions they must make about skills improvement. Other CIDS offer modules that can be tailored to the needs of business organizations for the development of career ladders and succession planning.

Although all CIDS offer the same general sorts of information, they differ greatly in how they present the information and in the types of self-exploration and searches they provide. In comparing CIDS, a counselor will notice variety in the number of occupations described. In general, this variety reflects a conscious decision regarding the level of detail appropriate to the audience. All CIDS attempt to capture the complete occupational structure of the United States. However, they differ in how they cluster and describe occupations. In addition, CIDS may offer special features such as files on entrepreneurship, Holland-code–related self-exploration, values-based self-exploration, military occupational information, and more. In selecting a CID, the counselor first needs to consider the nature and needs of the intended audience, the amount of time needed to move meaningfully through the modules in relation to the time generally available online, and the methods of delivery available in relation to the equipment and culture of the organization. In addition, the accuracy and comprehensiveness of the information needs to be evaluated. Some suggestions for information sources related to CIDS evaluation and research are presented in the last section of this chapter. Among these, the ACSCI (2002) standards are particularly important in evaluating the comprehensiveness, accuracy, and development of a CIDS. All of the CIDS listed earlier allow for an online tour, provide temporary passwords for full exploration of their systems, or both. CIDS are generally licensed to sites, although some may allow subscriptions by individual users, and some national CIDS are also used as the basis for state-based systems.

## State-Based CIDS

State-based CIDS have all the general information, self-exploration characteristics, and linkage characteristics as described for the national systems. They therefore have the same utility in working with clients. However, the state-based systems generally provide a deeper level of local data than the national systems. State-based systems provide wage and employment outlook information that is accurate for their state and often for regions within the state. Similarly, education information on institutions, programs of study, and financial aid within the state may be more detailed than in the national CIDS. In addition, state-based systems often provide information about employers and local job and training opportunities. Both state-based and national CIDS are responsible for collecting and presenting information with rigor, accuracy, and comprehensiveness.

A look at the sites on which state-based CIDS are offered shows the growth of the systems since their original use in high schools. The types of sites listed by the CIDS responding to the ACSCI survey include

- Elementary and junior high–middle schools
- Two- and 4-year colleges and universities
- Employment services offices
- Correctional institutions
- Rehabilitation agencies
- Counseling agencies
- Military bases
- Public libraries
- Private businesses.

In addition, state-based CIDS usually provide training customized to audiences, such as displaced worker programs, vocational rehabilitation programs, job centers, and equity programs. A number of CIDS offer newsletters or career tabloids on their sites.

State-based CIDS, like national CIDS, are in a state of perpetual development. The information with the systems is itself dynamic. Maintaining up-to-date information is the most important aspect of change. On a larger scale, technological advances, demands from existing and new audiences, and funding opportunities (or the lack thereof) lead to changes in delivery modes and design. Nevertheless, one should not expect that the turnaround time for changes in design is like that between new models of a laptop. Given the importance of the information and the need to validate any self-assessment changes, both national and state-based CIDS require adequate time for design and testing before changes can be implemented.

State-based CIDS generally license the systems to sites within the state. The costs vary with the nature of the funding for the CIDS. ACSCI (http://www.acsci.org/acsci_states.asp) is a good source of information as to whether your state has a CIDS.

## Occupational Information Systems

Unlike comprehensive CIDS, occupational information systems offer information, as their name suggests, only on occupations. However, that is not a limitation, but an increase in specialization. We discuss three government systems: O*NET, the *Occupational Outlook Handbook,* and the *Career Guide to Industries,* as well as one proprietary system from ERI Economic Research Institute.

### O*NET

O*NET (http://online.onetcenter.org), perhaps the most comprehensive source of occupational information, has been developed and is offered by the U.S. federal government online and at no cost to individuals and organizations. In fact, many of the CIDS described earlier use O*NET information either as the basis for their career information or as one element of their research. All one need do is go to the Web site. O*NET allows the client to access a searchable database of occupations using keywords, ordinary language, O*NET-SOC code numbers, job families, or the complete list of occupations included in the database. If you or the client have found occupations using another classification system, such as Military Occupational Classifications, you can use a cross-search tool to find matching O*NET occupations.

The O*NET occupational database has information on more than 900 occupations. For each occupation, information is provided on

- Tasks
- Knowledge
- Skills
- Work activities
- Work context
- Interests
- Work values
- Related occupations
- Job zones.

Interests are described in terms of Holland codes. *Job zones* refers to a method of grouping occupations by the level of overall experience, job training, and education required. There are five job zones, with Zone 5 requiring the highest levels. The work values are directly related to the Work Importance Locator. At the end of the description, a Wages and Employment link takes the client to a pull-down menu of states and, from there, to state information. All of this information is provided by selecting "Summary" under the "Reports" heading next to the list of relevant occupational titles. Summary is generally the most useful tool in working with clients. Selecting "Details" will, as the name suggests, give details, that is, numeric information related to each of the items under Summary. Selecting "Custom" allows the user to preset the levels for information that will be displayed. The Details and Custom reports are more useful to analysts or system developers than to individual counselors

The same Web page also takes the client to the skills search (http://online .onetcenter.org/gen_skills_page). By answering questions in one or more of six broad skills areas, the client will generate a list of occupations. The six skill areas are basic skills, social skills, complex problem-solving skills, technical skills, system skills, and resource management skills. The online directions suggest that the client begin by selecting one or more skill groups. Then, within the skill group or groups, the client is advised to select as many skills as he or she has or plans to acquire. In general, the fewer the skills selected, the larger the number of occupations that will be generated. The selected skills are compared with skill ratings for each occupation. If a selected skill is rated "very important" for a particular occupation, it is considered a match. "Very important" includes skills rated 69 or higher on a standardized scale. Occupations matching all the selected skills are shown first, followed by those matching all but one of the selected skills, and so on. Within these groupings, occupations are subgrouped by job zones.

O\*NET offers two other tools for searching the database of occupations. These are also offered without cost but they must be downloaded and unzipped to make them usable. At the top of the O\*NET site (http://www.onetcenter .org/tools.html) is a selection menu. From this menu, the Computerized Interest Profiler and the Work Importance Locator can be downloaded. The Computerized Interest Profiler uses the Holland hexagon system of realistic, investigative, artistic, social, enterprising, and conventional. The client is presented with a series of work activities. For each one, he or she must choose "like," "dislike," or "uncertain." On completion, a list of occupations for exploration is generated. The Work Importance Locator is based on the client's ranking of how important various values are to him or her on the job. The items refer, for example, to the desire to be busy all the time, to have fair supervision, to be innovative, to get steady employment, and to be recognized for one's achievement. The questions relate to six groups of values:

1. Achievement
2. Independence

3. Recognition
4. Relationships
5. Support
6 Working conditions.

On completion of the Work Importance Locator, a list of occupations for exploration is provided.

O\*NET provides the counselor with an ever-increasing array of tools and information. From the O\*NET home page, the counselor can go the Job Accommodation Network or the Searchable Online Accommodation Resource for assistance with working with clients who have a health problem or disability. A link to Career OneStop (http://www.careeronestop.org) provides services to job seekers such as a résumé posting service and services to employers such as a job posting service and links to America's Job Bank (http://www.ajb.org). America's Job Bank, a cooperative venture of the U.S. Department of Labor and state-operated public employment services, allows the client to search for job openings by category of work or job title and location, even down to zip code. USAJOBS (http://www.usajobs.opm.gov) offers searchable information on jobs in the federal government. In addition, the O\*NET database is now available in Spanish and can be requested directly from O\*NET or through its parent governmental agency. O\*NET is developed and supported by the U.S. Department of Labor's Employment and Training Administration (http://www.doleta.gov).

It is impossible to capture the myriad services offered by O\*NET. The counselor is urged to go to the site and begin exploring. We suggest that the counselor first explore the occupational information database and its search tools. The database will be useful to some clients, but many may find it overwhelming. Counselors need excellent facilitation skills as well as complete familiarity with the system. Although this is true of the use of all information, it is particularly true of O\*NET because of its complexity. An ancillary site to O\*NET (http://www.workforceaguirre.org) provides downloadable documents to help counselors use O\*NET. The O\*NET Online Desk Aid, a two-sided card that provides an overview of all the features and links, is recommended.

### Occupational Outlook Handbook

The *Occupational Outlook Handbook* (http://www.bls.gov/oco) is provided by the Bureau of Labor Statistics of the U.S. Department of Labor. The *Occupational Outlook Handbook* has been used for many years, predating the Internet, and many publishers have sold the *Occupational Outlook Handbook*, printing the information provided by the Bureau of Labor Statistics.

The *Occupational Outlook Handbook* contains narrative descriptions of approximately 275 occupational groups, including descriptions of what workers do on the job, working conditions, the training and education needed, earnings, expected job prospects, and sources of additional information in a wide range of occupations.

and off campus and employers offering jobs and internships. Subscribing colleges provide passwords to their students and alumni to use this site.

Another specialized job search site is IMDiversity.com (http://www.imdiversity.com). As its name suggests, it provides job search information and résumé posting services with particular emphasis on serving the needs of historically underrepresented populations, specifically, as stated on its Web site, "African Americans, Asian Americans, Hispanic Americans, Native Americans and Women." The Web site was founded by the *Black Collegian,* a magazine that has operated since 1970 to provide African American college students with information on career and job opportunities. The goals of IMDiversity are to provide access to a database of employers committed to workplace diversity and to help its users find jobs and the tools and information needed for job success. In addition, the Web site offers information specific to the needs of its targeted groups.

## Using Corporate Web Sites for Career Information

Corporate Web sites represent a focused and direct means of connecting to organizations that are currently hiring. They provide a level of specificity that is not available in any of the CIDS or specialized occupational information systems. In addition to looking at job listings on an Internet site created for that purpose, clients can also get information about organizations in general and, sometimes, about job vacancies by going directly to a company's Web site. Most companies, not-for-profit agencies, and government organizations have home pages on the World Wide Web. Web addresses are often part of companies' advertisements, or they can be found through Google or other search engines.

The information about an organization can be used in the job search in three ways. First, many companies now list their vacancies directly on their Web sites. Second, information about a company's direction and its products and services can be used in tailoring resumes and in planning for interviews. Finally, information about a company's mission and values, as stated on its Web site, can be used to assess the likelihood of finding harmony or a good fit between the client and the prospective employer.

Counselors can use Internet sites to help clients reach the person in the organization who can advance their chances of success in the hiring process. Once the counselor or the client has found the Web site, the counselor can help the client look for a link to company or organization news, which may include articles written about the company and published in newspapers, magazines, trade journals, and the like. The client can now use the Find command in the Edit menu of his or her Internet browser. Searching for words such as *said, commented,* and *noted,* the client will find the names, and often the titles or positions, of key people in the organization. The client may want to e-mail, telephone, or write to that person. Given the ever-present possibility of transitions, it is important that counselors teach their clients these skills rather than executing the searches themselves.

To help clients prepare for an interview, the counselor can ask them to go to the Web site of the organization for which they will interview. Once there, he or she can help them look at the listing for the specific job, if posted, and help them look beyond the listings. Look for publicity releases and news items, which often give clues as to directions the company plans to take or to problems they have solved. Look at mission statements or other general information. All of these are clues to what the company hopes to accomplish. They are also clues as to what clients can stress about the match between their backgrounds and an organization's needs.

Clients can use online indexes to newspapers such as the *New York Times* or the *San Jose Mercury News* and others to search for articles about the organization. The company's Web site will have only the information the company chooses to put there. News articles may present more objective information, both favorable and unfavorable, and information about changes in the organization that the company did not include in its Web site. Look for information about the industry as a whole and the company's competitors as well. The more prepared clients are with information, the better they can respond to the questions that will be asked.

Finally, counselors and clients can use online newsgroups and blogs to get the unofficial news, the "virtual water cooler" gossip about organizations. Because there are no organizational filters on the information, the material found through newsgroups may be more or less accurate than information from other sources. For this reason, counselors and their clients will need to exercise more caution in using newsgroup information. The purpose behind all of this searching is threefold: First, to ascertain whether this is an organization for which the client will want to work; second, to prepare the résumé and prepare for the interview in a way that shows a client's responsiveness to the organizational needs and requirements; and finally to identify organizations that need the client's skills but may not have posted or advertised a job.

### SIDEBAR 7.6  Tips for Organizing Your Online Job Search

Let's face it, organizing your online Web site visits during a job search can be daunting. An extended employment search may require the future employee to visit more than 100 sites in total, many of them multiple times a week. One way to make this task more manageable is to organize your online work before you get started using the bookmark function on your Internet browser. (The name of this function may vary depending upon the Internet browser software that you use. This sidebar uses the word "bookmark," which is the language used when exploring with the software Mozilla FireFox. Another example is "Favorite," the language used by Internet Explorer.) Follow these simple steps to make your job search more organized:

1. On a piece of paper, list the types of Web sites you think you will visit during your job search. These sites might include newspapers, career sites such as Monster.com, blogs, professional and social networking pages, corporate sites, and more. Beside each site, write the optimal number of times you will visit each type of site every week during your search.
2. Open your Internet browser and select the bookmarks option from your toolbar.
3. Select the "organize bookmarks" option from this menu. Using "organize bookmarks," you can create file folders to organize your Web pages.
4. Create a main folder titled "job search." In this folder, create seven subfolders, one for each day of the week (e.g., Monday).
5. When you identify a Web site you want to visit more often in your job search, simply select "Bookmark this page" from the bookmarks menu, and then save it in one or more day-of-the-week

folders depending on the type of site it is (see your original list). *Hint:* You can bookmark the same page in multiple folders so you visit it more often than once per week.

6. Each day of the week, simply go to your bookmark folder for that day and check in on updates in an organized, and less stressful, way.

7. Be prepared each day to capture and respond to new information as it is posted (e.g., new job posting, networking with a new contact).

## Using Technology to Respond to Résumé Requests

Whether responding to job postings on Internet sites or those that are found in newspapers and other traditional sources, more and more potential employers ask for faxed or e-mailed résumés. In this section, we examine four ways, other than mailing a printed copy, in which technology can be used to compile and submit a résumé.

### Creating a Scannable Résumé

Printed documents, such as a résumé, are easily converted into electronic computer files using a scanner. After the document image is read into the computer, optical character recognition software looks at the image and translates what it sees into letters and numbers. Additional software is then used to identify important information such as the client's name and address, work history, experience, skills, and key experiences.

Although more efficient than reading through a stack of resumes, optical character recognition software is imperfect, or perhaps too perfect. When the software is looking for perfect matches between the images being supplied and letters and numbers, it can only translate what it sees with the set of characters it has been given. If it has been given asterisks, for example, and the client uses bullets to highlight different responsibilities, the software, unlike a human, cannot think, "Oh yes, this person has used bullets." Instead, it will try to match the bullets with some character, perhaps periods, thereby creating strange sentences. Furthermore, it may not recognize or be able to translate italics or underlining, parentheses may be misinterpreted as part of the letter they adjoin or as some other symbol, smudges may become characters, and broken letters may be omitted altogether.

Once the résumé has been scanned, other software is used to place it in the potential employer's database and then to search it for the key words that the employer has identified for the job under consideration. Although a number of different programs for scanning and searching are available, the rules to increase the chances of being selected for the next step in the review process are generally the same.

The rules for creating a scannable résumé, then, are fairly simple. In fact, that is the rule: Keep it simple. Here are eight pointers to share with clients.

1. Use white, 8.5-inch × 11-inch paper, printed on one side only.
2. Use a standard font such as Arial, Optima, Universe, Times New Roman, or Courier in 12-point typeface. Do not condense or expand the type.

3. Avoid all fancy type—no italics, underlining, boxes, graphics, bullets, or columns. Do use capital letters and line spacing to help organize your résumé.
4. Be sure to put each of the following on separate lines: name, address, phone number, fax number, and e-mail address. Put only your name at the top of each additional page.
5. Use a structured résumé format, with clear headings.
6. Increase your use of key words, particularly nouns and industry jargon, to increase your chances that the key word search will select your résumé.
7. Be sure to print your résumé on a laser or ink jet printer. Dot matrix print and less-than-perfect photocopies do not scan well.
8. Do not staple or fold your résumé. Either of these can make marks that will confuse the optical character recognition software. Mail it in a large-enough protective envelope.

### Sending a Résumé by E-Mail

Employers in every field, not just those in high-tech industries, are asking for e-mailed résumés. Using e-mail has probably made counselors and clients aware of the limited ability to format the material they are sending. In addition, depending on the other party's software, an e-mail may arrive with even less style than it had originally. Although communication by e-mail improves almost daily, it is still difficult to know how well the text that is sent will resemble the text that is received. Very often, the first screen of an e-mail is taken up by the header that contains a raft of information about the machine-to-machine transmission of the letter. If the client sends a résumé in an e-mail, the only thing the employer may receive on the first screen will be the person's name. In addition, employers who want to print the résumé or store it in a database must find where it begins and separate that from the unneeded header.

The client can exercise some control over the appearance of the e-mailed résumé by sending it as an attachment to the e-mail rather than as a part of the e-mail itself. Because there is no way of knowing which word processing program the potential employer has, the best way to ensure compatibility of sending and receiving is to send the résumé as a PDF (Portable Document Format) file. PDF creates a representation of a document that is viewable independent of specific computer software or hardware, although an open-source program (downloadable from the Internet) is needed to open and view the document.

PDF files are simple images of the document, capturing the document as saved at the time it is made into a .pdf file.

### Using a Web-Based Résumé Listing Service

The Web sites identified in this section of the chapter—Monster.com, Hotjobs.com, Monstertrak.com, and IMDiversity.com—provide structures for posting a résumé. In addition, they allow the client to respond to a specific job listing as well as to post a résumé to a database that may be searched by prospective employers. The client can take advantage of both types of services.

The client can find other résumé-listing services that serve his or her field by using a search engine such as Google (http://www.google.com). or Dogpile (http://www.dogpile.com). In the search box, put the name of the job and the word *résumé*. For example, enter "sales resumes" or "accountant resumes" and then carry out the search. The disadvantage to this approach is that the client will also find many résumé-writing services available for a fee. Depending on the client's level of career sophistication and tolerance for frustration, you may want to facilitate the search.

Résumé-listing services generally provide forms that are completed by the client and that are then formatted to fit the database. The client may need assistance in being brief and to the point, stressing skills, and working within a rigid framework.

A word of caution: Some people prefer not to put their home address and telephone numbers on the Web. Remember, just as clients can get to the site to list their résumés and look at those of others, so can others get to clients' résumés. Some people will list their city, state, and e-mail address. Some prefer to list only their e-mail address and to include the location of the work they are seeking in the objective box. In fact, some résumé-listing services will provide a free e-mail address to aid in maintaining the security of one's identity.

### A Few Words on a Web Page Résumé

Clients can use the most sophisticated tools of the Internet including multimedia and links to other parts of the Web to create their own Web sites as an advertisement for their services. The techniques for creating a Web site are beyond the scope of this chapter; however, here are four simple tips for clients.

1. Remember that the purpose of the résumé is to get a job interview. Restrict the information provided to that which serves the purpose.
2. Consider that if readers follow links to other parts of the Web, they may never return. Consider how any links contribute to getting a job.
3. Be sure to make the information accessible. Consider how a potential employer will know that the Web site is out there advertising your services.
4. Do not include every graphic or auditory feature you can dream up. Do include those that demonstrate that you are the best person for the job you are seeking.

### Summary

We have explored the types of, purpose for, and means by which technology may enhance a career counseling practice. We encouraged readers to consider how their clients interact with technology, how this interaction informs choices about using technology in practice, and ethical means of doing so. Throughout the chapter, our emphasis has been on two aspects of the world in which we live, both exemplified by complexity theory. The first aspect of this theory is interconnectedness. The second aspect is change. Just as the lives of clients and counselors are affected by many circumstances and technological advances, so too are the systems. Even as we were writing this chapter, more was being added to the systems described, other systems began to decline, and still others were at the beginning of their design cycle. So our final advice is to stay abreast. Use the ACSCI and NCDA Web sites to watch for changes in the field, for conferences about career information, and for new statements of standards. Use search engines such as Google and Dogpile to identify new sources of information. Use ERIC to find research as it continues to be reported. We have included Web site URLs throughout this entire chapter. The next section lists Web sites with additional information mentioned in this summary.

## Useful Web Sites

- Dogpile search engine. http://www.dogpile.com/
- Economic Research Institute. http://www.erieri.com
- The Educator's Reference Desk. http://askeric.org/
- Google search engine. http://www.google.com
- National Career Development Association. http://associationdatabase.com/aws/NCDA/pt/sp/Home_Page
- O*NET OnLine occupational information. http://online.onetcenter.org
- U.S. Department of Labor, Bureau of Statistics, Career Guide to Industries. http://www.bls.gov/oco/cg/home.htm

## References

Association of Computer-based Systems for Career Information. (2002). *Standards implementation handbook*. Tulsa, OK: Author.

Bertot, J. (2009). Public access technologies in public libraries: Effects and implications. *Information Technology & Libraries, 28*, 81–92. Retrieved from EBSCO *host*.

Bloch, D. P. (1989). Using career information with dropouts and at-risk youth. *Career Development Quarterly, 38*, 160–171.

Bloch, D. P., & Kinnison, J. F. (1988). A method for rating computer-based career information delivery systems. *Measurement and Evaluation in Counseling and Development, 21*, 177–187.

Bloch, D. P., & Kinnison, J. (1989). Occupational and career information components: A validation study. *Journal of Studies in Technical Careers, 11*, 101–110.

Blowers, H. (2010). From realities to values. (cover story). *Computers in Libraries, 30*(4), 6–10. Retrieved from EBSCO*host*.

Brown, C. C., & Czerniewicz, L. L. (2010). Debunking the "digital native": Beyond digital apartheid, towards digital democracy. *Journal of Computer Assisted Learning, 26*, 357–369. Retrieved from EBSCO*host*.

Davis, F. D. (1989). Perceived usefulness, perceived ease of use, and user acceptance of information technology. *MIS Quarterly, 13*(3), 319–340.

Economic Research Institute. (2011). eDOT+ [Computer Software]. Redmond, WA: Author.

Gaddis, J. L. (2005). *The cold war: A new history.* New York, NY: Penguin Press.

Gallup, G., Jr., & Jones, T. (2000). *The next American spirituality: Finding God in the twenty-first century.* Colorado Springs, CO: Cook.

Guo, R. X., Dobson, T., & Petrina, S. (2008). Digital narratives, digital immigrants: An analysis of age and ICT competency in teacher education. *Journal of Educational Computing Research, 38*(3), 235–254.

Hohenshil, T. H., & Brott, P. (Eds.). (2002). Using the Internet for career development [Special issue]. *Career Planning and Adult Development Journal, 18.*

Hutchison, B., Niles, S. G., & Trusty, J. G. (2008). The evolution of career counseling in the schools. In G. Eliason & J. Patrick (Eds.), *Issues in career development: Career development in the schools.* Greenwich, CT: Information Age.

Ivey, A. E. (1994). *Intentional interviewing in counseling* (3rd ed.). Pacific Grove, CA: Brooks/Cole.

Jacobsen, S. (1997). *Heart to God, hands to work: Connecting spirituality and work.* Bethesda, MD: Alban Institute.

Kauffman, S. (1995). *At home in the universe.* New York, NY: Oxford University Press.

Kim, H., & Kankanhalli, A. (2009). Investigating user resistance to information systems implementation: A status quo bias perspective. *MIS Quarterly, 33*(3), 567–582.

Kim, T.-H., & Kim, Y.-H. (2001). The effect of a computer-assisted career guidance program on secondary schools in Korea. *Asia Pacific Education Review, 2,* 111–118.

Lapointe, L., & Rivard, S. (2005). A multilevel model of resistance to information system technology implementation. *MIS Quarterly, 29*(3), 461–491.

Mandelbrot, B. B. (1982). *The fractal geometry of nature.* San Francisco, CA: Freeman.

Mau, W.-C. (1999). Effects of computer-assisted career decision making on vocational identify and career exploratory behaviors. *Journal of Career Development, 25,* 261–274.

McCormac, M. E. (1988). The use of career information delivery systems in the states. *Journal of Career Development, 14,* 196–204.

McDaniels, C. (1988). Virginia VIEW: 1979–1987. *Journal of Career Development, 14,* 169–176.

National Board for Certified Counselors. (2007). *The practice of Internet counseling.* Greensboro, NC: Author.

National Career Development Association. (1991). *Preparation and evaluation of career and occupational information.* Tulsa, OK: Author. Retrieved from http://www.ncda.org

National Career Development Association. (1992). *Guidelines for the preparation and evaluation of video career media.* Tulsa, OK: Author. Retrieved from http://www.ncda.org (enter title into search box).

National Career Development Association. (1997). *Guidelines for use of the Internet for provision of career information and planning services.* Tulsa, OK: Author. Retrieved from http://www.ncda.org

Osborn, D. S., Peterson, G. W., Sampson, J. P., Jr., & Reardon, R. C. (2003). Client anticipations about computer-assisted career guidance system outcomes. *Career Development Quarterly, 51,* 356–367.

Prensky, M. (2001a). Digital natives, digital immigrants. *NCB University Press, 9*(5), 1–6.

Prensky, M. (2001b, November/December). Digital natives, digital immigrants, Part II: Do they really think differently? *On the Horizon, 9*(6), 1–6. Retrieved June 2, 2011, from http://www.marcprensky.com/writing/Prensky%20-%20 Digital%20Natives,%20Digital%20Immigrants%20-%20Part2.pdf

Remley, T. P., & Herlihy, B. (2007). Ethical, legal, and professional issues in counseling (2nd ed.). Upper Saddle River, NJ: Pearson.

Roof, W. C. (1999). *Spiritual marketplace: Baby boomers and the remaking of American religion.* Princeton, NJ: Princeton University Press.

Safron, J. D., & Muran, J. C. (2000). Resolving therapeutic alliance ruptures: Diversity and integration. *Journal of Clinical Psychology, 56*(2), 233–243.

Salajan, F. D., Schonwetter, D. J., & Cleghorn, B. M. (2010). Student and faculty inter-generational digital divide: Fact or fiction? *Computers & Education, 55,* 1393–1403. Retrieved from EBSCO*host*.

Sampson, J. P., Jr., Lumsden, J. A., Carr, D. L, & Rudd, E. A. (1999). *A differential feature-cost analysis of Internet-based career information delivery systems (CIDS): Technical Report Number 24.* Tallahassee, FL: Center for the Study of Technology in Counseling and Career Development. Retrieved from http://www.career.fsu.edu/documents/technical%20reports/Technical%20 Report%2024/Technical%20Report%2024.html

Stripling, B. (2010). Teaching students to think in the digital environment: Digital literacy and digital inquiry. *School Library Monthly, 26*(8), 16–19. Retrieved from EBSCO*host*.

Sue, D. W., Arredondo, P., & McDavis, R. (1992). Multicultural counseling competencies and standards: A call to the profession. *Journal of Counseling and Development, 70,* 477–485.

Thompson, S. D. (1988). Data—people—aspirations: The career information delivery system the Maine way. *Journal of Career Development, 14,* 177–189.

U.S. Department of Labor. (2010). *The career guide to industries.* Washington, DC: U.S. Government Printing Office.

U.S. Department of Labor. (2010). *The occupational outlook handbook.* Washington, DC: U.S. Government Printing Office.

U.S. Department of Labor. (2007). *O\*NET occupational database.* Washington, DC: Author.

CHAPTER **8**

# Designing Career Development Plans With Clients

Rich W. Feller and Jackie J. Peila-Shuster

**Contents**

> Career planning is "a straightforward process of understanding, explor-
> ing, and decision making, reflecting on your life, family, and work in
> a wider context. What complicates it is that careers and organizations
> are constantly changing. [Thus,] … careers have been defined as a set of
> improvisations based on loose assumptions about the future."

**Editors of Perseus Publishing (2000, p. 418)**

Helping clients assess and act on the interplay between their career decisions
and identity is the foundation of designing career development plans.
This book's authors have focused on important knowledge and skills needed
to gain insights about clients, the development process, and career counseling. Culled from our work with students, clients, and colleagues, this chapter
illustrates beliefs about partnering with clients to design career plans.

Stimulating clients to integrate insights and feedback leading to affirma-
tion and change is critical. Working alliances that articulate unmet needs,
identify remedies, and evaluate strategies are essential. Developing competencies that build on strengths, compensate for strength overuse, and

neutralize weaknesses are essential to planning. As clients explore development and gain feedback, motivating them to enhance lifestyle satisfaction, career adjustment, and performance takes center stage. Commitments tied to allies and timelines promote accountability. We attend to both in this chapter, using career development as a change strategy to serve individual clients and organizations.

Initially, we address career development's evolution to support thoughts on policy issues and opportunities. Throughout, we offer insights into perspectives and skills career counselors need to appropriately and adequately work with clients. To assist career counselors and consultants in understanding their pivotal roles, we introduce current thinking and research about individual and organizational motivations and goals and highlight challenges confronted by career development planning for organizational and individual success. Ultimately, we weave the practical and human dimensions of career development into an array of useful strategies and resources applicable to both individual clients and organizations.

## Evolution of Career Development

Writing this chapter 40 years ago would have meant focusing on how to build a supportive relationship with clients to fit them into jobs or traditional learning options through a rather mechanistic trait and factor approach. Many believed that career work could be separated from personal counseling and that vocational guidance was best done with youth than with adult clients, helping them to manage their career development throughout life. With the advent of portfolio careers, free agency, and downsizing expectations about jobs for life, matching people to jobs is much too narrow a perspective.

Thirty years ago, this chapter would have referenced the merits of fit models that included behavior modification methods and job clubs (Azrin & Besalel, 1980). Awareness about planning life roles beyond work for a more affluent society taught workers that no job could meet all needs. In 1972, Richard Bolles's *What Color Is Your Parachute?* popularized and expanded career development principles and exposed the hidden job market. Past achievement skill analysis, adapted from Haldane's (1960) success acknowledgment, helped clients break out of the "three boxes of life" (Bolles, 1978), and *Parachute*-related workshops paralleled creation of the career self-help book industry, which broadened perceptions of careers and vocational counseling. The changing nature of work, globalization and advanced technology, and the unraveling of the social employment contract between workers and employers moved counselors to advocate for lifelong learning and to challenge lifetime employment assumptions.

Vocational education legislation, the National Occupational Information Coordinating Committee, and the National Career Development Association stimulated a career development counselor training renewal by promoting occupational, career, and labor market information delivery systems and developing products to teach individuals the full range of career self-management skills. U.S. Department of Labor training programs, through partnerships among education, business, and workforce development councils, moved career development issues to the top of their agenda.

Today, we write this chapter with greater appreciation for holistic career development and promoting "mattering" as a replacement for occupational congruence. Taxonomies of school career development interventions have emerged (Dykeman et al., 2001). Moreover, local, national, and international crises—shootings in schools, wars in Iraq and Afghanistan, "jobless growth," economic downturns, calls for STEM Centric Career Development—have prompted self-reflection, resiliency, and reinvention at the most basic of levels. A sense of tentativeness or "positive uncertainty" (Gelatt, 1998), a renewed commitment to self-advocacy and self-management, and development of "possible selves" are now essential.

## Career Development Planning and Policy Implications

Career development is a complex field in which specialists freely interchange the words *career interventions*, *career assistance*, *career counseling*, *career planning*, and *career coaching* as proposed change models and techniques. It is increasingly accepted as a lifelong strategy for individuals, as talent management within organizations, and as a human resource issue within national economies. When "expressed in terms of measureable impacts on personal, community, economic and workforce development [it] can capture the attention of legislatures, policy makers and administrators" (Jarvis, Zielke, & Cartwright, 2003, p. 269), and it has the potential to foster efficiency in the allocation and use of human resources, as well as promote social equity through expanding educational and occupational access (Watts, Dartois, & Plant, 1986).

The extent to which workers fail to share in their organization's success, live in poverty, or have difficulty accessing education is directly proportionate to their need for external support. Reich (2002, 2010) argued that the most adversely entrenched workers need strong interventions from their companies and communities to stem a widening income gap. If individuals are neither infinitely nor readily malleable, especially as adults, and when work roles change more rapidly than the individual's capacity to adapt, Lowman (1996) suggested that there will be

> transitional casualties: persons will be unable to work at levels compatible with their economic wants and demands. Depression, anxiety, and other mental disorders related to work will accelerate under such circumstances, and mental health professionals will be increasingly called upon to address career and work-related issues. (p. 206)

Watts (1996) proposed that although the field of career counseling has been dominated by psychologists, career counseling is also a sociopolitical activity that

> operates at the interface between personal and social needs, between individual aspirations and opportunity structures, between private and public

identities.... [Thus], the rationale for public funding for such services stems from their value to society and the economy, as well as to individuals. (p. 229)

Although research has illustrated its value, national support for more comprehensive career development planning is presently hampered by shifts in political priorities and mounting government deficits. As employers place more responsibility on workers for managing their careers, health care, and retirement options, developing career plans has never been more important.

## Career Planning Makes a Difference

Individuals, organizations, and government policymakers are not easily convinced that comprehensive career development planning is a sound investment, despite evidence to the contrary. A report by America's Career Resource Network Association (2003) synthesized the existing research and found that comprehensive career counseling provides several benefits in educational, social, and economic areas. Educationally, career counseling has shown benefits such as improved educational achievement, better preparation and participation in postsecondary education, enhanced articulation among education levels, and higher graduation and retention rates. Socially, career counseling has been related to higher levels of worker satisfaction and career retention, shorter paths to primary labor markets for young workers, lower incidence of work-related stress and depression, and reduced likelihood of work-related violence. Economically, career counseling has been linked to lower rates and shorter periods of unemployment, lower costs of worker turnover, lower incarceration and criminal justice costs, and higher worker productivity.

Herr (1995, 1999), citing several studies, avowed career counseling's positive effects on eliminating both career information deficits and client needs for support, as well as assisting clients in identifying and selecting available options (Campbell, Connel, Boyle, & Bhaerman, 1983; Spokane, 1990; Spokane & Oliver, 1983). Complementing these findings, Holland, Magoon, and Spokane's (1981) meta-analysis showed that effective career interventions include (a) occupational information organized by a comprehensive method easily accessible to a client (e.g., using the Harrington-O'Shea Career Decision Making System; O'Shea & Feller, 2008); (b) assessment materials and devices that clarify a client's self-picture and vocational potentials (see Feller, 2003b); (c) individual or group activities that provide rehearsals of career plans or problems (see Barry, 2001); (d) support from counselors, groups, or peers (e.g., model reinforcement counseling session; see Krumboltz & Thoresen, 1964); and (e) a cognitive structure for organizing information about self and occupational alternatives (e.g., the communication–analysis–synthesis–valuing–execution cycle; see Sampson, Peterson, Lenz, & Reardon, 1992).

## Changing Perspectives and Skills for Career Counselors

As the comprehensiveness of career development increases, so does the need for counselor skills and strategies. To facilitate comprehensive development planning, counselors need to operate within well-defined roles, gain knowledge about the needs and idiosyncrasies of various groups of clients, and understand changes in learning and the workplace.

## Career Counselors: Developing Self

Learning about the value of diversity (Miscisin, 2001; Myers & McCaulley, 1985; Petersen & Gonzalez, 2000a), strength themes (Buckingham & Clifton, 2001), and career success strategies (Derr, 1986), coupled with courage to examine traditional career assumptions (Barry, 2001; Feller, 2003a; Feller & O'Bruba, 2009; Feller & Whichard, 2005; Gray & Herr, 2000; Hansen, 1997) and the willingness to question counseling conventions (Amundson, 2003), are all integral skills for career counselors to master. Moreover, creating development plans asks that counselors continually explore their own worldviews and expose themselves to experiences, models, and techniques that broaden their understanding and empathy. Accumulating varied experiences and practicing humility enhances counselor wisdom and openness to the ways others choose to live their lives (Dominguez & Robin, 1992; Whitmyer, 1994). By cultivating broader perspectives, counselors become effective at instilling hope (Snyder, Feldman, Shorey, & Rand, 2002) and belief in the self, in even the hardest client cases (e.g., "career stallers and career stoppers"; Lombardo & Eichinger, 2010, p. 415).

## Career Counselors: Providing More Than "Test and Tell"

To suggest that one can plan for a lifelong career by finding the perfect job is as naïve as thinking contemporary career counseling is driven by test administration. However, vocational or career counseling has often been introduced to counselors in training as a mechanistic, linear process of (a) meet and greet, (b) take charge of the process by administering interest and personality tests, (c) interpret the results to find congruence tied to labor market availability, and (d) measure success by level of client focus.

Helping clients fashion comprehensive plans requires approaches beyond individual talk therapy. Creativity, spontaneity, active engagement, and understanding how people make life transitions effectively are necessary counselor assets. Staying current with workplace learning tool, technological, and organizational changes prepares career counselors for the often daunting, and always unique, task of building client action plans.

The traditional trait–factor matching model seems most helpful when a person needs a job right away or simply needs a job to meet survival needs. However, it lacks comprehensiveness and does little to develop client competencies needed to build satisfying lifestyles and improve performance in newly assigned areas of responsibility. With workplace turbulence, pervasive learning and lifestyle choices, and a burgeoning appreciation for questions such as "What kind of person do I want to be?" "What am I doing with my life?" and "Am I living the way that I want to live?" career planning needs to be holistic. Particularly among clients without security and economic concerns, work has become an expression of meaning. Meeting needs tied to career satisfaction comes from evaluating, prioritizing, and developing life roles. Many clients are no longer satisfied with working for a living, but instead want to work at living (Boyatzis, McKee, & Goleman, 2002).

## Career Counseling: Integrating Humanistic Elements

Mental health practitioners have learned that a dichotomy between personal and career counseling rarely exists. Career counselors have learned that career counseling is not devoid of psychological processes. As Petersen and Gonzalez (2000b) noted, "It is impossible to separate vocational concerns from emotional factors, family interactions and social well-being" (p. 70). Herr (1999) suggested that work and mental health are interwoven, and Niles and Pate (1989) proposed that all counselors be trained in both the career and the noncareer domains. Feller and Whichard (2005) argued that counselors need to empathize with the differing traits of "knowledge nomads" and the "nervously employed."

### SIDEBAR 8.1   Creative Career Counseling

In *Getting Unstuck: How Dead Ends Become New Paths*, Timothy Butler (2007) eloquently demonstrated how one's personal life cannot be separated from career as he delves deeply into preverbal imagery and meaning. He challenged readers to experience whatever impasse they are at intentionally and deeply because although feelings of being stuck may be disquieting, "we must come to recognize them as signals that an important process is beginning" (p. 1). He provided information and activities to help clients recognize and move through impasses via work with imagery, patterns of meaning, and taking action. Visit http://www.careerleader.com/gettingunstuck for imagery exercises used in his book.

## Tools for Acquiring Counseling Skills

Counselors need a practical organizing tool that can help them acquire the skills necessary for their burgeoning roles. One option is offered by Hansen's (1997) integrative life planning approach. Combining accepted theories and proven practices about how people (a) choose jobs or educational pursuits, (b) make the transition through life stages and cycles, and (c) negotiate psychological and environmental barriers that can immobilize them during career changes, Hansen (1997) gave a comprehensive, interdisciplinary, and eminently practical template for working with clients. Subsuming fundamental and broad life-choice questions, it concentrates on six key life tasks: finding work that needs doing in changing global contexts, weaving one's life into a meaningful whole, connecting family and work, valuing pluralism and inclusivity, exploring spirituality and life purpose, and managing personal transitions and organizational change (Hansen, 1997, pp. 19–22).

Moreover, Hansen (1997) posed seven provocative questions to guide career counselors and consultants in strategizing individual or organizational change (p. 263). These questions explore living and working in a rapidly changing global society in the 21st century while honoring diversity and valuing individual uniqueness. They emphasize the need to negotiate the complexities of gendered lives and to achieve wholeness and balance when educational and occupational structures fail to keep up with human needs or erect barriers. Additionally, they promote self-directed change agency in negotiating and constructing life careers in meaningful ways. Unique in its comprehensiveness and incisiveness, integrative life planning encourages counselors to scrutinize pivotal life choices affecting career development. Career counselors benefit immeasurably in personal and professional growth by challenging themselves to ask and answer these questions.

## Career Development Planning: Its Myriad Challenges

Although the need for career planning assistance is well documented, many efforts fall short. Typically, such efforts are the result of well-intentioned, but misguided, plans affected by scarce resources, inadequately trained and informed professionals, disinterested systems, and competing priorities.

## Childhood Career Development: Providing the Foundation

Super (1980) supported the idea that career development is a lifelong process beginning in childhood. Gottfredson (2005) outlined the childhood process of career development with children orienting to sex roles and perceived social status with the possible outcomes of circumscription of career choices based on those orientations. Social cognitive career theory (Lent, Brown, & Hackett, 2002) emphasized social and cognitive factors and the role of learning in one's career development. However, much of the career development literature and research remains focused on adolescence and adulthood (Watson & McMahon, 2008).

Using these theories as a basis for research and application of career development programs with children would improve the understanding of childhood career development. Exploring childhood career development and interdisciplinary collaboration and research to develop new theories would improve knowledge of childhood career development processes. Schultheiss (2008) indicated that "discovery-oriented theory-building research could provide a window into the developmental realm of childhood career development as it naturally unfolds across diverse groups of children" (pp. 12–13). Childhood development literature has extensive information about social–emotional development, cognition, affect regulation, temperament, and personality characteristics, all of which complement career research that has focused on interests, abilities, skills, self-efficacy, and various contextual factors (Schultheiss, 2008).

Career development for children is about developing, exploring, and broadening interests, skills, and knowledge; it is not about focusing on and narrowing career choices. Harkins (2001) summarized career education goals as gathering information, learning about oneself, building positive attitudes and habits, exploring issues of equity, and increasing work and academic-related skills. Infusing these goals throughout school curriculums can help children build strong foundations useful to their career and educational futures.

### SIDEBAR 8.2  Childhood Career Development Case Study

Julie is a 9-year-old who loves writing, music, and science. Math used to be one of her favorite subjects, but she recently indicated that she no longer enjoys it as much. When explored further, she states that her current math group is boring and without challenge. Julie loves animals and has always stated that she wants to be a veterinarian, or maybe a teacher. Although previously very outgoing, Julie has recently become more withdrawn regarding her opinions. Julie's mother, a single parent and administrative assistant, shares concerns that her daughter is too worried about what others think of her.

- What messages might Julie be receiving regarding gender roles?
- What theories or constructs can help you as you conceptualize this case?
- What systemwide matters would you address to help facilitate career education goals?

## Career Planning With Students: Promoting Its Use

Despite its importance in life role success, career planning is not a major component in secondary education. Most students have little experience with comprehensive career guidance or computerized career planning systems. Those who do typically come from settings with more recently educated staff, significant technology support, integration of academic and career and technical education, and a high level of administrative commitment to a cohesive career development program. Additionally, career and technical education wanes as "educators assume that the changing economy simply requires more education, resulting in a misguided belief that all students should attend college" (Rosenbaum & Person, 2003, p. 252). Exploring where students can learn job skills, and how those not intending a college path can be motivated to learn in preparation for something in which they will not participate, is essential (Bailey, Hughes, & Moore, 2004; Gray, 2009). Mandated individual career plans for students with special needs offer models useful to all.

The Ferris State University Career Institute for Education and Workforce Development (2002) found that students perceive a lack of career guidance in their schools and often cannot name anyone other than their parents who has influenced their career choices. Moreover, most admit that parental guidance is limited to a few hours over a few months. The study also identified a pervasive bias toward a 4-year degree, even though only 28% of 25- to 29-year-olds obtain a bachelor's degree, ignoring those fields that need employees and require only technical training.

Parsad, Alexander, Farris, and Hudson (2003) found that helping students with their academic achievement in high school was the most emphasized goal of high school guidance programs (48% of all public high schools), and another 26% of programs reported that the most emphasized goal of their guidance program was helping students plan and prepare for postsecondary schooling. Helping students with personal growth and development was noted by only 17% as the most emphasized. Assisting students with planning and preparing for their work roles after high school was the least emphasized goal of school guidance programs (8%). Public Agenda (2010) suggested that most people who have graduated from public high schools in the past decade do not feel that their school guidance counselors provided them with any meaningful advice, and 48% of the former high school students indicated that they felt like their high school guidance counselors saw them as "just another face in the crowd" (p. 6).

### Student Presenting Problems

Most students entering career counseling begin with questions such as "I need to pick a college to attend" or "I don't know what to major in." Such questions are socially acceptable ways of saying "I'm confused about who I am," "I'm nervous I won't find a place in the adult world," "I'm afraid of letting my parents down," or "I feel my worth is tied to achievement." Developmentally, these questions are to be expected because most students experience little meaningful career development planning in schools, and most college courses offer little integration with career exploration experiences. Consequently, students often present with problems needing an imminent response. Unfortunately, resolution usually means longer term relationships, requiring developmental activities beyond quick fixes.

**SIDEBAR 8.3  Adolescent Career Development Case Study**

Josh is a 16-year-old boy in the 10th grade. He has shown excellent proficiencies in math and science but when asked about future plans, he states he has none and will probably "just get a job" upon graduating from high school. Neither of his parents has beyond a high school education. Josh must work after school at a fast food restaurant to help meet family expenses. He has been considering volunteering at a nursing home to help care for residents but has been teased about this by his male friends.

- What contextual issues, barriers, and supports come to mind as you consider this case?
- What theories or constructs help you as you conceptualize this case?
- What next steps would you take with Josh as you work with him to design a career plan?

## Career Planning With Nonschool Clients: Understanding Its Diversity

As individuals try to integrate life roles, seek balance, improve performance, and self-advocate for lifelong learning, they find that developing and managing careers takes on greater value. Regardless of age, carrying out development plans is indispensable because few individuals succeed in new roles by simply repeating past successful behaviors.

It is essential that employees understand the changing employment contract, hear a clear message about the requirements for success in the future, know clearly the business needs and competencies expected for contributions in the present job, and have the resources necessary for development to take ownership of their own careers and development (Simonsen, 1997, p. 196).

### Adults Want Career Planning

Gallup Organization (1989) surveys found that nearly two thirds of U.S. adults would seek more information about career options if they were starting their careers over again. The 1987 Gallup survey reported that 32.2% had no help in career development. The 41.2% of respondents who sought help typically did so through self-directed activities. Fewer than one in five sought assistance from school or college counselors, and fewer than 9% had used publicly supported employment counselors.

Unfortunately, 10 years later, little had changed. A 1999 Gallup survey found that 42% of adults indicated that friends or relatives were their most frequent source for career help, and 59% did not start their job or career through conscious choice. Only 2% were influenced by school, college, or career counselors, and 3% were influenced by a counselor, job or career specialist, or public service placement office. Just fewer than 10% of all adults reported that they needed help annually in career planning and making a career change. Herr, Cramer, and Niles (2004) observed that even when using professional services, clients typically have interactions with trained career counselors that are "short-lived and limited to points of crisis rather than to career planning and to helping an individual come to terms with the future" (p. 31).

### Job Satisfaction Matters

Palmore's (1969) findings that job satisfaction is the best predictor of longevity (better than a physician's ratings of physical functioning, use of tobacco, or even genetic inheritance) complement Dawis's (1984) comprehensive review of research on job satisfaction. Dawis noted that

> job satisfaction is a cognition, with affective components, that results from certain perceptions and results in certain future behaviors. As a cognition, it is linked to other cognitions, or cognitive constructs, such as self-esteem, job involvement, work alienation, organizational commitment, morale, and life satisfactions. (p. 286)

He also reported that job dissatisfaction is correlated with mental and physical problems including psychosomatic illnesses, depression, anxiety, worry, tension, impaired interpersonal relationships, coronary heart disease, alcoholism, drug abuse, and suicide.

### Adult Presenting Problems

Adults, who are often responsible for multiple life roles, may see few degrees of freedom when they present themselves in counseling. Issues related to burnout and stress, transitions in relationships, sudden loss of employment, conflicts at work, poor communication with significant others, unrealized career goals, or a sense of defeat are commonly interwoven with career counseling needs. Financial problems and caregiving responsibilities force a sense of urgency and necessitate a focus on immediate coping strategies rather than longer range objectives such as finding satisfaction and meaning in daily experiences, redefining success to match a preferred lifestyle, or living intentionally on the basis of clear priorities.

Weinrach (2003) and McDonald (2002) reminded counselors about the often overwhelming needs of welfare-to-work clients as they try to plan and integrate development needs, concrete goals, and action plans. One's social class generally determines economic realities, with higher social classes perceiving work as integrally tied to personal satisfaction and meaning and lower social classes viewing work primarily as a means to economic survival (Blustein et al., 2002). Often, immediate job opportunities are more important than personal interests to clients with basic survival needs. Crisis intervention methods and highly directive career counseling may be needed for such clients who have few internal resources from which to draw (Janosik, 1994; Sandoval, 2002; W. Stewart, 2001).

Research on work addiction (Fassel, 1990) provided insight into the personal costs of the inability to control compulsive work habits. Schlossberg's (1994) Transition Coping Guidelines; Leider's (1985) Purpose Profile; Krumboltz's (1991) Career Beliefs Inventory; Sampson, Peterson, Lenz, Reardon, and Saunders's (1996) Career Thoughts Inventory; Moris's (1988) Individual Life Planning; Richardson's (1999) What's Draining You? Inventory; and Simonsen's (2000) Career Compass all provide creative ways to help adult clients gain or regain mastery of self in work situations.

Herr et al. (2004) cited numerous studies suggesting that many workers are inadequately coping with typical life problems and need skill-building approaches organized around specific life crises to better manage themselves. Although employee assistance programs have had some measure of success in alleviating employee issues, they tend to focus on symptomatic mental health issues rather than encompass broader life and career development issues. Attending to job satisfaction as part of the intervention can often result in both career stimulation and enhancement opportunities within the employment setting and the consequent amelioration of social pathologies. Business's current performance review practices could be appreciably enhanced by providing meaningful and accountable development plans concomitant with employee assistance program support. Doing so would require a strong commitment from senior management to an employee development culture, including mentoring and coaching for managers.

Career counselors in workforce centers, private practice, community centers, or employee assistance programs serve heterogeneous populations at various life stages. Because of competing work–family priorities, career counselors need to help clients develop what the Families and Work Institute (Galinsky, 2003) called a "dual-centric" work life. Galinsky (2003) found that those who put equal priority on work and their personal and family life—who are dual-centric—have the highest ratings in feeling successful at both work and home, with appreciably less stress overall.

Adults will increasingly deal with skill obsolescence, age discrimination, and technological illiteracy. Seeking help in coping with feelings of loss, incompetence, job change, or voluntary or involuntary retirement is becoming more and more commonplace. Those who retire early, and aging clients with better health and a longer life span, may still want to work.

Preparing for what Curnow and Fox (1994) called the "Third Age"—that period of life beyond the career job and parenting, which can last as long as

30 years—presents additional challenges for career counselors. Often, individuals look toward retirement during this period of their life, but retirement is typically treated as a point in time rather than as a complex process (Siegel & Rees, 1992) and as an economic event rather than as a life event (Anthony, 2001).

By focusing on retirement as a point-in-time financial event, little attention is given to the preparation needed in multiple life facets. One indicator of this financial focus can be seen in preretirement education programs, many of which focus on the financial aspects of retirement, with topics such as benefits, insurance, and investments (Brady, Leighton, Fortinsky, & Crocker, 1996; Sharpley & Layton, 1998; Siegal, 1994). However, studies in the United States and other countries have revealed that other topics, such as hobbies and leisure activities, health issues, social participation, renegotiating relationships, and increasing one's sense of purpose in life, appeal to participants (Gee & Baillie, 1999; Marcellini, Sensoli, Barbini, & Fioravanti, 1997; Slowik, 1991).

Ageism is another overt and covert barrier that older adults may encounter as they plan for their next life chapter. As with other prejudices, ageism can cause individuals to feel invisible, ignored, and patronized (R. N. Butler, 2008). Unlike other prejudices, though, ageism is often very visible and accepted, as can be seen in the prevalence of advertisements and greeting cards that candidly and openly perpetuate ageism (Peila-Shuster, 2011). Additionally, in the workplace, ageism can become a factor as early as one's 40s, which is why the Age Discrimination in Employment Act of 1967 specifically prohibits age discrimination against employees ages 40 years and older.

### SIDEBAR 8.4  Adolescent Career Development Case Study

In addition to being the target of ageism from others, people may possibly internalize negative messages about aging throughout their lives and thus engage in self-directed ageist thoughts and behaviors (Peila-Shuster, 2011). This self-directed ageism hinders people from fairly and accurately assessing their own abilities and from recognizing unfair treatment or assessment from others (Bodily, 1991). Internalized ageism and being the target of more overt ageism may significantly interfere with retirement planning and transition processes. Palmore (1988) developed an aging quiz that can be very startling and enlightening in developing awareness regarding ageism in one's thoughts and attitudes. In addition, simply completing an Internet search for facts-on-aging quizzes will produce a variety of quizzes, many of them based on Palmore's (1988) work.

Acting as interpreters of "lives in progress rather than as actuaries who count interests and abilities" (Savickas, 1992, p. 338), career counselors find that their tasks include much more than working to help clients find a job that fits. Career counselors are in a prime position to partner with mature adults on a journey of self-exploration and discovery to facilitate a reidentification and clarification of values, interests, needs, desires, concerns, and fears. If confronting ageist thought processes on the part of the counselor and the client is done with care, this process of self-discovery can facilitate effective and meaningful identification of ways to go about living one's vision of the Third Age.

**SIDEBAR 8.5   Retirement Case Study**

JoAnne is a 64-year-old executive at a large international high-tech organization. She is Latina and married and has three grown children and two grandchildren. JoAnne has spent the past several years in charge of various areas such as talent management, diversity projects, and community outreach, all of which she has thoroughly enjoyed. However, she has decided that she will retire in 6 months, stating, "I don't know how I'll spend my time without work, but I know I'm ready to explore different avenues and spend more time with my grandchildren."

- What emotions, supports, and barriers might JoAnne encounter as she disengages from her work setting?
- What theories help you as you conceptualize this case?
- How will you go about helping her transition to her next life chapter?

## Career Planning and Development With Organizations

Organizations seek career development models when faced with the challenge of attracting and keeping talented people (Pink, 2001). They invest in employee development to induce performance, build employee strength at key positions, capture intellectual capital, foster innovation to drive patents, and define or enhance organizational identity (T. A. Stewart, 2001).

### Organizational Planning: Initiating the Process

Simonsen (1997) offered a comprehensive roadmap for creating a development culture in organizations.

1. First, employee development plans must be linked to, and driven by, business needs.
2. The organization needs to create and promote a vision and philosophy of career development.
3. Senior management must actively and publicly support all efforts.
4. Clear communication and comprehensive education for all employees across all organizational levels needs to precede and accompany the plan's implementation.
5. Management involvement in learning and mastering all phases of the plan is essential.
6. Employees must be given incentives and taught how to assume ownership of, and responsibility for, their own growth.
7. Adequate and appropriate career development resources must be available to all employees.

### Organizational Planning: Maximizing Employee Contributions

Clifton and Gonzalez-Molina (2002) highlighted the eight-step path to maximize individual employee contributions with positive business outcomes.

1. *Identify strengths:* Identifying an employee's dominant strength themes and refining them with knowledge and skills
2. *The right fit:* Placing the right people in the right roles with the right managers
3. *Great managers:* Developing managers who will (a) opt for talent, not simply experience, intelligence, or determination; (b) define the right

outcomes, not the steps to get there; (c) focus on the people's strengths, not their weaknesses; and (d) use the Gallup Q12 (discussed next) as a guide to understand and develop employees

4. *Engaged employees:* Developing employees so they can answer all the questions in the Gallup Q12 with strong affirmative responses

5. *Engaged customer:* Developing employees who engage customers to experience products or services in a superior fashion

6. *Sustainable growth:* Producing efforts that are metrically measurable, such as revenue per store, revenue per product, or number of services used per customer

7. *Real profit increase:* Producing sales growth tied directly to stock value

8. *Stock increase:* Sustaining profit increases that drive ongoing increases in stock value.

Moreover, this work offers career counselors and consultants 12 questions for organizations and their employees to tangibly measure their mutual effectiveness. Referred to as the Gallup Q12 (Harter, Schmidt, Killham, & Asplund, 2006), these questions evoke responses indicating satisfaction levels and delve into whether individuals know what is expected of them at work, why their work matters, and whether they have the correct resources to do it. It also explores whether individuals feel they are treated with dignity and respect at their work and are given the opportunity to learn and grow.

Career consultant Nicholas Lore stated that "approximately ten percent of people report that they love their work" (Rockport Institute, 2003). However, he noted that there are numerous indicators of better job satisfaction when one's "fit" with one's work is at an optimum level. Gallup's research indicated that as more of the Q12 questions are responded to as "strongly agree," work satisfaction grows, spurring on higher levels of organizational performance.

Career classes, workshops, and structured groups have been found to be useful career interventions that produce a variety of documented outcomes (Peterson, Long, & Billups, 1999, 2003; Reed, Lenz, Reardon, & Leierer, 2000; Spokane & Oliver, 1983; Whiston, Brecheisen, & Stephens, 2003; Whiston, Sexton, & Lasoff, 1998). These venues could easily be built around the Gallup Q12, because each question is both a developmental goal and a strategic objective for employee growth.

### Organizational Planning: Developing Human Capital With Performance Incentives

When career development interventions such as employee development plans are used by employers, evidence has indicated improved performance, a more engaged workforce, and more effective management (Wilms & Zell, 1993). As Michaels, Handfield-Jones, and Axelrod (2001) explained, career planning and management are becoming an important weapon in an employer's retention efforts, as well as a strategy for heightened competitiveness. In a knowledge-based, technology-enhanced, globally competitive workplace in which success hinges on human capital, there is no issue more important than developing people to increase performance. Product innovation, timeliness, and quality earn customer satisfaction as loyalty promotes brand recognition. These intangible assets are achieved chiefly through developing human capital.

However, what does developing human capital entail? Becker, Huseld, and Ulrich (2001) stated that "even when human resource professionals and senior line managers grasp this potential, many of them don't know how to take the first steps to realizing it" (p. 4). The most productive response seems to be dedication to developing people in three distinct ways: (1) presenting challenging tasks; (2) providing feedback before, during, and after; and (3) ongoing learning (Lombardo & Eichinger, 2002). If organizations and their workers are to prosper, a culture encouraging workers to plan and assume responsibility for their career development must be actualized (Simonsen, 1997).

### SIDEBAR 8.6 Performance, Image, Exposure (PIE)

Coleman (2005) asserted that performance, image, and exposure are keys to furthering one's career. Performing exceptionally well to advance oneself is essential, but image (the impression others have of one and one's performance) and exposure (people knowing one's results and image) are also crucial career drivers. Although Coleman (2005) discussed performance, image, and exposure for individual advancement in an organization, William Shuster (personal communication, September 23, 2010), College of Business faculty at Colorado State University, indicated that performance, image, and exposure are critical to managing one's career throughout life, to helping individuals see where their talents fit into the greater scheme, and to allowing them to develop their own style and reputation. In what ways can you enhance your own, and your client's, performance, image, and exposure?

## Developing Comprehensive Career Plans

Gysbers, Heppner, and Johnston (2003) noted, "Client presenting problems … are only a beginning point, and … as counseling unfolds, other problems emerge. Career issues frequently become personal-emotional issues, and family issues, and then career issues again" (p. 3). Amundson (2003) added that "most people come to counseling with life problems that do not fall neatly into the categories of career or personal: life just does not define itself that neatly" (p. 16). However daunting the individual's needs appear, career counselors assume responsibility for helping clients address issues of career satisfaction and adjustment resolved by initially identifying their desires, needs, competencies, and challenges. Ultimately, their alliance will construct concrete career development goals on which to build action plans.

### Identifying Career Competencies

Emerging career development assumptions are challenging traditional beliefs (Feller, 2003a) about competencies needed for navigating a career and are fostering progressive policies and practices to improve transitions from high school to college and then to jobs (Rosenbaum & Person, 2003). The National Occupational Information Coordinating Committee's (1996)

Career Development Competencies, the National Life/Work Centre's (2001) Blueprint for Work/Life Designs, and 40 developmental assets promoted by the Search Institute (1997) are powerful tools to help determine and focus on needed client competencies. Spawned by business leaders, attention to competencies helps clients prepare for greater career satisfaction and improved performance. Research has consistently noted that "to sustain superior performance, emotional competence matters—twice as much as IQ and technical skills combined" (Kivland & Nass, 2002–2003, p. 136). Dubois and Rothwell (2000) suggested that competencies are more enduring than jobs and are inherent to individuals rather than resident in the work employers do.

## Identifying Individual Strengths

Strengths models represent some of the more recent developments and thinking in career planning. Arguing that discovering and capitalizing on one's strength increases the potential of performance excellence, as well as work success and satisfaction in life, strength models have become available commercially. The Clifton StrengthsFinder 2.0, an online adult assessment from the Gallup Organization (Rath, 2007), helps clients identify their top five of 34 strength themes. It, and its youth counterpart, the StrengthsExplorer (Gallup Youth Development Specialists, 2007), help to uncover dormant, neglected, or emerging talents and serve as a foundation for goal setting and planning. Savickas (2003) offered a career adaptability framework to assess development delays and distortions in building human strengths and then offered interventions to build strengths needed to cope with newly encountered situations.

Lombardo and Eichinger (2002) have identified 67 competencies, falling into six factors: Strategic Skills, Operating Skills, Courage, Energy and Drive, Organizational Positioning Skills, and Personal and Interpersonal Skills. Their 2002 work provided a common language for assessing and developing individuals. It identified 10 performance dimensions and 19 career inhibiters and stoppers, while proposing client competencies in positive and straightforward language. Called the *Career Architect* (Lombardo & Eichinger, 2010), in its simplest application counselors ask clients to complete a forced-choice card sort of the 67 competencies into their highest, middle, and lowest skills. Counselors then recommend that clients validate the card sort with others who know them well. Counselors next review the sort and identify themes in the highest and lowest skills. Once the skills have been rated, the system offers the counselor and client a map to which each of the skills is tied, thus helping the client tangibly see the relative importance of each skill in successfully mastering career competencies.

In our experiences with these instruments, we have found that clients are able to gain tremendous insights into previously undiscovered proficiencies, aptitudes, and talents. Additionally, clients are helped to understand why some tasks come more readily than others and how they cannot compensate for more difficult-to-master or overused competencies. The concrete suggestions for competency enhancement, carefully couched in encouraging terms, allow clients to appreciate their inherent value while negotiating their intrinsic challenges.

## Developing Individual Competencies

Clients experience tension anytime a gap exists between a vision of what they want and their current reality. Feedback about a mistake, failing at something important, or seeing a need to learn are examples of instances in which gaps and consequent tension surface. Handled prudently, this tension can be used to motivate clients to master competencies at higher levels of effectiveness. However, where and when it occurs is pivotal. Lombardo and Eichinger (2010) stated,

> The odds are that [tension leading to subsequent] development will be about 70% from on-the-job experience, working on tasks and problems; about 20% from feedback or working around good and bad examples …; and 10% from courses and reading. (p. v)

Moreover, they argued that feedback, even when informed, is not adequate by itself for client development. Because tensions most often occur in situations in which counselors are not present, providing as many coping techniques and tools for skill mastery as possible that clients can use outside of sessions allows clients to maximize development opportunities.

Lombardo and Eichinger (2010) gave 10 "remedies" for overcoming skill weaknesses for each of the competencies, performance dimensions, and career stallers and stoppers that counselors can process with clients. Enhancing and developing strength themes are also critical to excellence with resources such as the results of the Clifton StrengthsFinder 2.0 and work by Marcus Buckingham (2007) providing numerous ideas and activities. We believe that such systems offer tremendous resources for counselors trying to help clients enhance strengths, develop middle skills into strengths, remedy weaknesses, work on untested areas, or compensate for overused strengths.

## Articulating Concrete Goals

Regardless of the client population, good counseling traits and strong working alliances (Bordin, 1979) are fundamental for successful counseling outcomes. Bordin (1979) suggested three essential parts needed to facilitate goal creation: (1) agreement between the client and the counselor on the outcomes expected in counseling, (2) agreement on the tasks involved to achieve the outcomes, and (3) a commitment between the client and the counselor on the importance of the outcomes and tasks to both of them.

In the *Career Counselor's Handbook*, Figler and Bolles (2007) listed key skills of the career counselor. They align with requirements needed to effectively move clients from presenting problems to identifying competency needs, to development plans, and to articulating goals and taking action. These skills include clarifying content, reflecting feeling, open-ended questioning, skill identification, value clarification, creative imagining, information giving, role playing, spot checking that the process is on track, summarizing with the purpose of moving forward, task setting, and establishing the "yes-buts" that reveal barriers, concerns, and obstacles.

### Goal Setting: An Iterative Process

Developing comprehensive career plans is seldom a sequential, linear process. Clients start and stop, reframe, and try out new thoughts, feelings, and behaviors as they explore feedback and options. Moreover, most client needs are not easily anticipated, as explained in Harrington's (2003) dual-track model. The dual-track model communicates the career counseling process to users, with Track 1 including the provision of career information with a cognitive orientation. Track 2 involves the integration of the information into self-awareness and the affective domain. The dual-track model allows professionals to personalize the process and "create a contract for specific services that may require an established time commitment with the client" (Harrington, 2003, p. 80), which helps the counselor and client mutually envision preferred outcomes at any specific point. Within Track 1, the counselor responds to client inquiries about informational aspects of career, self, job finding, and job preparation. Often, this omits

> bringing unconscious material to the conscious level such as integrating self-knowledge with career information [in order] to reflect a manifestation of the self-concept, developing the readiness to make decisions, and using self-knowledge of personality type with corresponding knowledge about work environments [Track 2]. (p. 83)

Thus, for a holistic understanding of a person, cognitive information-seeking behavior must be integrated with affective development. Understanding that clients move between the two tracks, counselors can keep focused on the overall goals while allowing clients room for exploration and experimentation.

Another approach to help clients articulate concrete goals is Figler's 1–2–3 career counseling system (Figler & Bolles, 2007). This model submits that the themes of career counseling are captured in three questions and woven together throughout the entire process (p. 106). The three questions are (1) What do you want to do? (2) What is stopping you from doing it? and (3) What are you doing about it?

Understanding human development, particularly age and stage, gender, and diversity issues, helps counselors negotiate the context within which goals are articulated. A useful acronym to guide goal selection, while keeping context in mind, is SMART (Doran, 1981). SMART proposes that goals should be kept specific, measurable, achievable, realistic, and time-bound. Creating goals within the SMART framework assists the counselor in integrating the client's unique contextual issues into a manageable development plan.

## Creating Action Plans

Helping clients look inward, outward, and forward helps move them toward developing action plans (Simonsen, 1993). Developing action plans is a dynamic, energy-driven process, and counselors must work hard to maintain client motivation. One strategy often used is encouraging clients to find "allies of support" to help keep them focused on completing tasks within the action plan. At times, the action phase will need to be modified and perhaps expanded. Counselors should be ready for such eventualities, preparing clients for the necessary flexibility while recognizing their need for closure. Providing homework assignments, Web sites, and additional resources are ways to keep clients continuously engaged between sessions. Renewing client commitments, following timelines, focusing on the ultimate outcomes, and measuring progress concretely are all effective tools for ensuring success throughout the action plan phase.

## Recent and Emerging Trends in Career Counseling

Herman, Olivo, and Gioia (2003) stated that "interest in career planning is at an all-time high and will become even stronger as we move into the future" (p. 108). Concurrently, they noted that individuals, particularly younger ones, do not trust employers to control their careers and are seeking ways to independently manage their professional and personal development. This demand has given rise to a proliferation of career development opportunities and choices—computerized, video-enhanced, Internet-based, and curriculum-based instruction; eCareer development programs on corporate Web sites; and career coaching, to cite just a few.

## Career Coaching Plays a Greater Role

Formerly provided only to executives, career coaching is now used at least as often as employee assistance programs or career counseling "by managers and employees in a variety of work settings" (Chung & Gfroerer, 2003, p. 141). Defined as strategists in

> promoting continuous resilience and performance in persons and organizations ... [career] coaches are often asked about personal evolving, succession planning, career shifting, work performance, high performance work teams, outplacement, burn-out, scenario building, leadership training, work-home balance, and individual and organizational renewal. (Hudson, 1999, p. 4)

Presently, professionally licensed counselors point out that little empirical research has attested to the effectiveness of the unregulated industry of coaching. However, as it grows in popularity, interest in defining its psychology is burgeoning (Grant, 2002). With traces of consulting and counseling in the coaching background, as well as the application of contemporary management theory (Whitworth, Kimsey-House, & Sandahl, 1998, p. xi),

Coach University (1999) suggested that career coaches are as much a part of life as personal fitness trainers.

## Career Development Facilitators: Expanding Career Counseling Accessibility

Responding to the need for career development training by staff other than professional career counselors, the National Career Development Association (2010) has implemented an advanced training program to develop career development facilitators. Designed for those working in diverse career development settings, this training prepares career development facilitators to serve as career group facilitators, job search trainers, career resource center coordinators, career coaches, career development case managers, intake interviewers, occupational and labor market information resource people, human resource career development coordinators, employment or placement specialists, or workforce development staff. Career development facilitators are trained in career planning techniques and development strategies commonly included in most professional career counselor programs. Although career counselors, coaches, and career development facilitators may differ in their emphasis on practices as well as on professional and ethical issues, many of the same career planning techniques and development strategies are used by all three, regardless of the helper's title.

## Emotional Intelligence: Its Emerging Role in Comprehensive Career Development

Emotional intelligence has increasingly been linked to success in school, family, and work. Goleman (1995) stated that emotional intelligence "is the ability to motivate oneself and persist in the face of frustrations, to control and delay gratification, to regulate one's moods, to empathize and to hope" (p. 34). His emotional competence framework, which includes self-awareness, self-regulation, and motivation as personal competence and empathy and social skills as social competence (Goleman, 1998, p. 26), has provided focus for counselors and human resource experts identifying and cultivating competencies for maintaining high-performance workers and workplaces (Dubois, 2002–2003). Groundbreaking emotional intelligence–based competency models, skills, strengths, and competency lists are currently available and are being used to enhance connections among lifelong learning, development plans, and performance improvement goals.

## Helping Clients Readily Access Career Planning

Many individuals are ready to change their lifestyles or set development goals or they want help in coping with searching for jobs in workplaces that change faster than they can adapt. Some landed in jobs and lifestyles with little planning; many lack awareness of their skills, abilities, and interests or have little experience making decisions. Some are self-directed learners, seeking permission and encouragement to plan for a new life direction. Others seek clarity on their internal motivation shaped by mastery, purpose, and autonomy (Pink, 2009).

One of the largest groups of clients increasingly stating their needs for career development is the group commonly referred to as the boomer population (Dychtwald, 2000). Many in this group have benefited from economic growth, medical advances, and significant educational opportunities, which have resulted in a different view on career development issues. Valuing their personal time, finding expression and meaning in multiple outlets, questioning their life purpose, and seeking connections through spirituality, they want relevant, succinct, but incisive career information. This need might well mean that career counselors implement career planning interventions in more creative ways, such as weekend workshops or retreats or ongoing onsite employee development trainings or through interactive multimedia projects such as Ellis's (2000) *Falling Awake*. Presenting engaging activities that help these clients capture insights into personal happiness, yet highlight the realities needed to attain their goals, surely demands heightened levels of counselor creativity.

## Summary

Fraught with a history of testing and telling clients what to do and fitting round pegs into square holes, career planning is evolving into a holistic approach through which clients design their careers to fit work into their lives, rather than fit themselves to jobs. No longer seen as merely job placement, career development has a growing presence in organizations promoting development cultures (Simonsen, 1997), giving and enhancing both corporate and individual purpose and meaning. It has moved from something done at key decision points with youth in search of a destination to a lifelong process using techniques from numerous disciplines. It has become a sociopolitical instrument, infusing economic vitality into communities, etching humanistic values into turbulent workplaces, and enhancing personal engagement and organization alignment.

The work of designing career development plans is more complex, exciting, and important than ever before. It attends to the very personal emotional domain of individuals on their journeys, searching for satisfaction, quality, and meaning in every choice. Helping to create and achieve these work-life designs, practitioners in a wider range of settings with greater variety in titles and levels of training are driven to keep pace with change. The only constant is that the number of individuals needing comprehensive career development plans will grow. This growth will spawn new and dynamic career counseling tools, career-planning strategies, and development opportunities needed to help clients achieve desired levels of excellence.

Comprehensive career development planning's value lies in the degree to which it helps clients make career decisions congruent with a healthy view of self and a sense of hope about future transitions.

When development is on schedule or career counseling succeeds, individuals approach occupational choices and work roles with a concern for the future, a sense of control over it, conceptions of which roles to play and conviction about what goals to pursue, confidence to design their occupational future and execute plans to make it real, commitment to their choices, and connections to their coworkers and organization (Savickas, 2003, p. 242).

We hope that this chapter provided useful insights, strategies, and resources to align client needs with comprehensive plans and supported career counselors' efforts to empower developmental progress. The Web sites listed in the next section provide additional information relating to the chapter topics.

## Useful Web Sites

- Blueprint for Life/Work Designs: http://www.blueprint4life.ca
- CDMInternet: http://www.cdminternet.com
- Center for the Study of Technology in Counseling and Career Development: http://www.career.fsu.edu/techcenter
- Customized career counseling programs: http://www.readyminds.com
- Falling Awake: http://www.fallingawake.com
- Families and Work Institute: http://www.familiesandwork.org
- Getting Unstuck Exercises, by Timothy Butler: http://www.career leader.com/gettingunstuck
- *Job Hunter's Bible*, by Richard Bolles: http://www.jobhuntersbible.com
- Jobs for the Future: http://www.jff.org
- Leadership Architect Sort Cards: http://store.lominger.com/store/lominger/en_US/pd/productID.128881600
- National Career Development Association: http://www.ncda.org
- National Research Center for Career and Technical Education: http://www.nccte.org
- New American Dream: http://www.newdream.org
- O*NET OnLine: http://online.onetcenter.org
- The Real Game Series: http://www.realgame.com
- Search Institute: http://www.search-institute.org
- Society for Human Resource Management: http://www.shrm.org
- STEM Career: http://stemcareer.com/
- StrengthsFinder: https://www.strengthsfinder.com
- StrengthsQuest: http://www.strengthsquest.com

## References

Age Discrimination in Employment Act of 1967, Pub. L. No. 90-202 § 621 et seq., 81 Stat. 602 (1967).

America's Career Resource Network Association. (2003). *The educational, social, and economic value of informed and considered career decisions.* Bismarck, ND: Author.

Amundson, N. E. (2003). *Active engagement: Enhancing the career counseling process.* Richmond, British Columbia, Canada: Ergon Communications.

Anthony, M. (2001). *The new retirementality: Planning your life and living your dreams … at any age you want.* Chicago, IL: Dearborn Financial.

Azrin, N. H., & Besalel, V. A. (1980). *Job club counselor's manual.* Baltimore, MD: University Park Press.

Bailey, T. R., Hughes, K. L., & Moore, D. T. (2004). *Working knowledge: Work-based learning and educational reform.* New York, NY: RoutledgeFalmer.

Barry, B. (2001). *The real game series* (Rev. ed.). St. John's, Newfoundland, Canada: Real Game.

Becker, B. E., Huseld, M. A., & Ulrich, D. (2001). *The HR scoreboard: Linking people, strategy, and performance.* Cambridge, MA: Harvard Business School Press.

Blustein, D. L., Chaves, A. P., Diemer, M. A., Gallagher, L. A., Marshall, K. G., Sirin, S., & Bhati, K. S. (2002). Voices of the forgotten half: The role of social class in the school-to-work transition. *Journal of Counseling Psychology, 49,* 311.

Bodily, C. L. (1991). "I have no opinions. I'm 73 years old!": Rethinking ageism. *Journal of Aging Studies, 5,* 245–264.

Bolles, R. N. (1972). *What color is your parachute? A practical manual for job-hunters and career-changers.* Berkeley, CA: Ten Speed Press.

Bolles, R. (1978). *Three boxes of life and how to get out of them: An introduction to life/work planning.* Berkeley, CA: Ten Speed Press.

Bordin, E. S. (1979). The generalizability of the working alliance. *Psychotherapy: Theory, Research, and Practice, 16,* 252–260.

Boyatzis, R., McKee, A., & Goleman, D. (2002). Reawakening your passion for work. *Harvard Business Review, 80,* 86–94.

Brady, E. M., Leighton, A., Fortinsky, R. H., & Crocker, E. (1996). Preretirement education models and content: A New England study. *Educational Gerontology, 22,* 329–339.

Buckingham, M. (2007). *Go put your strengths to work: 6 powerful steps to achieve outstanding performance.* New York, NY: Free Press.

Buckingham, M., & Clifton, D. O. (2001). *Now, discover your strengths.* New York, NY: Free Press.

Butler, R. N. (2008). *The longevity revolution: The benefits and challenges of living a long life.* New York, NY: Public Affairs.

Butler, T. (2007). *Getting unstuck: How dead ends become new paths.* Boston, MA: Harvard Business School Press.

Campbell, R. E., Connel, J. B., Boyle, K. K., & Bhaerman, R. (1983). *Enhancing career development: Recommendations for action.* Columbus: Ohio State University, National Center for Research in Vocational Education.

Chung, Y. B., & Gfroerer, M. C. A. (2003). Career coaching: Practice, training, professional, and ethical issues. *Career Development Quarterly, 52,* 141–152.

Clifton, C., & Gonzalez-Molina, G. (2002). *Follow this path: How the world's greatest organizations drive growth by utilizing human potential.* New York, NY: Warner Books.

Coach University. (1999). *Coaching University electronic media kit.* (Available from Y. Barry Chung: bchung@gsu.edu)

Coleman, H. J. (2005). *Empowering yourself: The organizational game revealed* (2nd ed.). Dubuque, IA: Kendall/Hunt.

Curnow, B., & Fox, J. M. (1994). *Third age careers.* Brookfield, VT: Gower.

Dawis, R. V. (1984). Job satisfaction: Worker's aspiration, attitudes and behavior. In N. C. Gysbers (Ed.), *Designing career counseling to enhance education, work and leisure.* San Francisco, CA: Jossey-Bass, pp. 275–301.

Derr, C. B. (1986). *Managing the new careerists.* San Francisco, CA: Jossey-Bass.

Dominguez, J., & Robin, V. (1992). *Your money or your life.* New York, NY: Penguin Books.

Doran, G. T. (1981). There's a S.M.A.R.T. way to write management's goals and objectives. *Management Review, 70*(11), 35–36.

Dubois, D. D. (Ed.). (2002–2003). Competencies from the individual's viewpoint [Special issue]. *Career Planning and Adult Development Journal, 18*(4).

Dubois, D. D., & Rothwell, W. J. (2000). *The competency toolkit.* Amherst, MA: Human Resource Development Press.

Dychtwald, K. (2000). *Age power: How the 21st century will be ruled by the new old.* New York, NY: Putnam.

Dykeman, C., Herr, E. L., Ingram, M., Wood, C., Charles, S., & Pehrsson, D. (2001). *The taxonomy of career development interventions that occur in America's secondary schools.* University of Minnesota, MN: National Research Center for Career and Technical Education.

Editors of Perseus Publishing. (2000). *Business: The ultimate resource.* Cambridge, MA: Bloomsbury.

Ellis, D. (2000). *Falling awake.* Rapid City, SD: Breakthrough Enterprises.

Fassel, D. (1990). *Working ourselves to death: The high cost of workaholism and the rewards of recovery.* New York, NY: HarperCollins.

Feller, R. (2003a). Aligning school counseling, the changing workplace, and career development assumptions. *Professional School Counseling, 64,* 262–271.

Feller, R. (Ed.). (2003b). Using career assessments with adults [Special issue]. *Career Planning and Adult Development Journal, 19*(2).

Feller, R., & O'Bruba, B. (2009). The evolving workplace: Integrating academic and career advising. In K. F. Hughey, D. B. Nelson, J. K. Damminger, & B. McCalla-Wriggins (Eds.), *The handbook of career advising* (pp. 19–47). Hoboken, NJ: Wiley.

Feller, R., & Whichard, J. (2005). *Knowledge nomads and the nervously employed: Workplace change and courageous career choices.* Austin, TX: Pro-Ed.

Ferris State University Career Institute for Education and Workforce Development. (2002). *Decisions without direction: Career guidance and decision-making among American youth.* Big Rapids, MI: Ferris State University.

Figler, H., & Bolles, R. N. (2007). *The career counselor's handbook.* Berkeley, CA: Ten Speed Press.

Galinsky, E. (2003). *Dual-centric: A new concept of work-life.* Retrieved from http://www.familiesandwork.org/site/research/reports/dual-centric.pdf

Gallup Organization. (1987). *A Gallup survey regarding career development.* Princeton, NJ: Author.

Gallup Organization. (1989). *Work in America.* Princeton, NJ: Author.

Gallup Organization. (1999). *National survey of working America.* Princeton, NJ: Author.

Gallup Youth Development Specialists. (2007). *Clifton youth strengths explorer: For ages 10–14* (2nd ed.). New York, NY: Gallup Press.

Gee, S., & Baillie, J. (1999). Happily ever after? An exploration of retirement expectations. *Educational Gerontology, 25,* 109–128.

Gelatt, H. B. (1998). Positive uncertainty: A new decision making framework for counseling. *Journal of Counseling Psychology, 36,* 2.

Goleman, D. (1995). *Emotional intelligence.* New York, NY: Bantam Books.

Goleman, D. (1998). *Emotional intelligence at work.* New York, NY: Bantam Books.

Gottfredson, L. S. (2005). Applying Gottfredson's theory of circumscription and compromise in career guidance and counseling. In S. D. Brown & R. W. Lent (Eds.), *Career development and counseling: Putting theory and research to work* (pp. 71–100). Hoboken, NJ: Wiley.

Grant, A. M. (2002). Towards a psychology of coaching: The impact of coaching on metacognition, mental health and goal attainment. *Dissertation Abstracts International: Section A, Humanities and Social Sciences, 63*(12), 6094.

Gray, K. (2009). *Getting REAL: Helping teens find their future.* Thousand Oaks, CA: Corwin Press.

Gray, K. C., & Herr, E. L. (2000). *Other ways to win: Creating alternatives for high school graduates* (2nd ed.). Thousand Oaks, CA: Corwin Press.

Gysbers, N. C., Heppner, M. J., & Johnston, J. A. (2003). *Career counseling: Process, issues, and techniques.* Boston, MA: Allyn & Bacon.

Haldane, B. (1960). *How to make a habit of success.* Englewood Cliffs, NJ: Prentice-Hall.

Hansen, L. S. (1997). *Integrative life planning: Critical tasks for career development and changing life patterns.* San Francisco, CA: Jossey-Bass.

Harkins, M. A. (2001). Using literature to establish career concepts in early childhood. *Reading Teacher, 55,* 29–32.

Harrington, T. F. (2003). Career counseling strategies. In T. Harrington (Ed.), *Handbook of career planning for students with special needs* (pp. 77–108). Austin, TX: Pro-Ed.

Harter, J., Schmidt, F., Killham, S., & Asplund, J. (2006). *Q12 meta-analysis.* Omaha, NE: Gallup.

Herman, R. E., Olivo, T. G., & Gioia, J. L. (2003). *Impending crisis: Too many jobs, too few people.* Winchester, VA: Oakhill Press.

Herr, E. L. (1995). *Counseling employment bound youth.* Greensboro, NC: ERIC/CAPS.

Herr, E. L. (1999). *Counseling in a dynamic society: Opportunities and challenges.* Alexandria, VA: American Counseling Association.

Herr, E. L., Cramer, S. H., & Niles, S. G. (2004). *Career guidance and counseling through the life span: Systematic approaches* (5th ed.). Boston, MA: Allyn & Bacon.

Holland, J. L., Magoon, T. M., & Spokane, A. R. (1981). Counseling psychology: Career interventions, research, and theory. *Review of Psychology, 32,* 279–300.

Hudson, F. M. (1999). *The handbook of coaching: A comprehensive resource guide for managers, executives, consultants and human resource professionals.* San Francisco, CA: Jossey-Bass.

Janosik, E. H. (1994). *Crisis counseling: A contemporary approach* (2nd ed.). Boston: Jones & Bartlett.

Jarvis, P., Zielke, J., & Cartwright, C. (2003). From career decision making to career management: It's all about lifelong learning. In G. W. R. Knowdell (Ed.), *Global realities: Celebrating our differences, honoring our connections.* Greensboro, NC: CAPS Press.

Kivland, C. M., & Nass, L. M. (2002–2003). Applying the use of emotional intelligence competencies: A business case report. *Career Planning and Adult Development Journal, 18,* 136–159.

Krumboltz, J. D. (1991). *Career Beliefs Inventory.* Palo Alto, CA: Consulting Psychologists Press.

Krumboltz, J. D., & Thoresen, C. E. (1964). The effect of behavioral counseling in groups and individual settings on information-seeking behavior. *Journal of Counseling Psychology, 11,* 324–333.

Leider, R. J. (1985). *The power of purpose.* New York, NY: Ballantine.

Lent, R. W., Brown, S. D., & Hackett, G. (2002). Social cognitive career theory. In D. Brown & Associates (Ed.), *Career choice and development* (4th ed., pp. 255–311). San Francisco, CA: Jossey-Bass.

Lombardo, M. W., & Eichinger, R. W. (2002). *The leadership machine: Architecture to developing leaders for any future.* Minneapolis, MN: Lominger.

Lombardo, M., & Eichinger, R. W. (2010). *The career architect development planner*. Minneapolis, MN: Lominger.

Lowman, R. (1996). Who will help us work more functionally? In R. Feller & G. Walz (Eds.), *Career transitions in turbulent times: Exploring work, learning and careers* (pp. 205–210). Greensboro, NC: ERIC/CASS.

Marcellini, F., Sensoli, C., Barbini, N., & Fioravanti, P. (1997). Preparation for retirement: Problems and suggestions of retirees. *Educational Gerontology, 23*, 377–388.

McDonald, D. L. (2002). Career counseling strategies to facilitate the welfare-to-work transition: The case of Jeanetta. *Career Development Quarterly, 50*, 326–330.

Michaels, E., Handfield-Jones, H., & Axelrod, B. (2001). *The war for talent*. Cambridge, MA: Harvard Business School Press.

Miscisin, M. (2001). *Showing our true colors*. Riverside, CA: True Colors.

Moris, A. (1988). *Individual life planning*. Seattle, WA: Sabah House/Individual Development Center.

Myers, I. B., & McCaulley, M. H. (1985). *Manual: A guide to the development and use of the Myers-Briggs Type Indicator*. Palo Alto, CA: Consulting Psychologists Press.

National Career Development Association. (2010). *Career development facilitator*. Retrieved from http://associationdatabase.com/aws/NCDA/pt/sp/facilitator_overview

National Life/Work Centre. (2001). *Blueprint for work/life designs*. Retrieved from http://www.blueprint4life.ca/blueprint/home.cfm/lang/1

National Occupational Information Coordinating Committee. (1996). *National career development guidelines: K-adult handbook*. Stillwater, OK: NOICC Training Support Center.

Niles, S. G., & Pate, P. H. (1989). Competency and training issues related to the integration of career counseling and mental health counseling. *Journal of Career Development, 16*, 63–71.

O'Shea, A., & Feller, R. (2008). *Harrington-O'Shea career decision making system*. Minneapolis, MN: Pearson.

Palmore, E. (1969). Predicting longevity: A follow-up controlling for age. *Gerontologist, 9*, 247–250.

Palmore, E. B. (1988). *The facts on aging quiz: A handbook of uses and results*. New York, NY: Springer.

Parsad, B., Alexander, D., Farris, E., & Hudson, L. (2003). *High school guidance counseling* (NCES 2003-015). Washington, DC: U.S. Department of Education, National Center for Educational Studies.

Peila-Shuster, J. J. (2011). Ageism: The "-ism" we will all face one day. In S. K. Anderson & V. A. Middleton (Eds.), *Explorations in diversity: Examining privilege and oppression in a multicultural society* (2nd ed.). Belmont, CA: Brooks/Cole.

Petersen, N., & Gonzalez, R. C. (2000a). *Career counseling models for diverse populations: Hands-on applications for practitioners*. Belmont, CA: Wadsworth.

Petersen, N., & Gonzalez, R. C. (2000b). *The role of work in people's lives: Applied career counseling and vocational psychology*. Belmont, CA: Wadsworth.

Peterson, G., Long, K., & Billups, A. (1999). The effect of three career interventions on educational choices of eighth grade students. *Professional School Counseling, 3*(1), 34.

Peterson, G., Long, K., & Billups, A. (2003). *How do career interventions impact the educational choices of eighth grade students?* (Research Brief 1.2). Retrieved from http://www.umass.edu/schoolcounseling/uploads/Research%20Brief%20 1.2.pdf

Pink, D. (2009). *DRiVE: The surprising truth about what motivates us.* New York, NY: Riverhead.

Pink, D. (2001). *Free agent nation: The future of working for yourself.* New York, NY: Warner Books.

Public Agenda. (2010). *Can I get a little advice here?* Retrieved from http://www .publicagenda.org/files/pdf/can-i-get-a-little-advice-here.pdf

Rath, T. (2007). *StrengthsFinder 2.0.* New York, NY: Gallup Press.

Reed, C., Lenz, J., Reardon, R., & Leierer, S. (2000). *Reducing negative career thoughts with a career course* (Technical Report No. 25). Retrieved from http:// career.fsu.edu/documents/technical%20reports/Technical%20Report%2025/ Technical%20Report%2025.htm

Reich, R. B. (2002). *I'll be short: Essential for a decent working society.* Boston, MA: Beacon Press.

Reich, R. B. (2010). *Aftershock: The next economy and America's future.* New York: Knopf.

Richardson, C. (1999). *Take time for your life.* New York, NY: Broadway.

Rockport Institute. (2003). *An interview with Rockport founder Nicholas Lore about career fit and satisfaction.* Retrieved from http://rockportinstitute.com/sites/ default/files/An%20Interview%20About%20Career%20Fit%20and%20 Satisfaction.pdf

Rosenbaum, J. E., & Person, A. E. (2003). Beyond college for all: Policies and prac- tices to improve transitions into college and jobs. *Professional School Counseling, 64,* 252–260.

Sampson, J. P., Peterson, G. W., Lenz, J. G., & Reardon, R. C. (1992). A cogni- tive approach to career services: Translating concepts into practice. *Career Development Quarterly, 41,* 67–74.

Sampson, J. P., Peterson, G. W., Lenz, J. G., Reardon, R. C., & Saunders, D. E. (1996). *Career Thoughts Inventory: Professional manual.* Odessa, FL: Psychological Assessment Resources.

Sandoval, J. (Ed.). (2002). *Handbook of crisis counseling, intervention, and prevention in the schools* (2nd ed.). Mahwah, NJ: Erlbaum.

Savickas, M. L. (1992). New directions in career assessment. In D. H. Montross & C. J. Shinkman (Eds.), *Career development.* Springfield, IL: Charles C Thomas.

Savickas, M. L. (2003). Toward a taxonomy of human strengths: Career counseling's contribution to positive psychology. In W. B. Walsh (Ed.), *Counseling psychology and optimal human functioning* (pp. 229–249). Mahwah, NJ: Erlbaum.

Schlossberg, N. K. (1994). *Transition coping guidelines.* Minneapolis, MN: Personal Decisions International.

Schultheiss, D. E. P. (2008). Current status and future agenda for the theory, research, and practice of childhood career development. *Career Development Quarterly, 57,* 7–24.

Search Institute. (1997). *The asset approach: Giving kids what they need to succeed.* Minneapolis, MN: Author.

Sharpley, C. F., & Layton, R. (1998). Effects of age of retirement, reason for retire- ment and pre-retirement training on psychological and physical health during retirement. *Australian Psychologist, 30,* 119–124.

Siegel, S. R. (1994). A comparative study of pre-retirement programs in the public sector. *Public Personnel Management, 23,* 631–647.

Siegel, S., & Rees, B. (1992). Preparing the public employee for retirement. *Public Personnel Management, 21,* 89–100.

Simonsen, P. (1993). *Managing your career within your organization.* Rolling Hills, IL: Career Directions.

Simonsen, P. (1997). *Promoting a development culture in your organization: Using career development as a change agent.* Palo Alto, CA: Davies-Black.

Simonsen, P. (2000). *Career compass: Navigating your career strategically in the new century.* Palo Alto, CA: Davies-Black.

Slowik, C. M. (1991). The relationship of preretirement education and well-being of women in retirement. *Gerontology & Geriatrics Education, 11,* 89–104.

Snyder, C. R., Feldman, D. B., Shorey, H. S., & Rand, K. L. (2002). Hopeful choices: A school counselor's guide to the hope theory. *Professional School Counseling, 5,* 298–307.

Spokane, A. (1990). Supplementing differential research in vocational psychology using nontraditional methods. In R. A. Young & W. A. Borgen (Eds.), *Methodological approaches to the study of careers* (pp. 25–36). New York, NY: Praeger.

Spokane, A. R., & Oliver, L. W. (1983). The outcomes of vocational intervention. In S. H. Osipow & W. B. Walsh (Eds.), *Handbook of vocational psychology* (Vol. 2, pp. 99–136). Hillsdale, NJ: Erlbaum.

Stewart, T. A. (2001). *The wealth of knowledge: Intellectual capital and the twenty-first century organization.* New York, NY: Doubleday.

Stewart, W. (2001). *An A-Z of counseling theory and practice* (3rd ed.). Hampshire, United Kingdom: T. J. International.

Super, D. E. (1980). A life-span, life-space approach to career development. *Journal of Vocational Behavior, 16,* 282–298.

Watson, M., & McMahon, M. (2008). Children's career development: Metaphorical images of theory, research, and practice. *Career Development Quarterly, 57,* 75–83.

Watts, A. G. (1996). The changing concept of career: Implications for career counseling. In R. Feller & G. Walz (Eds.), *Career transitions in turbulent times: Exploring work, learning and careers* (pp. 229–235). Greensboro, NC: ERIC/CASS.

Watts, A. G., Dartois, C., & Plant, P. (1986). *Educational and vocational guidance services for the 14–25 age group in the European Community.* Brussels, Belgium: Commission of the European Communities, Directorate-General for Employment, Social Affairs and Education.

Weinrach, S. (2003). A person-centered perspective to welfare-to-work services: In pursuit of the elusive and the unattainable. *Career Development Quarterly, 52,* 153–161.

Whiston, S. C., Brecheisen, B. K., & Stephens, J. (2003). Does treatment modality affect career counseling effectiveness? *Journal of Vocational Behavior, 62,* 390–410.

Whiston, S. C., Sexton, T. L., & Lasoff, D. L. (1998). Career intervention outcome: A replication and extension of Oliver and Spokane. *Journal of Counseling Psychology, 45,* 150–165.

Whitmyer, C. (1994). *Mindfulness and meaningful work.* Berkeley, CA: Parallax Press.

Whitworth, L., Kimsey-House, H., & Sandahl, P. (1998). *Co-active coaching: New skills for coaching people toward success in work and life.* Palo Alto, CA: Davies-Black.

Wilms, W. W., & Zell, D. M. (1993). *Reinventing organizational culture across international boundaries* (Working Paper 94-3). Pittsburgh, PA: Carnegie Bosch Institute for Applied Studies in International Management.

CHAPTER **9**

# Establishing a Thriving Career Development Program

Donald A. Schutt, Jr.

---

**Contents**

The effective management of organizational culture, processes, resources, and relationships—in career development programs or any setting—requires specific competence in the areas of human resource management, strategic planning and continuous improvement, budgeting resource management, and managing relationships through promotion and marketing. The particular combination of these elements is often influenced by the context in which the career development program resides. Understanding whom the career development program serves and how the services are delivered to meet their needs should guide program implementation. A one-person career center in a public library might demand a different blend of competencies and roles than a school counselor who is responsible for system-wide career development delivery targeted at kindergarten through high school students. "The effective design and use of career resources and services is a collaborative effort among a variety of public, not-for-profit, and private partners who deliver career, educational, training, employment, and social services" (Sampson, 2008, p. 3). In this chapter, I focus on the elements necessary to develop, plan, implement, and manage comprehensive career development programs in a variety of settings for diverse populations.

I begin the chapter with a discussion of management responsibilities and leadership characteristics that are critical to managing the organizational culture through effective relationship building between managers and staff in the workplace. After that, I discuss areas critical to effective program management: strategic planning and continuous improvement; managing resources, including budgeting; and managing relationships through marketing and promotions. The first area, strategic planning, is vital for establishing a foundation from which the other areas can build. The planning process I articulate in this chapter is very intentional and emphasizes the importance of systematic planning, which drives programmatic initiatives. Examples from different career development programs are interspersed to illustrate effective program management.

## Managing Organizational Culture

Regardless of the size and scope of the career development program, there are fundamental human resource roles and functions that must be performed. Vital to the success of any organization are the relationships between the key contributors in the workplace, which includes management, counseling, information technology, outreach, and operations. An appropriate staffing plan is congruent with priorities and initiatives identified through the planning process, described later in the chapter.

The management role is typically filled by an individual manager, coordinator, or director. That individual must

> have a strong understanding of the field of career development, as well as the components that are critical to developing and supporting comprehensive career development programs, and insights into successful management processes. Experience writing grants or soliciting funding would be additional desirable skills. Lastly, the manager should be competent in using technology and systems to manage the use and future needs of technology.
>
> The tasks of a manager/coordinator/director include: supervising staff, managing the day-to-day operations, searching for financial resources (when needed), developing collaborative partnerships with other organizations including schools and business/industry, and directing the continuous planning and improvement process guided by the mission and vision. (Schutt, 1999, p. 71)

The manager is also involved in the creation of positions, selection of staff, orientation, training, and performance management decisions. Wilder and Risher (2010) identified examples of critical manager competencies that included "strategic thinking, development of others, creativity and innovation. Professional expertise, problem solver, people management, interpersonal skills, resource management, customer service, [and] commitment to diversity" (p. 23). Finally, management staff are accountable to other staff for creating a positive and effective workplace environment that provides opportunities to work at one's highest level.

## What Managers Do Matters

Management practices are the foundation on which career development programs succeed or fail, regardless of program size or complexity. Effective management creates a workplace culture that is inclusive and welcoming; recognizes the contributions of others in the workplace as critical to the programmatic outcomes; is invested in the growth and development of the contributors; and fosters articulate and frequent communication among those working in the program and with those for whom the work is done. Ineffective management leads to negative feelings about the program, has a negative impact on quality and productivity, and instills negative feelings that employees have about their ability to do the work (Ryan & Oestreich, 1998). The manager, often supported by practices, policies, and procedures, establishes the climate and ultimately creates the culture in programs. This fact was reinforced by the Gallup Organization in its investigation of strong workplaces that attract and retain the most productive workers (Buckingham & Coffman, 1999), which discovered that "the manager—not pay, benefits, perks, or a charismatic corporate leader—was the critical player in building a strong workplace. The manager was the key" (p. 32). Clearly, how managers behave in the workplace matters.

This connection between culture and manager behavior is not just about what the manager does, it is also about who he or she is. Buckingham and Coffman (1999) described the key role of a manager:

> Great managers look inward. They look inside the company, into each individual, into the differences in style, goals, needs, and motivation of each person. These differences are small, subtle, but great managers need to pay attention to them. These subtle differences guide them toward the right way to release each person's unique talents. (p. 63)

The focus on individual differences as a strength invites employees to be "able to bring more of their whole selves to the workplace and identify more fully with the work they do" (Thomas & Ely, 1996, p. 80). In doing so, the workplace culture becomes a welcome and inviting environment for people from a variety of backgrounds and life experiences. It is clear that managers' behavior affects the ability of those with whom they work to succeed and for the career development program to succeed.

## Effective Management Behaviors

Being a manager requires skills in a number of different areas, typically outside of the education and training received in a discipline such as counseling or psychology. Often, technically competent employees are promoted into management positions because of their expert knowledge or technical skills rather than their ability to manage or lead. One challenge in facing circumstances that are unfamiliar (such as being in a management role for the first time) is the tendency to fall back on experience. Managers begin to manage as they have been managed—for better or for worse—on the basis of personal experiences with previous managers. In some cases, doing so can be very effective; however, in other cases it unintentionally sustains the cycle of poor management. The good news is that management and leadership skills can be taught and—through practice, self-reflection, and more practice—learned and integrated into the personal repertoire of the manager. The goal for managers is to develop effective skills that are used in an intentional and purposeful manner with the people, processes, and program in mind.

Zenger and Folkman (2002) captured the most critical elements of leadership. Those elements, summarized here, translate easily into areas in which managers also need to be effective:

1. Character, including treating people with respect, working collaboratively, and having emotional resilience or the ability to rapidly adjust to change
2. Personal capability, which includes technical competence, professional skills, and using information technology effectively
3. A focus on results, which consists of identifying and communicating important organizational goals that translate to the individual worker level
4. Interpersonal skills, such as communicating effectively, building positive relationships, and being an effective team member
5. The ability to lead organizational change, consisting of tactical changes such as process or facility improvements and also strategic changes such as creating a new vision for the program or changing the workplace culture.

Skills in these areas are necessary to effectively manage people, processes, and resources.

## Staff Responsibilities

The responsibilities of the manager are determined by the size and breadth of services. Typically, the smaller the staff is, the more the manager fills the role of generalist and is involved in all aspects of the program. As the size and breadth of the program grow, the manager may find that significant time is spent on personnel issues, budget discussions, and developing external partnerships and collaborations. If the program is actively engaged in grants or external funding or has a large internal budget produced through revenue streams, the management staff may be expanded to include a person with financial expertise, such as an accountant or bookkeeper, or these roles are outsourced. The disadvantage to having permanent management staff is cost; typically, individuals in management roles are the most highly paid, with the possible exception of information technology specialists.

The management staff are charged with ensuring that professional roles in the program are filled by staff who are qualified within their profession, appropriately prepared to work in career development, and committed to program success. Common professional roles in career development programs include professional counselors and psychologists, career development facilitators or global career development facilitators, information technologists, and administrative staff.

Professional counselors and psychologists are those who have been licensed at the state level, certified at the national level, or both. Professional counselors are certified by the National Board for Certified Counselors after meeting specific criteria (National Board for Certified Counselors, 2009). Professional psychologists are those who have graduated from American Psychological Association–accredited graduate programs that must be based, in part, on psychological scholarship such as a dissertation (American Psychological Association, 2010) and are current members of the American Psychological Association.

Career development facilitators and global career development facilitators receive 120 hours of classroom instruction before certification and are prepared to provide career development guidance and assistance. Career development facilitators have been endorsed by the National Career Development Association, the National Employment Counseling Association, and the National Association of Workforce Development Professionals and certified through the Center for Credentialing and Education, Inc., a subsidiary of the National Board for Certified Counselors. "A Career Development Facilitator (CDF) is a person who works in any career development setting or who incorporates career development information or skills in their work with students, adults, clients, employees, or the public" (National Career Development Association, 2010, para. 1). Career development facilitators provide service in a number of areas:

> This occupational title designates individuals working in a variety of career development settings. A CDF may serve as a career group facilitator, job search trainer, career resource center coordinator, career coach, career development case manager, intake interviewer, occupational and labor market information resource person, human resource career development coordinator, employment/placement specialist, or workforce development staff person. (National Career Development Association, 2010)

Information technology professionals are typically certified for the software in which they are proficient. Companies such as Microsoft, Cisco Systems, Oracle through Oracle University, and Novell offer a number of different certifications for the hardware and software they produce.

Administrative professional staff and office professionals can be certified as either a certified professional secretary or a certified administrative professional by the International Association of Administrative Professionals (2010). Each of these certifications requires passing an examination that covers finance and business law, office systems and administration, and management. The certified administrative professional certification also covers organizational planning, which includes team skills, strategic planning, and advanced administration. Other roles in the program may be filled by para-professionals, volunteers, or students.

In addition to professional preparation in program area expertise and in career development, management staff need to demonstrate a commitment to creating a diverse work environment through employment practices and policies. Moreover, expecting staff to be prepared to serve diverse populations requires a dedicated effort that may include professional development in different areas:

> Staff need to continually learn about topics related to diversity and to know how to use that information to create an informed and supportive environment that works for all clients (including students) and remains sensitive to the needs of each and every individual. (Ettinger, 2008, p. 105)

Understanding the needs of and societal influence on culturally diverse populations, including English-language learning populations, individuals with disabilities, students of all ages and developmental stages, and former offenders, offers ongoing opportunities for staff development. To meet the needs of diverse populations, Ettinger (2008, p. 118) proposed that staff be able to

- Learn to recognize and appreciate differences between self and clients;
- Create a multicultural environment for clients and value the backgrounds from which they come;
- Understand the importance of and need for positive role models who represent the client's background;
- Consider issues surrounding racism and stereotyping when they arise by addressing them directly;
- Read and research information about the historical, social, economic, and political factors affecting clients, including statistics related to workforce participation rates;
- Identify and promote full development of a client's potential; and
- Recognize when differences, whether related to culture, age, or gender, are affecting communication and make appropriate adjustments.

Management and career development program commitment to diversity may be achieved by continually asking, "What is in the best interest of the populations we serve?" and supported by ongoing self-, staff, and program evaluation.

When effective management behaviors are accompanied by strategic planning and continuous improvement skills, managers and the organization are positioned for success.

## Managing Processes: Strategic Planning and Continuous Improvement

The planning process is often viewed as having distinct beginning and end points. Effectiveness increases with intentionality; the greater the emphasis placed on the initial planning and ongoing improvement processes, the more likely it is that resources will be concentrated to areas most important to the program audience and other stakeholders. The approach described in this chapter offers a different and more dynamic framework. Planning and improvement are linked in a continuous process focused on enhancing service and operational excellence. Service excellence is seen as the "complex set of communication processes through which we create and maintain relationships with those with whom we interact" (Ruben, 2004, p. 24). Operational excellence is connected to the effectiveness and efficiency of how programs function (Ruben, 2004). Excellence is demonstrated in the policies, processes, and functions of the career development program.

At the foundation of the career development program strategic planning and improvement process are initiating a needs assessment, creating a mission statement, identifying the core values, setting a vision, and, ultimately, articulating organizational strategies, including objectives and measures. Kaplan and Norton (2001) defined these terms:

> The overall *mission* of the organization provides the starting point; it defines why the organization exists or how a business unit fits within a broader corporate architecture. The mission and *core values* that accompany it remain fairly stable over time. The organization's *vision* paints a picture of the future that clarifies the direction of the organization and helps individuals to understand why and how they should support the organization. In addition, it launches the movement from the stability of the mission and core values to the dynamism of strategy, the next step in the continuum. *Strategy* is developed and evolves over time to meet the changing conditions posed by the real world. (pp. 72–73)

These definitions are synthesized in Table 9.1.

The program planning approach (Figure 9.1) depicts the strategic planning process, moving from needs assessment to performance measures. These elements set the stage for providing effective career development services as well as guiding the evaluation of human resource management, budget, and marketing and promotional decisions. Understanding how these concepts are developed is critical to effectively assess progress and set the direction for ongoing improvement. The measure of success for strategic planning and

**TABLE 9.1   Definitions**

| Term | Definition |
|---|---|
| Mission | "A concise, internally focused statement of the reason for the organization's existence, the basic purpose toward which its activities are directed, and the values that guide employees' activities" (Kaplan & Norton, 2004, p. 34) |
| Core Values | Articulated or unexpressed principles or ethical guidelines that steer individual and organizational behavior; when unexpressed, individuals make decisions on the basis of what they think are the principles; articulating core values is more effective if the goal is to have individuals and the organization moving in the same direction and ensuring that decisions and behaviors are consistent with organizational principles |
| Vision | "A concise statement that defines the mid- to long-term (three- to ten-year) goals of the organization. The vision should be external and market-oriented and should express—often in colorful or 'visionary' terms—how the organization wants to be perceived by the world" (Kaplan & Norton, 2004, pp. 34–35) |
| Strategy | "Specific and detailed actions you will take to achieve your desired future" (Kaplan & Norton, 2001, p. 90) |

continuous improvement processes is finding that the needs of the program's target audience have been met or exceeded.

## Initiating a Needs Assessment

Developing an effective needs assessment process is essential. Needs assessments consider both organizational and individual needs, depending on the context of the career development program. The identification of needs gives direction to the strategic planning and continuous improvement process. "A need has been defined as the discrepancy between *what* is and *what ought to* be. Once identified, needs are placed in order of priority. They are the basis for setting program goals" (Isaac & Michael, 1984, p. 5). This gap analysis approach also considers what is or should be within the scope of the career development program.

Herr and Cramer (1996) described a multiphase process for needs assessment. The first phase is planning and designing the needs assessment, the second phase is conducting the needs assessment, the third phase is using the needs assessment results, and the fourth phase is determining the impact of the needs assessment process. Two steps are identified in the first phase:

**FIGURE 9.1**   Program planning process.

executing preliminary activities, and planning and designing the needs assessment.

The first step, executing preliminary activities, includes setting up a needs assessment committee, identifying external priorities or limiting factors, determining the scope of assessment, establishing the needs assessment schedule, and reviewing committee resources and obtaining commitment. The planning and designing step includes specifying process and product goals and defining process goals as the intervention process itself and product goals as student or employee outcomes resulting from the intervention process. The second step also includes developing statements of needs assessment program objectives with clarity, precision, measurability, feasibility, appropriateness, relevance, and logic; identifying what kind of data are to be gathered (performance, description, opinion, attitude, perception); identifying the sources of data, sampling methods (groups, sizes, strategies, methods), and quantitative and qualitative methods and instruments; and the strategy for analyzing variables.

### SIDEBAR 9.1 Case Study: Responding to the Needs

The challenge was to find a way to serve students enrolled in the largest academic unit on a university campus with 39 departments, five professional schools, and nearly 60 interdisciplinary research and teaching programs and a smaller college of five academic departments, with a total of nearly 20,000 students. The solution? Narrow the services to declared majors in these two colleges, allowing the career unit to identify appropriate marketing and image strategies. In addition, an organizational structural change meant a new home with an Advising Group in Student Academic Affairs in the College of Letters and Science and peer status with other academic support programs. The career program could participate as a partner in a seamless advising system for students with divisional support. Furthermore, the academic connection clarified reporting lines and, ultimately, clarified the target audience for services; it also meant the new director reported to an associate dean in an academic college.

The National Occupational Information Coordinating Committee identified a career guidance and counseling program model (Perry, 1995) that has relevance for process and product goals. Before moving to the second phase, conducting the needs assessment, career development and counseling programs may want to consider the content, processes, and structures outlined in this model as areas in which to gather needs assessment data. Aspects of content included self-knowledge, educational and occupational exploration, and career planning. The processes identified were outreach, instruction, counseling, assessment, career information, work experience, placement, consultation, referral, and follow-up. Structural components were leadership, management, personnel, facilities, and resources. These three areas may be useful when trying to decide where to begin the needs assessment.

The second phase described by Herr and Cramer (1996) involves implementing the assessment, a process that consists of obtaining, organizing, summarizing, analyzing, and interpreting the data collected, followed by an analysis of relationships to determine how the factors connect with needs and timing of the needs. The third phase, using the needs assessment results, involved selecting priorities as well as program planning and implementation.

Program planning and implementation are discussed in greater detail in this chapter, as is the fourth phase, determining the impact of the change process.

Whether beginning a new career development program or evaluating a program that has been in place for years, the needs assessment process is vital to overall program planning and management because it connects directly to the individuals and organizations served by the career development program. It gives definition to the direction of the organization. The case study provides insights into one process.

## Creating a Mission Statement

A program's mission statement answers the question "Why does the program exist?" and is driven by the results of the needs assessment. A mission statement helps to differentiate the program from others as well as to provide clarity regarding the target audiences, both internally and externally. Effective mission statements inspire change, are long term in nature, and are easily understood and communicated (Niven, 2002). One example of an effective mission statement is that of the U.S. Department of Labor's Employment and Training Administration:

> The mission of the Employment and Training Administration is to contribute to the more efficient functioning of the U.S. labor market by providing high quality job training, employment, labor market information, and income maintenance services primarily through state and local workforce development systems. (U.S. Department of Labor, Employment and Training Administration, 2010, para. 1)

Another example is from Career Services, University of Louisiana at Lafayette (2008, para. 2):

> The mission of Career Services is to assist students and alumni in developing and implementing their career goals by providing skill enhancement, career and employer information, and maintaining quality university-employer relationships which provide a link between students and potential employers.

Last, the Oakland University School of Education and Human Services Adult Career Counseling Center (2010, para. 1) has a straightforward, three-part mission:

> To provide career exploration and planning opportunities to adult members of the community at no charge.
>     To provide awareness of the use of computer-assisted career guidance programs.
>     To support research efforts for a better understanding of the career development needs of adults. (Oakland University School of Education and Human Services Adult Career Counseling Center, 2010)

The purpose of a mission statement is to orient the career development program staff, program participants, and other stakeholders to the central focus of one's work. As Niven (2002) stated, "It acts as a beacon for your work, constantly pursued but never quite reached. Consider your mission to be the compass by which you guide your organization" (p. 73).

**SIDEBAR 9.2   Case Study: Creating a Mission Statement**

An existing university career center had experienced leadership turnover, including a lengthy delay in filling the director position. One of the first jobs for the new director was to create a mission statement. Initially, the director turned to professional organizations for the answers. One source that guided her was the National Association of Colleges and Employers' (2010) Principles for Professional Conduct. Next, she investigated two career services operations in college settings. One was similar in terms of position within the institution and one was similar in terms of target audience (college majors) served. The new mission statement was created on the basis of the information collected from these sources, along with feedback from current staff and campus experts: "To educate and support L&S and human ecology students with their career development process, enabling them to integrate their academic and life experiences with their career goals, and transition to the world of work."

## Identifying the Core Values

Core values answer the question "For what does your program stand?" Niven (2002) defined values as "the timely principles that guide an organization. They represent deeply held beliefs within the organization and are demonstrated through the day-to-day behaviors of all employees. An organization's values make an open proclamation about how it expects everyone to behave" (p. 77). Collins and Porras (1997), in their study of visionary companies, described core values as "the organization's essential and enduring tenets—a small set of general guiding principles; not to be confused with specific cultural or operational practices; not to be compromised for financial gain or short-term expediency" (p. 73). They added,

> Visionary companies tend to have only a few core values, usually between three and six. In fact, we found none of the visionary companies to have more than six core values, and most have less. And, indeed, we should expect this, for only a few values can be truly *core*—values so fundamental and deeply held that they will change or be compromised seldom, if ever. (p. 74)

The Virtual Career Center (2006), which is a part of the Career Management Center at Old Dominion University, listed its core values as customer service, integrity, dependability, teamwork, accountability, and productivity. Core values are the unwavering principles supporting the mission and guiding the program through decision making.

## Setting a Vision

The value of a shared vision in the future direction of the career development program is enormous. "Vision statements inspire an organization to be more than what they are about now. Vision statements are all about what they will be in the future, not about what the organization will do to get there"

(Person, 2009, p. 20). The opportunity for people to consider creatively the future services and resources that a career development program might offer is exciting. Kotter (1996; as cited in Niven, 2002) described the purpose of shared vision, particularly during times of change:

1. By clarifying the general direction for change, the vision simplifies hundreds or thousands of more detailed decisions.
2. The vision motivates people to take action in the right direction, even if the initial steps are personally painful.
3. Actions of different people throughout the organization are coordinated in a fast and efficient way based on the vision statement. (p. 84)

A challenge is that there are many different definitions that try to capture the vision component of the strategic planning process, which creates an unclear picture of the importance of vision statements, as well as the process of creating one. Collins and Porras (1997) eliminated the confusion with their vision framework. The vision framework is created through a balance between preserving the core of what one's program is about while also stimulating new growth and progress. Vision:

> builds on the interplay between these two complementary yin-and-yang forces: it defines "what we stand for and why we exist" that does not change (the core ideology) and sets forth "what we aspire to become, to achieve, to create" that will require significant change and progress to attain (the envisioned future). To pursue the vision means to create organizational and strategic alignment to preserve the core ideology and stimulate progress toward the envisioned future. Alignment brings the vision to life, translating it from good intentions to concrete reality. (Collins & Porras, 1997, p. 221)

Effective vision statements are concise, appeal to all the stakeholders, are consistent with the mission and values, are verifiable and feasible, and are inspirational (Niven, 2002). One example taken again from the Web site of the U.S. Department of Labor, Employment and Training Administration (2010, para. 2), is

> Our vision is to promote pathways to economic liberty for individuals and families working to achieve the American Dream. On behalf of American taxpayers, the Employment and Training Administration will administer effective programs that have at their core the goals of enhanced employment opportunities and business prosperity.

Building a shared vision strengthens the relationship between the program and the stakeholders.

## Articulating Organizational Strategies

Strategy is the game plan through which a career development program implements the vision and, ultimately, the mission. Kaplan and Norton (2001) described the relationship between the vision and the strategy: "The vision creates the picture of the destination. The strategy defines the logic of how this vision will be achieved. Vision and strategy are essential complements" (p. 74). More specifically, strategy could be defined as "the specific and detailed actions you will take to achieve your desired future" (Niven, 2002, p. 90).

Niven (2002) reported the key principles of strategy as (a) generates understanding; (b) consists of programmatic activities that distinguish the program from others; (c) focuses the program to make decisions about what the program is to do and what the program will not do; (d) fits together with the other strategies to create an integrated whole; (e) provides continuity; and (f) combines conceptual as well as analytical components. The purpose of defining strategy is to align programmatic activities with the identified needs of a program's target audience or users.

Although strategy is the action-planning phase, it is also the vehicle through which program staff come to understand the vision and their contributions to the overall program. Kaplan and Norton (2001) made the point,

> Strategy does not (or should not) stand alone as management process. A continuum exists that begins in the broadest sense, with the mission of the organization. The mission must be translated so that the actions of the individuals are aligned and supportive of the mission. A management system should ensure that this translation is effectively made. Strategy is one step in a logical continuum that moves an organization from a high-level mission statement to the work performed by frontline and back-office employees. (p. 72)

Identifying the strategy or strategic themes is an important part of preparing to fully engage the strategic planning and continuous improvement process. One method to articulate the strategy is by creating a strategic destination statement (Person, 2009), described in Sidebar 9.3.

### SIDEBAR 9.3    Building Your Strategic Destination Statement

Implementing organizational plans and strategies eludes even those organizations with the best intentions. The failure, in part, may be the result of an inability to move the mission, values, and goals to action. Building a strategic destination statement is one tool that might work. "The Strategic Destination Statement is like a vision statement with specific details of what will be achieved in a specific timeframe with specific offerings to specific customer profiles," according to Person (2009, p. 29). Collis and Rukstad (2008) proposed three basic elements of a strategy statement: an objective that is specific, measurable, and time bound; a scope with clearly defined boundaries; and clarity about what makes the program distinctive from others. Person (2009) provided a formula for creating a statement:

Your program will _____ (action)
To _____ (result)
By _____ (timeframe)
By _____ (method)
Through _____. (means)

Combine these elements to create your strategic destination statement.

In terms of career development program strategies, one example at the national level is the National Career Development Guidelines Framework (2004). It provides broad domains—personal social development, educational achievement and lifelong learning, and career management—under which 11 specific goals are identified (Table 9.2).

TABLE 9.2   National Career Development Guidelines Framework Domains and Goals

| Domain | Goals |
|---|---|
| **Personal Social Development** | 1. Develop understanding of self to build and maintain a positive self-concept.<br>2. Develop positive interpersonal skills, including respect for diversity.<br>3. Integrate growth and change into your career development.<br>4. Balance personal, leisure, community, learner, family, and work roles. |
| **Educational Achievement and Lifelong Learning** | 1. Attain educational achievement and performance levels needed to reach your personal and career goals.<br>2. Participate in ongoing, lifelong learning experiences to enhance your ability to function effectively in a diverse and changing economy. |
| **Career Management** | 1. Create and manage a career plan that meets your career goals.<br>2. Use a process of decision making as one component of career development.<br>3. Use accurate, current, and unbiased career information during career planning and management.<br>4. Master academic, occupational, and general employability skills to obtain, create, maintain, and advance your employment.<br>5. Integrate changing employment trends, societal needs, and economic conditions into your career plans. |

*Source:* National Career Development Guidelines Framework (2004).

The structure provides for the integration of career development concepts into career counseling practice, curriculum, career services, and organizational structures (and has provided direction since initially released in 1986). Career centers and school career development programs organize materials around the domain areas. Career development activity books connect the activities to the National Career Development Guidelines domains and goals. Career counselors use the goals as a part of the intake interview. These strategic themes, framed as domains and goals, increase awareness of career development concepts and assist the delivery systems in moving down a common path. "Organizations don't execute unless the right people, individually and collectively, focus on the right details at the right time" (Bossidy & Charan, 2002, p. 33). The National Career Development Guidelines Framework supplies the necessary focus for career development programs to create and implement goal-directed activities and interventions.

### Fully Engaging Strategic Planning and Continuous Improvement Principles

Once the mission, values, and vision foundation have been set and the strategy areas identified, the strategic planning process is well underway. This process moves from strategy to performance objectives, to measures, and to initiatives and personal objectives that define the work of individuals. Kaplan and Norton (2001) noted an important caveat:

The strategic planning process should use initiatives to help the organization to achieve its strategic objectives, not as ends in themselves. Public sector and nonprofit organizations are especially guilty of often confusing initiative completion as the target rather than improvements in mission objectives and agency effectiveness. (p. 294)

Once the initiatives are identified, it is critical to identify the performance targets that will best demonstrate success relative to the objectives. The measure, in effect, becomes how well the initiative improves the program's ability to meet the strategic objectives, which is different than processes that assume success has occurred once the initiative is completed.

### Identifying Performance Objectives

Performance objectives "describe what you must do well in order to execute your strategy. Objective statements are just that—concise statements that describe the specific things you must perform well if you are to successfully implement your strategy" (Niven, 2002, p. 107). Objectives tell the story of one's strategy in action. The Career Connection to Teaching With Technology (2002) offered four objective statements, which I summarize:

- *Objective 1:* Identify reading, writing, mathematics, and science achievement standards, benchmarks, and accountability measures for students.
- *Objective 2:* Create a career connection to integrated core academic studies that increases the relevancy and authenticity of learning.
- *Objective 3:* Train teachers and students to access and use existing technologies, to create original instructional materials, and to collaborate with business partners in codevelopment of resources.
- *Objective 4:* Contribute to national educational networks using telecommunications to disseminate products and best practices.

Objectives link the strategy to the performance measures. Niven (2002) suggested conducting objectives and measures generation sessions with the goal of creating a number of objectives and measures.

Using the National Career Development Guidelines Framework (2004) goals to exemplify career-focused performance objectives, the domain of personal social development has four goals, and each of these goals connects to behavioral indicators delineated into three learning stages—knowledge acquisition, application, and reflection—thereby providing an extensive list of examples of measurable goals. In this case, each of the indicators serves as a performance measure. One example of an indicator from the personal social development domain (the goal "develop positive interpersonal skills including respect for diversity") is "recognize the benefits of interacting with others in a way that is honest, fair, helpful, and respectful." With the addition of indicators, the measure links to the strategy (domain and goals) through the objective.

### Performance Measures

Performance measures are the tools that gauge progress against the objectives. These tools come in varying forms, from informal measures such as short pen-and-paper evaluations at the end of events or traffic headcounts on a daily basis, to formal evaluations such as satisfaction surveys, transaction surveys, or user complaint management processes. The goal of any measure is to gather information and increase knowledge about the career development program's ability to meet the needs of clients and about the program's efficiency and effectiveness in managing processes, people, and resources.

Niven (2002) offered criteria to use when selecting performance measures. He recommended that performance measures be linked to strategy, quantitative, accessible, easily understood, counterbalanced against other measures, relevant to the area being measured, and clearly defined. If the target audience was veterans, the career development program could create a needs assessment based on the *National Career Development Guidelines Framework* (2004) indicators to gauge where each program participant was currently functioning, to develop initiatives based on the pattern of needs, and then to measure the growth or development of the individuals over time. A pattern that could emerge is that low self-concept appears when the veterans are interviewing for jobs. One initiative under this competency area—that would follow the pattern of needs identified—might be a workshop on effective interviewing techniques and mock interviews. If the veterans who took the workshop ultimately improved their skills in maintaining a positive self-concept (relative to the initial assessment), it could be inferred that the initiative (interviewing workshop) met the objectives (enhanced self-concept) as measured by the performance measures (mock interview). Furthermore, the success of meeting the objectives in the domain–strategic theme area (personal social development) thereby fulfilled the mission: strengthening career development programs at all levels and enhancing student and client achievement. This scenario emphasizes the links from the mission statement to the performance measures while also highlighting the importance of creating initiatives that are driven by the planning process rather by another source.

### Initiatives

Initiatives are the program components with which program staff and users are most familiar. Examples of initiatives include career fairs that connect job seekers with employers or a rescue helicopter landing on the elementary school playground to kick off "Careers in Health Care Day." Other examples of initiatives are Day 1 professional development plans, portfolio workshops, succession preparation courses, or workshops that enhance an employee's ability to be successful at work. Initiatives might also include working with managers or supervisors to help them understand the importance of ongoing professional development both for the career development needs of individuals and for the success of the organization. Initiatives should be driven by objectives. The landing of the rescue helicopter at the elementary school should have intentional connections back to the broader career development plan at that school. It should not be done just because the students love it and it has been done for the past 5 years. Initiatives that are most visible need to contribute to the results defined by the shared vision and mission for the career development program. The measure of success is not only at the programmatic level but also in the response to the question "How does this initiative positively contribute to the strategy?"

## Where to Begin?

Creating an effective strategic plan begins with selecting a planning committee. The initial steps are to identify the "individual who will oversee the process—the strategic planner—and to consider who should be the members of the committee," suggested Dolence, Rowley, and Lujan (1997, p. 6) in their discussion of strategic planning on a university campus. The strategic planner oversees the process and is responsible for organizing and making operational decisions about how the process unfolds. The committee

> should include people who are dedicated to the well-being of the institution and who also reflect the broad constituency base of the campus. This broadness is needed to assure that the major elements of the institution or unit are adequately represented while at the same time the size of the group is kept manageable. (Dolence et al., 1997, p. 6)

After the selection of and charge to the planning committee, the planner should begin the process of educating committee members on the process and expectations.

The process should flow in this manner: Select the initial committee; introduce the process; initiate the needs assessment process (with members of the planning committee participating on the needs assessment committee); identify the needs; review the mission, identify the values, and create the shared vision; establish broad-based support and understanding relative to the mission, values, and vision; determine the strategy, name the objectives and performance measures, and identify and execute the initiatives; continue to measure, reviewing the needs assessment findings and keeping track of changes in the economy, state, organization, community, and workplace; and evaluate and continue to make necessary adjustments.

## Strategic Planning and Continuous Improvement as the Foundation

The process of creating the components of the strategic plan and then using those components to continuously measure effectiveness and success, although time intensive, are critical as a map to guide management decisions in human resources, budgeting and resource management, and managing relationships, including marketing and promotion. One suggestion for keeping strategy in focus is to schedule strategy-centered management meetings (see Sidebar 9.4) or identify strategy as a recurring agenda item at existing meetings so strategy is embedded into the organizational structure. Van Mell (2008) described the process:

> As tasks are done and goals are met, the team should add or change them depending on how much time and money they've got. The first few meetings might be bumpy, because previously planless managers are used to coasting through progress reviews. However, in time and with a strong facilitator, people will learn it's much more satisfying to report on their own contribution than to avoid responsibility. (p. 34)

### SIDEBAR 9.4   The Strategy-Centered Management Meeting

One challenge to strategy implementation is tracking the progress toward the goals, and one way to achieve this is to schedule strategy progress reviews. Five questions to consider (Niven, 2005) are

1. Do we hold a strategy-centered meeting at least quarterly?
2. Do we open our strategy review meetings to anyone who is able to provide significant information on results, or do we limit attendance to management staff?
3. Are strategy-centered meetings strongly facilitated to achieve maximum effectiveness?
4. Have we established a tone in our strategy review sessions that balances the psychological safety of participants with a desire to aggressively learn about our strategy?
5. Do we track items raised during our meetings and ensure that they are reviewed at the subsequent session?

Earlier in the chapter, I described these elements as building on the foundation established in the planning and improvement process; the larger goal of strategic planning is to create alignment among the organization's staff and resources and move toward increased effectiveness and success.

## Managing Resources

There are a number of different budget management systems and fiscal management systems from which to choose. The allocation of resources receives direction, in part, from the strategy identified earlier. From the strategy, initiatives are identified, and each initiative requires resources to execute. Budgets can be used to prioritize which initiatives have the greatest impact on the objectives relative to the strategy. Kaplan and Norton (2001) described resource allocation as evolving from two different processes: the operational budget and the strategic budget. The operational budget recognizes that

> only a small percent of the spending and expenses in an annual (or quarterly) budget is discretionary. Most expenses are determined by the volume and mix of goods produced, services delivered, and customers served. The budget for such expenses reflects an expected level of spending based on forecasted revenue and the mix of products, services, and customers to generate the revenue. (Kaplan & Norton, 2001, p. 288)

Examples of the operational budget items are the costs related to the operations and infrastructure such as telephones, Web pages, salaries, benefits, heat, electricity, and other ongoing costs related to getting the work done.

Kaplan and Norton (2001) estimated those costs to be 65% of the total budget and resource allocations. Also in the operational budget are the costs of maintaining existing customers, with some adjustments for improvements or enhancements to existing services. They estimated that this portion of the operating budget constitutes an additional 25%, so the operational budget makes up 90% of the total budget, with the remaining 10% available for the strategic budget process.

The strategic budget returns to the idea that initiatives are not intended to be the endpoint of the funding but rather a means to explore a new level of service or to expand the program.

> The strategic budget authorizes the initiatives required to close the planning gap between desired breakthrough performance and that achievable by continuous improvement and business as usual. The strategic budget identifies what new operations are required; what new capabilities must be created; what new products and services must be launched; what new customers, markets, applications, and regions must be served; and what new alliances and joint ventures must be established. (Kaplan & Norton, 2001, p. 288)

In addition to managing financial resources, often overlooked are the areas of expanding information technology and effectively managing the scope of projects and time unintentionally given to areas outside of program or project scope, facilities and meeting spaces, and human resources as previously discussed. Kaplan and Norton (2004) identified strategy maps as a process to connect strategic priorities to objectives across four perspectives—the financial or fiduciary perspective, the customer perspective, the learning and growth perspective, and the internal business processes perspective—that offer organizations a way to consider how all the resources work together to achieve strategic goals (see Sidebar 9.4).

### SIDEBAR 9.5  Four Perspectives of the Strategy Map

A strategy map considers four different yet connected perspectives through which organizations can be viewed. Questions are used to guide the exploration of objectives for each perspective. The questions, by perspective, are

- *Financial or fiduciary perspective:* If we succeed, how will we look to our shareholders, taxpayers, or donors?
- *Customer perspective:* To achieve our vision, how must we look to our customers?
- *Learning and growth perspective:* To achieve our vision, how must our organization learn and improve?
- *Internal business processes perspective:* To satisfy our customers, which processes must we excel at (Kaplan & Norton, 2004, p. 8)?

Strategy mapping directly connects priorities and goals to objectives and to measures and to target goals that inform the creation of initiatives that support directly the goals and priorities, Applying these questions to your program or organization can provide insight into objectives for further development as well as an overall view to inform the management of program resources.

For a program manager, decisions regarding management of resources are challenging. The importance of working with the shared vision created through teamwork and open communication is felt during difficult budget times. Reallocating funding or reducing programs or positions is never easy, but the choices are less complicated when the pattern of decision making over time has been consistent with the mission, values, and objectives.

## Managing Communication and Relationships

Connecting career development programs and services to participants and users begins with the needs assessment. The needs assessment, if properly planned, creates awareness of the potential or current users' needs for services and programs. Understanding the needs of a target audience has always been critical to promoting and marketing career development programs effectively, yet marketing methods have changed recently. "The tools and strategies for communicating with customers have changed significantly with the emergence of the phenomenon known as *social media*, also referred to as *consumer-generated media*" (Mangold & Faulds, 2009, p. 357). The pervasive use of social media has shifted the traditional marketing interaction from providers simply sending promotional messages to customers to an extended, two-way conversation in which customers are able to voice their needs and wants in real time. The impact for career programs is that marketing efforts need to be more individualized and more immediate than ever before. Social media generate a new need to manage relationships and ensuing communications with existing and future customers. "Social media, where consumers communicate with each other across various platforms as diverse as discussion forums, blogs, wikis, social networks, and video-, photo-, and news-sharing sites, has witnessed explosive growth in recent years" (Gupta, Armstrong, & Clayton, 2010, p. 1). One example is Facebook, with more than 500 million active users, 50% of whom log on every day and join others to spend 700 billion minutes per month on Facebook (Facebook, 2010). Career development programs are not excluded from the social media phenomenon.

The influence of social media creates both a challenge and an opportunity. The opportunity is the ability to reach mass audiences. "Social media has amplified the power of consumer-to-consumer conversations in the marketplace by enabling one person to communicate with literally hundreds or thousands of other consumers quickly and with relatively little effort" (Mangold & Faulds, 2009, p. 361). The challenge is to use social media successfully. Specifically, career development professionals need to build relationships with career development program participants and establish trust and credibility around the sensitive life issues with them. Mangold and Faulds (2009) proposed nine methods to create hybrid campaigns drawing on social media elements: Provide networking platforms, use blogs and other social media tools to engage customers, use both traditional and Internet-based promotional tools to engage customers, provide information, be outrageous, provide exclusivity, design products with talking points and consumers' desired self-images in mind, support causes that are important to consumers, and last, use the power of stories. These methods, used in combination with a traditional marketing approach, enhance a career program's ability to develop strong relationships with its customers.

Developing a comprehensive marketing and promotion plan takes time. Effective marketing and promotion extends well beyond just pulling together a couple of flyers and handing them out to existing program participants. Marketing plans are about alignment between internal and external communications and the mission, values, goals, and objectives.

> Basic principles of marketing that do not change over time or with the application used include: (1) customer orientation, (2) creating your niche, (3) using promotional writing techniques, (4) promoting benefits, (5) being flexible, (6) focusing on readability, and (7) using what has been proven to work. (Edds, 2008, p. 37)

Middleton (2010) proposed a marketing strategy based on positioning, packaging, promotion, persuasion, and performance. Positioning communicates to potential users the unique aspects provided by the career development program. This area can tell the program's story to potential service users and program participants. Packaging is the plan for presenting the program's services to prospective users, generating interest and responses from potential users through marketing brochures, creating an image with a business identity package (such as letterhead and a logo), and identifying a way to connect with potential users. The purpose of packaging is to demonstrate to existing and potential users what the program is all about—the mission, the vision, the objectives, and how the program sees itself. Packaging also tells prospective users how they will be treated if they choose to use the career development program. Promoting career development services includes networking; well-crafted communications sent to existing mailing lists; a Web strategy (or at least a Web page); and getting out and speaking at community events or writing for community newspapers. One example is a workforce development center that partnered with a local newspaper to have them profile interesting and unusual jobs once a week. The newspaper ran the profile, and the workforce development center provided the occupational background information to the reporter. The persuasion process includes having a clear and concise description of the program prepared when asked "What is it that you do?" Persuasion emphasizes the value of sending consistent messages in incoming and outgoing communications and sharing success stories (when appropriate, always protecting the identity of individuals). Performance includes scheduling regular marketing meetings and making marketing a priority, keeping track of short-term and long-term marketing projects, and ensuring that programmatic actions match promises made to existing and new users.

A marketing and promotion plan is only as effective as the time and thought invested in its development, whether it involves or does not involve social media.

Effective marketing is a comprehensive and ongoing effort that includes research, program development, marketing strategy or plan, promotional activities, and customer feedback and assessment. While developing a marketing plan is a linear process, the whole process of marketing is best understood as a circular, comprehensive continuum where each part feeds important information into the other parts and where they are all integrated. (Edds, 2008, p. 37)

Effective marketing and promotion serve to showcase the results of effective management behaviors and planning processes.

## Evaluating Career Development

Comprehensive career development programs require the effective coordination of organizational culture and people, efficient and intentional planning processes, the effective management of resources, and thoughtful attention to developing and nurturing relationships within and outside the career development and counseling program. "Program design should be connected to the needs and expectations of those seeking career assistance, the support systems within the community, and the available resources" (Schutt, 2009, p. 108). Assessing and evaluating career development programs is important to sustaining and improving the services and, more important, in keeping pace with the needs of those served. Schutt (2009) articulated a process outlined by Isaac and Michael (1984) for assessing and evaluating career development programs:

There are four key steps in assessing and evaluating career development programs: needs assessment, program planning, formative (process) evaluation, and summative (outcome) evaluation. Needs assessment includes the identification of program participants. Program planning includes the mission statement, strategies, and outcome measures [as delineated in this chapter]. Formative evaluation assesses the program as an ongoing process. Summative evaluation assess the outcome of the activities, typically post program (Isaac & Michael, 1984). The evaluation of career development programs is integral and should be embedded into the planning and design process from the beginning. (Schutt, 2009, p. 108)

It is important to note that I have primarily focused on the needs assessment and program planning steps in the effective program design and evaluation plan. The outcomes from a strategy mapping process are also elements that could be included in a formal assessment and evaluation design as a part of the formative and summative steps. Planning for the assessment and evaluation of a career development program in the program establishment phase (and before implementation) ensures ongoing attention to program quality, effectiveness, and efficiency.

### SIDEBAR 9.6  Case Study: Measuring Effectiveness

Effectiveness in achieving the goals is enhanced through an assessment plan, developed annually to respond to critical issues that have emerged over the previous year, or based on the new initiatives introduced. This particular program had not created an ongoing plan for assessing success factors. The Career Services Office designed a twofold process for developing the plan: forming an internal assessment team and using an opportunity during a Web page redesign project. The traditional measures were tracking student traffic at events, tracking advising use, event and workshop evaluations, office traffic reports, and student satisfaction surveys. One tool used by the unit to measure major events was a Web-based product called Zoomerang (http://www.zoomerang.com) that offered free basic memberships. The results of the assessment plan were delivered through an annual report consisting of an update on the strategic planning goals, a staff activity report, and numerical data representing the three units within the Career Services Office.

## Summary

The process of planning, supported by strong management behaviors, can build effective and successful organizations that are aligned around mission, core values, and shared vision. Additional Web resources related to the areas discussed are listed in the next section.

Successful career development programs are based on many factors. In this chapter, I have demonstrated the importance of strategic planning and continuous improvement in all aspects of program planning. The skills of managing culture, processes, resources, and relationships are applicable to many settings; the ability of career development program managers to customize these concepts to the context in which they work and transfer this knowledge to program staff is essential.

## Useful Web Sites

- American Psychological Association: http://www.apa.org
- American School Counselor Association National Model: http://www.ascanationalmodel.org/
- California Department of Education Career Counseling: http://www.cde.ca.gov/ls/cg/cc/careercounsel.asp
- Career development facilitators: http://www.associationdatabase.com/aws/NCDA/pt/sp/facilitator_overview
- Center on Education and Work, University of Wisconsin—Madison: http://www.cew.wisc.edu/
- Cisco Systems: http://www.cisco.com/en/US/learning
- Global career development facilitators: http://www.associationdatabase.com/aws/NCDA/pt/sp/facilitator_overview
- International Association of Administrative Professionals: http://www.iaap-hq.org/
- Microsoft: http://www.microsoft.com/traincert/mcp/default.asp
- National Association of Colleges and Employers: http://www.naceweb.org/
- National Board for Certified Counselors: http://www.nbcc.org
- National Career Development Association Minimum Competencies for Multicultural Career Counseling and Development: http://www.associationdatabase.com/aws/NCDA/asset_manager/get_file/9914/minimum_competencies_for_multi-cultural_career_counseling.pdf
- National Center for Research in Vocational Education 1988–1999: http://ncrve.berkeley.edu/

- Novell: http://www.novell.com/training/certinfo/
- Oracle: http://education.oracle.com/
- University of Minnesota Career and Lifework Center: http://www .lifework.umn.edu/indicator/index.html
- University of Waterloo Career Development eManual: http://www .cdm.uwaterloo.ca/

## References

American Psychological Association. (2010). *Member.* Retrieved from http://apa .org/membership/member/index.aspx

Bossidy, L., & Charan, R. (2002). *Execution: The discipline of getting things done.* New York, NY: Crown Business.

Buckingham, M., & Coffman, C. (1999). *First, break all the rules: What the world's greatest managers do differently.* New York, NY: Simon & Schuster.

Career Connection to Teaching With Technology. (2002). *Objectives.* Retrieved from http://www.cctt.org/summaries/year5.asp

Collins, J. C., & Porras, J. I. (1997). *Built to last: Successful habits of visionary companies.* New York, NY: HarperBusiness. (Original work published 1994)

Collis, D. J., & Rukstad, M. G. (2008). Can you say what your strategy is? *Harvard Business Review, 86*(4), 82–90.

Dolence, M. G., Rowley, D. J., & Lujan, H. D. (1997). *Working toward strategic change: A step-by-step guide to the planning process.* San Francisco, CA: Jossey-Bass.

Edds, C. A. (2008). *How to market career development programs and services.* Broken Bow, OK: National Career Development Association.

Ettinger, J. (2008). Serving diverse populations. In D. Schutt (Ed.), *How to plan and develop a career center* (2nd ed.). New York, NY: Ferguson.

Facebook. (2010). *Press room statistics.* Retrieved from http://www.facebook.com/ press/info.php?statistics

Gupta, S., Armstrong, K., & Clayton, Z. (2010). *Social media* (Harvard Business School Case 9-510-09). Boston, MA: Harvard Business School.

Herr, E. L., & Cramer, S. H. (1996). *Career guidance and counseling through the lifespan: Systematic approaches* (5th ed.) New York, NY: HarperCollins.

International Association of Administrative Professionals. (2010). *The career advantage.* Retrieved from http://www.iaap-hq.org/prodev/certification/index.html

Isaac, S., & Michael, W. B. (1984). *Handbook in research and evaluation: A collection of principles, methods, and strategies useful in the planning, design, and evaluation of studies in education and the behavioral studies* (2nd ed.) San Diego, CA: EdITS. (Original work published 1981)

Kaplan, R. S., & Norton, D. P. (2001). *The strategy-focused organization: How balanced scorecard companies thrive in the new business environment.* Boston, MA: Harvard Business School.

Kaplan, R. S., & Norton, D. P. (2004). *Strategy maps: Converting intangible assets into tangible outcomes.* Boston, MA: Harvard Business School.

Mangold, W. G., & Faulds, D. J. (2009). Social media: The new hybrid element of the promotion mix. *Business Horizons, 52,* 357–365.

Middleton, R. (2010), September 4). *Why smart people don't know how to market.* Message posted to http://bpwebmarketing.com/tag/robert-middleton/2010/ 09/04/why-smart-people-don't-know-how-to-market

National Association of Colleges and Employers. (2010). *Principles for professional practice for career services & employment professionals.* Bethlehem, PA: Author. Retrieved from http://www.naceweb.org/Legal/Principles/Principles_for_Professional_Practice_(PDF).aspx

National Board for Certified Counselors. (2009). *The National Certified Counselor (NCC) credential and the National Counselor Examination (NCE).* Retrieved from http://www.nbcc.org/OurCertifications

National Career Development Association. (2010). *What is a career development facilitator (CDF)?* Retrieved from http://www.associationdatabase.com/aws/NCDA/pt/sp/facilitator_overview#1

*National Career Development Guidelines Framework: Understanding the NCDG framework.* (2004). Retrieved from http://associationdatabase.com/aws/NCDA/asset_manager/get_file/3384/ncdguidelines2007.pdf

Niven, P. R. (2002). *Balanced scorecard step-by-step: Maximizing performance and maintaining results.* New York, NY: Wiley.

Niven, P. R. (2005). *Balanced scorecard diagnostics: Maintaining maximum performance.* Hoboken, NJ: Wiley.

Oakland University School of Education and Human Services Adult Career Counseling Center. (2010). *Our mission.* Retrieved from http://www.oakland.edu/sehs/accc/

Perry, N. (1995). *Program guide—Planning to meet career development needs: School-to-work transition programs.* Washington, DC: National Occupational Information Coordinating Committee.

Person, R. (2009). *Balanced scorecards & operational dashboards with Microsoft Excel.* Indianapolis, IN: Wiley.

Ruben, B. D. (2004). *Pursuing excellence in higher education: Eight fundamental challenges.* New York, NY: Wiley.

Ryan, K. D., & Oestreich, D. K. (1998). *Driving fear out of the workplace: Creating the high-trust, high-performance organization.* San Francisco, CA: Jossey-Bass.

Sampson, J. P., Jr. (2008). *Designing and implementing career programs: A handbook for effective practice.* Broken Arrow, OK: National Career Development Association.

Schutt, D. A. (1999). *How to plan and develop a career center.* Chicago, IL: Ferguson.

Schutt, D. A. (2009). Innovative strategies for teaching career development program design and evaluation. *Career Planning and Adult Development Journal, 25,* 107–118.

Thomas, D. A., & Ely, R. J. (1996). *Making differences matter: A new paradigm for managing diversity. Harvard Business Review, 74*(5), 79–90.

University of Louisiana at Lafayette Career Services. (2008). *Mission.* Retrieved from http://careerservices.louisiana.edu/about/about_us.html

U.S. Department of Labor, Employment and Training Administration. (2010). *ETA mission.* Retrieved from http://www.doleta.gov/etainfo/mission.cfm

Van Mell, D. (2008). *Question-based planning: Business planning without mission, vision, strategy, tactics or objectives.* Madison, WI: Tranton Press Books.

Virtual Career Center, Career Management Center, Old Dominion University. (2006). *Core values.* Retrieved from http://www.odu.edu/ao/cmc/about/mission.shtml

Wilder, W., & Risher, H. (2010). Succession planning: It should make a difference. *HR News, 76*(9), 18–22.

Zenger, J. H., & Folkman, J. (2002). *The extraordinary leader: Turning good managers into great leaders.* New York, NY: McGraw-Hill.

CHAPTER **10**

# Supervision, Coaching, and Consultation

Laura R. Simpson and Matthew V. Glowiak

## Contents

Counseling, in general, is an incredibly multidimensional occupation. Career counseling is no exception. Meeting the various needs and interests of each client can be a counselor's greatest challenge. Thus, considering how to best meet those identified needs requires special attention. Career counselors may be asked to assume many diverse roles when working with individuals. Comprehending the similarities and differences among these assorted roles is the first step in determining how to best meet the needs of clients. This chapter was designed to explore some of the specific roles that career counselors may engage in while working with clients.

Too often, individuals try to fit themselves into a job and end up patterning their lives around it. According to Hayes (2001), a survey of 400 college-educated workers between the ages of 30 and 55 revealed that almost half would choose a different major if they could do it over. Career counselors can assist people in matching their values, interests, skills, and capabilities with occupations or professions that meet their personal needs. Career counselors are most appropriate for people who need encouragement to enter into, change, or reevaluate their career or life goals or who need to evaluate retirement career options. When tailoring an approach to assist a client, a career counselor may engage in many roles, including consultant, coach, and supervisor. Although these roles are similar, each is distinctly separate. In this chapter, we examine the roles of consultation, coaching, and supervision in relation to career counseling, as well as providing practical examples of how these roles might be applied to the counseling process.

### SIDEBAR 10.1   Did You Know?

In a survey conducted with college students, Wood (2004) found that more than 75% said they were in college "to get a good job" and "to make more money" (p. 71). What are the risks involved with making prestige and money one's top priority before entering the workforce? Take an honest look in the mirror and ask yourself whether these values are what drive your career choices. Matt is a high school student who refuses to consider any vocational choices unless they are going to make him "richer than God." Do you think you would experience bias if you were working with Matt? Would you grow weary of his constant emphasis on money in his career decision-making process?

## Variables Considered in Career Path Decision

Many factors may contribute to one's vocational selection. These factors include but are not limited to the jobs available, location, pay, ability, scholastic achievement, experience, personality, beliefs and values, work schedule, personnel, management, and benefits offered. Beyond these factors, consideration should also be given to diverse populations.

Clients of color are routinely targets of racism and discrimination. Best practices of career counseling would call for practitioners to consider cultural identity and contexts and environmental variables (Byars-Winston & Fouad, 2006, p. 188). For instance, living in poverty, lack of educational opportunities, and discriminatory interview practices create barriers that many dominant cultures do not face. As a result, finding work becomes significantly more complicated. Therefore, failure to acknowledge cultural constraints may lead eventually to the creation of overly simplified solutions that do not adequately fit the needs of such populations (Byars-Winston & Fouad, 2006, p. 189).

Women are also subject to difficulties in the workforce. Although social norms have shifted away from the traditional view of the man working while the woman stays home, barriers for women still exist, particularly in nontraditional lines of work (Quimby & DeSantis, 2006, p. 297). This phenomenon is a result of societal implications for both men and women—men to an extent still try to dominate the workforce, and women are still continuing to establish their place within these roles. Time and education continue to help women break through vocational barriers. Current theories, as proposed by Quimby and DeSantis (2006), suggest that female mentors in these roles advocate for further advancement in these types of careers (p. 297).

Mentorship, in this respect, may actually prove to be fruitful across all walks of diversity, even within the dominant culture.

Individuals with disabilities also face difficulties establishing a foothold in the workforce. Despite legislation protecting the worker with disabilities, career counselors must still make special considerations. "For persons with disabilities, a long-used strategy in job placement was to match the person's abilities and interests to those matching people in certain occupations" (Tansey, Mizelle, Ferrin, Tschopp, & Frain, 2004, p. 39). More recent literature has found that stress-related variables resulting from disability elicit a major impact on the careers that individuals with disabilities select (Tansey et al., 2004, p. 34). Once again, the theme here is that career counselors must take an individualized approach that goes beyond merely assessing one's abilities, motivations, or inclinations for a specific line of work.

Religious and spiritual variables are also important for the new age career counselor to consider. Newer research has begun to delve into discovering whether one's calling to a specific vocation exists. A *calling to a vocation* is the phenomenon of matching oneself with a line of work that is a perfect fit. Does this really exist? According to Dik, Duffy, and Eldridge (2009), one's calling is the result of three overlapping dimensions: (1) "a transcendent summons, experienced as originating beyond the self;" (2) "to approach a particular life role in a manner oriented toward demonstrating or deriving a sense of purpose or meaningfulness;" and (3) "that holds other-oriented values and goals as primary sources of motivation" (p. 625). Although little empirical evidence exists for this phenomenon, counselors may find themselves working with clients who feel quite strongly that it is at play in their vocational decision making.

## Many Roles of Career Counseling

### Consultant

Consultation frequently occurs within the hierarchical relationship between a supervisor and a supervisee, as well as in relationships between peers of equal status. There is little doubt that consultation activities are distinctly different from those that involve administrative or evaluative functions (Hays & Brown, 2004a). "It is essentially a problem solving process in which the two participants in the process identify the relevant difficulties, collaborate on some intervention, and then assess the results, making adjustments as needed" (Bradley & Kottler, 2001, p. 14). Consultation provides an indirect service to a client or group for whom the helping intervention is intended (Backer, 2003; Drapela, 1983).

Consultation as an activity and consultant as a career label became increasingly prevalent in the last decades of the 20th century. Although generally recognized as originating in the medical profession, today an endless variety of professions use the label *consultant*. The characteristics and models of consultation are easily applied to career counseling.

## Characteristics of Consultants

Regardless of the vocational arena, a variety of components characterize consultation. According to Brown, Pryzwansky, and Schulte (1991); Dougherty (2005); Gibson and Mitchell (2007); Gladding (2008); O'Roark (2002); and Scholten (2003), some components are as follows:

1. The consultant is considered an expert, whether a master counselor or, in the case of career consultation, an individual with extensive training and experience in the area of need.
2. The consultee is considered capable. Whether the individual is a counselor looking for assistance in dealing with a client or an employee seeking career intervention, he or she is accepted as potentially capable. If the consultant does not view the consultee as such, the effectiveness of the consultation may be threatened.
3. The consultant and consultee must be well matched and complementary. The role of the consultant is to help with personal and professional development, competency development, and the institution and continuation of accountability. The primary role of the consultee is to seek and benefit from the consultant's expertise in the attainment of responsible self-development.
4. A need exists that cannot be met by the individual or organization requesting the consultation.

Career consultants provide career counseling and placement services. The focus is generally on job search strategies and support. Consultants are typically degreed professionals with experience in business, industry, or the public sector. Executive placement consultants, or headhunters, work for employers, not the job seeker. Headhunters seek qualified people to fit existing positions, and they are paid by the employer. Although not useful for those changing careers, headhunters perform a valuable service for employers and those with recent and relevant transferable skills and experience.

**SIDEBAR 10.2  Consultation**

After building his business from the ground up, Rashad has finally moved up the ranks from small business to a full-blown Fortune 500 company. Although this achievement is certainly momentous for Rashad and his employees, he realizes that changes must be made to continue this forward momentum. New employees must be hired, new positions must be created, and select individuals will be promoted as more branches are opened. Recently, Rashad has been meeting with his executive team to make the best decisions for his company, but not all suggestions are being well received. Although Rashad realizes that not all of his suggestions will be perfect, he believes that because he conceived a business that has become successful so quickly, his ideas should weigh significantly more than anyone else's. In what ways would a consultant be able to help Rashad and his business continue to grow?

## Models of Consultation

Consultation and its application to counseling has been widely recognized and defined, although not nearly as well publicized as its business counterpart (Gibson & Mitchell, 2007). However, consultation as an activity for counselors has led to an examination of various models appropriate to the consultation process and their adaptation to counselor use. In this section, we examine a number of commonly used consultation models.

## Triadic Model

A traditional model that highlights the basic consultation process is the triadic model (Gibson & Mitchell, 2007; Newman, 1993). The triad is made up of a consultant, a consultee, and the consultee's client. In this model, consultation services are offered indirectly through an intermediary to target clients. The consultant has direct contact with the consultee, yet the issues discussed and the assistance offered is focused on a third party. All consultation efforts proceed to the third party through the consultee; none proceed directly from consultant to clients. The consultee derives some professional and personal benefits from the consultation process as well.

Kurpius (1978) and Kurpius and Fuqua (1993) suggested that the consultant can function effectively in several ways. The consultant may provide a direct service to a client by prescribing a solution to a specific problem identified by a consultee, assist a consultee in developing a plan for problem solving, or take a more directive approach by actually defining a problem and proposing a solution. These functions are organized into four consultation modalities.

### Provision Mode

The provision mode of consultation is used when a client finds her- or himself confronted with a problem and without the resources of time, interest, or competence to define the problem objectively, generate possible solutions, or implement a problem-solving strategy. In this case, a consultant is requested to provide a direct service to the client, with minimal or no intervention by the consultee after the referral is in place. For a career counselor functioning in this mode, the consultee could be an agency with a specific employee issue. For example, the board of a nonprofit organization might engage a career counselor to assist a new agency director in expanding fund-raising skills to better meet the needs of the position requirements.

### Prescriptive Mode

This mode is used when a consultee is looking for a specific solution or prescription for a specific problem. The consultant and consultee work together to ensure that all information needed to define and solve the problem is available and accurate and that the consultee accepts the plan prescribed and will implement the program as designed by the consultant. They also specify who will evaluate the process and outcomes. In this case, a career counselor might provide consultation to the board directly and prescribe specific training opportunities for the new director's development.

### Collaboration Mode

If this mode is used, the consultant functions more as a facilitator than as a technical expert. The consultant's efforts are aimed at assisting the consultee in maximizing his or her resources, realizing his or her abilities, and developing a plan for problem solving. This process may include providing feedback, making suggestions, and examining circumstances that may impede or assist with the resolution of the problem at hand. For a career counselor functioning in the collaboration mode, the consultation will involve meeting with the board (consultee) to explore potential resources among current staff to best meet the fundraising needs of the agency.

### Mediation Mode

Mediation is uniquely different from the previous three modes of consultation in which the consultee initiates contact and requests help for solving a problem. In mediation, the consultant recognizes a problem, gathers and interprets information, and determines an appropriate intervention, ultimately resulting in contacting the people who have the greatest potential for implementing change and sharing the proposed solution to the problem. Thus, the career counselor who has been working with the agency may recognize that the board and the director are not communicating and note a high employee turnover rate. The consultant approaches the board and makes suggestions on how to reduce turnover, bringing the two sides together to address the identified problem.

## Types of Consultation

Some models break down the consultation process into even more specific roles. Blocher (1987) identified seven models of consultation that help identify many of the specific roles of consultants.

1. *Triadic consultation:* Characterized by three distinct roles, this model uses a consultant who provides specific expertise, a mediator who applies the feedback of the consultant, and the client who is the focus of the service.
2. *Technical consultation:* Technical consultation is a narrow and specific intervention focused on a specific expert in relation to a specific problem. A career counselor with experience in a specific vocational arena might be used for technical consultation. For example, a career counselor with experience as a teacher might provide consultation for a school with teachers in need of classroom management techniques.
3. *Collaborative consultation:* Collaborative consultation is a cooperative relationship between a consultant and a consultee that combines the collective resources of the two; the pair work as equal partners. For example, a career counselor might provide collaborative consultation for a police department through the provision of assessment techniques to determine strengths and weaknesses of new officers.
4. *Facilitative consultation:* The consultant facilitates the consultee's access and use of resources. The consultant expresses legitimate interest in the functioning of the consultee.

5. *Mental health consultation:* The consultant assists a counselor in gaining better understanding of the interaction with a client through such means as analyzing the treatment approach, considering the consultee's responses to the client, and providing general education and support. This approach is the same as the consultation mode of Bernard's (1979) discrimination model of supervision, discussed later in this chapter.

6. *Behavioral consultation:* This model is focused on the consultant teaching the consultee behavior management techniques, which, when understood and implemented, influence the behavior of the consultee's clients. For example, a career counselor may provide consultation for a business to develop specific responses to customer issues on customer service lines.

7. *Process consultation:* The consultant provides services to an organization as a means of increasing the effectiveness of a work group in reaching its goals. This approach examines the interactions among groups of individuals who work with each other and their existing relationships. A career counselor may provide process consultation when two banks merge, retaining all employees. The consultation can assist employees who were formerly competitors with working together successfully.

Regardless of model choice, counselor consultants must recognize that they are involved in a process that provides structure and direction for their consultation efforts. It is naive to think that knowledge or experience in itself qualifies one to consult. An understanding of the process of consultation and the acquisition of skills for consultation are prerequisites to success as a consultant. Although experience is important, these skills and knowledge are typically acquired through special courses in consultation.

## Consultative Relationship

The consultative relationship is distinct from other relationships between counselor and client. A consultant is usually an expert in a field who consults with or offers expertise to others within and outside of the career area. Consultation occurs when the expertise is requested by another party or organization. The consultant's role is an advising or enhancing one, not a supervisory one. Unlike counseling, it is not a therapeutic relationship.

### SIDEBAR 10.3    Collaborative Efforts

"Teamwork makes the dream work." Okay, this saying might be a little cheesy, but it most certainly has merit. Problems in the workplace are generally a combination of both personal and external factors that may be taken into consideration. For instance, Sean is disgruntled with the fact that his employer has tacked an extra 5 hours onto the workweek to complete a project for a new customer, and he is struggling to balance the needs of his professional and personal lives. He understands the need to work the extra hours, but in doing this he will not be available for his children's immediate after-school needs. How would a consultant and counselor be able to work together to create a plan that will meet this employee's needs?

Although not traditional counseling, consultation does share certain special skills that are needed if the counselor is to function effectively as a consultant. Some skills include

- The expertise needed to address the identified need and provide effective intervention
- Knowledge of and experience in the consultation process
- The recognition and understanding of differing environments and their impacts on populations and organizations (Backer, 2003; Brown et al., 1991; Dougherty, 2005; Gladding, 2008).

The counselor who is functioning in the consultation role should possess and use those skills essential to the counseling process. Critical communication and specialized interpersonal skills such as attending, listening, questioning, and feedback are essential. Respect and understanding should be emphasized. Consultants should possess expertise in systematic problem-solving techniques and evaluation procedures as well. Skills in facilitating groups can be very helpful. These characteristics combine to equip the career counselor to transition from facilitator, mediator, planner, educator, and motivator, as needed.

Career counselors acting as consultants must be mindful that requests for consultation may be based on a foundation of the consultee's unresolved personal problems. For instance, a manager of a local business who wishes to consult about an employee may end up discussing her own personal problems. A counselor who realizes that the initial consultation is shifting toward counseling will likely respond to the personal needs of the manager but avoid losing sight of the primary professional responsibility to the employees of the business. After providing short-term assistance to the manager, the counselor may suggest additional counseling elsewhere and provide information regarding available counseling opportunities in the community. Such an approach will help the counselor uphold professional priorities and maintain an ongoing consulting relationship with the manager that will focus on the needs of the employees for whose benefit the helping intervention was initiated.

Counseling and consultation have an inherent overlap in the area of occupational issues. If occupational issues are closely linked to personal problems, they are dealt with through counseling. For example, an employee who experiences a reactive depression because of job-related pressures needs counseling assistance. If occupational issues are related to problems of a third party, they may fall within the perimeter of consultation. This situation could be the case if an employer asks for consultation because of employees' insubordination. In the process of consultation, it becomes evident that the problem lies with the employer, who lacks management skills and needs personalized instruction in this area.

The qualified career counselor will have multiple opportunities to consult. The effective consultant will always be mindful that for consultation to be effective, it must be wanted. Even when requested, the consultant should proceed with tact and understanding in providing ideas, opinions, and solutions to others.

## Ethical and Legal Concerns

Traditional counseling differs from consulting relationships in several primary ways. These differences require special deliberation in evaluating ethical considerations. The code of ethics for helping professionals provides only limited guidance for consultation practice, leaving clinicians to bear vast personal responsibility for their professional actions and decisions.

### Relationship Issues

At the most fundamental level, the triadic nature of consulting relationships must be considered. Ethical issues are complicated by the involvement of three parties in the relationship: the consultant, the consultee, and the consultee's client. Snow and Gersick (1986) said that it is

> conceptually awkward to consider clients of the consultee agency to be part of the consultation agreement since they are not present, do not have the opportunity to articulate their own priorities, and most often do not even know that a consultation is taking place. (p. 401)

Thus, the consultee's client is affected by the consultation process without the opportunity to participate in the process (Newman, 1993). Thus, it is generally agreed that the consultant's responsibility extends to these individuals (Backer, 2003; Brown et al., 1991; Newman, 1993; Newman & Robinson, 1991).

### Confidentiality

Confidentiality represents an individual's right to privacy and establishes the foundation of trust that is essential to successful outcomes. Although confidentiality has been widely addressed, the special circumstances of consultation require particular consideration.

"Given the practical limits of a consultant's ability to protect the confidentiality of information obtained during the consultation, individuals' rights to privacy may be difficult or even impossible to guarantee" (Newman, 1993, p. 150). Clearly, the consultant has an ethical responsibility to ensure that participants understand what information will be used as well as with whom it will be used and for what purpose. The limits of confidentiality must be plainly and unanimously understood by all participants. Consider this: A career counselor is called to provide consultation for a school interested in determining why a teacher is having difficulty disciplining her students. The teacher reveals to the consultant that she has a history of childhood abuse. Clearly, it would be important for the teacher to know on the front end that her employer will be informed of any information provided to the consultant.

### Power

Within the consultation process, power, or the ability to influence, is typically irregularly distributed among participants. Thus, the potential misuse or abuse of power is a concern in the consultation process (Hays & Brown, 2004b). This irregular distribution of power may exist between the consultant and the consultee organization or within the organization itself. Power differentials may be real or perceived, but they may exert substantial influence on the process and outcomes of consultation.

Because the consultant role is one of expert, the potential for an imbalanced power relationship exists (Tokunga, 1984). Consultants must make every effort to ensure their power is used to facilitate the goals and welfare of the consultee. "Collaborative definition of organizational interests and goals with the consultee will reduce the likelihood that the consultant will exploit this influence to facilitate unilaterally defined objectives" (Newman, 1993, p. 152). Power differentials within the organization itself may benefit from a positive influence of the consultant's own responsible use of power. Consultants are in a unique position to educate consultees in constructive methods for using power to extract cooperation from employees and for strengthening cooperative commitments to organizational goals (Merrell, 1991). The issue of power could be pertinent to a career counselor if consultation is requested for a situation in which the consultant has a personal interest. For example, perhaps the consultant called into an elementary school setting to assess student preparation for high school has a strong interest in foreign language. The consultant must be careful not to misuse power in the role of expert by pushing his or her personal agenda onto the consultee.

### Competence

It has been written that the most basic requirement for consultants wishing to ensure competent practice is a thorough understanding of their own limitations (Newman, 1993; Snow & Gersick, 1986). Consultants must develop the means to evaluate their own skills, knowledge, and expertise relative to the specific demands of the practice of consultation. They must recognize the margins of their competence and confine their practice accordingly. Equally as important, consultants must be aware of personal and interpersonal characteristics that might influence their perceptions, judgments, decisions, and actions (Schein, 2003). Consultants must maintain awareness to avoid defining organizational problems through the lens of their specific areas of expertise and resist pressure to provide services outside the boundaries of their competence (Gallesich, 1982; Scholten, 2003; Snow & Gersick, 1986). To assist in avoiding this risk, cautiously defining parameters of proficiency with the consultee before engaging in the consulting relationship is recommended. Finally, consultants have an ethical responsibility to be conscious of new developments in theory, research, and technology that might affect the quality of their services to consultees (Newman, 1993; O'Roark, 2002).

The complex nature of consulting relationships creates unique issues and challenges for career counselors. The need to balance the interests of multiple parties while maintaining awareness of personal strengths and limitations is imperative. Consultants must recognize and accept responsibility for the impact of their professional decisions and actions while adhering to professional and ethical standards (O'Roark, 2002).

## Career Coaching

Career coaching is a relatively new practice that combines the concepts of career counseling, organizational consulting, and employee development (Chung & Gfroerer, 2003). It is much less defined than consultation and involves considerable controversy among counseling professionals.

Think of a career coach as a job counselor. The coach helps people identify their sharpest skills, define their career goals, be more productive, set strategies to earn more money, and make them more valuable to their current or next boss (Chung & Gfroerer, 2003; Hube, 1996). A career coach can guide people's professional development, identifying and opening doors (Myers, 1996; Wasylyshyn, 2003). "You might even enlist a coach to help you become more creative, live with chemotherapy or attention-deficit disorder, resolve conflicts, market a book, or play in a rock 'n' roll band" (D. S. Campbell, 1999, para. 7).

Career coaches have been around for some time under other names such as mentor, management consultant, and human resource specialist (Hagevik, 1998). Career coaching has emerged as an individualized service to professionals who want to enhance their personal effectiveness by improving their communication and negotiating skills, professional presence, and other interpersonal abilities while remaining in their present job. Many career coaches provide their services via telephone or online.

There is considerable comparison between career coaching and career counseling as an occupation. Both address career planning, accomplishment of career alternatives, and the interaction of personal and vocational issues. Yet, the two specialties differ in some significant ways. Career counselors are trained professional counselors with a specialization in career interventions for which national and state credentialing is available. The field of career coaching is fundamentally unregulated, with only a few coaching institutions offering certificates and ethical codes (Chung & Gfroerer, 2003).

Initially, career coaching was an expansion of managers acting as coaches to their employees (Rich, 1998). However, the managers themselves found a need for improvement in management style and assistance with strategic planning or organizational development (Hudson, 1999b). Thus, career counselors found themselves with an extended role, and professional career coaches were an expansion of this need. Virtually nonexistent as recently as 1990, an estimated 1,500 coaches advised about 20,000 workers a year by 1996 (Hube, 1996). By 1999, with an estimated 10,000 coaches worldwide, coaches were helping to start businesses, straighten out finances, and improve personal and business relationships (D. S. Campbell, 1999).

The tasks of a career coach include facilitating continuity and change, clarifying core values and beliefs, identifying key social roles, tapping emerging developmental challenges, and developing a continuous learning agenda (Hudson, 1999a). Yet, what coaches often offer is common sense. Many people in stable work situations are so immersed in their day-to day job duties that they lack the perspective and objectivity to make major changes on their own. Hiring a coach can also be the route to moving up or even out. Career coaches make long-term commitments to work with clients as they move through job and life transitions, acting as an advisor during the transitions and helping clients reach full career potential (Myers, 1996). Coaches attend to specific problems through the implementation of strategies designed to bring about change (Grant, 2003). It has even been suggested that coaches are needed for clients "so someone will hold them accountable for taking action when they say they will" (D. S. Campbell, 1999, para. 29). An example of how a career counselor might function as a coach could be an insurance agent requesting assistance to improve sales. The coach would assist the agent in maximizing skills to increase productivity.

Coaches should have interpersonal, communication, team and group, and change mastery skills to assist clients in developing a new skill set, learn the culture, and build a new support network (Clarke, 1999). However, career coaching has no universal requirements. Depending on the state, some counselors must meet rigorous state licensing requirements and have an advanced degree in counseling or social work (Hayes, 2001). However, some coaches draw on years of work experience and simply hang out a shingle. Regardless of training, ethical coaches realize when clients fall out of their scope of practice and should be referred to other specialists. If an athlete tears a ligament, the coach does not fix it him- or herself; he or she sends the athlete to a doctor. Similarly, if stress on the job is caused by difficulties at home, a qualified counselor is in order.

Many dynamics within the career counselor's relationship with a client may call for the role of coach instead of counselor. Although both career coaches and career counselors work with clients in a confidential work relationship, career coaching is largely task and problem-solving oriented, as opposed to career counseling in which psychological interventions are often used. Counselors work with clients to achieve self-understanding and awareness in career planning, and they may use professional instruments to assess personality traits to aid in the awareness process. Conversely, career coaches who have not been trained as counselors generally do not have the skills or credentials to use professional assessment instruments and to work with mental health issues such as abuse, clinical depression, or addiction. Coaches suspecting damage or a need for healing within a client should be prepared to refer the client to a counseling professional.

Counseling and coaching can complement one another, and it is not uncommon for someone to work with both a coach and a counselor simultaneously. While working with a counselor, past experiences and patterns that cause blocks or challenges may be examined. A coach focuses on the future to assist the individual in defining what he or she wants to be and do and designs a step-by-step plan for accomplishment. Generally, career counselors assist clients in finding direction and focus; in coaching, clients arrive with certain goals and the coach helps them reach those goals. For example, a career counselor might work with a salesperson to condense a current level of sales from 6 days into 5 days.

Thus, career counselors are typically used by individuals who want to find a field to enter or by experienced workers trying to reevaluate their careers. Career coaches help clients achieve specific goals to improve their current career. Goals may include such issues as finding more time to spend with family, how to cultivate new business, and how to delegate duties to others. It is an individualized service to professionals who want to enhance their personal effectiveness by improving their communication and negotiating skills, professional presence, and other interpersonal abilities while remaining in their present job.

## Coaching Models

Although many career coaches do not have professional training, career counselors who are filling the role of coach should be familiar with coaching models. According to Price and Llevento (1999), the three major approaches to coaching are

1. Coaching for leadership, with focus on leadership support
2. Coaching for development and success, with an emphasis on current or future assignments and opportunities
3. Coaching for performance, with a focus on enhancement for current and future challenges.

Within each of these major approaches to coaching, there are specific models and techniques. One such coaching model is coactive coaching (Whitmore, Whitmore, Kimsey-House, & Sandahl, 2007). Developed by professional career coaches, this model is similar to person-centered counseling theory because it upholds the premise that the client has the answers and that the job of the coach is to listen and empower rather than inform and advise. This approach endorses that all people are naturally creative, resourceful, whole, and completely capable of finding their own answers to whatever challenges they face. On the basis of this assertion, strategies and techniques specifically target actions in the specific direction identified by the client. The intent is to deepen the client's life learning and enjoyment. The key outcome for this approach is to assist the client in creating genuine fulfillment and balance while engaging more fully in life as it unfolds. It is a holistic approach built on the principle that all parts of people's lives are interrelated. In contrast to a consulting model in which one person is an expert and the other is in need of expertise, participants using a coaching model recognize their complementary strengths and weaknesses. Thus, a career counselor functioning within this role might observe an employee at work to illuminate strengths that promote success and assist in identifying barriers that detract from success. Consider a fitness trainer. As a consultant, the trainer would write a workout plan. As a coach, the trainer would push the individual to run farther.

Another counseling model that is applicable to career coaching is Hershenson's (1996) model of work adjustment, which addresses relationships among three interacting intrapersonal domains and the individual's work environment. This model parallels career coaching because it takes an approach focusing on personality, work competencies, work habits, and work goals while considering the work setting.

According to Hershenson (1996), each individual has "three sequentially developing, interactive subsystems of work personality . . . , work competence . . . , and work goals" (p. 444). Work adjustment is accomplished through the interaction of these three subsystems in relation to the work environment. The three components of work adjustment are work role behavior, task performance, and worker satisfaction. These three components are connected to intrapersonal subsystems and work settings.

Three environments largely shape the development of the three intrapersonal subsystems. Initially, the family affects the development of work personality, which includes the individual's self-concept as a worker, system of work motivation, and system of work-related needs and values. Second, school experience primarily affects the development of work competencies, which consist of work habits, interpersonal skills, and physical and mental skills. Promptness, neatness, and reliability are examples of work habits. Finally, work goals are influenced by an individual's peer or reference group. Comprehensible, reasonable work goals should be consistent with the individual's work personality and competencies.

> In counseling for work adjustment, the counselor focuses on the relationship between the person and the work setting. The counselor must determine if the work problem is one of work role behavior, task performance, worker satisfaction, or some combination of the three. (Hershenson, 1996, p. 444)

On determining the specific nature of the problem, the role of coach may be useful in determining and implementing a solution-focused approach to improving the problem.

## Coaching Relationship

Because career coaches typically engage in a relationship that is longer than some career interventions, the dynamic between the coach and the client is critical. Work styles and backgrounds among career coaches differ. Thus, when choosing a coach, the client should verify that the knowledge and expertise are available to help develop the tools and strategies to achieve goals (Wasylyshyn, 2003).

The chemistry between the career coach and the client is important, because trust and commitment are key elements to predicting success. Additionally, because career coaches are less restricted by traditional boundaries and may assume a more active role in providing assistance, the relationship is critical. Career coaches "may interact with their clients in the clients' homes, places of employment, or over the telephone or Internet and may participate in the clients' work activities in order to observe, provide instant feedback, and implement career plans with clients" (Chung & Gfroerer, 2003, p. 142). Counselors typically configure their interactions with their clients in scheduled, face-to-face meetings in their counseling offices and tend to facilitate change rather than actively participate in the process of change.

As in the counseling relationship, career coaches depend on accurate interpersonal skills to facilitate a successful interaction. Listening and attending skills are emphasized as well as strengths in behavioral observations because coaches often observe clients functioning within their work environment. Because coaches tend to be more proactive in their interactions with clients, creativity and enthusiasm are necessary tools when assisting individuals in making personal change.

## Ethical and Legal Concerns

### Training

Of primary interest when considering the ethical issues inherent in the current practice of career coaching is the fact that no recognized professional organization exists that stipulates required guidelines for the training and practice of career coaching (Chung & Gfroerer, 2003). Although career counselors have nationally recognized bodies that accredit counselor training programs (e.g., Council for Accreditation of Counseling and Related Educational Programs), national certificates or state licenses for counselors or counseling psychologists (e.g., National Board for Certified Counselors), and relevant professional codes of ethics (e.g., American Counseling Association, American Psychological Association, National Career Development Association), the field of career coaching is limited to specific coaching institutes that offer specific training certificates. Thus, there is no national accrediting body to regulate training or continuing education, which is potentially hazardous for clients in need of specialized assistance because there are no guarantees of training or expertise. Approximately 90% of all career coaches hold at least a bachelor's degree, whereas only 50% hold a graduate degree (Chung & Gfroerer, 2003). Any individual who chooses to identify him- or herself as a career coach may do so. Many counseling professionals do not even recognize career coaching as a legitimate profession. Although the United States has many training programs for career coaches, none is accredited by a nationally recognized body. In addition, some training programs do not screen applicants for relevant educational background (Crockett 1996, as cited in Chung & Gfroerer, 2003). As a result of the lack of training and governing of credentials, it has been posited that standards of competence are called for when the goal is behavioral change (Brotman, Liberi, & Wasylyshyn, 1998). Wasylyshyn (2001) wrote, "Coaches who have not had training in psychology or in related behavior science are less likely to be successful in handling . . . a deeply entrenched and dysfunctional behavior pattern" (p. 17). This statement supports the concept that career coaching, as one of many roles of a career counselor, makes for better preparation for dealing with situations that arise during the coaching process. Without training in the multiple roles of career counseling, career coaches may lack the skill to deal with difficult and potentially dangerous situations that may leave both coaches and their clients at a critical disadvantage.

### Cultural Competence

Because one common goal of career coaching is to facilitate personal success and life satisfaction, sensitivity to individual values, beliefs, and cultural practices is imperative. Specialized training in cultural sensitivity—including the meaning and importance of work, the roles of family and significant others in an individual's career decision making, and the value of individual career development—is imperative to the success of career coaching and may be impeded by lack of exposure or training related to these issues.

Clear evidence exists of the importance of the role coaches can play in the career counseling process. Although some counseling professionals believe career coaches' training and ethical guidelines should be more regulated, the benefits of coaching are evident. Focusing on the individualized needs of employed individuals, coaches offer dynamic exploration of action-oriented solutions to specific problems in an effort to maximize potential, control careers, and manage personal and professional development. For example, a career counselor needs to be culturally sensitive in efforts to make a salesperson more productive. If a counselor coaches a salesperson on a hearty handshake and eye contact without taking into account that in his or her culture eye contact could be considered rude, the counselor may create feelings of inadequacy in the salesperson.

## Supervision

Counseling supervision has emerged as an increasingly important component of career counseling. Clinical supervision has been defined as "regular, ongoing supervision of counseling provided by another trained and experienced professional" (Remley, Benshoff, & Mowbray, 1987, p. 53). During the past decade, supervision has matured into a distinct specialty (Riordan & Kern, 1994). The importance of extensive, high-quality supervision has become recognized as critical to learning, maintaining, and improving professional counseling skills (Benshoff, 1994). Supervision is important to the ongoing professional development of counselors, as well as the counseling profession as a whole (Cobia & Boes, 2000). Supervision within the educational process coordinates a "major avenue of entry into the ranks of new professionals" (Pitts & Miller, 1990, para. 30). Additionally, empirical research has suggested that "supervision is an essential feature" of successful therapists (Emanuel, Miller, & Rustin, 2002, p. 581). Thus, supervision plays an essential role in the comprehensive development of practicing career counselors. Magnuson, Norem, and Wilcoxon (2000) reported that during the 1980s, authors asserted that the existing knowledge related to the counseling supervision process was insufficient. Contemporary supervisors now have an abundance of texts and journals to guide their work. Refinement of supervision theory and practice has been addressed by credentialing bodies such as the National Board for Certified Counselors with the implementation of the approved clinical supervisor credential (Magnuson et al., 2000). Relevant literature has identified specific roles and goals of supervisors, including supervision of career counselors (Bronson, 2001; H. A. Dye & Borders, 1990). Competent supervisors are able to convey their counseling knowledge and skills in a way that promotes a supervisee's effectiveness and professional identity. Clinical supervisors have the potential to positively or negatively influence students and clients with knowledge and life lessons. Clinical supervisors may influence students through relational trust, consultation, and collaboration, and counselors develop rapport to form a therapeutic alliance (Newgent, Davis & Farley, 2004). Clinical supervisors and counselors alike must understand the diversity and cultural issues of each student and client. Successful clinical supervisors are those who are approachable and will listen to and validate ideas. In other words, great clinical supervisors create an atmosphere of learning, collaboration, and consultation (Palmer, 2007). Primary functions of the supervisor include monitoring and evaluating, instructing and advising, modeling, consulting, and supporting and sharing (Bernard & Goodyear, 2009; Bronson, 2001). These functions encompass many tasks, including teaching counseling and intervention skills, case conceptualization, professional roles, emotional awareness, and self-evaluation (Bernard & Goodyear, 2009). Because supervision is concerned with the professional and personal growth of the counselors, it offers a direct service to professional staff members (Drapela, 1983). The American Association of State Counseling Boards (2010; http://www.aascb.org/associations/7905/files/AASCB_Supervision_Model-0607.pdf) stated that clinical supervision

> includes, but is not limited to, the supervisor's participation in the diagnostic evaluation, diagnosis, the development of a service plan, progress notes and other documentation, release of clinical information, appropriate referral, appropriate use of more experienced colleagues, adherence to applicable laws and ethics, and nurturing the therapeutic process. The clinical supervisor endeavors to insure competence of professional services, achieve and sustain appropriate standards of care, and to facilitate the supervisee's professional development.

Although both the supervisor and the supervisee are clinically responsible for the appropriate care of the client, the supervisor ultimately bears ethical and professional responsibility for the professional activities rendered by the supervisee during the course of the professional relationship. Hence, the supervisor is responsible for the planning, course of action, and outcome of the professional work of the supervisee. Chang, Hays, and Milliken (2009) indicated that supervision is different from counseling in that supervision includes evaluation of counselor competence and being a gatekeeper for the profession of counseling.

The blending of supervision theory with the goals of career counseling affords the practitioner the flexibility to function with other career counselors as well as clients in an effective and meaningful fashion.

## Models of Supervision

According to Bernard and Goodyear (as cited in Baker, Exum, & Tyler, 2002), "There has been considerable interest in developing models to explain the development of counselors and considerably less interest in models that attempt to explain the development of clinical supervisors" (p. 15). Research has suggested several reasons why experience is not sufficient preparation for clinical supervisors. Specifically, not only are accreditation bodies insisting on training in supervision, but clinicians are recognizing the importance of training in supervision (Baker et al., 2002). Leddick (1994) suggested, "Clinical supervision is the construction of individualized learning plans for supervisees working with clients. The specific manner in which supervision is applied is called a 'model'" (p. 1).

According to the literature, three specific types of models have emerged: developmental models, integrated models, and orientation-specific models (Leddick, 1994).

### Developmental Model

Developmental models approach supervision from the perspective that people are continuously growing. In combining their experience and hereditary dispositions, people develop strengths and growth areas. Stoltenberg and Delworth (1987) described a developmental model with three levels of supervisee: beginning, intermediate, and advanced. Particular attention is paid to self- and other awareness, motivation, and autonomy (Leddick, 1994).

### Integrated Model

Integrated models combine several theories into a consistent practice. Bernard's (1979) discrimination model combines attention to three supervisory roles with three areas of focus. Supervisors may take on the role of teacher, counselor, or consultant depending on the supervisory need within the session (Leddick, 1994).

## Orientation-Specific Model

Counselors who practice a particular type of therapy may engage in a supervision style that uses theory-specific premises. In this situation, it can be related to "the sports enthusiast who believes the best future coach would be a person who excelled in the same sport at the high school, college and professional levels" (Leddick, 1994, p. 2). Thus, psychoanalytic supervision approaches the process in stages. Behavioral supervision views client problems as learning problems. Supervision adheres to the theoretical principles specific to the approach.

### *Discrimination Model*

The discrimination model is one popular approach to supervision. Bernard's (1979) combination of the roles of teacher, counselor, and consultant effectively encompass the shifts that occur within any given session. This multidimensional model is both straightforward and adaptable (Bernard & Goodyear, 2009). This model works hand in hand with any career counseling theoretical perspective that embraces the idiosyncrasies of individuals and determines an approach on the basis of the individual needs of the client. Working within the discrimination model allows for shifting roles to best meet the needs of supervisees. According to Bernard and Goodyear (2009), it is called the discrimination model because it assumes that supervisors will modify their supervisory approach to the needs of each supervisee.

As described in Nelson, Johnson, and Thorngren (2000), this combination of roles results in "three foci for supervision: (1) intervention skills, (2) conceptualization skills, and (3) personalization skills of the trainee" (p. 48). Supervisors may take on the role of teacher, counselor, or consultant depending on the supervisory need within the session (Leddick, 1994). This approach allows for consideration of the skills of the supervisee in general and with specific types of issues. It allows for use with novice supervisees as well as with more skilled and confident supervisees. This model is synonymous with attention to the specific needs of supervisees. Any of the three roles may be used with each of the three foci, depending on the trainee's situational needs.

## SIDEBAR 10.4   Supervisory Roles

### TEACHER

Anna is a supervisor who uses the discrimination model. In her role as teacher, Anna identifies what her supervisee needs to increase his or competence and skills to become an effective counselor, for example, teaching student Austin how to use the Johari window as a tool for raising personal awareness of blind spots in identity.

### COUNSELOR

Wearing her counselor hat with supervisees requires Anna to facilitate personal growth and insight similar to that in a client–counselor relationship. Anna accomplishes this with Austin by exploring his worries, thoughts, and feelings about his sessions and providing an opportunity to process those emotions. Because counselors are never exempt from the potential to react strongly to a particular topic or client, the counselor role thus provides an opportunity to gain insight and awareness regarding the counselor's hot-button issues.

## CONSULTANT

Anna's role as consultant requires the least amount of external action because in this role she encourages Austin to work autonomously to conceptualize, analyze, and understand what he thinks is going on with his clients. She gently nudges Austin to brainstorm different intervention strategies, and when appropriate she provides him with alternate suggestions on how to intervene. This role is significant because it allows Austin to start to experience the transition from trainee to future colleague in the supervisor–supervisee relationship.

The three specified foci of the discrimination model also represent three of the primary areas of emphasis in counseling supervision. Intervention skills involve technique and strategy (Nelson et al., 2000). Depending on the supervisee's developmental level, the focus may be on the actual implementation of the skills than on treatment planning for their use. Supervisors routinely place emphasis on how supervisees draw conclusions and make choices in the development of treatment plans. For example, a career counselor providing supervision within the discrimination model might deal with assessment instruments as a teacher, counsel a supervisee if countertransference issues are affecting the supervisee, or serve as a consultant in development of vocational planning.

Conceptualization allows the supervisor to recognize cognitive skill that reflects deliberate thinking and case analysis (Nelson et al., 2000). How a supervisee understands what is occurring in the session, identifies patterns, and chooses interventions is imperative to understanding both areas of strength and issues of concern.

Personalization skills are critical because they involve a supervisee's comfort with self as he or she responds to the counseling experience (Nelson et al., 2000). One responsibility as a supervisor is to understand how well supervisees blend personal style in the counseling relationship while keeping their counselor–client relationships free from personal issues.

Because the discrimination model of supervision is incredibly flexible, one element of this approach includes establishing expectations at the outset of the supervision relationship. As noted by Ladany and Friedlander (1995), "Presumably, when supervisors and trainees discuss expectations, set goals, and agree on the tasks of supervision within the context of a positive relationship, trainees are less likely to experience confusion or conflict in supervision" (pp. 220–221). At the outset, it may be necessary to assume a teaching and counseling role because attempting to be a consultant sometimes results in confusion. Thus, initiating any supervisory relationship with a great deal of information can reduce misunderstanding. The tone and rapport established during this stage are critical, and the supervisor's role of counselor can be helpful in establishing a positive working relationship. In essence, according to Newgent et al. (2005), clinical supervision is a mentoring and tutorial relationship. Palmer (2007) suggested that the clinical supervisor is a catalyst to help the supervisee develop competence and professional identity. Regardless of which approach is used, it is vital to recognize that supervisees may possess latent resources within themselves that can be developed. "If, in addition to training, a supervisor accepts the challenge of facilitating a supervisee's development, the supervisor is more like a sculptor who is attempting to bring to the surface the supervisee's potential" (Presbury, Echterling, & McKee, 1999, p. 148).

## Supervisory Relationship

A discussion of the supervision process leads naturally to comparisons with the counseling process. Many comparisons can be drawn between the two processes, allowing counseling skills and techniques to translate well into supervision (Pearson, 2000). Despite the similarities between counseling and supervision, many differences are also evident. In the counseling relationship, the growth and welfare of the client is the primary concern. Similarly, in the supervisory relationship the professional growth and welfare of the counselor is a major concern. However, the focus on the counselor's growth must be balanced with protection of the client.

## Evaluation

Evaluation of the counselor by the supervisor is another factor that differentiates supervision from counseling (Pearson, 2000). Because the supervisor's purpose is to improve a supervisee's skills and ensure accuracy, evaluation of the supervisee's skill is imperative. This element of the relationship can be intimidating and create issues including anxiety, power, and games between the supervisor and supervisee (Borders et al., 1991). A structured approach to supervisee assessment and evaluation produces several beneficial outcomes (Harris, 1994). Supervisors can reduce their own and their supervisee's anxiety about the process, and when evaluation is viewed as a process of formative and summative assessment of the skills, techniques, and developmental stage of the supervisee, both supervisees and their clients benefit. A variety of strategies and methods are available to supervisors for use with counselors (Hart, 1994). Establishing a plan for supervision at the beginning of the supervisory relationship allows for insight into the supervisee's self-described strengths and weaknesses, as well as the supervisee's individual goals for supervision. Additionally, it allows an opportunity to initiate goals for the supervisee that can be evaluated, adjusted, and expanded throughout the supervision process.

Supervisor evaluation can also be of great importance to the growth and development of the supervisor in training. Having feedback from the supervisee can illuminate strengths and areas for improvement. Supervisee feedback may also assist in understanding the needs and perceptions of the supervisee. For a career counselor, this feedback translates into reinforcement for staying competent and up to date and creating a safe environment for honest exchange between the supervisee and supervisor.

## Diversity Issues

In addition to the challenges of power differential, the supervisory relationship is subject to influence by personal characteristics of the participants and by a great many cultural variables. Such factors include gender and role attitudes; supervisor's style, age, race, and ethnicity; and personality characteristics (A. Dye, 1994). Paisley (1994) suggested that cultural variables can affect issues the client brings to counseling, the perspective of the counselor, and the choice of interventions. The current literature has advocated discussing diversity issues early and often in supervision with the result of increasing supervisee satisfaction and developing trust and openness between the supervisee and the supervisor (Britton, Goodman, & Rak, 2002).

Because the supervisory relationship itself is taking place within the same societal context as other cultural issues, supervisors must be diligent in identifying any ways in which bias in expectations or actions might be occurring with supervision, such as identifying cultural influences on client behavior, counselor–client interactions, and the supervisory relationship (Fong, 1994). Supervisors must provide culturally sensitive support and challenge to the supervisee. Because all supervision is some form of multicultural supervision, supervisors will need to be proficient in multicultural competencies. The supervisor is responsible for addressing cultural biases and encouraging diverse thinking (Britton et al., 2002).

Cultural influences within the supervisory relationship can be managed to some extent by mutual respect. The complex goals of client and counselor development within a supervisory relationship require counselors to trust their supervisors and supervisors to trust the counselors being supervised. "Such a trusting relationship helps to increase the protection of the client, the professional growth of the counselor, and the assurance to the supervisor that ethical concerns are being addressed" (Pearson, 2000, p. 285).

### SIDEBAR 10.5 Diversity Is Not Just Color

Career counselors must always be sure to consider religious and spiritual variables when working with clients. Owing to a wide variety of beliefs, clients presenting career-related concerns will vary significantly in traditions and values. In some situations, clients may be hesitant to or refuse to work in certain fields that are not considered appropriate within this context. Attempting to steer a client in this direction may not only frustrate the client but also hinder the therapeutic alliance. However, counselors must also be sure not to jump to any conclusions without gathering enough facts from the client, because many individuals tend to vary in degrees of connectedness in regards to religion or spirituality. Take a moment to consider your religious and spiritual beliefs and how they differ from others around you, especially those with whom you are closest.

Numerous characteristics promote a positive supervisory experience. Some characteristics that prepare a student for growth within the supervisory relationship include demonstrating a capacity for openness to learning, curiosity, thoughtfulness, initiative, self-reflection, emotional and interpersonal self-monitoring, recognition of interpersonal patterns, flexibility, and motivation to change (Binder & Strupp, 1997; Kaufman, Morgan, & Ladany, 2001).

Characteristics of the effective supervisor include self-reflection and self-monitoring of the interpersonal process associated with supervisor–supervisee interactions, along with the ability to move between identifying with and observing the experiences of both supervisee and clients (Binder & Strupp, 1997).

## Ethical and Legal Concerns

The importance of supervision to the ongoing professional development of counseling is increasingly being recognized and regulated. Supervision is a complex professional endeavor that places participants at increased risk for involvement in ethical conflicts related to competence, conflicting roles, dual relationships, evaluation, and confidentiality (Cobia & Boes, 2000). As gatekeepers of the profession, supervisors must be diligent about their own and their supervisees' ethics. Role modeling is critical for supervisors hoping to instill a clear understanding of the ethical responsibilities expected of supervisees (Bernard & Goodyear, 2009). Supervisory arrangements increase legal exposure and pose unique ethical challenges for the supervisor (Sutter, McPherson, & Geeseman, 2002). Because supervision is a triadic relationship, the supervisor must always attend to the need for balance between the counseling needs of clients and the training needs of the counselor (Bernard, 1994). The supervisor's legal liability goes beyond the supervisee to include the supervisee's clients and even third-party individuals who would be considered potential victims of a client. The supervisor has the gatekeeping authority over the activities of a supervisee and can be held legally responsible for negligence on behalf of the supervisee (Remley & Herlihy, 2010). Vicarious liability can lead to a situation that could threaten a supervisor's license or even result in the process of litigation.

Supervisees working with dangerous clients can pose an ethical and legal challenge to the supervisor. The supervisor can be held liable for the supervisee's client, especially if that client has voiced a desire or intent to harm someone. As in *Tarasoff v. Regents of University of California*, the supervisor will need to determine the likelihood of third-party harm and the possibility of warning a potential victim (McClarren, 1987). The supervisor will need to weigh the option of breaking confidentiality to protect a foreseeable victim against the possibility of mislabeling the supervisee's client as dangerous and a direct threat to a third party.

Although there is no way to prevent ethical dilemmas, there are several ways to minimize the potential for their occurrence. One such method is the implementation of a professional disclosure statement. Risk to supervisees and potential ethical dilemmas related to misunderstanding about the expectations, goals, and evaluative aspects of supervision can be minimized by developing and adhering to a specific plan for supervision (Cobia & Boes, 2000).

Supervision is an invaluable tool in helping career counselors provide holistic, effective counseling. It is just one of many roles the counselor may choose to engage in to assist counselors in promoting clients' understanding of their interests, strengths, and weaknesses.

## Roles of the Career Counselor

Table 10.1 contrasts the three roles of career counseling we have examined on a number of dimensions.

### Many Roles in *Role Model*

As counselors explore the many possible roles that may become part of the process of career counseling, it is important not to lose sight of the impact an individual may have by modeling professional, ethical, competent practice. Being available and approachable for the questions and answers needed to assist young professionals in growth often facilitates mentoring among professionals.

Mentoring is considered to be an important element of career development in relation to career advancement. Mentor relationships develop slowly through mutual trust and commitment, patient leadership, and emotional maturity (Myers, 1996). Estimates have been that more than 90% of

**TABLE 10.1  Comparisons Among Three Roles of Career Counseling**

|  | Consultation | Coaching | Supervision |
|---|---|---|---|
| **Focus** | Focuses on developing a plan that will improve professional functioning with a specific client, program, or policy | Focuses on action-oriented, solution-focused intervention for an existing employee within a specific job | Focuses on reviewing service provision, including the skills and competencies of the counselor and the proposed treatment plan of the client |
| **Goal** | Advise and educate the consultee and assist in developing a program or policy to improve a problem | Actively engage in interaction with the client to identify skills, goals, and talents that will maximize potential | Provide feedback for career counselors to be better equipped to serve clients and grow as a professional |
| **Example** | Police chief asks for help in developing ongoing program to deal with interpersonal problems between veteran officers and new officers | A sales manager wants to own his own business and needs to chart a career course that will give him the experience he needs, including retail and marketing roles | A counselor needs assistance in working with Kathy, a 20-year-old depressed college sophomore having difficulty choosing a major |
| **Role and Responsibilities** | Responsible for assessing problem, recognizing the source of difficulty, and preparing a course of action | Observe the client's career situation, determine a plan of action, and assist the client in implementing the plan | Assist counselors in providing holistic career counseling and address the overlap and interplay of personal and career concerns |

executives have had mentors at some time in their career and that, of those, 80% considered their mentors to be important to their career advancement (Hagevik, 1998).

The ripple effect of mentoring spreads its benefits to mentees, mentors, and their organizations. Mentees benefit because someone cares enough to support them, advise them, and help them interpret inside information. That level of interest enhances mentees' sense of self-worth. The mentoring relationship is also a place for mentees to try out new ideas, skills, and roles in a real-world context.

Mentors experience the fulfillment of passing along hard-earned wisdom, influencing the next generation, and receiving appreciation from a younger worker, all of which enhance the sense of accomplishment. The relationship between a senior member of the profession and a more junior member of that profession also provides mentors a place to learn about generational and cross-cultural differences and about the benefit of giving.

The organization benefits when the optimism and energy of younger, more culturally, technologically, and ethically diverse employees intersects with the efficiency and confident decision-making skills of more experienced personnel. Ideally, mentoring of younger workers reduces turnover, helps mentees deal with organizational issues, and accelerates their assimilation into the culture. Figure 10.1 depicts the strengths and benefits of mentoring.

In the ever-turbulent world of work, the need for career development services is growing. New career specialties have emerged to meet the needs of

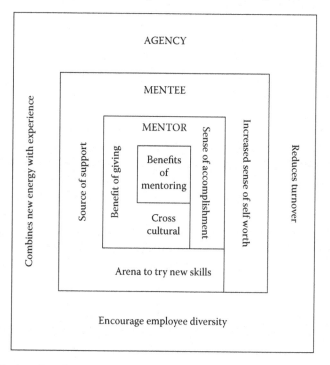

**FIGURE 10.1**  The benefits of mentoring.

adults in transition and young people preparing for work and may blend the roles of coach, consultant, supervisor, and mentor. For example, career development facilitators (CDFs) work in an organization that provides career services to its employees under the supervision of a qualified career counselor. CDFs are used to help individuals make informed career and job decisions, develop a career plan of action, and conduct a successful job search (Brawley, 2002). According to the National Career Development Association (1999), as cited in Kerka (2000), a CDF may

> serve as a career group facilitator, job search trainer, career resource center coordinator, career coach, career development case manager, intake interviewer, occupational and labor market information resource person, human resource career development coordinator, employment/placement specialist, or workforce development staff person. (p. 6)

CDFs serve as an example of the myriad functions a career counselor can serve in the world of work.

## Times Are Changing

The field of counseling as a whole is dynamic. To maintain professional status, counselors across all disciplines are required to partake in continuing education because they are expected to stay on top of the latest findings and information pertinent to the field. Should a counselor be out of the loop for some time, the risk of potentially harming clients by using out-of-date information emerges. This lack is a direct violation of the American Counseling Association's (2005) Code of Ethics. For this reason, many counselors choose to specialize in a specific domain or population as opposed to choosing to work in a general context. Through this rationale, specific domains such as career counseling are continuing to branch off and delve into topics that are specifically relevant to their discipline.

The fact of the matter is that the workforce is rapidly changing. In general, the economy is constantly in flux between cycles of expansion and decline. Any individual currently working or seeking employment is well aware of how an economic crisis may negatively affect not only one's line of work, but every other aspect of life as well. For example, major corporations are making cutbacks that include layoffs, small businesses are closing their doors, and some industries, such as travel and entertainment, are struggling to stay alive. During these crises, people lose their homes and their savings, cannot afford health care, cut back on luxury items and necessities, and often begin to struggle with simple expenses that were never of concern in the past. As a result, these individuals suffer from any variety of mental health issues that include but are not limited to anxiety, adjustment disorders, major depression, sleep disturbance, weight loss, weight gain, poor hygiene, rage, and suicidal ideation. Issues of this nature evolve from a vocational concern to complex, life-altering dysfunction (Tien, 2007).

Every year, new jobs are created and others are phased out. For instance, whatever happened to milkmen? "The changes have been fuelled by increasing globalization, advances in technology and information, and significant demographic shifts" (Amundson, 2006, p. 4). Just a mere 30 years ago, very few people would have imagined today's high demand for computer analysts and technicians. Because jobs such as these have become so common, colleges and universities are now offering new programs that cater to the modern job market because it would be illogical to educate students regarding professions that are no longer commonplace in today's society.

With all of these changes taking place in conjunction with an increasing population worldwide, the workforce has become more competitive. Now more than ever, employers are seeking individuals who are not only personable and intelligent but also educated and experienced in a given profession. Therefore, it is imperative that individuals be adequately prepared to choose the career path that best suits their needs to avoid potentially disastrous struggles in the future. One common misconception, however, is that individuals believe that just because they are skilled to perform a specific job, this job is what they are meant to do. In a survey of randomly sampled college students, Wood (2004) found that more than 75% said they were in college "to get a good job" and "to make more money" (p. 71). Although these factors are themselves valid and not necessarily a means for concern, it is disconcerting that college students listed these variables over discovering themselves or finding a job they considered meaningful. In this respect, money and prestige appear to be more highly valued than career satisfaction over the duration of one's life. However, because many people discover that money makes life more enjoyable in many respects but is not the end-all and does not compensate for other factors lacking in one's career choice, career counselors continue to serve an important function in promoting wellness among individuals.

Unless one receives a large inheritance, wins the lottery, or runs across some other source of fortune, a large percentage of time will be devoted to work. With such stress being placed on one's work and being a productive member of society, it seems only common sense that people would seek happiness in vocation, but unfortunately the evidence is quite contradictory (Wood, 2004). By keeping up with the latest advancements in career changes, career counselors will remain at the forefront of professionals assisting individuals with vocational needs and other related concerns.

## New Age Counseling Techniques

The world of work is changing, and so is the field of counseling. Postmodern approaches to career counseling focus on and account for changes inherent in postindustrial society (C. Campbell & Ungar, 2004, p. 17) Whereas merely a decade ago, there were more questions and concerns than positives surrounding the concept of online counseling, it is now something that has been taken into serious consideration. Despite issues concerning confidentiality and certain aspects of the counselor's ability to aptly deliver some of the traditional therapeutic techniques, there are many benefits to be experienced by the client.

As further technological advancements occur on the Internet, better and more efficient security systems may be put into place to protect confidentiality. Issues concerning therapeutic delivery by counselors may also be addressed in part by initiating a move toward the creation of interventions for use specifically in an online setting (Lewis & Coursol, 2007, p. 150). Such an endeavor may require the assistance of larger governing agencies including state boards, the National Board for Certified Counselors, American Counseling Association, and American Mental Health Counselors Association. Although traditional counselors share legitimate concerns about online counseling's changing the dynamic of the traditional counseling modality, they are correct that things will change drastically. In a changing society, however, counselors must also change because the potential benefits for clients cannot go unacknowledged. For instance, online counseling provides an environment that many clients find less intimidating (Lewis & Coursol, 2007, p. 150). This fact is significant in that clients may be more comfortable with and willing to open up more quickly to counselors. Other benefits for the client include cheaper cost of therapeutic services, the comfort of one's home, the lack of need to commute to the counselor's office, and more convenient hours of service. Each of the benefits, although secondary to the ultimate goal of successful treatment, is a factor that makes seeking out online therapeutic intervention more appealing. As more individuals become comfortable with such interventions, their popularity will grow, thus reaching more clients than could ever have been imagined via the traditional therapeutic setting of the counselor's office or an agency.

### SIDEBAR 10.6  Technology

With the Internet being so readily available these days via any number of devices ranging from a laptop computer to a smart phone, it is a means of communication that cannot go unnoticed. Web sites such as Facebook, MySpace, Twitter, LinkedIn, and Match.com all serve as a social medium for numerous people across the globe. For some individuals, this method of socialization is their most comfortable and therefore preferred one. Although ultimately getting the client to become more comfortable with socializing in a traditional fashion is often a goal of therapy, it may prove fruitful to conduct online counseling sessions for the client to become comfortable with the counselor and acclimate him- or herself to the therapeutic process. What other potential benefits can you think of, assuming that online counseling becomes a widely accepted means of treatment?

In conjunction with online therapy, various assessments may be administered via the online environment. Popular assessments that have already been conducted and proven successful include the Minnesota Multiphasic Personality Inventory–II and variations of Holland's Strong Interest Inventory. Grounded in motivational systems theory, the Assessment of Personal Goals measurement instrument is a newer assessment designed to determine an individual's motivations involving work (Henderson, 2009, p. 244). The Assessment of Personal Goals assesses 24 categories of motivation within the domains of task goals, self-assertive social relationship goals, cognitive goals, affective goals, and subjective organization goals (Henderson,

2009, p. 245). Assessments such as these are significant because they serve both counseling professionals and clients alike—counselors are able to learn more about what motivates people's work, and clients are able to receive some direction toward a specific line of work on the basis of their intrinsic and extrinsic motivations.

Online assessments are beneficial to both counselors and clients in that they are easy to administer, are cost efficient, and generally yield results more quickly than the traditional paper-and-pencil assessments that must be graded by a third party.

Failure to continue advancements along this line creates a major barrier to progress in the field—not only in the realm of career counseling but also in the field of counseling in general.

## Summary

*Career counseling* can be defined as an activity that helps individuals achieve greater flexibility, renew their self-definition, and live in a transformational relationship with themselves and the environment (Miller, 1995). Career counselors encourage people to transform limiting, dysfunctional conceptions of themselves into possibilities that reflect greater opportunities for self-expression, expand restricted roles, and become more responsive to fundamental needs and talents. Through a variety of roles, career counselors assist individuals in accumulating new information about themselves and their environment and help them to identify unarticulated fundamental values and needs, explore the competing beliefs that leave those values unexpressed, and translate the implications of this exploration into viable actions that are authentic responses.

Throughout this chapter, we provided conceptual awareness of and clarity on the diverse roles career counselors may need to engage in to operate as professionals. An integrated perspective of counseling, consultation, coaching, and supervision within counselor functioning is necessary to enhance professionalism and increase the overall effectiveness of career counselors. Between the ages of 21 and 65, people spend roughly 11,000 days of their lives at work (Koonce, 1995). With such an astounding amount of time spent on one activity, planning carefully to make the most of a career is imperative. Counselors who understand the relationship of their own helping functions are in a better position to select helping strategies for the various situations that they encounter. The Web sites listed in the next section provide additional information relating to the chapter topics.

## Useful Web Sites

■ The Association for Counselor Education and Supervision emphasizes the need for quality education and supervision of counselors in all work settings. The ultimate purpose of the association, in accordance with the purpose of American Counseling Association, is to advance counselor education and supervision to improve the provision of counseling services in all settings of society: http://www.acesonline.net/

- The online publication BoomerCareer provides access to dozens of articles written about career counseling issues: http://www.boomercareer.com/members/department19.cfm
- The International Coach Federation is the largest association of professional coaches, and its Web site provides an opportunity to search for coaches by race, business specialty, or region: http://www.coachfederation.org
- The National Career Development Association is a founding division of the American Counseling Association. The mission of National Career Development Association is to promote the career development of all people over the life span: http://associationdatabase.com/aws/NCDA/pt/sp/Home_Page
- The National Career Development Association Web site is sponsored by the National Career Development Association. It explains the functions of a CDF, describes the CDF training curriculum, and provides links to the National Career Development Association Registry of CDF Instructors/Programs: http://www.ncda.org/

## References

American Association of State Counseling Boards. (2010). *Welcome to AASCB.* Retrieved http://www.aascb.org/index.cfm

American Counseling Association. (2005). *ACA code of ethics.* Alexandria, VA: Author.

Amundson, N. (2006). Challenges for career interventions in changing contexts. *International Journal for Education and Vocational Guidance, 6*, 3–14.

Backer, T. E. (2003). Consulting psychology as creative problem solving: Lessons from my first 3 decades. *Consulting Psychology Journal: Practice and Research, 55,* 107–112.

Baker, S. B., Exum, H. A. & Tyler, R. E. (2002). The developmental process of clinical supervisors in training: An investigation of the supervisory complexity model. *Counselor Education & Supervision, 42,* 15–30.

Benshoff, J. M. (1994). *Peer consultation as a form of supervision.* Greensboro, NC: Clearinghouse on Counseling and Student Services. (ERIC Document Reproduction Service No. EDO-CG-94-20)

Bernard, J. M. (1979). Supervisor training: A discrimination model. *Counselor Education & Supervision, 19,* 60–68.

Bernard, J. M. (1994). *Ethical and legal dimensions of supervision.* Greensboro, NC: Clearinghouse on Counseling and Student Services. (ERIC Document Reproduction Service No. EDO-CG-94-17)

Bernard, J. M., & Goodyear, R. L. (2009). *Fundamentals of clinical supervision* (4th ed.). Needham Heights, MA: Allyn & Bacon.

Binder, J., & Strupp, H. (1997). Supervision of psychodynamic psychotherapies. In C. E. Watkins (Ed.), *Handbook of psychotherapy supervision* (pp. 44–62). New York, NY: Wiley.

Blocher, D. H. (1987). *The professional counselor.* New York, NY: Macmillan.

Borders, L. D., Bernard, J. M., Dye, H. A., Fong, M. L., Henderson, P., & Nance, D. W. (1991). Curriculum guide for training counselor supervisors: Rationale, development, and implementation. *Counselor Education and Supervision, 31,* 58–80.

Bradley, L. J., & Kottler, J. A. (2001). Overview of counselor supervision. In L. J. Bradley & N. Ladany (Eds.), *Counselor supervision* (3rd ed.; pp. 3–21). Philadelphia, PA: Brunner-Routledge.

Brawley, K. (2002). *"Working ahead": The national one-stop workforce system and career development facilitator curriculum training for instructors.* (ERIC Document Reproduction Service No. ED-465-911)

Britton, P. J., Goodman, J. M., & Rak, C. F. (2002). Presenting workshops on supervision: A didactic-experiential format. *Counselor Education & Supervision, 42,* 31–39.

Bronson, M. K. (2001). Supervision of career counseling. In L. J. Bradley & N. Ladany (Eds.), *Counselor supervision* (3rd ed., pp. 222–242). Philadelphia, PA: Brunner-Routledge.

Brotman, L. E., Liberi, W. P., & Wasylyshyn, K. M. (1998). Executive coaching: The need for standards of competence. *Consulting Psychology Journal: Practice and Research, 50,* 40–46.

Brown, D., Pryzwansky, W. B., & Schulte, A. C. (1991). *Psychological consultation.* Needham Heights, MA: Allyn & Bacon.

Byars-Winston, A. M., & Fouad, N. A. (2006). Metacognition and multicultural competence: Expanding the culturally appropriate career counseling model. *Career Development Quarterly, 54,* 187–201.

Campbell, C., & Ungar, M. (2004). Constructing a life that works: Part 1, blending postmodern family therapy and career counseling. *Career Development Quarterly, 53,* 16–27.

Campbell, D. S. (1999, October 20). Coaches also help put skills to work on job, in life! *Orlando Sentinel.* Retrieved from http://articles.orlandosentinel.com/1999-10-20/lifestyle/9910190236_1_coach-federation-international-coach-coaches-worldwide

Chang, C., Hays, D., & Milliken, T. (2009). Addressing social justice issues in supervision: A call for client and professional advocacy. *Clinical Supervisor, 28,* 20–35.

Chung, Y. B., & Gfroerer, M. C. A. (2003). Career coaching: Practice, training, professional, and ethical issues. *Career Development Quarterly, 52,* 141–152.

Clarke, R. D. (1999). Making the right moves. *Black Enterprise, 30*(1), 56.

Cobia, D. C., & Boes, S. R. (2000). Professional disclosure statements and formal plans supervision: Two strategies for minimizing the risk of ethical conflicts in post-masters supervision. *Journal of Counseling & Development, 78,* 293–296.

Dik, B. J., Duffy, R. D., & Eldridge, B. M. (2009). Calling and vocation in career counseling: Recommendations for promoting meaningful work. *Professional Psychology: Research and Practice, 40,* 625–632.

Drapela, V. J. (1983). Counseling, consultation, and supervision: A visual clarification of their relationship. *Personnel and Guidance Journal, 62*(3), 158–162.

Dougherty, A. M. (2005). *Consultation, practice and perspectives in school and community settings* (4th ed.). Pacific Grove, CA: Brooks-Cole.

Dye, A. (1994). *The supervisory relationship.* Greensboro, NC: Clearinghouse on Counseling and Student Services. (ERIC Document Reproduction Service No. EDO-CG-94-11)

Dye, H. A., & Borders, D. (1990). Counseling supervisors: Standards for preparation and practice. *Journal of Counseling & Development, 69,* 27–29.

Emanuel, R., Miller, L., & Rustin, M. (2002). Supervision of therapy of sexually abused girls. *Clinical Child Psychology and Psychiatry, 7,* 581–594.

Fong, M. L. (1994). *Multicultural issues in supervision.* Greensboro, NC: Clearinghouse on Counseling and Student Services. (ERIC Document Reproduction Service No. EDO-CG-94-14)

Gallesich, J. (1982). *The profession and practice of consultation.* San Francisco, CA: Jossey-Bass.

Gibson, R. L., & Mitchell, M. H. (2007). *Introduction to guidance and counseling.* Upper Saddle River, NJ: Prentice-Hall.

Gladding, S. T. (2008). *Counseling: A comprehensive profession* (6th ed.). Englewood Cliffs, NJ: Prentice-Hall.

Grant, A. M. (2003). The impact of life coaching on goal attainment, metacognition, and mental health. *Social Behavior and Personality, 31,* 253–264.

Hagevik, S. (1998). Choosing a career counseling service. *Journal of Environmental Health, 61*(4), 31–33.

Harris, M. B. C. (1994). *Supervisory evaluation and feedback.* Greensboro, NC: Clearinghouse on Counseling and Student Services. (ERIC Document Reproduction Service No. EDO-G-94-16)

Hart, G. M. (1994). *Strategies and methods of effective supervision.* Greensboro, NC: Clearinghouse on Counseling and Student Services. (ERIC Document Reproduction Service No. EDO-CG-94-09)

Hays, K. F., & Brown, C. H. (2004a). Consultant efforts that hinder performance. In K. F. Hays & C. H. Brown (Eds.), *You're on! Consulting for peak performance* (pp. 133–246). Washington, DC: American Psychological Association.

Hays, K. F., & Brown, C. H. (2004b). A good fit: Training, competence, and ethical practice. In K. F. Hays & C. H. Brown (Eds.), *You're on! Consulting for peak performance* (pp. 249–280). Washington, DC: American Psychological Association.

Hayes, C. (2001). Choosing the right path. *Black Enterprise, 31,* 109–112.

Henderson, S. J. (2009). Assessment of personal goals: An online tool for personal counseling, coaching, and business consulting. *Measurement & Evaluation in Counseling & Development, 41,* 244–249.

Hershenson, D. B. (1996). Work adjustment: A neglected area of career counseling. *Journal of Counseling and Development, 74,* 442–449.

Hube, K. (1996). A coach may be the guardian angel you need to rev up your career. *Money, 25*(12), 43–45.

Hudson, F. M. (1999a). Career coaching. *Career Planning and Adult Development Journal, 15,* 69–80.

Hudson, F. M. (1999b). *The handbook of coaching: A comprehensive resource guide for managers, executives, consultants, and human resource professionals.* San Francisco, CA: Jossey-Bass.

Kaufman, M., Morgan, K. J., & Ladany, N. (2001). Family counseling supervision. In L. J. Bradley & N. Ladany (Eds.), *Counselor supervision* (3rd ed., pp. 245–262). Philadelphia, PA: Brunner-Routledge.

Kerka, S. (2000). *Career development specialties for the 21st century.* (ERIC Document Reproduction Service No. ED-99-CO-0013)

Koonce, R. (1995). Becoming your own career coach. *Training & Development, 49*(1), 18–26.

Kurpius, D. (1978). Introduction to the special issue. *Personnel & Guidance Journal, 56,* 320.

Kurpius, D. J., & Fuqua, D. R. (1993). Fundamental issues in defining consultation. *Journal of Counseling and Development, 71,* 598–600.

Ladany, N., & Friedlander, M. (1995). The relationship between the supervisory working alliance and trainees' experience of role conflict and role ambiguity. *Counselor Education and Supervision, 34,* 220–231.

Leddick, G. R. (1994). *Models of clinical supervision.* Greensboro, NC: Clearinghouse on Counseling and Student Services. (ERIC Document Reproduction Service No. EDO-CG-94-08)

Lewis, J., & Coursol, D. (2007). Addressing career issues online: Perceptions of counselor education professionals. *Journal of Employment Counseling, 44,* 146.

Magnuson, S., Norem, K., & Wilcoxon, A. (2000). Clinical supervision of prelicensed counselors: Recommendations for consideration and practice. *Journal of Mental Health Counseling, 22,* 176–190.

McClarren, G. M. (1987). The psychiatric duty to warn: Walking a tightrope of uncertainty. *University of Cincinnati Law Review, 56,* 269–293.

Merrell, D. W. (1991). Back to basics: Things you have always known about consulting but tend to forget in the heat of battle. *Consulting Psychology Bulletin, 43,* 64–68.

Miller, M. J. (1995). A case for uncertainty in career counseling. *Counseling & Values, 39,* 62–168.

Myers, W. S. (1996). Finding a career coach. *Women in Business, 48*(6), 24–28.

Nelson, M., Johnson, P., & Thorngren, J. (2000). An integrated approach for supervising mental health counseling interns. *Journal of Mental Health Counseling, 2,* 45–59.

Newgent, R. A., Davis, H., Jr., & Farley, R. C. (2004). Perceptions of individual, triadic, and group models of supervision: A pilot study. *Clinical Supervisor, 23,* 65–79.

Newman, J. L. (1993). Ethical issues in consultation. *Journal of Counseling & Development, 72,* 148–157.

Newman, J. L., & Robinson, S. E. (1991). The best interests of the consultee: Ethical issues in consultation. *Consulting Psychology Bulletin, 43,* 23–29.

O'Roark, A. M. (2002). The quest for executive effectiveness: Consultants bridge the gap between psychological research and organizational application. *Consulting Psychology Journal: Practice and Research, 54,* 44–54.

Paisley, P. O. (1994). *Gender issues in supervision.* Greensboro, NC: Clearinghouse on Counseling and Student Services. (ERIC Document Reproduction Service No. EDO-CG-94-13)

Palmer, P. J. (2007). *The courage to teach: Exploring the inner landscape of a teacher's life.* San Francisco, CA: Jossey-Bass.

Pearson, Q. M. (2000). Opportunities and challenges in the supervisory relationship. *Journal of Mental Health Counseling, 22,* 283–295.

Pitts, J. H., & Miller, M. (1990). Coordination of supervision in practicum and internship programs. *Counselor Education & Supervision, 29,* 291–300.

Presbury, J., Echterling, L. G., & McKee, J. E. (1999). Supervision for inner vision: Solution-focused strategies. *Counselor Education & Supervision, 39,* 146–156.

Price, D., & Llevento, J. (1999). *License to sell: Professional field guide to selling skills & market trends.* New York, NY: Applied Business Communications.

Quimby, J. L., & DeSantis, A. M. (2006). The influence of role models on women's career choices. *Career Development Quarterly, 54,* 297–306.

Remley, T. P., Benshoff, J. M., & Mowbray, C. A. (1987). A proposed model for peer supervision. *Counselor Education & Supervision, 27,* 53–60.

Remley, T. P., Jr., & Herlihy, B. (2010). *Ethical, legal and professional issues in counseling* (3rd ed.). Upper Saddle River, NJ: Merrill.

Rich, G. A. (1998). The constructs of sales coaching: Supervisory feedback, role modeling and trust. *Journal of Personal Selling and Sales Management, 18,* 53–63.

Riordan, R. J., & Kern, R. (1994). Shazam!!! You're a clinical supervisor. *Family Journal, 2,* 259–261.

Schein, E. H. (2003). Five traps for consulting psychologists: Or, how I learned to take culture seriously. *Consulting Psychology Journal: Practice and Research, 55,* 75–83.

Scholten, T. (2003). What does it mean to consult? In E. Cole & J. A. Seigel (Eds.), *Effective consultation in school psychology* (2nd ed., pp. 87–106). Ashland, OH: Hogrefe & Huber.

Snow, D. L., & Gersick, K. E. (1986). Ethical and professional issues in mental health consultation. In F.V. Manning, E. J. Trickett, M. F. Shore, M. G. Kidder, & G. Levin (Eds.), *Handbook of mental health consultation* (pp. 393–431). Rockville, MD: National Institute of Mental Health.

Stoltenberg, C. D., & Delworth, U. (1987). *Supervising counselors and therapists.* San Francisco, CA: Jossey-Bass.

Sutter, E., McPherson, R. H., & Geeseman, R. (2002). Contracting for supervision. *Professional Psychology: Research and Practice, 33,* 495–498.

Tansey, T. N., Mizelle, N., Ferrin, J. M., Tschopp, M. K., & Frain, M. (2004). Work-related stress and the demand-control-support framework: Implications for the P x E fit model. *Journal of Rehabilitation, 70,* 34–41.

Tien, H. S. (2007). Practice and research in career counseling and development—2006. *Career Development Quarterly, 56,* 98–140.

Tokunaga, H. T. (1984). Ethical issues in consultation: An evaluative review. *Professional Psychology: Research and Practice, 15,* 811–821.

Wasylyshyn, K. M. (2001). On the full actualization of psychology in business. *Consulting Psychology Journal: Practice and Research, 53,* 10–21.

Wasylyshyn, K. M. (2003). Executive coaching: An outcome study. *Consulting Psychology Journal: Practice and Research, 55,* 94–106.

Whitmore, J., Whitmore, L., Kimsey-House, H., & Sandahl, P. (2007). *Co-active coaching: New skills for coaching people toward success in work and life* (2nd ed.). Palo Alto, CA: Davies-Black.

Wood, F. B. (2004). Preventing postparchment depression: A model of career counseling for college seniors. *Journal of Employment Counseling, 41,* 71–79.

# PART 3

# CONTEXTUAL PERSPECTIVES ON CAREER AND LIFESTYLE PLANNING

# CHAPTER 11

# Career Counseling
*Kindergarten Through Eighth Grade*

Rebecca M. Dedmond, Pat Schwallie-Giddis, and Shelby E. Strong

## Contents

Career planning has progressed through the years and is widely accepted as a developmental, sequential process that involves all students—all genders, all ethnicities, and all ages. Delivered as an integral component of a comprehensive school counseling program (American School Counselor Association [ASCA], 1995, 2005), career planning is dependent on the integration of a host of competencies, behaviors, and attitudes into all academic instruction that supports state and division standards of learning from kindergarten through Grade 12.

As society has become more complex, expectations that public schools will play a role in life and career preparation has increased to the point that career planning has become a more prominent component of school counseling programs throughout the United States (ASCA, 2005). Career planning reflects the changing needs of today's students. School counselors, educators, parents, and community members actively seek ways to engage youth in curriculum and activities designed to assist them to become productive, contributing citizens.

The ultimate goal of career planning is that students acquire and demonstrate competencies to recognize and analyze their own self-knowledge, behaviors, and attitudes, as reflected in self-esteem and self-worth. Systematic career planning facilitates the ability to learn to recognize, analyze, and exhibit abilities, interests, values, and personality traits compatible with job and career choices. As students progress through developmental, comprehensive school counseling programs, they learn to set goals and identify the process skills needed to achieve them. Learning to identify the relationship between academic content learned in school and how it applies to life and career choices is the cornerstone of the kindergarten through Grade 8 career planning system. We explore this concept more fully in the Interventions and Systemic Approaches sections.

The evolving concept of career counseling in schools is based on the continuous development of new theories, processes, and practices in career development and counseling. In this chapter, we highlight selected components of a career planning system. Throughout the chapter, we offer examples of what has worked and describe the importance of support groups and the roles they play in building a career planning system. A school counselor, given the myriad required tasks, cannot do the job alone. Closing comments support how the expectations of the 21st century will continue to require a balance between education and the delivery of student career planning.

## Career Planning System
### Foundation

Career development is an evolutionary process that begins in early childhood and extends through adulthood. Career development competencies and indicators are the basis for integrating career planning into the total school program. Exemplary education programs consistently place and reinforce career education and career planning within a framework of career and life skills. Many school systems have inaugurated career awareness efforts to equip all students with an understanding of what good work habits are and how to use them regularly (Hoyt, 2005, p. 139). Career planning provides youth with timely and accurate labor market and educational information, coupled with educational planning activities, to help them select the focused strategies necessary to become productive and contributing members of society.

### Guidelines

The guidelines set forth by the National Career Development Association, the *National Career Development Guidelines Framework* (National Career Development Association [NCDA], 2004), serve as broad general goals in three areas: personal social development, educational achievement and lifelong learning, and career management. The indicators describe specific knowledge, skills, and attitudes critical to lifelong career development tasks. Using them as a guiding framework, counselors and curriculum teams design curricula, programs, activities, and focus events to teach these skills throughout the kindergarten through Grade 8 years. Many educators believe that emphasizing the relevance of curriculum to the world of work provides depth of meaning to courses such that students are more likely to remember what they have learned.

The NCDA (2004) is not alone in serving as a foundation for career planning in schools. ASCA's (2005) National Model for School Counseling programs, which includes the ASCA (2004) National Standards for Students, centers around three domains: academic, career, and personal and social. The NCDA guidelines can be found on the NCDA Web site. The ASCA standards, competencies, and indicators can be found on the ASCA Web site.

## Career Development in Elementary Schools

Both the National Career Development Guidelines and the ASCA national model call for career programs that ensure that all students begin a developmental process of career awareness on entering the school system. In fact, in its position statement on academic and career planning, ASCA (2006, p. 1) stated, "By developing and maintaining an academic and career plan starting in elementary grades, students and parents can best plan for future opportunities."

## Developmental Theorists

The NCDA believes that career awareness begins even earlier than the elementary grades, positing that youth are first exposed to occupations within the home (NCDA, 2008). It has contended that preschool-age youth can be encouraged to engage in work experiences by being helpful to family members and being encouraged to have nonbiased views of occupations (NCDA, 2008).

Magnuson and Starr (2000) contended that career planning is a life skill that begins in infancy. Children begin to acquire job skills through their play activities and begin to make decisions about themselves and their potential that will last them a lifetime. This idea is heavily supported by many theories of child development, including those of Erikson and Vygotsky, as well as by career theorists, such as Super and Gottfredson. Developing a comprehensive career planning program involves first having a solid understanding of the developmental processes that children are undergoing in terms of their career development. We outline some of these developmental processes here.

### Erikson

Normally developing children entering school at around age 6 will already have passed through Erikson's first three stages of psychosocial development: trust versus mistrust, autonomy versus shame and self-doubt, and initiative versus guilt (Magnuson and Starr, 2000). Kindergarten-age children are usually struggling with Erikson's third stage, initiative versus guilt, and by 6 years of age will often move into the fourth psychosocial crisis, industry versus inferiority, which will continue until the child reaches puberty. The student's development through Erikson's initial stages has an impact on initial career awareness by determining the amount of trust they put in the adults around them at school and their degree of self-sufficiency. By adolescence, children enter into the stage during which they begin to define their identity. According to Erikson, if these earlier stages are not satisfactorily completed, it becomes very difficult for a young adult to acquire this next level of development. Thus, the attainment of trust, autonomy, and industry, with the support of school counselors and parental figures, is crucial to successful identity formation, not the least of which will become the student's identity within the world of work (Hoare, 2001; C. Hoare, personal communication, October 21, 2010).

### Vygotsky

Vygotsky believed that children's development and learning is the product of living in a social context (Sigelman & Rider, 2009). He believed that each child's culture affects how he or she thinks, not just what he or she thinks about. In Vygotsky's model, adults serve as mentors to children, who, through a zone of proximal development, guide, motivate, and channel a child's learning. The zone of proximal development, as Sigelman and Rider (2009) described, is the gap between what a learner can achieve on his or her own and what he or she can accomplish with the help of the mentor. By working with the mentor, the child is able to accomplish more than would be possible on his or her own and, in doing so, learns new skills and problem-solving techniques that can be used individually in the future. Children who are exposed to mentors who help them learn about the world of work early in elementary school years may increase their knowledge of career options.

## Career Theorists

### Super

A number of career theorists have also supported the importance of implementing career guidance in the kindergarten through Grade 8 years. One of the most prominent, Super, felt that people go through five developmental stages in their lifetime, starting with physical and psychological growth between birth and age 14 (Liptak, 2001). The major activities of this stage include identifying with activities occurring at home and at school as well as identifying one's own interests in and capacity for activities. Needs and fantasies govern during this stage. Substages of the growth stage during the elementary and middle school years include

- *Fantasy (4–10 years):* "Needs remain dominant aspects of the person's life, and role playing in fantasy takes place" (Liptak, 2001, p. 73).
- *Interest (11–12 years):* "Likes are the major determinant of the person's aspirations and activities. The person avoids activities that are not interesting" (Liptak, 2001, p. 73).
- *Capacity (13–14 years):* "Abilities take precedence in life, and the person begins to consider a variety of career requirements including training and salary" (Liptak, 2001, p. 73).

During these substages, the student is encountering four developmental tasks, including becoming concerned about the future, increasing personal control over one's life, developing an awareness of the importance of achieving in school and work, and acquiring competent work habits and attitudes (Schultheiss, 2005).

In addition to the growth stage, Super also proposed a model that consisted of nine dimensions, the successful completion of which would lead to effective problem solving and decision making. The dimensions included curiosity, exploration, information, key figures, interests, locus of control, time perspective, self-concept, and planfulness (Schultheiss, 2005). Development of self-concept is a central aspect of Super's theory and is centered on developing one's personality, needs, values, and interests. Thus, career interventions in elementary and middle schools should focus on developing youth's self-concepts by stimulating curiosity and exploration, developing an internal locus of control, and helping the students develop interests and an identity. Self-concept development is essential (Schultheiss, 2005).

### Ginzberg, Ginsburg, Axelrad, and Herma

Ginzberg, Ginsburg, Axelrad, and Herma (1951; as cited in Liptak, 2001) were some of the first theorists to argue that a client's career history must be looked at developmentally. They determined that career behavior begins and is rooted in early childhood and develops sequentially. They further believed that "occupational choice is a developmental process; it is not a single decision, but a series of decisions made over a period of years. Each step in the process has a meaningful relation to those which precede and follow it" (Ginzberg et al., 1951, as cited in Liptak, 2001, p. 70). Like Super, Ginzberg et al. also believed that there are distinct stages of career development that begin in the early stages of life. Beginning at birth and ending at age 11 is the fantasy stage, which is essentially the time children spend in play. By engaging in different types of play activities, children start to think about various types of work that they might like in the future. The second stage, the tentative stage, pertinent to middle school counseling, is where children start to make possible career choices on the basis of the information they have gathered throughout various substages. The first substage, which occurs most during the middle school years, ages 11 to 12, is the interest stage. During this substage, the student is focused on defining his or her likes or dislikes. Toward ages 13 and 14, the student will move into the capacity substage, in which he or she will focus more on abilities than interests. Ginzberg et al.'s model is mainly used in school settings because it focuses primarily on the stages a student will encounter throughout the kindergarten through Grade 12 years (Ginzberg et al., 1951, as cited in Liptak, 2001).

### Gottfredson

Lisa Gottfredson's (1981) theory of circumscription and compromise addresses the way in which children in particular make compromises in their career aspirations, particularly in the way these compromises relate to gender stereotyping and sex-typed learning experiences. Circumscription involves the process of eliminating certain unacceptable occupations on the basis of previous considerations about gender or prestige. Gottfredson's research indicated that most children's beliefs about occupations are based on their own self-beliefs rather than on factual information. Most children believe that an occupation is particularly feminine or masculine and has a particular level of prestige, and these beliefs affect the child's idea of compatibility or non-compatibility with the occupation based on the child's own view of him- or herself. This perceived degree of compatibility influences whether the child will eliminate the occupation as a viable future option. Early career planning can help rewrite these cognitive maps to allow students access to the greatest number of opportunities. Indeed, in a study by Auger, Blackhurst, and Herting Wahl (2005), fewer than half of the children reported the same career aspiration and career expectation, indicating that most of the children did not believe that they would be able to obtain the career they would most like to have.

Although theorists have argued that it is important to begin career interventions early, research has also supported this message. In one study by Seligman, Weinstock, and Heflin (1991), half of a group of 9- and 10-year-olds indicated that they had already made decisions in their lives that they felt would have an impact on their future careers. Another study by Trice and McClellan (1993, 1994; as cited in Auger et al., 2005) found that 23% of adults between the ages of 40 and 55 felt that they made decisions about their current career during their childhood. Auger et al. (2005) found that elementary-age children were making significant decisions in line with Gottfredson's (1981) theory of compromise and circumscription. They found that by age 9 these students had begun to eliminate career choices on the basis of elements of prestige or ability. Auger et al. pointed out that children at this age level may unknowingly be restricting their career options, and therefore it is important to explore with elementary school students both what they say they want to become and what they say they do not want to become. A 15-year longitudinal study by Helwig (2008) found results in line with Gottfredson's theory of child career development. According to Helwig's data, in second and fourth grade boys preferred masculine occupations and girls preferred feminine occupations. This sex typing continued into middle school for the boys but waned for the girls as the girls started to opt for prestige-granting occupations. Boys, who had always had more fantastical aspirations than girls, moderated their aspirations toward more realistic goals with age. In a 10-year longitudinal study, Helwig (2004) found that by eighth grade 96% of students aspired to high-social-value jobs.

The research has made it clear that elementary children do, in fact, start thinking and making decisions about careers early in life and that this has an impact on their future career planning processes. Therefore, it is important that school counselors and career practitioners remain up to date with career theories, current research, and interventions to start the developmental career process with elementary school students to help them consider their career choices.

In the next section, we present a variety of career interventions based on the aforementioned research that are applicable in elementary and middle school settings. Then, we discuss systemic approaches that will enhance the total school counseling program.

## Interventions

Teachers and counselors collaborate to create interactive and interdisciplinary hands-on experiences and simulations and to infuse career planning into the existing curriculum or into guidance groups and classes.

Career planning implementation can vary depending on the age group being addressed, where it is taking place, who is implementing it, and what definition and career theories are being used for an orientation. To help career practitioners in the field, the NCDA offered in 1993 and revised in 2008 their policy statement regarding career development across the lifespan, including career awareness in kindergarten through Grade 6 and career exploration in Grades 7 through 9 (NCDA, 2008).

According to NCDA (2008) policy, an important priority for every counselor implementing career development in elementary schools is to foster a partnership with parents. Counselors can encourage parents to promote curiosity in their child by encouraging play, magical thinking, and fantasy activities (NCDA, 2008).

In addition, the NCDA has promoted the activities discussed in the next sections at the elementary school level.

1. *Making the classroom a workplace.* The Secretary's Commission on Achieving Necessary Skills (SCANS; 1991) has encouraged the idea of moving from the concept of the workplace as an assembly line to the concept of a high-skills workplace.

   In the early 1990s, the commission was appointed to examine the skills that workers need to succeed in the workplace. The commission was asked to define the skills needed for employment, propose acceptable levels of proficiency, suggest effective ways to assess proficiency, and develop a dissemination strategy for the nation's schools, businesses, and homes (SCANS, 1991).

   Business leaders identified five workplace competencies, a foundation of skills and personal qualities, and eight core skills they deemed essential to successful preparation of all workers for the workplace. The SCANS (1991) articulated its view of how schools prepare young people for work:

   Schools do more than simply prepare people to make a living. They prepare people to live full lives—to participate in their communities, to raise families, and to enjoy the leisure that is the fruit of their labor. A solid education is its own reward. (p. v)

Expectations articulated in the SCANS (1991) report were that schools would teach youth to combine reading, writing, computing, and creative problem solving with personal work behaviors, attitudes, and skills (i.e., required workplace competencies). Career guidance and planning was expected to become an integral part of the education process to prepare youth for the world of work awaiting them; therefore, career planning programs were expected to be integrated with existing schoolwide policies. Revisiting the SCANS report (U.S. Department of Labor, 1999), more current assessment of business and industry needs remained unchanged. Employers continue to contend that the work of schools should be preparing youth for the world that awaits them.

2. *Teaching and reinforcing productive work habits.* Elementary school students should learn to recognize the work habits required by a highly productive society. These habits include coming to work (school) on time, doing assignments to the best of one's ability, finishing assignments on time, cooperating with others, problem solving, creative thinking, and following directions.

3. *Helping students understand the career applications of school subject matter.* Starting in elementary school, teachers should help students understand how what they are learning is applicable to and valuable "for success in a variety of occupational areas. This is especially true with regard to the basic academic skills of reading, mathematics, and oral/written communication to be learned at the K-6 level" (NCDA, 2008, p. 3).

4. *Using community resource people to emphasize both work and occupations.* It is important to encourage schoolwide involvement of community resource people representing the identified career clusters as a method for helping students understand the applications of various subject matters.

5. *Emphasizing career awareness but not specific occupational choice.* Elementary students benefit from being made aware of the wide array of occupational choices existing within and outside their communities.

6. *Reducing bias and stereotyping in career awareness.* Beginning at the elementary level, teachers and career development facilitators help students become aware of occupations without restrictions on gender, race, ethnic heritage, age, sexual orientation, religion, or disability.

Career awareness activities started in kindergarten through Grade 6 should be continued and expanded in the middle school years, Grades 7 through 9. In addition, as emphasized in the career theories explored previously, NCDA policy highlights that career planning in the middle school years should emphasize career exploration without a focus on making specific occupational choices. Youth in middle school should start to understand career interests, career aptitudes, and work values in terms of how they apply to the world of work and themselves. Middle school youth should begin to focus on tentative occupational choices based on this new self-understanding (NCDA, 2008).

Additionally, in accordance with NCDA policy, during the middle school years youth should engage in community volunteering and service learning projects to gain knowledge of the skills needed in the workplace. Through service learning, middle school students

> (a) better understand and value the concept of work; (b) increase understanding of their own occupational interests, aptitudes, and values; and (c) make tentative occupational choices that are acknowledged to be susceptible to change as self and environmental understandings increase. (NCDA, 2008, p. 4)

Finally, school counselors can help prepare middle school students for engagement in career preparation programs in high school such as youth apprenticeship, tech prep, internships, and work–study. Developmental career planning programs are, ultimately, intended to help maximize options available to students.

Although NCDA (2008) has delineated a model of expectations for implementation of career development at the elementary and middle school levels, a variety of other models and resources are available to help school counselors plan and implement comprehensive career development programs. The North Dakota Department of Career and Technical Education's Career Resource Network (2010) has released a document titled *Elementary Level Career Resources*, outlining 33 different career resources that can be used with elementary-age children. The resources range from free to paid and online to print.

## Classroom Instructional Strategies

The *Real Game* series (America's Career Resource Network Association, 2002) addresses the competencies of the National Career Development Guidelines (NCDA, 2004), the SCANS (1991) employability skills and competencies, and the ASCA (2005) national model. In the *Real Game* series, students assume work and life roles and learn about planning and setting goals; discovering and enhancing personal skills and talents; connecting school, work, and life roles; participating in teamwork situations; improving and exploring communication skills; and understanding local and global communities. The series is divided by grade level into five different topics. At the elementary level, students focus on building neighborhoods and looking at jobs in their local communities. As students develop, the game starts to focus on making lifestyle choices and learning about work roles. During the middle school years, students receive work roles with certain duties, a salary, work hours, and education requirements and are forced to make decisions regarding their lifestyle, budget, and future schooling (Jarvis & Keeley, 2003).

Another popular kindergarten through Grade 12 career intervention is the Kuder Career Planning System (2009). In the Kuder Galaxy, elementary students explore careers, play online games, watch videos about careers, download activity sheets, and participate in field trip excursions based on career development goals. The system is specifically designed to meet both the NCDA (2004) guidelines and the ASCA (2005) standards of early career awareness goals. At the middle school level, students are encouraged to engage in self-exploration through completion of research-based interest assessments in the Kuder Navigator.

Gibson (2005) and others (Heppner, O'Brien, Hinkelman, & Humphrey, 1994; Moon, Coleman, McCollum, Nelson, & Jensen-Scott, 1993; Okiishi, 1987) have found the career genogram to be a particularly effective career counseling tool when used with elementary and middle school students. Gibson found that the genogram "provides the child and counselor a non-threatening method of assessing and discussing the career patterns in the child's family" (p. 353). At the elementary school level, the career family tree is important because it helps facilitate engagement between the child and parent regarding familial work patterns. The child is given a tree template, something appealing at this level, and encouraged to add more information regarding parents' and grandparents' work and educational history, which requires a communication process about career-related beliefs and events to begin at home. As Gibson pointed out, "Parents may be the most influential role models for their children" (p. 354). Using the genogram helps parents to discuss careers with their children. This discussion, in turn, helps parents understand how influential they are in relation to their child's career awareness. At the middle school level, in addition to finding out what parents and grandparents have done, the students explore the why, who, what, and when questions. Middle school students are now encouraged to discuss with parents "'why' they chose their educational and career paths, 'what' factors influenced their decisions, 'who' influenced their decisions, and 'when' they made those decisions" (p. 359). Processing this information with parents or family members allows middle school students to garner greater self-understanding as they come to see how career preferences are related to their own family's values, interests, and opportunities.

Administered by the States' Career Clusters Initiative (2010), career clusters are becoming popular components of career development initiatives in elementary and middle schools. In 1999, the U.S. Department of Education divided occupations that make use of similar skills into 16 career clusters (States' Career Clusters Initiative, 2010): agriculture, food, and natural resources; architecture and construction; arts, audiovisual technology, and communications; business management and administration; education and training; finance; government and public administration; health science; hospitality and tourism; human services; information technology; law, public safety, corrections, and security; manufacturing; marketing; science, technology, engineering, and mathematics; and transportation, distribution, and logistics.

### SIDEBAR 11.1  Career Pathways Exploration

With the proliferation of career pathways, smaller learning communities, and academies in high schools across the United States, students today are being asked to make sophisticated choices regarding their future coursework. These choices often determine postsecondary and career options, and even potential earning power. So what can be done in the middle grades to provide students with a background on which to make informed decisions?

As part of the Middle School Career Exploration Program in Sonoma County, California, students have the opportunity to explore pathways of interest in step-up classes at local high schools. Step-up miniclasses are taught by high school career technical education teachers in a wide range of pathway areas and are offered as afterschool classes or as weeklong summer courses. In both cases, students experience hands-on exploration of a possible career pathway and a smoother transition from middle to high school. High schools have the opportunity to promote their valuable career technical education programs. (D. Blake, personal communication, November 9, 2010)

At the elementary and middle school levels, counselors use the career clusters as a curriculum framework to guide lesson planning and delivery and to help students explore their future opportunities. Career clusters are most often systematically implemented in secondary schools to help students link their academic knowledge with what they will need to succeed after graduation in a career. The Missouri Center for Career Education (http://www.missouricareereducation.org) has devised elementary career guidance lessons around the career clusters.

Other strategies that can be integrated into classroom instruction at the elementary and middle school levels include career journaling, resource speakers, classroom-of-the-future activities, creation of passports to the world of work, gender equity instruction, and minority achievement awareness. This curriculum can be further focused on addressing issues such as dropout prevention and cultural awareness. Field trips, career newsletters, internship programs, bulletin boards and showcase displays, and job-shadowing days should closely relate to the curriculum. School articulation programs create linkages with community and 4-year college programs.

## Alternative Curriculum Designs

Counselors coordinate programs that incorporate volunteering and service learning opportunities to introduce students to the world of work (Cobia & Henderson, 2003). These experiences provide the benefit of experiential learning to assess information related to self. Service learning projects and volunteering allow students to make a contribution to society and their community as they apply academic information and content of specific subject matter they are studying to a school or community issue or concern. Such opportunities are built on school and community collaboration in which students engage in projects and opportunities that address their own needs or the needs of schools, organizations, and communities while also meeting rigorous academic standards. These opportunities are as varied as the communities they serve. Through collaborative relationships, innovative practices are created that align with high academic rigor. Students try on jobs, create realistic goals, and take responsibility for their own actions to achieve them. Research projects, reports, and presentations become authentic assessments and evaluations (Dedmond & Kestler, 2010). Steen, O'Keefe, Griffin, and Routzahn (2010) studied elementary students who participated in three service learning projects focused on the school community, local community, and global community. They found that elementary students participating in service learning could express activities and jobs they took on during the service learning projects and had a greater understanding of the benefits of teamwork and taking risks. Also, elementary students participating in service learning could express activities and jobs they took on during the service learning projects and had a greater understanding of the benefits of teamwork and taking risks.

**SIDEBAR 11.2   Service Learning**

In Montana, Mary Ellen Earnhardt is constantly creating opportunities to increase learning and career planning opportunities for all youth. She has directed afterschool exploration programs in rural middle schools, engaging business partners in meaningful, hands-on projects including robotics and landscape and horticulture at the local botanical gardens. Soon after her move to the Montana Department of Education, where she oversees service learning projects, a business partner gave her a proposal for students to engage in green mining in Troy County. Students work to recycle mine waste into marketable materials for stream restoration in their community. (M.E. Earnhardt, personal communication, October 21, 2010)

> We look for supports around the school day. Expanding the quality of learning opportunities meets the array of interests, visions, and learning styles of our diverse student population. Transition and service-learning opportunities allow students to experience the world of work and find out what's beyond the classroom. They apply real skills to everyday life.

## Other Learning Strategies and Interventions

Other basic career planning strategies and interventions have been successfully implemented with students of all ages and at all stages of career awareness and exploration. Schwallie-Giddis and Kobylarz (2000) defined broad areas of interventions: outreach, classroom instruction, counseling, assessment, career information, career information delivery systems, work experience, placement, consultation, referral, and follow-up. Such interventions assist students in gathering, analyzing, synthesizing, organizing, and relating information to their future.

Building on the history and background of career awareness and exploration, and acknowledging the more recent national counseling models and guidelines, school counselors and educators have agreed on numerous practices in the process of building a system of career planning that need to be learned and achieved by all youth. We briefly discuss some of the more commonly accepted practices in elementary and middle schools here.

### Individual Planning

Career counseling, through individual or small-group sessions, provides a forum to help students examine ways to apply the information and skills they have learned to their personal plans and to the development of their individualized education and career plans.

Individual planning is the means that counselors use to help students make informed decisions by exploring many options, using many resources, and identifying probable outcomes. Students document the support, skills, and knowledge they need to use to set goals and to systematically monitor their progress toward the goals (Gysbers & Henderson, 2000; VanZandt & Hayslip, 2001). Individual learning plans are developed through group counseling, consultation with parents and teachers, coordination of community resources, classroom guidance focused on career education, and use of information in career resource and information centers. Career life plans that are consistent with students' personal and social, academic, and career goals are accomplished through student appraisal, advisement, placement, and follow-up (Gysbers & Henderson, 2000).

Commonly accepted activities include assessing one's skills and interests and learning to access education, career, and labor market information. The goal is that students learn to use the information they have gathered to design their own flexible, long-range, individualized education and career plan. Individual learning plans help students to prioritize their selected activities, delineate the purpose and expected outcome, and estimate the time needed to complete the activity (Sampson, Reardon, Petersen, & Lenz, 2004).

### Career Portfolios

A widely adopted strategy used for career planning is the development of a career portfolio. This valuable tool promotes informed career decision making and motivates students to become interested in and enthusiastic about career planning. Through structured creation and use of portfolios, students learn the techniques of assessing, recognizing, and developing their own abilities, interests, physical attributes, personal and social behaviors, values, and preferences.

Beginning at the elementary level and continuing through secondary school, students participate in counseling sessions and classroom and small-group guidance activities and use the resulting work and reflections for portfolio development. The portfolio then becomes the depository for samples of best work, achievements and skills, certificates, and letters of recommendation and a place to record short- and long-range plans. The process of working with teachers and counselors to design and keep career portfolios current ensures that students are well on the way to becoming self-directed achievers who create their own vision for their future, set priorities and goals, and take responsibility for pursuing them (Dedmond, 2005; Dedmond, Sherrod, & Bryant, 1994).

With computer and technology access, electronic portfolios have gained popularity. Current labor market and related economic information, data, and fact sheets and instructions are easily accessed, updated, and stored for individual and group use in counseling and career centers. Ease of access and the ability to continuously make entries and store electronic files is appealing to teachers, counselors, and students.

Creating portfolios, either hard copy or online, during middle school is becoming increasingly popular. Counselors recognize the importance of capturing students' goals, visions, and plans that are related to the subjects that they study and the activities in which they engage. Career exploration and planning facilitates students' assessing their activities and expanded learning and translating this information into the portfolio that can then be used to ease their transition from middle to high school. Then teachers and counselors at every grade level can review the online career portfolio and electronic files with students. Subsequently, they can continuously help students update and revise their plans. Armed with carefully explored, written, and quantifiable plans, students are far more likely to follow them and stay on track and graduate (Dedmond, 2005).

### Career Information

According to Sampson et al. (2004), career information is used to enhance knowledge of occupational, educational, training, and employment options. Students gain more information about career options, evaluate and narrow career options, and prepare for career implementation.

Counselors may choose to deliver career information through noninteractive formats (print, microform, audio, video, public presentations, and assessment) and interactive formats (CD-ROM or DVD, card sorts, programmed instruction, structured interview, role playing or games, instruction, simulated work environments, direct observation, direct exploration, social interaction). Interactive formats allow students to control selection and sequencing.

Career information is often disseminated through career days and career fairs. Although no single strategy is applicable to all communities, certain guidelines and procedures should be followed to ensure the success of the event. Degree of involvement by teaching staff, students, and community members is critical. Beale and Williams (2000) outlined specific strategies to successful implementation. Outlined strategies included establishing a planning committee, setting goals, identifying speakers and volunteers, creating a detailed schedule, and following up.

Many elementary schools make a commitment to career days and career fairs. According to Beale and Williams (2000), career fairs are particularly important at the elementary level because they expose elementary children to the world of work and help break down gender stereotyping. It is important to keep in mind that career information at the elementary level should be organized, focused, and introduced in small bits and segments.

At any level, organizing career days to feature a different career cluster each month is effective. Themes such as wellness works, math counts, heritage day, fitness and wellness awareness, communication counts, and motivating for success help students define who they are and build confidence in determining their strengths and abilities as they relate to career opportunities.

### Computerized Career Information

Students accessing computerized career information delivery systems gain a wealth of information to assist them in exploring career and educational options. Through interactive processes, they learn to set priorities, expand awareness of alternatives, and make short- and long-range plans. The most useful systems organize information around the National Career Development Guidelines (NCDA, 2004) and ASCA (2005) model domains and competencies. Most states have designed and adopted a system with specific state information. These systems are available through state career development supervisors, who are usually housed in either state education or labor departments.

### Work-Based Activities

Work-based learning experiences allow students to see the relation of their studies to the world of work. Some school districts begin job shadowing at the elementary level. Others encourage shadowing in the middle school–junior high school years. Through job shadowing, students can explore areas of interest, learn about careers they have never thought about, and combine that information with better course selection at the secondary level.

For middle-grade students, summer camps are gaining recognition as exploration experiences for youth. Popular themes today include leadership, entrepreneurism, cultural exploration, green careers, and science, engineering, technology, and math careers.

### Student Appraisal Inventories

Student appraisal inventories identify career interests and levels of career development and career maturity that are used in career planning. Standardized testing assists with individual appraisal and enables students to gather information to inform their decisions. More schools are using online career assessments to assimilate information on students' interests, skills, personalities, and aptitudes. This information is further used to research possible occupations, access Web sites on the basis of personal priorities (e.g., interests, salary, education level, outlook, favorite school subjects, and work conditions), and access additional online career assessments (e.g., interests, work values, aptitudes, and employability skills; Kobylarz et al., 2001).

Cobia and Henderson (2003) organized standardized career assessment instruments into four categories: (1) intelligence tests (to measure group or individual academic promise or as part of a battery to detect learning disabilities); (2) aptitude tests (to predict and consider student abilities to achieve, career potential, or both); (3) achievement tests (to assess academic progress, predict future learning, identify strengths and weaknesses in certain areas of learning, estimate amounts and rates of learning, and compare achievement); and (4) personality tests (to describe traits and characteristics of an individual's personality).

The NCDA (1997) delineated competencies for school counselors who conduct assessments. In brief, counselors must have knowledge of measurement principles such as scales, scoring systems, reliability, and validity; standardized tests such as intelligence, aptitude, achievement, interests, and personality instruments; nonstandardized assessment strategies such as card sorts, work samples, and observations; management of a school testing program; assessment issues such as invasion of privacy, test bias, and test anxiety; selection and administration of assessment instruments; and accurate communication of assessment information (Baker, 2000; Whitfield, Feller, & Wood, 2009).

### Student Reflection and Analysis

Student reflection on and analysis of career planning experiences is becoming a more widely accepted method that is critical to making the connection between learning and careers. This activity often includes an assignment (diary, journal, video, report, display, news article) that is reviewed with students. It is used for evaluation and to determine whether a second experience should be planned for comparison, contrast, and reinforcement of learning about different work roles and environments. Although they are sometimes considered time consuming, the advantages of an instrument to monitor and revise individual career plans are critical to the process.

### Referral

One of the strengths of a school and community partnership lies in referring and assisting students who have encountered barriers to career development. Partnerships that facilitate referral of students with needs requiring special assistance share a common working terminology, definitions, mission, and goals. The partnership facilitates developing a relationship with mentors and role models in community and work settings. In return, business partners are in a position to observe social, academic, and citizenship needs of youth. A partnership that addresses the needs of youth with special issues and concerns fosters positive public relations and, ultimately, demonstrates a common commitment to improving the quality of life of many who might otherwise remain unserved.

In summary, a number of ways exist to implement an effective comprehensive career development program for early grade levels. An excellent place to start is having a good understanding of the NCDA (1997) policies regarding elementary and middle school career development. As our review has shown, numerous resources are available for those wanting to reach out to younger students; whether through simulation projects, using online Web sites, or creating career portfolios along with individual career guidance, it is a matter of putting the resources to use in a comprehensive, systemic approach. In the next section, we expand on how to implement systemic approaches in career development to ensure successful programs.

## Systemic Approaches
### Assessing Needs

Although the NCDA (2004) national guidelines and ASCA (2005) national model movements provide a comprehensive framework for career counseling, career education, and career planning, a school is not expected to cover every competency and indicator at once. Counselors, as advocates for students, must ask themselves each school year what the focus of the career planning program should be. What are the most pressing needs of students, teachers, and community partners, that is, all stakeholders? What methods will be used to determine the needs? How will these identified needs be used to design the most effective career planning program?

In today's world, stakeholder needs change rapidly. When polled, stakeholders readily express and articulate their issues and concerns. Comprehensive career planning program designs are then based on the findings of formal needs assessments. The design considers and ensures that the needs of students, the concerns of parents, the requirements of the community and the workplace, and the economic and social trends affecting the community are all considered.

Career planning system design is accomplished when community leaders, school administration, counselors, teachers, and parents are in total agreement, understand, and endorse career planning, an integral part of the comprehensive school counseling program, being integrated into the elementary and middle school curriculum. The plan must be clear and concise, state desired outcomes for students, delineate roles of stakeholders, and be consistent with school policy and priorities that support learning competencies. The goals and objectives must be clear and achievable and be easily communicated to others. Successful program planning is dependent on the ability to listen to needs, to determine how the needs can best be met, to collaborate and determine how to best respond to the stated needs, and to document successes and impacts of the program.

### Process

Counselors take a lead role with administrators and faculty in planning the best way to administer the needs assessment instruments that are used to ascertain concerns. Needs assessment instruments can be found in the NCDA's (1997) Career Counseling Competencies or obtained from state departments of education, or they can be locally designed. Analyzed data are reported to administration, leadership, advisory groups, and curriculum specialists. Data are used to plan and improve career planning programs.

The assessment items correspond to the Career Counseling Competencies (NCDA, 1997). Using this companion instrument facilitates and validates program planning. After review, discussion, and consideration of collective stakeholder needs, a reasonable number of expressed items become the focus of instruction, learning, and school projects for the school year at the elementary school and the middle school levels. The curriculum and activities are designed to incorporate the selected career goals that correlate to and enhance state and local school division initiatives. To ensure total buy-in, the school vision statement may need to be rewritten to incorporate the new focus. The curriculum objectives and plan are highlighted in school communications, posted on the Web site, and shared with the local media.

The career planning goals that have been selected for the school year become the focus of curriculum and instruction for every student at every grade level. Consideration is given to the diversity of students in the schools. In the initial stages of planning, special consideration is given to students who learn differently and to those who are from different cultures. Counselors serve as advocates who ensure that resources are provided for every student to access appropriate levels of career planning information. For example, counselors determine whether interpreters are needed for students with hearing impairments; special software or recorded books are needed for students with visual impairments; or more time is needed for some students to participate in targeted learning activities. Counselors ensure that information and resources can be analyzed by different cultures. Careful assessment of the variety and suitability of materials and resources, speakers, and field trips must be made. A variety of speakers, placements, activities, and field trips should be considered.

## Advisory Councils

Career planning is clearly dependent on the interrelationship of the school with the community. Establishing an advisory council is the most tangible evidence of community collaboration and support. The council assists in gathering data that are used to ensure that a valid career planning program is built and sustained. It serves as the communications link between the community and the counselor. The counselor serves as the link among the advisory council, the school curriculum committee, and the school administration.

## Articulating the Vision

Involving the greater community in the educational process provides broad-based support for career planning. Relating curriculum to life and career needs makes academic content more concrete. Career awareness and exploration programs that build on basic academic competencies can be easily understood by students, parents, and community members. Career planning is a motivator for academic achievement as well as a means of building positive attitudes toward self, work, and lifelong learning. It provides an opportunity to extend classroom instruction into business, industry, and cultural worksites of the community.

Clear and constant communication with all stakeholders must be ongoing. Each group must see the benefits that can be derived. Articulation of benefits is used in program planning, in promotional materials, in gathering the support of the community, and in keeping parents informed of their child's educational program.

## Roles and Responsibilities of the School Team

Career planning is the responsibility of the whole school and involves counselors, teachers, administrators, parents, community, and employers working as a team.

### Role of Counselors

Counselors are the primary communications link between school personnel and share responsibility for planning and delivery of educational services. Although the extent of the counselor's involvement may vary from activity to activity, basic helping responsibilities usually include articulating the total career planning program focus with all educators so that expectations are mutual and achievable. Gysbers and Moore (1987) delineated the counselor's role within the educational services of career guidance, career information, staff development, curriculum infusion, instructional materials, community involvement, and services coordination. They saw counselors participating in implementation planning as it directly relates to school counseling and as it meets the local and state guidelines for career counseling.

The supportive services encompassed in comprehensive counseling programs have long been recognized as being critical to career planning implementation. Throughout the career planning process, the counselor acts as a resource to help teachers secure materials appropriate to the delivery of career guidance in the classroom setting, to use and promote resources that enhance guidance practices and program activities, and to facilitate an information exchange between guidance personnel and teachers regarding career guidance strategies and techniques. Counselors acquaint administrators and staff with the most current evaluation techniques and materials appropriate to the delivery of career guidance practices.

Increased attention is focused on preparation of students for the future in the context of the technological and information age. Students are faced with vast amounts of information to consider in the career planning process. Students seeking career assistance want easily accessible information about themselves and the world of work. Therefore, counselors attend to individual needs and develop and manage career information services that encourage independent self-exploration (Sampson et al., 2004).

Counselors identify and use appropriate instruments to help students explore interests, attitudes, and aptitudes relative to life roles and career choices, as discussed in the Interventions section. They take the evaluation of completed activities (internship, mentoring, apprenticeships, service learning) and conduct research on the career planning program and process. As discussed earlier, counselors assist middle school students with the development and updating of individual career plans and career portfolios and use them as tools to guide the seamless transition into high school.

### SIDEBAR 11.3   Self-Reflection: Role of the Counselor

Congratulations! You have just been selected Counselor of the Year for your district. You have only been a professional school counselor for 5 years and as the new counselor you were assigned the task that no one else wanted—overseeing the career planning program.

For the next 5 days, write in your personal journal about the satisfaction you have derived from your arduous task. What is it about directing the career planning program that won you this honor? What are the strengths you bring to the work? What satisfaction have you have derived? What were some of your hesitations or insecurities? How have you overcome them? On the last day, prioritize your reflections. How will you use these in your acceptance speech when you are honored? Most important, what story will you share with your students? And why?

#### *Counselor Competencies in Career Counseling*

The NCDA (1997) has identified competencies required for counselors. In addition, the NCDA (2003) has created ethical standards that govern the delivery of career services, including the counseling relationship, measurement and evaluation, research and publication, consulting and private practice, and procedures for processing ethical complaints.

### Role of Educators

With the ever-increasing demand to address the needs of students in a complex society and to attempt to meet those needs through existing courses of study and competency-based education, infusing career education and planning into the curriculum is both a cost-effective and a time-efficient delivery system. Integrating career planning into all academic content, at all levels, for all students is the philosophy that guides educators to raise expectations for students.

It is time for educators to rethink the way they instruct students. A more holistic approach to subjects and curriculum is required to help students see the relevance of what they are learning in school to the world of work that awaits them. Materials and resources, current information, and time for planning and coordination are necessary. Most important, to best understand how to integrate career awareness and career exploration concepts into the curriculum, staff must be provided with courses and encouraged to participate in professional development opportunities.

## Student Benefits

Students benefit from career planning and career counseling for many reasons. As the career planning program progresses in design and implementation, these reasons become readily apparent. Including students in the design and planning phases of career program development often highlights, focuses, and facilitates the career planning process at every step and every level. Students confirm that benefits they derive include but are not limited to

- Broadened academic program and application to life skills and career choices
- Heightened decision making, learning, and processes
- Increased understanding of economics and work
- Increased knowledge of job and career opportunities in locally and globally
- Added advantage of recording job and career insights and knowledge for future referral
- Documented experiences and activities that are incorporated into a self-marketing tool, often a portfolio
- Observed reality of women and men working successfully in traditional and nontraditional career fields.

### SIDEBAR 11.4  Self-Reflection: Advantages of Early Career Planning

You are an elementary counselor in an affluent school district. You are concerned that there is no career awareness program, and you believe that starting one will be good for the students. The school administration has been supportive of your ideas, but parents who believe that their child's education should focus exclusively on academics have pushed back. After all, no one helped them with their career planning.

You are afraid that the administration will cater to the wishes of the parents. Create a presentation for parents to outline the advantages of early career planning. Include concepts from developmental theorists. Couple these with the benefits of early career awareness. Be ready to shatter the myth that students who are going to college do not need career awareness now and career exploration in the middle schools. (Do not forget to include the important role of parents with children of this age.)

## Evaluation

Informal evaluation and continuous measurement of the effectiveness of the career planning program is critical to (a) the success of the program, and (b) student success. The purpose is to measure progress on current processes and activities. Data and information are used to make revisions to guidance strategies and the curriculum for increased student achievement. Evaluation findings and results are reported to the school board and to people in charge of budget decisions.

Whatever the means of collecting and analyzing data, the counselor's responsibility is to identify ways to optimally use the information. Career and educational information is shared with appropriate educators for curriculum planning and enhancement and with students and parents for incorporation into their individual short- and long-term career plans (Cobia & Henderson, 2003). Using an annual assessment or evaluation will assist in maintaining a high level of commitment to and involvement in career planning implementation strategies.

Well-designed reports are valuable in forging connections with additional business and community leaders. Findings facilitate discussion on the ways in which programs expose students to real-life environments and support consideration of additional ways to provide life skills and job and career information for student use. Data collection and assessment are useful in increasing community involvement and support. Including observations of community mentors and heightened areas of student interest should be considered for these purposes.

Findings can be useful in marketing the career planning and comprehensive counseling programs. Support can be verbal or written and delivered in a variety of media to a broad audience.

### SIDEBAR 11.5   Student Achievement

A comment frequently heard from middle school teachers and administrators today is "We'd love to provide more career awareness and exploration opportunities for our students, but we don't have time. Our focus is on raising student achievement." The truth is, the two goals are not mutually exclusive.

A large middle school in Santa Rosa, California, experienced the greatest single-year Academic Performance Index growth of any secondary school in the history of the Santa Rosa City School District in the same year as it began participating in the Middle School Career Exploration Program. The program focus, curriculum, and activities were carefully aligned to school and local standards for all students. Although quantifying the exact impact of the school's career exploration activities on the increased Academic Performance Index score is difficult, one thing is clear: A comprehensive career exploration program does not stand in the way of increased academic achievement. (D. Blake, personal communication, November 9, 2010)

### *Career Planning Program Evaluation*

Documentation should be gathered to show that programs are monitored through the review and updating of student education and career plans, include sequential plans and curriculum for all grades, and are assigned appropriate leadership and resources. A visible means of communicating and interpreting data to staff, students, parents, and community members enhances the program viability.

### Student Follow-Up

Follow-up studies determine students' needs and progress as they transition to high school. These studies can be effectively led by an advisory team that meets regularly to recommend and establish new directions for the program. The task of following graduates has improved as computerized data banks of contact information have been created. Important information that includes profiles of transitioning students can be compiled using both short- and long-term information. The ability to graphically portray goal attainment and perceptions of effective elements of career planning are important measures of program enhancement and improvement.

Findings can be analyzed and used to determine program strategies that have received the most positive and least positive reactions. This information empowers counselors to lead collaborative efforts to determine future commitment and plans for career planning programs for students, parents, educators, and the community.

## School Partnerships

Educators, parents, and business and community leaders work together to ensure that schools provide a variety of experiences that contribute to the development of informed, productive, and contributing citizens.

### Parent Involvement

As previously discussed, research has confirmed that parents are the number-one source children look to in planning their future (Gibson, 2005). They have a critical role to play in helping their child think about career goals and options. The vast number of career choices open to youth makes the selection process more complex. Many states have created parent resource information and parent guides for those who use the state-developed Web sites with their children and students. These resources and activities can usually be downloaded from state system Web sites. Career information specific to each state, such as financial aid, workforce projections, calendars and timelines, and worksheets, may be included. (See Classroom Instructional Strategies section on the theory of parental involvement and the research on parental involvement.)

### Business and Community Partners Working With Students

It is vital to continue to stress the importance of the involvement of the community surrounding the school and the critical and direct role it plays in the education of elementary and middle school students who will become future leaders. Leaders are in a position to provide accurate up-to-date information about labor needs in a given locality. They can help students see a direct relationship between academic instruction and life skills and career choices. Employers identify work sites where students can expand classroom instruction and experience involvement in tentative career interests.

Through such experiences, students are exposed to diversified career, job, and life roles.

Benefits of community education collaboration should be subject to continuous review from different perspectives. How will career planning be strengthened by sustained dialogue, relationships, and involvement with representatives from business, industry, labor, government, and human service agencies? How can career planning be enhanced through the cooperative goal setting of education and the community?

## Business and Community Partners Working With Educators

Business and community partners work collaboratively with educators to provide leadership, vision, and experiences that support education and ensure a better educated workforce. They assist teachers in providing educational experiences. These experiences often result in teacher motivation that enhances career awareness and career exploration program delivery.

Educators learn about their community, and the community, in turn, has the opportunity to become indirectly aware of the goals and aspirations, skills, and abilities of its future workforce. Partners provide educators with information about specific clusters of occupations. They advise on the types of knowledge, skills, and attitudes needed in the workplace. Partners offer assistance in locating appropriate awareness and exploration experiences for elementary and middle school students. Partners advocate for community service, volunteer, and service learning projects. Workplace learning for educators is a popular program that takes the educator out of the classroom and into the world of work in an experiential learning activity. It has long been recognized that if educators are to deliver the meaningful and relevant educational programs needed by today's students, they need the opportunity to develop their own knowledge of the world beyond the classroom so they can prepare their students to enter that world. Business and community partners are instrumental in the design of activities and strategies that connect the workplace skills needed to the classroom curriculum. Infusing this workplace information into the curriculum is a skill that can be quickly refined when the educator takes part in workplace activities.

Educators must model a commitment to lifelong learning to instill that value in students. The reward will be an enriched learning climate in which students are prepared to envision and plan for work in their chosen careers as a meaningful part of quality living.

Benefits of working with business and community partners are well documented. Students report that they understand the relevance of what they are learning to the world of work that awaits them. The benefits to educators are that students show more interest, are more motivated, and realize greater academic achievement when students make the connections between curriculum and work. Business and community partners benefit by gaining a platform and voice that serves to guide student preparation toward the competencies needed to become the next leaders.

**SIDEBAR 11.6  Self-Reflection: Comprehensive Program**

You have been a school counselor for 20 years. Your school division embraces a one-on-one personal and social counseling model. You worry that the needs of only a few students are being met. At a recent professional development presentation, a new comprehensive career planning program was announced. Although most counselors rolled their eyes, you were motivated to research career theory and program models.

Through the years, you have seen students who have succeeded and those who have missed opportunities. You know most of the parents and can relate to their hopes and dreams for their children. You make an appointment with your principal to discuss the new position that has been posted, seeking a qualified school counselor to lead the new guidance initiative.

Write a compelling one-page brief outlining the observations, beliefs, connections, knowledge, background, strengths, abilities, and accomplishments that make you the perfect candidate to design the comprehensive career planning program.

## Summary

Today's students and tomorrow's workers will be better able to make decisions about their future if they are given the opportunity to explore tentative interests and career choices while progressing through their formal education. Social skills, academic skills, and job and career information can be acquired through a variety of experiences, starting in elementary school and continuing through the middle school years. Students' interest in academic subject matter and career planning is stimulated through their awareness of personal development, life roles, and career path choices. When educators take students into the community and bring community resources into the school, students make the connections between work, learning, and career planning.

It is critical that all students participate in comprehensive career planning programs and activities starting in elementary school and continuing through middle school and high school. Career planning is the responsibility of all educators, counselors, parents, and community and business partners. Effective career education and career planning implementation are dependent on focused educational programs, services, and activities that are designed and delivered by counselors, administrators, teachers, parents, and community members at all education levels. The combined involvement and commitment of key participants is critical from system design to evaluation and continuous improvement. The desired results are skills, knowledge, attitudes, and competencies that help students make informed decisions about their life goals and how to reach them.

## References

America's Career Resource Network Association. (2002) *The Real Game series.* Retrieved from http://www.realgame.org

American School Counselor Association. (1995). *Get a life personal career planner.* Alexandria, VA: Author.

American School Counselor Association. (2004). *ASCA national standards for students.* Alexandria, VA: Author.

American School Counselor Association. (2005). *The ASCA national mode: A framework for school counseling programs* (2nd ed.). Alexandria, VA: Author.

American School Counselor Association. (2006). *The professional school counselor and academic and career planning*. Retrieved from http://homes.education. ucf.edu/~glambie/Streaming/ASCA%20Positions%20Statements%20as%20 of%202007.pdf

Auger, R. W., Blackhurst, A. E., & Herting Wahl, K. (2005). The development of elementary-aged children's career aspirations and expectations. *Professional School Counseling, 8,* 322–329.

Baker, S. B. (2000). *School counseling for the twenty-first century* (3rd ed.). Upper Saddle River, NJ: Merrill.

Beale, A. V., & Williams, J. C. (2000). The anatomy of an elementary school career day. *Journal of Career Development, 26,* 205–213.

Career Resource Network. (2010). *Elementary level career resources*. Bismarck, ND: Author. Retrieved from www.nd.gov/cte/crn/docs/ElementaryCareerCurriculum.pdf

Cobia, D. C., & Henderson, D. A. (2003). *Handbook of school counseling.* Upper Saddle River, NJ: Merrill.

Dedmond, R. M. (2005). A personalized plan for life. *Principal Leadership, 6,* 16–21.

Dedmond, R. M., & Kestler, E. T. (2010). Making a meaningful connection: Freshman transition and service learning. *Techniques, 85,* 30–32.

Dedmond, R. M., Sherrod, S. S., & Bryant, S. L. (1994). A quality approach to career development. In D. G. Burgess & R. M. Dedmond (Eds.), *Quality leadership and the professional school counselor* (pp. 73–99). Alexandria, VA: American Counseling Association.

Gibson, D. M. (2005). The use of genograms in career counseling with elementary, middle, and high school students. *Career Development Quarterly, 53,* 353–362.

Gottfredson, L. S. (1981). Circumscription and compromise: A developmental theory of occupational aspirations. *Journal of Counseling Psychology, 28,* 545–579.

Gysbers, N. C., & Henderson, P. (2000). *Developing and managing your school guidance program* (3rd ed.). Alexandria, VA: American Counseling Association.

Gysbers, N. C., & Moore, E. J. (1987). *Career counseling: Skills and techniques for practitioners.* Englewood Cliffs, NJ: Prentice Hall.

Helwig, A. A. (2004). *Lessons from a ten-year career development study.* Retrieved from http://www.associationdatabase.com/aws/NCDA/pt/sd/news_article/5255/_ PARENT/ layout_details/false

Helwig, A. A. (2008). From childhood to adulthood: A 15-year longitudinal career development study. *Career Development Quarterly, 57,* 38–50.

Heppner, M. J., O'Brien, K. M., Hinkelman, J. M, & Humphrey, C. F. (1994). Shifting the paradigm: The use of creativity in career counseling. *Journal of Career Development, 21,* 77–86.

Hoare, C. H. (2001). *Erikson on development in adulthood: New insights from the unpublished papers.* New York, NY: Oxford University Press.

Hoyt, K. B. (2005). *Career education: History and future.* Tulsa, OK: National Career Development Association.

Jarvis, P. S., & Keeley, E. S. (2003). From vocational decision making to career building: Blueprint, real games, and school counseling. *Professional School Counseling, 6,* 244–250.

Kobylarz, L., Miller, J. V. Pfister, L. A., Treichel, J. & the National Occupational Information Coordinating Committee. (2001). *Guidelines: National career development, K-adult handbook.* Des Moines, IA: National Training Support Center.

*Kuder Career Planning System.* (2009). Retrieved from http://www.kuder.com/ solutions/kuder-career-planning-system.html

Liptak, J. (2001). *Treatment planning in career counseling.* Pacific Grove, CA: Brooks Cole.

Magnuson, C. S., & Starr, M. F. (2000). How early is too early to begin life career planning? The importance of the elementary school years. *Journal of Career Development, 27,* 89–101.

Moon, S. M., Coleman, V. D., McCollum, E. E., Nelson, T. S., & Jensen-Scott, R. L. (1993). Using the genogram to facilitate career decisions: A case study. *Journal of Family Psychotherapy, 4,* 45–56.

National Career Development Association. (1997). *Career counseling competences: Revised version 1997.* Tulsa, OK: Author.

National Career Development Association. (2003). *Ethical standards.* Retrieved from http://www.ncda.org/pdf/EthicalStandards.pdf

National Career Development Association. (2004). *National career development guidelines framework: Understanding the National Career Development Guidelines framework.* Retrieved from Retrieved from http://associationdatabase.com/aws/NCDA/asset_manager/get_file/3384

National Career Development Association. (2008). *Career development: A policy statement of the National Career Development Association board of directors.* Retrieved from http://www.associationdatabase.com/aws/NCDA/pt/sp/guidelines

Okiishi, R. W. (1987). The genogram as a tool in career counseling. *Journal of Counseling & Development, 66,* 139–143.

Sampson, J. P., Jr., Reardon, R. C., Petersen, G. W., & Lenz, J. G. (2004). *Career counseling and services.* Belmont, CA: Thompson Brooks/Cole.

Schultheiss, D. E. P. (2005). Elementary career intervention programs: Social action initiatives. *Journal of Career Development, 31,* 185–194.

Schwallie-Giddis, P., & Kobylarz, L. (2000). Career development: The counselor's role in preparing K-12 students for the 21st century. In J. Wittmer (Ed.), *Managing your school counseling program: K-12 developmental strategies* (2nd ed., pp. 211–218). Minneapolis, MN: Educational Media Corporation.

Secretary's Commission on Achieving Necessary Skills. (1991). *What work requires of schools: A SCANS report for America 2000.* Washington, DC: U.S. Department of Labor.

Seligman, L., Weinstock, L., & Heflin, E. N. (1991). The career development of 10 year olds. *Elementary School Guidance and Counseling, 25,* 172–181.

Sigelman, C. K., & Rider, E. A. (2009). *Life-span human development* (6th ed.). Belmont, CA: Wadsworth.

*States' Career Clusters Initiative.* (2010). Retrieved from http://www.careerclusters.org/list16clusters.php

Steen, S., O'Keefe, A. L., Griffin, D., & Routzahn, K. (2010). *Service-learning and classroom guidance: A citizenship program for elementary students.* Unpublished manuscript, George Washington University.

U.S. Department of Labor. (1999). *Skills and tasks for jobs: A SCANS report for American 2000.* Retrieved from http://wdr.doleta.gov/opr/fulltext/document.cfm?docn=6140

VanZandt, C. E., & Hayslip, J. B. (2001). *Developing your school counseling program: A handbook for systemic planning.* Pacific Grove, CA: Brooks/Cole.

Whitfield, E. A., Feller, R., & Wood, C. (Eds.). (2009). *A counselor's guide to career assessment instruments* (5th ed.). Columbus, OH: National Career Development Association.

# CHAPTER 12

# High School Counseling

*Preparing Youth for College, Careers, and Other Alternatives*

Cheryl Holcomb-McCoy and Anita Young

## Contents

Determining one's postsecondary plans and goals is a critical milestone during the high school years. Students must ultimately decide what they will do or pursue after their senior year. Their choices typically range from entering the workforce to attending a 4-year college or university. Some students will join the military, and others will decide to attend vocational schools or begin apprenticeships. A significant number of students still believe that they have no options or that their futures are bleak and lack promise. Because the U.S. economy faces serious challenges from international competition and technology advances are booming, the United States cannot afford to have students graduate from high school unprepared for the workplace. Thus, the career and college readiness of U.S. youth is of critical importance.

Without a doubt, young people face many of life's most important decisions during high school. Unfortunately, too many students are unaware of their education and employment options. The path they follow to their careers, college, or both is often based on scant or faulty information. For instance, in 2002 Hurley and Thorp surveyed the attitudes and career plans of 809 high school juniors and seniors from across the United States and found that students perceive a lack of career guidance in their high schools and often cannot name anyone outside of their parents who have been helpful in career counseling or planning. Furthermore, most of the students reported that parental career guidance was limited to a few hours over multiple months. Students in the study also reported that their career choices were based on emotion rather than on career opportunity. Only 2.5% of the students cited job availability as the main reason they chose a particular career. The disconnect between the availability of jobs and the careers that young people choose is illustrated most clearly in computer-intensive fields; 47.6% of the students identified computers as one of the areas presenting the greatest career opportunities for young people, but only 6.8% planned to pursue a career in this field. Recognizing these hindrances, high schools have long played a role in designing, offering, or sponsoring experiences that further youth's preparation for their future careers (Phelps & Hanley-Maxwell, 1997).

Although the college- and career-ready agenda has recently taken on more urgency at the national level, many policymakers at the state and local levels have been hard at work on this agenda for years. The need for more college and career readiness in high schools is marked by the following statistics:

- The number of high school graduates in the United States reached a peak of 3.33 million in 2008 to 2009 after more than a decade of steady growth. An estimated 3.29 million students graduated in 2009 to 2010 (National Association for College Admission Counseling, 2010).
- High school completion and college enrollment rates vary substantially by both race–ethnicity and income. Only 58% of high school completers from the lowest income quartile transitioned to college in 2008, compared with 87% from the highest income quartile (National Association for College Admission Counseling, 2010).
- More than 80% of all jobs require at least some education after high school, but only about 70% of students graduate from high school (a percentage that drops considerably for minority and low-income students; Hurley & Thorp, 2002).
- Of students who graduate from high school, nearly 30% need remediation in English and mathematics before they can even begin to take classes for credit, significantly lowering their chance of earning a postsecondary degree (Hurley & Thorp, 2002).
- Only 28% of students at 2-year colleges earn a degree within 3 years (Hurley & Thorp, 2002).
- Of students at 4-year institutions, 56% earn a bachelor's degree within 6 years (Hurley & Thorp, 2002).

Clearly, many young people are not prepared for college or careers, and this fact has significant consequences for individuals and communities. Barton (2002) noted that many students, both graduates and dropouts, are deficient in career-planning skills as they enter the labor market or transition to postsecondary education. In a survey of high school counselors' career development competencies, Barker and Satcher (2000) found that counselors tended to overlook the need to implement career development programs, resulting in inadequate workplace training skills. They also noted that work-bound students received minimal counselor attention compared with college-bound students. In light of these findings, schools must provide career planning services to all students, including those who will be entering the job market immediately, with or without a diploma.

Previous chapters in this book have been concerned with theories and skills needed to implement career counseling. The application of those theories and skills to high school students (i.e., adolescents) was not overlooked in those chapters, but it was not dealt with at length. In this chapter, our purpose is to cover in more detail the career development of adolescents and the application of career counseling in the high school setting. This chapter is by no means exhaustive, because an entire book could be written on career and college counseling in high schools. Instead, we begin with an overview of the economic context in which high school students must begin their career trajectories. Next, we describe theories and models that are most often used to understand adolescents' career development. The remainder of the chapter includes an overview of factors that influence high school students' career development and counselor strategies and techniques that may be used to enhance career and college readiness.

## Economic Context

Regardless of background, younger generations are coming of age in an economic context in which work has been restructured to feature more episodic and insecure jobs with fewer benefits or guarantees (Farber, 2006; Flanagan, 2008). Job stability in the United States has been decreasing since the 1980s. The Bureau of Labor Statistics (2010) reported that Americans typically hold an average of 10.5 jobs between ages 18 and 40, suggesting very little job stability across early adulthood. A large share of jobs in the U.S. labor force consist of work that is independently contracted, temporary, on call, and part time. National data from 1995, 2001, and 2005 revealed that 32%, 29%, and 31% of the workforce during those years, respectively, were employed in such nonstandard jobs (Mishel, Bernstein, & Allegretto, 2010). The service industry represents a growing sector of the workforce, in which prerequisite job skills are minimal and employees are easily interchangeable. Nonstandard and service industry jobs tend to be characterized by lower pay, lower benefits, and less job security than full-time positions or positions in other sectors (Mishel et al., 2010). The increasing educational and occupational ambitions of high school seniors may, in part, be a response to these labor market shifts, because jobs not requiring higher education are fewer and less likely to offer economic security (Reynolds, Stewart, MacDonald, & Sischo, 2006).

Not surprisingly, individuals without college degrees and minorities are disproportionally burdened by the changing job market. Increases in job transitions may be an intentional choice by college graduates to explore career options, whereas for young people without college degrees, job transitions may be necessary to maintain employment and may indicate economic vulnerability (Farber, 2006). Moreover, declines in job stability are felt disproportionately by African Americans, especially African American men (Bluestone & Rose, 1997); less educated workers; and younger workers (Danziger & Gottschalk, 2004; Hill & Yeung, 1999). Compounding this issue is the already noted fact that young people with ethnic minority backgrounds, particularly African Americans and Latinos, are less likely to attend and graduate from college (Lopez & Marcelo, 2006).

Job loss and job transitions can be costly and anxiety provoking for workers, even in good economic times (Farber, 2005). Some have noted that the uncertainties of the economy produce uncertainty and anxiety in young people as well (e.g., Flanagan, 2008). The realities of work have certainly changed for the adult workforce given the increases in job instability. Less understood, however, are the changes over time in the work values of adolescents (i.e., the future labor force).

## Career Development of High School Students

Although much attention has been paid to adolescents' career development, little is known about when adolescents state their career choices or the number of them who are essentially decided about career or work commitments. More than 30 years ago, Fottler and Bain (1980) found that 18% of high school students in Alabama were undecided about their career or work choices. Bartol (1981) reviewed several studies and concluded that a majority of high schoolers are undecided about their future careers during high school.

Several theories related to career development have attempted to provide a better understanding of how students make career decisions and what elements may influence their choice of a proper career path. We present the patterns for students' process in choosing career paths from different points of view, including the developmental self-concept, self-efficacy, and the person–environment relationship (Brown & Lent, 2005; Lent, Brown, & Hackett, 1994; Super, 1980). In this section, we summarize Super's (1980) vocational development theory, Holland's (1973) vocational theory, Lent et al.'s (1994) social cognitive career theory, and Astin's (1984) sociopsychological causal model of career choice to provide a better understanding of the career development of high school students.

### Super's Vocational Development Theory

Super (1957) proposed that self-concept is a critical component of vocational development because vocational self-concept, which plays an important role in choosing a career that matches an individual's self-image, is formed by interaction between the person and the environment. He identified five stages of vocational development:

1. In the growth period (ages 0–14), children try out different experiences and develop an insight into and knowledge about work.
2. In the exploration period (ages 14–24), individuals explore different possible career choices and become aware of their interests and abilities. Individuals develop their vocational goals on the basis of interests and abilities and prepare to acquire necessary skills as well as experiences for employment.
3. In the establishment period (ages 25–44), individuals become competent in a career and in advancing it.
4. In the maintenance period (ages 45–65), individuals continue to advance their skills and knowledge to be productive while preparing for retirement.
5. In the decline period (ages 65 and older), individuals adjust their work on the basis of their physical capabilities and try to deal with resources to remain independent.

Super (1957) believed that the roles of individuals change over different life stages and that people have particular decision points over the course of the life span that reflect situational and personal determinants. Situational determinants are related to geographic, historic, social, and economic conditions, and personal determinants are related to the inherent foundation of the individual, such as home and the community.

When people take on a new role or make significant changes to their existing role, they encounter decision points, such as the decision to enter college (Super, 1980). Super (1980) attempted to portray lifelong occupational development by way of various roles, decision points, decision processes, and decision determinants within the life stages.

## Holland's Vocational Choice Theory

Holland (1996) believed that people make vocational choices on the basis of their personality types and their aspirations for career stability. He proposed six personality types: realistic, investigative, artistic, social, enterprising, and conventional. Holland believed that these personality types interact with work environments, and a person's type must represent the person's work environment. For instance, a realistic person's work environment would include concrete and practical activities, such as using machines, tools, and materials; an artistic person's work environment would be related to creative effort in music, writing, performance, sculpture, or unstructured intellectual endeavors; an investigative person's work environment would be related to analytical or intellectual activity aimed at troubleshooting or at the creation and use of knowledge; a social person's work environment would involve working with others in a helpful or facilitative way; an enterprising person's work environment would be focused on selling, leading, or manipulating others to attain personal or organizational goals; and a conventional person's work environment would be related to working with things, numbers, or machines to meet predictable organizational demands or specified standards (Holland, 1997). Holland (1997) asserted that an individual pursues a career that matches his or her personality type and that career choices of people on the basis of personality type could provide vocational satisfaction within the work.

## Social Cognitive Career Theory

Social cognitive career theory (Lent et al., 1994) was developed on the basis of Bandura's (1986) social cognitive theory. This theory addresses the interactive roles of personal, environmental, and behavioral variables in career interest development, career goal development, and actions to produce a particular goal. Lent et al. (1994) identified four basic elements as influencing factors in one's choice of career: self-efficacy, outcome expectations, goals, and contextual supports and barriers. Bandura (1986) proposed the view that people's belief about themselves is an important factor in controlling their sense of personal agency within their social system. He defined perceived self-efficacy as

> people's judgments of their capabilities to organize and execute courses of action required to attain designated types of performances. It is concerned not with the skills one has but with judgments of what one can do with whatever the skills one possesses. (p. 391)

In social cognitive theory, Bandura believed that a student's academic achievement is not determined solely by intellectual factors. Knowledge and skills do not necessarily guarantee a student's academic achievement in every situation. Students with high self-efficacy will interact better with teachers by adopting a positive attitude in school environments; that better interaction will in turn lead to better academic achievement in school work. Social cognitive career theory applies this theory to making career choices (Lent & Brown, 1996). Lent and Brown (1996) believed that self-efficacy is acquired through personal performance accomplishments, vicarious learning, social persuasion, and physiological states and reactions. Outcome expectations are shaped by the consequences of performing particular behaviors that are perceived through direct and vicarious learning experiences; personal goals may be defined as the intention to join in a certain activity. These variables interact with other environmental aspects in the career development of high school students.

According to social cognitive career theory, environmental factors, such as opportunities, resources, barriers, financial resources, parental behaviors, and school influences, play an important role in career development (Lent, Brown, & Hackett, 2000). Lent et al. (2000) interviewed 19 college students to examine career choice factors, rejected choices, barriers to choice pursuit, and supports for choice pursuit. They identified interests, direct exposure to work-relevant activities, vicarious exposure to work-relevant activities, work conditions or reinforcers, ability considerations, and leisure experiences as career choice factors. Also, they acknowledged negative social and family influences and excessive educational requirements as rejected choice and financial concerns as the barriers to make alternative choices rather than ideal choice.

## Sociopsychological Causal Model

Astin (1984) developed a sociopsychological model of career choice that includes both psychological factors (work motivation and work expectations) and cultural–environmental factors (gender role socialization and the structure of opportunity). This model of career development perspective asserts that perceptions of occupational opportunity play a critical role in an individual's career aspirations and choice (Turner & Turner, 1995). Also, Griffith (1980) argued that differential career opportunities influence how various racial and ethnic groups are socialized to work as well as the development of their work-related expectations, aspirations, and behavior. Astin's model illustrates that career opportunities are greatly influenced by perceptions of, as well as the reality of, the occupational opportunity.

## Factors That Influence Adolescents' Career Development

Contextual factors can foster progress in career development in youth, particularly youth of color and low-income youth. Career development researchers have found that perceived social support is related to high self-esteem, positive career expectations, and career certainty (Constantine, Wallace, & Kindaichi, 2005; Ferry, Fouad, & Smith, 2000; Kenny, Blustein, Chaves, Grossman, & Gallagher, 2003). In some cases, family members may not be able to provide career guidance (Blustein et al., 2002), but counselors, teachers, and other school personnel can be the main source of career development support for students.

Given the extent to which academic achievement and occupational attainment continue to vary along racial lines, the meaning of work continues to hold different meanings across groups as a function of their sociopolitical, historical, and political experiences (Chaves et al., 2004). Racial and ethnic minority students are entering into a labor market in which people of their own racial or ethnic group are concentrated in lower level positions and unskilled occupations, which in turn influences their perception of the opportunities available to them (Fouad & Byars-Winston, 2005). The continued existence of racism as manifested in pervasive differences in educational and occupational attainment and the prevalence of both macro- and micro-aggressions is a major challenge in the career decision-making process and career development of students of color. Considering educational and career development without accounting for the reality of racism in education and work neglects a significant challenge in students' lives. Existing research (e.g., Fine, Burns, Payne, & Torre, 2004) has revealed that poor and working-class youth are aware of inequities in the educational system related to race and social class and anticipate that they may not be prepared for higher education. Ogbu (1989) argued that awareness of the racial barriers in school and the workplace serves to undermine student engagement in school.

By ages 13 to 14, adolescents have developed two cognitive competencies related to career development: self-concept and perceptions about occupations (Gottfredson, 2005). During adolescence, students have also achieved an adult-level understanding of the sex type and prestige level of common occupations. Gottfredson (2005) argued that adolescents start to eliminate occupational choices on the basis of sex types and prestige levels. For example, female students might avoid choosing occupations that are generally perceived as too masculine (e.g., a career as a miner) and might also consider eliminating choices that are perceived as low social prestige status (e.g., a career as a housemaid).

In their effort to explain why women were underrepresented in science and math fields, Betz and Hackett (1981) argued that women avoid male-dominated occupations because of a lack of self-confidence in such occupations and that this lack of confidence is rooted in a lack of encouragement, role models, or similar experiences in the field. Several studies have found that career self-efficacy beliefs are critical to the choices made by and the persistence of women entering into mathematical, scientific, and technological careers (e.g., Zeldin & Pajares, 2000).

Thus, career self-efficacy is a significant factor for female high school students' career aspirations, particularly for nonfemale traditional occupations (Rainey & Borders, 1997). More than 15 years ago, Bonett (1994) found that women had lower self-efficacy than men for traditionally male occupations, and men had lower self-efficacy for traditionally female occupations. Similarly, male high school students demonstrated higher self-efficacy for male-dominated professions than did their female counterparts. Interestingly, Kelly (1993) found that female high school students who had been identified as gifted had higher self-efficacy in male-dominated careers but no difference in efficacy scores for sex-balanced occupations.

Research has also indicated that gender differences exist in other aspects of career development. For instance, studies have shown that women have different career patterns than men (Krakauer & Chen, 2003), and women have been found to have higher scores on career commitment than men (Chung, 2002). Pertaining to career interests, women and men were found to have differences on Holland's six interest types as well (Ryan, Tracey, & Rounds, 1996). Gender differences in interests were also found on another classification system of interests, the data–things and people–ideas dimensions. Several studies have confirmed that women are inclined to fall on the people side of the people–ideas dimension (Lippa, 1998; Tokar & Jome, 1998).

### SIDEBAR 12.1  Career Reflection Activity

Select a career development theory discussed in this chapter. Discuss the career development of students at all levels (elementary, middle, and high school) as it relates to your selected career theory. What societal or cogent factors may influence students' career decision making and postsecondary opportunities?

## Work Values

Value development takes place primarily during adolescence when youth also begin to think more deeply about work (Flanagan, 2003). Values are integral to identity development and help adolescents define who they are and make sense of their experiences. Values also guide present and future behaviors and are the resources that underlie adolescents' choices as they transition into adulthood and make decisions about careers (Eccles, Templeton, Barber, & Stone, 2003). As such, the active exploration of potential careers along with the exploration and identification of work values is important in adolescents' identity development (Vondracek & Porfeli, 2003). Research has indicated that adolescents' work values are in part derived from the perceived rewards of work and are associated with later work satisfaction (M. K. Johnson, 2002).

Recently, identity exploration has been noted to span a longer period for many U.S. youth. Therefore, the transition to adulthood has changed. The transition to adulthood once proceeded in an orderly sequence that included completing education, starting at the bottom of the career ladder, and working one's way up. Today, however, the path to adulthood for adolescents is characterized by diverse life trajectories that lack a predictable sequence (Settersten, Furstenberg, & Rumbaut, 2005). Recent trends have suggested that young people remain in school longer, combine work and education, and delay marriage and having children. Indeed, the occupational aspirations of today's adolescents are higher than those of any previous U.S. cohort, and adolescents are more likely than ever to aspire to graduate from a 4-year college (Schneider & Stevenson, 1999).

The transition to adulthood is not an experience of prolonged exploration and continued education for all, and the sequence of transitions into adult work roles varies across individuals with different opportunities and from different cultural backgrounds (Mollenkopf, Kasinitz, & Waters, 2005). Individuals who enter the full-time workforce directly after high school must often take on more responsibilities and experience fewer freedoms than those in college (Eccles et al., 2003). Moreover, non–college-bound youth are likely to experience several more years of job instability than those who attend college (Vondracek & Porfeli, 2003). Recent trends have indicated that ethnic minorities (particularly African American and Latino youth), economically disadvantaged youth, and men are less likely to attend college (National Association for College Admission Counseling, 2010). Of course, disparities in education and opportunities for minorities and disadvantaged youth are apparent long before the transition to adulthood (Jez, 2008). Accordingly, indicators of social location such as gender, race, parents' education, and educational aspirations point to diverging pathways in how adolescents experience the work world and may also illustrate differences in how adolescents make sense of work and value work as part of their identities.

Schulenberg, Bachman, Johnston, and O'Malley (1994) found that adolescent girls reported higher intrinsic work values (e.g., importance of creativity, decision making, and helping others at work), whereas boys reported higher extrinsic work values. Other aspects of individuals' cultural background also play a role in initial levels of adolescents' work values. In more recent studies, compared with Black women, White men and women reported lower extrinsic and job security values, and parents' educational attainment, a proxy for socioeconomic status, was also negatively associated with adolescents' extrinsic and job security values (M. K. Johnson, 2002). Using longitudinal panel data, M. K. Johnson and Elder (2002) examined the associations between work values and educational attainment across young adulthood (ages 18–32). They found that youth with no college education started with higher extrinsic values that declined substantially with age, whereas those with an associate's or bachelor's degree started with lower extrinsic values that declined less with age. In addition, adolescents most concerned with job security as high school seniors were least likely to continue their education in young adulthood.

## Work-Role Salience

Work-role salience represents the relative importance of work and career in an individual's life (Greenhaus, 1971; Nevill & Super, 1986). Super (1980) envisioned that the relative importance assigned by individuals to roles at different stages of their lives would determine their commitment to and involvement in tasks associated with the roles, as well as the rewards they expected to experience in the roles. For adolescents, this commitment is more affective and prospective because work and career have a more prominent role in the lives of adults than in those of adolescents. Work salience is particularly important for adolescents because it facilitates their career exploration, which is needed to make career and occupational decisions that are congruent with their occupational self-concept (Diemer et al., 2010). Diemer and Hsieh (2008) suggested that the vocational expectations and work salience of low-socioeconomic-status African American, Latin American, and Asian American youth are constrained by sociopolitical barriers because these youth often attend underresourced schools and live in impoverished communities that provide more limited access to quality vocational guidance, role models, and community support. Qualitative studies have also suggested that the structural racism's perceived effects on the work lives of family members, its effects on one's occupational aspirations, and the threat of random community violence may lead marginalized youth to disconnect from their vocational futures and reduce their vocational expectations (Sirin, Diemer, Jackson, Gonsalves, & Howell, 2004).

## School-to-Work Transition

Over the past 20 years, interest in the school-to-work transition for work-bound youth has grown (Blustein, 1997; Lent, O'Brien, & Fassinger, 1998). *The school-to-work transition* refers to that period of time before and after leaving high school for those youth intending to seek employment rather than pursue further education. Comprehensive and broad-ranging policy changes in education and training have been devoted to enhancing the process by which work-bound youth move from high school to work. The federal government attempted to stimulate the restructuring of the educational system that prepared students for the workplace and postsecondary education by enacting the School-to-Work Opportunities Act of 1994. Essentially, the law funds activities in three arenas: school-based learning, work-based learning, and connecting activities. A core theme of the act is the need to integrate academic and vocational learning, school-based and work-based learning, and secondary and postsecondary education. The act cites tech prep, youth apprenticeships, career academies, and cooperative education as promising school-to-work activities. Despite the passage of the School-to-Work Opportunities Act, significant and disconcerting gaps of knowledge still exist in understanding the processes by which high school students move into the world of work (Blustein, 2000). Central among these questions is the need to identify the antecedents and characteristics of an adaptive transition to the world of work. This knowledge is critically important to the development of counseling interventions, policy recommendations, and educational reform efforts.

## Career Maturity

The construct of career maturity consists of a readiness, attitude, and competency to cope effectively with career development tasks (Crites, 1978). Super (1980) defined career maturity as the place reached on the continuum of vocational development from exploration to decline. The assumption can be made that a career-mature person is more capable of making an appropriate and realistic career choice and decision. Career-mature individuals have the ability to identify specific occupational preferences and to implement activities to achieve their goals. Career maturity is thus the degree to which one has reached maturity in cognitive, emotional, and other psychological factors whereby one acquires the capacity to make realistic and mature career choices.

Salami (2008) highlighted the following aspects of career maturity:

1. Obtaining information about oneself and converting such information to self-knowledge
2. Acquiring decision-making skills and applying them in effective decision-making
3. Gathering career information and converting it into knowledge of the occupational world
4. Integrating self-knowledge and knowledge of the occupational world
5. Implementing the obtained knowledge in career planning.

*Career maturity* is conceptualized as an individual's readiness to make well-informed, age-appropriate career decisions and to shape one's career carefully in the face of existing societal opportunities and constraints.

As a construct, career maturity has been the subject of myriad studies and reviews. It is a well-established concept that is currently central to many career counseling and education programs in high schools. Career maturity is also the most commonly used outcome measure in career counseling. The literature is far from united on the presence of differences in scores of career maturity based on age and gender. Regarding age, although theoretical assumptions suggest uniform development in career maturity, practical considerations such as the planning activities needed for immediate decisions at transition points imposed by the education system suggest uneven development. Early work with the Career Development Inventory (Super, Thompson, Lindeman, Jordaan, & Myers, 1981) found significant differences in career maturity scores between Grades 9 and 10 and between Grades 9 and 11 and Grades 9 and 12 (Thompson & Lindeman, 1981). Early work with the Career Maturity Inventory (Crites, 1978) showed an incremental increase in career maturity from Grade 9 to Grade 12 (Herr & Enderlein, 1976). Other work has also shown that students in higher grades have higher career maturity scores than those in lower grades (e.g., Wallace-Broscious, Serafica, & Osipow, 1994). In contrast, in research reported by Fouad (1988) for a U.S. sample, ninth graders did not score lower than 12th graders.

## Need for Increased Access to Career and College Guidance Services

Given the inequities in career and college readiness among youth in high schools, a range of national reports and initiatives have argued for more college and career services for youth in schools, for more school–family–community partnerships on behalf of such needs, and for more career and college services designed specifically for the increasingly diverse population of students. These initiatives and reports include the Race to the Top Fund (U.S. Department of Education, 2009) and President Obama's *Blueprint for Reform* (U.S. Department of Education, 2010). Race to the Top is a competitive grant program of $4 billion that funds states that create innovative strategies for comprehensive education reform. The Race to the Top and *Blueprint for Reform* (U.S. Department of Education, 2010) both focused on four core areas that guided the reauthorization of the Elementary and Secondary Education Act: (1) Enhance and reward principal and teacher effectiveness; (2) build data systems that inform parents and educators about student achievement and guide instruction; (3) develop college- and career-ready standards and assessments aligned to those standards; and (4) implement effective interventions and support that will improve academic achievement in the lowest performing schools. In particular, the *Blueprint for Reform* emphasizes that high school graduates should be college and career ready and the importance of meeting the needs of students with the highest learning needs (i.e., culturally diverse learners, diverse English learners, children with disabilities, students of migrant workers, homeless students, and underprivileged children in rural and the highest need districts). Indeed, Title I, a central component of the Elementary and Secondary Education Act, ties funding for high-poverty schools to their ability to articulate and measure college and career readiness for students.

Interestingly, these current education reform groups and organizations are challenging school counselors' ability to meet the career and college needs of students. The recent Gates Foundation Public Agenda report *Can I Get a Little Advice Here* (Johnson, Rochkind, & Ott, 2010) highlighted college students' perceptions of school counselors' roles in the college-going process. Using a complex sampling design, Johnson et al. (2010) surveyed 614 individuals between 22 and 30 years old who had some postsecondary education experience. Between 54% and 67% of the young adults rated school counselors as only poor or fair in helping them decide what school was right for them, finding ways to pay for college such as financial aid and scholarships, thinking about different careers, and explaining and helping with the college application process. Almost 50% of the young adults felt that school counselors saw them as just another face in the crowd, and 47% felt that school counselors made an effort to get to know them as an individual. In addition, out of those who felt like a face in the crowd, 18% delayed going to college as opposed to 13% of those who felt as though counselors made an effort to get to know them.

In response, the American School Counselor Association (ASCA) asserted that the report illustrates what can go wrong when there are not enough school counselors to support students and when school counselors are placed in positions preventing them from performing the functions they were trained and hired to do. Although student–counselor ratios are high and school counselors have many non–counseling-related responsibilities, Public Agenda research has joined a body of research and literature that highlights school counselors' lack of attention to the college search, application, and enrollment process (e.g., Perez & McDonough, 2008). Lack of effective engagement in the college-going process by school counselors may hinder college access for students who need it most, particularly students from low-income and culturally diverse backgrounds. A national longitudinal study of high school seniors indicated that school counselors are an important source of social capital for students (Bryan, Holcomb-McCoy, Moore-Thomas, & Day-Vines, 2009). However, although student contact with school counselors for college information appears to increase college application rates, especially for students from low-income backgrounds, such student–counselor contact may be less useful for some groups of minority students.

## Implications for Career and College Counseling in High School

High school students have differing degrees of career maturity and diverse career development needs, and their career decisions are affected by varying contextual factors. As a result, the career and college guidance and counseling provided to adolescents must be varied as well. Herr and Cramer (1996) suggested that career guidance activities in high school must have three emphases: stimulating career development, providing treatment, and aiding placement (student movement to the next educational level or to the immediate life of worker, consumer, and citizen). The three emphases are implemented by counselors on the basis of where the individual student is in career development and what he or she needs most at a given time. It is important to remember that some high school students may need some of the same career awareness activities as elementary-age students (e.g., exploring careers). In the next section, we include an overview of career and college guidance activities that may be implemented by high school counselors.

## High School Career and College Counseling

Deciphering graduation requirements, understanding state proficiency test mandates, planning for college, or simply transitioning from middle to high school can be a timorous experience for a high school student. Although ideal, school counselors cannot assume that all students have developed an awareness of the vast of professional life roles, explored career choices, or engaged in postsecondary decision making before high school (McDonough, 2004; Stage & Hossler, 1989). Yet, one can assume that at a much earlier age students make life choices, knowingly or unknowingly, that affect their postsecondary options and career choices. School counselors can serve as conduits to help students from all socioeconomic backgrounds become independent thinkers by intentionally teaching and facilitating the career decision-making and goal-setting process (Hossler & Gallagher, 1987).

The ASCA (2005) national model recommends the development and implementation of comprehensive school counseling programs in three domains: academic, personal and social, and career counseling. The academic domain serves as a guide to implement strategies and activities that support and maximize student learning. Specifically, the academic standards emphasize (a) learning across the life span, (b) college and other postsecondary school preparedness, and (c) relating academics to life at home and in the community. The career counseling domain serves as a foundation for students to acquire the skills, attitudes, and knowledge to successfully transition from school to the world of work. The career counseling domain standards reinforce the importance of (a) self-awareness, (b) making informed decisions, and (c) achieving career goals. School counselors can teach students how to set postsecondary goals and make informed decisions by combining academic and career counseling during classroom guidance sessions, small groups, and individual sessions (Herr, Cramer, & Niles, 2004).

Herr and Cramer (1996) recommended the development of a five-stage model for implementing systematic educational and career intervention programs that reinforce the tenets of career development in the ASCA (2005) national model. The stages are

Stage 1: Develop a program rationale and philosophy.
Stage 2: State program goals and behavioral objectives.
Stage 3: Select program processes.
Stage 4: Develop an evaluation design.
Stage 5: Identify program milestones. (Herr & Cramer, 1996, p. 310)

The expected outcome of implementation will help students set aspirational goals, establish a plan, measure their progress, and reflect on individual accomplishments throughout the high school years. Most important, students will assume responsibility and accountability for their own destiny and learn how to integrate essential life skills in all aspects of postsecondary educational choices.

The process starts with teaching students how to identify and formulate goals in measurable terms by brainstorming questions about what they would like to achieve. For example, students may ask, "What are my interests? What are the graduation requirements? How do the courses I take prepare me for life after high school? How can I go to college? Which courses are honor courses? Which courses are Advanced Placement or International Baccalaureate? What does grade point average mean, and how does it influence going to college? To begin answering these questions, school counselors should review student enrollment data and evaluate current academic and career counseling program services available to all students and their parents or guardians. In this section of the chapter, we provide academic advisement and career counseling suggestions by grade level to address enhancing students' self-awareness, decision-making skills, understanding of graduation requirements, enrollment in courses of rigor, and college readiness.

## Ninth Grade

Developing a Freshman Transition School Counseling Program is one method to alleviate apprehension about a wide range of topics. To ensure information is not overwhelming to students and parents, if possible introduce program components before high school enrollment via rising ninth-grade communication such as student orientations, parent newsletters, and collaboration with middle school counselors. Working with freshmen throughout the ninth-grade school year, rather than in isolation, has a greater systemic impact and provides continuous support for all students. For example, ensuring all freshmen are introduced to information about individual learning styles, goal-setting strategies, transcript interpretation, time management skills, graduation requirements, and college readiness skills should be reinforced over time and in multiple ways. Interventions may be facilitated in large student orientations, classroom guidance lessons, small groups, and parent workshops. Assigning students to counselors alphabetically by last name allows collaborative interactions with and fluidity in family–school partnerships.

It is important to remember that although the school counselor may lead and coordinate a freshman transition program, seeking collaborative consensus with administrators, teachers, and parents is what will make the program a success. For example, using the management systems of the ASCA model as a guide, school counselors can collaborate with teachers to set aside scheduled times to facilitate goal-setting classroom guidance lessons (ASCA, 2005). As a result, teachers can integrate goal-setting concepts with instructional strategies that lead to increased focus on connecting learning to college readiness while exploring all postsecondary options. Administrators may also choose to provide information about school procedures and policies during a freshman orientation or introduction to high school classroom guidance lesson. Additional topics for a freshman orientation or introductory guidance lessons may include, but are not limited, to

- Transitioning: getting ready for high school and beyond
- People to know—your counselor, teachers, and assigned administrator
- Identifying your individual interests, skills, and values
- Exploring college and career paths
- Keeping track of assignments—time management and organization skills
- Technology resources and how to use them
- Coping with social and emotional stressors.

In other words, it is never too early for students to begin thinking about college selections and potential career paths and connecting the significance of the freshman grade point average and extracurricular participation to the college application process and other postsecondary options. Ninth-grade students should be continuously exposed to assessments and inventories that explore their skills, interests, and values. The school counseling office should become a familiar place to visit, and the school counselor should be perceived as an individual to help students interpret and reflect on assessments and inventory results. Counselors should even develop groups that offer students an opportunity to explore their feelings, thoughts, and fears about their future career and college experiences. Students should also be encouraged to seek learning through experiential opportunities (e.g., volunteering, job shadowing, mentoring).

Course selection, grades earned, school and community activities, and standardized testing are all factors colleges take into consideration when making admissions decisions. High school counselors should be knowledgeable about college requirements, assist students in course selection, and establish relationships with their school's regional college admission counselors when their assigned students are in the ninth grade. Preparing students for college readiness means preparing them for all postsecondary choices. Most important, they should ensure access to equitable course enrollment for all students, especially students of color and those from low-socioeconomic-status environments (Martinez & Klopott, 2003; McDonough, 2004).

## SIDEBAR 12.2  Ninth-Grade School Counselor Checklist

_____ During the spring of the ninth-grade year, communicate with middle school feeder counselors to share information about the Ninth-Grade Transition Plan.

_____ At the beginning of the school year, but before the first day of school, review data such as school report card and Individualized Education Program and 504 plans to ensure equitable placement and enrollment in rigorous courses.

_____ Review and prepare the Ninth-Grade Transition Plan for print and electronic posting.

_____ Send an introductory letter or e-mail to students and parents.

_____ Meet with ninth-grade students to introduce yourself and discuss services provided by the school counseling department.
_____ Plan and implement ninth-grade parent workshops.
_____ Review interim progress and end-of-quarter progress reports of students assigned to your caseload. Provide appropriate interventions to increase academic success.
_____ Provide comprehensive school counseling services as identified in your school counseling mission statement and accountability goals.

## Tenth Grade

As students enter the 10th grade, school counselors should begin to help students understand that choosing a post–high school pathway is a process that entails planning for life and that college readiness increases their chances for success. By 10th grade, students should be able to use the decision-making process steps to select rigorous courses and identify career interests, skills, and values. They should be able to articulate the steps to prepare themselves for college. It is here that students should develop a clear sense of the decision-making and goal-setting processes. Research (Herr & Cramer, 1996; Herr et al., 2004) has suggested that students who are able to make informed decisions and set goals are more likely to succeed in high school.

### SIDEBAR 12.3   Tenth-Grade School Counselor Checklist

_____ Review data such as school report cards and special education and 504 plans to ensure equitable placement and enrollment in rigorous courses.
_____ Encourage all students to take the PSAT.
_____ Facilitate test-taking strategies and classroom guidance lessons.
_____ Facilitate decision-making and goal-setting classroom guidance lessons.
_____ Review interim progress and end-of-quarter progress reports of students assigned to your caseload. Provide appropriate interventions to increase academic success.
_____ Plan and implement 10th-grade parent workshops.
_____ Provide comprehensive school counseling services as identified in your school counseling mission statement and accountability goals.

## Eleventh and 12th Grades

The college application process begins during the junior year; therefore, we combine 11th- and 12th-grade discussions in this section. Empowerment and informed decision making become essential as students approach their junior and senior years. Hossler, Schmidt, & Vesper, (1999) proposed that high school students make postsecondary educational decisions in three phases: (1) predisposition, (2) search, and (3) choice. During the predisposition stage, students develop aspirations through exposure to opportunities, peer interactions, and personal successes. School counselors can help foster positive experiences by creating a college-going culture at their school, initiating parental outreach, and ensuring students have access to rigorous courses that prepare them for college. The predisposition stage generally occurs during the underclassmen years of ninth and 10th grades.

During the second stage, search, students begin to identify posteducational goals. They may not know where they would like to attend college, but college is a vision. So what is the best way to prepare students and their parents for college? Unfortunately, one cannot wave a magic wand and have students be prepared. Students and parents need help to prioritize what criteria are important to them in the college search. What is most important—programs, size of school, public versus private, cost, location, competitiveness, residential facilities, or diversity? The search stage is very fluid and is the perfect time for school counselors to provide college information. Obstacles such as a large student caseload or noncounseling duties can limit individual student counseling sessions. Therefore, student orientations, classroom guidance lessons, and parent workshops become necessities. Sharing information in hard-copy format and electronically is an effective method to prepare upperclassmen for college and other postsecondary options. For example, a well-written and concise junior–senior handbook or pamphlet that details the college admission process in several languages can make the process manageable for students and serve as a checklist for school counselors. In addition, the school counselor should also create a personal system to organize information and meet deadlines.

The final stage of the Hossler–Gallagher (1999) model is choice. During the choice stage, students should be able to make informed decisions and determine which college is best for them on the basis of their strengths, interests, goals, and desires. Prior college exposure and readiness become apparent at this stage, and students who have not been equipped may experience difficulty. They can, however, be successful—school counselors simply need to use equitable resources and services to assist identified students and their parents. In this section, we outline suggestions for school counselors to help students successfully navigate the search and choice phases.

### SIDEBAR 12.4 Eleventh-Grade School Counselor Checklist

\_\_\_\_\_ Review data such as school report card and Individualized Education Program and 504 plans to ensure equitable placement and enrollment in rigorous courses.
\_\_\_\_\_ Develop and print junior–senior handbook or pamphlet.
\_\_\_\_\_ Collect student profile sheets from students to assist with writing letters of recommendations.
\_\_\_\_\_ Schedule junior student sessions and parent workshops.
\_\_\_\_\_ Communicate college admission test dates and remind students about registration deadlines.
\_\_\_\_\_ Communicate with college admission representative to arrange informational visits to your school.
\_\_\_\_\_ Ensure all students are registered for the PSAT.
\_\_\_\_\_ Remind junior athletes to send National Collegiate Athletic Association release form to National Collegiate Athletic Association Clearinghouse.
\_\_\_\_\_ Review interim progress and end-of-quarter progress reports of students assigned to your caseload. Provide appropriate interventions to increase academic success.
\_\_\_\_\_ Provide comprehensive school counseling services as identified in your school counseling mission statement and accountability goals.

## Getting Started

The school counselor should develop a system to inform students and parents about college entrance assessments, application deadlines, financial aid, and requests for recommendations and transcripts. The Internet provides a great deal of information about academic and career planning to assist with interest exploratory, college search, financial assistance, and work value inventories. Administrators should be encouraged to invest in comprehensive software tools that provide portals to store individual student information. Web-based products such as Naviance (http://www.naviance.com) and

Bridges (http://www.bridges.com) are postsecondary planning tools used by students, parents, and school counselors to develop and store career plans, explore college and career information, seek financial aid resources, and reflect on the process. Information sought and stored is password protected for later reference throughout the high school years.

## Prioritizing

School counselors should encourage students to attend college fairs, meet with college representatives, take virtual tours, and personally visit colleges to develop a college interest list. The career decision-making and goal-setting skills acquired during the ninth and 10th grades are useful tools for the development of a potential-college list. The list should include the student's must-haves and desires. A practical way to organize the list is by safety, comfort, and reach schools. *Safety schools* are colleges that students think are affordable and for which their scholastic records meet admission requirements. *Comfort schools* are colleges that students think are affordable and for which they may qualify for admission. *Reach schools* are colleges that students consider to be a stretch to both qualify and afford. Developing a matrix will help students to weigh the pros and cons of each college choice. If possible, students should tour as many colleges as possible on their potential list, eat in the cafeteria, visit a dorm room, and ask questions to help them make informed decisions.

### SIDEBAR12.5   Twelfth-Grade School Counselor Checklist

_____ Prepare and distribute college application information.
_____ Plan financial aid workshop.
_____ Plan and facilitate 12th-grade student academic and career sessions.
_____ Plan and facilitate 12th-grade parent academic and career workshops.
_____ Review data such as school report card and Individualized Education Program and 504 plans to ensure equitable placement and enrollment in rigorous courses. Identify students who may be in danger of not fulfilling graduation requirements.
_____ Schedule sessions with students to discuss how to complete college admission and financial aid applications.
_____ Complete letters of recommendations and required admission documents for students.

## Gathering Information

At the end of the junior year and no later than the beginning of the senior year, school counselors should remind students to accomplish two tasks: (1) complete a student profile list, and (2) gather college admissions information. The purpose of the student profile list is to allow students to share personal strengths and experiences that the school counselor may not know. Information from the student profile sheet can be used when writing letters of recommendations. The second task, gathering college admissions information, helps the student begin to target colleges of interest and develop a potential college list. Some applications may be posted in early summer but most will be available by August. School counselors should develop a working knowledge of application requirements and become familiar with admission categories. For example, regular admission requires students to apply by a specific deadline, generally in January. The applications are evaluated by college admission panels, and notifications are mailed to students in the spring. Rolling admission permits colleges to evaluate the application package on receipt and make decisions within 6 to 8 weeks. Open admission applications grant acceptance to potential students without regard to additional requirements such as test scores, grade point averages, and so forth. Early decision is a process that colleges use less frequently. This process requires students to submit their application in early November, and acceptance decisions are made by mid-December. If accepted, students must commit in writing to attend the college and withdraw considerations from other colleges. Early action is a process that requires students to submit the completed packet by early December. Early action is similar to early decision, except students are not committed to attend or respond until May. Students also have the option to apply to other colleges under the early action process.

### SIDEBAR 12.6   Five Tips for Writing Recommendation Letters

1. Ask students and their parents to complete a personal profile to enhance information provided on the letter of recommendation. Outline what you want to convey about the student.
2. Provide a solid introductory paragraph about how well you know the student. If you do not know the student well, explain your sources for gathering information.
3. Include three to four qualities that describe the student's strengths. Support your statements with examples. Highlight the student's potential for growth and accomplishing college expectations. Include extracurricular participation, leadership, honors, and service learning activities. Help the reader know the applicant.
4. End the letter by summarizing why you think the student is a perfect fit for the particular school.
5. Recognize the value of a school counselor recommendation. Proofread before sending.

Follow up with the college to ensure your letter was received as an e-mail attachment or by mail.

## College Admission Tests

Most colleges require some form of testing to determine students' readiness and potential for the college experience. Although taking the Preliminary SAT/National Merit Scholarship Qualifying Test (PSAT/NMSQT) is not required for admission to college, all 11th-grade students should take the PSAT on the national test date in October. The PSAT/NMSQT is the qualifying exam for national merit and commended scholars. To increase familiarity and improve test-taking strategies, ninth- and 10th-grade students should be highly encouraged to take the test before the 11th grade as a practice for the SAT. Many colleges use the SAT or ACT assessment as one of several admission requirements. Eleventh-grade students should take either the SAT or ACT or both during the spring of their junior year. If desired or needed, 12th-grade students may also take the SAT or ACT for a second or third time. Some colleges require additional information gained from assessments such as the SAT II. The SAT II assesses a student's knowledge in a particular academic discipline and may be used to determine placement in college freshman classes. If the SAT II is required, students should be encouraged to take the SAT II immediately on completion of the related course. To learn accurate information about registration deadlines, fee waivers, and test-taking strategies, school counselors should review http://www.collegeboard.org for PSAT and SAT information and http://www.act.org for ACT information and register to attend regional college workshops.

## Financial Assistance and Scholarships

In addition to learning about college admission requirements, school counselors should also be knowledgeable about financial obligations associated with admission to reassure students and parents that finances should never keep one from attending college. In addition to communicating electronically, school counselors should post financial aid information throughout the counseling office, library, and career center. Scheduling financial aid workshops for students and parents early in the senior year will also help streamline the process. Students and parents should also be exposed to the college financial aid process early in the eighth or ninth grade. Classroom advisory sessions or homerooms can be a place in which this information is discussed by counselors, teachers, or both on a regular basis.

Although many forms of financial assistance are available to students, deadlines and the cost of attendance may differ from college to college, but the expected family contribution remains the same. It is extremely important to inform students and parents to investigate specific required financial forms and costs. The Free Application for Federal Student Aid is required for federal funding; however, some colleges have additional applications.

Grants are usually awarded by the federal or state government and based on individual financial need. More often than not, grants do not require repayment. They are available to students attending 2- and 4-year colleges as well as technical educational institutions. There are various sources of local and national scholarships awarded by colleges, private donors, and the military. Loans, however, require repayment. Most federal loans can be deferred until after college graduation. To remain knowledgeable, school counselors should frequently refer to Web sites such as the U.S. Department of Education's Funding Education Beyond High School: The Guide to Federal Student Aid (http://www.studentaid.ed.gov).

## Apprenticeships

In the 1990s, youth apprenticeships emerged as a means to facilitate the transition between school and work. Apprenticeships allow students to become highly skilled employees with a combination of worksite experience and classroom learning. Generally, the apprentice is not only trained, but also paid; thus, students are assured a salary with regular increases while learning. The apprentice is trained and supervised by experts in the acquired profession and rotates throughout the industry to learn all required theoretical concepts and practical skills necessary to become proficient. Apprenticeships provide first-hand information about a student's commitment and passion. Although most apprenticeships require a minimum entry age of 16, programs may vary from state to state. Some programs may require enrollment or completion of specific high school courses as a prerequisite. The U.S. Department of Labor provides additional information at http://www.dol.gov/dol/topic/training/apprenticeship.

## Job Shadowing

Paris and Mason (1995) defined job shadowing as a work experience option through which students learn about a job by walking through the work day as a shadow to a competent worker. The job-shadowing work experience is a temporary, unpaid exposure to the workplace in an occupational area of interest to the student. Students witness firsthand the work environment, employability, and occupational skills in practice and the value of professional training and potential career options. Job shadowing is designed to increase career awareness, help model student behavior through examples, and reinforce in the student the link between classroom learning and work requirements. Almost any workplace is a potential job-shadowing site. Job shadowing is limited in that it only allows students to observe direct work experience; responsibility and skills are not acquired. Although integration of school and work is implied, there is little if any curriculum alignment between the school and occupational area.

Examples of assignments students may want to complete as a result of their job shadow are

- A written report on a specific career
- A compilation of the results of a worksite supervisor interview, including names and titles within the department or floor
- A journal entry describing the site, the people, the work, and the environment
- A classroom oral presentation or poster presentation on careers represented at the job-shadowing site
- An appointment with the school counselor about the career or careers.

## School to Work Transition Programs

Building school-to-work transition programs has been viewed as one means to increase adolescents' career or work readiness. Paris (1994) offered three approaches to developing successful school-to-work programs in high schools:

1. *Integrate the long-separated tracks of academic and vocational education.* From middle school on, schools should orient youth to work, help them explore different types of jobs, provide guidance about career paths, and assist them in finding work relevant to their needs and interests. Vocational education is considered too narrow and specific, outdated by modern technology, and ineffective in building language and math skills. Academic education is criticized for being too conventional, driven predominantly by standardized tests, and ineffective at motivating most students.

2. *Link schooling with the demands and realities of the workplace.* Through employment-related experiences and on-the-job learning, students can receive significant exposure to the workforce and can prepare for their future work environment.
3. *Develop programs to closely coordinate secondary and postsecondary education with employers.* Apprenticeships and school–business partnerships are just two of the many ways in which educators and businesspeople can produce a shared view of youth learning and development.

These changes have extensive learning implications, particularly for high schools, including developing new models that integrate vocational and academic education, from revamping the school counseling programs to creating a coherent sequence of courses related to broad occupational clusters.

## Career and College Counseling Activities and Resources

Career preparation components that are related to positive secondary and postsecondary school outcomes include (a) opportunities for both school-based and community-based experiences that expose youth to a broad array of career paths, experiences, and occupations; (b) opportunities for youth to build relevant skills, academic knowledge, and personal competencies required in the workplace and for continued education; and (c) opportunities for youth to tailor their career experiences to meet their individual needs (American Youth Policy Forum & Center for Workforce Development, 2000).

We next provide an inventory of career and college activities and resources for high school students and their counselors. These activities can be used individually or in groups, and they may be modified for use in schools, community agencies, or both.

1. Have students complete a college application, complete a job application, write a résumé, or role-play a job or college interview.
2. Have students read a biography of a person they admire. Next, have students describe how the person made career decisions.
3. Play career bingo.
4. Construct a career or occupational family tree or career genogram (http://counselingoutfitters.com/vistas/vistas06/vistas06.40.pdf).
5. Construct a career portfolio (http://www.ccd.me.edu/careerprep/career_portfolio.pdf).
6. Have students develop an educational plan that is aligned with their career or college goals.
7. Invite community members to discuss their career paths with students.
8. Have local university admissions officers speak to students about the admissions process (e.g., essays, recommendation letters).

9. Have a local employment administrator come to discuss local employment trends, unemployment rates, and so forth.

10. Have recent graduates come back to talk about work, college, apprenticeships, and so forth.

## Summary

Our purpose in this chapter was to cover, in more detail, the career development of adolescents and the application of career counseling in the high school setting. This chapter was by no means exhaustive, because an entire book could be written on career and college counseling in high schools. We began with an overview of the economic context in which high school students must begin their career trajectories. Next, we described theories and models that are most often used to understand adolescents' career development. The remainder of the chapter included an overview of factors that influence high school students' career development and counselor strategies and techniques that may be used to enhance career and college readiness.

## References

American School Counselor Association. (2005). *The ASCA national model: A framework for school counseling programs* (2nd ed.) Alexandria, VA: Author.

American School Counselor Association. (2010). *ASCA response to Public Agenda report.* Retrieved from http://www.publicagenda.org/pages/ASCA-Response

American Youth Policy Forum & Center for Workforce Development. (2000). *Looking forward: School-to-work principles and strategies for sustainability.* Washington, DC: Author.

Astin, H. (1984). The meaning of work in women's lives: A sociopsychological model of career choice and work behavior. *Counseling Psychologist, 12,* 117–126.

Bandura, A. (1986). *Social foundations of thought and action: A social cognitive theory.* Englewood Cliffs, NJ: Prentice-Hall.

Barker, J., & Satcher, J. (2000). School counselors perceptions of required workplace skill and career development competencies. *Professional School Counseling, 4,* 134–139.

Barton, P. E. (2002). *The closing of the education frontier?* Princeton, NJ: Educational Testing Service.

Bartol, K.M. (1981). Vocational behavior and Career Development, 1980: A review. *Journal of Vocational Behavior, 19*(2), 123–162.

Betz, N. E., & Hackett, G. (1981). The relationship of career-related self-efficacy expectations to perceived career options in college women and men. *Journal of Counseling Psychology, 28,* 399–410.

Blustein, D. L. (1997), A context rich perspective of career exploration across the life roles. *Career Development Quarterly, 45,* 260–276.

Bluestone, B., & Rose, S. (1997). Overworked and underemployed: Unraveling the economic enigma. *American Prospect, 31,* 58–69.

Blustein, D. L., Juntunen, CL, & Worthington, L. (2000). The school-to-work transition: Adjustment challenges of the forgotten half. In S. D. Brown & R. W. Lent (Eds.). *Handbook of Counseling Psychology,* (pp. 435–470). Hoboken, NJ: Wiley.

Blustein, D. L., Chaves, A. P., Diemer, M. A., Gallagher, L. A., Marshall, K. G., Sinn, S., & Bhati, K. S. (2002). Voices of the forgotten half: The role of social class in the school-to-work transition. *Journal of Counseling Psychology, 49,* 311–323.

Bonett, R. M. (1994). Marital status and sex: Impact on career self-efficacy. *Journal of Counseling and Development, 73,* 187–190.

Brown, S. D., & Lent, R. W. (2005). *Career development and counseling: Putting theory and research to work.* Hoboken, NJ: Wiley.

Bryan, J., Holcomb-McCoy, C., Moore-Thomas, C., & Day-Vines, N. (2009). Who sees the school counselor for college counseling? A national study. *Professional School Counseling, 12,* 280–291.

Bureau of Labor Statistics. (2010, September). Number of jobs held, labor market activity, and earnings growth among the youngest baby boomers: Results from a longitudinal survey. (U.S. Department of Labor Publication No. 06-1496). Retrieved on June 16, 2011, from http://www.bis.gon/news.release/archives/nlsoy_08252006.pdf

Chaves, A. P., Diemer, M. A., Blustein, D. L., Gallagher, L. A., DeVoy, J. E., Casares, M. T., & Perry, J. C. (2004). Conceptions of work: The view from urban youth. *Journal of Counseling Psychology, 51,* 275–286.

Chung, Y. B. (2002). Career decision-making self-efficacy and career commitment: Gender and ethnic differences among college students. *Journal of Career Development, 28,* 277–284.

Constantine, M. G., Wallace, B. C., & Kindaichi, M. M. (2005). Examining contextual factors in the career decision path of African American adolescents. *Journal of Career Assessment, 13,* 307–319.

Crites, J. O. (1978). *Theory and research handbook for the Career Maturity Inventory* (2nd ed.). Monterey, CA: CTB/McGraw-Hill.

Danziger, S. H., & Gottschalk, P. (2004). *Diverging fortunes: Trends in poverty and inequality.* New York, NY: Russell Sage Foundation.

Diemer, M. A., & Hsieh, C. (2008). Sociopolitical development and vocational expectations among lower-SES adolescents of color. *Career Development Quarterly, 56,* 257–267.

Diemer, M. A., Wang, Q., Moore, T., Gregory, S., Hatcher, K., & Voight, A. (2010). Sociopolitical development, work salience, and vocational expectations among low socioeconomic status African American, Latin American, and Asian American youth. *Developmental Psychology, 46,* 619–635.

Eccles, J. S., Templeton, J., Barber, B. L., & Stone, M. R. (2003). Adolescence and emerging adulthood: The critical pathways to adulthood. In M. H. Bornstein, L. Davidson, C. L. M. Keyes, K. A. Moore, & the Center for Child Well-Being (Eds.), *Well-being: Positive development across the life course* (pp. 386–406). Mahwah, NJ: Erlbaum.

Farber, H. S. (2005). What do we know about job loss in the United States? Evidence from the Displaced Workers Survey, 1984-2004. *Economic Perspectives, 29,* 13–28.

Farber, H. S. (2006). *Is the company man an anachronism? Trends in long term employment in the U.S. between 1973 and 2005* (Network on Transitions to Adulthood Policy Brief 38). Philadelphia, PA: MacArthur Foundation Network on Transitions to Adulthood and Public Policy.

Ferry, T. R., Fouad, N. A., & Smith, P. L. (2000). The role of family context in a social cognitive model for career-related choice behavior: A math and science perspective. *Journal of Vocational Behavior, 57,* 348–364.

Fine, M., Burns, A., Payne, Y. A., & Torre, M. E. (2004). Civic lessons: The color and class of betrayal. *Teachers College Record, 106,* 2193–2223.

Flanagan, C. A. (2003). Trust, identity, and civic hope. *Applied Developmental Science, 7,* 165–171.

Flanagan, C. A. (2008). Private anxieties and public hopes: The perils and promise of youth in the context of globalization. In J. Cole & D. Durham (Eds.), *Figuring the future: Children, youth, and globalization* (pp. 125–150). Santa Fe, New Mexico: SAR Press.

Fottler, M. D., & Bain, T. (1980). Managerial aspirations of high school seniors: A comparison of males and females. *Journal of Vocational Behavior, 16,* 83–95.

Fouad, N. A. (1988). The construct of career maturity in the United States and Israel. *Journal of Vocational Behaviour, 32,* 49–59.

Fouad, N. A., & Byars-Winston, A. M. (2005). Cultural context of career choice: Meta-analysis of race/ethnicity differences. *Career Development Quarterly, 53,* 223–233.

Gottfredson, L. S. (2005). Applying Gottfredson's theory of circumscription and compromise in career guidance and counseling. In S. D. Brown & R. W. Lent (Eds.), *Career development and counseling: Putting theory and research to work* (pp. 71–100). Hoboken, NJ: Wiley.

Greenhaus, J. H. (1971). An investigation of the role of career salience in vocational behavior. *Journal of Vocational Behavior, 1,* 216–295.

Griffith, A. R. (1980). Justification for black career development. *Counselor Education and Supervision, 19,* 301–309.

Herr, E. L., & Cramer, S. H. (1996). *Career guidance and counseling through the lifespan* (5th ed.). New York, NY: HarperCollins.

Herr, E. L., Cramer, S. H., & Niles, S. G. (2004). *Career guidance and counseling through the lifespan* (6th ed.) Boston, MA: Allyn & Bacon.

Herr, E. L., & Enderlein, T. E. (1976). Vocational maturity: The effects of school, grade, curriculum, and sex. *Journal of Vocational Behavior, 8,* 227–238.

Hill, M. S., & Yeung, W. J. (1999). How has the changing structure of opportunities affected transitions to adulthood? In A. Booth, A. C. Crouter, & M. J. Shanahan (Eds.), *Transitions to adulthood in a changing economy: No work, no family, no future?* (pp. 3–39). Westport, CT: Greenwood.

Holland, J. L. (1973). *Making vocational choices: A theory of careers.* Englewood Cliffs, NJ: Prentice-Hall.

Holland, J. L. (1996). Exploring careers with a typology: What we have learned and some new directions. *The American Psychology. 51,* 397–406.

Holland, J. L. (1997). *Making vocational choices: A theory of vocational personalities and work environments* (3rd ed.). Odessa, FL: Psychological Assessment Resources.

Hossler, D., & Gallagher, K. S. (1987). Studying student college choice: A three-phase model and the implications for policymakers. *College and University, 62,* 207–221.

Hossler, D., Schmidt, J., & Vesper, N. (1999). *Going to college: How social, economic and educational factors influence the decisions students make.* Baltimore, MD: Johns Hopkins University Press.

Hurley, D., & Thorp, J. (2002). *Decisions without direction: Career guidance and decision making among American youth.* Washington, DC: National Association of Manufacturers.

Jez, S. J. (2008). *The influence of wealth and race in four-year college attendance* (Research & Occasional Paper Series). Berkeley, CA: Center for Studies in Higher Education.

Johnson, M. K. (2002). Social origins, adolescent experiences, and work value trajectories during the transition to adulthood. *Social Forces, 80,* 1307–1340.

Johnson, M. K., & Elder, G. H. (2002). Educational pathways and work value trajectories. *Sociological Perspectives, 45,* 113–138.

Johnson, J., Rochkind, J. & Ott, A. (2010). Why guidance counseling needs to change. *Educational Leadership, 67,* 74–79.

Kelly, K. R. (1993). The relation of gender and academic achievement to career self-efficacy and interests. *Gifted Child Quarterly, 37,* 59–64.

Kenny, M. E., Blustein, D. L., Chaves, A., Grossman, J. M., & Gallagher, L. (2003). The role of perceived barriers and relational support in the educational and vocational lives of urban high school students. *Journal of Counseling Psychology, 50,* 142–155.

Krakauer, C., & Chen, C. P. (2003). Gender barriers in the legal profession: Implications for career development of female law students. *Journal of Employment Counseling, 40,* 65–79.

Lent, R. W., & Brown, S. D. (1996). Social cognitive approach to career development: An overview. *Career Development Quarterly. 44,* 310–321.

Lent, R. W., Brown, S. D., & Hackett, G. (1994). Toward a unifying social cognitive theory of career and academic interest, choice and performance. *Journal of Vocational Behavior, 45,* 79–122.

Lent, R. W., Brown, S. D., & Hackett, G. (2000). Contextual supports and barriers to career choice: A social cognitive anlaysis. *Journal of Counseling Psychology, 47,* 36–49.

Lent, R. W., Brown, S. D., Talleyrand, R., McPartland, E. B., Davis, T., Chopra, S. B., Alexander, M. S., … Chai, C.-M. (2000). Career choice barriers, supports, and coping strategies: College students' experiences. *Journal of Vocational Behavior, 60,* 61–72.

Lent, R., O'Brien, K. M., & Fassinger, R. E. (1998). School-to-work transition and the role of vocational counseling psychology. *Counseling Psychologist, 26,* 489–494.

Lippa, R. (1998). Gender-related individual differences and the structure of vocational interests: The importance of the people–things dimension. *Journal of Personality and Social Psychology, 74,* 996–1009.

Lopez, M. H., & Marcelo, K. B. (2006) *Youth demographics* (CIRCLE Fact Sheet). College Park, MD: Center for Information and Research on Civic Learning and Engagement.

Martinez, M., & Klopott, S. (2003). *Improving college access for minority, low-income, and first generation students.* Boston, MA: Pathways to College Network.

McDonough, P. M. (2004). *Choosing colleges: How social class and school structure opportunity.* Albany: State University of New York Press.

Mishel, L., Bernstein, J., & Allegretto, S. (2010). *The state of working America 2009-2010* (Economic Policy Institute Report). Retrieved from http://www.stateofworkingamerica.org

Mollenkopf, J., Kasinitz, P., & Waters, M. (2005). The ever winding path: Transitions to adulthood among native and immigrant young people in metropolitan New York. In R. A. Settersten, F. F. Furstenberg Jr., & R. G. Rumbaut (Eds.), *On the frontier of adulthood: Theory, research, and public policy* (pp. 454–497). Chicago, IL: University of Chicago Press.

National Association for College Admission Counseling. (2010). *2010 state of college admission.* Washington, DC: Author.

Nevill, D. D., & Super, D. E. (1986). *The Salience Inventory: Theory, application and research.* Palo Alto, CA: Consulting Psychologists Press.

Ogbu, J. U. (1989). The individual in collective adaptation: A framework for focusing on academic underperformance and dropping out among involuntary minorities. In L. Weis, E. Farrar, & H. G. Petrie (Eds.), *Dropouts from school: Issues, dilemmas, and solutions*, (pp.181–204). Albany: State University of New York Press.

Paris, K. (1994). *A leadership model for planning and implementing change.* Madison: Center on Education and Work, University of Wisconsin—Madison.

Paris, K. A., & Mason, S. A. (1995). *Planning and implementing youth apprenticeship and work-based learning.* Madison: Center on Education and Work, University of Wisconsin.

Phelps, L. A., & Hanley-Maxwell, C. (1997). School-to-work transition for youth with disabilities: A review of outcomes and practices. *Review of Educational Research, 67*, 197–226.

Perez, P. A., & McDonough, P. M. (2008). Understanding Latina and Latino college choice: A social capital and chain migration analysis. *Journal of Hispanic Higher Education, 7*, 249–265.

Rainey, L. M., & Borders, L. D. (1997). Influential factors in career orientation and career aspiration of early adolescent girls. *Journal of Counseling Psychology, 44*,160–172.

Reynolds, J., Stewart, M., McDonald, R., & Sischo, L. (2006). Have adolescents become too ambitious? High school seniors' educational an occupational plans, 1976–2000. *Social Problems, 53*, 186–206.

Ryan, J. M., Tracey, T. J. G., & Rounds, J. (1996). Generalizability of Holland's structure of vocational interests across ethnicity, gender, and socioeconomic status. *Journal of Counseling Psychology, 43*, 330–337.

Salami, S. O. (2008). Gender, identity status, and career maturity of adolescents. *Journal of Social Sciences, 16*, 35–49.

Schneider, B., & Stevenson, D. (1999). The ambitious generation. *Educational Leadership, 57*, 22–25.

School-to-Work Opportunities Act. (1994). School-to-Work Opportunities Act of 1994. *Public Law, 103*–239.

Schulenberg, J., Bachman, J. G., Johnston, L. D., & O'Malley, P. M. (1994). *Historical trends in attitudes and preferences regarding family, work, and the future among American adolescents: National data from 1976 through 1992.* Ann Arbor, MI: Institute for Social Research.

Settersten, R. A., Furstenberg, F. F., & Rumbaut, R. G. (2005). *On the frontier of adulthood: Theory, research, and policy.* Chicago, IL: University of Chicago Press.

Sirin, S. R., Diemer, M. A., Jackson, L. R., Gonsalves, L., & Howell, A. (2004). Future aspirations of urban adolescents: A person-in-context model. *Qualitative Studies in Education, 17*, 437–460.

Stage, F., & Hossler, D. (1989). Differences in family influences on college attendance plans for male and female ninth graders. *Research in Higher Education, 30*, 301–315.

Super, D. E. (1957). *The psychology of careers: An introduction to vocational development.* New York, NY: Harper.

Super, D. E. (1980). A life-span, life-space approach to career development. *Journal of Vocational Behavior, 16*, 282–298.

Super, D. E., Thompson, A. S., Lindeman, R. H., Jordaan, J. P., & Myers, R. A. (1981). *The Career Development Inventory.* Palo Alto, CA: Consulting Psychologists Press.

Thompson, A. S., & Lindeman, R. H. (1981). *Career Development Inventory: Vol. 1. User's manual.* Palo Alto, CA: Consulting Psychologists Press.

Tokar, D. M., & Jome, L. M. (1998). Masculinity, vocational interests, and career choice traditionality: Evidence for a fully mediated model. *Journal of Counseling Psychology, 45,* 424–435.

Turner, C., & Turner, B. (1995, April). *Race and sex discrimination in occupations: A 20-year replication.* Paper presented at the annual meeting of the Eastern Psychological Association, Boston, MA.

U.S. Department of Education. (2009). *U.S. Department of Education opens race to the top competition.* Retrieved from http://www2.ed.gov/news/pressreleases/2009/11/11122009.html

U.S. Department of Education. (2010). *ESEA reauthorization: A blueprint for reform.* Washington, DC: Author.

Vondracek, F. W., & Porfeli, E. J. (2003). The world of work and careers. In G. R. Adams & M. D. Berzonsky (Eds.), *Blackwell handbook of adolescence* (pp. 109–128). Malden, MA: Blackwell.

Wallace-Broscious, A., Serafica, F. C., & Osipow, S. H. (1994). Adolescent career development: Relationship to self-concept and identity status. *Journal of Research on Adolescence, 4,* 127–149.

Zeldin, A., & Pajares, F. (2000). Against the odds: Self-efficacy beliefs of women in mathematical, scientific, and technological careers. *American Educational Research Journal, 37,* 215–246.

# CHAPTER 13

# College Career Counseling
## Traditional, Hybrid, and 100% Online Campuses

Jeffrey D. Cook and Leanne Schamp

## Contents

The field of counseling continues to evolve just as do the arts, philosophy, and culture. This evolution demands that the different modalities of counseling continue to be evaluated and reevaluated. Our focus in this chapter is specific to counseling as it pertains to college students, with an emphasis on career discovery, or what has been traditionally referred to as *career counseling*. We use the terms *counseling* and *career counseling* interchangeably because both refer to processes of personal discovery and have more commonalities than differences. This distinction is important because it suggests the evolution of the field from career guidance that focuses on measureable traits, to career counseling that is person centered, to counseling that locates career discovery in the context of interpersonal experience.

Locating career discovery within interpersonal experience is a crucial distinction that aligns with developing postmodern constructivism and social constructivism theories. More important, as we suggest in this chapter, it aligns with the college student of today (Savickas et al., 2009). Further discussion of this shift is important because many college career services continue to function out of a modernistic framework (trait and factor or person-centered approach). Our intent is to continue the dialogue of revising career counseling in both theory and practice. In doing so, we broke the chapter into two major sections. The first section contrasts today's college student and traditional career work, and the second conveys the importance of the therapeutic alliance and a constructivist approach as it relates to counseling college students around the topic of career.

## Traditional Undergraduate College Students

For counselors to understand how to best serve prospective student clients in a campus career center, a review of the values and attitudes of today's traditional undergraduate college student is warranted. What follows is a brief discussion of how a generation is defined and how the experiences of a generation affect the values, attitudes, and expectations of the individuals who make up a particular generation. Additionally, we explore the characteristics identifying the current millennial generation.

Generations are defined by their placement in history and by common political and social events shared over roughly two decades (Zemke, Filipezak, & Raines, 2000, as cited in Gibson, 2009). These common experiences often result in the development of shared values among the members of a particular generation (Lancaster & Stillman, 2002, as cited in Elam, Stratton, & Gibson, 2007). As a generation evolves, those born in the later years reflect on the values of those born in the earlier years and determine which values they will retain, which values need adjustment, and which values are no longer relevant to the individual.

All generations develop particular characteristics that are directly influenced by the values and attitudes of their earlier-generation parents and by the historical and social events of their own lives. The millennial generation is no exception and in fact exhibits culture shifts comparable in degree to those associated with the movement of a generation from farm to city during industrialization. The challenge is to develop a guidance counseling paradigm that affords the best approach to integrating generational variations into career discovery. The literature has suggested (DeBard, 2004; Elam et al., 2007; Gibson, 2009; Pardue & Morgan, 2008) the following key characteristics and behaviors attributed to the millennial generation.

Millennials have grown up in a society that has become increasingly high tech, mobile, and globally aware and real-time connected. Unlike previous generations, this generation has grown up with personal computers, cell phones, and smartphones and the technological ability to access great amounts of information in an exceedingly short amount of time via Internet search engines. Their comfort with technology has helped to develop multitasking abilities. They expect feedback to be swift, if not immediate.

Millennial students were brought up by highly involved and protective parents who monitored and oversaw every aspect of their children's lives. They provided for high social and cultural involvement and extracurricular activities and stayed informed of their children's academic performance and progress. Parents of this generation expressed and reinforced to their children that they were special (DeBard, 2004, p. 35). Positive reinforcement was also provided to this generation via rewards not only for achievement, but simply for participation (DeBard, 2004). Although such positivism may have helped to shape the confidence found in millennials, it has also shaped their expectations about life and others' responses to them.

Millennials are accustomed to working in groups and enjoy group projects that they perceive as meaningful. They are identified as committed group members and also expect that each member of the group will follow through with individual responsibilities in completing a project. Having a positive impact and making a difference are important values to this generation. Comfortable with structure and amenable to clearly defined rules and procedures, millenials tend to respond well to structure and show respect for authority. They also expect fairness in the establishment and maintenance of rules and procedures.

Members of the millennial generation are said to reflect optimism and confidence about their lives, and they hold high expectations regarding personal success. However, given their experiences with highly involved parents, they may not feel comfortable making decisions without input and guidance from authority figures who may be considered to be experts. In the college setting, this discomfort may affect the expectations students have of faculty, administration, and staff such as career and mental health counselors (Elam et al., 2007).

Howe and Strauss (2000, as cited in DeBard, 2004) reported that millennials represent the highest degree of racial and ethnic diversity among generations in U.S. history. Many in this generation are biracial or multiracial, with some statistics indicating that one in five millennials have at least one immigrant parent. Because millennial students' relationships with parents may be close, their attitudes may reflect less of an individualistic perspective given particular cultural norms. Counselors who provide career and mental health services will need to consider their approaches with prospective millennial clients. Consideration of a student's cultural context and needs related to family structure and expectations of the student is critical.

The discussion regarding the millennial generation has to this point reflected general characteristics that have been observed and noted in the literature. It is important to note that there are always exceptions to generalizations, and these characterizations of a generation are not without exception. It is critical that stereotyping be avoided here, as in discussion about any particular group of people. Individuals in the millennial generation have had experiences that are very different than those described in extant literature and summarized here.

## Student Perspectives Regarding Career and Career Counseling

The literature has suggested that despite the majority of college students' perceived personal and career concerns and the seeming success of career counseling with college students, relatively small numbers of students seek professional help through college counseling services (Ludwikowski,

Vogel, & Armstrong, 2009). Evidence for precipitating factors contributing to student reluctance to seek out personal or career counseling services has revealed a number of student concerns.

A recent study (Ludwikowski et al., 2009) examined possible factors that could contribute to college students avoiding the use of career counseling services. The study considered student attitudes regarding career counseling and the possibility that attitudes are formed on the basis of factors of perceived personal and public stigmatization (external stigma) and the degree to which these result in self-stigmas (internal stigma). Ludwikowski et al. (2009) defined public stigma as occurring at the societal level, such as individuals being negatively perceived by society for seeking counseling. Personal stigma related to attitudes and opinions about counseling expressed by students' family members, peers, and teachers. An earlier study conducted by Vogel, Wade, Wester, Larson, and Hackler (2007, as cited in Ludwikowski et al., 2009) suggested that when family members or friends reflected positive views of counseling, students were more amenable to pursuing it. Internalized or self-stigma was defined as the student's personal perceptions regarding the acceptability of seeking counseling, based on personal and public stigmas.

Ludwikowski et al. (2009) found that students' internalization of external stigma may result in devaluating career counseling services, making it difficult for students to seek career development help. They found that students were more strongly affected by public stigma than by personal stigma. However, both public stigma and personal stigma were related to negative attitudes toward seeking career counseling. Men reported higher levels of stigma from close others if they were to seek career counseling than did women. Men also reported higher levels of perceived value from career counseling than did women.

Although public stigma seemed to have a greater impact on the participants in the study conducted by Ludwikowski et al. (2009), they illustrated the challenges involved in effecting change in public attitudes regarding career counseling. Because this process is slower, they recommended developing career-related interventions to address students' larger social systems, thus having an impact on personal stigma. Career outreach programs on campus could involve providing informative workshops regarding career counseling to clarify the effectiveness and benefits of these services. Addressing career help-seeking as a positive and empowering decision may help to alter projected attitudes that seeking career counseling reflects weakness or an inability to make decisions. Ludwikowski et al. also recommended early interventions with students and their families by providing workshops during new student orientation. Providing important information to parents and students related to the effectiveness of career planning and development could help to encourage positive attitudes toward career help seeking and positively influence students' internalized attitudes regarding the process.

Duffy and Sedlacek (2010) discussed varied influences affecting students when making career choices, which included environmental factors, the role of family or close others, various identity concerns, spiritual or religious beliefs, and other cultural considerations. In their study, which was designed to explore whether a sense of calling factored into students' career decision making, they considered how much a sense of career calling was related to gender, race, and education. They also examined whether spirituality or religious beliefs factored into career decision making for students. Results of their exploratory study revealed that more than 40% of their student participants ($n = 5, 523$) reported that having a sense of calling in their career decision-making process was accurate for them. Sense of calling was not necessarily related to spiritual or religious factors; however, the data suggested that the variable of career calling was somewhat correlated with participants' belief that life meaning was connected to career calling. In other words, those who experienced a sense of career calling also experienced their lives as being meaningful.

Given the values already discussed regarding millennial students' being desirous of making a difference in the world, accomplishing tasks that are meaningful to their lives and in society, some students may enter college with meaningful and purposeful career development plans in mind. Therefore, they may not perceive the need to seek career counseling services. It appears that as academic levels increase for some students, so does career calling (Duffy & Sedlacek, 2010). Again, if students experience increased clarity in their career calling as they advance through their academic careers, they may not find a need for formal career counseling.

It is important that a discussion on student attitudes related to career counseling include multicultural concerns. We consider these in the next section as we discuss the integration of personal counseling and career counseling.

## Career Counseling as Counseling

The counseling profession has its roots in career and vocational counseling (Gysbers, Heppner, & Johnston, 2009). Over the years, stereotypes have arisen regarding career counseling and other types of personal counseling, resulting in what may be an unnecessary divide within the profession (Imbimbo, 1994). More than 50 years ago, Donald Super (1957, as cited in Gysbers et al., 2009) stated, "The distinction between vocational and personal counseling seems artificial, and the stressing of one at the expense of the other seems uncalled for" (p. 5). A discussion regarding the perceived similarities among and distinctions between counseling and career counseling may assist in finding ways to view these forms of counseling in a more integrated, holistic fashion.

## Traditional Career Work Among College Students

Historically, vocational counseling served as the cornerstone on which the counseling profession was built (Gysbers et al., 2009). Frank Parsons, considered by many to be the father of counseling, responded to a shift in culture. In the early 1900s, the United States was undergoing an industrial revolution that led many workers to leave the farms their fathers worked and move to the cities for work. This move represented a cultural shift that led to identity crisis for many as they sought forms of work that were outside of their historical family context. In 1908, Parsons opened a vocational bureau in which he gave young people self-inventories to fill out and began the process of matching a young person's traits, interests, aptitudes, moral character, and motivations to vocational opportunities (Parsons, 1909).

Career services continue to engender some structure that moves students toward greater career awareness, greater self-awareness, and the integration of the two. This integration has, over the decades, continued to be primarily located in quantitative assessments and theories that support these assessments. Many of the theories emphasize what has commonly been referred to as a trait and factor approach—trait testing, expert status of the career counselor, and the concept of career as a rational, linear process (Peavy, 1997).

In response to this concept of a linear process, Donna Schultheiss (2005) wrote,

> An increasingly complex and dynamic 21st-century work and family life has led scholars and practitioners alike to search for new means to assist clients on life's journey. Decisions about work and career are no longer a straightforward matching process that leads one down life's path to happiness and success. Indeed for many individuals, this approach was never effective or even an option. The growing complexity of the world of work and the needs of people from diverse backgrounds has long raised concerns about the adequacy of strict trait and factor approaches. (p. 381)

Why is it that despite a culture that is radically different than the one before, so many career services continue to use an early 20th-century methodology? In part, the answer is simply because this approach worked in the early 20th century, and many career counselors were trained to work out of this linear lens. Perhaps it is also because career decision making is not an easy task (Gati & Amir, 2010), and it is much simpler to have a formal assessment to fall back on. Today's career counselor has the challenging task of bringing together each unique multicultural self, with an ever-changing global economy that requires a different skill set than what was required in the 20th century. In an effort to accomplish this task, we contrast a review of this linear approach with the multidimensional one demanded for the millennial student who now arrives at career counselor's office door.

## Construct of Self-Awareness

Career counselors have traditionally placed a heavy emphasis on self-awareness through the use of formal assessments with a few experiential opportunities recommended. Many different assessments are used; a few of the more common ones are the Strong Interest Inventory, the Myers-Briggs Type Indicator, and the Discover or Strength Indicator. These assessments are generally partnered with experiential opportunities such as internships, part-time jobs, and volunteer opportunities. This blend of qualitative and quantitative approaches with diverse college students created the foundation of career work in the 20th century. This foundation, which is still in place within much of career work, began to be challenged as early as the 1940s. Harry Kitson (1942) wrote, "Vocational counselors have generally been trying to discover ready-made vocational interests by giving interest tests, but without much success" (p. 567). The assumption is that students are born with an interest, but then interests develop out of personal experience. Counselors like formalized assessments because they offer occupational titles to discuss with students, which can be effective when working with a student who is ready to translate self-concept into an occupational calling (Savickas, 1998). The quandary is that many of the students with whom career counselors work do not have a strong sense of self-awareness and are given formal assessments prematurely.

### SIDEBAR 13.1   Case Study

Monica is a 21-year-old Latina student who attends a small liberal arts college in the southwestern United States. She is the eldest of three sisters and describes her family as being close. Her dad is the band teacher at the local high school, and her mom is an artist. Monica recently visited the career services center at her college, where she took several career assessments. She left career services discouraged because the inventories suggested that she should pursue a career as a musician, a bartender, or a substance abuse counselor. None of these jobs are of interest to her, and she now feels just as lost about her future career as when she arrived at career services. In addition, Monica was born with a hearing impairment and found school very challenging in her younger years, both academically and socially. She currently holds a 3.25 grade point average in her junior year of college and is anxious to come to some conclusion about her future career direction.

1. What themes are common to the three jobs?
2. What differing life experiences have shaped Monica?
3. How might the common job themes inform her of a career direction in light of her lived experience?

## Construct of Career Awareness

Many career counselors view career awareness and landing a job as the primary goal in their work with students. This perspective makes sense in the light of the development of vocational counseling at the turn of the 20th century. Donald Super, who was trained by Kitson, began moving toward a more holistic approach in the development of his career development theory (Super, 1957) and later his developmental self-concept theory (Super, 1981), both obviously developmental rather than reductionist (working with students as though they were born with a particular interest) but still focused primarily on career development. Not until the end of his life did Super develop the life span–life space theory (Super, 1990) that shifted the focus from career roles to life roles and in the view of many marked the death of the field of career counseling.

What is meant by "the death of the field of career counseling" is not that college students no longer need career services but that a reductionist view of self-awareness and career awareness no longer makes sense in the cultural context of the 21st century. According to Mark Savickas (1997), career counseling in the 21st century that cares for the spirit will seek to identify how students wish to spend their lives. Work is viewed as a social activity, one in which students will connect with and experience a sense of belonging that compels them to cooperate with people and contribute to community service and social justice efforts. It is the combining of a life story with work projects in a communal manner. According to Savickas (1997),

> to be fully alive means to share our unique contribution by joining spirit with other people in celebrating life through work, love, friendship and worship.... Career counseling that envisions work as a quest for self and a place to nourish one's spirit helps clients learn to use work as a context for self-development. (p. 3)

Nonetheless, many career counselors continue to focus on career awareness and job placement rather than on pursuing avenues into a deeper exploration of self-concept that will transcend any one job or career they land. Career development commonly involves formal assessments; a variety of Internet resources such as the *Occupational Outlook Handbook*, O*NET, the Riley Guide, and job Web sites specific to each state; experiential opportunities that may include informational interviews (interviewing someone in the workforce about the benefits and limitations of the particular job), job shadowing, internships, volunteering, hobbies, part-time jobs, and career fairs.

## Construct of Job Success

Traditionally, career counselors have been challenged with the task of helping students communicate their newfound career awareness into marketing and job success strategies. Most often, students prepare for the job market by preparing a résumé and cover letter. This preparation may involve a detailed and creative process of weaving newly discovered knowledge into a résumé and cover letter with a career counselor, or students may do this on their own and then visit career services during drop-in hours to have a career counselor or career assistant read over their materials.

Mock interviews have long been a successful component of preparing students because they present an opportunity to practice answering questions and to receive feedback on both their verbal and nonverbal communication. The interview allows students to become familiar with language that is specific to a particular career, dress for the part, and experience a degree of the anxiety that often accompanies an interview. Additionally, many students discover they are hesitant to talk about themselves, which provides a career counselor with the opportunity to help them explore the source of their hesitancy.

Many career services centers plan and implement career fairs. These highly energetic experiences bring employers onto campus one to three times a year and may have a specific focus (engineer fairs or nonprofit fairs) or a general focus (all major fairs). Career fairs provide students with an excellent opportunity to practice approaching employers and often include the development of what many in career work have referred to as the "30-second elevator pitch." The development of this pitch is often something a career counselor helps a student craft and involves the student's sharing something that attracts employer attention while illustrating what the student has to offer.

**SIDEBAR 13.2   Constructing a 30-Second Elevator Pitch**

Visit the Riley Guide at http://www.rileyguide.com and search on "30-second elevator pitch." Browse through the different suggestions for creating your own pitch. Imagine yourself as a career counselor, a school counselor, or a counselor starting a private practice. You are asked, "What do you do?" Create a 30-second pitch that is both intriguing and informative.

Additional services that a career counselor may offer include helping students prepare for a graduate admissions test, write a personal statement for graduate school, and build negotiating skills that will help with eventual job offers. Many of these topics, such as interview skills, résumé building, applying to graduate school, and so forth, are addressed through workshops that many career services offer. Career counselors and career assistants frequently have the opportunity to present any number of topics to classes and hence to enhance awareness of the importance of self-discovery as it pertains to career. Yet, students who begin to wrestle with career decisions often arrive at career services experiencing any number of emotions ranging from anxiety to depression.

## Impact of Career Decision Making

Aspiring career counselors may be surprised to discover that many students arrive with some degree of anxiety related to the pressure they feel to make a plethora of decisions. They must choose a major and a career, evaluate the need for an internship, manage feelings of inadequacy when it comes to their interview skills or résumé, and deal with pressure from parents to move in a specific direction, or they may simply have to face the fact that they have little idea what to do with their future. Campagna and Curtis (2007) stressed that deciding what to do with one's life is one of the most important decisions in life and that a variety of emotions and self-states inevitably accompany the process. The good news is that as career counselors make the shift to a life-design perspective, they will discover that each student has much in his or her lived experience that is needed to make the decision within that lived experience. In the next section, we further explore what this approach looks like. We take seriously the notion that when students are struggling to make decisions they often draw on formative life stories. We suggest that choosing a career allows for evolving mastery over many life concerns. Said differently, people need to do what they have been rehearsing for their whole life.

To this end, career counselors must acknowledge the importance of the therapeutic alliance so that a safe container is created for deeper work around the concept of self, family, and cultural expectations. Just as important, career services must be equipped with counselors who understand psychological process, how meaning is constructed in a person's life, and the concept that careers do not simply unfold; they are constructed (Savickas, 2002). In the next section, we suggest that career discovery pursued as personal discovery may increase the likelihood of flawed career choice; hence, the ability to develop a therapeutic alliance should be a component of the career counselor skill set.

## Therapeutic Alliance

A major key to success in the counseling process rests in the therapeutic alliance between counselor and client (Kern, Stoltz, Gottlieb-Low, & Frost, 2009). The therapeutic alliance, sometimes also referred to as the *working alliance* (Gysbers et al., 2009), has to do with the relationship or bond that develops between a client and a counselor. Although establishment of a solid alliance does not solely rest with the counselor, a number of foundational counseling skills contribute to forming a strong base from which to work.

Duff and Bedi (2010) defined the therapeutic alliance as "the client and counselor's subjective experience of working together towards psychotherapeutic goals in the counseling context, including the experience of and interpersonal bond that develops while engaged in this endeavour" (p. 91). Their study reflects the experiences of adult counseling clients who identified 15 counselor behaviors that they judged likely to have contributed to their experience of a successful therapeutic alliance. Eleven of these correlate in either a moderate or a strong way. Skills known as physical attending skills—facing the client, making eye contact, smiling when greeting the client, sitting without fidgeting—as well as counselor honesty and referring to information from past sessions were suggested to be moderately or strongly correlated with strong alliance (p. 101). Additionally, asking clients questions, identifying and reflecting client feelings, commenting positively about the client, and validating the client's experiences also contribute to the building of a solid therapeutic alliance (p. 99).

The perceived care and interest on the part of the counselor toward the client lays an important foundation on which to build trust in the counseling relationship. It is from this foundation of trust that clients are willing to disclose more of themselves and their circumstances. Skovholt and Ronnestad (1992) suggested that interpersonal engagement carries more influence than impersonal encounters, once again underscoring the importance of how the client perceives the counselor's care and concern and how this perception contributes to the change or healing process.

The results of a study conducted by Masdonati, Massoudi, and Rossier (2010) suggested that therapeutic alliance was positively associated with career clients' satisfaction with the career intervention. Results also suggested that therapeutic alliance was positively associated with client levels of life satisfaction. The quality of the working relationship between the counselor and the client contributed to the effectiveness of the career counseling, with the relationship between counselor and client contributing to client perception regarding career intervention quality.

The definition of the therapeutic alliance provided by Duff and Bedi (2010) makes it clear that the relationship between counselor and client is active and affects both parties. Although the client's perception of the counselor is one factor in establishing the alliance, another important factor is the counselor's experience of the client. When the counselor experiences the client's trust, it further allows the collaborative work of establishing goals and interventions that assist in achieving the desired goals.

Regardless of the type of counseling considered, without a strong therapeutic alliance, success for both client and counselor is diminished. How does this apply to career counseling, which has sometimes been referred to as "three interviews and a cloud of dust" (Crites, 1981, as cited in Gysbers et al. 2009, p. 4)? Further discussion reveals the integrated nature of personal and career counseling and the need for counselors to understand and implement treatment from a holistic framework.

Career counseling has been stereotyped as being directive and active; psychological or emotional counseling has been stereotyped as being facilitative and exploratory (Imbimbo, 1994). Although career counseling consists of a working relationship between a counselor and a client that focuses on career or work issues, psychological distress around those career and work issues may very well be present for the client. In personal counseling, a client may disclose a need or desire to discuss career- or work-related issues (Gysbers et al., 2009; Hinkelman & Luzzo, 2007; Imbimbo, 1994). To attempt to treat one set of client issues apart from the other neglects treatment of the whole person of the client. Although career- and work-related issues may call for direct attention and intervention, such issues are personal to the client and cannot be separated from the emotional experiences a client may encounter.

## Needs, Concerns, and Developmental Considerations of College Students

College students have unique needs and concerns related to personal, academic, and career issues. Having an understanding of college students' psychosocial development processes, as well as an awareness of the multiplicity of issues and concerns that might bring them into counseling, will aid counselors in assisting this population.

From a life span view of development, traditional college students in Western society are in a phase of "emerging adulthood" (Kail & Cavanaugh, 2010, p. 359). This term speaks to the idea that the rituals individuals go through that are identified as marking adulthood are indiscriminate for each person. Some of these rituals involve completing formal education, securing full-time employment, getting married, or having children. Role transitions are experienced at varied times and in diverse ways. Ivey (2004, as cited in Kail & Cavanaugh, 2010) illustrated that because rituals marking the transition to adulthood are limited to the types already mentioned here, college students have developed their own forms of initiation into adulthood.

These rituals are often manifested in drinking or in initiation into clubs or organizations. Some role transitions such as establishing independence apart from parents, developing committed relationships, and establishing oneself in work or career happen over several years and in different time frames.

Hinkelman and Luzzo (2007) highlighted the importance of psychosocial development in academic and work performance. Individuals who attend college directly after high school are engaged in building competence, learning how to become independent, and developing a greater level of maturity in interpersonal relationships. Increasing maturity in interpersonal relationships includes learning to negotiate conflicts and their resolutions, to manage emotions at deeper levels, and to make meaningful commitments. Exploring and establishing identity and developing purpose are also tasks facing college students. Successful negotiation of these tasks may result in higher academic success, as well as in more successful work performance (Hinkelman & Luzzo, 2007). Super (1980) suggested that at this stage in life span development, career and personal issues are of equal importance in an individual's career decision-making process. An integrated approach that addresses developing identity, sense of purpose, and interpersonal connections should be used.

College students may also find themselves dealing with adjustment to academic life as well as separation from family members and close others. Given the highly structured and parentally orchestrated lives of many in the millennial generation, transitioning to life apart from daily parental involvement may be welcomed; it may also present difficulties for some. Other students may negotiate successful adjustment to their 1st and 2nd years of college but may experience more distress related to career issues and decision making as they approach locating internship sites and postgraduate careers. It is not uncommon for college students to display symptoms of depression or anxiety when accessing campus counseling services (Hinkelman & Luzzo, 2007). Denise Jubber (personal communication, October 22, 2010), assistant director of career services at a small private university in the Pacific Northwest, has observed high anxiety in college students with whom she has worked, often because of a lack of direction regarding career goals. She has also worked with students whose difficulties in career decision making were related to unresolved personal distress. Jubber's experiences concerning psychological distress experienced by some college students, which may or may not have direct connection to career concerns but that affect career decision making, are supported in the literature (Hinkelman & Luzzo, 2007; Imbimbo, 1994). Although Jubber does not provide personal counseling to career counseling clients, she will make a referral for personal counseling when it is evident that psychological issues may be affecting career considerations.

Identity formation is an important developmental task for college students. The process of identity development and of establishing a stable identity is significant in the career decision-making process (Hinkelman & Luzzo, 2007). Because individuals develop within the context of multiple systems and experiences, career counselors must be able to explore a client's history and individual experiences. Anne Lapour (personal communication, October 21, 2010), a career counselor and coordinator of career development at a state university in the Pacific Northwest, emphasized the importance of context when working with college students around career issues.

In this period in history, career issues are becoming more complex, and counselors are living in a global economy and working with a diverse range of students entering college. This period of time requires collaborative work that is creative and takes context seriously. Taking context seriously means allowing students the space to talk about their cultural backgrounds and encouraging exploration of their unique family systems and of how the blend of culture and family is the blueprint for career construction.

Lapour (personal communication, October 21, 2010) also illustrated the need for a holistic approach to career counseling, because career exploration and choice are directly affected by other personal factors in an individual's life:

> Cultural sensitivity is absolutely important. I have met with many non-traditional students; we have many first-generation students whose parents are migrant workers. Context is everything. It's important for me to attune to what type of experiences and opportunities students have. This informs how we talk about networking, interviewing, etc. I frequently emphasize with our master's [counseling] students the importance of sitting with students and getting to know their stories before shuffling through paper in search of a career guide or interview questions.

Part of the process of forming identity relates to how one's perceptions and understandings of oneself are assumed into the self-concept. The developmental tasks of late adolescence and early or emerging adulthood (Kail & Cavanaugh, 2010) involve defining or striving for personal purpose, seeking connectedness with peers, and defining self-concept (Hinkelman & Luzzo, 2007). To accomplish these tasks requires self-awareness on the part of students. In individual interviews and discussions with us, Denise Jubber (personal communication, October 22, 2010) and Anne Lapour (personal communication, October 21, 2010) each talked about the ways in which they encourage a balance of self-reflection and action that assists students in defining themselves and their career interests and goals. In her work with college students, Jubber conducts professional development workshops, in addition to working with individual clients for anywhere from two to five sessions. She poses three questions to students to assist them in the process of increasing self-awareness and exploring career goals: (1) Who am I? (2) What is my purpose? and (3) How do the answers relate to my career? Jubber asserted that providing students with an opportunity for self-examination results in increased self-awareness. In addition, she stresses the importance of students' developing a mission statement for their lives so as to have a framework from which to create the various aspects of their personal lives, including career. She draws on the work of Laurie Beth Jones (1996) in providing a rationale and a model from which students construct their personal mission statements (D. Jubber, personal communication, October 28, 2010). According to Jones (1996), a mission statement, often used by corporations and organizations, is simply a "written-down reason for being" (p. x). Jones asserted that a mission statement provides a model from which one can move toward living life in accordance with individual purpose. It also provides a means for evaluating and fine-tuning activities and behaviors so that purpose and action are congruent (p. xi).

In her reflections on current-day career counseling and the foundation of self-reflection and self-awareness, Lapour (personal communication, October 21, 2010) pointed out the importance of these for both client and counselor.

> Self-awareness is crucial, both for the career counselor and for the student. What is not happening enough is self-awareness that is fostered through experiences, and the opportunity to reflect upon those experiences. College students are into process. We facilitate a process in which they are discovering themselves, giving them space to reflect on their histories, identities, and their career identities. It is very collaborative—a balance between reflection and action that leaves students feeling empowered.

### SIDEBAR 13.3  Constructing a Mission Statement

Self-reflection leading to greater self-awareness is critical in personal and career development. Self-awareness is necessary for counselors if they are to most effectively assist clients in their developmental processes. Read, reflect on, and answer the following questions:

1. Who am I?
2. What is my purpose?
3. How do the answers relate to my career?

According to Jones (1996), a mission statement is a "written down reason for being" (p. x). Consider your answers to these questions and create a personal mission statement.

Discussion of the needs and developmental processes of college students thus far has given further support to the idea that personal and career counseling are best approached in an integrative fashion. Historically, the integration of the two modalities has not been viewed in this way, taking into consideration the whole person of the client (Gysbers et al., 2009). Such an integrative and systemic approach provides for a holistic and contextual framework from which counselors will better serve their clients, including clients from diverse ethnic and cultural backgrounds.

## Multicultural Considerations in Counseling College Students

For ethnic, racial, and cultural minority students, career development and decision making include unique factors of which career counselors must be aware. As in any form of counseling, multicultural sensitivity and competency in working with diverse populations is critical. Arthur and McMahon (2005) proposed using the systems theory framework in assisting multicultural individuals in career counseling. This framework allows the career counselor to view clients within the contexts of their lives, taking into consideration the mutual impact of surrounding systems on the client and the client's influence on the surrounding systems. The client does not live isolated from the world around him or her but is affected by cultural forces in the social and environmental systems and subsystems that envelop him or her. These forces include family, friends, peers, educational and work environments, and religious systems, whose influences contribute to developing identity and cultural concerns. The systems theory framework allows career counselors to work individually with clients from a career development framework that is adaptable to multiple cultural groups, not just to the dominant culture.

Career counselors working with college students from diverse populations are encouraged to allow students to describe their experiences and to interpret the influences of social and environmental factors on their lives and career considerations (Arthur & McMahon, 2005). This statement echoes what we have already discussed in terms of building a trusting relationship between counselor and client; a strong therapeutic alliance is crucial in successful counseling outcomes (Duff & Bedi, 2010; Gysbers et al., 2009). As in personal or psychological counseling, career counselors need to empathically attend to and hear their clients, taking into consideration their clients' subjective experiences and the influences on their emotional and developmental processes.

### Gay and Lesbian Students

As many as 4 million adolescents and young adults in the United States may identify as gay or lesbian (Datti, 2009). Given this figure, it is critical that counselors who work in college and university settings have an understanding of the particular needs and challenges of this population.

As we have discussed, identity formation and development is a task young adults find themselves negotiating. How identity is assumed into the self-concept and the resulting perceptions individuals hold can contribute to mental and emotional distress or to a greater sense of well-being (Datti, 2009; Pope, Prince, & Mitchell, 2000). The literature has suggested that career development and career-related tasks may be suspended for some young adults as they find themselves investing more energy in working through identity development issues related to sexual orientation (Datti, 2009). Gay and lesbian students may experience distress in contemplating rejection or discomfort in work and social settings, as well as in what self-disclosure of their sexual orientation to family and close others might mean. They may deal with depression, experience shame, and in some cases become suicidal (Datti, 2009).

Pope et al. (2000) pointed out that gay and lesbian students may have been exposed to biased career information. They also illustrated the fear and skepticism that may accompany a gay or lesbian student's approach to career counseling when psychological and career inventories are used as part of the process. A student may not yet be ready to disclose his or her sexual orientation and may fear that answering honestly on an inventory will result in being exposed. Additionally, assessment tools have been used to diagnose gay and lesbian individuals as mentally ill (Pope et al., 2000).

Given these concerns, the skills counselors have to listen to a client's story and hear what is most important to the client are critical in the career counseling process. In addition to core counseling skills, career counselors need to understand the process gay and lesbian students negotiate in disclosing their sexual orientation (coming out), as well as identity confusion, self-esteem, and the role that cultural and family values play in the life of the client (Datti, 2009). They also have the added responsibility of knowing how to connect gay and lesbian students with other professionals, on and off campus, who can provide support in areas in which the counselor might be lacking.

### Collectivistic Versus Individualistic Cultures

Counselors must consider student issues revolving around values related to the family. Millennial students in general may have experienced highly involved parenting throughout their lives. Such involvement may also have affected college or university choice, as well as a student's particular area of study (Elam et al., 2007). Although some students might welcome the increased level of autonomy in living away from family, they may still be affected in their career development because of a perceived need to make career decisions on the basis of the expectations of parents and other family members. This need may be especially true for students whose cultural backgrounds are not grounded in an individualistic philosophy (DeVaney & Hughey, 2000).

According to DeVaney and Hughey (2000), Asian American college students seem to highly value financial success and job security and view education as a means to a vocational end. In addition, DeVaney and Hughey stressed that counselors should be aware that this student population may demonstrate a more dependent decision-making style, with an appreciation for tradition and traditional roles as they consider career choice. Along with a dependent decision-making style, counselors need to consider the deferential characteristics that Asian American students may display; these characteristics may lead students to avoid presenting personal issues in counseling, instead expressing concerns related to academic and career issues. To assist students in addressing the underlying interpersonal concerns that may be present, career counselors must build a therapeutic alliance with clients that will facilitate greater client trust.

In Latino culture, family members may exert a high level of influence over students' education, depending on the degree of assimilation of family members into the larger macroculture (DeVaney & Hughey, 2000). Counselors need to be aware that parental perceptions of job availability could have a greater influence on students' decisions related to major areas of study. DeVaney and Hughey (2000) recommended the inclusion of family members in student career development processes, as well as in discussions of life planning. They contended that family involvement may increase student retention in colleges and universities.

Native American culture also reflects a collectivistic philosophy over an individualistic one, and colleges and universities often show low enrollment by this population. For those Native American students who experience greater success in college, the communal support of their tribes may be crucial in their successes (DeVaney & Hughey, 2000). It is not uncommon for Native American young adults to have difficulty in adjusting to college life away from their tribal communities. Some may experience feelings of isolation; some may worry that they have abandoned their people. Tribal practices and customs are often at odds with those found in the dominant culture and within the world of work. Because manual labor is predominant on Native American reservations, students have little exposure to information regarding occupations, how to search for work, or how to maintain work if found. The high levels of poverty and unemployment are directly connected to a lack of understanding and exposure to the world of work.

Counselors must work with Native American students from an understanding of their culture and their subjective experiences. They must also be aware of specific ways to help Native American students navigate career development, such as being knowledgeable about available resources and how to direct students to others who are able to provide support (DeVaney & Hughey, 2000).

**SIDEBAR 13.4  Case Study**

Eric is a 20-year-old Asian American engineering major nearing the end of his 2nd year of college. He is from an upper-middle-class family; his father is an architectural engineer, and his mother teaches music. He has one older sister, who is preparing to graduate from a prominent art institute with a degree in fashion design. Eric has come into the career counseling center for help in determining specific areas of engineering toward which to direct his career path. As you talk with Eric, he discloses that although he has a solid 3.75 grade point average and a good group of friends and has adjusted well to college life in general, he has begun to experience what he calls "panic moments" when thinking about registering for classes for the fall semester and when he contemplates going home for the summer. As you encourage Eric to talk more about this anxiety, you learn that he is not really interested in becoming an engineer; he wants to study fine arts. He has been told by his father that he needs to have a career that is suitable to a man and that will support his future family. He has also been told that if he does not continue to pursue his degree in engineering, his father will cease paying for his college education. Eric is also questioning his sexual identity and believes he might be gay.

1. How would you proceed to help Eric on the basis of the information he has disclosed?
2. Given the information you currently have to work with, what knowledge and skills do you need to incorporate into helping Eric?
3. Considering multicultural issues, what are some key considerations in your work with Eric?

Historically, the personal concerns of individuals seeking career guidance have been viewed as being inextricably linked to career development and decision making (Gysbers et al., 2009; Imbimbo, 1994). Career counselors must be able to empathically hear their clients, be able to form a solid therapeutic alliance with their clients, and have knowledge of numerous counseling theories, developmental theories, and career development theories. Career counselors must demonstrate multicultural competencies in working with diverse client populations, as well as being familiar with career resources and the world of work (DeVaney & Hughey, 2000; Pope et al., 2000). Imbimbo (1994) suggested that the perceived differences between personal and career counseling rest with counselors rather than with clients. It may be that the stereotype that has evolved over the years of career counselors being directive and active and more about assessments and inventories has resulted in the area of career counseling being less attractive to counselors who are drawn to facilitating a healing process in clients' lives. However, to address career development and career decision making as disconnected from a client's personal issues and concerns is to fail to treat the whole person of the client.

Career counselors working with college students must be skilled in core counseling competencies in addition to theories related to human development and career development. They need to have an understanding of multiple generational influences on student populations, the impact of families of origin on students, and multicultural considerations. Additionally, they must be skilled in the use and interpretation of career assessments and inventories and have a clear understanding of the world of work. They must be able to move fluidly among all of these skills and areas of knowledge within the context of a well-developed working alliance with students if successful outcomes are to occur. It has been suggested that given the complex work of career counseling, it should be reserved for experienced counselors who can adjust counseling styles and approaches as needed (Imbimbo, 1994).

## Constructivist Career Work Among College Students

Having established the importance of a working alliance and the personal and, at times, distressing nature of career counseling work, we return to the millennial generation and ask what it means to engage in career work in a manner that is congruent with their overall cultural experience. If counselors are to take career work seriously, then they must take the cultural shifts that have occurred over the past several decades seriously. Industrialization led to the emergence of many new occupations and to a culture shift resulting from worker migration. The 20th-century worker lived in a period of history during which a loyal and dedicated worker could climb the ladder of success focused on one job and in return received occupational security. Today's job climate is less predictable and less enduring and requires the development of different skills. Workers today must become lifelong learners, be familiar with changing technology environments, embrace flexibility, and learn to create opportunities (Savickas et al., 2009).

Volatile and emerging markets represent cultural movements and are indicators that a revision of career counseling is needed both philosophically and practically (Peavy, 1997; Savickas, 2003). Many career services still maintain a basic paradigm that focuses on finding students jobs or internships or on fine tuning their résumés. This paradigm and these basic attitudes are proving to be insufficient in working with today's college student. Yet, for the shift toward a lifestyle integration paradigm to occur, career counselors must understand the cultural and philosophical shift that has occurred and led to a generation of students who require such a shift in thinking.

In the 21st century, careers are proving to be less defined and less predictable, and the jobs of the future will require different skill sets, flexibility, and high interpersonal and intrapersonal skills. These shifts can be attributed to globalization, technological advances, and demographic changes (Grier-Reed, Skaar, & Conkel-Ziebell, 2009). Peavy (1997) spoke to the philosophical shift that has occurred and that will lay the foundation for how career is approached:

> In the last decade there have been several important shifts within social science generally and to a lesser extent, in counseling and therapy … we now understand that we exist as a plurality of possible worlds, personal realities, and voices created by our own perceived distinctions. The concepts of external reality and objectivity are being replaced by self-referentiality and by the notion that human reality is constructed and participatory. (p. 122)

This movement is all but natural for the millennial generation as evidenced by the importance of Facebook, Twitter, and other online communities, not as hobby but as a way of being in the world. This movement in 21st-century culture is significantly different from the framework of the scientific age, which was an age of objectivity and linearity and, for the career counselor, of trait and factor assessments. This modernistic (linear) framework has been referred to by some as the "Cartesian mission" of the 17th century, in which people worked hard to establish objective truths about the world "out there," consequently downplaying the influence of two or more uniquely personal, interacting worlds of experience (Laetitia & Trasiewicz, 2002). This Cartesian mindset is a myth that permeates Western culture and has been referred to as the myth of the isolated mind (Stolorow & Atwood, 1996). This myth brings to bear a view of the individual as existing separately from the world of physical nature and also from engagement with others (Orange, 2001; Stolorow & Atwood, 1996; Stolorow, Orange, & Atwood, 2001). Overly simplistic for the 20th century, it certainly falls short for the millennial generation, which in addition to broadened interracial and multicultural underpinnings, brings technology-enabled social network and virtual reality gaming dynamics to the mix.

In understanding this cultural shift, career services can more accurately understand the notion that lives are constructed within the context of relationships, that careers are constructed within the context of relationship, and that each student who arrives at career services has made specific meanings of his or her life experiences, thus reinforcing that career counseling is more about life trajectories or life design than career development or vocational guidance (Savickas et al., 2009). Mark Savickas (1998) wrote, "They do not know themselves by their traits; instead they know themselves by their passions and purposes" (p. 8). The essence of the student, his or her unique spirit and personhood, can only be known as a whole person, not as traits.

The empirical tradition of rational career counseling does not encompass complex human qualities such as spirit, consciousness, and purpose. Science examines parts; personal stories explain the whole. Stories tell one the situation, the needs, the goals, the interests, and the outcomes. Through stories, counselors gain access to a person's spirit and life theme (Savickas, 1998, p. 9).

This constructivist approach allows students to construct their identities and careers by making sense of their lives holistically, within a uniquely subjective context and in a manner that emphasizes their unique multicultural self, all in the context of a relationship with a career counselor. A relationship so developed further signifies the importance of the counselor–client relationship and allows for the client to have a deeper understanding of self and how the self might continue to develop and be nourished within the world of work.

### SIDEBAR 13.5  Case Study

Ben is an 18-year-old Caucasian student at a large Midwestern university. He arrives at career services near the end of his first term of college. Ben reports that he is a business major, that his father is the CEO of a successful company on the East Coast, and that he has spent the past 2 summers as an intern at his dad's company. Ben is an only son and reports that his mother has just recently gone back to work after years of staying at home. When asked about the nature of his visit to career services, Ben responds that he really enjoys business, but that he is getting one C and two Ds in his three business courses. As Ben begins to suggest that he may not be cut out for business, he begins to tear up and states that he has not even had time to attend Mass since his arrival and that he must register for next semester by the end of the week.

1. As Ben's career counselor, what are you feeling at this point in the session?
2. How will you proceed with the session?

## Paradigm Shift Needed in Today's Career Services

Paralleling the approach to meaning making is the role of qualitative assessment within career work, which includes

> nonstandardized and nonquantitatively based measurement that provides an informal means of gaining more holistic and integrative understanding of personal meanings associated with life experiences.... A fundamental goal of constructivist career assessment is to assist clients in understanding personal patterns of meaning, or how one makes sense of life experiences over time. (Schultheiss, 2005, p. 382)

Constructive assessment is an active, dynamic, and cocreating process that occurs as new meanings are constructed within the counseling relationship. In constructivist assessment, both client and counselor are actively involved in the meaning making, moving the counselor out of the expert role and the client out of the passive responder role and into being a collaborative team (Schultheiss, 2005).

For this collaboration to occur, Savickas et al. (2009) suggested five philosophical shifts (Table 13.1) that must occur within the DNA of a career counselor and career services. These shifts create a new paradigm, or lens, and will result in a change in the very culture of career counseling.

According to Savickas et al. (2009), the five shifts in thinking shown in Table 13.1 allow for a basic framework that supports continual life design for students, a framework that encourages students to be lifelong learners and to

**TABLE 13.1   Five Philosophical Shifts Toward the Establishment of Constructivist Career Services**

| 20th-Century Career Development | 21st-Century Life Design |
|---|---|
| From a traits and states approach that was developed by the natural sciences … | To a context that seeks to understand life patterns and the lived experience of students |
| From prescription, or prescribing a career (when the average person has 9.6 jobs by age 36) … | To a process that helps to develop ways of coping and surviving for employability |
| From linear causality that is common in traditional scientific reasoning … | To nonlinear dynamics that accompany a more holistic life design |
| From scientific facts in which individual careers were shaped by societal norms … | To narrative realities that support students' own significant references for career |
| From career models that describe a single variable outcome … | To modeling a way of approaching career that leads to the discovery of personal patterns |

*Note:* Copyright © 2010 by Jeffrey D. Cook and Leanne Schamp.
*Source:* Adapted from Savickas, M. L., Nota, L., Rossier, J., Dauwalder, J.-P., Duarta, M. E., Guichard, J. Soresi, S., Van Esbroeck, R., & van Vianen, A. E. M. (2009). Life designing: A paradigm for career construction in the 21st century. *Journal of Vocational Behavior, 75,* 239–250.

view career from a holistic perspective that considers dominant life themes when constructing a career and the importance of social context in career decision making.

## Constructivist Interventions

We suggest four different approaches that a counselor might use with a student, although many more approaches can be found in the literature. In fact, by the very nature of the philosophical paradigm, the possible interventions are limitless. We briefly review the life design model as described by Savickas et al. (2009), the life line intervention as described by Brott (2005), the career-style interview (Savickas,1998), and a mixed-methods option.

### Life Design Model

The first intervention model is a life design model that has six general steps (Savickas et al., 2009).

### Step 1

In Step 1, the student and counselor define the problem and establish what the student hopes to accomplish with the counselor. In doing so, the therapeutic alliance begins to develop. During this step, the counselor and student work to accomplish two things around each problem. The student is encouraged to think on each problem and strive to communicate both the problem and the history of the problem through personal story. Once a problem has been put in story form, the counselor and student strive to discover the main context within which the problem is located.

## Step 2

This step is an exploration of how the student currently views him- or herself in relation to the issue at hand and in light of experiences and expectations, actions, relationships, and future aspirations as they relate to the student's story.

## Step 3

The intention of this step is to open perspectives, which occurs as counselor and student review the story; this review often allows students to see the story from new perspectives. The counselor asks whether any options were rejected, daydreams destroyed, or choices circumscribed. Through a retelling, the story often takes on new meaning that revitalizes the student and the story.

## Step 4

At this step, the student is to place the problem into the new story. The key moment during this step is when the problem is discovered to take on a new perspective. This new perspective allows the student to think about self with a new identity as it relates to the problem with which they arrived.

## Step 5

In this step, the student is encouraged to come up with an action plan. The student is encouraged to try on this new identity through participation in activities that seek to reconcile the problem. The plan should include methods for dealing with possible barriers and for communicating the newfound identity. Such actions may include visiting a specific class, participating in a job shadowing, volunteering for an organization, or scheduling a mock interview.

## Step 6

This step consists of short-term and long-term follow-up.

### Life Line

This intervention is designed to explore the student's past and present stories (Brott, 2005).

## Phase 1

Give the student a blank piece of paper and ask the student to draw a vertical line across it. Have the student write his or her birth date on the left side of the line and the current day on the right side of the line. The student is then instructed to create chapters that represent major life stages on the paper, such as elementary school, middle school, high school, college, first job, marriage, and children, and to note the year in which each stage began (Brott, 2005).

The counselor then asks questions about each chapter. What were the high and low points of this chapter? Who are the important people, and what is their significance in this chapter? Give a couple of adjectives that describe this chapter. Each chapter is given a title (Brott, 2005).

## Phase 2

The second phase of this intervention is a deconstruction of the life line. The counselor now probes to help the student define his or her beliefs and values. What themes does he or she see? What motivates the student in his or her differing roles? If the student could do anything different in life, what would he or she do? What parental messages did the student hear about life and work (Brott, 2005)?

## Phase 3

The last phase of this intervention includes a review of the life line followed by the creation of a future life line. The student begins the life line with the day's date and in collaboration with the counselor will establish an end date for this future chapter once the chapter has been constructed. A variety of questions may be asked when constructing this future chapter or self. Some possible questions may include, "What is the first step you can take to get you closer to where you would like to be?" "In what time frame would you be able to accomplish this goal?" "What other goals or action points are necessary for you to accomplish the stated goal for this chapter?" "What barriers do you foresee?" "What resources are needed?" "What values and beliefs will help in the completion of this chapter?" "What is the title of this chapter?" "What is the proposed closing date for this chapter?" At this point in time, the counselor tapes the two pieces of paper together and schedules a follow-up appointment appropriate to the timeline (Brott, 2005).

### Career-Style Interview

The career-style interview (Savickas, 1998) consists of a series of questions that reveal beliefs and experiences that point to life themes and career themes. The interview consists of eight questions that examine role models, books, magazines, leisure activities, school subjects, mottos, ambitions, and decisions. The first question is meant to examine the student's main predicament in life, which is illustrated through childhood role models. The counselor asks, "Who did you admire growing up?" This person may be a coach, teacher, cartoon character, musician, and so forth. Once a role model is named, the counselor asks for two more. Once they are named, the counselor asks, "What did you admire about … ?" The process of getting to know a student's role models reveals both the central issue of his or her life and the solution.

The seven interview questions listed in Sidebar 13.6 create a picture of what the student's central issue in life is, how others have dealt with the issue, what work environments will fit best, and what strategies the student uses for decision making. The strength of this interview is that it helps the student understand how his or her lived experience directly shapes career choice. Take a moment to answer the questions in the sidebar and see what life themes you come up with.

**SIDEBAR 13.6   Interview Questions**

Answer the following questions for yourself, looking for life themes and asking yourself how these themes have worked their way into your career direction.

1. Name three people, characters, or animals that you admired growing up. (Typically, your answers describe yourself and the central problem of your life.)
2. What were your favorite books growing up? (Portrays your central life problem and how characters in books dealt with the problem.)
3. What were your favorite magazines growing up? (Describes the environment that will fit your style.)
4. What leisure activities do you most enjoy? (Describes how you like to express yourself and what problem is being addressed.)
5. What were your favorite subjects in school? (Also speaks to your preferred work environment.)
6. What mottos were a part of your early years? (Speaks to what title may be appropriate for your life.)
7. What ambitions did your parents have for you as a child? (Informs occupations to which you have reacted.)
8. Describe an important choice you have made. (Reveals different decision-making strategies.)

### Mixed-Methods Approach

Another possible intervention is a mixed-methods approach in which the quantitative assessments are combined with qualitative story construction. The counselor begins by helping the client identify the problem, desired solution, and ways in which the problem has been addressed in the past. Any of the preceding interventions may be used to get a sense of what patterns are present and overlapping in the life of the client before administering an assessment such as the Strong Interest Inventory. During the interpretation phase, the counselor may ask the client to pay less attention to the particular jobs suggested and more attention to the particular themes suggested by the jobs and the characteristics required by the types of jobs. A discussion of how jobs themes make sense in the light of family history and specific roles within the family will further suggest job titles congruent with lived experience.

## Online Career Counseling

Providing online counseling services is a growing trend in the counseling profession. Ongoing research is required to determine the efficacy of this type of intervention, and continued discussion and examination of issues related to best practice are needed.

Arguments for the strengths and benefits of online counseling have been discussed in the literature (Herman, 2009; Maples & Han, 2008). Online counseling can provide services to individuals who have restricted access to face-to-face counseling services, whether such restrictions are geographical, financial, or the result of resistance or attitudes based on psychological or cultural concerns. Online counseling services have been suggested to serve college students well, reducing defense mechanisms and a sense of vulnerability experienced when faced with disclosing issues to a counselor in the more traditional setting of a counseling office (Maples & Han, 2008). Online counseling may also increase college students' motivation to seek help, especially in more collectivistic cultures. Traditionally trained counselors in South Korea have found online counseling to be valuable in delivering counseling services to South Korean students because of its accessibility, affordable and convenient services, and effectiveness of a more indirect approach to student issues rather than the more direct face-to-face method of counseling (Maples & Han, 2008).

Is online career counseling effective? The answer to this question may be directly related to the amount of involvement and availability of the counselor. One 4-week Internet-based career intervention was evaluated for effectiveness and client satisfaction (Herman, 2009). The intervention included automated integrative lessons, self-assessments, homework assignments, and group discussions. Although the results of the experiment suggested a positive impact on career decidedness, several deficiencies were found in the intervention. Participants reported the lessons were too long, and overall drop-out rates over 4 weeks were 80%. The online intervention was found to be less efficient than traditional individual career counseling. Herman (2009) pointed out that automated instruction is "less flexible than interventions in which a human being responds directly to an individual's concerns" (p. 343). Although the counselor did respond to online bulletin board queries, a greater level of direct involvement with clients may have been needed.

Masdonati et al. (2010) also suggested the importance of relational aspects in career counseling. In the examination of therapeutic alliance in career counseling, they found greater levels of client satisfaction based on perceptions of the relationship between counselor and client and suggested that the alliance may be one of the most salient explanations as to why counselor-free career counseling tends to be less effective than other modalities.

Although more research into the effectiveness of online counseling is needed, it appears clear that as relational beings, people will continue to benefit from a relationship with skilled, empathic counselors. The counselor's ability to join with a client to form a therapeutic alliance is critical. In addition, knowledge of multiple counseling, developmental, and career counseling theories and their practical applications to diverse populations is required.

## Summary

We have sought to inform future counselors of the importance of social context, the counseling relationship, and the complex process of helping traditional college students to discover their life theme and explore how this theme translates into a lifetime of career decision making. Career counselors facilitate a process that helps students to discover themselves by giving them space to reflect on their history, their identity, and their career identity in a manner that results in greater self-awareness. As in any type of counseling, career counseling is the interaction of two uniquely subjective individuals who come together in an effort to understand how students' lived experience informs their career choices and, more important, how career can meet the students' deepest longings. The Web sites listed in the next section provide additional information relating to the chapter topics.

## Useful Web Sites

- CampusCareerCenter. http://www.campuscareercenter.com
- CareerBuilder.com online job site. http://www.careerbuilder.com
- CareerVentures, LLC. http://www.careersite.com
- HigherEdJobs. http://www.higheredjobs.com
- Idealist. Career opportunities in the nonprofit sector: http://www.idealist.org
- Jobwich business network. Internships, full-time, and part-time jobs: http://www.bigapplehead.com
- Monster.com. http://www.hotjobs.com
- National Association of Colleges. Career Web site with job search and employer information and the National Association of Colleges and Employers' career student handbook, *Job Choices*: http://www.jobweb.com
- O*NET OnLine. http://online.onetcenter.org/
- The Riley Guide. Higher http://www.rileyguide.com
- University of Phoenix. http://www.collegegrad.com
- USAJOBS. U.S. government jobs: http://www.usajobs.opm.gov
- Vault.com Inc. http://www.vault.com
- Women for Hire. Women's career development job search: http://www.womenforhire.com

## References

Arthur, N., & McMahon, M. (2005). Multicultural career counseling: Theoretical applications of the systems theory framework. *Career Development Quarterly, 53*, 208–222.

Brott, P. (2005). A constructivist look at life roles. *Career Development Quarterly, 54,* 138–149.

Campagna, C., & Curtis, G. (2007). So worried I don't know what to be: Anxiety is associated with increased career indecision and reduced career certainty. *Australian Journal of Guidance and Counselling. 17,* 91–96.

Datti, P. A. (2009). Applying social learning theory of career decision making to gay, lesbian, bisexual, transgender, and questioning young adults. *Career Development Quarterly, 58,* 54–64.

DeBard, R. (2004). Millennials coming to college. *New Directions for Student Services, 106,* 33–45.

DeVaney, S. B., & Hughey, A. W. (2000). Career development of ethnic minority students. In D. A. Luzzo (Ed.). *Career counseling of college students; An empirical guide to strategies that work.* Washington, DC: American Psychological Association. (pp. 233–252).

Dikel, M. (1998-2011). *The Riley Guide.* Reviewed at http://www.rileyguide.com

Duff, C. T., & Bedi, R. P. (2010). Counsellor behaviours that predict therapeutic alliance: From the clients' perspective. *Counselling Psychology Quarterly, 23,* 91–110. doi: 10.1080/09515071003688165

Duffy, R. D., & Sedlacek, W. E. (2010). The salience of a career calling among college students: Exploring group differences and links to religiousness, life meaning, and life satisfaction. *Career Development Quarterly, 59,* 27–41.

Elam, C., Stratton, T., & Gibson, D. D. (2007). Welcoming a new generation to college: The millennial students. *Journal of College Admission, 195,* 20–25.

Gati, I., & Amir, T. (2010). Applying a systemic procedure to locate career decision-making difficulties. *Career Development Quarterly, 58,* 301–320.

Gibson, S. E. (2009). Intergenerational communication in the classroom: Recommendations for successful teacher-student relationships. *Nursing Education Perspectives, 30,* 37–39.

Greir-Reid, T., Skaar, N., & Conkel-Ziebell, J. (2009). Constructivist career development as a paradigm of empowerment for at-risk culturally diverse college students. *Journal of Career Development, 35,* 290–305.

Gysbers, N. C., Heppner, M. J., & Johnston, J. A. (2009). *Career counseling: Contexts, processes, and techniques* (3rd ed.). Alexandria, VA: American Counseling Association.

Herman, S. (2009). Career HOPES: An Internet-delivered career development intervention. *Computers in Human Behavior, 26,* 339–344. doi: 10.1016/j.chb.2009.11.003

Hinkelman, J. M., & Luzzo, D. A. (2007). Mental health and career development of college students. *Journal of Counseling & Development, 85,* 143–147.

Imbimbo, P. V. (1994). Integrating personal and career counseling: A challenge for counselors. *Journal of Employment Counseling, 31,* 50–59.

Jones, L. (1996). *The path: Creating your mission statement for work and for life.* New York, NY: Hyperion.

Kail, R. V., & Cavanaugh, J. C. (2010). *Human development: A life-span view* (5th ed.). Belmont, CA: Wadsworth.

Kern, R., Stoltz, K., Gottlieb-Low, H., & Frost, L. (2009). The therapeutic alliance and early recollections. *The Journal of Individual Psychology, 65*(2), 110–122.

Kitson, H. D. (1942). Creating vocational interests. *Occupations: The Vocational Guidance Magazine, 17,* 567–571.

Laetitia, L., & Trasiewicz, P. (2002). Can a rational agent afford to be affectless? A formal approach. *Applied Artificial Intelligence, 16,* 577–609.

Ludwikowski, W. M. A., Vogel, D., & Armstrong, P. I. (2009). Attitudes toward career counseling: The role of public and self-stigma. *Journal of Counseling Psychology, 56,* 408–416. doi: 10.1037a001618

Maples, M. F., & Han, S. (2008). Cybercounseling in the United States and South Korea: Implications for counseling college students of the millennial generation and the networked generation. *Journal of Counseling & Development, 86,* 178–183.

Masdonati, J., Massoudi, K., & Rossier, J. (2010). Effectiveness of career counseling and the impact of the working alliance. *Journal of Career Development, 36,* 183–203. doi: 10.1177/0894845309340798

Orange, D. (2001). From Cartesian minds to experiential worlds in psychoanalysis. *Psychoanalytic Psychology, 18,* 287–302.

Pardue, K. T., & Morgan, P. (2008). Millennials considered: A new generation, new approaches, and implications for nursing education. *Nursing Education Perspectives, 29,* 74–79.

Parsons, F. (1909). *Choosing a vocation.* Boston, MA: Houghton Mifflin.

Peavy, V. (1997). *Constructivist thinking in counseling practice, research, and training.* Danvers, MA: Columbia University, Teachers College.

Pope, M. S., Prince, J. P., & Mitchell, K. (2000). Responsible career counseling with lesbian and gay students. In D. A. Luzzo (Ed.), *Career counseling of college students: An empirical guide to strategies that work* (pp. 267–281). Washington, DC: American Psychological Association.

Savickas, M. L. (1997). The spirit in career counseling: Fostering self-completion through work. In D. P. Bloch & L. J. Richmond (Eds.), *Connections between spirit and work in career development* (pp. 3–25). Palo Alto, CA: Davies-Black.

Savickas, M. L. (1998). *Career style* assessment and counseling. In T. Sweeney (Ed.), *Adlerian counseling: A practitioner's approach* (4th ed.). Castelton, NY: Hamilton.

Savickas, M. L. (2002). Career construction: A developmental theory of vocational behavior. In D. Brown & Associates (Eds.), *Career choice and development* (4th ed., pp. 149–205). San Francisco, CA: Jossey-Bass.

Savickas, M. L. (2003). Advancing the career counseling profession: Objectives and strategies for the next decade. *Career Development Quarterly, 52,* 87–96.

Savickas, M. L., Nota, L., Rossier, J., Dauwalder, J.-P., Duarta, M. E., Duarta, M. E., Guichard, J., Soresi, S., Van Esbroeck, R., & van Vianen, A. E. M. (2009). Life designing: A paradigm for career construction in the 21st century. *Journal of Vocational Behavior. 75,* 239–250.

Schultheiss, D. E. (2005). Qualitative relational career assessment: A constructivist paradigm. *Journal of Career Assessment, 13,* 381–394.

Skovholt, T. M., & Ronnestad, M. H. (1992). *Journal of Counseling & Development, 70,* 505–515.

Stolorow, R., & Atwood, G. (1996). The intersubjective perspective. *Psychoanalytic Review, 83,* 181–194.

Stolorow, R. D., Orange, D. M., & Atwood, G. E. (2001). World horizons: A post-Cartesian alternative to the Freudian unconscious. *Contemporary Psychoanalysis, 37,* 43–61.

Super, D. E. (1957). *The psychology of careers.* New York, NY: Harper & Row.

Super, D. E. (1980). A life-span, life-space approach to career development. *Journal of Vocational Behavior, 16,* 282–298.

Super, D. E., & Knasel, E. G. (1981). Career development in adulthood: some theoretical problems and a possible solution. *British Journal of Guidance and Counselling, 9*(2), 194-201.

Super, D.E. (1990). A life-span, life-space approach to career development. In Brown, D., & Brooks, L. *Career choice and development: applying contemporary theories to practice* (2nd ed), San Francisco, CA: Jossey-Bass.

U.S. Bureau of Labor Statistics (2110-2011). *Occupational Outlook Handbook.* Reviewed at http://www.bls.gov/OCO

U.S. Department of Labor (2004). *O-Net.* Reviewed at http://www.onetonline.org

Vogel, D. L., Wade, N. G., Wester, S. R., Larson, L. M., & Hackler, A. H. (2007). Seeking help from a counselor: The influence of one's social network. *Journal of Clinical Psychology, 63,* 233–245.

CHAPTER **14**

# Career Counseling in Mental Health and Private Practice Settings

Mary H. Guindon and Francesca G. Giordano

**Contents**

Historically, career counseling has taken place in public schools, higher educational settings, the military, vocational rehabilitation centers, and more recently business and industry. The assumption has been that career-related issues are somehow separate from and qualitatively different from personal issues. More recently, there has been recognition that human beings must be viewed in a more holistic way. Self-knowledge about personality and other factors related to the self are seen as critical to career choice (Rottinghaus & Van Esbroeck, 2011). Research has indicated that clients' career and personal concerns, including their emotional issues, often appear together (Lewis, 2001). The processes of psychotherapy and career counseling are closely related (Niles, Anderson, & Cover, 2000), and "career is central to general life satisfaction and mental health" (McAuliffe, 1993, p. 13). Work for many Americans is the central organizing feature of life, and they spend more time at work than at any other single activity. It plays a significant role in mental well-being. Individuals exist in a dynamic relationship with their work environments, and they seek to develop satisfactory relationships by making continual adjustments. For some, the results are psychologically unhealthy. Mental health problems can result from the interaction of interests, personality characteristics, and such workplace issues as stress (Osipow, 2004). Yet, it is difficult to know whether some individuals bring mental illness into the workplace or if the workplace induces mental illness (Herr, Cramer, & Niles, 2003). The likelihood is that both influence each other. The challenges of job insecurity, balancing work and family roles, harassment, discrimination, underemployment, workplace stress, and unemployment can motivate individuals to seek counseling for mental health concerns.

It should be no surprise, then, that some clients in mental health and private practice settings need assistance with career development issues, whether or not the work domain is part of the presenting concern. In fact, clients may have career-related concerns in almost every setting in which counseling takes place (Niles & Harris-Bowlsbey, 2002). These clients, however, receive such services only insofar as the counselor's level of knowledge, comfort, and expertise in career counseling allow. In private settings, career-related issues and career life planning rarely receive the same kind of urgency that mental health–related issues do. As a rule, most mental health counselors are not well versed in career issues or may lack enthusiasm for career counseling. Conversely, career counselors may not have the expertise needed to assist clients for whom mental health issues are primary. Nevertheless, those private practice and mental health counselors who are well versed in both mental health and career counseling can offer a full range of counseling interventions to their clients. Herr (1992) suggested that unless one

> is willing to look at the interaction of career counseling and behavior health or mental health problems, there is little likelihood that [one] can be effective in assisting persons with job adjustment problems, dislocated workers, spouses of those experiencing job dislocations, or recovering alcoholics. (p. 26)

Many clients who present with career-related matters must often come to terms with issues related to their mental health; conversely, many clients who present with mental health concerns inevitably want to seek out and implement career-related goals once their mental health issues have been successfully resolved. In this chapter, therefore, we present information useful to those counselors who want to work in mental health and private practice settings. We discuss some of the mental health issues typically found in these settings and offer suggestions on how those with mental health concerns can be productively engaged in the workplace through career counseling interventions. A glossary of mental health terms is provided in Table 14.1.

### SIDEBAR 14.1  Self-Awareness: Need for Career Counseling With Mental Health Clients

So often, we miss the cues that our clients need career counseling as well as mental health counseling. How often have you heard, "My work is driving me crazy!" "If only I could find another job!" "I keep bringing my job stress home; it's negatively affecting everything," and "My new boss and I just don't get along, I know he is out to get me."

These client statements, as well as many others, can be signals that the client could benefit from setting goals and designing interventions that target workplace stress; career interests and skills assessment; balancing work and family roles; and other career interventions. It is easy to see these statements in the context of a client's anxiety or depression and to design interventions focused on insights, emotional expression, and replacing negative thoughts and behaviors. As a result, the occupational dissatisfaction expressed by clients can be ignored by mental health counselors who are inexperienced or uninterested in doing career exploration. Not only do these counselors deny clients important assistance, they also miss opportunities to use career interventions to achieve mental health goals.

## Nature of Mental Health Clients

A clinical or mental health counselor may work independently in a sole proprietorship or group practice, in a private mental health center, as a consultant in a nonprofit mental health clinic, in a community-based mental health agency, in an affiliated psychiatric hospital, in an employee assistance program as either a consultant or service provider, or in a vocational rehabilitation center. Each of these settings provides unique and different opportunities to offer direct career and lifestyle planning services to clients with mental health issues.

A number of considerations determine the necessity of and opportunity for career counseling with clients in each of these settings. In most cases, the presenting concern may not be directly work related. However, workers sometimes suffer from stress reactions, depression, anxiety, and other disorders for which they need treatment. Generally, clients who present with mental health concerns and who may also have job-related issues fall into several broad categories: (a) individuals with severe mental disorders (SMDs), usually chronic and of long-standing duration, such as schizophrenia, dissociative disorders, and the like; (b) those with personality disorders; (c) those who have various forms of depression; (d) those who exhibit symptoms of anxiety-related disorders including social phobia and posttraumatic stress disorder; and (e) those with substance-related disorders. Other clients may present directly with work-related issues that affect their mental health. Most common are those with mental health disorders resulting from job loss and those who seek help with occupationally related stress reactions. Each of these types of clients and their possible career-related issues are discussed with the understanding that these categories are not mutually exclusive. These concerns commonly present together; those experiencing anxiety, for example, may have stress-related disorders, exhibit symptoms of depressive disorders, have substance-related problems, or have lost a job. Individuals with SMDs often experience many other mental health problems as well. Because the purpose of this chapter is to discuss the career counseling process for those with mental health issues, we present only limited explications of these disorders. The reader is referred to the *Diagnostic and Statistical Manual of Mental Disorders* (4th ed., text revision, or *DSM–IV–TR*; American Psychiatric Association, 2000) for information about the diagnostic criteria for each mental health disorder.

## Typical Issues in Mental Health and Private Practice
### People With Severe Mental Disorders

Many individuals with severe, chronic psychiatric disorders may have interrupted training and educational opportunities, have fragmented work

### TABLE 14.1   Glossary of Mental Health Terms

| Term | Definition |
|---|---|
| **Anxiety Disorder** | A general term used to describe a number of related disorders distinguished by uneasiness, discomfort, worry, and fear that has no known basis or imminent threat. Physical symptoms may include sweating, trembling, heart palpitations, and other symptoms associated with stress. |
| **Cognitive–Behavioral** | A counseling approach in which counselors use a variety of techniques to bring clients' ineffective thinking and behavioral patterns into awareness. Direct, goal-oriented methods are used to assist the client in changing thoughts and actions. |
| **Depression (Depressive Disorder)** | A general term used to describe a number of related disorders distinguished by extreme sadness, hopelessness, despair, and low energy. Symptoms can range from mild to severe and be short term or chronic. |
| ***Diagnostic and Statistical Manual of Mental Disorders*** | The publication of the American Psychiatric Association that codifies and delineates mental disorders used in diagnosis and treatment planning. The most recent version is the text revision of the fourth edition (American Psychiatric Association, 2000). |
| **Dissociative Disorder** | A disorder in which the individual experiences an altered state of consciousness and includes a change in personality, memory loss, or both, usually of a traumatic or stressful nature that is not organic or psychotic in character. |
| **Dual Diagnosis** | The identification in an individual of two or more mental disorders, one of which is usually a substance abuse disorder (e.g., alcoholism and depression). |
| **Generalized Anxiety Disorder** | Excessive emotional fear, worry, and apprehensive expectation of a general nature about events or activities, usually involving the inability to control or turn off worrisome thoughts. |
| **Guided Imagery** | A technique in which the counselor assists the client in imagining various specific scenarios and the related feelings, thoughts, and behaviors that are evoked. |
| **Journaling** | A cognitive–behavioral technique used to bring thoughts, feelings, and behaviors into awareness and to recognize significant themes and patterns. |
| **Mood Disorder** | Mental disorders that have a predominantly excessive or inappropriate emotional basis. Included are depressive disorders. |
| **Personality Disorder** | An inflexible, enduring pattern of maladaptive thoughts, behaviors, or emotional responses that interferes with functioning across a broad range of social and work situations and causes impairment in interpersonal relationships and living. |
| **Posttraumatic Stress Disorder** | A type of anxiety disorder that may follow exposure to a traumatic event in which the individual experienced an actual threat or danger to self or others and responded with intense fear or horror. |

**TABLE 14.1 Glossary of Mental Health Terms (Continued)**

| Term | Definition |
|---|---|
| Rational Emotive Behavior Therapy | A type of cognitive–behavioral technique developed by Albert Ellis in the 1950s in which the counselor confronts the client about dysfunctional thoughts. Thoughts about events rather than the events themselves are seen as the cause of emotional difficulties and inappropriate behaviors. |
| Schizophrenia | A severe mental disorder in which the individual is out of touch with reality and experiences delusions, hallucinations, speech incoherence, disorganized behavior, and other thought abnormalities for a significant period of time. |
| Self-Esteem | The evaluative component of the self; the affective judgments placed on the self-concept consisting of feelings of worth and acceptance, awareness of competence, and sense of achievement. |
| Severe Mental Disorder | A general term used to describe any number of psychiatric disorders or mental illness, usually chronic and of long-standing duration, in which the ability to function normally is impaired or disrupted. |
| Social Phobia (Social Anxiety Disorder) | An extreme, unreasonable, and persistent fear of a social or performance situation in which the individual will be embarrassed, scrutinized, or humiliated by unfamiliar people. Exposure to the feared situation results in intense anxiety or distress. |
| Stress | A state of physiological tension caused by an imbalance between external demands in the environment and the individual's capacity to adequately respond to these demands. |
| Systematic Desensitization | A step-by-step and gradual behavioral technique in which the client's anxiety is reduced by pairing thoughts and fears with incompatible behaviors. Anxiety-provoking thoughts are paired with relaxation techniques and calming guided imagery. |
| Thought Stopping | A cognitive–behavioral technique in which clients are taught to use an external cue (such as snapping a rubber band on the wrist) that will interrupt an inappropriate or unproductive thought. |

histories, or lack work experience altogether and thus have limited understanding of the world of work and employment opportunities (Szymanski & Vancollins, 2003). A little more than 3 million adults, ages 18 to 69, have a serious mental illness. In a national survey by National Alliance on Mental Illness (n.d.), its members reported that 67% of individuals with mental illness are unemployed and another 17% are employed only part-time.

New drugs for treating severe mental illness have brought hope and possibility to these clients. As new techniques for managing severe mental illness and early interventions have been developed, a greater number of individuals are better able to manage their disorders and lead more productive lives. For some, career and life planning is now possible, whereas previously it was routinely out of the question.

Career development for those with any type of disability, including those with mental illness, can be described through five constructs (individual, contextual, mediating, environmental, and outcome) and six processes (development, decision making, congruence, socialization, allocation, and chance; see Szymanski & Hershenson, 2004). These constructs and processes are discussed in Chapter 12.

Early life experiences and expectations of others may determine how those with SMDs view themselves as workers, especially when the mental disability is central to the self-concept. Apathy is common in those with severe mental illness, who have all too often been the recipients of stigmatizing attitudes. Apathy and other consequences of stigma are one of many barriers counselors may experience when working with these clients (Caporoso & Kiselica, 2004). Human development theory suggests that expectations of parents, teachers, and counselors shape self-perceptions. Therefore, the positive expectation of counselors in the career and life planning process is essential in assisting those with SMDs in developing and maintaining their concepts as successful workers. According to Fabian (1999), three key counselor strategies affect the entry of those with SMDs into the labor force: endorsing the value of work, focusing on careers rather than just on obtaining jobs, and stressing client strengths rather than deficits.

### Americans With Disabilities Act

The elimination of barriers to employment has led to fuller and more productive lives for those with disabilities. Covered in the definition of a disability is an individual who has a mental impairment that substantially limits major life activities and includes those with SMDs who have recovered from a mental illness. Instrumental in breaking down barriers, the Americans With Disabilities Act (ADA) of 1990 has allowed society to benefit from the skills and talents of those with disabilities. Under ADA, employment discrimination against qualified individuals with disabilities is prohibited. Individuals are considered to have a qualified disability if they meet legitimate skill, experience, education, or other requirements of an employment position that they hold or seek and can perform the "essential functions" of the position with or without reasonable accommodation. The ADA prohibits discrimination in all employment practices, including job application procedures, hiring, firing, advancement, compensation, and training. This prohibition applies to all employment-related activities. Hence, career and employment counseling for individuals with mental illness is not only possible but is also mandated by law.

Career development is a complex, lifelong process of developing and implementing an occupational self-concept (Super, 1980). For those with severe and chronic mental disorders, this process is often irreparably compromised. The preponderance of career and employment counseling interventions for those with SMDs takes place in vocational rehabilitation centers (see Chapter 12) or in community-based mental health facilities in collaboration with vocational rehabilitation centers. Counselors in community mental health counseling centers are committed to providing preventive and developmental mental health programming to the general public. Counselors in these centers hold the belief that assessment, treatment, and consultation services should respond to the unique needs of individuals, families, and communities with the goal of promoting harmony among the psychological, emotional, physical, spiritual, interpersonal, and vocational elements of each person's life. Combining these services with career and employment-related counseling can be effective.

Numerous people with severe psychiatric disabilities are generally impaired significantly enough to prevent them from holding jobs without some kind of adaptation as required by the ADA. People with disabilities are in general a diverse group, and disability itself does not necessarily hinder career development (Szymanski & Hershenson, 2004). "Some individuals with marked pathology can manage work tasks quite well, often at high levels" (Spokane, 1991, p. 249). However, disability is a risk factor that may influence the course of career development. Many people with severe psychiatric disorders can initially only work in supported employment—highly supervised settings, most commonly sheltered workshops. These settings offer the opportunity for counselors to focus on vocational strategies and life-skills training to address individual performance within the limitations posed by the client's disorder. Common practices include either individual job placement and support or transitional placement during rehabilitation in anticipation of higher-level employment. Some have argued, however, that such an artificial separation between actual work and the nonwork domains found in sheltered community programs hinders opportunities for those with SMDs to explore possible appropriate careers, to develop self-efficacy, or to anticipate participation in the real world of work (Fabian, 1999). Consequently, counselors take care not to impose their own assumptions regarding the nature of meaningful work or the value of specific careers on those with SMDs. In fact, counselors understand that they are asking those with severe mental disabilities to manage two careers: employment and their mental illness (Fabian, 1999).

Combining vocational and mental health services to address on-the-job issues assists people with SMDs in making successful transitions to the workplace. Services that counselors typically offer include (a) assessing the client's level of vocational maturity, self-concept, and developmental life stage; (b) referring clients for formal vocational assessment through rehabilitation services; (c) facilitating the setting of realistic career plans and implementing them; and (d) addressing the impact of unrealistic or inappropriate career plans on the client's self-concept and level of success. Special care is taken to assist the client in understanding communications and overcoming communications barriers common to those with SMD. Counselors target interventions in which clients can form and maintain suitable relationships.

Clients can learn to respond to social cues correctly and to give and receive appropriate feedback. An expectation and conveyance of possible success on the counselor's part is essential. As an example, Kyle and Persinger (2000) described a community-based, integrated vocational life-planning model for people with chronic mental illness that focuses on the individual rather than the disorder to allow the client to exercise control over career choice. This model assesses "the client's intellectual abilities, his personality, and his educational achievement to identify areas of difficulties that need to be addressed in order to be successful" (p. 198). The intervention includes a thorough vocational assessment and an individualized plan to address needs and develop interests, skills, and abilities.

When work experience programs allow clients to experience success in a supportive environment, the client's confidence in his or her capacity for meaningful work increases (Caparoso & Kiselica, 2004). People with long-term mental illness can overcome barriers when programs offer speedy placement into real rather than sheltered work sites. Loughead and Black (1990) found that those with mental illness who participated in career development programs appropriate to them showed a significant change in vocational identity. Their findings supported the selection of Holland's (1994) Self-Directed Search and its concomitant activities as a feasible career development service. Other career interventions include helping clients with personal future planning and seeking out flexible educational programs, workplace mentorship, and interagency collaboration (Hagner, Cheney, & Malloy, 1999); implementing a developmental approach (Caparoso & Kiselica, 2004); and offering individual or group instruction and coaching in job-search skills. Ultimately, for this population job placement at the highest functional level possible is the goal.

## Personality Disorders

Personality can be a significant factor in workplace functioning and success. Personality is a pattern of cognitive, affective, and behavioral traits that endures over extended periods of time and manifests in a learned and predictable structure of overt and covert behaviors. A normal or healthy personality allows people to cope with and adapt to their environments effectively through individual, specific personality styles. In fact, Holland (1973) saw career and personality as interrelated and developed the Holland codes widely used as part of career counseling. Those with a personality disorder, however, attempt to cope with everyday activities and relationships with inflexibility and maladaptive behavior. Their perceptions of self and the environment are self-defeating and ineffective. In an informal study of clients in a career counseling practice, 18% exhibited sufficient criteria to indicate one or more personality disorders (Musgrove, 1992). Because of the prominence of work in the lives of most individuals, those with personality disorders experience many work-related difficulties and problematic career choices.

Personality disorders vary in level of dysfunctional behaviors. Millon and Everly (1985) differentiated personality behaviors along a continuum from normal personality style to mildly severe to moderately and markedly severe or dysfunctional. The more severe disorders are less amenable to treatment in general and can be categorized according to treatability as high amenability (dependent, histrionic, obsessive–compulsive, and avoidant personality disorders); intermediate amenability (narcissistic, borderline, and schizotypal personality disorders); or low amenability (paranoid, schizoid, and antisocial personality disorders; Stone, 1993). Those with low amenability and many with intermediate amenability would also be less amenable to career and life planning interventions than those with high amenability. Career counseling can be difficult with individuals with moderately severe personality disorders and is less effective with those with markedly severe personality disorders. Consequently, those with mildly severe personality disorders are more likely to benefit from career-related interventions.

Several behaviors are delineated in the *DSM–IV–TR* (American Psychiatric Association, 2000) as diagnostic criteria for personality disorders and include factors such as indecisiveness, dependence on others' advice, self-defeating behaviors, anxiety and perfectionism, instability, and difficulties in interpersonal relationships (Kjos, 1995). In the presence of personality disorder, career decision making and work performance are compromised. It is important to note that career counselors and mental health counselors do a disservice to their clients when they do not take into consideration the career implications of personality disorders in the counseling process (Kjos, 1995). Counseling interventions for those with personality disorders combine psychodynamic counseling with emotional, interpersonal, and cognitive–behavioral restructuring techniques. The goal is to facilitate movement from the personality disorder to a more functional personality style (Sperry, 1995). Career counseling is a cognitive–behavioral, psychoeducational modality and can be valuable in facilitating this move. Kjos (1995) pointed out that effective career counseling with those with personality disorders includes the ability to (a) recognize the traits that make up specific personality disorders that may inhibit (or enhance) career development; (b) develop treatment plans that capitalize on the positive aspect of individual client personality styles; and (c) work with such clients to maximize their strengths. She described interventions that are targeted toward those with dependent, borderline, and obsessive–compulsive personality disorders and discussed positive and negative characteristics of each of these disorders that should be considered in clients' career choices.

## Mood Disorders

Mood disorders include major depressive disorder, dysthymic disorder, and bipolar disorder. In a given year, almost 10% of the U.S. population age 18 and older, or approximately 20.8 million American adults, have a mood disorder. Forty-five percent of these cases (4.3% of adults age 18 or older) are classified as severe (National Institute of Mental Health, n.d. a). Depression is a widespread and costly disorder and is present to some degree in most mental health clients.

Depression is not one entity; it is several different but related mood disorders and can be susceptible to misdiagnosis. Depression can range in symptomatology from mild to actively suicidal. According to the *DSM–IV–TR* (American Psychiatric Association, 2000), the major symptoms of depressive disorders include depressed mood most of the day for a number of days, a diminished interest in activities, significant weight loss or weight gain, poor appetite or overeating, insomnia or sleeping too much, low energy level or fatigue, or psychomotor agitation, low self-esteem, feelings of worthlessness and inappropriate guilt, inability to concentrate, difficulty making decisions, feelings of hopelessness, and recurrent suicidal thoughts. When two or more of these symptoms are present during the same 2-week period, the existence of a minor depressive episode is likely. When five or more are present during the same 2-week period, a major depressive episode is probable. Mild, chronic depression of long-standing duration is known as dysthymia and affects approximately 1.5% of the U.S. population age 18 and older in a given year (National Institute of Mental Health, n.d. b). The symptoms are similar to but less severe than those of other depressive disorders. Major depressive disorder, single episode, is a common type of depression encountered among those who lose their jobs. It is situational in nature and often but not always lifts when the situation changes. Stress is a significant contributor to depression, and threats to career can precipitate both stress and depression. Occupational stress and job loss are discussed later in this chapter.

Research has indicated a significant positive relationship between depression and career indecision and between depression and dysfunctional career thought, and a negative relationship between depression and vocational identity (Saunders, Peterson, Sampson, & Reardon, 2000). Engagement in work is problematic for some depressed clients, and stress in this population can lead to either temporary or long-term inability to work. Typically, depressed clients who are not able to work began their work lives expecting failure and rejection and "react[ed] to the inevitable setbacks of work life with some combination of confusion, frustration, anger, and demoralization" (Axlerod, 1999, p. 71).

Because inability to make decisions is a common symptom in depressed clients, career counseling strategies associated with decision making can be effective. A significant component of career indecision is dysfunctional career thought. Crites (1969) differentiated indecision from indecisiveness. *Career indecision* is the inability of a person to commit to a course of action that will result in preparation for and entering into a specific career or occupation. Career indecision is addressed by using techniques common to career development and life-planning interventions such as facilitating the discovery of skills, interests, abilities, and values and teaching the client goal setting, world-of-work information, and, again, decision-making skills. Indecision is ameliorated through gaining information about careers, job search and the like, and the knowledge of how to make decisions to sort through alternatives. Indecisiveness, however, is a personality dysfunction and generally involves pain and anxiety in making any decision. An indecisive person is incapable of making a decision even after career counseling, and interventions of a more psychotherapeutic nature are indicated. Working with depressed clients to make career decisions has been linked to improvement in their overall well-being (Uthayakumar, Schimnack, Hartung, & Rogers, 2010).

The counselor working with a depressed client on career issues must first attend to the depression either through personal counseling or by referral for therapy or medications, or both. Counseling is required before career development techniques are indicated. Most important is conveying to the depressed client that satisfaction and pleasure in work activities are real possibilities. The implementation of skills, talents, and interests in and of itself can have a therapeutic effect (Axelrod, 1999).

Self-esteem and depression are highly correlated. Therefore, interventions targeted toward self-esteem enhancement may also improve depressive symptoms and prepare the client for career and life planning when appropriate. Low self-esteem affects individuals' perceptions of their abilities and their willingness to take action and make healthy choices in their lives. Self-esteem is significantly related to physical and mental well-being, functional behavior, and life satisfaction (Guindon, 2010). Self-esteem is that part of the individual that makes a judgment about all the constituent pieces of the self; it is the evaluative component of the self-concept. Self-esteem can be described in terms of attitudes of approval or disapproval people hold about themselves and all their many characteristics. It appears to vary across different areas of one's experience and fluctuates depending on the different roles one plays (see Guindon, 2010). What this means is that, in different situations, individuals' feelings about their self-worth will change. They might have high self-esteem in one situation and low self-esteem in another. Therefore, the counselor first ascertains in which situations low self-esteem predominates and on which elements of the self the depressed client places the most importance. He or she assists the client in realistically evaluating the various constituent elements of the self through assessment of authentic interests, values, and the like and by challenging irrational thought processes and helping the client bring these thought processes into awareness. Thought stopping, journaling, and other cognitive–behavioral techniques are commonly prescribed. Group work is especially helpful, and career and life planning workshops are structured around life skills training as well as job search skills.

### SIDEBAR 14.2 Case Study: Should Jane Change Careers?

Jane is 23 years old and works as a project manager. She has symptoms of both anxiety and depression. She finds herself obsessively worrying about how her boss and coworkers view her contributions to their group projects. Her worry causes her to inappropriately seek feedback from those she supervises, which often undermines her authority. She then receives negative feedback from her supervisor, which leads to perfectionist thinking and difficulties sleeping. She is caught in a negative cycle, and she does not see a way out. She often thinks about changing jobs, but because she has always had difficulties making decisions, she has never been able to decide and just feels increasingly overwhelmed and sad. Can you identify Jane's dysfunctional career thinking? How does this distorted thinking affect her decision-making ability? How can her counselor help her decide whether to change jobs?

## Anxiety Disorders

The diagnostic category of anxiety disorders includes panic attack, agoraphobia, specific phobia (of an object or situation), social phobia, obsessive–compulsive disorder, posttraumatic stress disorder, acute stress disorder, and generalized anxiety disorder. Counselors in mental health and private practice may find that people with any of these disorders may have career-related concerns because of the nature of anxiety itself. Anxiety produces feelings of apprehension and fearfulness and may be severe enough to limit everyday workplace behaviors. The work environment itself can be predictive of generalized anxiety disorder (Smith, 1989). Bordin (1986) suggested that clients can best confront career-related problems only when anxiety is minimized.

We discuss social phobia and posttraumatic stress disorder (PTSD) here because of their prevalence in mental health settings and their impact on workplace functioning, with the understanding that there may be a need to facilitate career and life planning skills with people experiencing other kinds of anxiety as well.

### Social Phobia (Social Anxiety Disorder)

Approximately 6.8% of American adults age 18 and older have social phobia in a given year (National Institute of Mental Health, n.d. c), and thus it poses a significant mental health threat. Those with social phobia fear meeting new people, situations in which they must be assertive, and performance appraisal. Consequently, work situations can be difficult for them. Research has indicated that people with social phobia are underemployed and more anxious than healthy people about beginning a job but show no less job satisfaction than their healthier counterparts (Bruch, Fallon, & Heimberg, 2003). Yet the anxiety felt by people with social phobia significantly interferes with occupational functioning (Rosenberg, Ledley, & Heimberg, 2010).

### Posttraumatic Stress Disorder

Unique among anxiety disorders, PTSD is a condition that can manifest at any age in those with no predisposing conditions. It is distinguishable from other anxiety disorders because symptoms develop only after exposure to a traumatic event or extreme stressor. However, personality characteristics, social support, and the nature of the trauma itself can affect the duration and severity of the disorder. Estimates of its prevalence vary widely. The *DSM–IV–TR* (American Psychiatric Association, 2000) stated that community-based studies indicate a lifetime prevalence of PTSD of approximately 8% of the adult population. Highest rates of PTSD are found among victims of rape, internment, and genocide and among military combat veterans. Workplace violence is a risk factor as well. The National Institute of Mental Health (n.d. d) has reported that approximately 3.5% of American adults age 18 and older have PTSD in a given year. About 19% of Vietnam veterans experienced PTSD at some point after the war. Veterans returning from the Iraq and Afghanistan wars have been reported to have high levels of unemployment and PTSD (Bullock, Baud, Lindsay, & Phillips, 2009).

Symptoms of PTSD can affect understanding and memory, concentration, persistence, social interaction, and adaptation and can significantly reduce tolerance of stress. Each of these factors can have a significant influence on workplace functioning and can result in difficulty in completing long-term tasks or weaken the ability to complete standard work-week activities, meet deadlines, and handle stressors. These clients may have trouble working closely or interacting socially with coworkers. Even mild impairments may affect the person's capacity to respond effectively to changes, to match skills and abilities to suitable work settings, and to set appropriate goals independently.

Individual counseling first addresses these clients' realistic self-image and person–environment fit congruence. Introducing standard self-exploration career assessment to ascertain interests, skills, and values and using more objective aptitude testing are interventions of choice. Counseling addresses the clients' understanding of the disorder and knowledge of mental health and rehabilitation services available to them. Because support is critical for clients with PTSD, group counseling can be especially effective. Full-service career counseling groups that include job search skills for those who are out of work can be effective. With those who are appropriately employed but experiencing difficulties at work, cognitive–behavioral techniques (e.g., systematic desensitization, thought stopping, rational emotive behavior therapy, guided imagery, and music) commonly used in addressing a range of other anxiety disorders, along with communications skills and assertiveness training, can be effective, as can some alternative counseling techniques.

## Substance-Related Disorders

Alcohol and other drugs (AOD) pose a serious health risk, including a risk to mental health. The impact of substance abuse and addictions on education, career development, and employment is well documented, as is the relationship between AOD and workplace stressors. A substance abuse problem is present if "a client's use of alcohol or another mood-altering drug has undesired effects on his or her life or on the lives of others," whereas addiction is a problem "only when physical symptoms of withdrawal or tolerance to the substance are present" (Lewis, Dana, & Blevins, 2010, p. 4). Those with problems with AOD manifest in nearly every counseling setting, and counselors must be prepared to facilitate their treatment through their own interventions or by referral to qualified substance abuse counselors. The Center for Substance Abuse Treatment (2000) has recommended that "an individual needing treatment will be identified and assessed and will receive treatment, either directly or through appropriate treatment no matter where he or she enters the realm of services" (p. 14).

Alcohol continues to be the most common problem in the general population and in counseling settings. According to the ADA, people with alcoholism are considered to have a disability and thus, as is the case with those with SMDs, are protected under the law if they are qualified to perform the essential functions of the job. In fact, an employer may be required to provide an accommodation to a person with alcoholism but can require that employees not be under the influence of alcohol. However, a person who is actively using alcohol is not automatically denied protection. Nevertheless, an employer can discipline, discharge, or deny employment to a person with alcoholism whose use of alcohol adversely affects job performance or conduct. Uses of illegal drugs are not protected under the provisions of the ADA.

Those with problems with AOD may present in counseling settings at any point along a continuum of abuse and thus may need a variety of services along a prevention–intervention continuum as well. General categories of use of AOD are "nonuse; moderate, nonproblematic use; heavy, nonproblematic use; heavy use associated with moderate life problems; heavy use associated with serious life problems; and substance dependence/addiction associated with life and health problems" (Lewis et al., 2010, p. 7). Depending on the category of use, counseling programs are targeted toward preventing use of or intervention with AOD, and many of these programs combine at least some elements of career or employment counseling. The point is that counseling services for this population are multidimensional, individualized, and targeted toward ameliorating life problems across many domains. Because substance abuse can permeate all aspects of life, addressing as many life domains as are relevant is part of appropriate and necessary intervention.

Career and life planning for these clients includes setting and implementing career goals, usually after the client is committed to recovery or, in the case of early intervention, in conjunction with other activities. Job search skills and other employment-related services are common in AOD treatment settings. Such interventions can assist the client in meeting immediate financial and survival needs and may be instituted early in counseling. At the same time, a more comprehensive career development and life-planning process may be undertaken for long-term goals. A common perspective is that those who are addicted to AOD stopped growing developmentally at about the time that AOD became a problem. Thus, these clients must work through the developmental tasks that have not yet been accomplished. This perspective applies to the area of career knowledge and awareness as well. Many of these clients, regardless of age, lack vocational identity and are stuck somewhere between two of Super's (1980) developmental stages: the growth stage, with its need to develop a realistic self-concept, and the exploratory stage, wherein the individual learns about world-of-work opportunities. These clients may need assistance with the vocational developmental tasks associated with the crystallization stage (ages 14–18; Super, Starishevsky, Matlin, & Jordan, 1963). At this stage, clients set a general vocational goal by learning about possible interests and values, learning about available resources, and beginning to plan for preferred occupations. Thus, it is not unusual, for example, to see a mid-life recovering person with alcoholism with the same career identity issues and lack of world-of-work knowledge as a typical adolescent. Thus, the same career counseling strategies used with secondary school students can be effective with this population. AOD issues are discussed in greater detail in Chapter 18.

The National Institute on Alcohol Abuse and Alcoholism (2010) has reported the co-occurrence of incidents of *DSM–IV–TR* psychiatric disorders and alcohol use disorders. People with co-occurring substance abuse and mental disorders make up a portion of client populations, especially in the publicly supported mental health care system. In any given year, at least 10 million people in the United States have a combination of mental and substance abuse disorders, and this number may be significantly higher (Substance Abuse and Mental Health Services Administration, 2003). Although some of these dually diagnosed clients may have substance abuse disorders along with the less severe personality disorders, most are those with SMDs who need a plethora of services. Unfortunately, many settings are inadequately prepared to help people with both substance abuse and mental health disorders, which means that many of these clients do not get the full care they need but receive treatment for only one of their disorders (Substance Abuse and Mental Health Services Administration, 2003). Moreover, they make up a disproportionate number of people who are homeless and who are in the criminal justice system. Unfortunately, no single social service or care system is equipped to provide these individuals with the range of services they need. Career and life planning, when appropriate, are most often absent in any systematic meaningful way.

**SIDEBAR 14.3  Case Study: Using Job Search Interventions to Help Harvey in His Recovery**

Harvey has struggled with bipolar disorder and cocaine addiction for many years. His mood swings, especially his manic episodes, have fueled his use of cocaine and alcohol. He works in an auto repair job. After 10 years of marriage, his wife divorced him, so the men he works with are his major source of support. He has used cocaine with them, and as part of his recovery, he knows he must find a new set of friends. He works nights as a bouncer in a local bar. He loves the excitement and aggression of this work. Harvey reports that he is feeling very bad about himself and the ways his addiction has hurt others. He reports that his only sources of self-esteem are the relationships he has with his buddies, his ability to fix cars, and his skill as a bouncer. How has Harvey's addiction affected his vocational developmental tasks? What job search strategies might help Harvey manage his bipolar symptoms and aid in his recovery?

## Job Loss and Mental Health

Job loss and unemployment are significant factors in the U.S. labor force. Throughout the 20th century, the mental health consequences of unemployment were constant and unchanged (Liem & Liem, 1996). The fallout from the events of September 11, 2001, has resulted in significant disruptions to local and national economies and continues to have long-term employment consequences (Bureau of Labor Statistics, 2010). Recent survey results have documented the negative effects of unemployment and economic upheaval on the mental health of U.S. citizens (Vetzner & Lodato, 2009). Many workers are unemployed or have been downsized into jobs well below their skill level. They continue to search for employment at pre–job-loss levels.

Unemployment takes an emotional toll. Research has shown that loss of employment is connected to a number of mental health concerns. People who involuntarily lose their jobs can be psychologically harmed in various ways.

Evidence has suggested that "absence of work ... [is] reflected in behaviors which suggest various problems in living, or, indeed, mental illness" (Herr, 1989, p. 5). In a study of the employment status of private practitioners' mental health clients, 64.7% of those treated by psychiatrists and 80.5% of those treated by psychologists were unemployed during treatment (Taube, Burns, & Kessler, 1984). Of course, many of these mental health clients are those with severe and chronic mental disorders. However, a significant number suffer from emotional trauma because of recent job loss. In fact, admissions to psychiatric hospitals can be associated with unemployment and economic decline (Brenner, 1973; Hanisch, 1999), and high levels of unemployment have been associated with increased rates of chemical dependency (Herr et al., 2003).

Feelings of isolation, rejection, and shame are common in clients experiencing job loss. Among the most frequent presenting concerns are stress reactions, depression, and anxiety (Guindon & Smith, 2002), each of which is discussed elsewhere. Crites (1981) noted that when counseling unemployed people, traditional assumptions that career counseling takes place only after mental health counseling is established must be discarded. He viewed the relationship between career and mental health counseling as dynamic and interactive. He went further to suggest that career counseling often goes beyond personal counseling and is more effective and more difficult than psychotherapy and that the need for career counseling is greater than the need for psychotherapy.

Borgen and Amundson (1987) compared the loss of employment with an emotional rollercoaster. They applied the stages of grieving delineated in the Kübler-Ross (1969) model of grief and loss to this population and described feelings of denial, anger, bargaining, depression, and frustration after job loss. In the job-loss process, the client may experience all or some of the stages of grieving. Mental health and private practice counselors help their clients work through these emotional stages so that they successfully reach the acceptance stage, at which point the client is ready to undertake an effective job search and career life planning can begin.

Unlike employed individuals, who tend to engage in group activities as part of their work day, those who are unemployed experience minimal engagement. Employment offers opportunities for external social and internal work group activities. Unemployed people tend to have less contact with coworkers and engage in social activities less often or not at all, contributing to the experience of latent deprivation (Waters & Moore, 2002). Because self-esteem may plummet during job loss, self-esteem interventions should be instituted.

Gender is an important consideration; men and women react to job loss in different ways. Gender differences in symptoms of stress have been widely reported. Women report higher levels of depression, psychological distress, and anxiety than do men (Nelson & Hitt, 1992), as do gay, lesbian, and bisexual individuals. Malen and Stroh (1998) found that male and female managers who are unemployed have different styles for managing their loss of employment. Men were found to use networking more and to rely more extensively on support systems than were women. Unfortunately, "societal norms for 'masculinity' and 'femininity' remain firmly embedded in our collective psyche" (Herlihy & Watson, 2010, p. 175). Hence, women may need additional assistance in identifying support systems to help them with tasks associated with an employment search.

## Occupational Stress

In 1987, a Gallup survey partially sponsored by the National Career Development Association found that more than 30% of those surveyed ($N = 1,006$) reported that job stress interfered with their ability to do their jobs and with their personal relationships and also affected their physical health (Smith, 1989). Stress can be a threat to mental health in the workplace. Feelings of hopelessness and powerlessness, racial anger, disparity in earnings, and rapid change can be stressors (Parmer & Rush, 2003). The turbulence of the work world and possibility of violence in and out of the workplace further contribute to stress.

Although stress itself is neither good nor bad, there are optimal levels of stress. The nature, intensity, and duration of stress can vary, as can the resources with which the individual responds (Selye, 1956). Stress occurs when an imbalance occurs between perceived external demands and the individual's perceived capability to adequately respond to these demands. The individual may be unable to muster the internal and personal resources necessary to counteract stress effectively.

Stressors such as role overload, role ambiguity, interpersonal conflict, underemployment, and job loss are major causes of psychological and physiological strain. Caplan, Cobb, French, Harrison, and Pinneau (1975) defined strain as resulting "from discrepancies between either environmental demands and an individual's abilities to meet them or between an individual's needs and environmental supplies to meet those needs" (p. 47). Strain manifests itself in an array of symptoms, including such common conditions as headaches, sleep disorders, anxiety and depression, lowering of self-esteem, substance abuse, and family disruption and abuse (Guindon & Smith, 2002). Physiological problems such as many cardiovascular and digestive disorders are commonly attributed to stress reactions. Accidents, interpersonal conflicts, marital and family discord, apathy, and dissatisfaction are often attributable to strain. Many of these symptoms may also be indicative of depression and anxiety. Thus, many of the disorders discussed in this chapter are interrelated and appear together, during the intake and treatment planning stages or manifesting during stages of treatment.

Mental health practitioners and career counselors alike can play a major role in helping their clients manage stress in the workplace. Initially, they can assist their clients in recognizing symptoms of stress. This role is perhaps one of the most important ones counselors can assume. Stress is so closely related to other mental health disorders that managing stress may serve as preventative intervention. Stress management techniques can be incorporated into career and life planning programs for people with the disorders discussed in this chapter. Table 14.2 delineates common stress reactions.

**TABLE 14.2   Some Common Reactions to Stress**

| Domain | Symptom |
|---|---|
| **Behavioral** | Increased use of alcohol, prescriptions, or illegal drugs |
| | Difficulty sitting still |
| | Frequent frowning |
| | Tight or hunched shoulders |
| | Nail biting |
| | Teeth grinding |
| | Increased speech and rate of speech |
| | Short temper and mood swings |
| | Impulsive or pressured actions |
| | Lashing out verbally or physically |
| | Withdrawal from normal activities |
| | Family disruption |
| | Prone to accidents |
| **Physical** | Upset stomach |
| | Diarrhea |
| | Frequent need to urinate |
| | Hives |
| | Headache or neck pain |
| | Chest pain |
| | Cardiovascular concerns |
| **Cognitive** | Forgetfulness |
| | Mental block |
| | Nightmares |
| | Inward preoccupation and ruminating |
| | Difficulty organizing thoughts |
| | Apathy |
| **Emotional** | Feelings of hopelessness |
| | Feelings of helplessness |
| | Decreased interest in sex |
| | Feelings of being overwhelmed |
| | Impatience |
| | Urge to lash out at others |
| | Resentment toward others or fate |
| | Anxiety about the future |
| | Anxiety about being disapproved of by others |

**SIDEBAR 14.4   Self-Awareness: Compassion Fatigue and Occupational Stress**

Compassion fatigue is a common result of occupational stress for mental health professionals. It is a physical, emotional, and spiritual fatigue or exhaustion that takes over a person and causes a decline in his or her ability to experience joy or to feel and care for others. Review Table 14.2 for the stress reactions you may experience as a result of compassion fatigue. As your own career counselor, what treatment goals would you set for yourself?

# Intake, Assessment, Treatment Planning, and Intervention

## Intake and Assessment

Whether counselors work in career or mental health settings, they use assessment methods in making sound decisions so that their interventions fit the needs of their clients. By using objective and subjective methods of appraisal, counselors in either setting are better able to develop plans that aid their clients in identifying problems and discovering effective problem-solving strategies. Regardless of whether the presenting concern is related to mental health or career, assessment can promote discussion about the direction and goals of counseling and encourage independent thinking and reflection. Hohenshil (1995) pointed out that counselors cannot establish the best treatment interventions unless they diagnose effectively. This is especially true when career and life planning concerns are not evident at the outset of counseling. Use of assessment instruments not only allows the counselor to gain information on the client's presenting concern but can help identify the contributing factors associated with the problem (Cormier, Nurius, & Osborn, 2008). It can diagnose those factors that may hinder developmental growth and evaluate individual strengths and weaknesses. Assessing interpersonal and academic skill deficiencies can aid in identifying the need for treatment, remedial training, or skills development (Osborn & Zunker, 2005).

An intake interview is a routine procedure in mental health and private practice settings. Standard procedures such as administering a mental status exam are undertaken to ascertain the presenting concern, the major issues, and appropriate treatment planning. Medical, personal, and family history information is gathered. The counselor takes note of appearance, speech, behavior, emotions, concentration and attention, orientation to reality, thought processes and content, memory and intelligence, perception, and insight and judgment. Whether or not the presenting concern is work related, the intake procedure should include some assessment of the client's capacity to work (Lowman, 1993). Life-span issues are included to help the counselor better understand the client's personal and vocational identity. When a career issue is indicated, the counselor should assess vocational and career maturity and consider the inclusion of appropriate career assessments instruments as needed.

Lowman (1993) stated that the initial task of the counselor is to

> (a) assess the type of work problems, if any, presented by the client and (b) determine the relation of such problems to other aspects of personality and psychopathology for purposes of (c) formulating a diagnosis and (d) developing an initial intervention strategy. (p. 40)

For further information on intake and diagnosis, several guides are available. Spokane (1991) offered a thorough diagnostic taxonomy of adult careers concerns that can be incorporated into the intake assessment stage in either career or mental health settings. Campbell and Cellini (1981) offered another useful taxonomy of problem categories and subcategories of work dysfunctions.

## Treatment Planning and Interventions

Treatment for mental health disorders can be classified as primary, secondary, or tertiary. *Primary treatment* means that through promoting healthy behaviors, many disorders may be prevented altogether before problems reach a critical point and before they exact a psychological toll. Prevention as a psychological goal gained acceptance when the negative effects of mental disorders became clearer (Spokane, 1991). *Secondary treatment* means that existing disorders can be minimized by early identification and treatment. *Tertiary treatment* means providing interventions for fully developed disorders so that their effects and symptoms can be managed.

Albee (1982) suggested a competency model of mental disturbance instead of a mental illness model. Career counseling and life planning offer such a competency model. Table 14.3 delineates the threats to mental health described in this chapter and relates them to possible appropriateness or suitability of career interventions in mental health and private practice settings.

Assisting individuals to gain career competence through implementation of authentic career-related goals is a mental health modality—a primary treatment intervention. For example, those who have lost a job may experience feelings of sadness and despair. Many feel at least temporarily without hope. It is not unusual, and is even expected, that many will experience symptoms of loss and grieving. Providing the many interventions and techniques associated with career and life planning and assisting clients in performing activities necessary to a thorough job search may prevent some forms of depression and anxiety from reaching psychopathological levels. Thus, to provide interventions that lead to employment and career satisfaction is to address significant and important mental health areas. When

**TABLE 14.3  Typical Presenting Concerns of Clients in Mental Health and Private Practice Settings and Suitability of Career and Life Planning**

| Presenting Concern | Level of Career Treatment or Intervention | | |
| --- | --- | --- | --- |
| | Primary | Secondary | Tertiary |
| Severe Mental Disorders | | X | X |
| Personality Disorders | | X | X |
| Depressive Disorders | X | X | X |
| Anxiety Disorders | X | X | X |
| Substance-Related Disorders | | X | X |
| Job Loss Issues | X | X | |
| Occupational Stress Reactions | X | X | |

*Note:* Primary = career and lifestyle planning may prevent threats to mental health; secondary = career and lifestyle planning may moderate effects of existing mental health disorders and minimize severity of disorder through early identification and treatment of work–life issues; tertiary = career and lifestyle planning techniques may be possible and suitable in concert with mental health counseling for full developed disorder.

depression, anxiety, or other mental health issues exist, career counseling can ameliorate the severity of these threats through early identification and treatment of work–life issues.

For those with personality disorders, career counseling may be an appropriate secondary treatment objective. Because personality disorders are long-standing and enduring patterns of thoughts, behaviors, and emotional responses, they are less likely to be amenable to primary intervention. However, career and life planning techniques can assist these individuals so that the severity of their disorder may be minimized. For example, these clients can learn more effective ways of interacting in the world of work, or how to minimize the effects of their disorders through life skills training. Tertiary treatment may also be appropriate with individuals diagnosed with severe personality disorders.

People with schizophrenia, people with long-standing substance abuse disorders, and others with SMDs that keep them from functioning normally in society may benefit from career counseling at either a secondary or a tertiary level. Vocational counseling can be a secondary treatment intervention when it assists clients to maximize their potential through suitable work and may moderate the effects of some disorders early in identification and stages of some disorders. We mentioned earlier the importance of sheltered workshops for those who cannot work in more traditional settings. For these individuals, experiential programs that provide opportunities for practicing appropriate workplace behaviors offer a tertiary treatment intervention.

### SIDEBAR 14.5  Case Study: Goal Setting for Jane and Harvey

A critical aspect of effective treatment planning is goal setting. When appropriate goals are set, interventions and outcomes tend to flow naturally from them. Treatment for mental health disorders can be classified as primary, secondary, or tertiary. Each of these levels reflects a symptom-based treatment goal. Primary goals are set to keep symptoms from developing; secondary goals are set to keep symptoms from getting worse; and tertiary goals are set to manage the disorders associated with the symptoms. Career interventions can be used to develop treatment goals at each of these levels. Determine which level of treatment is appropriate for Jane and Harvey. Once you have determined the level of treatment (primary, secondary, tertiary) necessary to manage their symptoms, develop career-based goals, interventions, and outcomes that might aid in the necessary symptom management for them.

## Career and Life Planning for People With Mental Health Concerns

Career and life planning programs in mental health and private practice settings have much in common with standard programs offered by career counselors in more traditional settings. With clients who do not possess cognitive clarity, counselors should postpone addressing career concerns until cognitive clarity is attained (Brown & Brooks, 1991). The exceptions are those whose best career-related option is work in sheltered workshops. Individuals with SMD or those recovering from addictions to AODs are provided opportunities to work despite this lack of cognitive clarity. For others whose disorders do not require a supported work environment and for whom career and workplace concern are a legitimate area of treatment, career counseling looks very much as it does for clients without mental health problem. Mental health, of course, is always the treatment goal, and career counseling is the vehicle toward that goal. Individual career and mental health assessments are administered, interpreted, and integrated into overall diagnosis and treatment planning.

Hands-on experiential programs provide many mental health clients with opportunities to assess and reevaluate their current belief systems and self-concepts, to challenge outdated and dysfunctional values, and to reduce those beliefs and values that prevent progress toward a more fulfilling career and personal life. Some programs focus on challenges to mental health and provide clients with opportunities for emotional healing and growth. Clients can thus reevaluate their self-defeating behaviors and perceptions to gain an understanding of themselves as successful workers. They learn that, although their mental health problems are real, some barriers to success are self-imposed. They begin to clearly define and work toward achieving realistic long- and short-term goals and learn the decision-making process. Personal step-by-step action plans prepare clients to move toward their own, pragmatic self-defined goals.

Group work is useful for those who are ready to undertake career and life planning as part of their mental health treatment goals. Screened for suitability, members of these preestablished, closed groups serve as a support for each other as they make lifestyle changes and reinforce continued growth under the direction of the properly trained counselor. In the process, external and internal barriers to employment are identified. Where external goals are present, participants can be assisted with workplace modifications as mandated by the ADA. Most important, internal barriers are challenged. Examples of topics facilitated by the counselor include managing mental illness, developing and refining effective communication skills, understanding and using community resources, risk taking, goal setting, problem solving and decision making, learning about world-of-work information and resources, developing life skills, and ultimately practicing job search skills. Life skills training contributes to empowerment and self-sufficiency and may include stress management, time management, assertiveness training, education on AOD, work–life balance strategies, budgeting and financial management, self-esteem enhancement, and coping with transitions. Job skills training consists of employment counseling activities and may include résumé and job application preparation assistance, interview preparation sessions, dress-for-success workshops, practical world-of-work speakers, and when appropriate, field trips, informational interviewing, job shadowing, and referrals.

Job retention groups are effective for those who are currently employed or who begin employment during the course of their mental health treatment. Additional topics covered in these psychoeducational groups include employer expectations, work-related communications skills, sexual harassment and discrimination, customer service skills, conflict resolution skills, and many more.

Because the nature of mental illness may preclude some individuals from reaching the level of career achievement that others may accomplish, it is important to bear in mind that the definition of *career* includes not only work but all other life roles as well. Niles and Harris-Bowlsbey (2002) stated, "When work is lacking in personal satisfaction, other life roles may be useful in offsetting this lack of meaning and satisfaction" (p. 6). Attending to the place and significance of other life roles can assist these clients in living fuller, more meaningful lives even when the worker role is limited.

## Importance of Diversity Issues

Counselors should understand clients and their needs in context. Career and life planning interventions in private practice or community mental health settings must attend to issues of diversity. The National Career Development Association's (2008) *Minimum Competencies for Multicultural Career Counseling and Development* address the need for knowledge about and skills with diverse populations that affect career counseling and include the demonstrated ability to identify the developmental needs unique to populations with regard to gender, sexual orientation, ethnic group and race, and physical and mental capacity. Counselors must take these differences into account in each of the areas of mental health concern discussed earlier. The deleterious effects of racism on mental health are well documented. Institutional racism is an issue. For example, in 2008, only an estimated 21.9% of noninstitutionalized U.S. Blacks and African Americans with a cognitive disability, ages 18 to 64, were employed (Erickson, Lee, & von Schrader, 2010). Certainly, "institutional racism and the ripple effect of White privilege are so embedded in our society that many Whites are unaware of racism's existence and thus, its negative impact" (Bailey & Bradley-Bailey, 2010, p. 164).

The multicultural counseling movement has

> revolutionalized the ways that counselors have traditionally been trained to think about mental health, psychological disorders, and the types of helping strategies that result in positive counseling outcomes when working with persons from diverse cultural groups and backgrounds. (D'Andrea & Heckman, 2008, p. 259)

For those from nondominant cultures and minority groups, traditional career counseling, grounded as it is in the Eurocentric worldview, can be problematic. Career counselors must be trained in alternative methods. Byars-Winston and Fouad (2006) suggested incorporating metacognition processes to address counselor-related cultural factors. Chope and Consoli (2007) recommended narrative therapy as a tool useful in career decision making and planning with minority clients, and Toporek and Flamer (2009) viewed résumé writing as helpful in addressing barriers and increasing employability potential. These techniques could assist diverse populations with mental health needs as well. Consequently, multicultural and contextual factors, although beyond the scope of this chapter, must be incorporated into any treatment plan. Refer to Chapters 15 through 17 for additional information.

## Collaboration and Referral

Few counselors are skilled in offering services to all clients with all disorders. Consequently, counselors skilled in mental health issues as well as counselors skilled in career development issues must be willing to make appropriate referrals when their clients' concerns are beyond the scope of their own expertise and training. Their ethical codes demand it. (Ethical issues are discussed in detail in Chapter 4.)

Although it is true that career counselors need to broaden their conception of career counseling to consider their clients' mental health concerns and that they should become more aware of the relationship between mental health and employment conditions (Zunker, 2008), it is essential that they receive adequate training and credentialing to provide some mental health services. The same applies to mental health counselors with regard to career issues. Unless the professional counselor is skilled in both areas, he or she must cultivate relationships with colleagues in all the related helping professions and work collaboratively to offer a full range of necessary services to the betterment of clients. Clients deserve nothing less.

### SIDEBAR 14.6   Self-Awareness: Barriers to Working With Career Professionals

There are many different types of career counseling professionals who work in a variety of different settings, including licensed counselors with career counseling specializations, unlicensed career counselors, and career and life coaches. These professionals are not often found in community counseling or private practice settings, so mental health counselors must often work to find them. Additionally, many mental health professionals may have a bias against career interventions or career development professionals that may help to inhibit collaboration. Additionally, reimbursement practices for counseling services may also serve to negatively affect efforts to aid clients in accessing the services they need. How many barriers to collaboration can you think of? What can you personally do to overcome them? What can counseling associations do to help support collaboration among various types of counseling professionals?

## Summary

Decisions about work affect the totality of one's life. The need to assist individuals trying to effectively manage the influence of work in their lives is great (Niles & Harris-Bowlsbey, 2002). Career counseling interventions in mental health and private practice settings are similar to those services provided by career counselors in more conventional settings and include activities such as clarifying values, determining interests, imparting world-of-work information and resources, setting career goals, and providing coaching about how to achieve them. Counselors in mental health practice who offer these services do so in concert with the mental health services they provide and only when career-related needs arise as a focus of treatment.

In formulating career interventions, the counselor should keep in mind that vocational development is a normal developmental process. Those with mental health issues "have had significant physical, mental, or emotional barriers to normal development ... [and may] experience difficulty in choosing and implementing work that is satisfying and interesting to them" (Musgrove, 1992, p. 47). Consequently, counselors must strive to discover the factors that interfere with the normal process of career development. As mental health counseling progresses, clients can try new behaviors in the workplace if they are employed and risk fresh behaviors in the job search process if they are not. Both types of clients can benefit from implementation of a new self-concept, redefinition of workplace roles, and personal change management.

Mental illness and career development are not mutually exclusive and counselors in all settings must be aware that clients may need assistance in both parts of their lives, either through referral or through the interventions of the counselor trained and experienced in both domains. Professional counseling is one profession with many subspecialties. Mental health counseling and career counseling are complementary specialties that, when practiced together, offer many clients fuller opportunities for positive change and life satisfaction. The Web sites listed in the next section provide additional information relating to the chapter topics.

## Useful Web Sites

- Partnership for Workplace Mental Health, a program of the American Psychiatric Foundation (under APA), provides topics on mental health issues, resources, surveys, and a subscription link to their magazine, *Mental Health Works*: http://www.workplacementalhealth.org
- The Anxiety Disorders Association promotes the early diagnosis, treatment and cure of anxiety disorders: http://www.adda.org
- The International Foundation for Research and Education on Depression offers information and promotes diagnosis, treatment, and management of depressive disorders: http://www.ifred.org/
- The Job Stress Network Web site offers public dissemination of information about and related to job strain and work stress: http://www.workhealth.org
- The National Institute of Mental Health is the lead federal agency for research on mental and behavioral disorders: http://www.nimh.nih.gov
- The National Mental Health Association is the country's oldest and largest nonprofit organization addressing all aspects of mental health and mental illness through advocacy, education, research, and service: http://www.nmha.org
- The purpose of the National Alliance on Mental Illness is the eradication of mental illnesses and the improvement in the quality of life of all whose lives are affected by these diseases. It offers articles and links to related sites: http://www.nami.org
- The Substance Abuse and Mental Health Services Administration is part of the National Mental Health Information Center; it provides information about mental health: http://www.mentalhealth.samhsa.gov

- Mental Health America is the country's leading nonprofit dedicated to helping all people live mentally healthier lives: http://www.nmha.org
- Mental Health Matters supplies information and resources to mental health consumers, professionals, and students and provides links to other related sites: http://www.mental-health-matters.com

## References

Albee, G. W. (1982). Preventive psychopathology and promoting human potential. *American Psychologist, 37,* 1043–1050.

American Psychiatric Association. (2000). *Diagnostic and statistical manual of mental disorders* (4th ed., text rev.). Washington, DC: Author.

Americans With Disabilities Act of 1990, Pub. L. 101–336, 42 U.S.C. § 12101.

Axelrod, S. D. (1999). *Work and the evolving self: Theoretical and clinical considerations.* Hillsdale, NJ: Analytic Press.

Bailey, D. F., & Bradley-Bailey, M. (2010). Promoting the self-esteem of adolescent African American males. In M. Guindon (Ed.), *Self-esteem across the lifespan: Issues and intervention* (pp. 159–172). New York, NY: Routledge.

Bordin, E. S. (1986). The effectiveness of psychotherapy: An introduction. *American Journal of Orthopsychiatry, 56,* 500.

Borgen, W. E., & Amundson, N. E. (1987). The dynamics of unemployment. *Journal of Counseling & Development, 66,* 180–184.

Brenner, M. H. (1973). *Mental illness and the economy.* Cambridge, MA: Harvard University Press.

Brown, D., & Brooks, L. (1991). *Career counseling techniques.* Boston, MA: Allyn & Bacon.

Bruch, M. A., Fallon, M., & Heimberg, R. G. (2003). Social phobia and difficulties in occupational adjustment. *Journal of Counseling Psychology, 48,* 109–117.

Bullock, E., Braud, J., Lindsay, A., & Phillips, J. (2009). Career concerns of unemployed U.S. war veterans: Suggestions from a cognitive information processing approach. *Journal of Employment Counseling, 46,* 171–181.

Bureau of Labor Statistics. (2010). *Employment situation summary.* Retrieved from http://www.bls.gov/news.release/empsit.nr0.htm

Byars-Winston, A. M., & Fouad, N. A. (2006). Metacognition and multicultural competence: Expanding the culturally appropriate career counseling model. *Career Development Quarterly, 54,* 187.

Campbell, R. E., & Cellini, J. V. (1981). A diagnostic taxonomy of adult career problems. *Journal of Vocational Behavior, 19,* 178–180.

Caplan, R. D., Cobb, S., French, J. R. P., Jr., Harrison, R. V., & Pinneau, S. R., Jr. (1975). *Job demands and worker health: Main effects and occupational differences.* Washington, DC: U.S. Government Printing Office.

Caporoso, R. A., & Kiselica, M. S. (2004). Career counseling with clients who have a severe mental illness. *Career Development Quarterly, 52,* 235–245.

Center for Substance Abuse Treatment. (2000). *Changing the conversation: Improving substance abuse treatment: The national treatment plan initiative* (Vol. 1). Rockville, MD: Author.

Chope, R. C., & Consoli, A. J. (2007). A narrative approach to multicultural career counseling. *Vistas 2007 Online.* Retrieved from http://counselingoutfitters.com/vistas/vistas07/Chope.htm

Cormier, S., Nurius, P., & Osborn, C. (2008). *Interviewing and change strategies for helpers: Fundamental skills and cognitive behavioral interventions* (6th ed.). Pacific Grove, CA: Brooks/Cole.

Crites, J. O. (1969). *Vocational psychology.* New York, NY: McGraw-Hill.

Crites, J. O. (1981). *Career counseling: Models, methods, and materials.* New York: McGraw-Hill.

D'Andrea, M., & Heckman, E. F. (2008). Contributing to the ongoing evolution of the multicultural counseling movement: An introduction to the special issue. *Journal of Counseling & Development, 86,* 259–260.

Erickson, W., Lee, C., & von Schrader, S. (2010). *Disability statistics from the 2008 American Community Survey (ACS).* Ithaca, NY: Cornell University Rehabilitation Research and Training Center on Disability Demographics and Statistics. Retrieved from http://www.ilr.cornell.edu/edi/disabilitystatistics/reports/report.cfm?fips=2042000

Fabian, E. (1999). Rethinking work: The example of consumers with serious mental health disorders. *Rehabilitation Counseling Bulletin, 42,* 302–317.

Greenberg, P. E., Stiglin, L. E., Finkelstein, S. N., & Berndt, E. R. (1993). Depression: A neglected major illness. *Journal of Clinical Psychiatry, 54,* 419–424.

Guindon, M. H. (2010) What is self-esteem? In M. H. Guindon (Ed.), *Self-esteem across the lifespan: Issues and intervention* (pp. 3–24), New York, NY: Routledge.

Guindon, M. H., & Smith, B. (2002). Emotional barriers to successful reemployment: Implications for counselors. *Journal of Employment Counseling, 39,* 73–82.

Hagner, D., Cheney, D., & Malloy, J. (1999). Career-related outcomes of a model transition demonstration for young adults with emotional disturbance. *Rehabilitation Counseling Bulletin, 42,* 228–242.

Hanisch, K. A. (1999). Job loss and unemployment research from 1994–1998: A review and recommendations for research and intervention. *Journal of Vocational Behavior, 55,* 188–220.

Herlihy, B., & Watson, Z. E. P. (2010). Self-esteem of African-American adolescent girls. In M. Guindon (Ed.), *Self-esteem across the lifespan: Issues and interventions* (pp. 173–185). New York, NY: Routledge.

Herr, E. L. (1989). Career development and mental health. *Journal of Career Development, 16,* 5–18.

Herr, E. L. (1992). Types of career counseling practices. In A. A. Hafer (Ed.), *The nuts and bolts of career counseling: How to set up and succeed in private practice* (pp. 23–32). Garrett Park, MD: Garrett Park Press.

Herr, E. L., Cramer, S. H., & Niles, G (2003). *Career guidance and counseling through the lifespan: Systematic approaches* (6th ed.). New York, NY: HarperCollins.

Hohenshil, T. (1995). Editorial: Role of assessment and diagnosis in counseling. *Journal of Counseling & Development, 75,* 64–67.

Holland, J. L. (1973). *Making vocational choices: A theory of careers.* Englewood Cliffs, NJ: Prentice-Hall.

Holland, J. L. (1994). *Self-Directed Search.* Odessa, FL: Psychological Assessment Resources.

Kjos, D. (1995). Linking career counseling to personality disorders. *Journal of Counseling & Development, 73,* 592–597.

Kübler-Ross, E. (1969). *On death and dying.* New York: Macmillan.

Kyle, M. T., & Persinger, S. (2000). Chronic mental illness and work: An integrated vocational life-planning model. In N. Peterson & R. C. Gonzalez (Eds.), *Career counseling models for diverse populations: Hands-on applications by practitioners* (pp. 197–204). Belmont, CA: Brooks/Cole.

Lewis, J. (2001). Career and personal counseling: Comparing process and outcome. *Journal of Employment Counseling, 38,* 82–90.

Lewis, J. A., Dana, R. Q., & Blevins, G. A. (2010). *Substance abuse counseling* (4th ed.). Pacific Grove, CA: Brooks/Cole.

Liem, R., & Liem, J. H. (1996). Mental health and unemployment: The making and unmaking of psychological casualties. In M. B. Lykes, A. Banuazizi, R. Liem, & M. Morris (Eds.), *Myths about the powerless: Contesting social inequalities* (pp. 105–127). Philadelphia, PA: Temple University Press.

Loughead, T. A., & Black, D. R. (1990). Selection criteria for a career development program for the mentally ill: Evaluation of the Self-Directed Search (SDS). *Journal of Counseling & Development, 68,* 324–326.

Lowman, R. L. (1993). *Counseling and psychotherapy of work dysfunctions.* Washington, DC: American Psychological Association.

Malen, E. A., & Stroh, L. K. (1998). The influence of gender on job loss coping behavior among unemployed managers. *Journal of Employment Counseling, 35,* 26–39.

McAuliffe, G. (1993). Career as imaginative quest. *American Counselor, 2,* 12–16, 36.

Millon, T., & Everly, G. S. (1985). *Personality and its disorders: A biosocial learning approach.* New York, NY: Wiley.

Musgrove, M. (1992). Psychological aspects of career counseling. In A. A. Hafer (Ed.), *The nuts and bolts of career counseling: How to set up & succeed in private practice* (pp. 45–52). Garrett Park, MD: Garrett Park Press.

National Alliance on Mental Illness (n.d.). Data snapshot from Triad: Employment. Retrieved from http://www.nami.org/Content/NavigationMenu/Inform_Yourself/About_Public_Policy/Policy_Research_Institute/TRIAD/TRIAD_Data_Snapshot_Employment.htm

National Career Development Association. (2008). *Minimum competencies for multicultural career counseling and development.* Alexandria, VA: Author.

National Institute of Mental Health (n.d. a). *Statistics: any mood Disorders among adults.* Retrieved from http://www.nimh.hih.gov/statistics/1ANYMOODDIS_ADULT.shtml

National Institute of Mental Health (n.d. b). *Statistics: Dysthymic disorders among adults.* Retrieved from http://www.nimh.hih.gov/statistics/1DD_ADULT.shtml

National Institute of Mental Health (n.d. c). *Statistics: Social phobia among adults.* Retrieved from http://www.nimh.hih.gov/statistics

National Institute of Mental Health (n.d. d). *Statistics: Post-traumatic stress disorder among adults.* Retrieved from http://www.nimh.hih.gov/statistics/1AD_PTSD_ADULT.shtml

National Institute on Alcohol Abuse and Alcoholism. (2010). Mental and physical health. Retrieved from http://www.niaaa.nih.gov/Resources/DatabaseResources/QuickFacts/MentalPhysicalHealth/Pages/default.aspx

Nelson, D. L., & Hitt, M. A. (1992). Employed women and stress: Implications for enhancing women's mental health in the workplace. In J. C. Quick, L. R. Murphy, & Hurrell, J. J., Jr. (Eds.), *Stress and well-being at work* (pp. 164–177). Washington, DC: American Psychological Association.

Niles, S. G., Anderson, W. P., Jr., & Cover, S. (2000). Comparing intake concerns and goals with career counseling concerns. *Career Development Quarterly, 49,* 135–145.

Niles, S. G., & Harris-Bowlsbey, J. (2002). *Career development interventions in the 21st century.* Upper Saddle River, NJ: Prentice Hall.

Osborn, D. S., & Zunker, V. G. (2005). *Using assessment results for career development* (7th ed.). Pacific Grove, CA: Brooks/Cole.

Osipow, S. H. (2004). *Theories of career development* (4th ed.). Englewood Cliffs: NJ: Prentice-Hall.

Parmer, T., & Rush, L. C. (2003). The next decade in career counseling: Cocoon maintenance or metamorphosis? *Career Development Quarterly, 52,* 26–34.

Rosenberg, A., Ledley, D. R., & Heimberg, R. G. (2010). Social anxiety disorder. In D. McKay, J. S. Abramowitz, & S. Taylor (Eds.), *Cognitive–behavioral therapy for refractory cases: Turning failure into success* (pp. 65–88). Washington, DC: American Psychological Association.

Rottinghaus, P. J., & Van Esbroeck, R. (2011). Improving person–environment fit and self-knowledge. In P. J. Hartung & L. M. Subich (Eds.), *Developing self in work and career: Concepts, cases, and contests* (pp. 35–52). Washington, DC: American Psychological Association.

Saunders, D. E., Peterson, G. W., Sampson, J. P., & Reardon, R. C. (2000). Relation of depression and dysfunctional career thinking to career indecision. *Journal of Vocational Behavior, 56,* 288–298.

Selye, H. (1956). *The stress of life.* New York, NY: McGraw-Hill.

Smith, R. L. (1989). Work and mental health: Stress as a major factor. In D. Brown & C. W. Minor (Eds.), *Working in America: A status report on planning and problems* (pp. 82–96). Alexandria, VA: National Career Development Association.

Sperry, L. (1995). *Handbook of diagnosis and treatment of the DSM-IV personality disorders.* New York: Brunner/Mazel.

Spokane, A. R. (1991). *Career intervention.* Englewood Cliffs, NJ: Prentice-Hall.

Stone, M. (1993). *Abnormalities of personality: Within and beyond the realm of treatment.* New York, NY: Norton.

Substance Abuse and Mental Health Services Administration. (2003). *Strategies for developing treatment programs for people with co-occurring substance abuse and mental disorders* (SAMHSA Publication No. 3782). Rockville, MD: Author.

Super, D. E. (1980). A life-span, life-space approach to career development. *Journal of Vocational Behavior, 16,* 282–298.

Super, D. E, Starishevsky, R., Matlin, N., & Jordan, J. P. (1963). *Career development: Self-concept theory.* New York, NY: College Entrance Examination Board.

Szymanski, E. M., & Hershenson, D. B. (2004). Career development of people with disabilities: An ecological model. In R. M. Parker & E. M. Szymanski (Eds.), *Rehabilitation counseling: Basics and beyond* (4th ed., pp. 327–278). Austin, TX: Pro-Ed.

Szymanski, E. M., & Vancollins, J. (2003). Career development of people with disabilities: Some new and not-so-new challenges. *Australian Journal of Career Development, 12,* 9–16.

Taube, C. A., Burns, B. J., & Kessler, L. (1984). Patients of psychiatrists and psychologists in office-bound practices: 1980. *American Psychologist, 39,* 1435–1447.

Toporek, R. L., & Flamer, C. (2009). The résumé's secret identity: A tool for narrative exploration in multicultural career counseling. *Journal of Employment Counseling, 46,* 4–17.

Uthayakumar, R., Schimnack, U., Hartung, P., & Rogers, J. (2010). Career decidedness as a predictor of subjective well-being. *Journal of Vocational Behavior, 77,* 196–204.

Vetzner, S., & Lodato, L. (2009). Economic downturn taking toll on Americans' mental health. In Mental Health America. Retrieved from http://nmha.org/index.cfm?objectid=2A7E7943-1372-4D20-C8B93 FIEE)6C70A

Waters, L. E., & Moore, K. A. (2002). Reducing latent deprivation during unemployment: The role of meaningful leisure activity. *Journal of Occupational and Organizational Psychology, 75,* 15–32.

Zunker, V. G. (2008). *Career, work, and mental health: Integrating career and personal counseling.* Thousand Oaks, CA: Sage.

CHAPTER **15**

# Career and Lifestyle Planning in Vocational Rehabilitation Settings

Mark D. Stauffer, David Capuzzi, and Jerry A. Olsheski

## Contents

One of the core values of U.S. society is that everyone has the right to work. For individuals with disabilities, however, this value has been more of a dream than a reality. Individuals with disabilities have substantially higher unemployment rates than those who are not disabled. According to the President's Committee on the Employment of People With Disabilities (1992), 31% of people with disabilities were employed or actively seeking employment, whereas more than 78% of Americans without disabilities worked or were actively seeking work (Kaye, 2010). The lack of participation of people with disabilities in the world of work is of major concern to society because the human and financial costs associated with disability continue to escalate. This concern is not new; it was expressed in the congressional findings contained in the Workforce Investment Act of 1998 (Elinson, Frey, Li, Palan, & Horne, 2008). Congress concluded that people with disabilities, as a group, experience very high rates of unemployment and that reasons for this chronic unemployment include discrimination, lack of accessible and available transportation, fear of losing health care benefits under Medicaid or Medicare, and a lack of education, training, and supports to secure, retain, or advance in employment (Andrew, 2000; Gervey, Ni, Tillman, Dickel, & Kneubuehl, 2009).

SIDEBAR 15.1   Employment and Representation

A growing body of research has substantiated the fact that people with disabilities continue to be over-represented in lower-paid service jobs. In addition, they are underrepresented in better-paid managerial, leadership, and professional positions. Can you identify some reasons why these circumstances exist?

Vocational adjustment is a complex process that involves the interaction of the individual's physical, educational, academic, psychosocial, and cultural traits with the physical, social, and cultural dimensions of the work environment. The presence of a disability complicates the interactive relationship of these important work adjustment components (Szymanski & Parker, 2003). The disabling condition may result in functional limitations that hinder the person's ability to perform job tasks or restrict his or her exposure to specific types of work settings. A number of environmental barriers—for example, discrimination—can restrict and undermine career development and vocational functioning. The negative stereotype of the person with a disability in the employment community has been well documented (Bordieri, Drehmer, & Comninel, 1988; Hallock, Hendricks, & Broadbent, 1998; Nordstrom, Huffaker, & Williams, 1998). Some of the stereotypical beliefs regarding employers' attitudes toward hiring people with disabilities include anticipation of high accommodation costs, difficulty in supervising and communicating with the employee, problem behavior, poor attendance, low productivity, and problems with coworker acceptance (Blessing & Jamieson, 1999; B. Lee & Newman, 1995).

People with disabilities have unique career needs and face challenges in securing and maintaining employment. Interventions must not only address personal issues but also be sensitive to the contextual and environmental factors that affect the person's career development and opportunities for employment.

In this chapter, we present information that may be useful in providing career and life planning services to people with physical disabilities, including information on career development issues for people with disabilities; the use of functional capacity and job analysis information in vocational planning and job accommodation; the impact of the Americans With Disabilities Act of 1990 on the employment of people with disabilities; and vocational rehabilitation services that may be useful in facilitating career development and employment of people with disabilities.

## Career Development and Disability
### Relevancy of Career Theory to People With Disabilities

Because *disability* is often defined in U.S. society as the inability to work, it is of little surprise that career development researchers have largely ignored the career and vocational needs of people with disabilities. Consequently, the relevancy of mainstream career development theory and research to the career development issues that are typically experienced by people with disabilities and other minority groups has been questioned (Gysbers,

Heppner, & Johnston, 2003; Hershenson, 2005; Lent, Brown, & Hackett, 2000; Syzmanski, Enright, Hershenson, & Ettinger, 2003). Osipow (1976) noted that people with disabilities have largely been omitted from career research because most of the participants in this research are middle-class White men. The systematic, linear model of career development that emerged from this type of class-biased research was based on the assumption of freedom of choice in career decisions, and little attention was given to the role that contextual and environmental factors play in hindering or restricting career development. Consequently, these theories were not relevant to people with disabilities whose career and vocational experiences were more often characterized by discontinuous development, constricted choices, limited employment opportunities, chronic unemployment, and a variety of contextual and environmental barriers to career development (Szymanski et al., 2003). Conte (1983) and Curnow (1989) concluded that many theories are insensitive to the unique career development issues faced by people with disabilities. They noted that people with disabilities often have experiences related to their career development that people without disabilities do not encounter. Disability may limit the individual's early vocational development, restrict vocational exploration, and hinder the development of career decision-making skills and a positive self-concept (Winn & Hay, 2009).

### SIDEBAR 15.2   Career Development Question

It is interesting to note that during recent years, a number of calls have been made for research on the impact of disability on the early career development of youth. This call has resulted in increased awareness on the part of school faculty, staff, and administrators of the importance of facilitating a more positive transition from high school to postschool-related career opportunities. Given the information you read in Chapter 2 about career development theories, what do you think might be different about the career development of a young person with a disability in comparison to a youth of the same age without a disability?

Szymanksi and Trueba (1994) cautioned that most theories incorporate the basic trait and factor philosophy of matching people to jobs. This mechanical matching may result in a type of "castification" of minority groups in which people are relegated to stereotyped occupations because of their membership in a particular group, for example, matching the functional limitations of people with disabilities to certain stereotypical occupations.

## More Appropriate Models for Individuals With Disabilities

More recently, alternative models of career theory and research have emerged that recognize the unique career development experiences of women and other minority groups. These models are more ecologically sensitive and consider the effects of cultural or environmental factors on career development as well as the impact of bias and discrimination (Arbona, 1996; Beveridge, Heller Craddock, Liesener, Stapleton, & Hershenson, 2002; Gysbers et al., 2003; Hershenson, 1996, 2005; Lent et al., 2000; Szymanski et al., 2003).

### Hershenson's Theory

Hershenson (1996) developed a model of work adjustment that is useful in understanding career development issues of people with disabilities. He emphasized the developmental nature of work adjustment and identified the personal and environmental components of work adjustment that dynamically interact in the developmental process. The personal domains of work adjustment include work personality, work competencies, and appropriate work goals. These domains develop sequentially within the person, and each domain is influenced by a specific formative environment. The first domain to develop is the work personality. The work personality includes two components: the person's self-concept as a worker and the person's system of work motivation. The work personality develops during the preschool years when the family is the primary environmental influence. The second domain involves the development of work competencies. Work competencies include work habits, physical and mental skills used in jobs, and interpersonal skills required in the work setting. Work competencies develop during the school years and are mainly influenced by both positive and negative experiences in meeting the demands of the school environment (Szymanski et al., 2003). The last domain to develop is appropriate work goals. This domain, which is developed as the person prepares to make the transition from school to work, is mostly influenced by the individual's peer or reference group.

In the sequential development of the work adjustment domains, each domain is influenced by the others. The domains that emerge earlier in the developmental process influence the level of development achieved in the domains that subsequently emerge. Thus, a negative self-concept (work personality domain) may hinder success in school (work competency domain). There is also a reciprocal relationship among the domains, and subsequent domains may influence those that developed earlier. For example, success in school (work competency domain) may result in the modification of a negative self-concept (work personality domain) that developed in a dysfunctional family environment (Szymanski et al., 2003).

Work personality, work competencies, and appropriate work goals continue to develop over the individual's life span and establish a dynamic balance so that changes in one domain effect changes in the others (Hershenson, 1996). Individuals achieve positive work adjustment by fulfilling the task performance requirements of the job (work competency), maintaining appropriate behavior in the workplace (work personality), and feeling a sense of satisfaction or gratification from one's work (appropriate work goals). Disability may limit the development of the work adjustment domains and disrupt the balance among them. The effect of disability in the early years of development may restrict the development of the work personality as the result of exposure to a nonsupportive family environment. Likewise, the onset of disability in mid-career may affect the person's work competencies and necessitate a reevaluation of work goals. Hershenson (1981) observed that disability typically affects the work competency domain of work adjustment by imposing functional limitations that restrict the person's physical or mental abilities. The changes in work competencies may spread to the work personality (i.e., self-concept, motivation to work), and vocational goals may no longer be appropriate. The degree of spread to the other domains depends on the level of development of the domains and the degree to which the disability disrupts the compatibility between the person and his or her current or planned occupation.

Counselors may find Hershenson's (1996) model useful in guiding assessments and designing interventions to serve the career needs of the person with a disability. Problems with the development of the work personality may require an assessment of the individual's career maturity (Crites, 1978) or interventions that promote the development of appropriate work behaviors and skills. Specific vocational rehabilitation services such as work adjustment programs, vocational evaluation, and supported employment may be useful interventions in addressing problems related to the development of the work personality. A need to provide interventions to enhance work competencies may also exist. Vocational and academic training programs, physical conditioning, and other services that strengthen the physical, cognitive, and psychological abilities of the individual to perform work may be appropriate. In addition to providing a framework to conceptualize the personal components of work adjustment, Hershenson's model allows for the analysis of potential environmental factors that may pose barriers to work adjustment and career development. Interventions may be designed to modify the various environments of the work adjustment domains. Examples of these types of interventions include family counseling (family environment), special education interventions (school environment), and modifications to the work setting (peer group and coworker environment). Hershenson's model of work adjustment is outlined here:

| Personal Domain | Domain Elements | Work Adjustment Behaviors | Primary Environment |
|---|---|---|---|
| Work Personality | • Self-concept<br>• Motivation<br>• Needs and values | Work-role behaviors | • Preschool<br>• Family |
| Work Competencies | • Work habits<br>• Physical and mental skills | Task performance | School education |
| Appropriate Work Goals | | Work satisfaction | Peer groups |

More recently, Hershenson (2005) has been exploring how the INCOME model, first proposed by Helms in 1995, enabled researchers, and ultimately the career counselor, to integrate constructs from a variety of career development theories into their approach to counseling diverse clients (including clients with disabilities). Helms (1995) posited the concept of statuses, or dynamic processes, through which an individual's career behavior can be understood. The INCOME model includes five statuses—imagining, informing, choosing, obtaining, maintaining, and exiting. Imagining is the status that involves awareness that jobs or occupations exist about which the individual was not formerly aware. Informing involves the individual's understanding of aptitudes, abilities, interests, limitations, and so forth connected with a job or occupation. Choosing, the third status in the framework, is that in which the individual is able to integrate information about self and the world of work. In the obtaining status, the individual seeks and obtains a position. This status is followed by the maintaining status, in which the individual maintains or adapts to and performs in an occupation or job well enough to sustain that particular job. Finally, the exiting status has to do with the individual thinking about or actually leaving a job situation.

In applying the INCOME model, the counselor must first ascertain the status in which the client is engaged and in which of these statuses the problem is located (it is possible for a client to be experiencing simultaneous problems in more than one status). After status is determined, the counselor can apply interventions to assist the client with issues connected to a particular status. For example, if a client is experiencing a high level of stress because he or she is considering exiting a position and applying for a new position, the counselor may first need to teach the client some stress management skills before the client develops the confidence to do a job search and actually accept a position that is somewhat different from the position being exited. The INCOME model is not intended to become a comprehensive career development theory but to integrate numerous theories and interventions in a way that facilitates the career development of clients.

### Ecological Model of Vocational Behavior

Szymanski and Hershenson (1998; Szymanski et al., 2003) incorporated Hershenson's (2005) developmental model of work adjustment as well as the theories developed by Lent and Hackett (1994) and Fitzgerald and Betz (1994) in their ecological model of vocational behavior. This model is composed of five constructs and six processes. Career development is organized around common theoretical constructs organized into five interrelated groups: individual, context, mediating, environment, and outcome. The model also contains six processes that affect the interaction among the constructs: development, decision making, socialization, allocation, congruence, chance, and labor market forces. Particular attention is given to the influence of disability and other minority group factors that influence the interactions of concepts and processes.

Individual constructs include the physical and psychological traits of the person. Factors such as race, gender, values, interests, needs, and limitations are classified as individual constructs. The personal, not social, aspects of disability are also viewed as individual constructs. Context constructs include factors that are external to the person such as socioeconomic status, family, and educational opportunities, as well as non-normative influences such as natural disasters, war, and relevant legislation. Mediating constructs describe individual, cultural, and social beliefs that affect the interaction of people with their environments. Individual mediating constructs include personal beliefs about abilities, self-efficacy, self-concept, adjustment to disability, and work personality. Cultural mediating constructs consist of beliefs that are influenced by the individual's larger cultural group. These cultural beliefs influence how the person perceives and acts on his or her environment. Examples of these beliefs include a person's worldview, racial and ethnic identity, religious orientation, and minority group status (e.g., deaf culture, disability rights advocacy). Social mediating constructs describe the societal belief structures that influence the interaction of the person and environment. These beliefs include stereotypes, discrimination, marginalization of certain groups, and attitudes toward people with disabilities.

Environmental constructs describe characteristics of the work environment. These characteristics include task requirements, organizational factors, interpersonal requirements, and issues concerning disability-related access and accommodation. Outcome constructs refer to the product of the interaction among the other construct groups and processes. These outcomes may include a positive work adjustment characterized by job satisfaction, tenure, productivity, and competitiveness or negative outcomes including chronic unemployment, underemployment, job dissatisfaction, and termination.

The processes of the ecological model of vocational behavior are used to describe factors that influence the interaction among the construct groups. These processes include congruence (the degree of fit between the person and environment); development (systematic changes in the person over time); decision making (the person's ability to process information and make career decisions); socialization (how people learn about work and life roles); allocation (how societal gatekeepers such as parents, teachers, and employers direct individuals toward or away from specific career directions); chance (unforeseen events or encounters); and labor market forces (health of the economy, technological changes, changing corporate structures).

According to the ecological model, career development is viewed as the interaction of the individual, mediating, contextual, environment, and outcome concepts with the processes of congruence, decision making, development, socialization, allocation, chance, and labor market forces (Szymanski et al., 2003). The ecological model is useful in conceptualizing the career development process for people with disabilities. Assessment questions and interventions may be organized around the constructs or the processes of the model that serves as a framework for analyzing individual, contextual, and environmental factors that influence career development. For example, it may be necessary to evaluate the work skills and functional capacities of the client with a disability and to provide additional vocational training or physical conditioning to enhance these individual traits. Evaluating an individual's skills and providing vocational training are illustrations of possible client assessments and interventions that are related to the individual construct.

Individuals with disabilities may also face a number of contextual and environmental issues that limit their career development, and the ecological model is useful in guiding both assessments and interventions that are designed to remove or minimize these types of barriers. From a contextual standpoint, it may be important to assess the influence of the family and socialization processes on the person's perceptions of career opportunities and use such interventions as exposure to role models or mentors and participation in supported employment experiences to overcome contextual barriers. Evaluating the need for job accommodations and implementing job modifications are examples of assessment and intervention methods related to the environmental construct. It may also be appropriate to evaluate the impact of such mediating factors as discrimination and stereotyping the person with a disability may experience in the career development process and world of work.

The applicability of career development theories to people with disabilities remains a concern. However, more recently developed approaches, such as the ones discussed earlier, provide models that are sensitive to the unique developmental, contextual, individual, and environmental experiences of individuals with disabilities. These ecologically oriented approaches provide a conceptual framework that is useful for evaluating the impact of disability on career development and for designing interventions aimed at removing individual and environmental barriers to the developmental process. Components of the ecological model of vocational behavior are outlined in Table 15.1.

### SIDEBAR 15.3   An Auto Accident Case

Your 22-year-old male client was recently involved in an accident such that he must use a wheelchair most of the time. Although he is able to stand for limited periods of time with the support of crutches, he cannot take more than one or two steps at a time without extreme effort and pain. Before the accident, the client was actively involved in home remodeling and design and carried out the renovations himself. He is licensed by the state licensing board as an architect and builder and has a degree from a local community college. Using either the INCOME model or the ecological model, discuss how you might begin assisting this client.

## Implications of the Americans With Disabilities Act

As with other minority groups, people with disabilities face discrimination and limited participation in many aspects of social life, particularly the world of work (Wilson-Kovacs, Ryan, Haslam, & Rabinovich, 2008). In the 1960s, civil rights legislation was passed to protect women and racial and ethnic minority groups. Although previous legislation such as the Rehabilitation Act of 1973 afforded civil rights protection for people with disabilities, this protection was limited in the private sector to employers who had contracts with the federal government and public agencies that were recipients of federal funds. Not until 1990 was civil rights protection extended to essentially all of the private sector and state and local governments, regardless of their status as either federal

**TABLE 15.1 Ecological Model of Vocational Behavior**

| Construct | Construct Component | Process |
|---|---|---|
| **Context** | Socioeconomic status<br>Family<br>Education<br>Non-normative events | Development |
| **Individual** | Gender<br>Race<br>Physical and mental abilities<br>Impairments | Decision making<br>Congruence |
| | Individual<br>• Work personality<br>• Self-efficacy<br>• Outcome expectations<br>• Adjustment to disability<br>• Career maturity | Socialization |
| | Cultural<br>• Beliefs and values<br>• Acculturation<br>• Racial identity | Allocation |
| | Societal<br>• Discrimination<br>• Prejudice<br>• Stereotypes<br>• Castification | |
| **Environment** | Organizational culture<br>Task requirements<br>Reinforcement systems<br>Physical structure | Labor market forces<br>Chance |
| **Outcome** | Job satisfaction<br>Satisfactoriness<br>Job stress<br>Occupational attainment<br>Productivity<br>Competitiveness | |

contractors or fund recipients, when the ADA was passed. Just as women and members of racial and ethnic minority groups advocated for laws to protect their civil rights, people with disabilities began to perceive themselves as members of a marginalized minority group in U.S. society (Fabian, Ethridge, & Beveridge, 2009). As noted in the congressional data gathered to document the need for disability-related civil rights legislation, people with disabilities, as a group, occupy an inferior status in U.S. society and are severely disadvantaged socially, vocationally, economically, and educationally (see Rubin & Roessler, 1995). The passage of the ADA was viewed as a major victory in the long-fought battle of the disability rights movement and the advocacy organizations representing people with disabilities. Because of the discrimination that people with disabilities face in the workplace, it is important for career counselors to have a basic understanding of the ADA.

## Five Titles of the Americans With Disabilities Act

The ADA (1990) contains five separate titles that guarantee equal access to employment, public accommodations, transportation, state and local government resources, and communication services. The enforcement provisions of the ADA are the same as those used to enforce Title VII of the Civil Rights Act of 1964 (Montgomery, 1996). The Equal Employment Opportunity Commission (EEOC) is the agency that receives and investigates allegations of discrimination. If unlawful discrimination occurs, possible relief may include reinstatement to a job, accommodations, compensatory damages, payment of legal fees, and punitive damages.

The basic provisions contained in the five titles of the ADA are described here:

1. Title I prohibits discrimination in access to employment. This section of the law applies to private sector employers, unions, employment agencies, and all government bodies, with the exception of the federal government, who employ 15 or more employees for 20 or more calendar weeks during a calendar year. Because Title I pertains to employment rights, we discuss it in further detail later.
2. Title II prohibits discrimination by any public entity in providing public services, including transportation, to individuals with disabilities. Public entities include agencies, special-purpose districts, departments, and other instrumentalities of state and local government.
3. Title III prohibits discrimination on the basis of disability in places of public accommodation, which includes such places as restaurants, lodging facilities, places of exhibition or entertainment, places of public gathering, retail establishments, educational institutions, and places of commerce.
4. Title IV contains the telecommunication provisions that require common carriers of wire or radio communications to provide accommodations such as telephone operator relay services for individuals with hearing and speech impairments.
5. Title V contains miscellaneous provisions of the act, such as prohibiting retaliation against an individual who takes action to exercise his or her rights under the ADA and the relationship of the ADA to other federal and state laws.

### SIDEBAR 15.4 What Would You Do?

Have you ever witnessed an individual with a disability face discrimination? If so, what was the nature of the discrimination, and do you think it was connected with any of the five titles of the ADA? If this happened to one of your career counseling clients, what would you do? What would be the rationale for your actions?

The five titles of ADA provide a comprehensive safeguard for protecting the civil rights of individuals with the most severe disabilities. On January 1, 2009, the ADA Amendments Act of 2008 went into effect, thus changing some important key definitions related to disability. It shifted the general emphasis from a burden on the individual to prove disability to the act of discrimination itself. People with disabilities, disability advocates, and lawmakers pushed passage of the ADA Amendments Act by means of social advocacy on several critical points, but mostly that the term *disability* was too strictly defined as a result of U.S. Supreme Court rulings and other legal precedence, thus limiting the rights of individuals.

According to the ADA, an *individual with a disability* is defined as someone who has a physical or mental impairment that substantially limits one or more major life activities. *Major life activities* include walking, seeing, speaking, breathing, hearing, thinking, performing manual tasks, learning, caring for oneself, and working and were expanded by the ADA Amendments Act to include other items such as reading, bending, communicating, and so forth (EEOC, 2009b). Individuals may also be protected by the ADA if they have a record of some disability, for example, they are in recovery for alcoholism, or if they are regarded as having a disability even though it is not functionally limiting in nature, for example, facial disfigurement. Title I of ADA, which prohibits discrimination in the workplace, is of particular importance in career service programs that serve people with disabilities. Title I is discussed in more detail in the next section.

### Title I: Prohibiting Discrimination in the Workplace

Title I prohibits discrimination in all phases of the employment process, including job application procedures, hiring, advancement, compensation, training, and other terms, conditions, and privileges of employment. The provisions contained in Title I also provide certain safeguards during the job application process. For example, it is now unlawful for an employer to ask questions about a person's disability or medical status on application forms or during the pre–job offer interview. These include questions about previous hospitalizations, workers' compensation claims, medications, and so forth. These types of questions may only be asked after a conditional job offer has been made. Once the job has been offered to the individual, disability-related questions are permitted. An employer may condition a job offer on the satisfactory result of a post–job offer medical examination or medical inquiry if this information is required of all entering employees in the same job category. If it appears that the person may have difficulty performing the essential functions of the job, the employer may ask about the type of reasonable accommodations needed or the person may request accommodations. If an individual is not hired because of a postoffer medical exam or medical inquiry, the reasons for not hiring must be job related and consistent with business necessity. The employer must also demonstrate that no reasonable accommodation that would enable the person to perform the essential job functions was available or that implementing the accommodation would pose an undue hardship.

It is important for counselors who serve the career needs of people with disabilities to be familiar with the provisions of Title I of the ADA. Specifically, Title I prohibits discrimination against a qualified individual with a disability who can perform the essential functions of a job with or without reasonable accommodations. *A qualified individual with a disability* is one who not only meets the ADA definition of disability but also satisfies the requisite skill, experience, education, and other job-related requirements of the employment position that the individual holds or desires and can perform the essential functions of the position with or without reasonable accommodations (Olsheski & Breslin, 1996). In addition, the ADA Amendments Act "provides that an individual subjected to an action prohibited by the ADA (e.g., failure to hire) because of an actual or perceived impairment will meet the 'regarded as' definition of disability, unless the impairment is transitory and minor" (Southeast DBTAC, 2009, p. 2).

Determining whether an individual with a disability is qualified under Title I of the ADA involves a series of steps. First, the presence of a disability that substantially limits one or more major life activities must be documented by collecting the appropriate medical or psychological information. Second, the traits of the individual must be evaluated to determine whether he or she possesses the necessary skills, education, certifications, and other traits to perform the essential functions of the job. Next, an assessment is needed to determine whether the person can perform the essential functions of the job with or without a reasonable job accommodation. Included in this step is a comparison of individuals' functional capacities with the physical and environmental demands of the job. Information specifying the demands of the job is obtained using job analysis data or the performance of an on-site job analysis (Weed, Taylor, & Blackwell, 1991). By synthesizing this information, the degree of compatibility between the person's capacities and job requirements may be determined. If discrepancies between the person's capacities and job requirements are identified, an evaluation of potential reasonable accommodations that may be implemented to remove or reduce the discrepancies is conducted.

### SIDEBAR 15.5  A Possible Lawsuit

While interviewing a 26-year-old female applicant for a position as a crisis counselor for a crisis line, the interviewer noticed that the applicant received her GED at the age of 20. He asked her why she did not earn a traditional high school diploma at about age 18. Initially, the applicant made a vague response to the inquiry but, when asked for a more concrete response, conveyed that she spent time in a rehabilitation center after a car accident resulting in a head injury. The applicant did not receive a job offer to work at the crisis line even though she had completed a BA in human services and an MS in counseling. Could she file a lawsuit on the basis of discrimination related to Title I of the ADA?

General guidelines in the ADA regarding the job accommodation process are to

- Analyze the job to determine its purpose and essential functions.
- Evaluate the physical and mental functioning of the individual.

- Consult with the individual who needs the accommodation to ascertain the precise job-related limitations and how those limitations could be overcome with certain accommodations.
- Identify the potential accommodations and assess the effectiveness that each would have in giving the individual the opportunity to perform the essential functions of the job.
- Consider the preference of the individual to be accommodated and determine the reasonable solution that would be most appropriate for both the employee and the employer.
- Make the accommodation.
- Determine the effectiveness of the job accommodation (EEOC, 2009a).

Saab (2008) described a five-step process: (1) define the situation; (2) perform a needs assessment; (3) explore alternative placement options; (4) redefine the situation; and (5) monitor accommodations (see Figure 15.1). In addition, Blanck, Anderson, Wallach, and Tenney (1994) proposed the following guidelines for assessing reasonable accommodations: Get the facts regarding essential job functions and the capacities of the employee with a disability; identify what specific disability-related limitations need to be accommodated; assess the need for expertise and objective review; assess costs and undue hardship; engage in a problem-solving dialogue; develop an accommodation plan; and evaluate the effectiveness of the accommodation.

### Reasonable Accommodations

*Reasonable accommodations* are modifications or adjustments to the job or work environment that allow the person with a disability the opportunity to perform the job (Hutchinson, Versnel, Chin, & Munby, 2008). The ADA mandates reasonable accommodations in all phases of the employment process, including job application procedures. Reasonable accommodations in the application process may involve assistance to an individual who is unable to complete the application form because of manipulative or visual impairments. Examples of reasonable accommodations cited in the ADA include restructuring a job by reallocating or redistributing marginal job functions; altering when or how an essential function is performed; working part time or modifying work schedules; modifying equipment; using assistive technological devices; and reassigning the person to another job (EEOC, 1991).

### Examples of Reasonable Job Accommodations

These examples of actual job accommodations have been provided by the U.S. Department of Labor (2002). *See* North Carolina Department of Human Services (2001). *Accommodating employees with disabilities*. Retrieved June 1, 2011 from http://www.ncdhhs.gov/dvrs/newspubs/pubs/Accommodating_Employees_with_Disabilities.pdf:

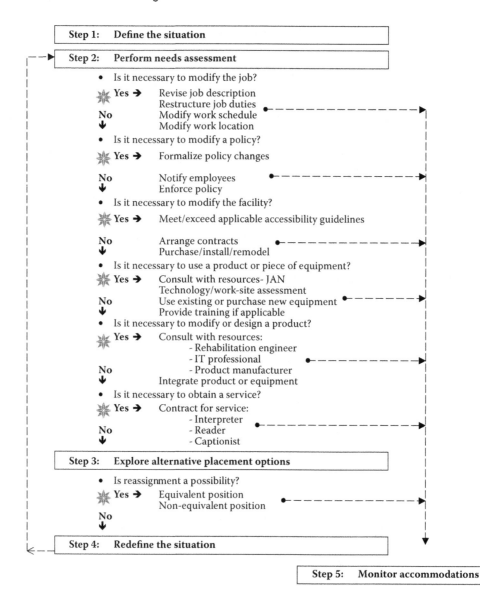

| Step 1: | Define the situation |
| --- | --- |

**Step 2:    Perform needs assessment**

- Is it necessary to modify the job?

  **Yes →**  Revise job description
             Restructure job duties
  **No**      Modify work schedule
  ↓        Modify work location

- Is it necessary to modify a policy?

  **Yes →**  Formalize policy changes

  **No**      Notify employees
  ↓        Enforce policy

- Is it necessary to modify the facility?

  **Yes →**  Meet/exceed applicable accessibility guidelines

  **No**      Arrange contracts
  ↓        Purchase/install/remodel

- Is it necessary to use a product or piece of equipment?

  **Yes →**  Consult with resources- JAN
             Technology/work-site assessment
  **No**      Use existing or purchase new equipment
  ↓        Provide training if applicable

- Is it necessary to modify or design a product?

  **Yes →**  Consult with resources:
             - Rehabilitation engineer
             - IT professional
  **No**      - Product manufacturer
  ↓        Integrate product or equipment

- Is it necessary to obtain a service?

  **Yes →**  Contract for service:
             - Interpreter
  **No**      - Reader
  ↓        - Captionist

**Step 3:    Explore alternative placement options**

- Is reassignment a possibility?

  **Yes →**  Equivalent position
             Non-equivalent position
  **No**
  ↓

**Step 4:    Redefine the situation**

| Step 5: | Monitor accommodations |
| --- | --- |

**FIGURE 15.1** The job accommodation process. Saab, T. D. (2008). *Job accommodation process.* Morgantown, WV: Job Accommodation Network, U.S. Department of Labor (p. 5).

- *Example 1:* An assembler for a furniture manufacturer has spinal degeneration, which results in an uncoordinated gait and problems with balance that limit her abilities to walk, carry materials, and balance. This worker was accommodated by installing a plywood platform to raise part of the workstation; tools were suspended from the ceiling to balance their weight; and a cart was provided to move materials and prevent carrying. The cost of this accommodation was $200.
- *Example 2:* A well-drilling rig operator with a low back condition is having difficulty performing his job because of the constant

vibration of the standard seat in the rig. This worker was accommodated by removing the seat in the rig and installing an ergonomically designed, mechanical seat that allowed him to adjust his position and avoid most of the vibration. The cost of this accommodation was $1,100.

■ *Example 3:* An administrative assistant with amyotrophic lateral sclerosis is having difficulty with using the phone, typing, computer input, completing forms and reports, and filing. Accommodations for this worker included providing a cordless headset for the telephone; using arm rest extensions from the edge of the desk to reduce strain on arms and wrists; and installing a new effortless lock and handle on the restroom door. The cost of the accommodation was $450.

■ *Example 4:* An airline programmer with postpolio fatigue brought on by stress cannot be on call 24 hours a day and work overtime as needed. This worker was accommodated by waiving the requirements of the 24-hour on-call duty and overtime work. This change in policy cost the company nothing to implement.

As illustrated by these examples, accommodations often do not involve considerable cost. Information from research on employers from 2004 to 2010 by the Job Accommodation Network (2010, p. 3) found that 58% of accommodations needed by employees cost absolutely nothing, and 37% incurred a one-time cost averaging around $600. Similarly, Sears, Roebuck and Company reported that for the period of 1978 to 1992, a total of 436 employees were provided with job accommodations. Of these accommodations, 69% involved no cost, 28% cost less than $1,000, and only 3% cost more than $1,000 (Cameron & Sharp, 1998).

**SIDEBAR 15.6   A Reasonable Accommodation**

A department of counselor education denied admission to an applicant with quadriplegia who also had a severe speech impediment. This applicant had to employ an attendant to be with her during the admissions interview to help operate her wheelchair and to interpret her response to questions during the admissions interview because she was so difficult to understand. The applicant disclosed that she would need the assistance of a full-time attendant during the time period she would be a graduate student at the university but did not have the finances to do so. She made it clear, via the attendant, that she felt the university should accommodate her by paying for the attendant. Would doing so be considered a reasonable accommodation? Do you think the counselor could function as a counselor after graduation even if she was able to complete academic and practicum–internship requirements?

### Undue Hardship or Direct Threat

Although Title I of the ADA mandates reasonable accommodations in the workplace for people with disabilities, the issue of what is considered reasonable may be unclear or subject to debate among the employee and the employer. Therefore, the ADA contains some criteria that address situations in which the proposed accommodations are not reasonable. These provisions are expressed by the concepts of undue hardship and direct threat. In general, employers may defend their decision to not accommodate a particular worker by alleging that the accommodation would impose an undue hardship. The nature of the undue hardship could involve the cost of the proposed accommodation or that the accommodation would be disruptive or fundamentally alter the nature or operation of the business.

The determination of whether a particular accommodation constitutes an undue hardship is done on a case-by-case basis. Cameron and Sharp (1998) outlined the following factors that should be considered in determining whether an accommodation poses an undue hardship: the nature and cost of the accommodation; the overall financial resources of the employer, including the number of employees, type of business, number of locations, and other company resources; and the type of operation or operations of the employer, including the composition, structure, and functions of the workforce.

Another defense that employers may use to refuse an accommodation for a person with a disability is the concept of direct threat. A direct threat exists if it can be established that the presence of the individual in the work setting would cause a significant risk to his or her own safety and health or the safety and health of others and this threat cannot be eliminated by reasonable accommodation. The factors that must be considered in determining whether an individual would pose a direct threat include the duration of the risk, the nature and severity of the potential harm, the likelihood that the potential harm will occur, and the imminence of the potential harm (EEOC, 1991).

## Using Functional Capacity and Job Analysis Data in Career Planning

Career planning for individuals with disabilities requires an assessment of how their particular illness or disease affects the ability to function in an actual or desired work environment. This analysis involves a comparison of the person's functional capacities with job analysis data and is similar to the trait and factor approach that is central to many theories of career development. Therefore, an accurate assessment of the person's functional capacities and accurate job analysis information are essential in selecting appropriate vocational goals and identifying reasonable job accommodations. Without this type of information, the chances of achieving a positive work adjustment or implementing effective accommodations are greatly reduced. In this section of the chapter, we discuss the use of functional capacity information and job analysis information in the career planning process for people with disabilities.

### Functional Limitations

*Functional limitations* refer to the hindrance or negative effect on the performance of tasks or activities and other adverse or overt manifestations of a mental, emotional, or physical disability (Delfs & Campbell, 2010; Wright, 1980). A clear understanding of how the individual's disability affects his or her functional capacities is essential to the career and vocational planning process (Buys & van Biljon, 2007). It is important to differentiate between the concepts of disability and functional limitation. *Disability* describes a physiological, anatomical, mental, or emotional impairment resulting from disease or illness. *Functional limitations* describe the impact that the disability has on the person's abilities to perform certain tasks in a life adjustment context (Wright, 1980). For example, an individual with a below-the-knee amputation of the left leg (disability) is limited to standing for no more than 1 hour at time and cannot ambulate on uneven surfaces or maintain balance on ladders (functional limitations). These limitations may preclude working in certain occupations unless they could be removed or minimized via reasonable accommodations. Vocational and career planning, therefore, require an understanding of how the person's disability affects his or her ability to perform specific job tasks and tolerate certain work conditions.

Although the functional limitations that arise from disabilities are many and varied, there have been some attempts to group the most common into general categories (Mueller, 1990; Wright, 1980). Brodwin, Parker, and DeLaGarza (2003) developed a list of functional limitation categories that expanded previous classification models and included these 19 categories:

1. Difficulty in interpreting information
2. Limitations in sight and total blindness
3. Limitations in hearing and total deafness
4. Susceptibility to fainting, dizziness, and seizures
5. Incoordination
6. Limitations in stamina
7. Limitations in head movement
8. Difficulty in reaching, lifting, and carrying
9. Difficulty in handling and fingering
10. Inability to use the upper extremities
11. Difficulty in sitting
12. Difficulty in using the lower extremities
13. Poor balance
14. Cognitive limitation
15. Emotional limitation
16. Limitation because of disfigurement
17. Substance abuse
18. Pain limitation
19. Limitation of sensation

Next, we provide a brief overview of the more common categories.

### Difficulty in Interpreting Information

Individuals with this limitation have an impaired ability to read or understand written or verbal communication (Naik, Dyer, Kunik, & McCullough, 2009). This limitation may result from a variety of disabilities including stroke, learning disabilities, traumatic brain injury, mental retardation, and other neurological impairments. The individual may experience limitations in expressive and receptive communication abilities. Impairment in interpreting information affects a large number of occupations ranging from jobs that have information processing as an essential job function (secretary, computer programmer) to less skilled jobs that require the employee to follow written or verbal instructions (assembler, order filler). Counselors must evaluate the specific job functions that are affected and implement accommodations or the use of assistive technology to facilitate job performance. For example, if the employee's limitation is primarily related to expressive communication skills, an attempt could be made to rely more on written communication than on verbal communication, or complicated communications may be reduced to more understandable units for an individual with cognitive impairment.

**SIDEBAR 15.7    Repetitive Steps**

Sometimes individuals with a cognitive disability that makes it difficult to assimilate and retain a complex set of directions can function quite well if a supervisor can write out directions that are presented in a step-by-step fashion or are provided verbally one step at a time. If a job-related task requires the repetitive use of the same set of directions, the steps often become second nature to the employee.

### Limitations of Sight and Blindness

This limitation includes a variety of visual impairments including total blindness. Visual impairments are related to such disabilities as glaucoma, periocular disease, macular degeneration, diabetic retinopathy, corneal diseases, optic nerve damage, central nervous system damage, and other conditions.

As noted by Brodwin et al. (2003), the functional limitations of an individual with a visual impairment are related to the amount and type of the impairment, environmental conditions such as lighting and contrast, the individual's degree of motivation to function in a particular environment, and the individual's ability to use remaining vision. From a vocational standpoint, it is important to evaluate the specific nature of the vision loss in conjunction with specific work tasks. Panek (2002) noted that the functional limitations caused by a visual disability are best described in a visual task–related manner. This approach focuses on the individual's ability to perform different types of visual tasks. Colenbrander (1977) developed a model for classifying the degree of functional limitations for visual disability. The model is based on the degree of ability to perform various visual tasks, such as reading. A person with a *slight disability* performs visual *tasks without special aids, often with glasses alone. Moderate visual disability* indicates that the person cannot perform fine tasks without special aids. *Severe disability* indicates that the person needs visual aids to function even with difficulty. *Profound visual disability* indicates that the person cannot perform most detailed tasks such as reading and has difficulty with gross visual tasks such as mobility. *Total visual disability* means the individual must rely on other senses and vision contributes nothing to functional ability.

Accommodations for employees with residual vision may include changes in illumination, color and contrast, size (enlarged print), distance, and space arrangements. Assistive technology in the form of low-vision devices such as magnifiers and telescopes are also commonly used. Computers may also be modified to include large-print magnification, speech output, and optical scanning features. For individuals with total blindness, accommodations rely on tactile and auditory senses. These types of accommodation include the use of Braille printers and labels, speech output on computers, talking calculators, and the use of speech synthesizers combined with both a Braille and a regular printer. An orientation and mobility specialist may also be used to teach a person with blindness or low vision how to safely move about in the work environment. Services for people with visual impairment are also available in each state's public rehabilitation program. These agencies provide a variety of vocational rehabilitation and independent living services for individuals who are legally blind.

### Limitations of Hearing and Deafness

People with hearing impairments have difficulty comprehending usable speech with or without amplification. *Deafness* is defined as a hearing impairment that limits the ability to understand normal conversation. The level of functional limitation depends on the degree of impairment in auditory discrimination of speech frequencies and the age of onset (Harvey, 2002). Functional limitations associated with hearing problems are rated in severity by the degree of decibel loss associated with the impairment. These problems exist on a continuum of severity and range from conditions involving a slight hearing loss to a profound hearing loss or deafness (Moores, 2001). For example, a moderate hearing impairment involves a loss of between 26 and 40 decibels. With a moderate loss, the person can hear conversation at a distance of 3 to 5 feet, but understanding speech is difficult and the full-time use of a hearing aid is necessary. A severe hearing impairment involves a loss of 71 to 90 decibels, and the person can hear only very loud speech from about 1 foot from the ear. Hearing aids may be of limited use for a person with a severe loss, and lip reading and sign language may also be necessary. Workplace accommodations include the use of interpreters, amplified telephones, flashing lights and alarms, communication aids, and telecommunication devices for people who are deaf. Environmental restrictions related to hearing impairments may include avoiding loud noise work settings or exposure to hazards such as moving machinery.

### Limitations in Lifting, Reaching, and Carrying

These types of limitations may be related to a variety of disabling conditions that result in decreased range of motion and strength in the upper extremities and back, including spinal cord injuries, musculoskeletal injuries, multiple sclerosis, arthritis, neurological diseases, and other permanent injuries. Limitations may involve the magnitude, frequency, and duration of a person's ability to lift, carry, push and pull, and reach. In severe cases, paralysis of one or both of the upper extremities requires substantial modification to work tasks that require handling, reaching, lifting, and carrying. Ergonomic evaluation of the workstation may be needed to identify job accommodations for limitations involving the upper extremities (Olsheski & Breslin, 1996). The use of worksite physical and occupational therapy may also be useful in transitioning individuals who have these types of functional limitations back to work (Breslin & Olsheski, 1996).

### Difficulty in Using the Lower Extremities

Functional limitations associated with impairments of the lower extremities include slowness of gait and impairment of the ability to walk, stand, kneel, and climb stairs or ladders. These limitations may be related to spinal cord injuries, degenerative joint disease, arthritis, stroke, peripheral neuropathy, congenital deformities, amputation, cardiovascular or pulmonary diseases, and other neurological impairments. Functional limitations include impaired ability to ambulate, stoop, bend, lift, balance, kneel, climb, carry, and stand (Andrews, 2000). Workplace accommodations may involve the use of wheelchairs or other motorized vehicles for mobility and minimization of job tasks that require prolonged periods of standing, use of foot controls, and bending (Brodwin et al., 2003).

### Limitations Related to Fainting, Dizziness, and Seizures

These limitations involve conditions in which the person experiences periods of unconsciousness from fainting or seizures and a loss of balance because of dizziness. People with these types of limitations may have epilepsy, cerebral palsy, brain injury, vertigo, migraine headaches, hypertension, and other various neurological or cardiac impairments (Brodwin et al., 2003). These types of impairments may restrict the individual from being exposed to certain environmental risk factors, for example, unprotected heights, hazardous machinery, and extreme temperatures. For individuals with epileptic seizures, the severity and frequency of the seizure, the effectiveness of antiseizure medication, and the time needed to recover after having a seizure will influence the degree of environmental restriction and need for accommodation. Individuals who have problems with dizziness may need such accommodations as supportive grab bars and avoiding exposure to unprotected heights, slippery surfaces, and hazardous machinery (Mueller, 1990).

### SIDEBAR 15.8   A Case of Seizures

Matt is 32 years old and works in a small travel agency consisting of the owner, himself, and two other employees. He is seizure prone but has been evaluated a number of times and is on medication to control the onset of seizures. During the past 2 or 3 weeks, he has reported feeling strangely, and he took a day off earlier in the week to check in with his physician. He asked about the possibility of being reevaluated so that his medication could be adjusted if needed but was discouraged from scheduling another evaluation because of the cost to the insurance carrier and the amount of his copay. The day after he returned to work, he had a grand mal seizure in the office at a time when two potential clients were meeting with colleagues. An ambulance had to be called, and the office was disrupted for more than an hour. Both clients left and said they would call back for another appointment; neither of them did so. Matt returned to work 3 days later and had another seizure that disrupted the office; this incident also resulted in clients leaving. Matt's boss found out that no changes had been made in Matt's medication after the first episode. Matt has been in counseling with you for the past year and calls you to tell you he is desperately afraid that he will lose his job. What should you do to be of assistance to your client?

## Functional Capacity Evaluation

To make appropriate educational and vocational decisions, people with disabilities must have an accurate understanding of their functional assets and limitations. This information is essential in all phases of the career planning process, including the development of vocational goals, selection of appropriate training or educational programs, and identification of the need for potential accommodations. Functional capacity evaluations may be conducted by physical and occupational therapists who also have expertise in job analysis methods (Chen, 2007). This information quantifies the person's functional capacities by measuring standing tolerance, sitting tolerance, lifting capacity, ability to assume various postures, pushing and pulling capacity, fine and gross manipulation abilities, reaching, range of motion, strength, endurance, and ability to tolerate exposure to various work environment conditions (Lynch & Lynch, 1998; Wind, Gouttebarge, Kaijer, Sluiter, & Frings-Dresen, 2009). Chen (2007) noted that by comparing information about the person's functional capacities with job analysis data, the degree of compatibility between the worker's capacities and the requirements of the job can be determined. Reasonable accommodations may be used to remove or reduce specific areas of incompatibility between the worker's capacities and the job requirements.

**SIDEBAR 15.9    Ten Different Types of Commonly Used Functional Capacity Evaluations (Chen, 2007)**

1. Key
2. Blankenship
3. Ergos
4. Ergos Work Simulator and Ergo-Kit variation
5. Isernhagen Work System
6. WEST-EPIC
7. Hanoun Medical
8. Physical Work Performance Evaluation (Ergoscience)
9. ARCON
10. AssessAbility.

## Job Analysis Information

Job analysis is the gathering, evaluating, and recording of accurate, objective, and complete job data (Materials Development Center, 1992). Job analysis describes in a systematic manner what the worker does; how the work is done; results of the work; worker characteristics; and the context of the work in terms of environmental and organizational factors (U.S. Department of Labor, 1982). Job analysis data include the essential job tasks performed by the worker and the tools, equipment, or work aids that are used on the job. In addition, job analysis data describe the general educational development, training, aptitudes, interests, and skills that are required to perform a job. Job analysis data are used to classify the physical demands of the occupation and assign it to a strength category; specify the frequency and duration of various physical traits such as handling, reaching, bending, climbing, and so forth; and describe various factors in the work environment such as exposure to hazardous machinery, dust, fumes, or temperature extremes.

Occupations may be classified in various strength categories on the basis of the amount of standing, sitting, walking, lifting and carrying, and pushing and pulling. These factors are used to define the five physical demand categories defined in the *Dictionary of Occupational Titles* (U.S. Department of Labor, 1991): sedentary work, light work, medium work, heavy work, and very heavy work. Sedentary work requires the worker to lift up to 10 pounds occasionally and to work primarily in a seated position. Light work requires the worker to lift items weighing up to 20 pounds occasionally and items weighing 10 pounds or less on a frequent basis. Medium work requires the worker to lift up to 50 pounds occasionally and up to 25 pounds frequently. Heavy work requires the worker to lift up to 100 pounds occasionally and up to 50 pounds frequently. Very heavy work requires the worker to occasionally lift 100 pounds or more and to lift up to 50 pounds or more on a frequent basis. Most of the occupations that exceed the sedentary classification typically require standing or walking for approximately 6 of 8 hours.

Having a physical disability affects not only the individual's physical capacities for meeting the physical demands or strength factors required to perform a specific occupation but also the type of work environment in which the individual is able to function. Job analysis data are useful for evaluating environmental factors that workers may be exposed to in the course of performing job duties. These factors may hinder successful job performance and pose a threat to safety. For example, a person who experiences epileptic seizures may not be able to tolerate extremely hot temperatures in the workplace if the seizures are precipitated by exposure to high heat. Similarly, individuals with pulmonary impairments may be restricted to work environments that are free of dust and fumes. *Environmental conditions* are defined as specific physical working conditions to which the worker is exposed while performing assigned work tasks (Materials Development Center, 1992). Environmental conditions include exposure to weather; extreme cold; extreme heat; wet conditions, humid conditions, or both; noise; vibration; atmospheric conditions; moving mechanical parts; electric shock; high, exposed places; radiant energy; explosives; toxic or caustic chemicals; and dust, fumes, gases, and odors. Noise intensity is rated on the Occupational Safety and Health Administration decibel continuum ranging from quieter exposures (10 decibels) to very loud exposures (115 decibels and higher).

Although the most accurate job analysis data are obtained from performing an onsite analysis of the job, several generic sources of job analysis information are also useful in career planning. A number of U.S. Department of Labor publications contain valuable job analysis information, including the *Dictionary of Occupational Titles* (U.S. Department of Labor, 1991), the *Revised Guide to Job Analysis* (U.S. Department of Labor, 1991), and the Internet tool known as the Occupational Information Network, or O*NET

(Peterson et al., 1997). The O*NET is designed to replace the *Dictionary of Occupational Titles,* which was last updated in 1991. The *Dictionary of Occupational Titles* contained descriptions of more than 12,000 discrete occupational titles. However, O*NET groups a number of similar occupations into 1,172 occupational units. The O*NET database is relational in nature and is more useful in evaluating transferable work skills. The O*NET model merges information from the *Dictionary of Occupational Titles* and other U.S. Department of Labor publications such as the *New Guide for Occupational Exploration* (Farr, Shatkin, & Ludden, 2006) and the *Occupational Outlook Handbook* (U.S. Department of Labor, 2010–2011; the pdf can be downloaded at http://www.bls.gov/oco). Information contained in the O*NET model includes experience requirements (training, experience, licensing); worker requirements (basic skills, cross-functional skills, general knowledge, education); worker characteristics (abilities, interests, work styles); occupational characteristics (labor market information, occupational outlook, wages); occupational requirements (generalized work activities, organizational context, work conditions); and occupation-specific requirements (occupational knowledge, occupational skills, tasks, duties, machines, tools and equipment). The O*NET offers easy access to job analysis data and vocational information that is useful in career planning, assessing transferable skills, and identifying reasonable accommodations (Olsheski & Schelat, 2003).

Vocational and career planning for individuals with physical disabilities requires an accurate assessment of their functional capacities and an integration of this information with job analysis information (i.e., the physical demands, job requirements, and work conditions). By synthesizing these two important sets of data, appropriate vocational choices and career paths may be selected that enhance the likelihood of a successful work adjustment. In addition, this information is critical in identifying reasonable accommodations that may be implemented to minimize or eliminate any discrepancies between the worker's abilities and the requirement of the job.

## Vocational Rehabilitation Services

*Vocational rehabilitation services* are defined as continuous and coordinated services that are designed to enable a person with a disability secure and retain suitable employment (Wright, 1980). In the United States, vocational rehabilitation services have developed over time as new models of service delivery have emerged, and federal legislation has broadened the scope of services as well as the types of disabling conditions served (Jenkins, Patterson, & Szymanski, 1998). Originally, vocational rehabilitation services were limited to veterans. The passage of the Soldiers Rehabilitation Act of 1918 authorized vocational training and placement for World War I veterans with disabilities. Rehabilitation services for civilians began in 1920 with the passage of the Smith-Fess Act. Permanent funding for vocational rehabilitation services was not established until the passage of the Social Security Act in 1935. Other key legislative acts included the Barden-LaFollette Act of 1943, which made services available to people with mental illness, mental retardation, and blindness.

In 1956, the Social Security Administration initiated cash disability payments for workers older than age 50 who were considered permanently and totally disabled. Today, the Social Security Administration provides medical and financial disability benefits for totally disabled workers, regardless of their age, through two major disability benefits programs: Social Security Disability Insurance Title II (SSDI) and Supplemental Security Income Title XVI (SSI). The SSDI program provides medical and cash benefits to disabled workers who are insured as a result of their contributions (Federal Insurance Contributions Act payroll deductions) to the Social Security trust fund. The SSI program provides medical and cash benefits to disabled individuals who have not earned insured status but are unable to engage in substantial gainful activity. Unlike the SSDI program, the person with a disability must also meet financial need criteria to be eligible for SSI benefits. There may also be individuals who are simultaneously eligible for both SSDI and SSI benefits. Vocational rehabilitation services for SSDI and SSI recipients are available through both public and private rehabilitation programs. The passage of the Ticket to Work and Work Incentives Improvement Act in 1999 expanded vocational rehabilitation services for beneficiaries and provided safeguards for continued health care coverage and income during employment attempts (Robertson, 2005; Social Security Administration, 2008).

The passage of a number of rehabilitation- and disability-related legislative acts has shaped the structure and function of today's comprehensive public (state–federal partnership) vocational rehabilitation program. This system is implemented through state rehabilitation agencies and is referred to as the state–federal program. Federal funding is provided to state vocational rehabilitation agencies in the form of grants under the authority of the Rehabilitation Act of 1973 (Brabham, Mandeville, & Koch, 1998). A federal–state matching formula is used in the funding process, with the federal contribution amounting to nearly 80%. The program is administered by the U.S. Department of Education's Rehabilitation Services Administration, a federal agency that monitors state program operations, oversees requirements for program implementation, and interprets legislation.

Counselors who provide career services to people with disabilities should become familiar with their local public vocational rehabilitation agency and the many services that are available. To be eligible for public vocational rehabilitation services, it must be demonstrated that the individual has a physical or mental impairment that constitutes or results in substantial impediments to employment. Furthermore, it must be determined that the individual is able to benefit in terms of employment outcomes as a result of vocational rehabilitation services and that vocational rehabilitation services are necessary to prepare for, secure, or retain employment (Andrew, 2000). Vocational rehabilitation services may include funding for academic or vocational training programs, physical restoration services, vocational counseling, vocational assessment, rehabilitation engineering, job search and placement assistance, and other interventions that help the individual achieve his or her vocational objectives.

Besides public sector vocational rehabilitation programs, a number of private programs have also emerged. Vocational rehabilitation services are often provided by private insurance carriers who underwrite compensable occupational disability policies such as workers' compensation, short-term disability, and long-term disability (Rasch, 1985). Additionally, a number of employers have developed their own disability management programs and use vocational rehabilitation services to prevent or minimize lost work time and control disability-related costs (Olsheski, 1996). Some larger companies employ rehabilitation specialists as part of their internal human resources staff, and others contract services with external providers (Rosenthal & Olsheski, 1999).

The primary objective of private-based vocational rehabilitation services is to return the individual to suitable employment in an expeditious manner. Therefore, private-based vocational rehabilitation services tend to be more time limited than public sector interventions and place more emphasis on physical conditioning, disability case management, job placement, job accommodation, and the development of early return-to-work programs (Lynch & Lynch, 1998).

A number of specialized vocational rehabilitation services have emerged in both the public and the private sectors. These services are designed to meet the unique career and vocational development needs of people with disabilities. We discuss some of the major types of vocational rehabilitation services in the next section.

## Vocational Rehabilitation Services

### Work Adjustment Training

Work adjustment training consists of a series of activities designed to teach people appropriate work behaviors (Rubin & Roessler, 2007). Work adjustment training is a type of behavior modification program that emphasizes eliminating undesirable work behaviors and reinforcing appropriate behaviors in areas related to job responsibilities, task production, and social–vocational competence (McCuller, Moore, & Salzberg, 1990; Minarovic & Bambara, 2007). Marr and Roessler (1994) noted that work adjustment interventions are useful in ameliorating problems related to fluctuating production output, social skills deficits, and poor responses to coworkers and supervision. Work adjustment training is used for people with various disabilities including cognitive impairments resulting from mental retardation, brain injury, mental illness, or other neurological impairments.

Inappropriate work behaviors may also be the result of developmental problems. Individuals with severe disabilities may experience problems in developing a healthy work personality, vocational self-efficacy, and career maturity (Hershenson, 1996). These developmental problems may have impeded the development of appropriate work behaviors and impaired the person's ability to achieve a positive work adjustment. Work adjustment training is useful as a remedial intervention that may help restore the person's work personality, enhance their motivation to work, develop feelings of self-efficacy, and learn appropriate work behaviors.

Marr (1982) recommended the development of an individualized work adjustment treatment plan that would take into consideration the person's behavioral assets and limitations. The treatment plan should specify the problems and objectives in terms of observable behaviors and the products of these behaviors. Other components of the work adjustment treatment plan include measuring behaviors before interventions; selecting intervention procedures on the basis of research evidence; continually measuring the target behavior to evaluate success; and attributing any failure of the intervention to the technique used, not to the person.

Work adjustment training occurs in different settings ranging from rehabilitation facility–based programs to professionally supervised programs in competitive work settings (Rubin & Roessler, 2007). Facility-based programs use either real-work tasks, which are developed by contracting work from local businesses and industries, or simulated work activities in the training process. The most effective programs are those that occur in actual competitive work settings and use supported employment interventions (Wehman & Kregel, 1992). Supported employment approaches to work adjustment training involve the use of job coaches who supervise and train the workers with disabilities in integrated work settings.

**SIDEBAR 15.10  Client Troubles at Work**

You are the case manager for a 57-year-old woman with developmental disabilities who lives in a group home with six other residents. Your client is able to work part time in a store that sells a variety of merchandise and is responsible for keeping the displays of seasonal items orderly. The director of the group home has been noticing some erratic behavior and memory loss that seems to occur on an intermittent basis. One day, you receive a call from the director of the group home, saying that the store manager called to complain that your client had scolded customers on two different occasions for moving items in the display she had organized, and that one of these incidents was followed by the client reporting that she could not remember which bus to take to return to the group home after work. The store manager is not sure she can continue to work in her current capacity. What should you as the case manager do?

### Work Evaluation

Work evaluation represents an approach to vocational assessment that combines the principles of psychometric testing with performance-based techniques (Rubin & Roessler, 2007). Work evaluation allows for observation of the individual's performance on actual or simulated work tasks in real or simulated work settings. Caston and Watson (1990) noted that the purpose of work evaluation is to provide reliable and valid data concerning the person's ability to work, preferences for different jobs and work activities, need for training in specific and general skills, and capacity to perform in various vocational roles (Brady, Duffy, Frain, & Bucholz, 2010).

The three basic work evaluation methodologies include work samples, the situational approach, and on-the-job evaluation (Rubin & Roessler, 1995).

Work samples involve the use of real or simulated work tasks that are used in various occupations. Simulated work samples are designed by professionals and include work activities of specific occupations (G. K. Lee et al., 2008). Work samples include a sample of the procedures, tools, and materials used in actual jobs. By using real tools, materials, and tasks, the individual's vocational exploration is facilitated and the evaluator is provided with the opportunity to observe important work behaviors. Work sample testing allows for a comparison of the individual's performance with performance standards that have been developed from competitive or industrial norms. Test results indicated whether the individual is performing tasks in terms of quantity and quality at the competitive employment or noncompetitive employment levels.

Several commercial work evaluation systems have been developed, including the Jewish Employment and Vocational Services System developed by Philadelphia's Jewish Employment and Vocational Services, the Singer/ Graflex Work Sample System, and the Valpar Component Work Sample Series (Power, 1991, 2006). Many of these systems are available in rehabilitation facilities that provide work evaluation services.

The situational approach to work evaluation involves an assessment of the individual who is performing either contract or simulated work in a rehabilitation facility. The individual's performance is evaluated regarding the quality and quantity of work tasks performed as well as the behaviors demonstrated during task performance. In situational assessment, the individual responds to the realistic expectations of a work supervisor and productivity demands, which enables the evaluator to assess a wider range of work behaviors and employability characteristics (Power, 1991, 2006). The individual's work potential may be evaluated concerning such work behaviors as getting along with coworkers and supervisors, staying on task, maintaining production, and tolerating frustration (Neff, 1985).

On-the-job evaluation consists of evaluating the person under the real conditions of the worksite (Rubin & Roessler, 2007). This approach allows the evaluator to observe how the person responds to the environment and how the environment affects the person. The on-the-job approach gives the individual an opportunity to self-evaluate task performance and work behaviors in a work setting that is presumed to be compatible with their interests and skills. The evaluator rates the performance of tasks and work behaviors. In addition, work supervisors may provide supplemental information on the individual's suitability for the job.

Work evaluation services are provided to individuals with a wide range of disabilities including mental retardation, psychiatric impairments, orthopedic impairments, brain damage, and educational deficiencies and to individuals having more than one type of disability (Rubin & Roessler, 1995). Work evaluation is appropriate for individuals with disabilities who have little occupational information and who learn best by direct exposure to work activities. Nadolsky (1983) observed that the experiential nature of work evaluation enabled many individuals to develop more concrete images of a job or jobs and to seek more occupational information.

The work evaluation report contains important information regarding the nature of the person's disability and background information; a discussion of why the person was referred for evaluation; vocational history and transferable skills analysis, if applicable; vocationally significant behavioral observations; results of psychometric tests and work samples; information related to activities of daily living and social skills; recommendations for vocational rehabilitation services; and appropriate job options for the person to consider (Cutler & Ramm, 1992).

### Supported Employment

Supported employment is a vocational rehabilitation service for individuals with severe disabilities who would otherwise not be able to obtain or maintain competitive employment (Brady et al., 2010; Hanley-Maxwell, Szymanski, & Owens-Johnson, 1998). The supported employment model is based on the principles that job preparation for many people with severe disabilities should take place in a competitive setting and that intensive follow-along interventions at the worksite should be provided to the client (Ottomanelli et al., 2009; Wehman & Kregel, 1985). This approach departs from the traditional train-and-place model of vocational rehabilitation for individuals with severe disabilities that operates on the belief that job readiness and other types of skills training should occur before placement in a competitive job. The supported employment approach allows individuals who do not possess all of the required skills and behaviors required for immediate occupational success to be placed in competitive jobs. Using professional support services at the worksite, the individual becomes job ready by performing tasks in a competitive, integrated work setting. This place–train–follow-up approach to supported employment includes four major components: job placement, job-site training and advocacy, ongoing assessment, and job retention (Wehman, 1986, p. 23).

The most common form of support is job coaching (Rubin & Roessler, 2007). Job coaching may be provided in either individual or group models. Job coaches function as trainers and supervisors by helping the person acquire the vocational skills required of the job as well as critical work behaviors, including appropriate relationships with coworkers and supervisors. The duration of supported employment services varies according to the needs of the individual. Some individuals may need support for a specified amount of time and professional interventions may be systematically faded out as natural supports in the workplace emerge through enhanced social and physical integration. Coaching can be overt or covert (i.e., covert audio coaching) in format to suit the psychosocial needs of the client (Bennett, Brady, Scott, Dukes, & Frain, 2010). With improved integration, coworkers and supervisors may assume the supportive functions that the job coach provided. However, other individuals with significant disabilities may need long-term or permanent support to maintain competitive employment (Hanley-Maxwell et al., 1998). Although supported employment was initially used with individuals with developmental disabilities, it has proved valuable for other types of disabilities including chronic mental illness, traumatic brain injury, deafness, and visual impairments (Wehman & Kregel, 1992).

### Job-Seeking Skills Training

Job-seeking skills training programs are used to address skill deficiencies that people with disabilities have in the job-search process.

> [Job seeking skills training] helps a person prepare for the job search process by reviewing and learning topics such as preparing resumes and cover letters, creating a job search plan, preparing for an interview, finding job leads, networking, negotiating salary, and learning about disability disclosure issues. (Vision and Vocational Services, 2011, p. 1)

Some common problems experienced by job seekers with disabilities include difficulties in explaining skills to employers, completing applications properly, dealing with issues related to a marginal work history with gaps in periods of employment, and discussing or disclosing the nature of their disability or need for accommodations during the interview (Roessler, Hinman, & Lewis, 1987).

Job-seeking skills training is usually offered in a group format, and most programs follow an established curriculum of instruction. Specific training methods include the use of videotapes, instruction manuals, computer resources, occupational and labor market information, counseling, and supervision of job search activities (Roessler & Rumrill, 1994). Training involves the use of video equipment for developing appropriate interviewing skills and the development of résumés, cover letters, and other documents related to the job search. Participants also receive instruction in using labor market information and learning how to identify job leads. An important aspect of the training involves helping the person respond appropriately to disability-related issues, including an understanding of employment rights and strategies for requesting job accommodations (Rubin & Roessler, 1995).

### Assistive Technology and Rehabilitation Engineering

The Technology-Related Assistance for Individuals With Disabilities Act of 1988 (Tech Act) authorized financial assistance to the states to plan and implement a consumer-responsive assistive technology service delivery system for individuals with disabilities (Rehabilitation Services Administration, 1998). Assistive technology devices are defined in the Tech Act as "any item, piece of equipment, or product system, whether acquired commercially off the shelf, modified, or customized, that is used to increase, maintain, or improve functional capabilities of individuals with disabilities" (DeWitt, 1991, p. 315). By extending or replacing the capacities of the person, assistive technology removes barriers to participation in various social, personal, and vocational environments (Rubin & Roessler, 2007).

Categories of assistive technology applications have been defined by the Rehabilitation Services Administration's (1998) Institute on Rehabilitation Issues. These categories include aids for daily living, augmentative communications, computer applications, environmental control systems, home and worksite modifications, prosthetics and orthotics, seating and positioning, aids for vision and hearing impairments, wheelchairs and mobility aids, and vehicle modifications (Martin, 2009).

Assistive technology devices used to enhance capacities for activities of daily living typically include low-tech, self-help tools that provide assistance with such activities as preparing food, cleaning, bathing, and dressing. Augmentative and alternative communication devices include picture or letter communication boards or electronic speech synthesizers to assist people who have difficulty speaking or who are unable to speak. Environmental control units help a person with mobility limitations operate and control home appliances and other equipment. Vision aids include devices such as magnifiers, Braille labels, voice synthesis computers, and audio clocks and alarms.

Rehabilitation engineers are qualified technologists that assist people with disabilities and counselors in assessing the need for assistive technology services and in selecting or designing the devices to be used. The Rehabilitation Engineering and Assistive Technology Society of North America conducts exams for licensing and certification of qualified professionals (Rehabilitation Services Administration, 1998). Rehabilitation engineering has been defined by Reswick (1980) as a combination of engineering technology and medicine designed to improve the life of people with disabilities. In addition to their expertise in the application of assistive technologies, the skills of the rehabilitation engineer are also useful in evaluating environmental modifications that can remove or minimize barriers to participation in the home, community, or workplace. Workplace applications may include an ergonomic evaluation of the workstation for the purpose of fitting the job to the person and modifying tools and equipment used by the worker (Olsheski & Breslin, 1996).

### Physical Restoration Services

A number of vocational rehabilitation services involve those that are designed to enhance the physical capabilities of people with disabilities. Many of these services are provided by medical and allied health care professionals. Physical medicine and rehabilitation physicians, also known as physiatrists, specialize in the treatment and rehabilitation of people with disabilities. Physiatrists establish treatment goals and collaborate with various health care specialists including physical therapists, occupational therapists, nurses, other physician specialists, speech pathologists, audiologists, prosthetic and orthotic specialists, and others related to the physical restoration of the individual (Rubin & Roessler, 1995).

Physical therapy is used to increase and maintain range of motion, strength, stamina, and balance and to teach proper body mechanics such as lifting techniques (Falvo, 1991). Occupational therapy services are designed to rehabilitate the functional deficits of the individual with a disability. Occupational therapy services include training and therapy to help improve the person's ability to function in activities of daily living, the community, and the workplace. Occupational therapists are also useful in designing orthotic devices such as splints and braces and for consultation concerning the adaptation of the physical environment. Occupational and physical therapists can also perform functional capacity evaluations, make recommendations for job accommodations, and provide clinical supervision of workers who are transitioning back to employment (Olsheski & Breslin, 1996).

Specialists in prosthetics and orthotics provide services related to the design, modification, and maintenance of artificial devices that increase a person's functional capacities (Rubin & Roessler, 2007). Orthotists specialize in fitting people with braces to provide support and stability for weakened parts of the body. These may include braces for the lower extremities, upper extremities, or spine. Prosthetists provide care for people by fitting them with prosthetic devices to replace missing limbs or parts of missing limbs (Clawson, 2002).

Speech therapy services are provided for individuals with various speech–language pathologies. These services may include evaluating, diagnosing, and treating various disorders of speech, including problems of articulation, fluency, and voice, and developing augmentative and alternative communication systems. Conditions may include disorders of the oral–pharyngeal functions and cognitive communication disorders (Rubin & Roessler, 1995). Speech therapy services have been used for such disabilities as stroke, brain injury, degenerative diseases, learning disabilities, cerebral palsy, and autism (Rehabilitation Services Administration, 1992). Audiologists evaluate hearing impairments and make recommendations for using residual hearing ability. Audiologists also provide assistance in the selection and fitting of hearing aids or other listening devices as well as training the person in the proper use of the device (Harvey, 2002).

## Summary

As with other minority groups, people with disabilities continue to be underrepresented in many aspects of social and economic life. The negative stereotyping and discrimination experienced by people with disabilities is perhaps most poignant in the world of work. Restricted opportunities for participation in meaningful work not only result in high poverty rates among people with disabilities but also contribute to their exclusion from other life activities in the context of where they live.

To better meet the career development needs of people with disabilities, counselors need to be aware of the person's unique developmental experiences and the influence of contextual or environmental factors that make it difficult to obtain, maintain, and advance in the world of work. The information presented in this chapter may be useful in helping people with physical disabilities overcome both personal limitations and environmental barriers to career development and work adjustment. The Web sites listed in the next section provide additional information relating to the topics discussed in this chapter.

## Useful Web Sites
### Rehabilitation Agencies

- Rehabilitation Services Administration (information on the Office of Special Education and Rehabilitation Services; Rehabilitation Services Administration organization, programs, grants, state plans, monitoring, and policy): http://www.ed.gov/about/offices/list/osers/rsa/index.html
- WorkWorld. State Vocational Rehabilitation Agencies (provides links to all state vocational rehabilitation agencies): http://www.workworld.org/wwwebhelp/state_vocational_rehabilitation_vr_agencies.htm

### Disability Policy and Legislation

- Americans With Disabilities Act Document Center (contains information on statutory law, regulations, accessibility guidelines, federally reviewed technology checklists, and other assistance documents): http://askjan.org/links/adalinks.htm
- Center for the Study and Advancement of Disability Policy (provides information on advocacy training, ADA, Individuals With Disabilities Education Act, court decisions, Rehabilitation Act, Temporary Assistance for Needy Families, Ticket to Work and Work Incentives Improvement Act, vocational rehabilitation, and Workforce Investment Act): http://www.disabilitypolicycenter.org
- National Council on Disability (an independent federal agency that makes disability-related policy recommendations to the president and congress): http://www.ncd.gov

### Job Accommodations, Assistive Technology, and Employment

- AbleData (AbleData Bulletin provides information on vendors and organizations that design and manufacture custom made products; AbleData Fact Sheets on various types of assistive technology describe components, accessories, applications, and manufacturers; AbleData Informed Consumer Guides presents information on assistive technology from a consumer's standpoint): http://www.abledata.com
- Job Accommodation Network (provides practical information on accommodating a specific person with a disability in a specific work situation; also provides information on ADA and employment tips for individuals with disabilities): http://www.jan.wvu.edu/
- Rehabilitation Engineering and Assistive Technology Society of North America Technical Assistance Project (provides information on the Technical Assistance Project funded by the U.S. Department of

Education's National Institute on Disability Rehabilitation Research; the grant provides technical assistance and information to 56 assistive technology projects located throughout the United States): http://resna.org
■ President's Committee on Employment of People With Disabilities (provides information on the costs and benefits of accommodations; a business guide for hiring people with disabilities; and the use of job analysis as an employment tool): http://www.icdri.org/Employment/pcepd.htm
■ ADA Amendments Act of 2008: http://www.adabill.com

## References

Americans With Disabilities Act of 1990, Pub. L. 101–336, 42 U.S.C. § 12101.

Americans With Disabilities Act Amendments Act of 2008, Pub. L. 110–325.

Andrew, J. (Ed.). (2000). *Disability handbook.* Fayetteville: University of Arkansas, Department of Rehabilitation Education and Research.

Arbona, C. (1996). Career theory and practice in a multicultural context. In M. L. Savickas & W. B. Walsh (Eds.), *Handbook of career counseling theory and practice* (pp. 45–54). Palo Alto, CA: Davies-Black.

Bennett, K., Brady, M. P., Scott, J., Dukes, C., & Frain, M. (2010). The effects of covert audio coaching on the job performance of supported employees. *Focus on Autism and Other Developmental Disabilities, 25*(3), 173–185. Retrieved from EBSCO*host.*

Beveridge, S., Heller Craddock, S., Liesener, J., Stapleton, M., & Hershenson, D. (2002). INCOME: A framework for conceptualizing the career development of persons with disabilities. *Rehabilitation Counseling Bulletin, 45,* 195–206.

Blanck, P., Anderson, J., Wallach, E., & Tenney, J. (1994). Implementing reasonable accommodations using ADR under the ADA: The case of a white-collar employee with bipolar mental illness. *Mental and Physical Disability Law Review, 18,* 458–464.

Blessing, L., & Jamieson, J. (1999). Employing persons with a developmental disability: Effects of previous experience. *Canadian Journal of Rehabilitation, 12,* 211–221.

Bordieri, J., Drehmer, D., & Comninel, M. (1988). Attribution of responsibility and hiring recommendations for job applicants with low back pain. *Rehabilitation Counseling Bulletin, 32,* 140–149.

Brabham, R., Mandeville, K., & Koch, L. (1998). The state-federal vocational rehabilitation program. In R. M. Parker & E. M. Szymanski (Eds.), *Rehabilitation counseling: Basics and beyond* (3rd ed., pp. 41–70). Austin, TX: Pro-Ed.

Brady, M. P., Duffy, M. L., Frain, M., & Bucholz, J. (2010). Evaluating work performance and support needs in supported employment training programs: Correspondence between teachers' ratings and students' self ratings? *Journal of Rehabilitation, 76,* 24–31.

Breslin, R., & Olsheski, J. (1996). The impact of a transitional work return program on lost time. *NARPPS Journal, 11*(2), 35–40.

Brodwin, M., Parker, M., & DeLaGarza, D. (2003). Disability and accommodation. In E. M. Szymanski & R. M. Parker (Eds.), *Work and disability: Issues and strategies for career development and job placement* (2nd ed., pp. 201–246). Austin, TX: Pro-Ed.

Buys, T., & van Biljon, H. (2007). Functional capacity evaluation: An essential component of South African occupational therapy work practice services. *Work, 29*(1), 31–36.

Cameron, D., & Sharp, T. (1998). *ADA resource manual.* Columbus: Ohio Rehabilitation Services Commission.

Caston, H., & Watson, A. (1990). Vocational assessment and rehabilitation outcomes. *Rehabilitation Counseling Bulletin, 34,* 61–66.

Chen, J. J. (2007). Functional capacity evaluation and disability. *Iowa Orthopedic Journal, 27,* 121–127.

Clawson, L. (2002). Orthotics, amputation, and prosthetics. In M. Brodwin, F. Tellez, & S. Brodwin (Eds.), *Medical, psychosocial, and vocational aspects of disability* (2nd ed., pp. 305–316). Athens, GA: Elliott & Fitzpatrick.

Colenbrander, A. (1977). Dimensions of visual performance. *Transaction—American Academy of Ophthalmology and Otolaryngology, 83,* 332–337.

Conte, L. (1983). Vocational development theories and the disabled person: Oversight or deliberate omission. *Rehabilitation Counseling Bulletin, 26,* 316–328.

Crites, J. (1978). *Theory and research handbook for the career maturity inventory.* Monterey, CA: McGraw-Hill.

Curnow, T. (1989). Vocational development of persons with disability. *Vocational Guidance Quarterly, 37,* 269–278.

Cutler, F., & Ramm, A. (1992). Introduction to the basics of vocational evaluation. In J. Siefker (Ed.), *Vocational evaluation in private sector rehabilitation* (pp. 31–66). Menomonie: Materials Development Center, Stout Vocational Rehabilitation Institute, University of Wisconsin—Stout.

Delfs, C. H., & Campbell, J. M. (2010). A quantitative synthesis of developmental disability research: The impact of functional assessment methodology on treatment effectiveness. *Behavior Analyst Today,* 11(1), 4–19.

DeWitt, J. (1991). Removing barriers through technology. In J. West (Ed.), *The Americans With Disabilities Act: From policy to practice* (313–332). New York: Milbank Memorial Fund.

Elinson, L., Frey, W. D., Li, T., Palan, M. A., & Horne, R. L. (2008). Evaluation of customized employment in building the capacity of the workforce development system. *Journal of Rehabilitation, 28,* 141–158.

Equal Employment Opportunity Commission. (1991). *The Americans With Disabilities Act: Your responsibilities as an employer.* Washington, DC: U.S. Government Printing Office.

Equal Employment Opportunity Commission. (2009a). *The job accommodation process: Steps to a collaborative solution.* Retrieved January 21, 2011 from http://www.dol.gov/odep/pubs/misc/job.htm

Equal Employment Opportunity Commission. (2009b). *Notice concerning the Americans With Disabilities Act (ADA) Amendments Act of 2008.* Retrieved from http://www.eeoc.gov/laws/statutes/adaaa_notice.cfm

Fabian, E. S., Ethridge, G., & Beveridge, S. (2009). Differences in perceptions of career barriers and supports for people with disabilities by demographic, background and case status factors. *Journal of Rehabilitation, 75,* 41–49.

Falvo, D. (1991). *Medical and psychosocial aspects of chronic illness and disability.* Gaithersburg, MD: Aspen.

Farr, M. J., Shatkin, L., & Ludden, L. L. (2006). *New guide for occupational exploration* (3rd ed.). Indianapolis, IN: Jist Works.

Fitzgerald, L., & Betz, N. (1994). Career development in cultural context: The role of gender, race, class, and sexual orientation. In M. L. Savickas & R. W. Lent (Eds.), *Convergence in career development theories: Implications for science and practice* (pp. 103–117). Palo Alto, CA: Consulting Psychologists Press.

Gervey, R., Ni, G., Tillman, D., Dickel, K., & Kneubuehl, J. (2009). Person-centered employment planning teams: A demonstration project to enhance employment and training outcomes for persons with disabilities accessing the one-stop career center system. *Journal of Rehabilitation, 75*(2), 43–49.

Gysbers, N., Heppner, M., & Johnston, J. (2003). *Career counseling: Process, issues, and techniques* (2nd ed.). Boston, MA: Allyn & Bacon.

Hallock, K., Hendricks, W., & Broadbent, E. (1998). Discrimination by gender and disability status: Do worker perceptions match statistical measures? *Southern Economic Journal, 65,* 245–263.

Hanley-Maxwell, C., Szymanski, E., & Owens-Johnson, L. (1998). School-to-adult life transition and supported employment. In R. Parker & E. Szymanski (Eds.). *Rehabilitation counseling: Basics and beyond* (3rd ed., pp. 143–180). Austin, TX: Pro-Ed.

Harvey, E. (2002). Hearing disabilities. In M. Brodwin, F. Tellez, & S. Brodwin (Eds.). *Medical, psychosocial, and vocational aspects of disability* (2nd ed., pp. 143–156). Athens, GA: Elliott & Fitzpatrick.

Helms, J. E. (1995). An update of Helm's White and people of color racial identity models. In J. G. Ponterotto, J. M. Cass, L. A. Suzuki, & C. M. Alexander (Eds.), *Handbook of multicultural counseling* (pp. 181–198). Thousand Oaks, CA: Sage.

Hershenson, D. (1981). Work adjustment, disability, and the three r's of vocational rehabilitation: A conceptual model. *Rehabilitation Counseling Bulletin, 25,* 91–97.

Hershenson, D. (1996). Work adjustment: A neglected area in career counseling. *Journal of Counseling and Development, 74,* 442–448.

Hershenson, D. (2005). INCOME: A culturally inclusive and disability-sensitive framework for organizing career development concepts and interventions. *Career Development Quarterly, 54,* 150–161.

Hutchinson, N. L., Versnel, J., Chin, P., & Munby, H. (2008). Negotiating accommodations so that work-based education facilitates career development for youth with disabilities. *Work, 30,* 123–136.

Jenkins, W., Patterson, J., & Szymanski, E. (1998). Philosophical, historical, and legislative aspects of the rehabilitation counseling profession. In R. Parker & E. Szymanski (Eds.), *Rehabilitation counseling: Basics and beyond* (3rd ed., pp. 1–40). Austin, TX: Pro-Ed.

Job Accommodation Network. (2010). *Workplace accommodations: Low cost, high impact.* Morgantown, WV: U.S. Department of Labor.

Kaye, H. S. (2010). The impact of the 2007–2009 recession on workers with disabilities. *Monthly Labor Review, 133*(10), 19–30.

Lee, B., & Newman, K. (1995). Employer responses to disability: Preliminary evidence and a research agenda. *Employee Responsibilities and Rights Journal, 8,* 209–229.

Lee, G. K., Tansey, T. N., Ferrin, J. M., Parashar, D., Frain, M. P., Tschopp, M. K., & Adams, N. (2008). Assessment of functional capacity: An investigation on the benefits of combining ability-predicted and work-simulated work samples. *Australian Journal of Rehabilitation Counselling, 14*(1), 26–35.

Lent, R., Brown, S., & Hackett, G. (2000). Contextual supports and barriers to career choice: A social cognitive analysis. *Journal of Counseling Psychology, 47,* 36–49.

Lent, R., & Hackett, G. (1994). Sociocognitive mechanisms of personal agency in career development: Pan theoretical prospects. In M. Savickas & R. Lent (Eds.), *Convergence in career development: Implications for science and practice* (pp. 77–101). Palo Alto, CA: Consulting Psychologists Press.

Lynch, R. K., & Lynch, R. T. (1998). Rehabilitation counseling in the private sector. In R. Parker & E. Szymanski (Eds.), *Rehabilitation counseling: Basics and beyond* (3rd ed., pp. 71–106). Austin, TX: Pro-Ed.

Marr, J. (1982). Behavioral analysis of work problems. In B. Bolton (Ed.), *Vocational adjustment of disabled persons* (pp. 127–148). Baltimore, MD: University Park Press.

Marr, J., & Roessler, R. (1994). *Supervision and management: A guide to modifying work behavior.* Fayetteville: University of Arkansas Press.

Martin, C. P. (2009). Assistive technology to improve transition, career, and vocational rehabilitation services for postsecondary students with disabilities. *Journal of Instruction Delivery Systems, 23*(4), 5–9.

Materials Development Center. (1992). *A guide to job analysis.* Stout, WI: Author.

McCuller, G., Moore, S., & Salzberg, C. (1990). Programming for vocational competence in sheltered workshops. *Journal of Rehabilitation, 56,* 41–44.

Minarovic, T. J., & Bambara, L. M. (2007). Teaching employees with intellectual disabilities to manage changing work routines using varied sight-word checklists. *Research and Practice for Persons With Severe Disabilities, 32*(1), 31–42.

Montgomery, J. (1996). Legal aspects of ergonomics. In A. Bhattacharya & J. McGlothlin (Eds.), *Occupational ergonomics: Theory and applications* (pp. 685–698). New York, NY: Marcel Dekker.

Moores, D. (2001). *Educating the deaf: Psychology, principles, and practices* (5th ed.). Boston, MA: Houghton Mifflin.

Mueller, J. (1990). *The workplace workbook: An illustrated guide to job accommodation and assistive technology.* Washington, DC: Dole Foundation.

Nadolsky, J. (1983). The development of vocational evaluation services. In R. Lassiter, M. Lassiter, R. Hardy, & J. Cull (Eds.), *Vocational evaluation, work adjustment, and independent living for severely disabled persons* (pp. 5–17). Springfield, IL: Charles C Thomas.

Naik, A. D., Dyer, C. B., Kunik, M. E., & McCullough, L. B. (2009). Patient autonomy for the management of chronic conditions: A two-component re-conceptualization. *American Journal of Bioethics, 9*(2), 23–30.

Neff, W. (1985). *Work and human behavior.* New York, NY: Aldine.

Nordstrom, C., Huffaker, B., & Williams, K. (1998). When physical disabilities are not liabilities: The role applicant and interviewer characteristics on employment interview outcomes. *Journal of Applied Social Psychology, 28,* 283–306.

Olsheski, J. (1996). Contemporary issues in disability management. *NARPPS Journal, 11*(2), 5–7.

Olsheski, J., & Breslin, R. (1996). The Americans With Disabilities Act: Implications for the use of ergonomics in rehabilitation. In A. Bhattacharya & J. McGlothlin (Eds.), *Occupational ergonomics: Theory and applications* (pp. 669–684). New York, NY: Marcel Dekker.

Olsheski, J., & Schelat, R. (2003). Reasonable job accommodations for people with psychiatric disabilities. In D. Moxley & J. Finch (Eds.), *Sourcebook of rehabilitation and mental health practice* (pp. 1–76). New York: Plenum.

Osipow, S. (1976). Vocational development problems of the handicapped. In H. Rusalem & D. Malikin (Eds.), *Contemporary vocational rehabilitation* (pp. 51–60). New York: New York University Press.

Ottomanelli, L., Goetz, L., McGeough, C., Suris, A., Sippel, J., Sinnott, P., … Cipher, D. J. (2009). *Journal of Rehabilitation Research and Development, 46,* 919–930.

Panek, W. (2002). Visual disabilities. In M. Brodwin, F. Tellez, & S. Brodwin (Eds.), *Medical, psychosocial, and vocational aspects of disability* (2nd ed., pp. 157–170). Athens, GA: Elliott & Fitzpatrick.

Peterson, N., Mumford, M., Borman, W., Jeanneret, P., Fleishman, E., & Levin, K. (1997). *ONET final technical report, Vol. II.* Salt Lake City: Utah Department of Workforce Services.

Power, P. (1991). *A guide to vocational assessment* (2nd ed.). Austin, TX: Pro-Ed.

Power, P. (2006). *A guide to vocational assessment* (4th ed.). Austin, TX: Pro-Ed.

President's Committee on the Employment of People With Disabilities. (1992). *Report.* Washington, DC: Author.

Rasch, J. (1985). *Rehabilitation of workers' compensation and other insurance claimants.* Springfield, IL: Charles C Thomas.

Reswick, J. (1980). Rehabilitation engineering. *Annual Review of Rehabilitation, 1,* 55–79.

Rehabilitation Act of 1973, Pub. L. 93–112, 29 U.S.C. § 701 *et seq.*

Rehabilitation Services Administration. (1992). *Rehabilitation-related professions.* Washington, DC: Office of Special Education and Rehabilitation Research.

Rehabilitation Services Administration. (1998). *Achieving successful employment outcomes with the use of assistive technology: Twenty-fourth institute on rehabilitation issues.* Menomonie: University of Wisconsin—Stout.

Robertson, R. E. (2005). Social Security Administration: Better planning could make the ticket program more effective (GAO Rep. GAO-05-248). Washington, DC: Author. Retrieved from EBSCO*host.*

Roessler, R., Hinman, S., & Lewis, F. (1987). Job interview deficiencies of "job ready" rehabilitation clients. *Journal of Rehabilitation, 53,* 33–36.

Roessler, R., & Rumrill, P. (1994). *Enhancing productivity on your job: The "win-win" approach to job accommodations.* New York, NY: Multiple Sclerosis Society.

Rosenthal, D., & Olsheski, J. (1999). Rehabilitation counseling and disability management: Present status and future opportunities. *Journal of Rehabilitation, 65,* 31–38.

Rubin, S., & Roessler, R. (1995). *Foundations of the vocational rehabilitation process* (4th ed.). Austin, TX: Pro-Ed.

Rubin, S. E., & Roessler, R. T. (2007). *Foundations of the vocational rehabilitation process* (6th ed.). Austin, TX: Pro-Ed.

Saab, T. D. (2008). *Job accommodation process.* Morgantown, WV: Job Accommodation Network, U.S. Department of Labor.

Smith-Fess Act of 1920, Pub. L. 66–236.

Social Security Act of 1935, Pub. L. 74–271.

Social Security Administration. (2008). *The ticket to work program and other work incentives* (SSA Publication No. 05-10060, ICN 463261). Washington, DC: Author.

Soldiers Rehabilitation Act of 1918, Pub. L. 65–178.

Southeast Disability and Business Technical Assistance Center (DBTAC, 2009). *ADA amendments act of 2008: Summary and resources.* Retrieved June 1, 2011 from http://www.sedbtac.org/ada/publications/adaaa_resources.doc

Szymanski, E., Enright, M., Hershenson, D., & Ettinger, J. (2003). Career development theories, constructs, and research: Implications for people with disabilities. In E. Szymanski & R. Parker (Eds.), *Work and disability: Issues and strategies for career development and job placement* (2nd ed., pp. 91–153). Austin, TX: Pro-Ed.

Szymanski, E., & Hershenson, D. (1998). Career development of people with disabilities: An ecological model. In R. Parker & E. Szymanski (Eds.), *Rehabilitation counseling: Basics and beyond* (3rd ed., pp. 327–378). Austin, TX: Pro-Ed.

Szymanski, E., & Parker, R. (Eds.). (2003). *Work and disability: Issues and strategies in career development and job placement* (2nd ed.). Austin, TX: Pro-Ed.

Szymanski, E., & Trueba, H. (1994). Castification of people with disabilities: Potential disempowering aspects of classification in disability services. *Journal of Rehabilitation, 60*(3), 12–20.

U.S. Department of Labor (1982). *Handbook for analyzing jobs.* Washington, DC: U.S. Government Printing Office.

U.S. Department of Labor. (1991). *Dictionary of occupational titles* (4th ed.). Indianapolis, IN: Jist Works.

U.S. Department of Labor (1991). *Revised Handbook for Analyzing Jobs.* Washington, DC: Government Printing Office.

U.S. Department of Labor. (2002). *Accommodations get the job done.* Washington, DC: Author.

U.S. Department of Labor. (2010–2011). *Occupational outlook handbook.* Washington, DC: U.S. Employment Services.

Vision and Vocational Services. (2011). *Qualified people with disabilities perform assembly, packaging, and inspection tasks for local employers.* Retrieved on from http:// visionandvocationalservices.org/service/30/job-seeking-skills-training/

Weed, R., Taylor, C., & Blackwell, T. (1991). Job analysis for the private sector. *NARPPS Journal, 6,* 153–158.

Wehman, P. (1986). Competitive employment in Virginia. In F. Rusch (Ed.), *Competitive employment issues and strategies* (pp. 23–33). Baltimore, MD: Paul H. Brooks.

Wehman, P., & Kregel, J. (1985). A supported work approach to competitive employment of individuals with moderate and severe handicaps. In P. Wehman & J. Hill (Eds.), *Competitive employment for persons with mental retardation* (pp. 20–45). Richmond: Virginia Commonwealth University, Rehabilitation and Training Center.

Wehman, P., & Kregel, J. (1992). Supported employment: Growth and impact. In P. Wehman, P. Sale, & W. Parent (Eds.), *Supported employment: Strategies for integration of workers with disabilities* (pp. 3–28). Stoneham, MA: Butterworth-Heinemann.

Wilson-Kovacs, D., Ryan, M. K., Haslam, A., & Rabinovich, A. (2008). Just because you can get a wheelchair in the building doesn't necessarily mean you can participate: Barriers to the career advancement of disabled professionals. *Disability and Society, 23,* 705–717.

Wind, H., Gouttebarge, V., Kuijer, M., Sluiter, J. K., & Frings-Dresen, M. (2009). Complementary value of functional capacity evaluation for physicians in assessing the physical work ability of workers with musculoskeletal disorders. *International Archives of Occupational and Environmental Health, 82,* 435–443.

Winn, S., & Hay, I. (2009). Transition from school for youths with a disability: Issues and challenges. *Disability and Society, 24,* 103–115.

Wright, G. (1980). *Total rehabilitation.* Boston, MA: Little, Brown.

CHAPTER **16**

# Career Counseling With Couples and Families

Kathy M. Evans

## Contents

Until very recently, career planning has been directed toward a single individual and his or her specific personality characteristics, values, interests, skills, and desires. Family issues may have been considered, but they were seldom treated as central to the individual's career planning needs. The counseling profession has evolved over the years and has moved from conceptualizing clients as isolated individuals to viewing clients in the context of their environment (e.g., their families, partners, and other significant people in their lives). This move has been heavily influenced by (a) multicultural counseling, which introduced the notion that the Anglo American value of the rugged individualist is contrary to the values of many ethnic and cultural minority groups; (b) feminists who pointed out that women tend to be more relationship oriented and that use of individualism as the norm pathologizes women's experiences; (c) postmodern philosophy, which asserts that individuals make their own meaning of their experiences and that counselors should honor their clients' perception of the world; and (d) family therapy that purports that an individual is part of a family system and that there is a reciprocal influence between an individual and his or her family.

## Systems Theory

Although family influencing the careers of its members is an ancient process, the more research that is conducted, the more researchers are aware of the reciprocal influences between family and individuals on career planning. Children have been going into the family business for centuries. It is not uncommon for a family to produce generations of doctors, lawyers, farmers, teachers, and business owners (Evans & Rotter, 2000). Research has shown that most people seek family support and approval for their career decisions, and in fact, rather than lose that family support, individuals are willing to compromise their career aspirations (Gottfredson, 1981; Keller & Whiston, 2008; Whiston & Keller, 2004). When a family member does choose an occupation without family support, upheaval may occur in some families and stress may be placed on the defector (Chope, 2006).

### SIDEBAR 16.1   Exercise 1: Identifying Your Family Influences

Write a two-page essay identifying the family influences on your career decisions. Please include some historical information as well as the results of your self-exploration. Ask family members on both sides of your family about the careers of family members. Try to go back a couple of generations or as far as you can. Analyze the results, looking for any trends that seem to emerge. Be sure to comment on the family members from your generation and discuss how many, if any, have gone into a career related to that of previous family members.

What careers were you encouraged to and discouraged from entering when you were a child? A teenager? A college student? Whose opinion held the most weight for you within the family? Did you choose a career because it was what your family desired? How do you think future generations of your family will make career decisions?

The reciprocal influences of individuals and their families is a concept from general systems theory, adapted to family therapy to understand family dynamics. General systems theory was originally a mathematical theory developed by Norbert Wiener (1948) and extended to biology and medicine by Von Bertalanffy (1968). Simply put, the first part of general systems theory asserts that systems are made up of many parts that interact and relate to one another. The interrelationships between parts affect the functioning of the entire system. A change in any one of these parts results in a change in all the other parts as well as in the entire system. Any change in the system affects all of its parts. This process is called *circular causality*. Second, the system works to maintain homeostasis—stability and equilibrium. That is, the system works to maintain the status quo. Goldenberg and Goldenberg (1994) used the thermostat as an example of homeostasis, stating that the thermostat will maintain a constant temperature, keeping the house from getting too hot or too cold.

To relate general systems theory to family therapy, each member of the family is part of the larger family system. When one family member displays problematic behavior, this behavior is understood to be a manifestation of a change in the interactional process of the family system as a whole (circular causality); the problematic behavior is an attempt to regain stability and equilibrium (homeostasis) in the family. If Tyreeq suddenly starts to pick fights with fellow classmates, he may be reacting to the decreased attention he is receiving from his parents, who spend most of their time arguing over the new addition to their home. His behavior is an attempt to regain his parent's attention and return family interaction to the status quo. The family is also affected by other, even larger systems (e.g., ethnic group, neighborhoods, schools, communities, workplaces, economic and political institutions), and changes in those systems affect the family and, in turn, its individual members (Goldenberg & Goldenberg, 1994).

Systems theory has gained general acceptance in counseling and psychology as a way to better understand individuals. However, it is not without its critics. Feminists have criticized systems theory because it assumes that everyone in the family has equal power and can affect the system equally when change occurs (Melito, 2003; Walters, Carter, Papp, & Silverstein, 1988). Less powerful individuals (women and children), they say, cannot be equally as responsible for what happens as those who are more powerful. Multicultural counselors have stated that systems theory is based on a White, middle-class model of the family and does not take into account different family configurations and the effects of race, gender, ethnicity, and culture (Evans & Rotter, 2000; Sciarra, 1999). Given these caveats, systems theory helps counselors to understand the workings of many families and may help them develop interventions that will be useful for their clients. Before counselors can really understand families, they need to have an understanding of the meaning of *family* in the 21st century.

## Twenty-First-Century Family

Chope (2006) declared that the complexity of today's families is reflected in the "revolutionary changes in the structure of the family" (p. 64). The notion of family has changed so much over the past few decades that it is not surprising that Paniagua (1996) recommended that counselors ask their clients to identify who is family to them. Carter and McGoldrick (1999b) and Chope described the contemporary U.S. family as having various configurations: (a) two-parent families in which parents may be heterosexual, gay, lesbian, or transgender, married or unmarried, and may or may not be the biological parents of their children; (b) single-parent families, in which the parent may be heterosexual, gay, lesbian, or transgender and may or may not be the biological parent of the child; (c) extended families that may or may not be biologically related to one another; (d) couples (heterosexual, gay, lesbian, or transgender) without children; (e) single adults (heterosexual, gay, lesbian, or transgender) without children; and (f) grandparents raising grandchildren without the biological parents being present. Family configurations are often determined by cultural influences; however, even within cultural groups, there is diversity. For example, Billingsley (1992) was able to identify 32 different configurations of African American households. Carter and McGoldrick (1999b) said it best when they wrote, "It is high time we gave up on our traditional concept of family and expanded our very definition of the term" (p. 10).

## Connection Between Family and Work

Sigmund Freud described a healthy individual as one who has the ability to love and work. The wisdom of that observation is not lost on today's researchers and practitioners (Bernas & Major, 2000; Erickson, Martinengo, & Hill, 2010; Stevens, Ninotte, Mannon, & Kiger, 2007). Zedeck and Mosier (1990) stated that family and work are the two central institutions in life, and Burke (1996) stated that the major life roles for most employed adults are worker and family member. Individuals in the United States spend, on average, two thirds of their lives (Dawis & Lofquist, 1984) and 36% of their days doing work (Bureau of Labor Statistics, 2010a). It is not surprising that many people spend the better part of their lives juggling the responsibilities of work and family.

A great deal of the research that has been conducted on family and career connections has supported the belief that a predictable relationship exists between how well a person functions at work and how well he or she functions in familial relations. Most of the research has been driven by one or more theories that have evolved regarding the work and family connection. These theories include spillover theory, compensation theory, conflict theory, instrumental theory, and segmentation theory (Gysbers, Heppner, & Johnston, 1998).

Compensation theory purports that individuals compensate for what is missing in their families by increasing their commitment to work or vice versa.

> *With a bachelor's degree in marketing, Marie is underemployed as an administrative assistant at an advertising firm and compensates by spending more time on leadership activities involving her children. She has taken on the tasks of Little League baseball coach, Sunday school teacher, and president of the parent–teacher organization.*

According to segmentation theory, individuals are able to compartmentalize their lives, keeping family life and work life completely separate.

> *At work, Johnny does not have pictures of his family on his desk, nor does he discuss family problems or issues with his coworkers. Johnny also refuses to take work home and does not discuss his work with his family. He concentrates on only one facet of his life at a time because he believes he would be less effective in his role as a worker if he were to let his family interfere at work and less effective as a parent and spouse if he were to let his work interfere at home.*

Instrumental theory purports that individuals work to provide their families not only with what they need but also with luxuries.

> *By putting in overtime and weekends during the winter months, Annie is able to buy a wide-screen television, send her children to camp for 2 weeks in the summer, take a family vacation, and have a membership in the local recreation club.*

Most of the research today on family and work is devoted to spillover theory and conflict theory. In spillover theory, boundaries between work and family are very fuzzy. Spillover theory is the opposite of segmentation theory.

*Bill shares his frustrations with his family with his coworkers and shares his disappointments in his work with his family. He conducts family business during work hours and frequently takes work home.*

Most of the work done in this area has focused on the negative effects of work on family life or vice versa.

However, recent research has investigated the positive effects of spillover—how good things that happen at work can influence good things happening at home and vice versa (McNall, Nicklin, & Masuda, 2010; Stevens et al., 2007). Much of this research involves work-to-family enrichment or family-to-work enrichment or facilitation and how enriching the quality of the work (or family) experience can have a positive influence on worker attitudes, behavior, and productivity (Greenhaus & Powell, 2006; Grzywacz & Butler, 2005; McNall et al., 2010).

Conflict theory describes how conflict can arise from the roles that individuals play at work and at home. They are often forced to choose one role over the other because of the conflict. Much of the research today is focused less on spillover and more on work-to-family conflict and family-to-work conflict, and terminology in this research includes *work–family interface* (Bianchi & Milkie, 2010).

*As a supervisor, Thea must work evenings to oversee a special project that has a critical deadline. Thea's daughter, Shani, has the lead in the school play that takes place on the very evenings Thea must work.*

These theories illustrate very clearly that work and family are intertwined and that to work out these problems, counselors may have to work with more than one member of the family. Therefore, family counseling skill competencies are indeed essential for career counselors. In fact, Blustein (2001) stated that

the artificial barriers between work and relationships are finally beginning to be understood and perhaps diminished in scope. Once we can fully internalize the fact that work and relational functioning are integrated aspects of human life, we may be able to generate theory, research, and practice models that truly embrace the full scope of human life in the 21st century. (p. 189)

## Family Life Cycle

One of the ways in which counselors have been able to internalize the relationship between work and relational functioning is to take a close look at the family life cycle. The family life cycle illustrates the development of the traditional nuclear family by describing six stages of development and the emotional processes that the family experiences during these stages (Carter & McGoldrick, 1988). Carter and McGoldrick (1988) offered developmental examples of each stage as well as the changes that the family needs to make to continue to develop. The stages are leaving home, joining families through marriage, families with young children, families with adolescents, launching children, and families in later life. They primarily reflect major transitions that mostly coincide with the age of the children in the family. As the child grows, the interactions and relationships that the parents have with that child and with each other change, resulting in changes in other family members as well. Families that do not make the adjustment from one stage to another effectively tend to have difficulties that may result in a need for counseling. These adjustments that the family makes are referred to as *second-order change*, in which the generations must shift their status in the relationship and reconnect in a new and different way. Recent research on the family life cycle by Erickson et al. (2010) has confirmed that having children in a family is influential on the work and careers of the caregivers and that the age of the children affects both work and family demands.

What is clearly apparent from the family life cycle is that it was developed on the model of a nuclear family—two married heterosexual parents and their biological children, with the mother staying at home and working full time as a homemaker and the father working outside the home. In 1999, Carter and McGoldrick (1999b) stated that in current U.S. society, the idea of the traditional family needs to be abandoned because it does not describe the majority of households. "It is becoming increasingly difficult to determine what family life cycle patterns are 'normal,' causing great stress from family members, who have few consensually validated models to guide them through the passages they must negotiate" (Carter & McGoldrick, 1990b, p. 1).

Because the stages are based on the traditional White (Anglo) middle-class family of old, Hines, Preto, McGoldrick, Almeida, and Welman (1999) have warned that to understand how families move through their life cycles, counselors have to determine the importance of their cultural and ethnic backgrounds. Different ethnic and cultural groups may place more importance on some stages and transitions than they do others. For example, Irish American and African American families place a great deal of importance on the wake after the death of a family member. Italian American and Polish American families emphasize weddings, and Jewish families stress the bar mitzvah. Ethnic groups often have different generational patterns that may call in to question the timing of the life cycle stages. In some cultures, launching does not take place until marriage; in others, interdependence lasts a lifetime. When second and third generations of a cultural group are in close contact, conflict often occurs when the younger generation wants to adopt the dominant culture's traditions and the older generation wants to pass on its legacy. The traditional family life cycle would not explain the struggles of a family from every cultural group, so it is important for counselors to have an understanding of their clients' cultural traditions and create the unique family life cycle of a particular cultural group. Hines et al. (1999) warned that "any life cycle transition can trigger ethnic identity conflicts, since it puts families more in touch with the roots of their family traditions" (p. 70).

Other very important transitions that modern-day families encounter are not included in the Carter and McGoldrick (1988) model. Some examples include open adoption, artificial means of conceiving, reunions of families separated by social services, separation of nonmarried couples, gay and lesbian marriage or commitment, and biracial and bicultural marriages. One of the largest issues in most of these transitions is that they involve alternative lifestyles that the larger society has rejected, and as such, the families involved are seldom likely to get the kind of support that is available in more traditional transitions (Imber-Black, 1999). Carter and McGoldrick's family life cycle is not predictable for all families and needs to be reconfigured to reflect culturally different families and families with different lifestyle patterns. Consider the Connor family.

## Connor Family

*Judy Connor is a 23-year-old African American woman who has an 8-year-old daughter, Taylor. Judy and Taylor live with Judy's parents and two siblings, Troy, 15 and Ricky, 17. Judy has limited contact with Taylor's biological father, Joe, 30, who is employed at a local discount store and who sends child support payments to Judy only sporadically. Judy became pregnant while she was in high school but was able to finish and go on to study computer graphic design at the community college. Her parents have been very supportive and have helped her with her tuition as long as she takes care of her child and works full time while she is in college.*

*Although Judy was able to take on the responsibilities of an adult by becoming a parent, she remained financially and emotionally dependent on her parents. The extended family support will enable her to become truly independent in the near future. Judy has not married, although she shares parenthood with Joe. The two families are related through Judy's daughter and, on occasion, interact. Judy's parents are also involved in several other family life stages at this time. They have teenage boys (families with adolescents) and a grandchild (launching). Grandparenthood, too, came earlier for the elder Connors than called for in the original family life cycle.*

The career issues reflected in the family life cycle model are implied and may need further explanation. Juxtaposing Super's (1990) career development stages with the family life cycle, one can begin to see the impact of career issues (see Table 16.1).

Young adults leaving home are not only testing out their independence from their family of origin, they are also examining their initial career choices. As they marry and join with their spouse's family, they are solidifying their career choices and beginning to make advances in their careers. Once they start to have children, their careers may begin to soar, and the

**TABLE 16.1  Comparison Between Carter and McGoldrick's (1999b) Family Life Cycle Stages and Super's (1990) Career Development Stages**

| Carter and McGoldrick's Family Life Cycle Stages | Super's Career Development Stages |
|---|---|
| *Leaving home:* Young adult begins life on his or her own. | *Exploration:* Young adult tries out career opportunities. |
| Marriage: Young adult commits to a new family system. | *Exploration and establishment:* Young adult completes exploration of careers and begins to establish him- or herself. |
| *Families with young children:* Young adult takes on responsibility of parenthood. | *Establishment:* Parents grow and develop in their careers. |
| | *Growth:* Children begin to learn and fantasize about careers and try out new abilities. |
| Families with adolescents: Parent grants children more independence. | *Maintenance:* Parents settle into their careers. |
| | *Growth and exploration:* Children begin to learn interests and abilities through participation in academic work, extracurricular activities, and part-time work |
| Launching children: Parent accepts family members leaving; both new beginnings and endings. | *Maintenance:* Parents continue to work in careers and begin to think about retiring |
| | *Exploration:* Children try out career opportunities. |
| *Families in later life:* Parent/Grandparent accept new generation roles. | *Disengagement:* Retirement or reduced hours for parents. |

role conflicts become critical. Their children, however, are just beginning to understand what careers are about as well as what they are capable of doing. When the children become adolescents, the parents' careers are beginning to level out and do not rise as quickly. Some have reached as high as they will go by this time. The children, however, are beginning to explore careers through part-time work and extracurricular activities at school. As the children leave home and parents begin to lose their own parents, the parents are settled in their careers and attempting to maintain what they have gained. The children have started exploring their own careers at this point and are trying out their first jobs. Finally, when the parents reach later life, they enjoy being grandparents and scale down work or retire altogether while their children are climbing their own career ladders.

Some of the current career issues individuals may encounter with the family life cycle are

1. *Leaving home:* Many young people today find it difficult to find their first job, especially if they leave formal education before or right after completing high school. If they do find a job, it may be difficult for them to earn enough to live on their own. Therefore, leaving home is occurring later and later for many adult children (Fulmer, 1999).

2. *Joining:* This lifestyle stage is also being delayed because young people are leaving home later in their lives. Also, once they get married, most couples find it necessary for both spouses to work. The couple will need to decide on the lifestyle they want to live on the basis of their income and the commitment they want to make to their careers.

3. *Young children:* Because both parents are likely to work, decisions have to be made about childcare and how parental roles are to be shared. One or both spouses will start to experience role conflicts between work and family obligations. Decisions will need to be made regarding chores for school-age children.

4. *Adolescent families:* Work and family role conflicts lessen as adolescents become more independent. The teenager may begin work to earn his or her own money or be frustrated by the lack of available jobs.

5. *Launching children:* Parents may see that retirement may not occur as soon as they thought because of financial need. Children remain dependent longer as they enroll in higher education or stay at home until they can afford to move or get married. Children may be starting their own careers and discovering that they may have made a poor career decision.

6. *Later life:* More and more retired people are returning to work to supplement their income and to remain physically and mentally active.

The family life cycle and related career development issues will become even clearer as I explore the specific career issues of families and couples.

### SIDEBAR 16.2  Exercise 2: Alternative Stage Model

Using the Carter and McGoldrick (1988) family life cycle as a model, create new life stages that need to be developed for a blended, extended family such as the one described here:

1. A heterosexual couple, both of whom have been previously married with school-age children from those marriages living in the household.
2. The couple also have a child in common living with them.
3. The wife's parents also live in a first-floor apartment in their home. Her father has Alzheimer's disease.

Insert the new life stages where you believe they would be most appropriate.

## Two-Income Families

The literature on issues for heterosexual dual-career and dual-earner couples is vast. It is the most researched area for family- and career-related issues. For the purposes of this discussion, I define two-income families as two heterosexual, married or unmarried parents and their children. I also include blended families in which parents have remarried; the children may be the biological children of one parent and stepchildren of an otherwise childless stepparent, biological children of each parent, biological children of both parents, or some or all of these. The most recent data available showed that 20% of U.S. children live in homes that are blended in some way (U.S. Census Bureau, 2001–2002). In today's society, it is often necessary for both parents to earn an income, although two-parent families make up only 30% of the total population of families in the United States (U.S. Census Bureau, 2011). Overall, in at least 58.1% of two-parent families, both parents work (Bureau of Labor Statistics, 2010b).

It is necessary to distinguish between two groups of two-income families. The first group is dual-career families, in which both members of the couple are engaged in a managerial or professional position that (a) requires high levels of effort and energy for success, (b) commands a high commitment to excel, and (c) offers advancement in responsibility and pay status (Cooper, Arkkelin, & Tielbert, 1994; Duxbury & Higgins, 1994). Dual-earner couples, however, are involved in jobs rather than careers. They tend to have gainful employment with no expectation of a high degree of commitment or advancement and to involve lower levels of energy and effort. A couple could be considered a dual-earner couple even if one spouse was in a pursuit of a career. Many of the problems encountered by dual-earner couples are felt by dual-career couples, but they also have different issues.

Gysbers et al. (1998) suggested that it is helpful to develop a vocabulary of family and work problems to clarify any potentially fuzzy issues. They suggested categorizing problems into life roles (worker role, family role), life events (work-related events, family-related events), and life setting (home or work). I use these categories in the following discussion of the issues of two-income families.

### Problems With Life Roles

When two parents work, there are many concerns—childcare, household duties, and managing spillover from work to home and from home to work. However, the overarching theme for dual-career and dual-earner families is gender role expectations and socialization. Women have been socialized to be the caretakers of the young and men have been socialized to be the providers. Although these roles have been evolving (especially because the majority of women now work outside the home), little has changed as to society's expectations of mothers and fathers (Duxbury & Higgins, 1994; Higgins, Duxbury, & Lyons, 2010). When young men and women prepare for a career, women are more likely to consider their future family in their career decision making. They have the expectation of subordinating, and for many the desire to subordinate, their career interests for the sake of raising their children. McGoldrick (1999) stated that the three marital types of dual-career families are (1) traditional–conventional, (2) modern–participant, and (3) egalitarian–role sharing. In traditional–conventional families, parenting and household work are the wife's duties. In modern–participant families, parenting is shared, but the wife does the housework. In egalitarian–role-sharing families, both spouses do the parenting and the housework; however, only a few of all dual-career couples have this kind of division of labor. McGoldrick (1999) stated that the difference in how the family is divided is the result of a variety of factors of which gender role socialization is one and cultural factors are another. When couples have difficulty agreeing on what is a fair division of work and power, there will be disharmony in the relationship. If they agree, there is satisfaction (Goldenberg & Goldenberg, 1994).

On average, women work more hours per week on home-related activities than do men (Bureau of Labor Statistics, 2010a). Today's men, however, are placing more importance on family and relationships than ever before, and they are spending more time caring for children. The work that is done in the home is, however, typically divided by gender (Bianchi & Milkie, 2010; Higgins et al., 2010). Women do more meal preparation, and men do yard-work and home repairs (Bureau of Labor Statistics, 2010).

In dual-earner families, many women work to supplement the family income. Although Brines (1994) found that women are more likely than men to downgrade career or work concerns and Bianchi and Riley (2005) found that mothers more often cut back their employment to take care of the family, Higgins et al. (2010) found that both members of the couple tended to put work first and were less likely to cut back on work when they felt overloaded. This change may reflect the dependence on dual incomes many families now feel since the deep recession in 2008 through 2009. In their research on dual-earner couples, Becker and Moen (1999) found that some couples try to buffer their families from the demands of work by scaling back their career pursuits. Some of the strategies they use include deciding on a one-career marriage, limiting work hours and travel, or trading off who has the job and who has the career. Part-time work may be another of the scaling-back strategies that may be practiced by women with children younger than 6 whose husbands earn a high income. Most of these wives worked fewer hours than career women with higher pay (Risman, Atkinson, & Blackwelder, 1999). This strategy was supported in more recent research by Reynolds (2005), who found that women from affluent households were more willing to reduce hours when there was conflict between work and family responsibilities.

Professional women's commitment is expected to mirror that of professional men whether or not they have a family. Stone (2007) found that women who took time off from high-status careers ended up not returning to those careers because of the demands of the work setting. Often, employers' policies toward families were favorable for the birth or adoption of a child, but few were willing to negotiate flex time, work from home, or leave time when children got older. However, couples pay the price for sharing the work both at home and outside the home (Mackey, 1995). Men with children and a working spouse earn about the same as single men and married men with no children but less than men with children and a stay-at-home spouse. Women with children and a working spouse made more than single women but about the same as married women with no children (Schneer & Reitman, 1993).

Child care, of course, is of concern whether parents work full time or part time. Although more affluent couples may have their choice of child care providers, child care is often a challenge to those with lower incomes. In fact, part of the scaling down that lower income couples may decide to make is for one spouse (usually the wife) to stay at home with the children because it is less costly than going to work (Baum, 2002).

### Problems With Life Events

Job stress is likely to have a negative impact on marital relationships and the worker's mood at home, which may be more true for women than it is for men. Barnett (1994) found that women in dual-career couples experience stress when their marital or family experiences are negative. Women are also more likely to suffer stress from spillover and role conflict when things are not going well at home (Byron, 2005; Higgins et al., 2010; Nomaguchi, Milkie, & Bianchi, 2005). Things going well at home tended to buffer stressful situations at work for both men and women. Conversely, family demands tended to result in role overloads for men, perhaps because men perceived that family time demands took away from their traditional role as breadwinner (Higgins et al., 2010).

Another life event that may have a major effect on the couple and the family is the need to care for aging or disabled parents. Dual-income couples with dependent children at home and the responsibility of caring for aging parents, whether or not the parents reside with the family, have been dubbed the "sandwich generation." The number of this particular type of family has grown over the years. In fact, Bond and Wise (2003) found that 35% of the working population cared for an older relative. The work–family demands on the sandwiched couple can create a special kind of conflict, given the multiple roles these couples face (Cullen, Hammer, Neal, & Sinclair, 2009). However, little research has been done on this population, and those studies that do exist were published more than a decade ago (Buffardi, Smith, O'Brien, & Erdwins, 1999; Chapman, Ingersoll-Dayton, & Neal, 1994). In a recent study, Cullen et al. (2009) created a typology for dual-income sandwiched couples that includes three basic types—high parent care demands, high child care demands, and high work demands. Their research determined the work–family conflict these couples experience. They found that both women and men in these couples differed in terms of work–family conflict. The women with high child care and high parent care demands and the men with high work demands experienced more work–family conflict than their partners. Interestingly, no differences were found among the groups in the work–family conflicts of men or women. Cullen et al. suggested that perhaps couples were hesitant to report that family interfered with work or that their work was beneficial to those they cared for (e.g., providing need income). In the high work-demands group, the men had high work demands (putting in 17 hours more per week than their partners) and more family–work conflicts.

Other life events that can be problematic for dual-career couples occur in their relationship. At times, there is competition between the individuals in a couple because they are both chasing a career (Goldenberg & Goldenberg,

1994). Resentment may arise if one partner is advancing more quickly than the other or if one's salary is higher than the other's. Also, equity in the relationship may become an issue because it is closely related to money. If the male partner makes more money, then he is likely to assume more power. Because women typically earn less than men even if they are employed in the same career, men will maintain the power. However, competition issues may arise if the woman makes more than her partner because such a situation defies gender socialization.

### Problems in Life Settings

One of the most difficult issues for dual-career couples is geographical mobility. Typically, the goal is for each partner to find an ideal position in the same city. However, in many dual-career couples, one partner's career is at a higher level than the other's and there are only a few opportunities at the highest levels and more opportunities at the medium and lower levels (Rhodes, 2002). More often than not, the man's career is the one at the higher level, so the geographic moves are based on his career.

When both spouses are intensely career minded and committed to their respective careers and their relationship, a commuter marriage may result. One spouse chooses to stay in City A, and the other spouse goes to City B. They are together on weekends or during monthly visits (depending on time and distance). Commuter marriages require a great deal of sacrifice because the couple is separated most of the time and carry the cost of running two households. It is particularly stressful if children are involved. The parent who stays with the children is virtually a single parent while the other parent is out of town. More often than not, commuting is temporary. Most couples prefer not to be separated or uproot their families for advancement. Even when companies were willing to assist couples in finding work for both partners, it is difficult to get employees to leave their positions and move their families.

Employers are slowly responding to the family needs of their employees. These adjustments include flex time, telecommuting, onsite day care centers, parental leave for fathers and mothers, financial assistance for day care, job sharing, and part-time options for workers (Goldenberg & Goldenberg, 1994). Unfortunately, the United States lags behind other Western countries in providing such work flexibility (Bianchi & Milkie, 2010). However, IBM is one U.S. company that has offered flexibility to employees through virtual offices (doing work anytime, anywhere) and telecommuting (working from home). Hill, Ferris, and Martinson (2003) found that telecommuting helped IBM workers to balance work and family lives but that virtual offices had a negative effect on family life balance. Previous studies have found that men are less likely to take advantage of these benefits even when they are available. Interestingly, even when men are self-employed, an avenue many tend to take to gain work-time flexibility and autonomy, they do not tend to use this flexibility and autonomy to put more balance in their work–family life as do women (Loscocco, 1997). That phenomenon may be changing but probably not rapidly. Warner, Winer, and Mansfield (2007) studied the attitudes of college students about family leave, and although both college men and women rated family leave for children as important, women rated it as significantly more important than did men.

### Counseling Two-Income Families

Before counselors begin to work with two-income families, they should recognize that each family is unique in terms of its ethnicity and culture. To connect with their clients, counselors need to understand clients' perspectives on the cultural expectations that the family attempting to meet. Goldenberg and Goldenberg (1994) have suggested a number of strategies for counseling dual-income families. They recommended that counselors involve couples in what Hazard and Koslow (1992) called *conjoint career counseling*, in which the counselor treats each partner evenhandedly. It defeats the purpose of counseling if one person perceives that the counselor is on the other person's side and feels ganged up on. Couples should be encouraged to revaluate their career expectations and, if necessary, redefine success in their careers if they are having problems with role conflict and spillover. Often, conflicts that parents experience may be improved by stress and time management strategies. Sometimes it will be necessary for the couple to resolve any unfinished business that they have with their family of origin that seems to be repeating itself in their current family relationships. Gender role socialization is one area in which counselors will need to examine both partners to help them find the source of their conflicts (Forrest, 1994). Remarried couples may need attention to mourn the loss of their previous lifestyle and adjust to their present situation. Stepparenting can be a challenge to a previously childless stepparent, and couples have to negotiate stepparent involvement not only in disciplining but in taking on parental responsibilities that will influence their work.

In addition, it is essential to draw on the couple's positive assets (commitment to one another, extended family, cultural values, etc.) to help them work through relationship problems that occur as a result of stressful work and family experiences. Couples should be encouraged to approach their respective employers about making family-friendly changes in their policies. Sometimes, just working out a flexible schedule will go a long way toward smoothing out families' rough edges.

## Single-Parent Households

The term *single-parent households* is preferred to *single-parent families* because it avoids the exclusion of the noncustodial parent that the term *single-parent families* tends to imply (Amato, 2000). Although these families, too, may have myriad configurations, for the sake of this discussion, single-parent households include parents who are widowed, divorced, or never married or partnered. Single-parent households make up 8% of the total households with children (Bureau of Labor Statistics, 2010b). The increase in the number of single-parent households is the result of divorce as well as of the increased number of affluent, never-married career women either delivering their own children or adopting children (Gottfried, 1991; Okun, 1996).

Traditionally, single-parent households were considered broken homes, and children were believed to be damaged by having only one parent in the home. Research has shown that this is a myth. The truth is that the difficulties encountered by single parents have more to do with socioeconomic status than with the number of parents the child has at home. When poverty is factored out, researchers have found that children from single-parent households have no more problems adjusting than those from two-parent households (Anderson, 1999). Unfortunately, in 2009 the poverty rate for children in the United States was 20.7%. Nearly 29% of all families headed by a single woman and 16% of those headed by a single man live in poverty (DeNavas-Walt, Proctor, & Smith, 2010).

### Challenges for Single-Parent Households

The most common concerns of single parents include child care, role overload, financial strain, and negative perceptions of society. Child care for single working parents needs to be reliable and flexible. Finding such child care can be elusive, so single parents must develop a primary support system that can assist with child care as well as provide social support and adult connections (Jackson, 1993). Bianchi and Milkie (2010) cited research that found that the cost of affordable and reliable child care was the reason why low-income women who were heads of households dropped out of the workforce. Women heading single-parent households are prone to be more vulnerable to financial strain than their male counterparts. Women typically earn less than men and use more of their time for child care and other nonpaid labor, making it difficult for them to increase their income by working longer hours, getting a second job, or training for a better, higher-paying job.

It may seem reasonable to expect that in the 21st century, societal taboos against single parenting would be a distant memory, but this is not the case. Single parents are still the targets of stereotypes and bias (Anderson, 1999; Goldenberg & Goldenberg, 1994; Usdansky, 2009). The typical stereotype of a single parent is a young, unwed, African American woman living on welfare with several children under the age of 5. The assumption is that she is lazy and that rather than find employment, she will just have more babies. The children of such families are assumed to be juvenile offenders and dangerous to society. Bias regarding single-parent households is often based on these negative stereotypes, and society is loath to provide financial assistance or other types of support for them.

### Divorce

Divorce accounts for most of the increase in single-parent households over the past 20 years. On the scale of stressful life events, divorce is ranked highest (Ahrons, 1999). The trauma of divorce may go on for months and years even though the divorce decree has a day and date. Divorce lowers the income of both parents; however, mothers typically take longer than fathers to recover from the financial effects of divorce, and households led by women likely experience greater hardships and are more likely to be poor (Barber & Eccles, 1992; Peterson & Gonzalez, 2000). When divorce occurs after the children have grown, women often find themselves with limited income and limited or no retirement or social security (Ahrons, 1999; Hilton & Anderson, 2009). Single-father households have different problems. They may have more money than female-headed households, but the drop in income may be more pronounced because they typically buy housekeeping and childcare services.

Women who held part-time work or who were stay-at-home mothers while they were married are likely to struggle with finding work after a divorce and having to shoulder the burden of keeping a job to support their family. The older a woman is, the more difficulty she may have and the more desperate she may feel. Women who have been employed full time and have children may find it necessary to seek better jobs to compensate for lost income.

The divorce process is a highly emotional one, and the anger, despair, anxiety, loneliness, and helplessness that each person experiences are likely to affect his or her job performance (Carter & McGoldrick, 1999a). Employers are also challenged to have patience to adjust to the change in the availability of employees who are attempting to survive this process.

### Counseling for the Single-Parent Household

Society tends to frown on single-parent households, but not those of the public in general. Because of the high percentage of single-parent households among African Americans, the bias is often twofold—racial and family configuration. Counselors must be willing to explore their own biases toward these families and work with supervisors and other counselors to overcome any biases that they may have. Acceptance of the client is the first priority.

Counseling the newly divorced client is a challenging task, and the client will need to seek counseling just to work on divorce issues. Career counselors may focus on work-related stressors of the newly divorced and single-parent head of household. The most important task is to help parents develop a sense of confidence in their abilities as parents and workers. They will need to develop problem-solving skills and learn to draw on existing supports and develop new ones. Because money is an overarching problem in many single-parent households, counselors may want to focus on debt management skills and work with the client on the depression and hopelessness that often accompany money worries. Equally as important is helping the newly single parent to assess his or her ability to prepare for crises such as illness or death.

### SIDEBAR 16.3  Case Study 1

Alisha is a 22-year-old single mother of four children younger than age 6. She is a second-generation teenage mother. Alisha is biracial—one of two biracial children in her family of origin, although her biracial sibling is a half sister. The father of Alisha's children no longer cohabitates with them, nor is he giving her child support. She is no longer eligible for welfare assistance, and she has just lost her job for the third time in less than a year. Alisha says it is because she cannot get reliable child care, especially when one of the children is sick. Alisha, who dropped out of high school, has been referred to you for career counseling.

Discuss your first reaction to meeting Alisha and any biases against her or prejudices toward her you may have. What help is available in your area for clients such as Alisha?

## Families Headed by Gay Men and Lesbians

Although gay men and lesbians are more visible than ever in U.S. society, acceptance of their lifestyle has been slow in coming. Only after gay rights advocates challenged discriminatory practices and laws have gay men and lesbians been able to improve their lives and reduce some of the risks of coming out of the closet (Goldenberg & Goldenberg, 1994). However, hostility toward and discrimination against gay men and lesbians is still widespread and often socially acceptable (Gysbers et al., 1998; Perrone, 2005). Lack of acceptance by the larger society colors all of the experiences of gay and lesbian couples and their families. To begin with, joining together as a couple is complicated by each partner's level of disclosure of his or her sexuality. One partner may be completely open about his or her sexual orientation at work and with family members, and the other may not have revealed his or her sexual orientation to anyone. Typically, once couples cohabitate, they have both revealed their sexual orientation to some extent. However, because gay men and lesbians are still discriminated against in the workplace, many will stay closeted to coworkers and employers. If they decide to stay closeted, they may live in fear of being outed, fired, or both. Those who are out at work risk harassment or dismissal from their jobs.

Moreover, in most states, gay and lesbian couples are prohibited from getting married. Without marriage, they are deprived of spousal privileges ranging from family insurance coverage to spousal considerations in job relocation. For those who are not out at work, employers may perceive them to be single and expect a greater commitment to the job than heterosexual married employees (Johnson & Colucci, 1999).

### Parenting Issues

Lesbian and gay couples become parents in a number of ways: via (1) children from a previous heterosexual marriage or relationship, (2) artificial insemination, (3) surrogate mothers, or (4) adoption. Regardless of how they become parents, nonbiological parents must legally safeguard their parental rights. It is not always a given that lesbian and gay couples can depend on their family of origin to support their relationship with their partners or their children. The families of origin of gay men and lesbians provide varying levels of support, reflective of homophobia in U.S. society. The parents of gay men and lesbians often do not know how to handle the grandchildren and partners of these unions. Although societal bias against lesbian motherhood has led the general public to believe that children of lesbian parents are damaged by the experience, research has shown that children of lesbian parents develop as normally as children of heterosexual parents (Patterson, 1996; Perrone, 2005). As a result of the unpredictable nature of familial assistance, it is not uncommon for gay and lesbian parents to garner support from a network of close friends. Weston (1991) referred to this network as the *chosen family*.

Most gay and lesbian couples are dual-earner or dual-career couples and tend to be committed to their work and their relationships (Eldridge & Gilbert, 1990). They share problems with child care, role conflict, and spillover with heterosexual dual-career couples, but their gender role restrictions differ (Mock & Cornelius, 2003). Although heterosexual couples may haggle over gender-appropriate tasks at home, lesbian and gay couples are more likely to share household duties equally (Esmail, 2010). The gender differences that have been found are those between lesbians and gay men. Lesbians tend to strive for equality in their relationships more than do gay men (Blumstein & Schwartz, 1983). Esmail (2010) found that lesbian couples use justification (e.g., expectations for cleanliness) and comparison (to heterosexual couples' division of labor) to determine how labor is divided in their families.

Other gender differences are related to income. Although gay couples may have high combined incomes, lesbian couples do not often share that privilege. As women, they often hold lower-paying jobs and are more likely to face poverty if one partner has an extended illness or loses her job (Perrone, 2005).

### Counseling Gay and Lesbian Couples and Families

The most challenging problem for counselors of gay and lesbian clients is the counselor's own homophobia. Research has shown that a large percentage of counselors are homophobic and before they can be successful with their gay and lesbian clients, they need to be free of it. This challenge may be more difficult for some counselors because homosexuality goes against the very core of their value systems and beliefs.

The most challenging problem for gay men and lesbian women as individuals and couples is coming out. Counselors can assist the couple in this process and help them to accept each other's current stage in that process. In a recent study on dual-career lesbian and gay couples, O'Ryan and McFarland (2010) concluded that the stages couples go through to successfully negotiate career–relationship boundaries are (a) planfulness (deciding when and where their relationships will be revealed to work colleagues), (b) creating positive networks (deciding which colleagues to include in their personal lives), and (c) shifting from marginalization to consolidation and integration (finding safety in combining their work and personal lives).

Counselors can also assist gay men and lesbian women in finding support networks and groups that will help them along the way. Networks can also be helpful in locating safe, gay-friendly employers. If that fails, clients will also need to learn strategies for coping with discrimination and hostility in the workplace.

### SIDEBAR 16.4 Case Study 2

Marvin, a White man, and Charlie, his Latino partner, have just been approved to adopt a 4-week-old mixed-race baby girl. However, Marvin's sister, who is a stay-at-home mother and who was slated to provide day care, backed out of their arrangement. Her husband did not believe gay men could adopt a baby, which is why he agreed to it. But now he does not want her to take care of "any half-Black baby." Charlie is only out to select people at work and nervous about being outed. He may need to take family leave to provide child care for awhile, and he fears losing his job if he takes too much time off. Marvin is looking for ways to supplement their income if Charlie loses his job.

Can you work effectively with this couple? Have you explored your own homophobia? What are some strategies you would use to assist these clients?

## Other Challenges Affecting Families and Work

### Unemployment

Unemployment, underemployment, and low-paying unskilled and semi-skilled jobs all contribute to a family's financial distress. Unemployment has skyrocketed in recent years as a result of the worst recession the United States has known in decades. The growth in the number of homeless families may say more about the extent of the U.S. unemployment problem; however, even that figure is hard to pin down. The economic uncertainty that has plagued the country in recent years has had devastating effects on many families. Unemployment affects all the family types discussed so far. Since the start of the recession in 2007, unemployment has risen almost uncontrollably (Bureau of Labor Statistics, 2010c). Traditionally, unemployment was experienced by low-level employees, those involved in seasonal work, and part-time workers, most of whom were ethnic minorities. However, in the past 15 years, companies have been downsizing to compensate for the fluctuating economy, and for the first time the White middle class has experienced layoffs in large numbers that have continued throughout the recession. Moreover, the racial breakdown of the unemployed population continues to be unevenly distributed among racial groups. The October 2010 unemployment percentage for all races was 9.6%. When race is factored in, 8.8% of Whites, 12.6% of Hispanics, and 15.7% of African Americans were unemployed (Bureau of Labor Statistics, 2010).

Families cope with unemployment in a variety of ways, but they start by cutting back buying luxuries and soliciting assistance from family and friends. The first thing the counselor must attend to is any crisis that the family faces because of the layoff. Counselors can also help clients with feelings of anger toward the employer and themselves, feelings of loss and shame, and the doubt in their abilities that accompanies job termination. They need to help clients focus on solutions rather than on their loss.

Once crisis issues have been addressed, counselors can help clients to develop job search strategies that might improve their chances of finding a new position. In addition, the counselor might want to discuss financial issues with the client for future planning. The discussion can be as simple as asking children to give 10% of their money to charity or to the community (e.g., nonprofits or church) and saving 10%.

### Poverty

One of the most far-reaching and disturbing trends in the United States is the poverty of its people (Rank, 2000). Recent census figures have reported that 14% of the total population live below the poverty line (which is adjusted every year on the basis of a number of factors). Again, 25.8% of African Americans (the highest percentage); 25.3% of Hispanic families; and 12.3% of White families live below the poverty level. Families headed by single women are overrepresented among those who are poor. Although only 14% of the total population lives in poverty, as stated earlier, 29.9% of households headed by single women are considered poor (DeNavas-Walt et al., 2010). The 2009 U.S. poverty rate was the highest since these figures began being reported. The racial breakdown of individuals living in poverty is telling. Of the 14.3% of the total population living below the poverty line, 9.5% were non-Hispanic Whites, 25.8% were African American or Black, 25.3% were Hispanic, and 12.5% were Asian.

The gap between those who are affluent and those who are struggling to survive is steadily increasing and difficult to ignore. Although the middle and upper classes tend to dismiss and rebuke those who are on welfare, arguments of laziness and fraud cannot be applied to the plight of the working poor. These individuals are employed in low-wage, low-security jobs that do not supply sufficient income to raise the family's income over the poverty level. The numbers of this population have risen, primarily as a result of the welfare-to-work programs instituted in the 1990s (Corcoran, Danziger, Kalil, & Seefeldt, 2000; Hong & Wernet, 2007). The working poor struggle to meet even the most basic family needs of food, clothing, and shelter, and health care is nonexistent for them. Often, they must sacrifice meeting one need in favor of another. The working poor defy the U.S. value of meritocracy—that if you work hard, you will get ahead. These families work hard and have little to show for it. Many of these families would not think of welfare as an alternative, but welfare is the one way in which many single-parent households can keep food on the table. The early reports on welfare reform were encouraging. It seemed that poor families were able to raise their family income a fraction higher than it had been, and many were able to leave welfare. However, some of these families did not move out of poverty, they simply moved off the welfare lists. Hong and Wernet (2007) found that the working poor were distinguished from the working nonpoor in that they were usually younger, unmarried with children younger than 18, and non-White and had only their earnings to support them financially.

In addition, Hong and Wernet (2007) found that their working-poor respondents had less education and on-the-job training and more health problems than the working-nonpoor respondents. One of the saddest results of the increasing large population of working poor is that they often are not covered by health insurance at the jobs they are able to secure.

## Homelessness

Lindsey (1994) stated that extreme poverty resulting from reduced need for unskilled workers is responsible for homelessness in the United States. Because of the reduction in welfare payments, the scarcity of low-income housing, and increases in housing costs, unemployment, even welfare, can deteriorate into homelessness. Families with children are the fastest growing group of homeless people in the country today (Mihaly, 1991). The National Center on Family Homelessness (2009) reported that approximately 2% of all U.S. children are homeless, and half of those children are younger than age 5. Most of these families are headed by single women, who typically have inconsistent work histories and higher rates of mental illness, substance abuse, and family violence (National Center on Family Homelessness, 2007; Swick & Williams, 2010). The rate of substance abuse and psychiatric history among homeless mothers is similar to that of other homeless people, and other reasons for their homelessness include leaving abusive relationships, condemned and fire-damaged buildings or buildings used for drug sales, or being asked to leave by friends or relatives.

Counseling poor and homeless clients may often require crisis intervention strategies, depending on how dire the client's circumstances are. The homeless client will need to find shelter and a job that pays enough to afford housing. Poor clients may need to explore more ways to increase their income. It is imperative that counselors focus on the strengths and resourcefulness of their clients and explore clients' extended network of support (family, church). As with unemployed clients, the counselor's knowledge of the labor market and employment opportunities is essential. Equally as important is the counselor's involvement in advocacy for those who are poor and homeless. The most effective way to assist those who are poor is to change the system that is designed to support them (Hong & Wernet, 2007).

### SIDEBAR 16.5  Homeless Shelter

One of the most valuable experiences you can have to appreciate your own privilege and understand the experiences of others is to visit or, more important, to volunteer at a homeless shelter. Choose a shelter that is designed to house families, and spend some time there volunteering and talking to the residents. After your visit, reflect on what you have learned and share it with your colleagues and friends.

## Overall Counseling Strategies

Gysbers et al. (1998) suggested that counselors separate work and family problems into life roles, life settings, and life events and then identify underlying dynamics in family or work that affect the problem. They suggested 11 tasks that career counselors complete in addressing work–family issues. They range from helping clients to see the connection between family and work to helping them to turn frustration into positive solutions. Hazard and Koslow (1992) suggested that counselors use family systems theory as well as a career stage theory in their work with couples. What occurs in counseling will depend on each partner's career stage (apprenticeship, independence–specialization, interdependence–managerial, director of organization) and the couple's family stage (early, middle, late).

Strategies for career and lifestyle planning for couples and families overlap family counseling and career counseling specialty areas. Theories of family counseling and theories of career counseling do not adequately address the family and career connection. Clearly, the counseling field needs more complex and comprehensive theories to accommodate today's families (Forrest, 1994). Two models have been proposed that have some promise in integrating these theories—those of Hansen (2001) and of Gold, Rotter, and Evans (2002).

Hansen's (2001) integrative life planning model takes a "holistic approach by encouraging people to connect various aspects of life" (as cited in Niles & Harris-Bowlsbey, 2002, p. 85). The assumptions of the model are that (a) new ways of knowing for career development are needed because the nature of knowledge has seen so many changes, and (b) an expanded view of career requires broader self-knowledge in addition to interests, abilities, and values such as multiple roles, identities, and critical life tasks in diverse cultures. The integrative life planning model is based on six career development tasks that reflect social justice, social change, connectedness, diversity, and spirituality:

1. Finding work that needs doing in a changing global context
2. Weaving one's life into a meaningful whole
3. Connecting family and work
4. Valuing pluralism
5. Managing personal transitions and organizational change
6. Exploring spirituality and life purposes.

The model is designed to help not only individuals but also partners and families in exploring the way the various priorities in their lives fit together and in developing an awareness of how life choices and decisions are affected by the changing contexts of one's life.

Gold et al. (2002) introduced the out-of-the-box model for synthesizing family, culture, and career counseling. Rather than being a theoretical model, it is a practice model that is designed to get counseling practitioners to see the importance of family, culture, and career issues in their clients' lives, to give each of these areas equal attention in assessing clients' problems, and then to focus on the issue of the greatest importance to the client when counseling is started.

The out-of-the-box model has the following assumptions: (a) The notion that there is one truth for all people is not feasible, (b) the stories of families and cultural groups that explain their common social reality are imprinted on individuals, (c) the building blocks of an individual's worldview are his or her family and cultural stories, (d) the individual's personal worldview is confirmed or amended through interaction with family and significant others, (e) individuals develop their own stories through their own experiences while incorporating family and cultural group stories into their own reality, and (f) the individual's story reveals the person's knowledge of self, symbols, and meanings that the individual values about the world. Stories make meaning of an individual's life; it is imperative,

**TABLE 16.2   Counseling Process for the Out-of-the-Box Model**

**Step**

1. Counselors determine how well they understand the client's worldview.
   a. Counselors assess client problems from multiple perspectives.
   b. Counselors listen to clients' priorities with an open mind.
   c. Counselors become aware of clients' lifestyle focal point.
2. Counselors determine how their own cultural values and biases affect their approach to the client.
   a. Counselors are aware of their theoretical biases.
   b. Counselors are aware of their cultural biases.
   c. Counselors works on letting go of biases.
3. Counselors evaluate the usefulness of their interventions.
   a. Counselors base intervention on clients' lifestyle focal point.
   b. Counselors move easily into the sphere of counseling that best fits the clients' needs.

therefore, from a conceptual and interventional perspective, that counseling reflect narrative approaches to helping. The out-of-the-box model was designed to help counselors help their clients tell their whole stories and encourage clients to reauthor their stories to overcome the pressures of society. Through a process of finding a truer career and life direction, one begins to connect with one's true career dreams, values, beliefs, and commitments. Table 16.2 describes the process for using the out-of-the-box model with clients.

**SIDEBAR 16.6   Case Study 3**

Glenn, 35, was a grocery store manager for 11 years. Judy, Glen's wife, 33, is a stay-at-home mother who has an associate's degree in restaurant management, although she has never worked outside the home. They have two children, ages 7 and 12. They lost their dream home as a result of creative financing. Shortly after moving into a rental apartment, Glen's store closed, and he was unable to find a job of any kind and collected unemployment. However, the rent for their apartment was too high, and they ended up moving twice to smaller and smaller apartments using older and less reliable cars. Finally, they moved in with relatives for 6 months until they found housing in the homeless shelter where they are now.

Using the out-of-the-box model, discuss how you would work with this family to help them get back on their feet.

## Summary

The changing family dynamics and changing work environments in the United States have made it evident that counselors need to address a significant family–work relationship. There are many configurations of households in this country, each of which is defined as a family. The systems perspective of the family emphasizes circular causality—that is, individual members have an effect on the family, and as they change, the family changes. Changes from larger systems have an effect on the family and thus change individuals in that family. Work influences the different configurations of families in different ways, and counselors need to keep those influences in mind when they work on family issues. In addition, poverty, violence, and unemployment can affect any family configuration, and each of these issues cuts across all family configurations. Life planning for couples and families is a developing area for counselors, and although no comprehensive theories are available at this time, work is being done to fill the void. The Web sites listed in the next section provide additional information relating to the chapter topics.

## Useful Web Sites

- A Great Life—Brought in Color: http://www.aglbic.org
- Association for Multicultural Counseling and Development: http://www.amcdaca.org/amcd/default.cfm
- Familyresource.com: http://www.familyresource.com
- International Association of Marriage and Family Counselors: http://www.iamfconline.com
- National Career Development Association: http://ncda.org

## References

Ahrons, C. R. (1999). Divorce: An unscheduled family transition. In B. Carter & M. McGoldrick (Eds.), *The expanded family life cycle: Individual, family, and social perspectives* (pp. 381–398). Boston, MA: Allyn & Bacon.

Amato, P. R. (2000). Diversity within single-parent families. In D. H Demo, K. R. Allen, & M. A. Fine (Eds.), *Handbook of family diversity* (pp. 149–172). New York, NY: Oxford University Press.

Anderson, C. J. (1999). Single-parent families: Strengths, vulnerabilities, and interventions. In B. Carter & M. McGoldrick (Eds.), *The expanded family life cycle: Individual, family, and social perspectives* (pp. 399–416). Boston, MA: Allyn & Bacon.

Barber, B. L., & Eccles, J. S. (1992). Long-term influence of divorce and single parenting on adolescent family- and work-related values, behaviors, and aspirations. *Psychological Bulletin, 111,* 108–126.

Barnett, R. C. (1994). Home-to-work spillover revisited: A study of full-time employed women in dual-earner couples. *Journal of Marriage and the Family, 56,* 647–656.

Baum, C. L. (2002). A dynamic analysis of the effect of child care costs on the work decisions of low-income mothers with infants. *Demography, 39,* 139–164.

Becker, P. E., & Moen, P. (1999). Scaling back: Dual-earner couples' family strategies. *Journal of Marriage and the Family, 61,* 995–1007.

Bernas, K. H., & Major, D. A. (2000). Contributors to stress resistance: Testing a model of women's work–family conflict. *Psychology of Women Quarterly, 24,* 170–178.

Bianchi, S. M., & Milkie, M. A. (2010). Work and family research in the first decade of the 21st century. *Journal of Marriage and Family, 72,* 705–725.

Bianchi, S. M., & Raley, S. B. (2005). Time allocation in families. In S. M. Bianchi, L. M. Casper, & R. B. King (Eds.), *Work, family, health, and well-being* (pp. 21–42). Philadelphia, PA: Erlbaum.

Billingsley, A. (1992). *Climbing Jacob's ladder: The enduring legacy of African-American families.* New York, NY: Simon & Schuster.

Blumstein, P., & Schwartz, P. (1983). *American couples: Money, work, and sex.* New York, NY: Morrow.

Blustein, D. L. (2001). The interface of work and relationships: Critical knowledge for 21st century psychology. *Counseling Psychologist, 29,* 179–192.

Bond, S. & Wise, S. (2003). Family leave policies and devolution to the line. *Personnel Review, 32,* 58–72.

Brines, J. (1994). Economic dependency, gender, and the division of labor at home. *American Journal of Sociology, 100,* 652–688.

Buffardi, L. C., Smith, J. L., O'Brien, A. S., & Erdwins, C. J. (1999). The impact of dependent-care responsibility and gender on work attitudes. *Journal of Occupational Health Psychology, 4,* 356–367.

Bureau of Labor Statistics. (2010a, June 22). American Time Use Survey summary [News release USDL-10-0855]. Retrieved from http://www.bls.gov/news.release/atus.nr0.htm

Bureau of Labor Statistics, (2010b). *Employment characteristics of families.* Retrieved from http://www.bls.gov/opub/ted/2011/ted_20110328.htm

Bureau of Labor Statistics. (2010c, October). Employment situation October 2010 [News release USDL-10-1519]. Retrieved from http://www.bls.gov/news.release/archives/empsit_11052010.pdf

Burke, R. J. (1996). Work experiences, stress and health among managerial and professional women. In M. J. Schabraca, J. A. M. Winnubst, & C. L. Cooper (Eds.), *Handbook of work and health psychology* (pp. 205–230.). New York, NY: Wiley.

Byron, K. (2005). A meta-analytic review of work-family conflict and its antecedents. *Journal of Vocational Behavior, 67,* 169–198.

Carter, B., & McGoldrick, M. (1988). The changing family life cycle: A framework for family therapy (2nd ed.). Boston, MA: Allyn & Bacon.

Carter, B., & McGoldrick, M. (1999a). The divorce cycle: A major variation in the American family life cycle. In B. Carter & M. McGoldrick (Eds.), *The expanded family life cycle: Individual, family, and social perspectives* (3rd ed., pp. 373–380). Boston, MA: Allyn & Bacon.

Carter, B., & McGoldrick, M. (1999b). *The expanded family life cycle: Individual, family, and social perspectives* (3rd ed.). Boston, MA: Allyn & Bacon.

Chapman, N. J., Ingersoll-Dayton, B., & Neal, M. B. (1994). Balancing the multiple roles of work and caregiving for children, adults, and elders. In G. P. Keita & J. J. Hurrell, Jr. (Eds.), *Job stress in a changing workforce* (pp. 283–300). Washington, DC: American Psychological Association.

Chope, R. C. (2006). *Family matters: The influence of the family in career decision making.* Austin, TX: Pro-Ed.

Cooper, S. E., Arkkelin, D. L., & Tielbert, M. J. (1994). Work-relationship values and gender role differences in relation to career-marriage aspirations. *Journal of Counseling and Development, 73,* 63–68.

Corcoran, M., Danziger, S., Kalil, A., & Seefeldt, K. (2000). How welfare reform is affecting women's work. *Annual Review of Sociology, 26,* 241–269.

Dawis, R. V., & Lofquist, L. H. (1984). *A psychological theory of work adjustment.* Minneapolis: University of Minnesota Press.

Cullen, J. C., Hammer, L. B., Neal, M. B., & Sinclair, R. R. (2009). Development of a typology of dual-earner couples caring for children and aging parents. *Journal of Family Issues, 30,* 458–483.

DeNavas-Walt, C., Proctor, B. D., & Smith, J. C. (2010). *Income, poverty, and health insurance coverage in the United States: 2009* (Current Population Reports P60-238). Washington, DC: U.S. Government Printing Office. Retrieved from http://www.census.gov/prod/2010pubs/p60-238.pdf

Duxbury, L., & Higgins, C. (1994). Interference between work and family: A status report on dual-career and dual-earner mothers and fathers. *Employee Assistance Quarterly, 9*, 55–80.

Eldridge, N. S., & Gilbert, L. A. (1990). Correlates of relationship satisfaction in lesbian couples. *Psychology of Women Quarterly, 14,* 43–62.

Erickson, J. J., Martinengo, G., & Hill, E. J. (2010). Putting work and family experiences in context: Differences by family life stage. *Human Relations, 63,* 955–979.

Esmail, A. (2010) "Negotiating fairness:" A study on how lesbian family members evaluate, construct, and maintain "fairness" with the Division of Household Labor. *Journal of Homosexuality, 57,* 591–609.

Evans, K. M., & Rotter, J. C. (2000). Multicultural family approaches to career counseling. *Family Journal: Counseling and Therapy for Couples and Families, 8,* 67–71.

Forrest, L. (1994). Career assessment for couples. *Journal of Employment Counseling, 31,* 168–187.

Fulmer, R. (1999). Becoming an adult: Leaving home and staying connected. In B. Carter & M. McGoldrick (Eds.), *The expanded family life cycle: Individual, family, and social perspectives* (pp. 215–230). Boston, MA: Allyn & Bacon.

Gold, J. M., Rotter, J. C., & Evans, K. M. (2002). Out of the box: A model for the twenty-first century. In K. M. Evans, J. C. Rotter, & J. M. Gold (Eds.), *Synthesizing family culture and career: A model for counseling in the twenty-first century* (pp. 3–15). Alexandria, VA: American Counseling Association.

Goldenberg, H., & Goldenberg, I. (1994). *Counseling today's families* (2nd ed.). Pacific Grove, CA: Brooks/Cole.

Gottfredson, L. S. (1981). Circumscription and compromise: A developmental theory of occupational aspirations. *Journal of Counseling Psychology, 28,* 545–579.

Gottfried, A. E. (1991). Maternal employment in the family setting: Developmental and environmental issues. In: J. V. Lerner & N. L.Galambos (Eds). *Employed mothers and their children.* pp. 63–84. New York: Garland Publishing.

Gottfried, A. E., & Gottfried, A. W. (1996). A longitudinal study of academic intrinsic motivation in intellectually gifted children: Childhood through early adolescence. *Gifted Child Quarterly, 40,* 179–183.

Greenhaus, J. H., & Powell, G. N. (2006). When work and family are allies: A theory of work-family enrichment. *Academy of Management Review, 31,* 72–92.

Grzywacz, J. G., & Butler, A. B. (2005). The impact of job characteristics on work-family facilitation: Testing a theory and distinguishing a construct. *Journal of Occupational Health Psychology, 10,* 97–109.

Gysbers, N. C., Heppner, M. J., & Johnston, J. A. (1998). *Career counseling: Process, issues, and techniques.* Boston, MA: Allyn & Bacon.

Hansen, S. (2001). Integrating work, family, and community through holistic life planning. *Career Development Quarterly, 49,* 261–274.

Hazard, L., & Koslow, D. (1992). Conjoint career counseling: Counseling dual-career couples. In H. D. Lea & Z. B. Leibowitz (Eds.), *Adult career development: Concepts, issues, and practices* (pp. 218–233). Alexandria, VA: National Career Development Association.

Higgins, C. A., Duxbury, L. E., & Lyons, S. T. (2010). Coping with overload and stress: Men and women in dual-earner families. *Journal of Marriage and Family, 72,* 847–859.

Hill, E. J., Ferris, M., & Märtinson, V. (2003). Does it matter where you work? A comparison of how three work venues (traditional office, virtual office, and home office) influence aspects of work and personal/family life. *Journal of Vocational Behavior, 63*(2), 220–241.

Hilton, J. M., Anderson, T. L. (2009) Characteristics of women with children who divorce in midlife compared to those who remain married. *Journal of Divorce & Remarriage, 5,* 309–329.

Hines, P. M. (1999). The family life cycle of African American families living in poverty. In B. Carter & M. McGoldrick (Eds.), *The expanded family life cycle: Individual, family, and social perspectives* (pp. 327–345). Boston, MA: Allyn & Bacon.

Hines, P. M., Preto, N. G., McGoldrick, M., Almeida, R., & Welman, S. (1999). In B. Carter & M. McGoldrick (Eds.), *The expanded family life cycle: Individual, family, and social perspectives,* 3rd ed. (pp. 69–87). Boston, MA: Allyn & Bacon.

Hong, P. Y., & Wernet, S. P. (2007). Structural reinterpretation of poverty by examining working poverty: Implications for community and policy practice. *Families in Society, 88,* 361–373.

Imber-Black, E. (1999). Creating meaningful rituals for new life cycle transitions. In B. Carter & M. McGoldrick (Eds.), *The expanded family life cycle: Individual, family, and social perspectives* (pp. 202–214). Boston, MA: Allyn & Bacon.

Jackson, A. P. (1993). Black, single, working mothers in poverty: Preferences for employment, well-being, and perceptions of preschool-age children. *Social Work, 38,* 26–34.

Johnson, T. W., & Colucci, P. (1999). Lesbians, gay men and the family life cycle. In B. Carter & M. McGoldrick (Eds.), *The expanded family life cycle: Individual, family, and social perspectives* (pp. 346–361). Boston, MA: Allyn & Bacon.

Keller, B. K., & Whiston, S. C. (2008). The role of parental influences on young adolescents' career development. *Journal of Career Assessment, 16,* 198–217.

Lindsey, E. W. (1994). Homelessness. In P. C. McKenry & S. J. Price (Eds.), *Families and change: Coping with stressful events* (pp. 281–302). Thousand Oaks, CA: Sage.

Loscocco, K. A. (1997). Work-family linkages among self-employed women and men. *Journal of Vocational Behavior, 50,* 204–226.

Mackey, W. C. (1995). U.S. fathering behaviors within cross-cultural context: An evaluation by an alternate benchmark. *Journal of Comparative Family Studies, 26,* 443–458.

McGoldrick, M. (1999). Women and the family life cycle. In B. Carter & M. McGoldrick (Eds.), *The expanded family life cycle: Individual, family, and social perspectives* (pp. 106–123). Boston, MA: Allyn & Bacon.

McNall, L A., Nicklin, J. M., & Masuda, A. D. (2010). A meta-analytic review of the consequences associated with work-family enrichment. *Journal of Business and Psychology, 25,* 381–396.

Melito, R. (2003). Values in the role of the family therapist: Self determination and justice. *Journal of Marital and Family Therapy, 29,* 3–11.

Mihaly, L. (1991). Beyond the numbers: Homeless families with children. In J. H. Kryder-Coe, L. M. Salamon, & J. M. Molnar (Eds.), *Homeless children and youth: A new American dilemma* (pp. 11–32). New Brunswick, NJ: Transaction.

Mock, S. E., & Cornelius, S. W. (2003). The case for same-sex couples. In P. Moen (Ed.), *It's about time: Couples and careers* (pp. 275–287). New York, NY: Cornell University Press.

National Center on Family Homelessness. (2007). *National Center on Family Homelessness: Resources: Fact sheets.* Retrieved from http://www.familyhomelessness .org/families.php?p=ts

National Center on Family Homelessness. (2009). Working to end family homelessness.: Annual Report. Retrieved from http://www.familyhomelessness.org/ media/88.pdf June 26, 2011

Niles, S. G., & Harris-Bowlsbey, J. (2002). Career development interventions in the 21st century. Upper Saddle River, NJ: Merrill Prentice Hall.

Okun, B. F. (1996). *Understanding diverse families: What practitioners need to know.* New York, NY: Guilford Press.

Nomaguchi, K. M., Milkie, M. A., & Bianchi, S. M. (2005). Time strains and psychological well-being: Do dual-earner mothers and fathers differ? *Journal of Family Issues, 26,* 756–792.

O'Ryan, L. W., & McFarland, W. P. (2010). A phenomenological exploration of the experiences of dual-career lesbian and gay couples. *Journal of Counseling and Development, 88,* 71–79.

Paniagua, F. A (1996). Cross-cultural guidelines in family therapy practice. *The Family Journal: Counseling and Therapy for Couples and Families, 4,* 127–138.

Patterson, C. (1996). Lesbian mothers and their children. In J. Laird & R. Green (Eds.), *Lesbians and gays in couples and families: A handbook for therapists* (pp. 420–437). San Francisco, CA: Jossey-Bass.

Perrone, K. M. (2005). Work-family interface for same-sex, dual-earner couples: Implications for counselors. *Career Development Quarterly, 53,* 317–324.

Peterson, N., & Gonzalez, R. C. (2000). *The role of work in people's lives: Applied career counseling and vocational psychology.* Belmont, CA: Brooks/Cole.

Rank, M. R. (2000). Poverty and economic hardship in families. In D. H. Demo, K. R. Allen, & M. A. Fine (Eds.), *Handbook of family diversity* (pp. 293–315). New York, NY: Oxford University Press.

Reynolds, J. R. (2005). In the face of conflict: Work family conflict and desired work hour adjustments. *Journal of Marriage and Family, 67,* 1313–1331.

Rhodes, A. R. (2002). Long-distance relationships in dual-career couples: A review of counseling issues. *Family Journal: Counseling and Therapy for Couples and Families, 10,* 398–404.

Risman, B. J., Atkinson, M. P., & Blackwelder, S. P. (1999). Understanding the juggling act: Gendered preferences and social structural constraints. *Sociological Forum, 14,* 319–344.

Schneer, J. A., & Reitan, F. (1993). Effects of alternate family structures on managerial career paths. *Academy of Management Journal, 36,* 830–843.

Sciarra, D. T. (1999). *Multiculturalism in counseling.* Itasca, IL: F. E. Peacock.

Stevens, D. P., Ninotte, K. L., Mannon, S. E., & Kiger, G. (2007). Examining the "neglected side of the work-family interface": Antecedents of positive and negative family-to-work spillover. *Journal of Family Issues, 28,* 242–262.

Stone, P. (2007). *Opting out: Why women really quit careers and head home.* Berkeley: University of California Press.

Super, D. E. (1990). A life-span, life-space approach to career development. In D. Brown, L. Brooks, & Associates (Eds.) *Career Choice and Development: Applying contemporary theories to practice.* 2nd ed., (p. 212). Hoboken, NJ: John Wiley and Sons, Inc.

Swick, K. J., & Williams, R. (2010). The voices of single parent mothers who are homeless: Implications for early childhood professionals. *Journal of Early Childhood Education, 38,* 49–55.

U.S. Bureau of Census (2001–2002). American Community Survey, Marital status and living arrangements, Washington, DC: Government Printing Office.

U.S. Census Bureau. (2011). Table 59. Households, families, subfamilies, and married couples 1980–2009. In *Statistical abstract of the United States: 2011* (p. 54). Washington, DC: Author. Retrieved from http://www.census.gov/compendia/statab/2011/tables/11s0060.pdf

Usdansky, M. L. (2009). Ambivalent acceptance of single-parent families: A response to comments. *Journal of Marriage and Family, 71,* 240–246.

Von Bertalanffy, L. (1968). *General systems theory: Foundation, development, application.* New York, NY: George Braziller.

Walters, M., Carter, B., Papp, P., & Silverstein, O. (1988). *The invisible web: Gender patterns in family relationships.* New York, NY: Guilford Press.

Waner, K. K., Winter, J. K., & Mansfield, J. C. (2007). Family benefits:What are students' attitudes and expectations by gender? *Journal of Education for Business, 82,* 291–294.

Weston, K. (1991). *Families we choose: Lesbians, gays, kinship.* New York, NY: Gardner.

Whiston, S., & Keller, B. (2004). The influences of the family of origin on career development: A review and analysis. *Counseling Psychologist, 32,* 493–568.

Wiener, N. (1948). *Cybernetics, or control and communication in the animal and the machine.* Cambridge, MA: Technology Press.

Zedeck, S., & Mosier, K. L. (1990). Work in the family and employing organizations. *American Psychologist, 45,* 240–251.

# CHAPTER 17

# Gender Issues in Career Counseling

Barbara Herlihy and Zarus E. P. Watson

## Contents

Throughout human history, there has been "women's work" and "men's work," although the relative worth accorded them by society has not remained constant. A clear division of labor existed in societies of the Old Stone Age: Men were the hunters and women were the gatherers of vegetables and grains. In these primitive clan societies, women had equal economic and social status with men, because women contributed equally to the group's subsistence as food gatherers and as bearers of the children who would ensure the clan's continued existence (Leavitt, 1971).

Gender equity began to erode with the dawn of the New Stone Age. As a result of agricultural advances and the domestication of animals, women's contributions to the food supply grew less important and their economic value to society gradually diminished. At that time, occupational gender equity was lost, never to be regained. As civilization advanced, women were further marginalized. In ancient Greece, women were regarded as inherently inferior and evil, and 80% of them were slaves. In the late medieval period, some women began to achieve a measure of independence as merchants and producers of textiles, although women were still perceived as evil, as was exemplified by the practice of witch burning (Atkinson & Hackett, 2004).

In the colonial United States, women had few rights. They did not exist legally apart from their husbands and could not own property. Not until the frontier era did women begin to gain a rough equality that was born of necessity (Atkinson & Hackett, 2004). During the latter half of the 19th century, the women's movement resulted in some significant gains for women, such as securing the right to control the wages they earned. Despite further advances made by women in the 20th century, inequalities remained and were embedded in a context of social myths such as "the happy housewife." Job discrimination persisted despite the passage of the Equal Pay Act and civil rights legislation in the mid-1960s.

In the United States of the 21st century, occupational segregation still exists, with men and women being concentrated in different clusters of occupations. Women today are overrepresented in low-paying, low-status, "pink collar" jobs, and men dominate the ranks of the high-paying, high-status upper echelons of corporate management. Wage discrimination based on gender has been against the law in the United States for nearly 50 years, yet women earn an average of $0.80 for every dollar earned by men (Bureau of Labor Statistics, 2010).

In this chapter, we examine the underlying causes of gender inequities in the world of work and describe problems that contemporary women and men encounter in their careers and occupations. Suggestions for gender-aware career counseling are offered, and two case studies are presented to give readers an opportunity to apply the concepts and strategies that have been discussed.

## Gender Role Socialization

To understand the profound effect of gender on the occupational and career decision making of women and men, it is essential to recognize that gender is socially constructed. Gender is not synonymous with sex, which refers to biological differences. A considerable body of research has shown that biological differences between the sexes are few, whereas learned differences are great. These learned differences are a result of gender role socialization, which is based on assumptions about women and men that have been conditioned into people's thinking over multiple generations.

Gendered behaviors are learned from birth. From the beginning of life, boys and girls are socially supported and encouraged in very different characteristics and behaviors. This pervasive gender role socialization is carried out, often unconsciously, by virtually every significant force in a child's life, including parents, teachers, peers, schools, and religious organizations. Stereotypical beliefs about what is "masculine" and "feminine" are reinforced in myriad ways, through language, clothing, toys, games, movies, books, gendered play experiences, and television and other mass media. Children's experiences with these influences form the foundation for complex cognitive schemas they then use to organize the world into gendered categories. Over time, an individual's gender schemas become a powerful, unconscious mechanism for processing information (Bem, 1993).

Gender role socialization has a cumulative effect on boys and girls, to which parents and teachers alike contribute by expecting boys to be more active and aggressive and girls to be more passive and dependent (Atkinson & Hackett, 2004). Throughout their school years, boys are typically reinforced for competition, skill mastery, achievement, and ambition, and girls are rein-forced for connectedness, nurturing, emotiveness, and cooperation (Gilligan, 1982; Niles & Harris-Bowlsbey, 2002).

Even very young children have already acquired stereotypical views of masculinity and femininity and of the occupational choices open to each gender (Enns, 2000, 2004; Gilbert & Sher, 1999). Occupational stereotyp-ing begins so early that 2- and 3-year-old children are able to identify gen-der-stereotyped occupations for women and men (Gettys & Cann, 1981). By the time children are 6 to 8 years old, they have developed what Gottfredson (1996) has called their "tolerable sex type boundary," which is a set, narrow range of perceived occupational choices. Children's perceptions of acceptable career options for their gender become increasingly rigid from kindergar-ten to fourth grade (Matlin, 1996). As girls and boys mature, these socially conditioned occupational gender stereotypes become deeply engrained. They also interact in complex ways with other cultural variables that must be con-sidered along with gender to understand the context in which people engage in the career and occupational planning process.

### SIDEBAR 17.1 Gender Role Socialization Self-assessment

Reflect on your own gender role socialization and jot down the gender-related messages that you received when you were a child and teenager. In what ways might you have internalized these messages? How might these internalized messages affect your ability to conduct career counseling effectively with female clients? With male clients?

## Gender, Culture, and Individual Differences

Although gender has a powerful influence on occupational and career aspi-rations, it is not the only force that operates to shape people's occupational development. Race, ethnicity, social class, and culture are also extremely influential. All people have multiple cultural identities, and the relevance and importance of these identities vary according to the situation. In some contexts, gender is likely to be a highly salient cultural variable, and in other situations it may have a secondary role. As an example, for a 50-year-old man who is contemplating a return to college to gain further education to make a career change, age may be a primary consideration. If he is thinking about a traditionally female-dominated occupation such as elementary school teach-ing, gender may have a more prominent role in his deliberations.

At the same time, it is important to keep in mind that individual differ-ences play an equally crucial role. If gender and other cultural variables were the sole determinants of career choice, it would be difficult to explain how we made the same career choice to become counselor educators. Zarus E. P. Watson is an African American man and was reared in a middle-class home in an urban area in the southern United States. His family structure included two working parents. He was expected to attend college and earn a degree. College, although intimidating, was seen as almost the sole path to economic and social success both for him and for his family.

Barbara Richter Herlihy is a White woman and was raised in an upper middle class family in the Northeastern and Midwestern regions of the United

States. Her family structure was a traditional one in which her mother did not work outside the home and her father, a corporate executive, was the sole income provider. Although she was expected to attend college, she was not expected to persist and earn a degree. College was primarily a venue for ensuring that she would find a well-educated man who would be a good provider.

That two such disparate sets of influences could converge at the same career choice is a testament to the complexity of the interactions among myriad factors in career decision making. Gender role socialization is a powerful force but it cannot be isolated from other aspects of identity, nor can individual differences be ignored.

## Outcomes of Gender Role Stereotyping

With an understanding of the pervasive influence of gender role socialization, we can now look more closely at the effects of gender role stereotyping on the occupational and career development of girls and boys. The consequences of gender role stereotyping are profound. Girls and boys internalize societal messages regarding gender expectations, and as a result, their career decision-making processes are shaped while they are still very young (Worell & Remer, 2003). For girls, well-documented outcomes include math avoidance, fear of failure, and lowered expectations for success. For boys, consequences that have lifelong effects include an intense need to compete and succeed and a concomitant restriction of career choices.

### Consequences for Girls

One of the most devastating outcomes of gender role stereotyping for female career attainment is math avoidance (Gysbers, Heppner, & Johnston, 1998). In elementary school, girls outperform boys on math tasks, report liking math more than do boys, and believe they are better at math than boys (Boswell, 1985). By late high school, however, boys have gained a clear advantage in math skills. Evidence has suggested that, even when girls enter high school with confidence in their math ability, teachers and other adult figures communicate a stereotyped belief that girls are not as competent as boys in this realm of learning. As these messages become internalized, girls come to have lower self-efficacy for math even when their actual performance is higher than that of boys (Fassinger, 2001). This lower self-efficacy strongly affects their willingness to pursue math-related careers (Eccles, 2001). Thus, mathematics becomes a critical filter (Farmer, 1976) that operates to narrow women's career choices. As Gysbers et al. (1998) have pointed out, math will become an increasingly important prerequisite for high-paying, high-status jobs as society continues to become more technologically advanced.

A second consequence for girls of growing up in a gendered context is that they learn to consistently underestimate their abilities and develop a fear of failure and lowered expectations of success. Even when girls earn good grades in school, they get less attention and fewer comments on the intellectual quality of their work (Barnett & Rivers, 1996). By the time they enter college, they have lower expectations of success on exams (Matlin, 1996) and lower estimates of their present abilities and future success even when their objective performance exceeds that of men (Meece, Parsons, Kaczala, Goff, & Futterman, 1982). These underestimates seem to be particularly true when women assess their ability to succeed in nontraditional careers; women have been shown to have lower career self-efficacy for nontraditional occupations than for traditional ones (Eccles, 2001). Because many fields that are nontraditional for women require math and science backgrounds, it becomes evident that external and internalized forces interact with each other to compound their impact.

### Consequences for Boys

Because theories of career development and normative work patterns were all developed from a male perspective, little attention has been paid to the effects on men of a gendered career decision-making context (Gysbers et al., 1998). Only recently has gender role stereotyping been recognized as taking a significant toll on boys as well as girls. From early childhood, boys are socialized to be more aggressive and competitive than girls. A clear example is the influence of sports as a major socializing experience for boys (Gysbers et al., 1998; Skovholt, 1990). In football, basketball, baseball, wrestling, and other sports there are winners and losers, and boys are taught to compete and win. Winning is perceived as necessary to maintain the masculine role (Smith & Inder, 1993); therefore, when boys grow up they translate the values of the sports field into the workplace and judge their success on their ability to compete, win, and acquire status. Of course, not every boy can win, and the outcome of failure often can be a diminished sense of self-worth.

Along with the expectation to compete and succeed comes a parallel societal message to boys that they must be tough and avoid showing weakness. Thus, adolescence becomes a time of restricted emotionality for boys, which results in a narrowing of their range of coping behaviors when faced with stressful situations (Gysbers et al., 1998) and can lead to stress-related health problems in adulthood. The fear of femininity, of being seen as weak or as a sissy, influences boys to avoid anything that might be considered feminine (Slattery, 2004). They internalize and come to avoid expressing feelings of grief, sadness, pain, or uncertainty because such expressions are perceived as unmanly. Not only do they learn to avoid self-disclosing and admitting their vulnerabilities, they become reluctant to consider careers that are traditionally female dominated or to seek help, including career guidance (Rochlen & O'Brien, 2002).

## Gender Differences in Career Decision Making

By young adulthood, when choosing an occupation or career is a major life task, the influence of deeply embedded gender role socialization of men and women is so profound that there are marked differences in their career decision-making processes (Gilligan, 1982). The pattern that is more characteristic of women's decision making is contextual and embedded in relationships with others. Women often make decisions on the basis of relationship and connectedness, considering the effects of their decisions on others. With respect to occupational and career development, women's decisions have been described as dichotomous (A. P. Jackson & Scharman, 2002). Women are socialized to perform the primary family role of nurturer and caregiver. This role is expressed through interactions within the family. Thus, women's perspective is that family and career do not run parallel with each other; rather, they are in conflict. When women frame their career issues in this dichotomous way, they are forced to choose between family and career, or they may lower their career aspirations to maintain a balance between the two responsibilities. Women tend to assign lower importance to the centrality of work in their lives than do men (Harpaz & Fu, 1997).

Although women tend to emphasize relatedness, the pattern more characteristic of men is based on separation, logic, and individuality. The isolated decision presented to men is quite different from the dichotomous choice presented to women. Male gender role socialization has taught men that their identity is defined primarily through work (Skovholt, 1990). Historically, men were socialized to be the family financial provider or breadwinner, a role expressed through career endeavors. Thus, men's family and career obligations ran parallel and were synchronous rather than in competing positions. Career decision making simultaneously fulfilled both family and career imperatives for men. Today, however, there is increasing recognition that men pay a price for working long hours and expending so much of their energy in fulfilling the breadwinner role. They may become isolated from the family and come to resent their peripheral status. Thus, men's decisions have become more dichotomous, too, in that success in the work role may compete with meaningful involvement in family life.

These decision-making patterns have deleterious effects on both women and men; the perceived dichotomy forces women to make career compromises to fulfill their nurturing roles, and the isolated decision making experienced by many men places them under tremendous pressure to succeed in their careers, often at the expense of family inclusion. In addition, external reality operates to reinforce stereotypical perceptions of occupational choice. The world of work does not present the same opportunities to men and to women.

### SIDEBAR 17.2  Gender Differences in Choosing a College Major

Ronnie is a college sophomore who needs to declare a major before beginning the junior year. Ronnie's friends all have said that Ronnie's excellent grades in the sciences would be a great fit for a career in junior or senior high school teaching. Ronnie is engaged to be married to someone who is several years older than Ronnie and is already a successful small business owner. If Ronnie is a woman, what factors would you expect her to consider in choosing a major? If Ronnie is a man, what factors would you expect him to consider?

## Gendered Workplace

In this section of the chapter, we explore gender-based issues inherent in the world of work, including occupational segregation, the earnings gap between the sexes, and barriers to women's advancement. Each of these issues affects both women and men, although women generally bear the brunt of the associated costs.

## Occupational Segregation

Women and men tend to be concentrated in different clusters of occupations (Moen, 1992). Men are overrepresented in craft, laborer, and senior executive jobs in corporations, and women are overrepresented in clerical, sales, and services jobs (Maume, 1999; Moen, 1992). Some traditionally masculine jobs are physician (especially surgeon), those involving math and science, electrician, plumber, and teamster. Traditionally female jobs are almost always lower paying and lower status pink-collar (Howe, 1977) jobs such as beautician, secretary, nurse, elementary school teacher, child care worker, and waitress. The gender disparities in many of these stereotyped job categories are distinct: In 2008, only 8% of construction workers (a traditionally male occupation) were women, whereas 79% of social workers (a traditionally female occupation) were women (Bureau of Labor Statistics, 2010). Although women have made inroads into some traditionally male-dominated occupations such as accountant or police officer, these inroads have not been as great in many occupations that pay well. For example, in 2009 only 9% of female professionals, as compared with 43% of male professionals, were employed in the relatively high-paying computer and engineering fields (Bureau of Labor Statistics, 2010).

Occupational segregation has become further entrenched as the United States has moved toward a service economy (the vast majority of workers—between 80% and 92%—are now in the service sector) and as more women with young children have entered the work force. In 2008, 71% of women with children younger than age 18 were in the labor force (Bureau of Labor Statistics, 2010). Along with the growth of the service economy, the number of part-time and temporary jobs (more than two thirds of which are held by women) has increased significantly. Employers recruit this "contingent work force" because it is less costly. This situation creates a double bind for women: Part-time jobs offer the flexibility to better manage home and work responsibilities, but they also tend to be low-wage positions with little or no opportunity for advancement and few fringe benefits. The proliferation of mothers of young children in the work force also has led to an increased need for child care workers, restaurant workers, and sales clerks to staff expanded retail business hours—all low-paying, "female" occupations (Moen, 1992). This situation, in which low-paying jobs generate more low-paying jobs, has produced a chronic condition of poverty that is very difficult to escape. All these factors have led to a "feminization of poverty" (Pearce, 1978, p. 30): In 2009, 25% of families maintained by a woman with children younger than age 18 were living in poverty, and female heads of household are twice as likely as men to be classified among the working poor (Bureau of Labor Statistics, 2010).

These occupational disparities are not the result of a natural inclination of women and men toward certain types of occupations, although occupational segregation is often justified on the basis of women's and men's different strengths or as a result of choices they have made. Occupations that are stereotypically viewed by society as male or female can in fact be gender equitable. For example, in the United States only 6.6% of university faculty in physics are women (American Association of University Professors, 2004), whereas in Hungary approximately half of physics professors are women (Hyde, 1997).

## Earnings Gap

In the United States, the overwhelming majority (nearly 99%) of women will work for pay at some time in their lives (Bureau of Labor Statistics, 2010; Costello & Stone, 2001). Most work out of economic need. Wage discrimination based on gender has been against the law for nearly half a century. The Equal Pay Act of 1963 prohibits employers from paying women less than men for substantially equal work. Title VII of the Civil Rights Act of 1964 prohibits paying women less than men even when their jobs are different if the reason for the pay difference is gender. Title VII also prohibits discrimination against women in hiring, promotion, training, and discipline and makes sexual harassment against female workers illegal (http://www .aflcio.org/issues/jobseconomy/workerrights/disc_sex.cfm). Despite the existence of these laws, women still do not receive equal pay for equal or similar work. In 1979, women working full time earned $0.62 for every dollar that men earned; by 2002, it had risen to $0.76 and then peaked at $0.81 in 2005 and 2006. In recent years, the wage gap has remained stable, with women in 2008 earning $0.80 for every dollar earned by men. When race or ethnicity is factored in, the disparity is even greater: African American women in 2007 were earning $0.68 and Latina women were earning $0.60 for every dollar earned by White men (U.S. Census Bureau, 2008). Levels of workforce participation often have been higher for women of color than for White women. For many women of color, the need to balance personal and work lives is a given (Atkinson & Hackett, 2004). Their income is especially important to the family because African American and Latino men earn less than White men (Bureau of Labor Statistics, 2010).

The median salary for men in 2008 was approximately $42,600, whereas for women it was just more than $34,150 (Bureau of Labor Statistics, 2008). This difference can be explained in large measure by occupational segregation by gender. The earnings gap is wider in traditionally female occupational categories; managerial and professional women earn 72% of what men in those occupations earn, but they earn only 60% of what men earn in sales occupations. Men earn more than women even in female-dominated occupations (Bureau of Labor Statistics, 2008).

## Barriers to Advancement for Women

Gender discrimination in the workplace often occurs when a woman is hired for a job. "The inequality of level and compensation experiences between women and men is early written in stone, because comparable male and female candidates enter the field at different levels" (Canning & Kaltreider, 1997, p. 246). When married women interview for jobs, they may be perceived as having less economic need for a position and as unlikely to be geographically mobile. They may be offered a lower starting salary than men hired into comparable positions, a practice that persists in part because many women are reluctant or unprepared to negotiate wages (Canning & Kaltreider). Rather, they focus on getting hired and then expect to be promoted when they prove themselves (Gilbert & Kearney, 2006; Hymowitz, 2004).

Once hired, women are penalized in their career trajectories for taking time off because of pregnancy and childcare responsibilities, for moving because of their spouse's career, and for lack of geographic mobility. Women who take time off to attend to family responsibilities are seen as lacking commitment to the organization. Additionally, they are subjected to many subtle workplace "microinequities" (Rowe, 1990), such as holding meetings at the end of the day when female employees may have to pick up children at day care, not mentioning women as likely candidates for promotion, and not giving women high-profile assignments.

Women who aspire to leadership positions often are penalized by a lack of mentors. Not only do men prefer to mentor men (Garland, 1991; Hymowitz, 2004), but there are few women in leadership positions to provide the needed mentorship. In addition to a dearth of mentors, a lack of institutional resources such as secretarial help or technical assistance and exclusion from the old boy network are especially problematic for women in nontraditional careers (Worell & Remer, 2003). As these external barriers become internalized, some women adjust their career aspirations and seek occupations that are viewed as consistent with their (present or future) responsibilities as parents and spouses (Gilbert & Kearney, 2006).

More women are in the professions and in management positions today, but they are still disproportionately absent from the top echelon. Fewer than 1% of CEOs of Fortune 500 companies are women, despite the fact that women represent a large percentage of the talent pool from which high-level executives are drawn (Burke & Richardson, 2009). Institutional power structures, values, and promotion policies create a glass ceiling composed of artificial barriers that prevent women from advancing into mid-level and senior management positions (Vega, 1993).

Women who aspire to advancement have to contend with a double-bind situation. On the one hand, they need to counter the gender role expectation that women do not know how to play hardball (Spielvogel, 1997). On the other hand, they are often penalized for exhibiting the very characteristics and behavior that would be valued in a male leader (Fassinger, 2001). A woman might be called arrogant, abrasive, and overbearing, whereas a man who displayed the same behaviors would be called self-confident, outspoken, and assertive.

Women, far more than men, have to contend with sexual harassment in the workplace. Sexual harassment has been called the single most widespread occupational hazard for women (Gilbert & Kearney, 2006). According to various estimates, 35% to 70% of women have experienced sexual harassment on the job (Barnett & Rivers, 1996; Fitzgerald, 1993). In nontraditional occupations, the percentage is much higher (Gutek & Done, 2001). The consequences of sexual harassment can be pervasive. They can affect a woman's career advancement via disrupted work history, absenteeism, loss of seniority, and changing jobs (Worell & Remer, 2003) and can take a toll on women's psychological and physical health as well.

The effects of embedded systemic discrimination in the workplace present particular challenges to women of color. Structural barriers to career advancement may be especially difficult for them to surmount. If they are heads of household, they may find themselves holding several jobs to make ends meet and then coming home to still more responsibilities (Lum, 2007). At work, women of color must contend with both racism and sexism, even though acts of discrimination may not always be conscious or deliberate. Those who are in positions of power in the workplace may have benefitted from White, male, middle-class privilege all their lives and may subscribe to the myth of meritocracy, the belief that choice and opportunity are equally available to all (M. A. Jackson, Leon, & Zaharopoulos, 2010). They may fail to understand why some women do not avail themselves of opportunities for advancement, such as tuition-paid evening courses at a local college or weekend management training seminars.

### SIDEBAR 17.3  Balancing Career and Family

Maria's employer has offered her a promotion from secretary to office manager. The new position would require that she work extended hours but within 6 months could lead to a significant raise in pay. Maria has two children, ages 2 and 4, and is married to Phil, who is an offshore oil rig worker. The nature of Phil's work is that he is gone 2 weeks and then home for 1 week. If you were Maria's career counselor, how would you help her navigate the decision-making process regarding the offered promotion?

## Contemporary Issues

In this section of the chapter, we explore issues that today's men and women commonly confront as they establish and negotiate their career paths. For many, balancing work and family responsibilities, including child and elder care, is an ongoing struggle. Women who are reentering the workforce face particular difficulties as they attempt to restart their careers. Male socialization, with its emphasis on achievement and competition, can exact a heavy toll on men's health. Dual-career couples, both heterosexual and same sex, often have to make tough sacrifices to maintain both careers. Men and women alike have adopted new roles, and employers who have historically ignored or misunderstood these sacrifices are beginning to adopt new policies (Burke & Richardson, 2009).

### Work–Family Conflicts

Building a life that includes both family and career is a challenge for contemporary Americans, particularly for women. Young women who aspire to have successful lifelong careers and to have children often end up being doubly penalized. Taking time out of the labor force or working part time while the children are young can wreak havoc on a long-term career trajectory. "The difficulty is that the child-nurturing years are also the career nurturing years. What is lost in either case cannot be 'made up' at a later time" (Moen, 1992, p. 133).

Some young women with children get shunted onto a "mommy track," an alternative career path for women who are committed to both raising children and having a career. These women often are held in less esteem in the workplace and are sidetracked for advancement. Other young women choose to delay child bearing, a decision that has particular consequences for professional women in front-loaded careers (Denmark, 1992) such as medicine, law, academia, and business management. Because the education and training for these professions is lengthy and because the early years in the profession require a great investment of time and commitment to establish oneself, women who decide to postpone child bearing can find themselves in a race with their biological clocks.

Despite evidence that has suggested that men increasingly participate in household work and that women have decreased the amount of time they devote to household tasks, the division of household labor has not even begun to approach equity. Women continue to bear most of the responsibility for managing time-consuming, routine household tasks and child care (Steil, 2001; Worell & Remer, 2003). Balancing the demands of work and family can cause role overload, which occurs when the demands of a role exceed a person's resources.

This superwoman ideal of having and managing both career and family has been fostered by women's perception that they need to "do it like a man." Self-help books and seminars on how to dress for success, handle confrontation, and learn to be assertive are a growth industry with a largely female audience, despite the fact that the ideal of a woman who can do it all has been attacked as impossible and even life threatening to women who attempt it (Ponton, 1997). Many women who start out with the expectation that they can manage children and a career are forced to modify these expectations and reevaluate their priorities. As they cut back on their personal time for exercise, pleasure reading, hobbies, friends, and time alone, they may begin to wonder whether career success is worth the price.

A growing body of evidence has suggested that career–family conflict is no longer primarily women's problem. Studies have indicated that contemporary men experience their family life as more psychologically significant than their jobs, and they want to spend more time with their families and are willing to adapt their working lives considerably to do so. Many contemporary men struggle equally with women with difficulties related to child care (Luzzo & McWhirter, 2001), dual careers, and balancing work and family life (Barnett & Rivers, 1996). Younger men (of Generations X and Y) are increasingly placing greater importance on family than on career (Ebenkamp, 2001).

## Child and Elder Care

A lack of adequate child care may be the biggest unresolved issue for working couples (Reardon, Lenz, Sampson, & Peterson, 2000). The percentage of working women with children younger than age 3 held steady at approximately 60% between 1998 and 2007 (Pew Research Center, 2007). Despite growing evidence that employer-provided child care is actually cost effective in that it reduces absenteeism and tardiness and increases productivity (Burud, Aschbacher, & McCroskey, 1984; Lambert, Hopkins, Easton, & Walker, 1992; Stewart & Burge, 1989), a growing number of women and men must coordinate their work demands with their spouses' job and child care (Moen, 1992).

In respond to this need, more employers are now offering parental leave, which can be an important asset in managing work and family commitments. However, taking paternity leave is a "tricky area for men" (Barnett & Rivers, 1996, p. 67). Gender stereotypes still exist, and the cultural message remains in force that it is somehow "unmasculine" for men to take time off work to care for children. Because paternity leave requires formal approval and is often unpaid, men often take sick leave or vacation time (Barnett & Rivers).

For members of the sandwich generation, childcare concerns may be compounded by the need to care for elderly parents. Estimates are that more than half of baby boomers will find themselves caring for children and elders at the same time (Michaels & McCarty, 1993). Elder care can take a toll on worker productivity: One study showed that the elder care responsibilities of employees at a large insurance corporation cost an estimated $2,500 annually per worker (Scharlach, Lowe, & Schneider, 1991). Nonetheless, employers do not seem to be addressing this need.

Some divorced women and men have children who depend on them emotionally, physically, and financially. Both women and men who have dependent children are challenged to balance the responsibilities of parenthood and household management with work demands (Zunker, 1998).

Reentry women, who are returning to the labor force after a lengthy absence, face some unique difficulties. Broadly defined, reentry women range in age from 35 to 55 and are married with children still in the home, single parents, empty nesters, or displaced homemakers. Among those who are the most disadvantaged are displaced homemakers, women older than 35 who have been out of the labor force for an extended period of time (Zunker, 1998). Their occupational problems are acute because they often lack job search skills and current training that would be useful in the modern work world. For example, a woman who worked 15 years ago as a secretary and was skilled at taking dictation by shorthand would now need computer skills instead.

## Stress and Health Concerns

Through traditional male socialization, boys learn that they are expected to work outside the home throughout their lifetimes and provide for their families. The most powerful gender stereotype or schema for males has been suggested to be the concept of breadwinner (Reardon et al., 2000). Work becomes the primary means for them to achieve an identity. Internalized messages to achieve and succeed put pressure on men to strive to get ahead and be on top, even though there is very little room at the top (Blustein, Kenna, Gill, & DeVoy, 2008; Gysbers et al., 1998). Because men have few other avenues for their identity, failure to succeed in the work role can lead to discouragement, stress-related physical illnesses, psychological distress, and even a shortened life span (Pedersen, Draguns, Lonner, & Trimble, 2002). Gysbers et al. (1998) have suggested that differences in longevity (on average, women live 7 years longer than men) are largely attributable to gender role behaviors of men.

An intense drive to compete and succeed is often associated with Type A behavior and workaholism. Workaholism has been described as an addiction to work or a need to work that is so excessive that it negatively affects a person's physical health and marital and family relationships (Seybold & Salomone, 1994). Similarly, people with Type A personalities have been described as being overcommitted to their work and highly achievement oriented. Although Type A behavior is more common among men than among women, many professional women display Type A behavior patterns as well (Greenglass, 1991). There appear to be strong links among workaholism and competitiveness, Type A behavior, and heart disease (Booth-Kewley & Friedman, 1987; Machlowitz, 1980). Although the consequences of a workaholic lifestyle include marital failure and family estrangement (Klaft & Kleiner, 1988; Spruell, 1987), workaholism is still the addiction that is most rewarded in U.S. society (Spruell, 1987).

## Dual-Career Couples

Dual-career couples or dual wage-earning couples are more the norm than the exception today. These couples have developed strategies for managing work–family conflicts such as buying services (e.g., hiring a housekeeper); learning to negotiate both at home and at work; and developing support systems with partners, friends, relatives, and colleagues. Still, they face many stressors as they attempt to negotiate the complexities of their lives. Relocation is very stressful for dual-career couples who face difficult decisions when the career of the husband or wife requires them to relocate. The expectation is still that the man will be mobile and the woman will follow him. Typically, the woman sets aside her career or consciously alters her career aspirations. A man's decision to refuse to relocate is still nontraditional, and he is likely to be seen as lacking professional commitment (Kaltreider, 1997).

Issues of family management, negotiation of roles, and social support are salient for same-sex couples as well as heterosexual couples. Same-sex couples may face the same difficult decisions regarding relocation, career dominance, or both, and these decisions can place stress on relationships.

Commuter marriages are becoming more common as increasing numbers of wives and husbands choose to maintain their own employment even though this requires them to live in geographically separate locations. Dual-career relationships, in all their permutations, often require sacrifices. However, many couples have reported that the rewards are substantial, including personal fulfillment and increased income (Kaltreider, Gracie, & Sirulnick, 1997).

## New Roles for Women and Men

Jobs traditionally allocated to men are now more available to women (Zunker, 1998). In 2009, women made up nearly half (44.7%) of workers in management and professional occupations (Bureau of Labor Statistics, 2010). Men have been more reluctant to move into occupations that are nontraditional for them (Reardon et al., 2000), possibly because they face the double disincentive of low wages and a socialized fear of being perceived as feminine. Nonetheless, it is no longer startling to encounter a male nurse or a male elementary school teacher.

As more women have entered the workforce and as women have increasingly pursued full-time careers, the relatively new role of househusband has emerged. Although how many men are now staying at home while their wives work outside the home is unknown, the range has been estimated to be between 325,000 and 2 million (Rauch, 1996). This reversal of the stereotypical marital roles may start out as a temporary arrangement that stretches into years, as a logical division of labor when the wife is making more money than the husband or when adequate child care is not available at the workplace or in the community. It may also occur because the father wants the opportunity to watch his children grow. Whatever the reasons are for a man's taking on the househusband role, he can expect that friends and family may find it odd and wonder what he does all day.

More women are taking responsibility for the breadwinner role in the family. In 2008, women were the primary breadwinner in 39.3% of households and the cobreadwinner in an additional 24% of households (Center for American Progress, 2008). Men married to successful businesswomen may find themselves in the uncharted role of first husband. Although traditional male socialization may make it difficult to men to share the limelight with their wives, relinquish the provider role, be a subordinate earner, and be a more involved parent (Reardon et al., 2000), these new configurations afford both men and women opportunities to move away from traditional gender roles. Recent career development literature has provided some support for the existence of a trend toward changing gender role ideology (Abowitz & Knox, 2003).

Entrepreneurship among women and couples is increasing. Women own approximately half of small businesses. The number is growing despite barriers not usually faced by men, such as discrimination by lenders, exclusion from informal old boy networks, and lack of information on how to obtain capital (Worell & Remer, 2003). Advantages for women of owning their own businesses may include flexible work schedules and the opportunity to take control of their economic lives (Reardon et al., 2000). Shared entrepreneurship—husbands and wives running their own businesses—is one of the fastest growing areas in the business world (Granfield, 1993). Although making such an arrangement work has obvious challenges, successful couples seem to share a common vision, have distinct roles, and make a strong effort to protect their private lives (Granfield, 1993).

## Changing World of Work

Over the past 25 to 30 years, employers have become more responsive to the needs of the changing workforce. The federal government, the nation's largest employer, provides flextime in many of its agencies and is more likely than private-sector employers to provide employer-sponsored day care. Flextime is used regularly by mothers and fathers alike to deliver and collect children and to spend time with the family (Lewis & Lewis, 1996). Private sector initiatives, led by several large corporations (such as IBM, Xerox, Kodak, and Corning) have adopted new policies including assistance for child care, part-time employment, work-at-home options such as telecommuting, job sharing, flextime, flexible time off, parental leave, and relocation support for trailing spouses (Moen, 1992). Still, these workplace accommodations are by no means routinely available.

In conclusion, ample evidence exists that the world of work is changing, although it still has far to go to be gender equitable. Women and men are finding new, creative ways to accommodate their desire to have both a family and a meaningful career. Career counselors will need to be creative, as well, if they are to serve their clients effectively and in a gender-fair manner.

## Strategies for Gender-Aware Career Counseling

In this concluding section of the chapter, we focus on strategies to help counselors ensure that their career counseling practices are gender aware. As a first step, it is essential for counselors to realize that they are not immune to society's gender-conditioning messages. Counselors are products of their gender role socialization processes and have developed their own deeply embedded gender schemas. Because the forces of gender role socialization operate at an unconscious level, they can lead counselors to see gender differences when none exist and to pay attention to behavior that conforms to gender expectations while ignoring behavior that is inconsistent with their beliefs about gender. On the basis of this awareness, our recommendations for gender-fair career counseling those discussed in the following sections.

### Career Counselors Need to Constantly Check Their Assumptions

Research has confirmed the existence of gender-biased attitudes and practices in career counseling (Fitzgerald & Cherpas, 1985; Haring & Beyard-Tyler, 1984; Robertson & Fitzgerald, 1990). Thus, counselors need to be aware of how their own internalized gender schemas, as well as the gender stereotyping that exists in the larger social system, may limit the perspectives and choices of women and men (Atkinson & Hackett, 2004). This awareness points to the need for career counselors to constantly self-monitor and check the assumptions they are making. The goal is to develop a culturally competent, nonassumptive stance.

### SIDEBAR 17.4  Inner Conflict and Gender

Joey is a division manager of a large Fortune 500 company. She demonstrated impressive expertise in her former position as lead accountant. Now, as division manager, she is in charge of promotions. Recently, a vacancy arose for a lead position in marketing; two men and one woman are vying for the position. The decision rests solely with Joey. She has met with all three candidates. The female candidate seems to be the best qualified, but Joey is hesitant. What factors (both external and internalized) might affect Joey's ability to make the best decision for the company?

It is equally as important to not lose sight of individual differences, both within and between genders (Betz, 1994). All women are not alike, nor do they all share the same value of willingness to compromise their careers for family reasons. This principle also applies to men; for some men, family considerations are as important as the stereotypical motivators of power and prestige in their career choice process (Pedersen et al., 2002).

Although it is true that women generally are relational in their orientation and that men are more achievement oriented, not all women are relationally oriented nor are all men driven to compete and achieve. Counselors should inquire into the meaning of work for their female and male clients alike and ascertain what needs these clients hope to meet through their career or occupational choices. Even when clients conform to gender role expectations, some women will be relationally oriented but choose to fulfill their relational needs outside the work arena, just as some men will choose to channel their needs to compete and win into sports and other nonwork activities.

Another assumption to be avoided is that women who have young children must choose between pursuit of a full-time career (which would entail leaving child care to others) and being part-time employees with little opportunity for advancement or career development. Women studied by A. P. Jackson and Scharman (2002) were able to creatively construct their careers to allow them to work less than the standard 40-hour week, thus striking a balance between work and child care. Joint decision making with their spouses and children was a key component in making arrangements work. For career counselors, such studies have highlighted the importance of including spouses and even entire families in the career counseling process when appropriate.

### Gender-Aware Career Counseling Should Begin Early, in the Elementary School Years

Because occupational gender stereotyping starts very early in life, school counselors have unique opportunities to help boys and girls move out of their traditional gender boxes. Children at the elementary school level can be exposed to a wide range of career options and can be encouraged to explore jobs that are nontraditional for both sexes. They can be connected with mentors and role models who have been successful in careers and occupations that are nonstereotypical. School counselors are well positioned to address the barriers of insufficient career exploration, gender role expectations, and restrictive internalized beliefs that work to limit the career development of boys and girls (Perusse & Goodnough, 2004).

### SIDEBAR 17.5   Planning a Career Workshop

Assume that you have been given the opportunity to develop and deliver a half-day career awareness workshop at a local elementary school (you might be a school counselor or you may work for a community agency that does outreach with the schools). Outline the major topics you would want to cover and the primary lessons you would want your audience to acquire.

## Counselors Should Work From Career Development Theories That Apply Equally to Women and Men

Traditional models of career development need to be examined with a critical eye. Historically, career development theories were patterned on life-stage models created from studying the experiences of men. They were based on assumptions such as (a) career choices are made autonomously, (b) equal opportunity is open to all, (c) work is the most important aspect of people's lives, (d) career decisions are made through a rational matching of a person's traits to the characteristics of occupations, and (f) career development progresses in linear stages, moving upward toward greater responsibility, rank, and financial reward (Betz, 1994; Gysbers et al., 1998). Well into the 1960s, descriptions of women's career paths were based on the premise that women's normative life role was that of homemaker. Women who gave equal or greater emphasis to their careers were described as innovative (Ginzberg, 1966) or unusual (Zytowski, 1969).

In more recent decades, awareness has been growing that neither women's nor men's occupational life cycles follow a rigid progression but rather are influenced by events such as marriage, child rearing, financial resources, and cultural values. It has become evident that counselors need to consider barriers to career development as well as interests and aptitudes (Farmer, 1976; Harmon, 1977). Some of these barriers are internal (psychological) and include (primarily for women) fear of success, home–career conflict, math avoidance, and low expectations of academic success and (primarily for men) fear of failure, avoidance of occupations that are traditionally feminine, and restricted emotional expressiveness. Other constraints are external (societal), such as sex discrimination, sexual harassment on the job, lack of child care, and gender-biased counseling (Herlihy & Watson, 2003).

Researchers (Byars-Winston & Fouad, 2006; Cook, Heppner, & O'Brien, 2002) have suggested that ecological models (such as feminist and multicultural) can help counselors broaden their perspectives by focusing on both individual and environmental interventions. Individual interventions can be targeted toward helping clients analyze, understand, and develop skills for dealing with socioenvironmental barriers (M. A. Jackson et al., 2010; Luzzo & McWhirter, 2001). Environmental interventions can focus on creating supportive networks that include mentors and role models, working to create change in child care policies, and designing educational strategies to reduce sexual harassment and increase gender equity in the workplace. Counselors can function as change agents as well as providers of individual counseling services.

Betz (2002) has cautioned that although ecological models may improve career counseling, attention must be given to individual differences within as well as between genders. All women are not alike, nor do they all share the same willingness to compromise their careers for family reasons. Neither are all men alike; for some men, family considerations are as important or more important in career choice as are the stereotypical motivators of power and prestige. Whatever the counselor's approach to career development, that approach may need to be adapted so that it is free of gender-role stereotyping (Miller & Brown, 2005), considers internal and external barriers, and accounts for individual differences as well as differences between women and men.

## Counselors Should Take a Holistic Approach to Career Counseling

It is important to remember that cultural issues, including gender, are inextricably interwoven with career planning issues. This fact is particularly evident when clients need assistance in achieving a balance between work and family. Work–family conflicts are common among heterosexual and same-sex working couples. Rather than concentrating exclusively on career and workplace issues, interventions can address broader goals that would consider the interplay among career, family, society, and self (M. A. Jackson et al., 2010). For example, Tennent and Sperry (2003) focused on optimizing clients' physical health by combining physical activities with family time. They found such interventions to be effective. There was a positive spillover in both the family and work spheres when clients' physical health was increased. Family members were positively affected, and clients' productivity at work increased.

## Counselors Should Use Caution in Interpreting Career Interest Inventories

Most career assessment inventories have been revised to be more gender sensitive, but counselors still need to be alert to inherent biases (Fouad & Kantamneni, 2010). For example, most women tend to score high on the artistic, social, and conventional scales of Holland's (1994) hexagon, and men are more likely to score high on the realistic, investigative, and enterprising scales. When these typical scoring patterns are accepted without question, the ghettoization of women in clerical and service occupations is perpetuated, and men lose the opportunity to explore careers that are nontraditional and potentially self-fulfilling for them. Before test interpretation, counselors can incorporate a self-reflection phase, during which clients are encouraged to explore the impact of their gender role socialization on their career interests and goals (Pieterse & Miller, 2010).

### SIDEBAR 17.6 Culturally Sensitive Career Counseling

You have administered a series of career interest and personality inventories to a client who is a 23-year-old Korean American woman. You review the printed results with the client and explain to her what career interests she might pursue on the basis of these results. Can you see any potential problems with this strategy?

What factors, other than test results, do you think it would be helpful to consider to increase your effectiveness in assisting this client?

## Counselors Need to Be Prepared to Assist Women and Men With the Gender-Based Concerns That They May Bring to Career Counseling

Male clients (and some female clients) might benefit from learning (a) how the gender role socialization process influences their career behavior, (b) how to increase their emotional expressiveness, (c) strategies for managing and reducing stress, and (d) ways to participate more fully in family life and other nonwork roles (Niles & Harris-Bowlsbey, 2002). Female clients (and some male clients) might find it helpful to (a) explore and learn how to transcend restrictive gender role messages about careers, (b) increase their self-efficacy and expectations for success, (c) develop skills for challenging workplace and home inequities, (d) find ways to achieve a satisfying balance between work and family roles (Atkinson & Hackett, 2004), (e) find mentors, and (f) deal with sexual harassment. Both men and women might benefit from assistance in finding adequate and affordable child care and garnering support for their aspirations to enter nontraditional occupations.

In closing, we offer two case examples and invite you, the reader, to think about how you might apply the concepts in this chapter in conducting career counseling with these clients.

### Case Example 1: Maria

Maria Rodriguez is a 24-year-old unmarried woman who lives at home with her parents and her two younger siblings. She seeks counseling because she wants to learn to be less self-critical and figure out "some goals in my life." She works in a technical support staff position at a cellular communications company. She says she enjoys her work, but that she just took the first job she was offered after she graduated from a community college and has stayed there ever since. She would like to pursue a 4-year degree but questions whether she would be able to succeed academically. When asked how she fared with her grades at the community college, she replies that she graduated with a 3.7 grade point average but that a "real university would be much harder." Besides, even if she could do well in her studies, she has no idea what major she would pursue or what career goal might suit her.

Maria adds that it would be difficult for her to juggle the demands of her job, college studies, and her household responsibilities. Her youngest brother, age 16, has cystic fibrosis, and her mother depends on her to help with his physical care as well as with the cooking, cleaning, and other household chores. Her other brother, age 19, works at a full-time job and is rarely home when he is off work. She describes her father as the dominant force in the family, even though he is sometimes absent for extended periods of time as a result of "getting into trouble when he starts drinking." She states that she realizes she would have more control over her time if she were to move out on her own, but that would not be possible because "my mother could never manage without me during the times when my father is gone."

In our view, a holistic approach is indicated in Maria's case, one that considers cultural issues along with career exploration. Maria seems to have internalized several gender role expectations, such as the belief that women are responsible for caregiving and household chores. She also appears to have lowered self-efficacy expectations with respect to her academic abilities. She questions her ability to succeed in a 4-year university despite having achieved a 3.7 grade point average at the community college. She may also lack assertiveness skills because she has remained in the same position at work since she was hired.

Maria's career counselor needs to remain sensitive not only to gender issues in working with Maria, but also to expectations associated with Latino culture that may be influencing her decision making. If her counselor is culturally different from Maria (e.g., Caucasian, male), the counselor might assume she could benefit from learning to be more independent, moving out on her own, and pursuing her baccalaureate degree. If her counselor is culturally similar to Maria (e.g., Latina, female), the counselor will need to remain alert to the possibility that cultural differences are present even though counselor and client are trait-factor matched. In any event, the counselor must understand and respect Maria's cultural values.

The counselor should explore Maria's self-efficacy beliefs with her. Cognitive–behavioral techniques might be used to help her identify her cognitive distortions with respect to her ability to succeed academically. Feminist therapy strategies such as gender role analysis and power analysis, as well as a narrative approach to careers, might be useful to increase Maria's awareness of her competencies and personal power. Then Maria will be able to choose which of her internalized gender role expectations she wants to continue to live by and which ones she may wish to modify.

Maria's counselor needs to ascertain the role of work in Maria's life. Does Maria envision that she will get married and have children? If so, how will her work role relate to her roles as wife and mother? Depending on her answers to these questions, she may or may not want to focus her career exploration on jobs that have flexibility to allow her to balance work and family responsibilities.

Career counseling with Maria needs to include helping her explore her interests. Because she enjoys her work providing technical support services, a career in the technology field, although nontraditional for women, might be an option she would want to investigate. At age 24, with her academic talents, Maria has a vast world of possibilities open to her. The counselor's task is to help her become aware of her choices and make decisions that are in accordance with her values.

## Case Example 2: Richard

Richard Johnson, age 52, has sought counseling at the suggestion of an emergency room physician. Richard has made four trips to the hospital emergency room within the past 3 months, each time because he was certain he was having a heart attack. Each time, his electrocardiographs and other medical tests were normal, and he was discharged.

In his first session with the counselor, Richard described the symptoms that had led the physician to refer him. They were textbook symptoms of a panic attack. Richard's wife accompanied him to the counselor's office, and she was included in the first 15 minutes of the session while initial information was gathered. She appeared to be very supportive of Richard's decision to seek counseling and provided this occupational information about herself: She works part time in a small Hallmark shop, taking care of sales, inventory, and general store management duties.

The counselor noted that Richard is highly verbal and articulate. He is well read and can quote entire passages from Kafka and Tolstoy. He did not finish high school. At age 20, he enrolled in several courses to complete his GED but quit because they were boring. He has been employed for 18 years as a forklift machine operator in a warehouse. He and his wife have been married for 24 years, and they have no children.

Richard describes his work as dull and unchallenging but adds that it compensates him well financially. He says he is lucky to have such a good job despite his lack of education. When he is asked about what he does for enjoyment, he talks at length about his love of woodworking. His wife chimes in, stating that he does beautiful work with refinishing old furniture and has designed and created many small wooden objects as gifts for friends. Richard's goals for counseling, other than to "stay out of emergency rooms," are ill defined. He feels as though his life has no meaning and that he is just "drifting through."

If we were counseling Richard, we would want to deal with his immediate presenting problem first. Cognitive–behavioral techniques could be applied to reduce the frequency and severity of his panic attacks. Then, Richard and his counselor would be able to focus on longer term goals. The counselor, working from a holistic framework, would want to understand what brought on Richard's series of panic attacks at the age of 52. They may be related to his sense of meaninglessness and his belief that he has no alternative work options to his dull and unchallenging job. He may be feeling trapped, not only by his lack of formal education but also by gender-stereotyped thinking that he must be a good breadwinner even though he does not enjoy his job. His physical problems could also be a result of long-suppressed emotions.

A positive asset search would reveal that Richard has some important strengths: He is intelligent, is a steady and reliable employee, and has a stable and supportive marital relationship. Despite his intelligence, returning to school may not be a viable option for Richard, given his experience with GED courses. He and the counselor might instead work from his demonstrated interests and talents and explore ways he could convert his love of woodworking into a paying occupation. He might be interested in entrepreneurship. Possibly, he could take a course or two in small business ownership at a community college without having to enroll for course credit. Opening a business that would offer a service (restoration of antique and old furniture) and a product (his own creations) might give him a sense of control over his life and provide him with work that he loves to do. It is possible, too, that he and his wife would want to consider making the business a shared entrepreneurship, as she already has skills in sales and small business management.

## Summary

The gender role socialization of men and women profoundly affects their career decision making. The world of work is not gender equitable, despite significant gains made by women over the past 50 years. Both women and men face numerous challenges as they attempt to establish successful and fulfilling careers. Gender-aware career counselors are uniquely suited to helping them meet these challenges. The Web sites listed in the next section provide additional information relating to the chapter topics.

## Useful Web Sites

- ABC News, *Good Morning America*. A list of companies that have developed model family-friendly programs: http://www.abcnews.go.com/GMA/Careers/story?id=1838423
- AFL-CIO. Information on what workers can do if they believe their rights have been violated, up-to-date statistics on wages: http://www.aflcio.org/issues/jobseconomy/workersrights/
- Business and Legal Resources. Gender discrimination resources, links, and information: http://www.blr.com/HR-Employment/Discrimination/Sex-Discrimination
- Equal Rights in Employment [Equal Rights in Employment Commission]: http://www.eeoc.gov/
- International Labour Organization, Bureau of Library and Information Services. Gender issues in employment: http://www.ilo.org/public/english/support/lib/resource/subject/gender.htm
- Jean Baker Miller Institute, Wellesley Centers for Women. Listings of women's and gender resources: http://www.jbmti.org/Links-to-Resources/resources/
- Jobseekers Advice. Information and advice for job seekers: http://www.jobseekersadvice.com
- The U.S. Department of Labor–Women's Bureau: http://www.dol.gov/wb/

## References

Abowitz, D., & Knox, D. (2003). Goals of college students: Some gender differences. *College Student Journal, 37,* 550–557.

American Association of University Professors. (2004). Women underrepresented on science faculties. *Academe, 90,* 3. Retrieved from http://www.aaup.org/AAUP/pubsres/academe/2004

Atkinson, D. R., & Hackett, G. (2004). *Counseling diverse populations* (3rd ed.). Boston, MA: McGraw-Hill.

Barnett, R. C., & Rivers, C. (1996). *He works, she works.* San Francisco, VA: HarperCollins.

Bem, S. L. (1993). *The lenses of gender: Transforming the debate on sexual equality.* New Haven, CT: Yale University Press.

Betz, N. E. (1994). Basic issues and concepts in career counseling for women. In W. B. Walsh & S. H. Osipow (Eds.), *Career counseling for women* (pp. 1–42). Hillsdale, NJ: Erlbaum.

Betz, N. E. (2002). Explicating an ecological approach to the career development of women. *Career Development Quarterly, 50,* 335–338.

Blustein, D. L., Kenna, A. C., Gill, N., & DeVoy, J. E. (2008). The psychology of working: A new framework for counseling practice and public policy. *Career Development Quarterly, 56,* 294–308.

Booth-Kewley, S., & Friedman, H. S. (1987). Psychological predictors of heart disease: A quantitative review. *Psychological Bulletin, 101,* 343–362.

Boswell, S. L. (1985). The influence of sex-role stereotyping on women's attitudes and achievement in mathematics. In S. F. Chipman, L. R. Brush, & D. M. Wilson (Eds.), *Women and mathematics: Balancing the equation* (pp. 175–198). Hillsdale, NJ: Erlbaum.

Bureau of Labor Statistics. (2008). *Employment and earnings.* Washington, DC: U.S. Government Printing Office.

Bureau of Labor Statistics. (2010). *Women in the labor force: A databook* (2009 ed.). Washington, DC: U.S. Government Printing Office.

Burke, R. J., & Richardson, A. M. (2009). Work experiences, stress and health among managerial women: Research and practice. In C. L. Cooper, J. C. Quick, & M. J. Schabracq (Eds.), *International handbook of work and health psychology* (3rd ed., pp. 147–161). West Sussex, England: Wiley-Blackwell.

Burud, S. L., Aschbacher, R., & McCroskey, J. (1984). *Employer-supported child care: Investing in human resources.* Dover, MA: Auburn House.

Byars-Winston, A. M., & Fouad, N. A. (2006). Metacognition and multicultural competence: Expanding the culturally appropriate career counseling model. *Career Development Quarterly, 54,* 187–201.

Canning, M., & Kaltreider, N. B. (1997). Heads up: Strategies to deal with gender discrimination and harassment. In N. B. Kaltreider (Ed.), *Dilemmas of a double life: Women balancing careers and relationships* (pp. 237–252). Northvale, NJ: Jason Aronson.

Center for American Progress. (2008). *The Shriver report.* Retrieved from http://www.shriverreport.com/awn/economy.php

Cook, E. P., Heppner, M. J., & O'Brien, K. M. (2002). Career development of women of color and White women: Assumptions, conceptualization, and interventions from an ecological perspective. *Career Development Quarterly, 50,* 291–305.

Costello, C. B., & Stone, A. J. (Eds.). (2001). *The American woman, 2001–2002: Getting to the top.* New York, NY: W. W. Norton.

Denmark, F. L. (1992). The thirty-something woman: To career or not to career. In B. R. Wainrib (Ed.), *Gender issues across the life cycle* (pp. 71–76). New York, NY: Springer.

Ebenkamp, B. (2001). Chicks and balances. *Brandweek, 42*(7), 16.

Eccles, J. S. (2001). Achievement. In J. Worell (Ed.), *Encyclopedia of women and gender* (Vol. 1, pp. 43–53). San Diego, CA: Academic Press.

Enns, C. Z. (2000). Gender issues in counseling. In S. D. Brown & R. W. Lent (Eds.), *Handbook of counseling psychology* (3rd ed., pp. 601–638). New York, NY: Wiley.

Enns, C. Z. (2004). Counseling girls and women: Attitudes, knowledge, and skills. In D. R. Atkinson & G. Hackett, *Counseling diverse populations* (3rd ed., pp. 285–306). Boston, MA: McGraw-Hill.

Farmer, H. S. (1976). What inhibits achievement and career motivation in women? *Counseling Psychologist, 6,* 12–14.

Fassinger, R. E. (2001). Women in non-traditional occupational fields. In J. Worell (Ed.), *Encyclopedia of women and gender* (Vol. 2, pp. 1269–1280). San Diego, CA: Academic Press.

Fitzgerald, L. F. (1993). The last great open secret: The sexual harassment of women in the workplace and academic. Washington, DC: Federation of Behavioral, Psychological, and Cognitive Sciences.

Fitzgerald, L. F., & Cherpas, C. C. (1985). On the reciprocal relationship between gender and occupation: Rethinking the assumptions concerning masculinity and career development. *Journal of Vocational Behavior, 27,* 109–122.

Fouad, N. A., & Kantamneni, N. (2010). Cultural validity of Holland's theory. In J. G. Ponterotto, J. M. Casas, L. A. Suzuki, & C. M. Alexander (Eds.), *Handbook of multicultural counseling* (3rd ed., pp. 703–714.) Thousand Oaks, CA: Sage.

Garland, S. D. (1991, August 19). Throwing stones at the glass ceiling. *Business Week,* p. 29.

Gettys, L. D., & Cann, A. (1981). Children's perceptions of occupational sex stereotypes. *Sex Roles, 9,* 597–607.

Gilbert, L. A., & Kearney, L. K. (2006). Sex, gender, and dual-earner families: Implications and applications for career counseling women. In W. B. Walsh & M. J. Heppner (Eds.), *Handbook of career counseling for women* (pp. 193–218.). Mahwah, NJ: Erlbaum.

Gilbert, L. A., & Sher, M. (1999). *Gender and sex in counseling and psychotherapy.* Boston, MA: Allyn & Bacon.

Gilligan, C. (1982). *In a different voice.* Cambridge, MA: Harvard University Press.

Ginzberg, E. (1966). *Lifestyles of educated American women.* New York, NY: Columbia University Press.

Gottfredson, L. S. (1996). A theory of circumscription and compromise. In D. Brown, L. Brooks, & Associates, *Career choice and development* (3rd ed., pp. 179–281). San Francisco, CA: Jossey-Bass.

Granfield, M. (1993, June). Till debt do us part. *Working Woman,* pp. 33–35.

Greenglass, E. R. (1991). Type A behavior, career aspirations, and role conflict in professional women. In M. J. Strube (Ed.), *Type A behavior* (pp. 277–292). Newbury Park, CA: Sage.

Gutek, B. A., & Done, R. S. (2001). Sexual harassment. In R. Unger (Ed.), *Handbook of the psychology of women and gender* (pp. 367–387). New York, NY: Wiley.

Gysbers, N. C., Heppner, M. J., & Johnston, J. A. (1998). *Career counseling: Process, issues, and techniques.* Boston, MA: Allyn & Bacon.

Haring, M. J., & Beyard-Tyler, K. C. (1984). Counseling with women: The challenge of nontraditional careers. *School Counselor, 31,* 301–309.

Harmon, L. W. (1977). Career counseling for women. In E. Rawlings & D. Carter (Eds.), *Psychotherapy for women* (pp. 197–206). Springfield, IL: Charles C Thomas.

Harpaz, P. J., & Fu, L. (1997). Work centrality in Germany, Israel, Japan, and the United States. *Cross-Cultural Research, 31,* 171–200.

Herlihy, B. R., & Watson, Z. E. (2003). Ethical issues and multicultural competence in counseling. In F. D. Harper & J. McFadden (Eds.), *Culture and counseling: New approaches* (pp. 363–378). New York, NY: Allyn & Bacon.

Holland, J. L. (1994). Self-directed search. Odessa, FL: Psychological Assessment Resources.

Howe, L. K. (1977). *Pink collar workers.* New York, NY: Avon.

Hyde, J. S. (1997). Gender differences in math performance. In M. R. Walsh (Ed.), *Women, men, and gender: Ongoing debates* (pp. 283–287). New Haven, CT: Yale University Press.

Hymowitz, C. (2004, 3 February). Women put noses to the grindstone, and miss opportunities. *Wall Street Journal*, p. B1.

Jackson, A. P., & Scharman, J. S. (2002). Constructing family-friendly careers: Mothers' experiences. *Journal of Counseling & Development, 80,* 188–196.

Jackson, M. A., Leon, C. A., & Zaharopoulos, M. (2010). Multiculturally competent career counseling interventions with adolescents vulnerable to discrimination. In J. Ponterotto, J. M. Casas, L. A. Suzuki, & C. M. Alexander (Eds.), *Handbook of multicultural counseling* (3rd ed., pp. 715–730). Thousand Oaks, CA: Sage.

Kaltreider, N. B. (Ed.). (1997). *Dilemmas of a double life: Women balancing careers and relationships.* Northvale, NJ: Jason Aronson.

Kaltreider, N. B., Gracie, C., & Sirulnick, C. (1997). Love in the trenches: Dual-career relationships. In N. B. Kaltreider (Ed.), *Dilemmas of a double life: Women balancing careers and relationships* (pp. 121–140). Northvale, NJ: Jason Aronson.

Klaft, R. P., & Kleiner, B. H. (1988). Understanding workaholics. *Business, 38,* 37–40.

Lambert, S., Hopkins, K., Easton, G., & Walker, J. (1992). *Added benefits: The link between family responsive policies and work performance at Fel-Pro, Inc.* Chicago, IL: University of Chicago Press.

Leavitt, R. R. (1971). Women in other cultures. In V. Gornick & B. K. Morgan (Eds.), *Woman in sexist society* (pp. 393–427). New York, NY: New American Library.

Lewis, S., & Lewis, J. (1996). *The work-family challenge.* Thousand Oaks, CA: Sage.

Lum, D. (2007). *Culturally competent practice* (3rd ed.). Belmont, CA: Brooks/Cole.

Luzzo, D. A., & McWhirter, E. H. (2001). Sex and ethnic differences in the perception of educational and career-related barriers and levels of coping efficacy. *Journal of Counseling & Development, 79,* 61–67.

Machlowitz, M. (1980). *Workaholics: Living with them, working with them.* Reading, MA: Addison-Wesley.

Matlin, M. (1996). *The psychology of women.* New York, NY: Holt, Rinehart & Winston.

Maume, D. J. (1999). Glass ceilings and glass escalators. *Work & Occupation, 26,* 483–510.

Meece, J. L., Parsons, J. E., Kaczala, C. M., Goff, S. B., & Futterman, R. (1982). Sex differences in math achievement: Toward a model of academic choice. *Psychological Bulletin, 91,* 324–348.

Michaels, B., & McCarty, E. (1993). Family ties and bottom lines. *Training & Development, 47,* 70–72.

Miller, M. J., & Brown, S. D. (2005). Counseling for career choice: Implications for improving interventions and working with diverse populations. In S. D. Brown & R. W. Lent (Eds.), *Career development and counseling: Putting theory and research to work* (pp. 441–465). Hoboken, NJ: Wiley.

Moen, P. (1992). *Women's two roles: A contemporary dilemma.* New York, NY: Auburn House.

Niles, S. G., & Harris-Bowlsbey, J. (2002). *Career development interventions in the 21st century.* Upper Saddle River, NJ: Prentice Hall.

Pearce, D. (1978). The feminization of poverty: Women, work, and welfare. *Urban and Social Change Review, 30,* 28–36.

Pedersen, P. B., Draguns, J. G., Lonner, W. J., & Trimble, J. E. (Eds.). (2002). *Counseling across cultures* (5th ed.). Thousand Oaks, CA: Sage.

Perusse, R., & Goodnough, R. (2004). *Leadership, advocacy, and direct service strategies for professional school counselors.* Belmont, CA: Brooks/Cole.

Pew Research Center. (2007). *Fewer mothers prefer full-time work.* Retrieved from http://www.pewresearch.org/pubs/536/working-women

Pieterse, A. L., & Miller, M. J. (2010). Current considerations in the assessment of adults: A review and extension of culturally inclusive models. In J. G. Ponterotto, J. M. Casas, L. A. Suzuki, & C. N. Alexander (Eds.), *Handbook of multicultural counseling* (3rd ed., pp. 649–666). Thousand Oaks, CA: Sage.

Ponton, L. E. (1997). Career and parenting: Women make it work. In N. B. Kaltreider (Ed.). Dilemmas of a double life: Women balancing careers and relationships (pp. 141–164). Northvale, NJ: Jason Aronson.

Rauch, S. (1996, January 9). Dads at home. *Tallahassee Democrat*, pp. 3D, 6D.

Reardon, R. C., Lenz, J. G., Sampson, J. P., & Peterson, G. W. (2000). *Career development and planning: A comprehensive approach.* Pacific Grove, CA: Brooks/Cole.

Reskin, B. F., & Hartmann, H. D. (Eds.). (1986). *Women's work, men's work: Sex segregation on the job.* Washington, DC: National Academies Press.

Robertson, J., & Fitzgerald, L. F. (1990). The (mis)treatment of men: Effects of client gender roles and life-style on diagnosis and attribution of pathology. *Journal of Counseling Psychology, 37,* 3–9.

Rochlen, A. B., & O'Brien, K. M. (2002). Men's reasons for and against seeking help for career-related concerns. *Journal of Men's Studies, 11,* 55–64.

Rowe, M. (1990). Barriers to equality: The power of subtle discrimination to maintain unequal opportunity. *Employees' Responsibilities and Rights Journal, 3,* 153–163.

Scharlach, A. E., Lowe, B. F., & Schneider, E. L. (1991). *Eldercare and the work force.* Lexington, MA: Lexington Books.

Seager, J., & Olson A. (1986). *Atlas: Women in the world.* New York, NY: Simon & Schuster.

Seybold, K. C., & Salomone, P. R. (1994). Understanding workaholism: A review of causes and counseling approaches. *Journal of Counseling & Development, 73,* 4–9.

Skovholt, T. M. (1990). Career themes in counseling and psychotherapy with men. In D. Moore & F. Leafgren (Eds.), *Men in conflict* (pp. 39–54). Alexandria, VA: American Association for Counseling and Development.

Slattery, J. M. (2004). *Counseling diverse clients: Bringing context into therapy.* Pacific Grove, CA: Brooks/Cole.

Smith, A. B., & Inder, P. M. (1993). Social interaction in same and cross gender preschool peer groups: A participant observation study. *Educational Psychology, 13,* 29–42.

Spielvogel, A. M. (1997). Women in leadership. In N. B. Kaltreider (Ed.), *Dilemmas of a double life: Women balancing careers and relationships* (pp. 189–208). Northvale, NJ: Jason Aronson.

Spruell, G. (1987). Work fever. *Training and Development Journal, 41,* 41–45.

Steil, J. M. (2001). Family forms and member well-being: A research agenda for the decade of behavior. *Psychology of Women Quarterly, 25,* 344–363.

Stewart, D. L., & Burge, P. I. (1989). *Assessment of employee satisfaction, stress, and childcare at Dominion Bankshares Corporation.* Blacksburg: Virginia Polytechnic Institute and State University Press.

Tennent, G. P., & Sperry, L. (2003). Work-family balance: Counseling strategies to optimize health. *Family Journal, 11,* 404–408.

U.S. Census Bureau. (2008). *Census 2008.* Washington, DC: U.S. Government Printing Office.

Vega, J. (1993, Spring). Crack in the glass ceiling? *Career Woman,* pp. 43–45.

Worell, J., & Remer, P. (2003). *Feminist perspectives in therapy: Empowering diverse women* (2nd ed.). Hoboken, NJ: Wiley.

Zunker, V. G. (1998). *Career counseling: Applied concepts of life planning* (5th ed.). Pacific Grove, CA: Brooks/Cole.

Zytowski, D. (1969). Toward a theory of career development of women. *Personnel and Guidance Journal, 47,* 660–664.

# CHAPTER 18

# Career Counseling and Lifestyle Planning for Clients With Addictive Behaviors

Chris Wood and Sibyl Camille Cato

## Contents

## Case Example

John is a 29-year-old Caucasian man who has come to see you for career counseling. He is currently employed full time as a tester for a computer company. Additionally, he works part time as a DJ for weddings and other social events on evenings and weekends. After high school, John started college at a local community college, taking primarily general courses in math, English, and computer technology to complete the requirements for an associate's or bachelor's degree. He quickly became disinterested in classes and left to work full time.

For the past several years, John has been steadily employed in several different dot-com and Web-based companies, moving from one company to the next when each company subsequently went out of business. In general, he has been satisfied with the standard of living his vocation has provided him, but he finds the nature of his work at his current company stifling. The part time job as a DJ has given him a more creative outlet and provided him with a needed social context outside of work.

John is currently very dissatisfied with the rut in which he has found himself and feels that he needs to make some changes in his life. Although he likes the financial rewards of his tester position, he cannot imagine himself staying in that vocation for the rest of his life. John finds his work an increasing drudgery and is concerned about the lack of long-term stability in the industry. Although he finds his work as a DJ much more interesting, his employment there is sporadic at best, and he believes the hectic party pace and atmosphere would wear on him if he were to try doing it full time.

John has also revealed to you that he currently copes with his job stress and dissatisfaction through recreational drug use. He has been an infrequent marijuana user for years and has recently started using cocaine regularly after being introduced to it through his work as a DJ. He says that marijuana helps him escape the intense pressure of his work as a tester and cocaine helps him become energized for his work as a DJ. Although he is aware of an increase in his drug usage in recent months, his primary anxiety concerns his current job situation.

### SIDEBAR 18.1   Personal Reflection

Have you ever been unhappy in a job? Why were you unhappy in that job? What maladaptive behaviors did you develop (or begin to develop) as a result of your dissatisfaction with the job?

In 2010, the Substance Abuse and Mental Health Services Administration (SAMHSA) published results from the 2009 National Survey on Drug Use and Health. The findings of the survey indicated that an estimated 21.8 million Americans age 12 or older, or 8.7% of this population, were current illicit drug users (SAMHSA, 2010). From 2002 to 2009, the rate of current nonmedical use of prescription type drugs increased from 5.5% to 6.3% in young adults ages 18 to 25 (SAMHSA, 2010). Also, heavy alcohol use was reported by 6.8% of those ages 12 and older, which is an estimated 17.1 million people (SAMHSA, 2010). "One dramatic and frightening estimate of the scope of substance use problems in the United States was offered by Wilens (2004a, b), who suggest that between 10% and 30% of adults have a substance use disorder" (Doweiko, 2008, p. 3). With this level of prevalence, the chances of career counseling a client with addictive behaviors seems highly likely. Counselors in agencies, college counseling centers, employee assistance programs, and even schools need to be prepared to help clients struggling with both their career development and addictive behaviors.

### SIDEBAR 18.2   Discussion Questions

What do you make of the incredible pervasiveness of addictions? Does it surprise you or confirm your expectations? Discuss these questions in pair share (discuss in groups of two) and then prepare to contribute to a large-group discussion.

Counseling individuals with career concerns and addictive behaviors is in one sense an issue of dual diagnosis. Although at one time the predominant thinking regarding dual diagnosis was to treat addictions separately from other client problems, current professional literature has encouraged addressing such issues together (Drake, Mueser, Clark, & Wallach, 1996; Ford, Russo, & Mallon, 2007; Greenbaum, Foster Johnson, & Petrila, 1996; N. S. Miller, 1994). Moreover, because an inherent relationship between a client's career concerns and his or her addictive behaviors is likely, it seems only logical that these respective issues be dealt with concurrently.

**SIDEBAR 18.3   Learning Extension**

Conduct a review of the research literature on workplace substance abuse. Answer the following questions: (a) How prevalent is workplace substance abuse? and (b) What workplace problems are associated with workplace substance abuse?

To counsel clients with addictive behaviors, one must first have an understanding of both (a) how addictions develop, and (b) how people change behaviors. The process of developing addictions and the process of changing addictive behaviors involve essentially the same stages of change. As changing careers and lifestyles also involve behavioral change, this process too follows the same stages of change.

## Stages of Change

Prochaska and DiClemente (1984) have developed a transtheoretical model of behavioral change. This model posits six segments in the process of intentional behavior change that can be described as the stages of change (DiClemente, 2003): precontemplation, contemplation, preparation, action, maintenance, and termination. Movement through these stages of change is generally recursive and cyclical (see Figure 18.1). Each stage has a unique character and an identifiable goal to be achieved. Similarly, the individual engaged in the process of change must successfully complete the necessary tasks of the subsequent stage to successfully progress in the change process. Counselors assisting individuals with the process of change can benefit from being aware of the six stages of change, the goals for each stage, and the necessary tasks for each stage.

### Precontemplation

As Figure 18.1 shows, precontemplation is the stage before entering the wheel of change. The precontemplation stage is characterized by a lack of consideration of change. Individuals in the precontemplation stage do not feel the need to change current patterns of behavior or see no convincing reasons to consider behavioral change. Clients in this stage do not believe that the negative aspects of the current behavior outweigh the costs of actively engaging in behavior change. "As long as the current pattern of behavior seems functional for the individual or no compelling reason arises to disrupt this pattern, an individual can remain in precontemplation for extended periods of time, even a lifetime" (DiClemente, 2003, p. 26).

The precontemplation stage has four categories of individuals: reluctant, rebellious, resigned, and rationalizing (DiClemente, 1991; DiClemente &

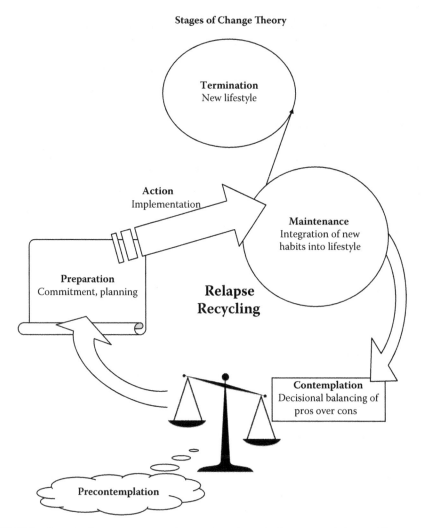

**Stages of Change Theory**

**FIGURE 18.1** A cyclical representation of movement through the stages of change. From *Addiction and Change: How Addictions Develop and Addicted People Recover* (p. 30), by C. C. DiClemente, 2003, New York: Guilford Press. Copyright 2003 by Guilford Press.

Velasquez, 2002). Individuals in the precontemplation stage regarding their addictive behaviors are sometimes labeled *resistant*. Understanding the four categories of precontemplators, however, can allow a counselor to use specific strategies to assist clients in changing problematic behavior.

Reluctant precontemplators are individuals who lack full awareness of their problematic addictive behavior and are therefore passively resistant. They do not want to risk change because they do not see any potential benefits to changing their current status quo.

Rebellious precontemplators, however, are actively resistant to change. They often have strong feelings against change and may have a heavy investment in their current addictive behavior. They do not like being told what to do and may even be hostile toward the proposal of a specific strategy for change.

The resigned precontemplator lacks the energy to invest in change and is prepared to accept that her or his current behavior is inevitable. The problem seems overwhelming, and the barriers to change are too great to warrant an investment of time or energy into the change process.

The fourth category of precontemplators is the rationalizing precontemplator. "These clients are not considering change because they have figured out the odds of personal risk, or they have plenty of reasons why the problem is not a problem or is a problem for others but not for them" (DiClemente, 1991, p. 193). Rationalizing contemplators sometimes like to debate their rationale for their current behavior, thus reinforcing their position against change.

The primary goal in the precontemplation stage is for the individual to begin to seriously consider the possibility of change. Because there has been little or no consideration of change of behavior in the foreseeable future, reaching this goal can be a formidable achievement. For the precontemplating client to envision change as a possibility requires successful completion of the major tasks in this stage.

The necessary tasks of the precontemplation stage include increasing client awareness of the need to change. Multiple internal and environmental influences have an impact on the individual's reasons for considering change: social pressure, human development, relationships, values, economic pressure, and so forth. Consideration of the current behavior within the context of these influences can compel an individual to explore the possibility of changing current patterns of behavior.

Increasing concern about the current pattern of behavior is another task for the precontemplation stage. Again, this task involves an awareness of potential reasons for change as well as those factors that may positively or negatively affect the client's ability to even begin to consider change.

Instilling hope is perhaps the most profound task for the precontemplation stage. Generally, it initially involves exploring the barriers to change and generating productive strategies for overcoming such obstacles. Clients in the precontemplation stage may lack hope as a result of previously unsuccessful change attempts in the current or alternate patterns of behavior. It is important for the client in this stage to realize that a setback in the change process is expected and inherently different than a complete failure.

## Contemplation

In the contemplation stage, the client is engaged in a cost versus benefit analysis. The client is weighing the risks associated with change against the potential benefits. This analysis becomes a period of instability for the client. Individuals may struggle with ambivalent or confusing thoughts and feelings about a given behavior pattern as they consider the possibility of change. "The contemplation stage involves a process of evaluating risks and benefits, the pros and cons of both the current behavior pattern and the potential new behavior pattern" (DiClemente, 2003, p. 28).

Contemplators are not yet ready to actively commit to the process of change. They are still gathering information and considering options.

"Contemplation is the stage when clients are quite open to information and decisional balance considerations. Yet it is also the stage where many clients are waiting for the one final piece of information that will compel them to change" (DiClemente, 1991, p. 195). In a sense, contemplators are still testing the waters to decide whether they are ready to wade into the sea of change.

The goal for this stage, then, is a thoroughly reasoned evaluation that reinforces a client's decision to change. This evaluation should consist of the carefully considered risks and benefits of change.

The task for the contemplation stage is to conduct a thorough analysis of the advantages and disadvantages of the current behavior. This analysis needs to include both the affective and the cognitive rewards of the current behavior and the stake involved in change. At the same time, the client needs to fully realize the costs of continuing the current behavior and the potential return on investment of an endeavor to change.

## Preparation

Clients in the preparation stage are ready to make a change in the near future. "Preparation takes you from the decisions you make in the contemplation stage to the specific steps you take to solve the problem during the action stage" (Prochaska, Norcross, & DiClemente, 1994, p. 146). The decisional balance in the contemplation stage has been tipped in favor of change, and it is time to get ready. In the preparation stage, clients must solidify a commitment to change and operationalize their energy by developing a plan of action.

The primary goal for the preparation stage is to formalize a plan of action. The plan of action needs to be a specific, detailed list of the steps necessary to engage in active change. The plan of action must include those crucial elements necessary to mobilize client energy through initiating action.

Inherent in a plan of action are several critical elements. Clients must believe in the feasibility of the plan. They need to see the plan as possessing a strong likelihood for bringing about the desired outcome (the new behavior). Moreover, clients need to believe in their own ability to successfully engage in the steps necessary to complete their plan of action. The tasks of the preparation stage involve reinforcing the client's commitment to change and determining the best plan of action.

Reinforcing the commitment to change is an important task in the preparation stage. In this stage, the client will still be resolving feelings of ambiguity about change. He or she is still engaged in the decision-making process of considering his or her current behavior and other alternatives. A commitment to change is crucial to mobilizing energy and formulating a plan for action.

Several important considerations are part of the task of developing a plan of action. The previous experiences with change should be considered to strategize a plan that has optimal potential for success. Similarly, considering the potential difficulties in a plan is also useful in preparing for action. Finally, as mentioned previously, the client's courage and competency to be successful in a plan are key components of the client's potential to implement any plan of action.

## Action

The action stage is the implementation of the plan of action. In this stage, most people make the move toward altering their behavior. This stage of change requires the greatest commitment of time and energy. For these reasons, this stage is also characterized by an attraction to the old patterns of behavior. It is often easier to return to the previous behavior than to follow through on the plan and begin to sustain a new behavior.

The goal for this stage is to establish a new pattern of behavior. In addition to the major task of implementing the plan of action, additional tasks include sustaining commitment in the face of obstacles to the plan and revising the plan as necessary to maintain the enterprise of change.

## Maintenance

As Figure 18.1 illustrates, maintenance is the final stage before exiting the wheel of change. In this stage, "the new behavior must become integrated into the lifestyle of the individual" (DiClemente, 2003, p. 29).

The maintenance stage is distinguished by the clear absence of the previous behavior and the sustained presence of the new behavior. Still present, however, may be the urges and temptation to return to the previous behavior. "In the maintenance stage the person works to consolidate the gains made during the action stage and struggles to prevent relapse" (DiClemente & Velasquez, 2002, p. 212).

### SIDEBAR 18.4   Experiential Assignment

Interview a significant other about his or her current job. Ask the person what she or he likes and dislikes about the job. What stage of change (in respect to the person's job) do you see him or her in? Why is the person in this particular stage? Encourage the person to describe how the job influences their avocation (hobbies, time for leisure, relationships outside work, etc.). What statements of change do you hear?

It is important to note that relapse is not a collapse of the change process. People often re-cycle through one or more stages in the wheel of change before successfully negotiating the maintenance stage and exiting the wheel of change into termination.

Success in the maintenance stage allows the new behavior to become automatic and the new status quo (DiClemente, 2003). Ultimately, then, the client is able to exit the wheel of change (termination) with the new behavior as an integral part of a new lifestyle.

## Termination

Termination is characterized by the final exit from the cycle of change. It is not a stage as such but rather a new state of being in which a new behavior has replaced the old behavior and it would, in fact, take a substantial amount of effort to go back to the old behavior. In reference to addictive behaviors, this state is sometimes referred to as recovery. The goals and tasks of termination focus on the new way of being that does not include the previous behavior. "The entire gestalt of life now supports a new lifestyle committed to not engaging in the addictive behavior" (DiClemente, 2003, p. 201).

In the preceding discussion of the stages of change, we primarily addressed the change process for addictive behaviors. As may already be apparent, however, the stages are indicative of any behavioral change. This process also applies to those behaviors that make up career change.

### SIDEBAR 18.5   Reflection

What are your own personal views about addictive behaviors? Which addictive behaviors would be most difficult for you to address in a career counseling setting? Why?

## Case Example and the Stages of Change

The case example introduced at the beginning of the chapter demonstrates how career and lifestyle planning clients with addictive behaviors can be conceptualized using the transtheoretical model stages of change. John is discerning two simultaneous and interrelated processes of change. In one respect, he is exploring a career change, and interconnected issues of drug use are also worthy of consideration in career and lifestyle planning.

In the case example, both John's career concerns and the addictive behaviors can each be conceptualized within the transtheoretical stages of change framework. This conceptualization can help a counselor understand John's situation and develop a strategy to help him. Which stage or stages of change is John negotiating?

John has come to see the counselor voluntarily. He was not mandated to see a counselor for a drug or alcohol problem, nor has he sought career assistance as part of a severance package from a job loss. He is seeking career counseling and seems open to exploring different options. He is clearly not in the precontemplation stage regarding his career concerns.

Although he has in one sense taken some action by seeking career counseling, he has no substantial plan beyond that initial step. Moreover, he has no definite commitment to change beyond just the initial counseling session. Perhaps the following exchange between John and his counselor will help illuminate the stage of change regarding his career behavior.

> *Counselor:* You wish you had greater opportunity for creativity at work and you're wondering if it is time for a career change.
>
> *John:* Yes, but I make pretty good money, especially for someone my age. I do much better financially than most of my friends. I'd be stupid to give up a sweet deal like this.
>
> *Counselor:* You like the financial rewards your job offers and you're thinking it might be a mistake to leave your present position.
>
> *John:* Yeah, but I don't know how long this company's even going to last; I mean, I've already been at two different places that went under, and each time it was really tough finding a new position.

Note that although the counselor is accurately paraphrasing the different messages from the client, each time John takes an opposing perspective. This exchange is indicative of the ambiguity present in the contemplation stage. John sees certain advantages to his present position and specific risks to change. At the same time, he is cognizant of the drawbacks of remaining in his current situation and considering the potential benefits of devoting energy to change. Clearly, John is in the contemplation stage regarding his career behavior.

What about John's drug behavior? This statement may make John's stage of change clearer:

> *John:* When we have a product launch deadline, everyone gets really stressed. We put in 10- to 12-hour days. Sometimes I smoke some pot after I get home so that I can unwind before going to bed. And then sometimes I just don't have the energy to get geared up for work. I might do a line of coke as a pick-me-up. I don't drink coffee, so for me it's just a quick albeit expensive pick-me-up.

John does not appear to be overly concerned about his drug use. He states that his use of marijuana and cocaine currently serves a useful purpose in his life. For the most part, John does not seem to be interested in changing his behavior in this area of his life.

These characteristics suggest that John is in the precontemplation stage. Although John does mention the expensive nature of his behavior, he has convinced himself of its necessity. For these reasons, John would most aptly be categorized as a rationalizing precontemplator.

Understanding the stage of change for John's career concern and his drug behaviors allows a counselor to select a strategy and specific techniques. The general principles of motivational interviewing (MI; W. R. Miller & Rollnick, 1991, 2002) provide a guiding character as well as specific strategies for counselors to use in helping clients with addictive behaviors in the different stages of change. Following these principles and the specific strategies for the stages of change can assist counselors in helping clients with both their addictive behaviors and their career development.

### SIDEBAR 18.6   Personal Application

Reflect on a change (a habit, behavior, job, lifestyle, etc.) you made at some point in your life. What factor or factors contributed to your change? Relate your process of change to the guiding principles of MI. What or who helped you to negotiate the change?

## Motivational Interviewing

MI is a counseling approach developed by W. R. Miller and Rollnick (1991, 2002) to assist individuals with the process of change. Although originally conceptualized as an approach to working with clients with addictive behaviors, it has been used successfully with a range of behavioral changes, including physical exercise (Harland et al., 1999), weight reduction (Smith, Heckemeyer, Kratt, & Mason, 1997; West, DiLillo, Bursac, Gore, & Green, 2007), bulimia and other eating disorders (Treasure et al., 1999; Wilson & Schlam, 2007), marijuana use (Stephens, Roffman, & Curtin, 2000), and alcoholism (Project MATCH Research Group, 1997, 1998; Vasilaki,

Hosier, & Cox, 2006). Burke, Arkowitz, and Menchola (2003) conducted a meta-analysis of 30 controlled clinical research trials that investigated MI or adaptations of motivational interviewing (AMI). They determined that the research supported the efficacy of AMI for problems involving alcohol and drugs, as well as diet and exercise. Additionally, Rubak, Sandbæk, Lauritzen, and Christensen (2005) conducted a systematic review and meta-analysis of 72 randomized controlled trials and found that "motivational interviewing in a scientific setting effectively helps clients change their behavior and that it outperforms traditional advice giving in approximately 80% of the studies" (Rubak et al., 2005, p. 309). No studies, according to their research, reported MI to be harmful or have any adverse effects (Rubak et al., 2005).

### SIDEBAR 18.7  Small/Large Group Discussion

MI is not often thought of in relationship to career change. We suggest MI as an approach to help clients negotiate change in vocation and addictive behaviors. The case study exemplifies the connectedness of the two. How are addictive behaviors and vocations different? How are they similar? Discuss these questions in pair share, and then prepare to contribute to a large-group discussion.

MI posits four guiding principles to underscore the counselor's orientation toward the client. These four principles emphasize the character of the MI approach and the subsequent strategies for each stage of behavioral change. The principles are (1) express empathy, (2) develop discrepancy, (3) roll with resistance, and (4) support self-efficacy.

## Express Empathy

The first principle is to consistently express empathy immediately and throughout the change process. The emphasis should be on understanding the client's perspective free of blame or judgment. Although a counselor may not agree with the client's behavior or approve of the client's choices, it is still possible to maintain a climate of acceptance.

A climate of acceptance facilitates change. Conversely, judgment and blame tend to immobilize the change process. One way to conceptualize this process is viewing a climate of acceptance as freeing people to change rather than forcing them to devote energy to resisting judgment.

Related to the notion of acceptance is the understanding that ambivalence is normal and even a healthy part of the change process. "Ambivalence is accepted as a normal part of human experience and change, rather than seen as pathology or pernicious defensiveness" (W. R. Miller & Rollnick, 2002, p. 37). Counselors often have a tendency to see ambivalent feelings and thoughts as unhealthy manifestations of an unwillingness to engage in positive change—denial or resistance. An important element of the principles of MI, however, is to view ambivalence as a normal part of the change process, to be honored with empathy as are all client experiences and perspectives. Understanding and accepting a client's ambivalence about change, then, becomes an essential component of being an empathic counselor.

The principle of expressing empathy is demonstrated through the use of counseling skills. Counseling skills are used to develop an awareness and understanding of client experiences. Through skillful reflective listening, the counselor is able to step into the client's phenomenal space and thus empathically share his or her perspective. Moreover, counseling skills are also used to express the empathic understanding of the client's perspective through paraphrasing of messages and feelings.

Consider the opportunities for expressing empathy with John, the client described in the case example. Recall that John's last statement expressed ambivalence over his current job:

*John:* Yeah, but I don't know how long this company's even going to last; I mean I've already been at two different places that went under, and each time it was really tough finding a new position.

*Counselor:* You feel exhausted by the thought of having to search for a new vocation and at the same time you are frightened that your current position may be eliminated.

Although other empathic statements are certainly possible, the counselor's response provides an example of skillful reflective listening that expresses understanding of the client's perspective.

The same empathy could be expressed to John relating to his other behaviors.

*John:* And then sometimes I just don't have the energy to get geared up for work. I might do a line of coke as a pick-me-up. I don't drink coffee, so for me it's just a quick albeit expensive pick-me-up.

*Counselor:* Your job is extremely stressful and leaves you physically and mentally drained. Sometimes you use cocaine to rejuvenate. Although a part of you feels this is a quick energizer, another part of you is concerned about the expense involved with the use of cocaine.

Again, although there may be alternate ways of reflecting the client's thoughts and feelings, this counselor statement demonstrates a specific counselor response expressing empathy for the client.

### SIDEBAR 18.8 Discussion: Cultural Competency

If the client, John, was a member of a racial–ethnic minority group or a sexual minority group, what additional empathic awareness might be required for a culturally competent counselor? Discuss these questions in pair share, and then prepare to contribute to a large-group discussion.

## Develop Discrepancy

The second principle that underlies MI is to develop discrepancy between a client's present behavior and his or her goals and values. It is important to note that the counselor is to develop or amplify this discrepancy as initiated by the client and within the context of the client's perspective—not to artificially create the discrepancy by imposing the counselor's perspective or value system. In one sense, the counselor is helping the client to identify and clarify the client's personal goals and values. Concurrently, the counselor is helping to bring to the client's awareness the conflict between the client's current behavior and client's preferred state of being.

This discrepancy is of course the motivation for change. For change to occur, clients must be aware of the discrepancy between their current behavior and their desired self. Moreover, the awareness of this discrepancy and the client's belief in his or her ability to successfully bring about change is what fuels the client's energy to actively continue the process of change.

In using the principle of developing discrepancy, the counselor places the responsibility for change on the client. "When motivational interviewing is done well, it is not the counselor but the client who gives voice to concerns, reasons for change, self efficacy, and intentions to change" (W. R. Miller & Rollnick, 2002, p. 39).

In the case example, the counselor's last paraphrase to the client is an example of beginning to develop discrepancy.

> *Counselor:* Although a part of you feels this is a quick energizer, another part of you is concerned about the expense involved with the use of cocaine.

Here, the counselor is using a paraphrase of message from the client and structuring the paraphrase so as to highlight the client's concerns about his present behavior. It is important to note the nonconfrontational style of the counselor's response.

The interrelationship of career and lifestyle planning and addictive behaviors presents a unique opportunity to develop discrepancy within a client. Consider the following exchange between counselor and client:

> *John:* I don't want to feel so exhausted all the time. I want to have the kind of job that is both fun and creative. My job is so stressful that I really need to go out and cut loose once in awhile. Sometimes after I DJ at a wedding, I'll still be pumped up and need to go out with coworkers to clubs or a party. When I have to work at my regular job the next day, though, I'm usually exhausted and pretty hung over. It's tough to just get through the workday. I can't imagine trying to find the time to look for a new job, take classes, or go out and interview for a job or anything like that. Still, I can't see myself staying a tester for the rest of my life either.
>
> *Counselor:* You'd like to see yourself making a move toward finding a career that is more enjoyable than your present job. Right now, the cycle of two jobs and partying with coworkers keeps you exhausted most of the time.
>
> *John:* Exactly! I feel like all my energy is being sucked away, and although I can get it back for a while when I go out, the next day it's gone again.
>
> *Counselor:* You would like to get out of this pattern of being drained at work and feeling exhausted and hung over so that you can begin to start on changes you want to make in your lifestyle. However, something keeps you stuck in this present pattern.

The counselor is developing discrepancy between the client's current addictive behavior and the client's goal for changing careers. Similarly, the counselor is developing discrepancy between the client's current vocational behavior and his wish to explore vocational options. In the broader sense, each of these changes involve altering the client's lifestyle. Developing discrepancy when career counseling clients with addictive behaviors, then, means developing discrepancy between their current behaviors (that keep them trapped in an undesirable lifestyle) and their goals for developing the lifestyle they would like to have.

It is important to remember that the reasons for change ultimately come from the client, not the counselor. The counselor is helping the client see the discrepancies between the client's present behavior and the client's goals or values. "When motivational interviewing is done well, it is not the counselor but the client who gives voice to concerns, reasons for change, self efficacy, and intentions to change" (W. R. Miller & Rollnick, 2002, p. 39).

## Roll With Resistance

The third foundational principle of MI is to roll with resistance. Counselors sometimes conceptualize resistance as an attribute of the client—an unwillingness to engage in positive growth. In MI, however, resistance is more appropriately conceptualized as a function of the counselor–client dynamic. In one sense, resistance is created by confrontational encounter with another person or an interaction that engenders defensiveness on the part of the client.

One way to deal with resistance or defensiveness is to try to overpower it with convincing arguments. This approach may just cause the client to become increasingly entrenched in his or her present position. Another approach, however, is to avoid arguing or trying to convince the client of the need to change; rather, to roll with resistance and allow the client to be the primary impetus for change.

Rolling with resistance calls for a counselor to take several stances with a client. One, the counselor should not argue for specified change or try to convince the client of the need to change. Similarly, the counselor should not directly oppose resistance or defensiveness when presented by the client. Rather, the counselor should interpret the presence of resistance as a directive to change approaches. The counselor must consistently maintain the attitude that the client is the primary resource for generating solutions to the current situation. It is not the counselor's responsibility to find all the answers, and attempting to do so may cause a client to find fault in each suggestion proposed. Ultimately, it is the client who will be living with the new lifestyle, so it only makes sense that changes be built on the strategies determined by the client.

> *Counselor:* Although a part of you feels this is a quick energizer, another part of you is concerned about the expense involved with the use of cocaine. (Develop discrepancy)
>
> *John:* I don't think I'm an addict or anything. I mean, I've never hurt anybody else or myself, and I've never had any legal trouble or anything like that.
>
> *Counselor:* I'm not here to label you as addict, diagnose any problem, or convince you to do anything you don't want to do. I'm just here to help you

take a look at your current situation and how you'd like things to be. One thing you feel proud about is that your cocaine use has never hurt anyone. (Express empathy) Tell me more about the things you feel good about in your current lifestyle. (Roll with resistance)

## Support Self-Efficacy

Perhaps the most important guiding principle undergirding the MI approach is the conviction to support self-efficacy. "Perceived self efficacy refers to beliefs in one's capabilities to organize and execute the courses of action required to produce given attainments" (Bandura, 1997, p. 3). Obviously, the belief in one's ability to successfully bring about change is a key motivator. Individuals who do not believe they are able to go through the process of change and successfully achieve a new lifestyle are less likely to even attempt change. Thus, a counselor must consistently support the self-efficacy of clients throughout the change process.

The following dialogue highlights supporting self-efficacy in the process of career change.

> *John:* I don't know, I've never really been good at job interviews.
> *Counselor:* You mentioned before that you see communication as one of your strengths.
> *John:* That's true, I'm as good or better than anyone at any of the places I've worked.
> *Counselor:* And you've certainly been very articulate in describing your strengths to me.
> *John:* Yeah, that's true too. I'm just so used to having my pot as a way to deal with stress and a little coke to get energized that it scares me to go into a job interview straight.
> *Counselor:* It really frightens you to think about having to deal with stressful situations without marijuana or cocaine. (Express empathy)
> *John:* When I flew home for Christmas to visit my folks, I was too scared to take pot or coke with me through security. It was tough for awhile, but I did okay without it. I even started jogging again, and sleeping better.
> *Counselor:* Although it was tough, you were able to go an entire week without using drugs. The Christmas holidays can be a very stressful time, and you were able to deal with them drug free.
> *John:* Yeah, that's true, my parents were just about enough to drive me over the brink, but I made it through the visit.
> *Counselor:* And even started yourself on an exercise regimen.
> *John:* Yeah, now that I think about it, I'm pretty proud at not letting everything get to me.

### SIDEBAR 18.9   Discussion: Intersection of Identity

If the client, John, was a member of a marginalized population (such as a racial or ethnic minority group, a sexual orientation minority group, a fleeing political refugee, a transgender person, or the intersection of any of these identities), how might this influence the person's self-efficacy?

Following the previously described guiding principles of MI, additional strategies can assist a client with change. Facilitating change talk, responding appropriately to resistance, and strengthening the commitment to change are MI strategies that use specific counseling techniques to assist clients.

## Change Talk

Change talk is dialogue between counselor and client that is oriented toward the advantages of behavioral change. This dialogue tends to fall into four categories: (1) disadvantages of the status quo, (2) advantages of change, (3) optimism about change, and (4) intention to change (W. R. Miller & Rollnick, 2002).

To facilitate change talk, a counselor will want to ask specific, open-ended questions in the order of the four categories given.

Consider how these open-ended questions can be used with the case example.

### Disadvantages of Status Quo

*Counselor:* What worries you about your current situation—both your career and your drug use?

*John:* I don't see myself lasting long term in either of my jobs. The DJ job is fun and it gave me some friends, but I wouldn't want to do it full time and it's too expensive to party all the time. My tester job pays well but I don't think it will be stable in the long run and it's not really me. The drug use is really just an offshoot of two jobs—if I had a job that I really loved, I wouldn't need to party so much for relief.

*Counselor:* You like the friends you have made through your DJ job and the money you make as a tester. You don't want to be a DJ full time and the tester job doesn't suit you. You'd like to find a career you enjoy more. You'd like to have a lifestyle where you don't party to deal with stress.

*John:* Yeah.

The counselor used an open-ended question to elicit the client's perspective on the disadvantages of the status quo. Then the counselor carefully paraphrased the disadvantages expressed by the client.

*Counselor:* Why do you think you need to do something about your job situation and your drug use?

*John:* I guess I think working two jobs and my partying are really starting to wear me out.

*Counselor:* In what ways does this concern you?

*John:* Well, I'm really tired a lot of the time. And . . . the partying is really getting expensive. I can afford it because I make pretty good money, but I could be putting that money away to help with a job change.

*Counselor:* What do you think will happen if you don't change anything?

*John:* I'm either going to be let go at my tester job and have no savings to fall back on or I'll just quit some day down the line because I can't take it anymore!

The preceding discussion between client and counselor illustrates how open-ended questions can be used to evoke a discussion of the disadvantages of the status quo. The dialogue presented here is an accelerated example of a discussion that likely needs to be conducted in much greater depth with the client. It is important to note that in this example, as with discussions in general, the disadvantages of the status quo are described by the client, not argued by the counselor.

**SIDEBAR 18.10  Personal Reflection**

Think about a time when you stuck it out in a job longer than you would have liked. Why did you stay as long as you did? Did you develop any bad habits—interpersonally or intrapersonally—as a result of your unhappiness in the job situation?

### Advantages of Change

*Counselor:* How would you like things to be different?

*John:* I wish I had a better job. I wish I wasn't so tired all the time.

*Counselor:* Describe how your job could be better.

*John:* Well, I'd like a job where I can brainstorm a little … be creative. Whenever I have an idea about something now it doesn't really matter because that's not my role. I have to put all my time and energy into just making sure things work as they're supposed to—and it doesn't really matter if I have ideas on how to improve features of the products. And I'd like to have more positive contact with customers. Instead of just troubleshooting things for problems, I'd like to talk with people about the possibilities of products.

*Counselor:* Describe how you'd like to be less tired all the time.

*John:* Well, if my work were more stimulating, I'd be more energized. I wouldn't spend most of my day thinking about how I can't wait to get out and party or how I just wish I were at home trying to forget about work.… And if I weren't so tired at work all the time, then the day wouldn't drag so much—then maybe I'd have some energy to change careers.

*Counselor:* What would be the advantages of making a lifestyle change?

*John:* I think I'd be happier if I weren't in this cycle of too much stressful work and then too much wild partying. I'd bet I could get through tough days at work much easier, even if I just knew there were some change in sight.

## Optimism About Change

*Counselor:* What makes you think that if you decide to make a change you could do it?

*John:* Well, I'm that not sure I can, really. But I've lost my job twice before and been able to find a new one in the same area pretty quickly. It's just that switching to a different area could be pretty tough, I don't know.… And with the partying, well I've cut back on that off and on at different times. I think it would be even easier to cut back on that stuff if my job situation were better.

*Counselor:* How confident are you—say on a scale from 0 to 10 where 0 is
not at all confident and 10 is extremely confident—regarding this
lifestyle change?

*John:* Probably a 5 for changing my partying and a 4 for changing my career …
maybe a 4.5 overall.

*Counselor:* Why a 4.5 and not a 0?

*John:* Well, I know I need to do something. I've changed jobs before and I
have cut back on partying before. I think working on each will
help the other.

*Counselor:* You think working toward a career change will help you cut back
on your partying and you believe that cutting back on your drug
use will help your efforts toward changing careers.

Here the counselor has used an open-ended question to explore the client's optimism toward change. To further this understanding, the counselor
asks the client to rate his confidence on a 1-to-10 scale, which is another
MI technique (sometimes called a "ruler") designed to assess the client's
confidence and to further elicit change talk. It is interesting to note that
in the case example, the ruler technique elicited the client's first expression
of a perceived connection between addictive behaviors and career concerns.
Also, notice that the counselor asked why the client's assessment was not
lower (and not the opposite). This question encourages the client to express
strengths toward change. Asking the client, "Why is it 4.5 and not 10?"
would force the client to argue against change. The ruler technique can be
used further as shown in the next section.

### Intention to Change

*Counselor:* What would it take for you to go from 4.5 to a 5 or a 6?

*John:* If I had some sort of plan, I mean, if I knew what sort of steps I was
going to take … and if, if I'd started the steps … then I'd feel more
like an 8 or a 9, maybe even a 10 if I'd already started initiating
the plan.

*Counselor:* What do you think you might do?

*John:* Well, I could look through the want ads for a different job, but I've done
that before and nothing there interested me much … and I could
try to quit smoking dope, drinking, and coke total cold turkey, but
then I wouldn't know what to do when I go out with friends.… I
guess I can't really think of any other ways.

Here the counselor builds on the ruler technique by asking the client to
describe how he might further progress toward change. Moreover, the counselor is tapping into the client's current change strategies and the client's estimated probability of success for those strategies. In this respect, the counselor
has determined what the client believes is necessary to move toward change
and has ascertained that the client lacks constructive strategies for effecting
a change in lifestyle.

The case example illustrates some strategies for eliciting change talk.
Equally as important is how the counselor responds to change talk.

W. R. Miller and Rollnick (2002) encouraged the use of specific counseling skills as a means of furthering change talk and enhancing intrinsic motivation. These skills include (a) elaborating change talk, (b) summarizing change talk, (c) affirming change talk, (d) clarifying ambivalence, and (e) clarifying values.

Elaborating change talk is accomplished when a counselor encourages a client to expound on statements of change. The counselor helps the client explore change talk by using furthering responses such as "Tell me more about … [client's change statement]," "What are some other reasons you might want to make a change?" or "Give me an example of …" (W. R. Miller & Rollnick, p. 87). The intent of these directive counseling responses is to help the client to explore his or her intentions toward change.

Equally as important in responding to client statements of change is reflecting change talk. This counseling skill can help clients clarify ambivalence about change and continue exploration of client intentions toward change. Recall the previous counselor responses in the case example:

> *Counselor:* You'd like to see yourself making a move toward finding a career that is more enjoyable than your present job. Right now, the cycle of two jobs and partying with coworkers keeps you exhausted most of the time.

The counselor's response reflects client change talk around both the career and the addictive behaviors. It is important for counselors to be aware that reflecting client statements of change can sometimes engender psychological reactions in a client and elicit client statements against change.

> *Counselor:* You'd like to end your pattern of partying and being exhausted or hungover at work.
> *John:* Well, going out with friends gives me relief from the stresses of work.

In such cases, it is necessary to use what W. R. Miller and Rollnick (2002) referred to as double-sided reflection. Double-sided reflection can help a counselor avoid being caught in the position of arguing for change while the client argues against it.

> *Counselor:* You like the stress relief you feel going out with friends and you hate feeling physically bad the next day after having been out partying with drugs and alcohol.

Summarizing change talk is also another way for counselors to assist clients in exploring their feelings and thoughts about change. "In general, summaries are collections of change statements the person has made: disadvantages of the status quo, reasons for change, optimism about change, and desire to change" (Miller & Rollnick, 2002, p. 90). As with double-sided reflection when reflecting change talk, including both sides of ambivalence can be effective in facilitating client movement toward change.

Affirming change talk is also an important counselor response to clients' self-motivational change statements. Selective counselor responses such as

"That sounds like a good idea" and "That's a good point" (W. R. Miller & Rollnick, 2002, p. 91) can serve to reinforce a client's commitment to change and facilitate client movement through the stages of change.

Clarifying ambivalence involves helping a client to examine each side of the conflict surrounding change, which might mean the counselor and client evaluate separately the pros and cons for each of the change alternatives as well as the status quo. It is important that the counselor and client complete this process for each alternative separately as well as the current behavior or status quo.

Clarifying values is equally as important and intrinsically related to clarifying ambivalence. Clients must be aware of their personal values to evaluate the advantages and disadvantages of change. Helping to discern what is truly important can help a client resolve ambivalence around change. Consider the following discussion:

> *Counselor:* Let's talk about some of the options you have been considering regarding changing your lifestyle. We can evaluate the advantages and drawbacks of each. Let's start with your current lifestyle.
>
> *John:* Okay, I make good money. I can afford to go out when I want.
>
> *Counselor:* You like the salary of your current job and having money for social activities. What else?
>
> *John:* I get along well with my boss. She trusts me to work independently, I mean, I don't have to report in on how I'm going to do everything.
>
> *Counselor:* You like to work independently, and autonomy is important to you.
>
> *John:* Yes, exactly, I don't like it when someone is overseeing you all the time. I just wish I had more room to be creative in my work.
>
> *Counselor:* So the ability to express creativity is important to you too. What else do you like about your present lifestyle?
>
> *John:* Well, in my other job I like interacting with people—the people who hire me as a DJ. And I like going out with coworkers after work; my second job has helped me make friends.
>
> *Counselor:* An advantage of your job as a DJ is that it allows you to interact more with people—which you enjoy. Okay, what else?
>
> *John:* That's all that I can think of. I think that if I had more opportunity for creativity and more autonomy I'd be much happier. My sister is a teacher, and she is in total control of her classroom on a daily basis with a lot of ways to be creative. I have no desire to be a teacher, but I think if I had that kind of situation the money and the social extras would matter a lot less to me.
>
> *Counselor:* So creativity and autonomy are more important to you than financial rewards.
>
> *John:* I believe so, yes.
>
> *Counselor:* What are some of the disadvantages of your current lifestyle?
>
> *John:* Well I'm exhausted all the time. I'm either so wound up I can't relax or so drained I can barely function, but either way I feel totally empty on steady energy.
>
> *Counselor:* What about your current lifestyle exhausts you?
>
> *John:* Well, the stress when we have a deadline, say a product launch. Then there's a lot of pressure on everyone. And when I work pretty hard,

then I tend to party pretty hard, too. I'd like to have time and
energy to do some of the things I used to do like hobbies. (Laughs)
Some more clean-living type things like golf and taking my sister's
kids out for pizza.

*Counselor:* So feeling physically good is important to you. You also value family and having time to pursue personal interests.

*John:* Yes, I do value family; in fact, I'd like to get married and have kids of my
own someday. I just can't seem to meet anyone really nice. Most
of the women I meet are at bars. That's one of the reasons I was
thinking about going back to college; I mean, it could be a way to
meet new people.

*Counselor:* Okay, so one of the changes you're considering is going back to
school, let's talk about some of the advantages and disadvantages
of that.

In the preceding discussion, the client and counselor are exploring some
of the pros and cons of the client's current lifestyle. Moreover, they are discerning the client's values and how those values relate to the client's current
lifestyle and potential changes.

### SIDEBAR 18.11   Discussion: Cultural Values

The case study client presented in this chapter does not belong to a visible racial or ethnic minority group.
What additional considerations would a multiculturally competent counselor take into account if the client,
John, were a member of any of these groups? What cultural values might need to be explored as a part of
the change process? Discuss these questions in pair share, and then prepare to contribute to a large-group
discussion.

Clearly, values play a central role in career development and lifestyle planning. Similarly, values are imperative to the change process for clients with
addictive behaviors. As with other facets of career counseling, it is important
that counselors explore with their clients the relevancy of their personal values to their career and lifestyle choices.

## Dealing With Resistance

Some counselors find that the most challenging aspect of counseling clients with addictive behaviors is encountering resistance. As mentioned
previously, the MI approach takes a somewhat nontraditional view of
resistance in the counseling relationship. Rather than interpreting resistance as a client trait that needs to be defeated, MI views resistance as
a function of the counseling relationship. More specifically, resistance is,
in a sense, psychologically engendered reactions from the counselor and a
signal to defer the current tactic in favor of another approach. Although
this view of resistance is in and of itself a strategy for working with resistance in the process of change, a counselor might use additional strategies
when encountering resistance. Simple reflection, double-sided reflection,
reframing, and agreeing with a twist are four techniques posited by MI
to diminish resistance and foster progress through the stages of change
(W. R. Miller & Rollnick, 2002).

### Simple Reflection

One response to resistance is a reflective listening statement (W. R. Miller & Rollnick, 2002). By acknowledging the client's disagreement, disbelief, doubts about change, or differing perception, a counselor can avoid fostering increased defensiveness.

For example, regarding addictive behaviors, consider this exchange:

*John:* Who are you to be pointing out how I'm doing drugs? You've probably never had to put up with the kind of stress I'm dealing with. You've probably never even tried pot.

*Counselor:* It's hard for you to imagine that I could possibly understand what you're dealing with.

Or this exchange:

*Counselor:* You're very angry at me for asking about your drug use.

Regarding career behaviors, consider this exchange:

*John:* I don't know—if I went back to community college or technical college, I'd probably just blow it.

*Counselor:* You don't see yourself being successful in community college or technical college.

Or

*Counselor:* You feel frightened, then disheartened when you think of not being successful in school.

**SIDEBAR 18.12   Learning Extension**

Explore the emerging position of career coach. What does this position offer clients? Does a career coach use any of the guiding principles or techniques from MI?

The principles of MI continue to apply when dealing with resistance and giving simple reflection. It is imperative that the counselor continue to express empathy and also support self-efficacy in subsequent work with the client. Similarly, a counselor may see an opportunity to deal with resistance and continue to develop discrepancy through double-sided reflection.

### Double-Sided Reflection

Sometimes resistance may manifest itself in the counseling relationship through a client's continued exploration of only one side of the change argument. In response to this type of resistance, it is helpful to use the previously discussed technique of double-sided reflection. Double-sided reflection is a technique that can assist counselor and client in exploring both sides of ambivalence (W. R. Miller & Rollnick, 2002).

*John:* Yes, I use a lot more than I used to, but it's not like I'm getting stoned or jacked up on coke all the time; I mean, I've only used it a few times at work and no one really sees me as an addict.

*Counselor:* Part of you is concerned about your increased drug use, and in another part it's also important to you that people don't view you as an addict.

When career counseling clients with addictive behaviors, double-sided reflection might also incorporate the facets of ambivalence that relate to career and lifestyle planning.

> *John:* I know it makes sense to cut back on my partying and the drugs if I'm going to start saving money and look at going back to school, but I don't think you realize how much stress I'm under at work; it's like a vise squeezing all the life out of me!
>
> *Counselor:* You'd really like to decrease your drug use, and you are afraid of how you'll cope without drugs to help you deal with stress.

As with other strategies suggested throughout this chapter, double-sided reflection has potential application to both career and lifestyle planning with clients and for counseling clients struggling with addictive behaviors. Just as client choices and behaviors in the career and lifestyle realm are inherently connected with client addictive behaviors, counseling interventions in one area can be used to assist with facilitating change in the other as well.

### Amplified Reflection

Another potentially effective method for responding to resistance is amplified reflection. "A related and quite useful response is to reflect back what the person has said in an amplified or exaggerated form—to state it in an even more extreme fashion" (W. R. Miller & Rollnick, 2002, p. 101). It is important to note that this be done in a serious, straightforward tone that does not suggest sarcasm on the part of the counselor. Such a negative reflection from the counselor would likely only elicit greater resistance.

> *John:* I couldn't give up my partying with friends; I mean, what would they think—that I'm some kind of loser?
>
> *Counselor:* You can't even imagine not doing drugs with your friends. You couldn't handle their reaction if you quit.

Or

> *John:* You make it sound like I'm a raging alcoholic or a total drug addict! I didn't even come here to talk with you about that stuff!
>
> *Counselor:* You don't see any negative consequences from your drug and alcohol use, and you resent that I brought it up. In fact, you really see no connection at all between your drug and alcohol use and your career choices.
>
> *John:* Well, I know I need to take a look at how that stuff is affecting where I want to go. . . . I mean, the drugs and partying aren't making it any easier to get out of my present job situation.

In each of these two examples, the counselor used amplified reflection to respond to resistance in the counseling relationship. In the second example, the counselor responded specifically to the issue of exploring addictive behaviors simultaneously with career concerns. The counselor's response using amplified reflection elicited the client's arguments for exploring the relationship between addictive behaviors and career and lifestyle planning.

## Reframing

Sometimes clients express resistance through a self-defeating, problematic, or counterproductive view of a situation. "A persistent use of a false or problematic perceptual frame indicates that the client is 'stuck' and likely to continue unless a change in perception can be engineered" (Gerber, 2003, p. 144). Reframing is the process of helping a client to alter the maladaptive frame into a new perceptual frame. More specifically, reframing in MI may mean helping to generate a more adaptive perception of the process of change.

Reframing is another useful response to resistance.

> *John:* I've tried to cut back on doing coke before, but I always get back into it.
> *Counselor:* You're very persistent. You're not afraid to try again when you aren't successful initially.

Or

> *John:* I don't know why I should bother trying to build a new lifestyle. I clearly blew it when I chose this career.
> *Counselor:* You've done a great job noticing some of the mistakes you've made in developing your current lifestyle—now you'll be able to avoid a lot of problems as we go through the process together.

## Agreeing With a Twist

W. R. Miller and Rollnick (2002) proposed another technique for rolling with resistance that they called agreeing with a twist. This technique involves initially concurring with a client by reflecting his or her message coupled with a slight twist or modification of resistant momentum. "Agreement with a twist is basically a reflection followed by a reframe" (W. R. Miller & Rollnick, 2002, p. 105).

> *John:* You're probably going to tell me I need to do some AA program or something and that I need to go back to school and get some exercise. It wears me out just thinking about it.
> *Counselor:* You're exactly right—if I were to make out a giant to-do list for you it would likely just disable you. It's paradoxical, isn't it? When you're told what you "have" to do, it can actually prevent you from doing the very things you want to do.

**SIDEBAR 18.13**

Look at the front page of a current copy of a national newspaper. What socioeconomic issues do you identify? How would these events affect the client, John, in this chapter's case study?

## Summary

So what has become of the case example and the client, John? The counselor has developed discrepancy between John's current addictive behaviors and his lifestyle objectives. John has moved from precontemplation to contemplation. He is ready to explore his ambivalence toward his use of drugs and alcohol further. Because he has already noted several disparaging aspects of his current behavior, he is already beginning to tip the scale in favor of positive change. Soon he will be ready to explore options for beginning to alter his addictive behaviors and develop a plan of action, as the preparation stage necessitates.

Regarding his career concerns, John seems ready to access career and educational planning information in an effort to develop an action plan for a career change. It may be logical for the counselor and John to formulate a plan for his career development and altering his addictive behaviors concurrently because both involve a similar commitment of time and energy. Additionally, the resources obtained for one may be relevant to the other. John may want to take advantage of intervention programs he can access as a returning student, and John's investment in education and retraining will likely have financial implications for his use of drugs and alcohol in his current lifestyle.

It is imperative that the counselor and John consider all potential implications of his plan of action. It may be useful for the counselor and John to generate a menu of options as to various potential plans and then evaluate each for its advantages and disadvantages and the probability of success. The counselor will continue to foster John's sense of self-efficacy by reviewing the substantial progress he continues to make in improving his lifestyle by changing his addictive behaviors and cultivating his career development.

Career development is sometimes defined as "the total constellation of psychological, sociological, educational, physical, economic, and chance factors that combine to shape the career of any given individual over the life span" (Herr & Cramer, 2004, p. 139). Career counseling and lifestyle planning, then, should take into account those salient factors that affect a client's career development—including a client's addictive behaviors.

**SIDEBAR 18.14**

Using the Internet, search for career counseling agencies or career centers in your area (local, regional, or national). Do any of the agencies also offer counseling for addictive behaviors? Do any of the agencies or career centers use an MI approach?

Understanding the stages of change for behaviors can assist counselors in working with clients struggling with addiction. Knowledge of a client's current stage of change can help a counselor conceptualize the tasks necessary for clients to continue on the path toward positive change. Moreover, the four guiding principles of MI—express empathy, develop discrepancy, roll with resistance, and support self-efficacy—can provide a solid foundation for career counseling clients with addictive behaviors. The specific MI counseling techniques introduced in this chapter provide counselors with a repertoire of tools to help them further positive change in clients and avoid the potential pitfalls posed by resistance.

**SIDEBAR 18.15**

Relate the case example in the chapter to the American Counseling Association's Advocacy Competencies. What additional advocacy or social justice interventions could be conducted at the individual, community, and public arena levels? Discuss these questions in pair share, and then prepare to contribute to a large-group discussion.

Finally, although the case example demonstrates the stages of change and the use of specific counseling techniques, it is of course a parsimonious example. The process of change is often long and arduous and riddled with frequent setbacks. It is important that counselors not give up on the process of change just as they ask clients not to give up on themselves.

We must become the change we want to see.

—**Gandhi**

## Useful Web Sites

- Addictive Behaviors Research Center, University of Washington: http://depts.washington.edu/abrc/
- Addiction Technology Transfer Center: http://www.nattc.org/
- *Journal of Occupational Health Psychology*: http://www.apa.org/journals/ocp.html
- Motivational Interviewing Web site: http://www.motivationalinterview.org/
- National Center on Addiction and Substance Abuse at Columbia University: http://www.casacolumbia.org
- National Clearinghouse for Drug and Alcohol Information: http://www.health.org/
- National Institute of Mental Health: http://www.nimh.nih.gov/
- National Institute on Alcohol Abuse and Alcoholism: http://www.niaaa.nih.gov/
- National Institute on Drug Abuse: http://www.nida.nih.gov/ and http://www.drugabuse.gov
- Practitioner resources on substance abuse: http://www.athealth.com/Practitioner/particles/FR_SubstanceAbuse.html
- *Psychology of Addictive Behaviors*: http://www.apa.org/journals/adb.html
- Substance Abuse and Mental Health Services Administration: http://www.samhsa.gov

## References

Bandura, A. (1997). *Self efficacy: The exercise of control.* New York, NY: W. H. Freeman.

Burke, B. L., Arkowitz, H., & Menchola, M. (2003). The efficacy of motivational interviewing: A meta-analysis of controlled clinical trials. *Journal of Consulting and Clinical Psychology, 71,* 843–861.

DiClemente, C. C. (1991). Motivational interviewing and the stages of change. In W. R. Miller & S. Rollnick (Eds.), *Motivational interviewing: Preparing people to change addictive behavior* (pp. 191–202) New York, NY: Guilford Press.

DiClemente, C. C. (2003). *Addiction and change: How addictions develop and addicted people recover.* New York, NY: Guilford Press.

DiClemente, C. C., & Velasquez, M. (2002). Motivational interviewing and the stages of change. In W. R. Miller & S. Rollnick (Eds.) *Motivational interviewing: Preparing people for change* (pp. 201–216). New York, NY: Guilford Press.

Doweiko, H. E. (2008). *Concepts of chemical dependency* (7th ed.). Pacific Grove, CA: Brooks/Cole.

Drake, R. E., Mueser, K. T., Clark, R. E., & Wallach, M. A. (1996). The course, treatment, and outcome of substance disorder in persons with severe mental illness. *Journal of Orthopsychiatry, 66,* 42–51.

Ford, J. D., Russo, E. M., & Mallon, S. D. (2007). Integrating treatment of posttraumatic stress disorder and substance use disorder. *Journal of Counseling & Development, 85,* 475–490.

Gerber, S. K. (2003). *Responsive therapy: A systematic approach to counseling skills* (2nd ed.). New York: Lahaska Press.

Greenbaum, P. E., Foster Johnson, L., & Petrila, A. (1996). Co-occurring addictive and mental disorders among adolescents: Prevalence research and future directions. *American Journal of Orthopsychiatry, 66,* 52–60.

Harland, J., White, M., Drinkwater, C., Chin, D., Farr, L., & Howel, D. (1999). The Newcastle Exercise Project: A randomized controlled trial of methods to promote physical activity in primary care. *British Medical Journal, 319,* 828–831.

Herr, E. L., Cramer, S. H., & Niles, S. G. (2004). *Career guidance and counseling through the lifespan: Systematic approaches.* (6th ed.) Boston, MA: Allyn & Bacon.

Lewis, J., Arnold, M. S., House, R., & Toporek, R. (2003). Advocacy competencies [Electronic version]. Retrieved June 10, 2011, from http://www.counseling.org/Files/FD.ashx?guid=680f251e-b3d0-4f77-8aa3-4e360f32f05e

Miller, N. S. (1994). Psychiatric comorbidity: Occurrence and treatment. *Alcohol Health and Research World, 18,* 261–264.

Miller, W. R., Benefield, R. G., & Tonigan, J. S. (1993). Enhancing motivation for change in problem drinking: A controlled comparison of two therapist styles. *Journal of Consulting and Clinical Psychology, 61,* 455–461.

Miller, W. R., & Rollnick, S. (1991). Motivational interviewing: Preparing people to change addictive behavior. New York: Guilford Press.

*Miller, W. R., & Rollnick, S. (2002). *Motivational interviewing: Preparing people for change.* New York, NY: Guilford Press.

Prochaska, J. O., & DiClemente, C. C. (1984). *The transtheoretical approach: Crossing the traditional boundaries of therapy.* Malabar, FL: Krieger.

Prochaska, J. O., Norcross, J., & DiClemente, C. C. (1994). *Changing for good: The revolutionary program that explains the six stages of change and teaches you how to free yourself from bad habits.* New York, NY: William Morrow.

Project MATCH Research Group. (1997). Matching alcoholism treatments to client heterogeneity: Project MATCH posttreatment drinking outcomes. *Journal of Studies on Alcohol, 58,* 7–29.

Project MATCH Research Group. (1998). Matching alcoholism treatments to client heterogeneity: Project MATCH three year drinking outcomes. *Alcoholism: Clinical and Experimental Research, 23,* 1300–1311.

Rubak, S., Sandbæk, A., Lauritzen, T., & Christensen, B. (2005). Motivational interviewing: A systematic review and meta analysis. *British Journal of General Practice, 55,* 305–312.

Smith, D. E., Heckemeyer, C. M., Kratt, P. P., & Mason, D. A. (1997). Motivational interviewing to improve adherence to a behavioral weight control program for older obese women with NIDDM: A pilot study. *Diabetes Care, 20,* 53–54.

Stephens, R. S., Roffman, R. A., & Curtin, L. (2000). Comparison of extended versus brief treatments for marijuana use. *Journal of Consulting and Clinical Psychology, 68,* 898–908.

Substance Abuse and Mental Health Services Administration. (2010). *Results from the 2009 National Survey on Drug Use and Health: Volume I. Summary of national findings* (HHS Publication No. SMA 10 4586). Rockville, MD: Author.

Treasure, J. L., Katzman, M., Schmidt, U., Troop, N., Todd, G., & de Silva, P. (1999). Engagement and outcome in the treatment of bulimia nervosa: First phase of a sequential design comparing motivation enhancement therapy and cognitive behavioural therapy. *Behavioural Research and Therapy, 37,* 405–418.

Vasilaki, E. I., Hosier, S. G., & Cox, W. M. (2006). The efficacy of motivational interviewing as a brief intervention for excessive drinking: A meta analytic review. *Alcohol and Alcoholism, 41,* 328–335.

West, D. S., DiLillo, V., Bursac, Z., Gore, S. A., & Greene, P. G. (2007). Motivational interviewing improves weight loss in women with type 2 diabetes. *Diabetes Care, 30,* 1081–1087.

Wilson, G. T., & Schlam, T. R. (2004). The transtheoretical model and motivational interviewing in the treatment of eating and weight disorders. *Clinical Psychology Review, 24,* 361–378.

# Index

Lightning Source UK Ltd.
Milton Keynes UK
UKOW07n1133080317
296139UK00014B/111/P